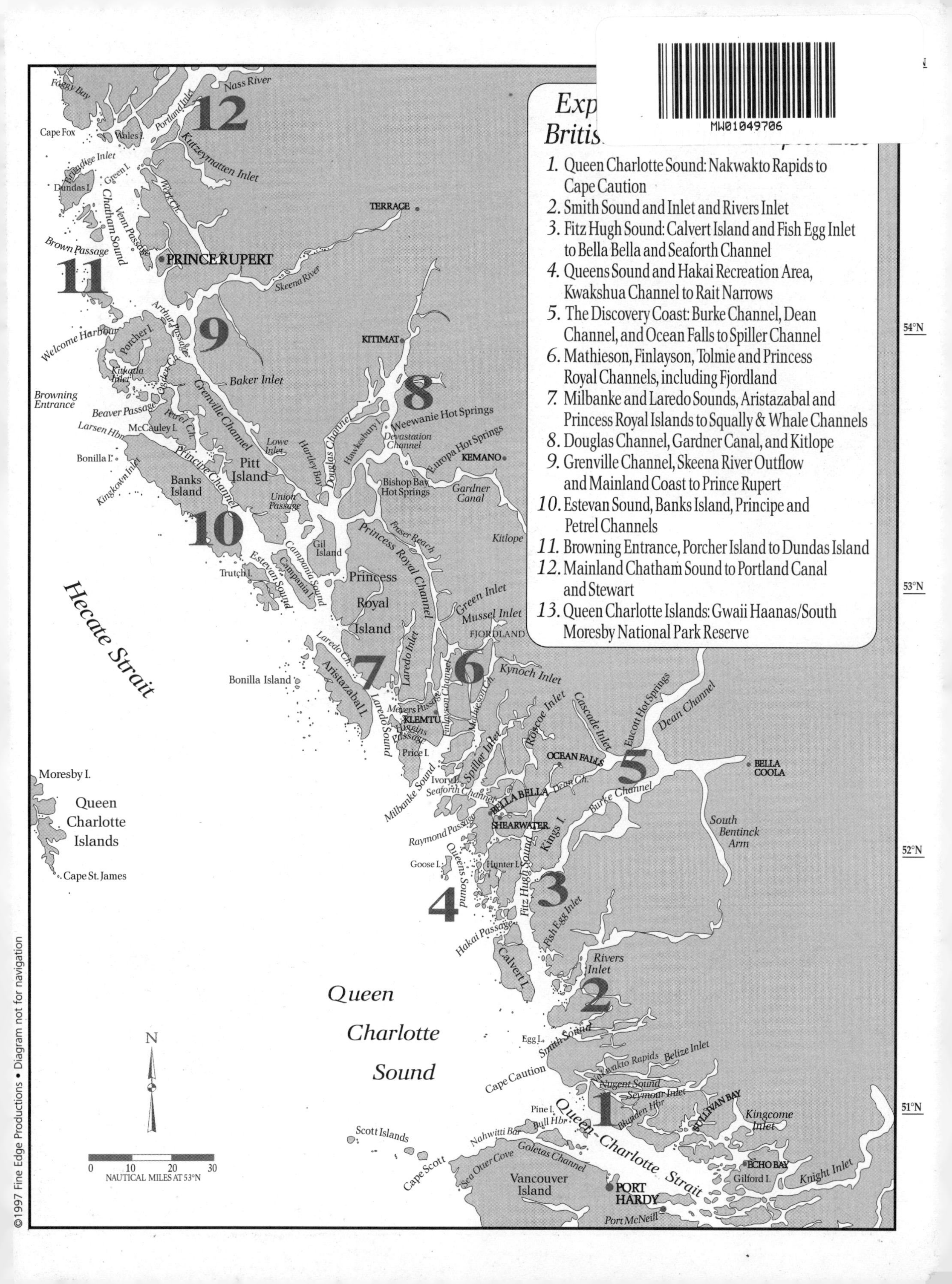

Exp
Britis
1. Queen Charlotte Sound: Nakwakto Rapids to Cape Caution
2. Smith Sound and Inlet and Rivers Inlet
3. Fitz Hugh Sound: Calvert Island and Fish Egg Inlet to Bella Bella and Seaforth Channel
4. Queens Sound and Hakai Recreation Area, Kwakshua Channel to Rait Narrows
5. The Discovery Coast: Burke Channel, Dean Channel, and Ocean Falls to Spiller Channel
6. Mathieson, Finlayson, Tolmie and Princess Royal Channels, including Fjordland
7. Milbanke and Laredo Sounds, Aristazabal and Princess Royal Islands to Squally & Whale Channels
8. Douglas Channel, Gardner Canal, and Kitlope
9. Grenville Channel, Skeena River Outflow and Mainland Coast to Prince Rupert
10. Estevan Sound, Banks Island, Principe and Petrel Channels
11. Browning Entrance, Porcher Island to Dundas Island
12. Mainland Chatham Sound to Portland Canal and Stewart
13. Queen Charlotte Islands: Gwaii Haanas/South Moresby National Park Reserve
PRINCE RUPERT
TERRACE
KITIMAT
KEMANO
Hecate Strait
Queen Charlotte Islands
Queen Charlotte Sound
Queen Charlotte Strait
Vancouver Island
PORT HARDY
Port McNeill
OCEAN FALLS
BELLA BELLA
SHEARWATER
BELLA COOLA
KLEMTU
SULLIVAN BAY
ECHO BAY
54°N
53°N
52°N
51°N
0 10 20 30
NAUTICAL MILES AT 53°N
©1997 Fine Edge Productions • Diagram not for navigation

Ninstints, Sgaan Gwaii World Heritage site, Queen Charlotte Islands

EXPLORING THE NORTH COAST OF BRITISH COLUMBIA

Blunden Harbour to Dixon Entrance Including the Queen Charlotte Islands

BY DON DOUGLASS & RÉANNE HEMINGWAY-DOUGLASS

FOREWORD BY CAPTAIN KEVIN MONAHAN

GUEST ESSAY BY RODERICK FRAZIER NASH

Quotations from the *Canadian Sailing Directions,* Vol. 1 and 2 are used with permission of the Canadian Hydrographic Service. Reproduction of information from Canadian Hydrographic Service Sailing Directions in this publication are for illustrative purposes only, they do not meet the requirements of the Charts and Publication Regulations and are not to be used for navigation. The appropriate Sailing Directions, corrected up-to-date, and the relevant Canadian Hydrographic Service charts required under the Charts and Publications Regulations of the Canada Shipping Act must be used for navigation.

Contact the Canadian Hydrographic Service to obtain information on local dealers and available charts and publications or to order charts and publications directly:

Chart Sales and Distribution Office,Canadian Hydrographic Service
Department of Fisheries and Oceans, Institute of Ocean Sciences, Patricia Bay
9860 West Saanich Road, Sidney B.C., V8L 4B2 Telephone (250) 363-6358; FAX (250) 363-6841

Important Legal Disclaimer

This book is designed to provide experienced skippers with cruising information on the coast of British Columbia. This book is not to be used for navigation, nor does it replace official Canadian resources, nor the constant need for vigilant navigation. The user must accept full responsibility for all consequences arising from use of this book. Every effort has been made, within limited resources, to make this book complete and accurate. Much of what is presented in this book is local knowledge, based upon personal observation and subject to human error. There may well be mistakes, both in typography and in content; therefore this book should be used only as a general guide, not as the ultimate source of information on the areas covered. The authors, publisher and local authorities assume no liability for errors or omissions, or for any loss or damages incurred from using this information.

Credits:
Cover charts from 3747 and 3853 by permission of CHS
Computer graphics by Sue Irwin
Front cover by Robin Hill-Ward: *Baidarka* and crew at Ellerslie Falls
Back cover photo by Ron Thiele
Frontispiece photo by Réanne Hemingway-Douglass
All other photos not credited are by the authors
Cover design by Laura Patterson

Library of Congress Cataloging-in-Publication Data

Douglass, Don, 1932–
Exploring the north coast of British Columbia : Blunden Harbour to Dixon Entrance, including the Queen Charlotte Islands / by Don Douglass & Réanne Hemingway-Douglass : foreword by Kevin Monahan.
p. cm.
Includes bibliographical references (p.) and index.
ISBN 0-938665-45-6
1. Pilot guides—British Columbia. I. Hemingway-Douglass, Réanne, 1933– II. Title.
VK945.D684 1997 96-48468
623.89'29711—DC21 CIP

ISBN 0-938665-45-6

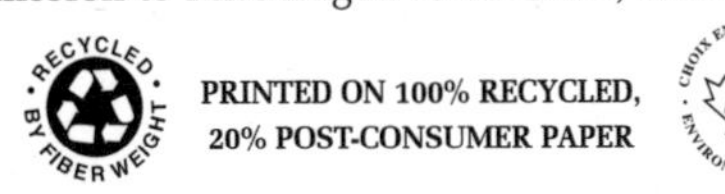

Contents

Acknowledgments . . . 6

Foreword by Captain Kevin Monahan . . . 7

Using This Book . . . 9

Guest Essay: The Last Great Place by Roderick Frazier Nash . . . 15

Chapter 1 Queen Charlotte Sound: Nakwakto Rapids to Cape Caution . . . 18

Chapter 2 Smith Sound and Inlet and Rivers Inlet . . . 46

Chapter 3 Fitz Hugh Sound: Calvert Island and Fish Egg Inlet to Bella Bella and Seaforth Channel . . . 74

Chapter 4 Queens Sound and Hakai Recreation Area, Kwakshua Channel to Rait Narrows . . . 106

Chapter 5 The Discovery Coast: Burke Channel, Dean Channel, and Ocean Falls to Spiller Channel . . . 136

Chapter 6 Mathieson, Finlayson, Tolmie and Princess Royal Channels, including Fjordland . . . 184

Chapter 7 Milbanke and Laredo Sounds, Aristazabal and Princess Royal Islands to Squally and Whale Channels . . . 206

Chapter 8 Douglas Channel, Gardner Canal, and Kitlope . . . 246

Chapter 9 Grenville Channel, Skeena River Outflow and Mainland Coast to Prince Rupert . . . 274

Chapter 10 Estevan Sound, Banks Island, Principe and Petrel Channels . . . 296

Chapter 11 Browning Entrance, Porcher Island to Dundas Island . . . 322

Chapter 12 Mainland Chatham Sound to Portland Canal and Stewart . . . 342

Chapter 13 Queen Charlotte Islands: Gwaii Haanas/South Moresby National Park Reserve . . . 380

Appendices and References

A. Distance Tables . . . 420

B. Procedures Used in Documenting Local Knowledge . . . 422

C. Sources for Fishing Regulations . . . 422

D. Canadian Holidays . . . 422

E. Sources of Charts, Books, & Information . . . 423

F. Key VHF Radio Channels . . . 424

G. Summer Wind Reports . . . 425

Bibliography and References . . . 425

Index . . . 427

About the Authors . . . 431

Nautical Titles from Fine Edge Productions . . . 431

Acknowledgments

Over the years of cruising the waters of the beautiful North Coast, we have met many wonderful people whose help, encouragement, and contributions played an important part in the making of this guidebook.

We would like to thank, in particular, those who took time to review parts of the manuscript and provide invaluable comments, and those who provided informative report or sidebars: Neil Carey, author of *Guide to Queen Charlottes* and his wife Betty, pathfinders of the coast; Andy Macdonald, Hakai Recreation Ranger, for sharing his knowledge and comments; fellow explorer Captain Kevin Monahan, who has more year-round experience on this coast than anyone we know; Roderick Frazier Nash, for his insightful Guest Essay and help in documenting Spiller Channel; Linda Murray-Nash, for co-authoring Bears and Boats; Iain Lawrence, Prince Rupert, author of *Faraway Places* for his perceptive suggestions; Bob Waldon, for his piece on coastal birds; Don and Merilyn Baldwin, owners of SeaSport Marine, Prince Rupert; Ian Douglas, Quadra Island, for allowing us to use excerpts from his article on *Hakai Ranger*; Jim Henly and Bryce Gillard, Fisheries and Oceans, Bella Bella for their inputs on Central Coast; David Scharf, Portland, for his kayaker's viewpoint; Don Pearson, Moon Bay Marina, for sharing his local knowledge of Douglas Canal; Ron Thiele, Kitimat, for information on the Kermodei bear and his excellent photographs; Norm Wagner, Kitimat, for his sidebar on Jesse Falls and inputs on Gardner Canal and the Kitlope; Robin Hill-Ward and Steve Ward, *Charisma*, for contributions and photographs; Lach McGuigan, *Landfall,* for his sidebar on diving in icy waters; Linda and Jack Schreiber, *Sanctuary,* for their sidebar on whales; Glen Craig, Kemano, for his information on anchor sites in Gardner Canal; John De Boeke, captain of *Clavella,* for sharing his notes on Moresby Island; Don Radford, Division of Forestry, Prince Rupert, and Tom Tabacco, Victoria, for information on the Griffin Passage *Mayday*. Thanks also to Canadian Hydrographic Service, especially Dick MacDougall, Ottawa, and Brian Watt, Sidney, for their support and timely responses.

To the many boaters and residents along the waterways who volunteered information or checked our observations: Lizzie Tullis and John Herchenrider, *Sara;* Warren and Laurie Miller, *Sacalaurie;* Bob and Anne Reeves, *Seabird;* Bobbie and Keith Bracht, *Dixie Ann II*; Bill Swaine, *High Flight III*; Terry Jack, *Seasons in the Sun*; John and Randi Sanger, *Starlite;* Harry and Barbara Patton, *Neuron II;* Joe and Doris Harlacher, *Camelot;* Gwen and Don Burton, *Endymion;* Heine Dole, *Evening Star;* the skipper and crew of the *Narwhal*; Jim Robinson, Hartley Bay; Dan and Danielle Pollock, Langley Passage; Wendy and Mike Clark, Stewart; Tonnae Hennigan, Vancouver. And to the many boaters along way the whose names may have escaped our attention, we thank you, too!

A special thank you to our lightstation friends Stan and Judy Westhaver, Egg Island, Sherrill and Rene Kitson, Ivory Island, and the crew of the MAREP stations at Cape Scott and Bonilla Island—all of whom do a fantastic job for the benefit of *every* boater; and to the staff of Prince Rupert Coast Guard Radio Station whose high standards and superior abilities match any we have encountered in 150,000 miles of world cruising.

To our *Baidarka* crew members who offered valuable insights of their own and endured long work days as we carried out our research: Geza Dienes, Rusty O'Brien, Herb Nickles, Wendy Shepherd, Tom and Gloria Burke, Bob and Annamae Botley, and Al Ryan. An additional thanks to Herb Nickles for supplying photos used in the Spiller Channel chapter. In addition, we would like to honor crew members and veteran cruising boaters, Frank and Margy Fletcher, whose enthusiam for the North Coast encouraged our explorations.

And last, but never least, we owe our deepest thanks to our shore crew, without whose long "watches" we would never have been able to bring this project to a conclusion: Pat Eckart, Cindy Kamler, Bernadine Whitmore, Sue Irwin, Melanie Haage, and Laura Patterson.

Foreword

by Kevin Monahan

Throughout my time at sea, it has been the tiny harbours that appealed to me the most. No matter how stimulated by the drama of the coast, one must eventually find refuge. Diminutive but secure, such places are scattered throughout this coastline in vast numbers, providing privacy and contentment for the spirit. Indeed, after beating my way through gale-force winds or worse, weaving my boat into a quiet anchorage brings on a kind of euphoria, a joy that cannot be understood without the experience.

Though the North Coast of British Columbia provides numerous protected passages and anchorages, let there be no doubt that these waters can be as hazardous as any. While it may seem that a benevolent creator has scattered numerous islands to protect the inner coast from the Aleutian low and its devastating weather systems, this comforting shield of forested rock also focuses the power of wind and sea into narrow confines. To anyone who has experienced the frigid outflow of gales in Douglas Channel or the treacherous tide rips of Nahwitti Bar, these conditions will come as no surprise. As is true of any waters, those of the British Columbia coast are at times placid and nurturing (a truly *Pacific* ocean), or deadly and menacing. Yet, for those of us who go down to the sea in boats, it is precisely these qualities that attract us. I have made my living in West Coast waters for more than twenty years; first as a fisherman and later as a professional mariner. At times I have been terrified. At other times I have been astonished by the sublime beauty and power of this place. And sometimes I have felt all those emotions at once. But never have I grown tired of the spectacle.

In the remoter parts of the North Coast, some areas have not been charted at all, while other areas are charted only at small scale, so that many sheltered bays and coves barely show, and it is only local knowledge that can bring us safely out of the weather. True, one can plan one's cruising so that well charted harbours break up the journey, but then one misses the truly unique and refreshing places, many of which are used only by fishermen in season and a few locals who live in these remote areas. Some are sacred to native communities; all are populated by waterfowl and marine and terrestrial mammals. Yet others are punctuated by waterfalls and tidal rapids, or by salmon runs and white Kermodei bears.

In my first meeting with Don Douglass I recognized a fellow mariner. In Réanne Hemingway-Douglass I subsequently discovered another. While I was surveying a herring spawn in Smith Inlet, I steered my inflatable boat into a small bay. A trim little powerboat turned in from the opposite point. I approached the boat and came face-to-face with Baidarka and her crew who were gathering information for their books. One small boat, exquisitely neat and seemingly so roomy, could barely contain the force of Don's enthusiasm. Indeed, he fills his own personal space to overflowing and his presence is generous enough to enfold all those with whom he comes in contact. Since that time, I have seen Baidarka at work in many out-of-the-way places.

In this book, *Exploring the North Coast of British Columbia—Blunden Harbour to Dixon Entrance, Including the Queen Charlotte Islands,* as in their previous publications, Don and Réanne present an atlas of local knowledge for the amateur and professional alike. Together, with uncommon skill and integrity, they have systematically observed and recorded the exacting details of local knowledge for this very complex area.

This guidebook captures the North Coast like never before. Designed to be a constant wheelhouse companion, it easily fills our expectations. The local knowledge found inside helps us understand the North Coast waters, and more importantly, helps us safely to our destination. And may you all have safe and eventful voyages!

Kevin Monahan, is a Master and Fishery Officer for Canadian Coast Guard. He lives in Victoria

Writing a guidebook on location

Northwest Anchoring

Northwest cruising is all about anchoring, and once we get beyond marinas and fishing resorts, the feeling of being safely anchored in our own secluded cove is unforgettable. Nothing gives us a good night's sleep like a well set, oversized anchor. A conventional cruising anchor (not a lightweight folding version), a boat-length of chain, and good stretchable nylon rode are indispensable equipment. In addition, we carry a smaller lunch hook to use for temporary stops or to restrict our swinging room. Sometimes—in close quarters or in deep, steep-to anchorages—we use a stern tie to shore. Although we usually prefer to swing on a single CQR anchor, in marine parks or popular anchorages we try to minimize our impact by matching the mooring technique and swinging radius of other boats. Choosing our site carefully and setting our anchor well assures us that *Baidarka* will rock us to sleep even in occasional downslope winds or williwaws. Finding a secluded anchorage is one of the challenges and pleasures of Northwest cruising, and we hope this book will help you find your *own* special site!

Using This Book

The North Coast of British Columbia is an enchanted cruising ground; many experienced mariners consider it the best in the world. The guest essay by Roderick Frazier Nash speaks eloquently about this unique environment which touches all those fortunate enough to visit its pristine waterways and gaze upon its magnificent scenery. We agree that the North Coast is a "Great Place," a place to admire and respect which must be saved for future generations.

The goal of this guidebook is to help you explore and enjoy these remote waters by sharing "local knowledge." While the beautiful, convoluted coastline of the North Coast is, for the most part, a user-friendly boating environment, it is wilderness none-the-less and requires careful and vigilant navigation. Boaters must respect its wild and unpredictable nature and be prepared to handle whatever comes. On the North Coast, response time for assistance in an emergency can be hours or even days, rather than the minutes found in urban cruising areas. VHF radio coverage is good, but there are a number of blind spots, like the east end of Gardner Canal, where neither weather forecasts nor maydays can be heard. Preparation, self-sufficiency, and constant vigilance are required to make a visit to the North Coast incident-free as well as carefree.

In providing up-to-date pilothouse information, we have tried to anticipate both general and navigational concerns that might arise as you plan and execute your cruise. While our information does not replace official publications and is not to be used for navigation, it reports useful information discovered in personally visiting the more than 1,000 sites described.

In addition to popular Inside Passage destinations, we have included many alternative anchor sites; in thousands of miles of coastline, you are seldom more than an hour away from a place to drop your hook. You can quickly find shelter if the fog sets in, the chop picks up, or you need somewhere to wait for favorable current.

We have a 32-foot diesel trawler that draws 40 inches, and we prefer to keep "one foot on the beach" to get the feel of a cove, be near the beach, and enjoy the sights, sounds and smells of the land. We always post at least one alert lookout on the bow when we approach narrow passages or anchor sites. At all times, we work at knowing our exact position and identifying any potential threats.

Some of the narrow passages or intimate coves cited in this book may be too small for larger vessels. Some may involve risks you are not prepared to take, or require such demanding skills you may not feel comfortable sailing there. Some anchor sites may be too close to shore if you have a larger boat or are short-handed. More swinging room may be desirable, especially in foul weather. Each skipper must exercise judgment, and choose what is appropriate for the vessel and the given circumstances.

If you are unsure of your cruising skills or the suitability of your vessel, we recommend that you consult local experts—cruising instructors, the Coast Guard, yacht clubs, experienced North Coast sailors, commercial fishermen—and that you read many of the texts listed in the bibliography.

In discussing local knowledge concerning routes, coves or anchoring, this book makes the assumption that each skipper has the proper large-scale chart for the area visited, the proper edition of Canadian Tide and Current Tables (Volumes 5 and 6), and is skilled in using them. Also needed are the latest *Sailing Directions* and Marine Weather Hazards Manual. Not only is it prudent to be familiar with them, but you are also required by Canadian Hydrographic Service regulations to have these official references aboard. (Please refer to the bibliography for further information and to the publisher's page for the legal disclaimer.)

By knowing your own abilities and interests and matching them to the unlimited cruising opportunities for exploring the North Coast, you can enjoy the trip of a lifetime.

How to Use this Book

Each chapter in this book covers a separate cruising area (proceeding usually from south to north). An area map is included at the beginning of each chapter to serve as a quick reference to location of channels, passages, and coves found within the text.

The following short example, taken from Chapter 8, illustrates our layout:

Kiltuish Inlet

Chart 3745; entrance:
53°24.40′ N, 128°31.70′ W;
anchor (outside narrows):
53°23.82′ N, 128°30.23′ W (NAD 27)

> *Kiltuish Inlet, 2 miles SE of Europa Point, has a narrow entrance encumbered with rocks . . .*
> (p. 113, SD)

Anchor in 3 to 5 fathoms deep in the inlet, over a sticky mud bottom with . . .

Paragraph titles

Each cove or destination is identified by bold-face type. Since this guidebook documents many small, unnamed coves and bays for the first time, we have tried to use local names. Where we could find no reference to a name in either Canadian charts or in C.H.S. sources *(Sailing Directions)*, we used a new name that seemed appropriate. Local names and new names are shown in quotation marks the first time they are mentioned.

Canadian Chart number(s)

The first chart listed is always the largest scale available and the one we have used to determine the latitude and longitude of a place. Where additional charts are listed, they are smaller-scale charts which cover the area. Metric charts are noted as such.

Information following the chart number(s) identifies:

a general **position**, a specific **anchor** site, a mid-channel **entrance** point, a **buoy**, or a navigational **light.** Latitude and Longitude to the nearest one-hundredth of a minute are specified. (The term "position" is used for a general site or an anchor site that we have not personally checked or are unsure about.) Buoy and light positions are taken from the latest Canadian Coast Guard *Light List* (1992 edition), with seconds of arc converted to decimal minutes.

The Lat/Long of an anchor site is just that; it is not the entrance to a cove. GPS receivers set to an anchor site—or to any other position given—will take you directly there, whether there is an intervening land mass or not.

Italicized text

Quotations are excerpted and abridged from the latest edition of Canadian Hydrographic Service *Sailing Directions,* 1990 edition (SD, Vol. 1 & 2). The referenced page number is given at the end of a quotation. Where no quotation is used, we could find no reference in *Sailing Directions.*

Body of text

The local knowledge we have personally observed and recorded (or in a few cases, learned from other experienced skippers) may include general information, special entrance information, a description of the general anchor area, hazards known to us, details about the degree of shelter, etc.

Anchoring information

The final information given is always the anchor information for the GPS position stated in the paragraph title. Depths at zero tide are listed, followed by specific bottom matter (sand, mud, clay, rocks, gravel, kelp), and our estimate of the relative anchor holding power.

Where depth, bottom type and holding of an anchor site are specified, we have personally anchored there and this information is from our log. In places where we have not personally anchored, or where our records were incomplete, we have stated the bottom or its holding power as *unrecorded.* (See Appendix for details on how Local Knowledge was obtained and for definitions of holding power.)

Anchor diagrams

We have included anchor diagrams for places where we felt they would be helpful. *Please note:* these are non-representational diagrams, *not* nautical charts, and are *not to be used for navigation.* The diagrams are not exact scale drawings and do not include all known or unknown hazards—they simply show the approximate routes we took, the typical depths we found, and the places where we anchored.

Key to Detailed Diagrams

Shoal (dries)
Land mass
Reef
Rock(s) below or above water; small islet(s)
Anchor site
Mooring buoy
Aid to navigation
Peak or high point
Trails

Please Note: *Because this book lists in the text or shows a particular anchor site in diagrammatic form does not mean to imply that the site is suitable either for temporary or overnight anchorage or that it is safe to leave your boat unattended in that site. Whenever faced with critical judgments involving navigation or anchoring, a skipper should consult official primary sources of data. The individual skipper is the sole judge of what is appropriate under each circumstance and assumes full responsibility for using this book.*

Canadian Metric Charts

Canada is in the process of converting its navigational charts from traditional British naval units, using fathoms and feet, to the metric system. Because of Canadian Hydrographic Service budget limitations, this conversion may take several decades to complete. Anyone navigating the North Coast must pay close attention to every chart used, since many still use fathoms and the older horizontal datum of NAD 27. The new charts have "Metric" printed in red in the lower right-hand corner. In general, the new metric charts are being introduced south to north, so charts for the North Coast are still predominately in the old style. Please note that several of the metric charts issued in the late 1980s and 1990s do not use the new 1983 horizontal datum.

Changes on metric charts involve more than just a substitution of depth numbers—the *symbols* for depth and height have changed as well. For instance, $[1_3]$ on old Canadian and American charts means a depth of 1 fathom and 3 feet, for a total depth of 9 feet (1.5 fathoms). An islet shown as (45) means a height of 45 feet. On the new metric charts, the symbol $[1_3]$ means 1.3 meters or about 4 feet. An islet shown as $\overline{45}$ means 45 meters (150 feet) in height. These differences (1.5 fathoms versus 1.3 meters, 45 meters versus 45 feet) can be particularly confusing if you are accustomed to the British naval system. Please purchase and study Canadian Chart 1 for all current Canadian symbols.

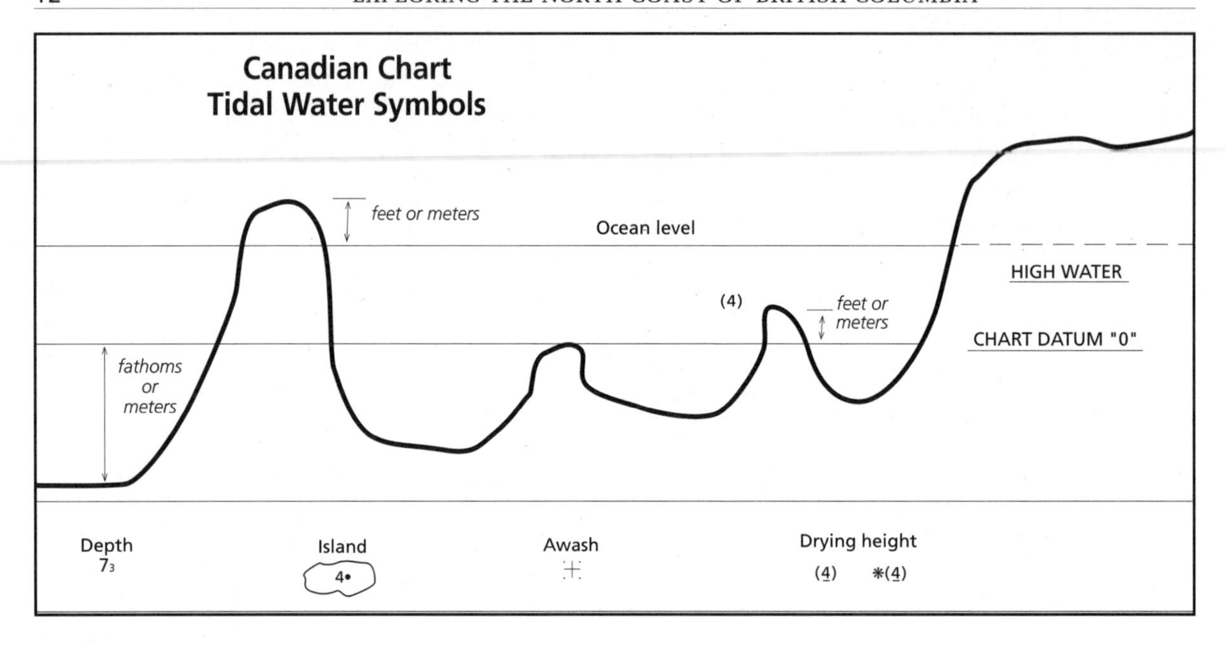

Measurements and Other Conventions Used in this Book

Spelling and usage of place names follow, as closely as possible, local tradition and the lead of the Canadian *Sailing Directions.*

The authors have chosen to continue, for the time being, the use of fathoms, nautical miles, yards, feet, degrees in Fahrenheit, etc. (Canadians are more adept at making conversions than Yankees are.) We urge both local and visiting navigators to double-check each chart, echo sounder readings, and GPS initial settings for consistent use of measurement units.

Unless otherwise noted, depths listed in the text or shown on diagrams are always given in fathoms, regardless of the measurement units on cited charts; depths are reduced to approximate zero tide. You should add the amount of tide listed in the corrected tide tables when you use these numbers. In Canada, zero tide data is given as the lowest expected tide for the year; therefore tide tables almost always appear as a positive number rather than the frequent minus tides of the United States. The depths shown on diagrams or mentioned in the text are typical of what we found and do not represent exact minimums for any given area.

Bearings and courses, when given, are generally magnetic and identified as such. Courses are taken off the chart compass rose; they are approximate and are to be "made good." No allowances have been made for deviation, possible current or drift. When compass cardinal points are used (example NW or SE), these refer to true bearings and should be taken as approximate only.

Distances are expressed in nautical miles, and speed is expressed in knots unless otherwise stated. Scales on the diagrams are expressed in yards, meters, and miles as noted and are approximate only. Time is given in four-digit 24-hour clock numbers, and all courses are given in three digits.

Unnamed islands and islets are referred to in the text by the height of the island enclosed in parentheses [e.g., island (45)]. In some cases, where more than one chart covers an area, the numbers in parentheses may be either in feet or meters and may change from chart to chart.

Global Positioning System

GPS is an excellent tool for navigating the North Coast. Nav-Aids are rare and many passages and islets can be confusing. GPS will help locate the proper entrances, detect cross-track errors, provide speed over the ground, and hence determine tidal currents.

Latitude and longitude for anchor sites and way-points in this book are given to the nearest one-hundredth of a minute of latitude. These Lat/Longs (GPS positions) are to be treated as approximate only. Many of the referenced charts are not accurate (nor can they be read accurately) to one-hundredth of a minute. We have approximated this last digit to provide as complete a picture as possible.

Because of inherent random-induced error (Selective Availability), we derived the latitude and longitude reading from the specified charts, rather than relying on GPS output. We generally found good correlation between the charts and GPS readings, if we took the average of a series of readings. Differential GPS does not have universal coverage on the North Coast so vigilance is required in critical places.

It is necessary to set your GPS receiver to the correct horizontal datum for the chart you are using if you want optimum accuracy. The horizontal datum for Canadian charts for the north coast of British Columbia are either NAD 27 or NAD 83, and you must be alert for changes in the horizontal datum between different editions of a given chart. (NAD 27 differs from NAD 83 at some latitudes by about 0.011 minutes in latitude and 0.089 minutes in longitude, a difference of about 300 feet.)

The default datum in GPS receivers is generally WSG 84 which, for all practical purposes, is equivalent to NAD 83. We have been told by C.H.S. that if horizontal datum is not specified on a particular chart, then it can *generally* be assumed to be NAD 27. However, for some Queen Charlotte Islands and West Coast charts, C.H.S. is unsure of what datum was used. To minimize the chance of error, we have given the horizontal datum appropriate for each Lat/Long we use in this book.

Public floats in British Columbia

At public floats where space is limited, rafting, three-wide, is obligatory. In crowded harbors, you should *always* put fenders on the outer side of your boat to protect your hull. Fishing boats frequently enter a harbor late, and it is an unfriendly practice to leave your dinghy along the outer side of your boat, thereby preventing their rafting to your boat.

Free Supplement Available for this Guidebook

The authors seek your corrections or comments and will incorporate them into our free supplement and errata sheets. Write us at the address below. We will try to make acknowledgments whenever possible.

Supplements will be sent at no cost to any guide purchaser who sends a stamped (U.S. postage or international reply coupons), self-addressed, business-sized envelope to:

Fine Edge Productions
Route 2, Box 303
Bishop, California 93514

Fueling time!

Photo by Robin Hill-Ward

Starlight *takes a break*

GUEST ESSAY

The Last Great Place

by Roderick Frazier Nash

From a mariner's point of view, the most significant landmarks are called "capes." Horn, Good Hope, Cod, Hatteras . . . the list is well known. Cape Caution marks the most significant passage on the British Columbia coast; rounding it is a nautical coming of age. Weekend warriors and two-week charterers don't make it this far. Serious cruisers who do, enter a fraternity of mutual respect where they experience the space, the solitude, and the silence of one of the world's wildest coastlines. Cape Caution is a gateway to the last great place—British Columbia's North Coast.

Time was, and not so long ago, that one of the largest conifer forests on the planet stretched in an unbroken green carpet from the Gulf of Alaska all the way south to the central California coast. Salmon and steelhead runs occurred in rivers as far as Southern California. Grizzly bears and wolves roamed the entire North American coastline.

People lived here too, but their lifestyle centered on complementing, rather than conquering nature. These First People saw nature as a community to which they belonged, rather than a commodity to possess. Their numbers, however, were small, and their impact on the environment could be sustained in perpetuity—over thousands of years.

Change came to the west coast with the arrival of Europeans. Capitalism, Christianity and industrial civilization quickly ripped the fabric of the primeval ecosystem. Dams blocked rivers and ended salmon runs; old-growth forests disappeared; highways and railroads paralleled the coast; and subdivisions and airports replaced nutrient-rich saltwater wetlands. From Los Angeles to Vancouver, we are now dealing with fragments of ecosystems. In the United States, the vast coastal temperate rain forest has dwindled to a few tiny preserves.

For historical perspective, think of the biological richness and beauty of San Francisco Bay or Puget Sound just 150 years ago. Think of the food chains involving salmon, bears, eagles and native peoples along rivers like the Sacramento and the Columbia. It is twilight for those miracles now. Wild salmon seem headed on the same course as the buffalo. Management efforts have been too little, too late and piecemeal.

But on its central and northern coast, British Columbia has an opportunity to protect what California, Oregon and Washington squandered. The intricate, wild coastline north of Cape Caution is a remnant, a reminder and, hopefully, an inspiration. Thousands of miles of island and mainland coastline have changed little since the glaciers rolled back 15,000 years ago. The massive old-growth Sitka spruce, western red cedar and eastern hemlock crowd the water's edge as they did for Vancouver's crew in the 1790s. The largest virgin timber stands in North America are here. Although the last grizzly (the fabled "golden bear") disappeared from California in 1922, the big carnivores thrive on the north coast, as do whales, salmon, and eagles. First Nations People are still here too, some of them trying to cling to the shreds of their traditional and splendid cultural heritage.

The north coast is a land hanging in the balance between wilderness and civilization. While there is vast wilderness, there is also intense pressure for environmental transformation. British Columbian policy is still driven by the old frontier land-use priorities. Clearcutting is a way of life. Moving up from the south coast and Vancouver Island, giant lumber companies have laid bare huge tracts of land, sometimes entire watersheds, from the mountain ridges right down to salt water. Of course, not just the trees disappear. Entire ecosystems unravel; biodiversity takes a heavy beating.

The full scale of this war against the Earth may not be apparent to the casual observer. The cutting is often cleverly done and not visible from the decks of cruise ships on the Inside Passage. But get in a smaller boat and look behind the "tourist fringe" of waterline trees, back into the bays, and you see a war between wilderness and civilization. Here are the simple numbers: British Columbia has 25% of all the coastal temperate rain forest in the world; 39% of that has been logged. There is intense pressure to extract the rest of the prime old growth. Others feel it is time to establish a balance between human needs and the natural ways.

Of course, the lumber companies say the forest will recover, and demonstration reforestation projects support the idea of tree farming. But farms are not wilderness, either ecologically or spiritually.

For its part the British Columbia government proudly claims that it is committed to placing 12% of the province in protected status by the year 2000. However, most of the established and proposed parks are or will be swamps, scrub forest and snow peaks. The critical low elevation temperate rain forest is notable for its absence in the province's plans. There is a shortage of large habitats so critical to free-ranging creatures like bears, wolves and salmon. Also lacking are the corridors or bridges from one protected sanctuary to another which conservation biologists believe are vital to the health of wildlife populations.

In particular, friends of wildness in British Columbia covet a chain of environmental reserves extending from Tweedsmuir Provincial Park in the interior, through the Kitlope and Fjordland protected areas, and on to the proposed Spirit Bear Park. It is this last that is the most exciting. While Kitlope and Fjordland touch a small portion of the mainland coast, Spirit Bear is *all* marine oriented. Included in the 265,000 hectare proposal are Campania, Princess Royal, and Swindle islands, as well as a substantial reach of the mainland coast centered on Green and Khutze inlets with their extensive saltwater marshes. The final link in the chain is Gwaii Haanas National Park Reserve on South Moresby Island, Queen Charlotte group. Taken together, this is a preservation vision that does justice to the scale and variety of this immense land.

Spirit Bear, the common name for the *Kermodei Ursus*, was the focus of an exploratory cruise we made in the summer of 1996 when we circumnavigated the fabulous Princess Royal Island. The island is huge (over 100 miles long) and, except for its north end fronting Whale Channel where clearcutters have been at work, it is pristine.

The star of the wildlife show in this region, and namesake of the proposed park, is the Kermodei (spirit bear). Its coat ranges from a dazzling white to a rich caramel, but it is not an albino. Rather, biologists think this white phase of the black bear results from occasional manifestations of a recessive gene that has persisted since the ice age when it had an evolutionary advantage. Although there are only an estimated 100 spirit bears alive, patient study by Charles Russel and Jeff and Sue Turner has brought international attention to the animal. Russel's book *Spirit*

Bear: Encounters with the White Bear of the Western Rain Forest (1994), and the Turner's outstanding documentary film, will enrich any cruise in the Princess Royal area.

Although few in number, the spirit bear has come to symbolize the fragile wilderness of the northern coast and its uncertain future. The white bear lives only on the islands and the mainland north of Bella Bella. If this area continues to be logged, the bear will go, along with the giant trees. Also at stake in the Spirit Bear proposal is the economic and cultural vitality of the Kitasoo First People, centered in the village of Klemtu on Swindle Island. Along with the Heiltsuk of Bella Bella and the Haida of the Queen Charlotte Islands, the identity of the Kitasoo is tied closely to the wildness of their coastal environment. True, some natives welcome the logging that is moving north from Roderick Island and Griffin Passage, but increasing numbers are aware that logging jobs are ephemeral. Sustainability lies in a productive ecosystem and eco-tourism. Moreover, if the Kermodei country and the spectacular Spiller Channel-Ellerslie Lake region is clearcut, deep-rooted spiritual values are jeopardized.

The big picture shows that a corridor of protection—from the interior plateaus, over the coastal ranges and down to the ocean islands—could be a splendid monument to the human capacity for restraint, and a gesture of planetary modesty. Wilderness holds the answers to questions we have not yet learned how to ask. If we destroy the last of the planet's great wild places, we cut ourselves off from the evolutionary path that ours and all species have followed. On the large scale of time, technological civilization is a perilous new experiment. In the sea of monumental changes in which we will live during the next millennia, wilderness, like that of the northern British Columbia coast, is both an ecological and psychological anchor.

Roderick Frazier Nash, Professor Emeritus, University of California Santa Barbara, is an envirnomental historian. His works include the well known, Wilderness and the American Mind.

(For more information about Spirit Bear sources, please see the Appendix.)

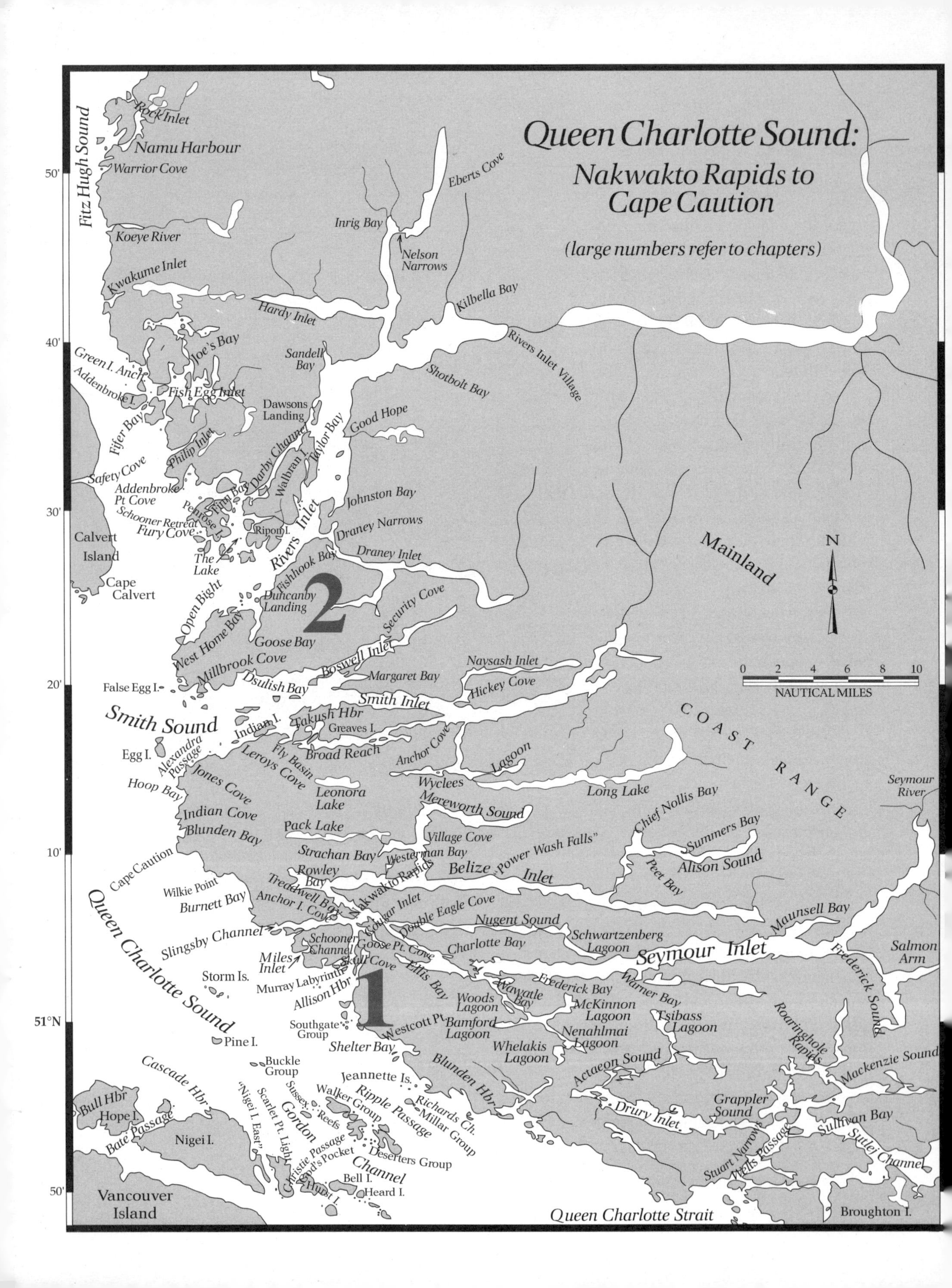

Queen Charlotte Sound:
Nakwakto Rapids to Cape Caution
(large numbers refer to chapters)
Rock Inlet
Namu Harbour
Warrior Cove
Fitz Hugh Sound
Eberts Cove
Inrig Bay
Nelson Narrows
Koeye River
Kwakume Inlet
Hardy Inlet
Kilbella Bay
Rivers Inlet Village
Joe's Bay
Green I. Anch.
Addenbroke I.
Fish Egg Inlet
Sandell Bay
Shotbolt Bay
Dawsons Landing
Good Hope
Fifer Bay
Philip Inlet
Darby Channel
Taylor Bay
Walbran I.
Safety Cove
Addenbroke Pt Cove
Penrose I.
Finn Bay
Johnston Bay
Schooner Retreat
Fury Cove
Ripon I.
Rivers Inlet
Draney Narrows
Draney Inlet
Calvert Island
The Lake
Fishhook Bay
Cape Calvert
Open Bight
Duncanby Landing
2
Security Cove
Mainland
N
West Home Bay
Goose Bay
Boswell Inlet
Naysash Inlet
Millbrook Cove
Margaret Bay
Hickey Cove
False Egg I.
Dsulish Bay
Smith Inlet
0 2 4 6 8 10
NAUTICAL MILES
Smith Sound
Takush Hbr
Indian I.
Greaves I.
COAST RANGE
Egg I.
Alexandra Passage
Fly Basin
Broad Reach
Anchor Cove
Lagoon
Leroys Cove
Jones Cove
Hoop Bay
Leonora Lake
Wyclees
Long Lake
Seymour River
Chief Nollis Bay
Mereworth Sound
Indian Cove
Blunden Bay
Pack Lake
Village Cove
Summers Bay
Cape Caution
Strachan Bay
Westerman Bay
"Power Wash Falls"
Alison Sound
Rowley Bay
Nakwakto Rapids
Belize Inlet
Peet Bay
Wilkie Point
Treadwell Bay
Burnett Bay
Anchor I. Cove
Cougar Inlet
Double Eagle Cove
Maunsell Bay
Queen Charlotte Sound
Slingsby Channel
Nugent Sound
Schooner Channel
Goose Pt. Cove
Charlotte Bay
Schwartzenberg Lagoon
Seymour Inlet
Salmon Arm
Miles Inlet
Skull Cove
Ellis Bay
Frederick Sound
Storm Is.
Murray Labyrinth
Frederick Bay
Warner Bay
Allison Hbr
1
Woods Lagoon
Wawatle Bay
McKinnon Lagoon
Tsibass Lagoon
Roaringhole Rapids
51°N
Southgate Group
Westcott Pt.
Bamford Lagoon
Nenahlmai Lagoon
Pine I.
Shelter Bay
Whelakis Lagoon
Actaeon Sound
Mackenzie Sound
Buckle Group
Cascade Hbr
Blunden Hbr
Jeannette Is.
Bull Hbr
Hope I.
"Nigei I. East"
Scarlet Pt. Light
Sussex Reefs
Walker Group
Ripple Passage
Richards Ch.
Millar Group
Drury Inlet
Grappler Sound
Sullivan Bay
Bate Passage
Nigei I.
Gordon Channel
Christie Passage
God's Pocket
Deserters Group
Stuart Narrows
Wells Passage
Sutlej Channel
Bell I.
Heard I.
Hurst I.
Vancouver Island
Queen Charlotte Strait
Broughton I.
50'
40'
30'
20'
10'

1

Queen Charlotte Sound: Nakwakto Rapids to Cape Caution

The area between Wells Passage and Cape Caution, some of the most fascinating and little known waters of British Columbia, is often ignored by northbound cruising boats that want to cross Queen Charlotte Sound as quickly as possible. However little by little, adventurous boaters are beginning to discover the beautiful fjords that lie behind swift Nakwakto Rapids in Seymour and Belize inlets, as well as the fantastic fishing grounds or remote, quiet lagoons in Smith Sound, Rivers and Fish Egg inlets. Some boaters have also discovered that, in addition to being destinations in themselves, these inlets offer sheltered steppingstones to Fitz Hugh Sound that break up the "dreaded crossing."

For years, the standard northbound route along the Inside Passage followed the eastern shore of Vancouver Island to its very tip; Port Hardy was the traditional last stop for provisioning and fueling, with God's Pocket or Bull Harbour the jumping-off sites for an early morning crossing of Queen Charlotte Sound. For powerboats, this was the shortest distance to the lee of Calvert Island in Fitz Hugh Sound; for sailboats it was just a close-hauled reach. Because so many boats took the standard route, the area between Wells Passage and Cape Caution remained one of the last on the coast to be explored and charted.

These days, greater numbers of cruising boats leave Port McNeill and head for Blunden Harbour; or they use the Broughton archipelago for shelter as far as Wells Passage, then Blunden Harbour, Miles Inlet, and Fury Cove as steppingstones to Cape Caution and Fitz Hugh Sound.

With the new charts available, you can now safely expand your cruising itineraries to include the seldom-visited waters east and north of Egg Island along the mainland shore of British Columbia, well beyond the northern tip of Vancouver Island.

Combing the shores of Blunden Harbour

Blunden Harbour

Chart 3548 metric (inset); entrance: 50°54.07′ N, 126°16.00′ W; anchor: 50°54.42′ N, 127°17.37′ W (NAD 83)

> *Blunden Harbour, entered between Shelf Head and Edgell Point, is separated into two arms by the Augustine Islands which are connected to one another and joined to the north shore by a drying mud flat on which there are numerous boulders. An abandoned Indian village is on the north shore, NW of Augustine Islands. A narrow channel, suitable for small craft, lies to the west and north of these islands [Jula Island and Frost Islands] and leads to rapids at the entrance to Bradley Lagoon. This rapids can only be passed at HW slack. Anchorage in the outer part of Blunden Harbour can be obtained south of the north Augustine Island in a depth of about 13 m (43 ft), mud bottom. In the inner part a good anchorage is SW of Moore Rock in 6 m (20 ft), mud bottom. Both anchorages afford good shelter. If proceeding to the inner anchorage care must be taken to avoid the drying reefs and rock with less than 2 m (6 ft) over it extending south from Augustine Islands and the drying reef close north of Bartlett Point.* (p. 258, SD, Vol. 1)

Blunden Harbour, a wonderful, well-sheltered anchorage, is a favorite of cruising boats that follow the mainland coast. Upon entering, follow a midchannel route. Although the bay is shallow, holding is good.

A thriving native culture once existed in this area and, in addition to a lengthy midden along the beach, you can find giant logs on shore, the remains of an old longhouse.

You can visit the narrow entrance to Brady Lagoon by dinghy. Slack water at the rapids lasts for just a short time before reverting to rapids and a waterfall once again, and turning room is restricted.

Anchor in 1½ fathoms, mud bottom with very good holding.

Marsh Bay

Chart 3548 metric; position: 50°55.35′ N, 127°22.00′ W (NAD 83)

> *Marsh Bay, 1.5 miles NW of the Browning Islands, does not afford anchorage as it is exposed SE and encumbered with drying rocks on its NE side.* (p. 258, SD, Vol. 1)

Marsh Bay, tucked in behind the islet east of Stuart Point, appears to offer protection from prevailing westerlies and can be useful as a lunch stop.

Jeannette Islands

Charts 3548 metric, 3574; south entrance: 50°55.32′ N, 127°24.04′ W; anchor: 50°55.72′ N, 127°24.24′ W (NAD 83)

> *Jeannette Islands are two thickly wooded islands. Anchorage for small craft can be obtained in the bay between Robertson Island and Leading Hill. Reefs lie in its approach and the anchorage is foul in places; local knowledge is necessary.* (p. 260, SD, Vol. 1)

Jeannette Islands are well-placed for a temporary stop but not recommended for overnight anchorage since they receive chop from prevailing northwest

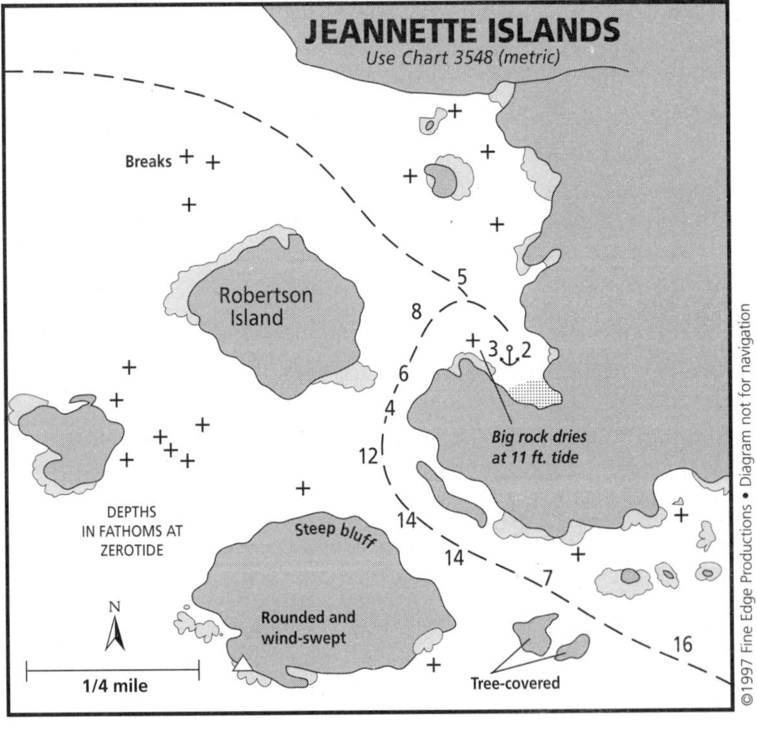

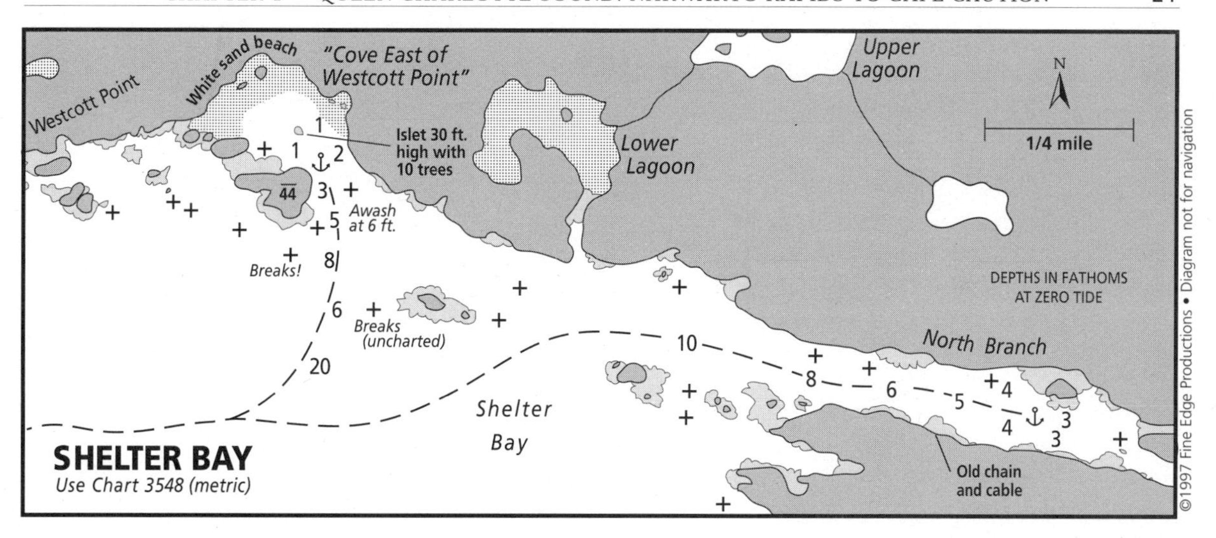

winds. Avoid the large drying rock off the cove point, and favor the north wall for a less rocky bottom. We have found Jeannette Islands calm and comfortable in moderate southerly winds.

Anchor in 3 fathoms over a mixed bottom with fair holding.

Wallace Islands

Chart 3548 metric; entrance:
50°57.44′ N, 127°27.57′ W; anchor:
50°57.56′ N, 127°27.37′ W (NAD 83)

At the Wallace Islands, you can find temporary relief from northwest chop in a small nook on the east side of island (47) and south side of island (70). The nook is partially protected by a kelp bed; however, surge exists. Enter by going north of the unnumbered island, staying close to it, and avoiding the rocks near island (47).

The bottom, about 5 fathoms deep, is rocky with poor holding so we use this as a lunch stop only.

Shelter Bay North

Chart 3548 metric; entrance:
50°58.21′ N, 127°26.73′ W; anchor:
50°58.08′ N, 127°25.33′ W (NAD 83)

> *Shelter Bay...is entered between Wallace Islands and Westcott Point.... In its most sheltered parts the bay is encumbered with rocks and should only be used by those with local knowledge.*
> (p. 260, SD, Vol. 1)

The north branch of Shelter Bay offers good protection in almost all weather and excellent shelter from southerly storm winds. The northwest swell is greatly diminished by the nearly landlocked entrance. The lack of driftwood indicates that the bay is not greatly affected by storms, and the lower branches of the trees are cut evenly along the high tide line, suggesting a lack of chop or swell. Shelter Bay's north branch is strategically located halfway between Blunden Harbour and Miles Inlet, the two main anchorages for cruising boats along this part of the coast.

We have found good anchoring a quarter mile from the head of the bay, on a line from the rock on the south shore to the tree-covered island on the north shore.

Contrary to *Sailing Directions*, we found the bay easy to enter; the fairway to the north branch is a flat 10 fathoms with no sign of rocks except along shore. We recommend this as an overnight anchorage if you need one in the area. The biggest drawback is that, deep in the bay, you can't see or guess conditions outside.

Anchor in 4 fathoms over a soft mud and clay bottom with good holding.

"Cove East of Westcott Point"

Chart 3548 metric; entrance:
50°58.25′ N, 127°27.30′ W; anchor:
50°58.52′ N, 127°27.27′ W (NAD 83)

The small, scenic cove east of Westcott Point makes a great lunch stop or an overnighter in prevailing northwest conditions. We enjoy its lovely sand beach and lack of swell or chop. From here, you can easily determine outside conditions by hiking over the spit for a view.

The entrance to Cove East of Westcott Point lies between two rocks across which swells occasionally break. The uncharted southern rock is particularly dangerous. Anchor on a line between the small 30-foot high islet with ten trees on it and island (44) to the south. Avoid the rock on the east side of the cove, which dries on a 6-foot tide.

Anchor in 2 fathoms over a sand bottom with good holding.

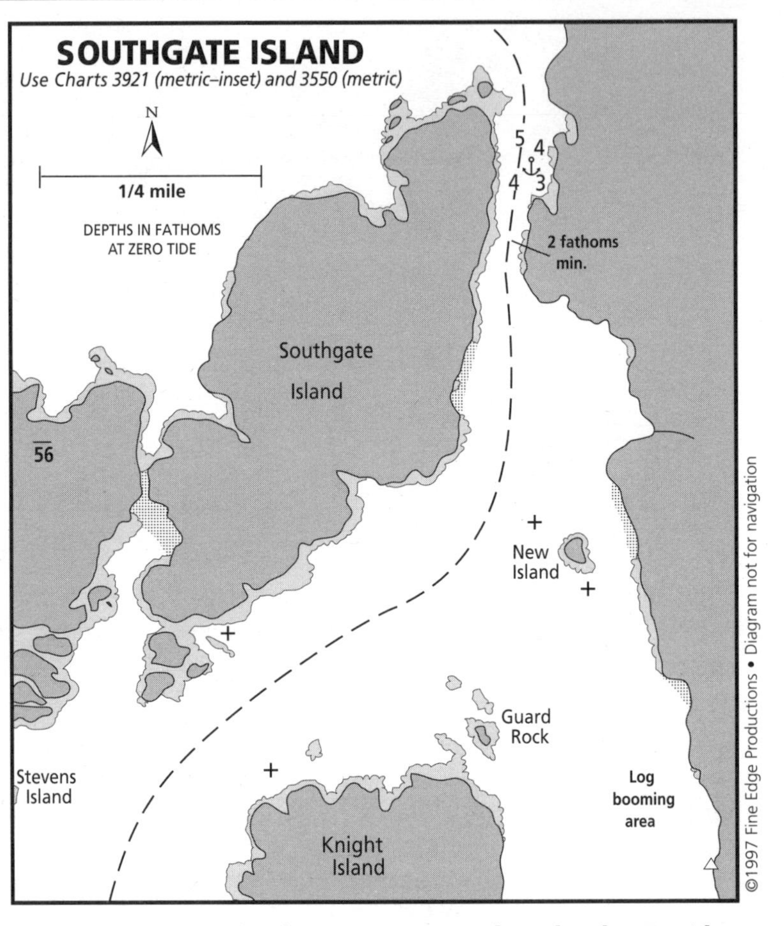

Southgate Island

Chart 3921 metric (inset)
or 3551; south entrance:
51°00.15′ N, 127°32.25′ W; anchor:
51°00.94′ N, 127°31.37′ W (NAD 83)

> *Knight Island and Southgate Island are the two largest islands in Southgate Group. The passage between Knight Island and Arm Islands to the SE is encumbered with islets and rocks and only suitable for small craft; local knowledge is required. Anchorage can be obtained between Knight Island and the mainland; it is completely sheltered but suitable only for small vessels owing to dangers within the entrance. The best position in which to anchor is with Guard Rock bearing 250°, distant 0.1 mile, in 14 fathoms (26 m), mud and sand.* (p. 264, SD, Vol. 1)

Southgate Island offers a "flat-water" shortcut of sorts for boats heading to Allison Harbour. It can also be used in fair weather as a lunch stop or an overnighter since it is near Queen Charlotte Strait. Sheltered anchorage can be found on either side of the narrows, but the north end is our preference.

The area east of Knight Island is a log storage area for the operations inside Nakwakto Rapids.

Anchor in 3 fathoms over a mixed bottom of unrecorded holding power.

Allison Harbour

Chart 3921 metric; entrance:
51°02.15′ N, 127°31.23′ W; anchor head of bay:
51°03.47′ N, 127°30.38′ W; anchor east cove:
51°02.94′ N, 127°30.50′ W (NAD 83)

> *Allison Harbour . . . extends nearly 2 miles NNE. Anchorage with mud bottom can be obtained in 8 fathoms (15 m) just north of the former settlement, or in 7 fathoms (13 m) about 0.1 mile north of the 8 foot (2.4 m) drying rock, or in 4 fathoms (7 m) near the head of the Harbour.* (p. 264, SD, Vol. 1)

Allison Harbour, a long north-south inlet, provides good shelter in most weather. The entrances to Allison Harbour and Schooner Channel are encumbered with rocks and reefs offshore, and in

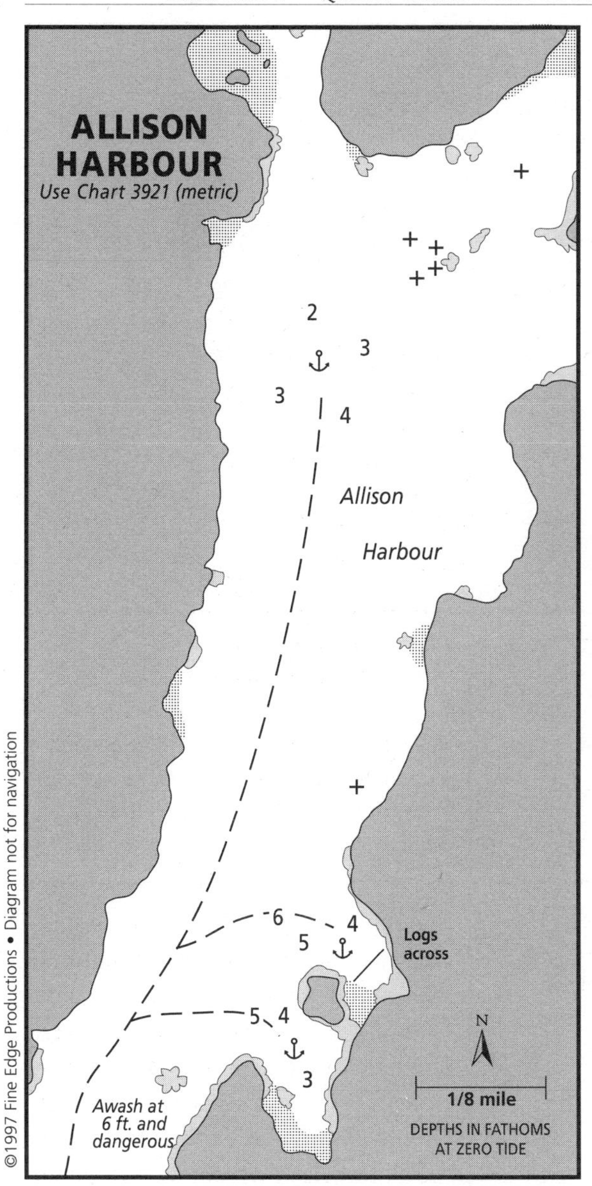

foul weather or limited visibility entering can be risky.

Halfway into the harbor there's a dangerous rock awash on a 6-foot tide which you can easily avoid by staying to the west. In stable weather, anchor at the head of the bay favoring the west side. In unsettled weather, anchor in one of the two small coves, and set your anchor well—it's sometimes hard to get a good hold on the clay bottom.

Anchor at the head of the bay in 3 to 4 fathoms over clay and mud with good holding.

Anchor in the east cove in 3 to 4 fathoms over a soft mud bottom with poor-to-fair holding.

Murray Labyrinth

Chart 3921 metric; entrance:
51°02.59′ N, 127°32.38′ W; anchor:
51°02.81′ N, 127°31.88′ W (NAD 83)

Murray Labyrinth, NE of Deloraine Islands, consists of many islands and islets. The passage between Deloraine Islands and Murray Labyrinth and the passage along the north side of Murray Labyrinth, are suitable for small craft. (p. 264, SD, Vol. 1)

Murray Labyrinth is truly a maze of islands, islets and rocks, well sheltered in a pristine setting. The new large-scale Chart 3921 is helpful for exploring the area and for avoiding the shoals and reefs.

There's a protected spot right in the center of Murray Labyrinth where you can anchor and make it your base from which to explore the area by dinghy or kayak. Be skeptical of the chart, however, since the bottom is more irregular than indicated on the chart, and not all the hazards are noted.

Anchor in 1.5 fathoms over soft bottom with good holding.

Skull Cove

Chart 3921 metric; entrance:
51°02.95′ N, 127°33.30′ W; anchor (north):
51°03.23′ N, 127°33.68′ W (NAD 83)

Skull Cove, NW of Deloraine Islands, affords good shelter for small craft; it is entered NE of the island lying in the entrance. (p. 264, SD, Vol. 1)

Skull Cove, just west of Murray Labyrinth, is another favorite well-sheltered anchorage that makes a good base camp for exploring the nearby island complex. Small boats can anchor in many places in Skull Cove since the water is quite shallow. Midden Hill, on the east side of the bay, composed of a large heap of shells, indicates that this was an important harvesting area. As in the case of Murray Labyrinth, the bottom is somewhat irregular and not all hazards are shown on the chart. Particularly avoid the rock in the center, just west of Ten Tree Islet.

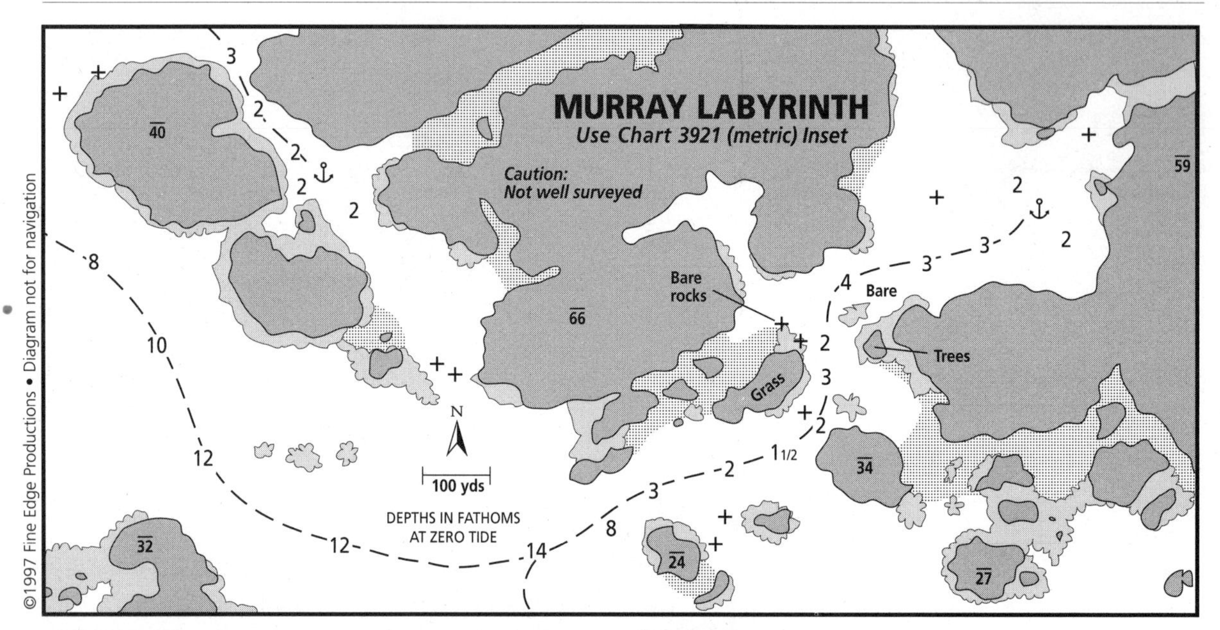

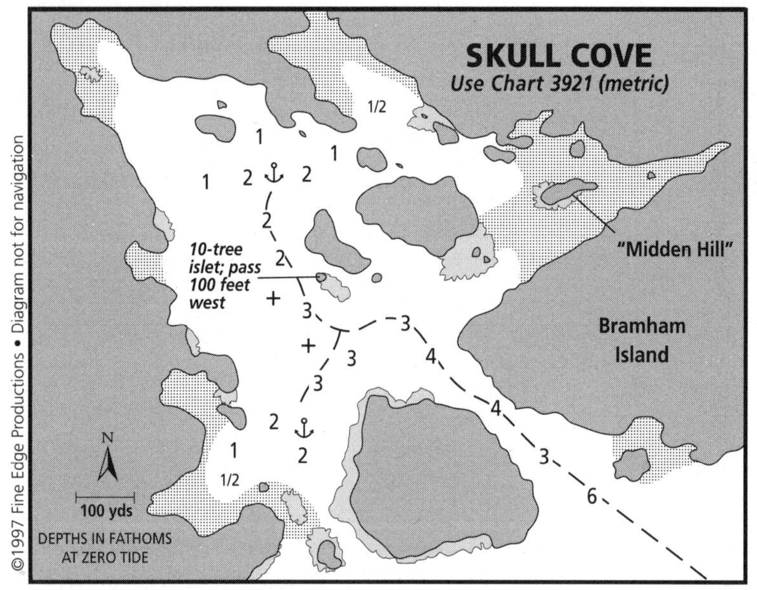

Anchor in 1 to 2 fathoms over a mud and sand bottom with good holding.

Schooner Channel

Chart 3921 metric; south entrance: 51°02.25′ N, 127°31.95′ W; north entrance: 51°05.08′ N, 127°31.24′ W (NAD 83)

Schooner Channel, entered from the south between Ray Island and the dangers off the south extremity of Murray Labyrinth, leads north into the east end of Slingsby Channel. The fairway through Schooner Channel is narrow with several dangers and is reduced to 200 feet (61 m) wide west of a reef and some islets which lie 1.8 miles north of Ray Island. The channel should not be attempted without local knowledge. Tidal streams through Schooner Channel attain 5 kn on the flood and 6 kn on the ebb. (p. 264, SD, Vol. 1)

Schooner Channel is a 3-mile-long, narrow channel between Bramham Island and Allison Harbour. To navigate it safely requires constant vigilance. Although we have been able to transit Schooner Channel and Nakwakto Rapids twice in fog under radar and GPS, we don't recommend it; the current can easily set you on the rocks or on shore, and log tows may be encountered on the turn to ebb.

Logging tugs frequently use Schooner Channel to tow log booms out of Seymour Inlet to the storage area at Southgate Island. They have limited maneuverability when the current is flowing, so stay clear!

Tiny Goose Point Cove on the east shore, 0.8 mile south of the point, can be used as an anchorage. Avoid two uncharted rocks a quarter-mile south of Goose Point close to the west shore.

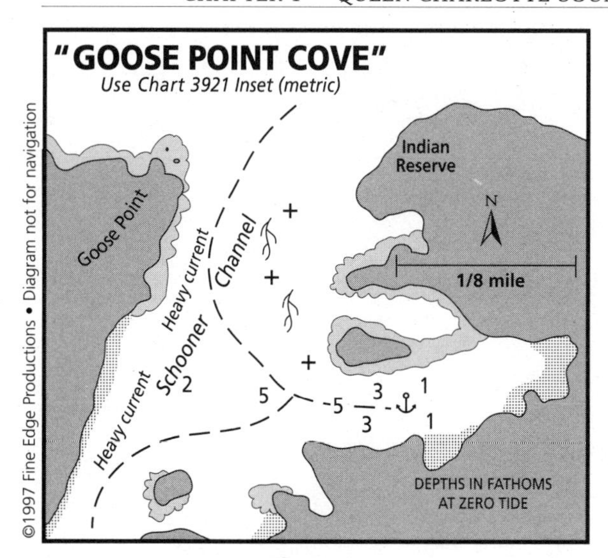

"Goose Point Cove"

Chart 3921 metric; anchor:
51°04.92′ N, 127°30.58′ W (NAD 83)

> *Anchorage for small craft is reported to be excellent in the bay at the NE end of the channel, SE of Goose Point.* (p. 264, SD, Vol. 1)

We call the small cove described above Goose Point Cove. Well protected from all weather, it is removed from the heavy currents that flow outside. It is a good place to stay overnight and catch slack water if you plan to visit Nakwakto Rapids or Seymour Inlet.

There is room for two boats to anchor in mid-channel south of the islet just before the drying shoal to the east. You can leave your boat in Goose Point Cove if you want to explore Nakwakto Rapids by high-speed inflatable.

Anchor in 1 to 2 fathoms over a mud bottom with good holding. Consider using a second anchor if there are other boats in the cove.

Cougar Inlet

Chart 3921 metric; entrance:
51°05.18′ N, 127°30.56′ W (NAD 83)

> *Cougar Inlet, SE of Butress Island, has a narrow entrance and is suitable only for small craft.* (p. 264, SD, Vol. 1)

The entrance to Cougar Inlet is the closest anchor site to Nakwakto Rapids, and over the years many

Cougar Inlet, boat names on outer wall

vessels have painted their names on the vertical wall of the north shore just east of Barrow Point. Boats that stay here get out of the current and enjoy the relative calm compared to water and foam surging past outside.

Small boats can anchor in shallower water closer to the narrows or deep inside the inlet for full protection with no current. Larger vessels can anchor in 12 fathoms and use a stern tie to the steep-to vertical wall (note the piton driven into one of the cracks).

Minimum fairway depth in Cougar narrows is about 2 feet at zero tide, with current of about 3 knots; width is about 45 feet. The current changes to flood about the time of high water at Alert Bay, and 2 hours before slack at Nakwakto Rapids. Prior reconnoitering is advisable in order to avoid uncharted rocks. At the west entrance, favor the south shore, staying within about 15 feet of one of the rocks to avoid kelp on the north shore. In the center of the narrows there is a dangerous rock on the north shore which can be avoided by favoring the south shore.

"Chappell Cove"

Chart 3921 metric; anchor (north of spit):
51°04.68′ N, 127°29.33′ W; anchor (head of inlet): 51°04.80′ N, 127°28.53′ W (NAD 83)

Anchorage can be taken 0.4 mile inside Cougar Inlet on the north shore, just above a spit that extends out from shore. We call this Chappell Cove in honor of John Chappell, who in his

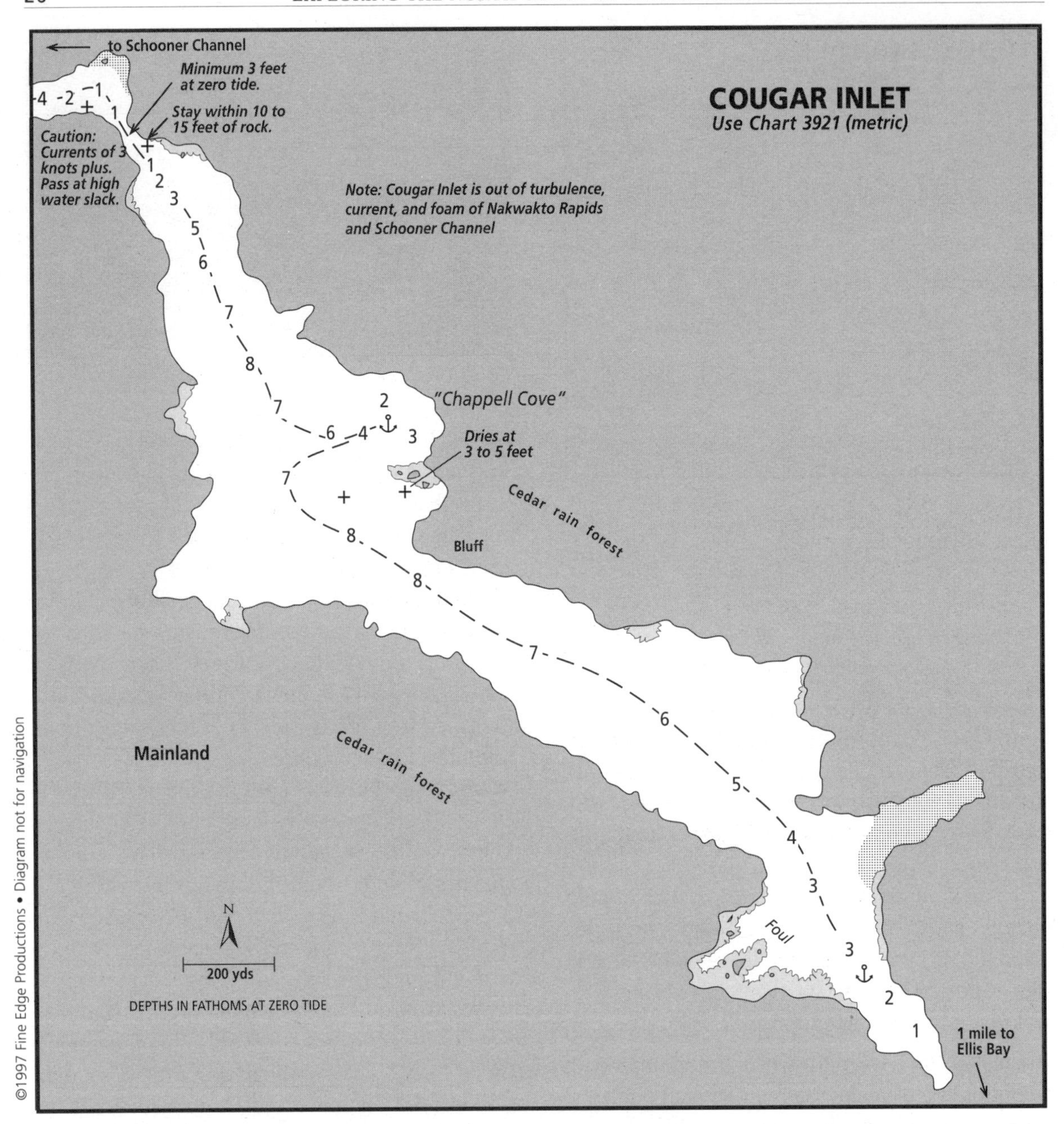

wonderful book, *Cruising Beyond Desolation Sound,* speculated that this inlet might be an interesting place to explore. If his sailboat had had a shallower draft, he, too, might have been able to enjoy the wild nature of Cougar Inlet. Here you are surrounded by old-growth rain forest in which time stands still and the quiet is overpowering.

Anchor (north of spit) in 4 fathoms, soft mud and sand with good holding.

Anchor (head of inlet) in 3 fathoms, soft mud and sand with good holding.

Nakwakto Rapids

Chart 3921 metric; position (Turret Rock): 51°05.79′ N, 127°30.18′ W; north entrance: 51°06.00′ N, 127°30.20′ W (NAD 83)

Nakwakto Rapids . . . connects Slingsby and Schooner Channels to Seymour Inlet. Turret Rock, known locally as Tremble Island, lies in the middle of the rapids and has dangerous reefs extending up to 0.1 mile SSW of it. Turret Rock can be passed on either side but the west channel is preferred. Caution. Mariners are strongly advised to navigate Nakwakto Rapids only at slack water for at no other time is it possible to navigate this rapids safely. Tidal streams in Nakwakto Rapids attain a maximum 14 kn on the flood and 16 kn on the ebb, one of the highest rates in the world, their main strength impinging on Turret Rock. The duration of slack is about 6 minutes. Daily predictions for the times of slack water, and the times and rates of maximum flood and ebb streams, are tabulated for current station Nakwakto Rapids in the Tide Tables, Volume 6. (pp. 264, 266, SD, Vol. 1)

Nakwakto Rapids, one of the world's fastest rapids, should set your adrenaline pumping, and if the descriptions about the rapids don't do it, check out the pictures in *Sailing Directions*, page 265. *Caution*: Extremely hazardous eddies and turbulence are encountered in Nakwakto Rapids when the current exceeds more than a few knots. During neap tides and near slack water, Nakwakto Rapids is not difficult to cross at either high or low water. This opens up a cruising world seldom visited except by a few intrepid loggers and fishermen. On spring tides a large area of foam obscures much of the rapids, and transit must be closely timed to slack water. In his book, *Secrets of Cruising, . . . The Undiscovered Inlets,* Anderson writes that the preferred route through the rapids leads west of Tremble Island. However, we generally approach the rapids from the south and find the wider and slightly more shallow route east of Tremble Island to be perfectly acceptable.

We stumbled across another strategy to enjoy the incredible sight of the rapids in full ebb. From Treadwell Bay or Goose Point Cove, with a dependable high-speed inflatable, you can land on a rock shelf on the northwest corner of island (49) (Indian Reserve on the west side), 0.18 mile due west of Turret Island. Tie your boat well and follow the primitive trail southeast across the top part of the island to a 10-foot-square viewing platform 100 feet above the seething rapids! As you approach the haul-out rock, be careful not to get sucked into the extremely narrow 4-foot-wide slot at the north end of the island, where water rushes through, creating waterfalls of 3 feet or more in either direction!

Dive boat waiting for just the right moment, Nakwakto Rapids

Note the light boards and signs with the names of ships nailed to the trees on Turret Island—including that of *Baidarka!*

Seymour Inlet

Chart 3552 metric

Seymour Inlet, one of the major fjords of the British Columbia coast, cuts deep into the mainland mountains. It extends from Lassiter Bay, northwest of Nakwakto Rapids, 12 miles southeast to Harriet Point where it turns east for 21 miles to Eclipse Narrows, then north for another 13 miles to its head at the outlet of Seymour River, a total of 42 miles.

Eclipse Narrows marks the beginning of Frederick Sound, a deep and scenic fjord that cuts 7 miles to the southeast. For several miles Seymour Narrows has depths in excess of 2,000 feet, particularly impressive because the narrows is a mile wide or less.

The tidal range in Seymour Inlet is seldom more than 4 feet, or less than one-third that found west of Nakwatko Rapids. The waters although generally calm are subject to occasional up- or

Baidarka's sign on Tremble Island, Nakwakto

downslope williwaws, especially in winter. The water is a muskeg brown with limited underwater visibility, particularly in the nearly stagnant lagoons. Tidal currents are generally weak except at a few narrows.

We describe Seymour Inlet from the northwest to the southeast before venturing into the other inlets.

Lassiter Bay

Chart 3552 metric (inset); position:
51°08.60′ N, 127°36.60′ W (NAD 27)

> *Lassiter Bay, NW of Helm Island, has a mud bottom and forms the NW end of Seymour Inlet. Jezzard Rock lies 0.5 mile NW of Helm Island and about 0.1 mile off the south shore of the bay.* (p. 267, SD, Vol. 1)

Lassiter Bay, immediately north of Rowley Bay, appears to be a collection point for all logs,

Planning tomorrow's route

stumps, and trees that drift down Belize and Seymour Inlets and are blown ashore by southeast storm winds. Bleached silver logs lie piled deep, one on top of another, all around the head of Lassiter Bay. We did not find suitable anchorage here; however, temporary anchorage can be taken off the wood piles as desired.

Rowley Bay

Chart 3552 metric (inset); anchor:
51°07.65′ N, 127°36.55′ W (NAD 27)

> *Rowley Bay, entered south of Helm Island, has a mud bottom.* (p. 267, SD, Vol. 1)

Rowley Bay, at the northwest corner of Seymour Inlet, offers protection from all but easterly winds. The head of the bay widens slightly and has a 2- to 4-fathom bottom. The shore at the head contains a number of drift logs, and isolated rocks lie under water along both the north and south shores.

There is swinging room for one small boat, or two to three boats using stern ties. Larger boats can anchor farther east in deeper water with more swinging room.

Anchor in 2 to 4 fathoms over a mixed bottom of sand and mud; fair-to-good holding.

"King Bay"

Chart 3552 metric; position:
51°06.71′ N, 127°31.02′ W (NAD 27)

One mile west of Nakwakto Narrows on the north

shore there is a small indentation known locally as King Bay. In season, a resort with float houses completely fills the head of the bay. You can anchor in the middle of the bay in about 5 fathoms with good protection from all but southwest winds. Avoid the charted rock on the west side of entrance.

Anchor in 5 fathoms over an unrecorded bottom.

Harvell Islet Cove

Chart 3921 metric (inset) for vicinity of Nakwakto Rapids; Chart 3552 metric; anchor (north of Harvell Islet and the reefs): 51°06.19′ N, 127°29.08′ W (NAD 83)

> *Above-water, drying and sunken rocks lie about 0.1 mile north of Harvell Islet and NE of Holmes Islets. A rock with 6.2 m (20 ft) over it lies 0.1 mile SSE of Harvell Islet and a rock with 2.1 m (7 ft) over it lies about 0.1 mile west of Holmes Islets. The fairway lies to the south of Harvell Islet and Holmes Islets.* (p. 266, SD, Vol. 1)

Anchorage can be taken to the northeast of Nakwakto Rapids in the small cove 0.3 mile north of Harvell Islet; it's a good place to wait for slack water and watch the rapids.

Anchor (north of Harvell Islet and the reefs) in 2 fathoms over a sand and mud bottom with good holding

"Double Eagle Cove"

Chart 3552 metric; anchor: 51°03.94′ N, 127°25.20′ W (NAD 27)

Double Eagle Cove on the west shore, 2 miles west of Charlotte Bay, is a convenient lunch stop protected by several islets. You may have the good fortune to observe the eagles that sometimes use this spot as a strategically-located lookout with good visibility up and down the inlet.

Anchor in about $1\frac{1}{2}$ fathoms with a gravel bottom and some kelp with fair holding.

Charlotte Bay

Chart 3552 metric; anchor: 51°03.55′ N, 127°22.40′ W (NAD 27)

> *Charlotte Bay is entered south of a group of islands that front its north entrance point. A rock, with 0.4 m (1 ft) over it, lies close off the north shore, east of the islands. A drying flat with boulders forms the head of the bay. Anchorage for small vessels can be obtained in Charlotte Bay in 8 m (26 ft), mud.* (p. 266, SD, Vol. 1)

Charlotte Bay is out of most of the east wind; however, the many drift logs on shore indicate that strong westerlies blow here.

Anchor in 4 to 6 fathoms over sand and gravel bottom with fair holding.

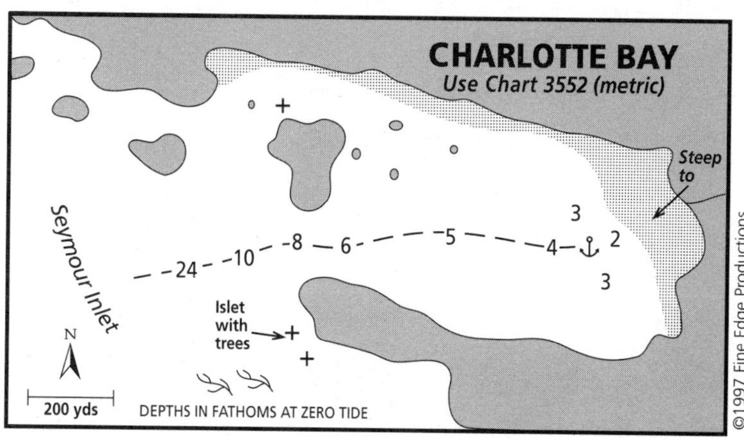

Ellis Bay

Chart 3552
metric; entrance:
51°03.08′ N,
127°24.22′ W; anchor:
51°02.92′ N,
127°25.05′ W
(NAD 27)

Ellis Bay, SW of Charlotte Bay, has several islands and drying rocks in its approach. Its narrow entrance with numerous drying rocks has a twisting

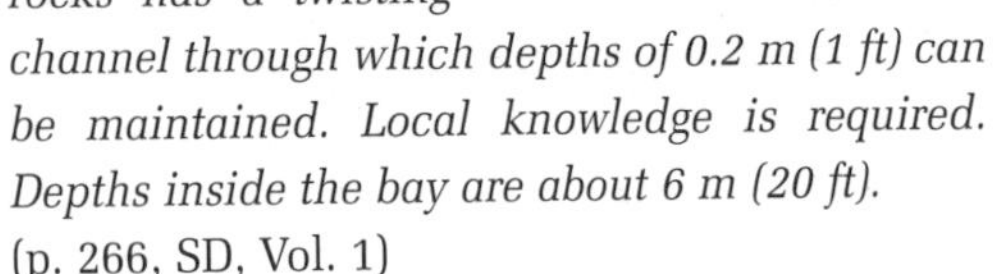

channel through which depths of 0.2 m (1 ft) can be maintained. Local knowledge is required. Depths inside the bay are about 6 m (20 ft).
(p. 266, SD, Vol. 1)

Ellis Bay is a good introduction to the fascinating lagoons that lie along the south shore of Seymour Inlet. Extra caution or prior reconnoitering by dinghy is advised in these shallow, rocky waters. Very good protection from all weather may be obtained in Ellis Bay on the south shore just west of the narrows. The upper end of Ellis Bay is less than a mile away from the bitter end of Cougar Inlet.

Dixon Ann II *at anchor, Westerman Bay*

Anchor in 2 fathoms over a soft mud bottom with isolated rocks; fair-to-good holding.

Wawatle Bay

Chart 3552
metric; narrows:
51°02.06′ N,
127°18.04′ W;
anchor: 51°02.04′ N,
127°16.65′ W
(NAD 27)

Wawatle Bay, entered south of Harriet Point, has depths of about 50 m (164 ft) with a mud bottom. A rock awash lies close off the north shore, about 0.5 mile inside its entrance.
(p. 266, SD, Vol. 1)

Wawatle Bay, good shelter in southerly or downslope weather, makes a good base for larger boats to explore, by dinghy or kayak, the wonderful lagoons to the southeast.

A shoal area extends out into midchannel midway down the bay and boats should favor the south shore, perhaps 200 feet off, at this point. The water in Wawatle Bay is brackish (muskeg brown)

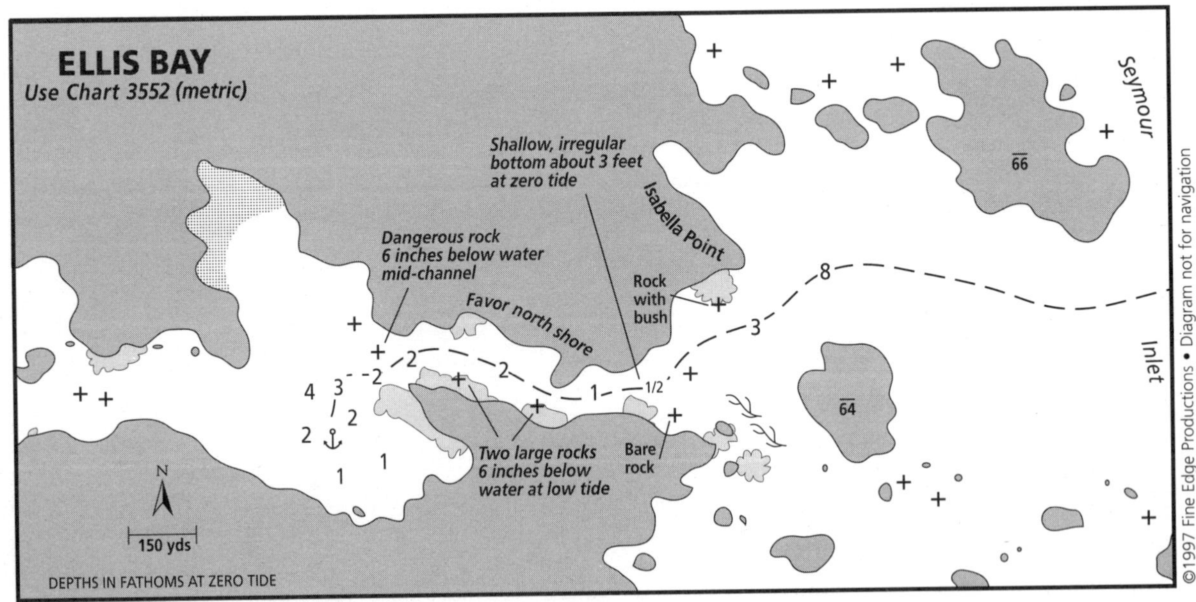

limiting visibility to 2 to 3 feet. Anchor directly off creek outlet and south of the islet with trees and a rock that extends about 60 feet to the west.

Anchor in 5 fathoms over a mud bottom with good holding.

Frederick Bay

Chart 3552 metric; position:
51°02.20′ N, 127°14.82′ W (NAD 27)

> *Frederick Bay, entered between Henry Point and Nea Point, is too deep for anchorage. A small cove on its west side has depths of about 30 m (98 ft) and offers shelter for small craft.*
> (p. 266, SD, Vol. 1)

Frederick Bay has a small bay on its west shore that offers shelter in shallow water. Since swinging room is limited, a stern tie to shore is a good idea.

Anchor in 4 to 6 fathoms over an unrecorded bottom.

Warner Bay

Chart 3552 metric; entrance:
51°02.78′ N, 127°05.50′ W (NAD 27)

> *Warner Bay, 5 miles east of Frederick Bay, has a low islet and some drying rocks close off its east entrance point. A rock that dries 1.2 m (4 ft) lies in the centre of the bay about 0.2 mile from its head. Booming grounds with a large shed and float are at the head of the bay and a wreck is on its east shore.* (p. 266, SD, Vol. 1)

Warner Bay is frequently used by loggers working Seymour Inlet, but good shelter can be found in shallow water near the head of the bay, avoiding whatever logging may be going on. From here, it is less than 2 airline miles to the head of Tsibass Lagoon in Actaeon Sound but a very long boat ride!

Anchor in about 8 fathoms over an unrecorded bottom.

Safe Cove

Chart 3552 metric; position:
51°05.00′ N, 126°55.00′ W (NAD 27)

> *Safe Cove, about 5 miles east of Stripe Bluff, can offer temporary anchorage to small vessels in depths of about 30 m (90 ft) within 0.1 mile of shore; outside this distance depths drop off steeply.* (p. 267, SD, Vol. 1)

Safe Cove, little more than a bight in the north side of Seymour Inlet, can be used as an anchorage in fair weather tucked in near shore. Jesus Pocket, just to the east, offers better protection from wind and chop for small boats.

Jesus Pocket

Chart 3552 metric; anchor:
51°05.03′ N, 126°53.77′ W (NAD 27)

> *Jesus Pocket is the local name for the small cove midway between Safe Cove and Maunsell Bay. The cove is entered to the east of the islet lying in its entrance. Anchorage for small vessels can be obtained in Jesus Pocket in 7 m (23 ft), sand.*
> (p. 267, SD, Vol. 1)

Jesus Pocket was probably named by someone who was thankful for finding good shelter in an

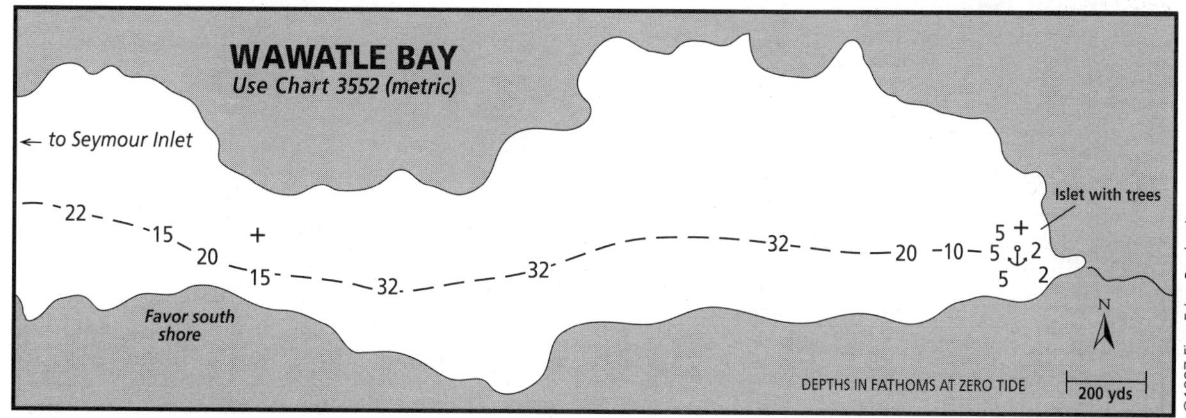

otherwise deep and steep fjord. It reminds us of the size and shape of Cathedral Point Cove in Burke Channel. There is room for just one or two boats and swinging room is limited.

Anchor in about 4 fathoms over an unrecorded bottom.

Towry Point West Cove

Chart 3552 metric; anchor:
51°03.71′ N, 126°54.19′ W (NAD 27)

> *Towry Point is a hook shaped point south of Jesus Pocket. The small cove west of the point has depths of 6 m (20 ft) in it and offers shelter for small craft.* (p. 267, SD, Vol. 1)

A small boat can find shelter from east winds squeezed in close to shore, 0.35 mile west of Towry Point in what we call Towry Point West Cove.

Towry Point East Cove

Chart 3552 metric; anchor:
51°03.71′ N, 126°53.74′ W (NAD 27)

> *The cove on the east side of the point has a treed islet near its head, close off its north shore. Depths south of the islet are about 5 m (16 ft); outside the islet depths drop off steeply.* (p. 267, SD, Vol. 1)

Towry Point East Cove is a more sizeable cove than the west cove and provides good protection in most stable weather.

Anchor in 5 to 10 fathoms over a mud bottom with good holding.

Maunsell Bay

Chart 3552 metric; entrance:
51°05.00′ N, 126°51.75′ W; anchor:
51°05.86′ N, 126°47.54′ W (NAD 27)

> *Maunsell Bay, entered between Dine Point and Martin Point, has a bottom of sand, mud and shells but is too deep for satisfactory anchorage. The inlet at its NE end has a narrow entrance with depths in excess of 20 m (66 ft). A conspicuous waterfall is near the south entrance point to the inlet.*
>
> *Anchorage for small vessels can be obtained near the head of the above-mentioned inlet in 24 m (79 ft), mud and gravel.* (p. 267, SD, Vol. 1)

The tiny inlet on the east end of Maunsell Bay offers welcome shelter for small boats, although it has limited swinging room. However its plus side is that any wind entering this well-hidden spot can only flow lengthwise in the inlet while you're tethered nicely into it.

Anchor in 12 fathoms over a mud and gravel bottom with good holding.

Eclipse Narrows

Chart 3552 metric (inset); entrance:
51°04.13′ N, 126°45.48′ W (NAD 27)

> *Eclipse Narrows . . . is about 90 m (295 ft) wide with a fairway depth of 11 m (36 ft). It is the entrance to Frederick Sound. An old log dump is 0.2 mile SW of its south entrance point. Tidal streams in Eclipse Narrows attain 5 kn. Secondary current station Eclipse Narrows, referenced on Nakwakto Rapids, is given in the Tide Tables, Volume 6.* (p. 267, SD, Vol. 1)

Eclipse Narrows is the stunning hole-in-the-wall where Seymour Inlet turns abruptly northeast to its head at Seymour River. Behind Eclipse Narrows there is another complete fjord system in which the narrows is simply the terminal moraine.

Frederick Sound

Chart 3552 metric (inset); entrance:
51°04.13′ N, 126°45.48′ W; anchor (basin)
50°59.27′ N, 126°44.48′ W (NAD 27)

> *Frederick Sound extends east and then south for about 5.5 miles from Eclipse Narrows. About 1 mile east of Eclipse Narrows the sound curves south and depths increase to greater than 200 m (656 ft). Several waterfalls and slide areas are on both sides of the sound. The head of the sound curves sharp west then opens into a basin with depths of 50 to 60 m (164 to 197 ft), mud bottom.* (p. 267, SD, Vol. 1)

Although Frederick Sound has seen the effects of loggers' saws, the views of the high coastal peaks are magnificent. You are a long way from anywhere here; however, the narrow end of Frederick Bay is only 1.5 air miles from Nepah Lagoon north of Sullivan Bay!

The western curve of Frederick Sound forms its own landlocked basin which, thankfully, shoals gradually to its head and offers very good protection from any weather.

Anchor (basin) in 10 fathoms over a mud bottom with good holding.

Salmon Arm

Chart 3552 metric (inset); entrance:
51°02.55′ N, 126°42.70′ W (NAD 27)

Salmon Arm, entered between Nose Point and Taaltz Point, extends about 2.5 miles from Frederick Sound and has waterfalls and slide areas on both sides. Depths gradually decrease up the arm and the bottom is mud. (p. 267, SD, Vol. 1)

Hugo Anderson reports good anchorage at the head of Salmon Arm in the northeast corner in about 10 fathoms. He experienced some uncomfortable chop here during upslope winds but considers this one of his and Rachel's favorite anchorages.

Seymour River

Chart 3552 metric (inset); position:
51°11.35′ N, 126°40.00′ W (NAD 27)

Seymour River flows into the head of Seymour Inlet across a steep-to drying flat composed of stones and boulders. A logging camp with extensive booming grounds is on the east side of the river entrance. (p. 267, SD, Vol. 1)

Hugo Anderson reports that he has anchored on the west side of the river outlet across from the large logging camp on the east shore. The bottom is steep-to and there is little shelter from upslope winds except what you can find behind the shallow point. He reports taking his dinghy 2 miles up the river in plenty of water and snags before encountering a 50-foot waterfall.

Nugent Sound

Chart 3552 metric; west entrance:
51°05.52′ N, 127°27.95′ W (NAD 27)

Nugent Sound, entered between Holmes Point and Nugent Point, extends 10.5 miles east from Seymour Inlet. (p. 266, SD, Vol. 1)

Time to reconnoiter

Nugent Sound, more of an inlet than a sound, is the first major indentation east of Nakwakto Rapids. Narrow and picturesque, it offers two coves for exploration.

"Holmes Point Cove"

Chart 3552 metric; anchor:
51°05.66′ N, 127°27.69′ W (NAD 27)

The first cove east of Holmes Point (IR), where there is an abandoned native village, has its access to shore blocked by a big drift logjam. The two small bights just east of Holmes Point are full of driftwood, their bottom rocky, and they are subject to current that comes down the sound. Unless you are in a dugout which can be pulled up onto shore, this is a marginal anchorage and should be used in calm weather only.

Anchor in 3 to 6 fathoms over a rocky bottom with poor holding.

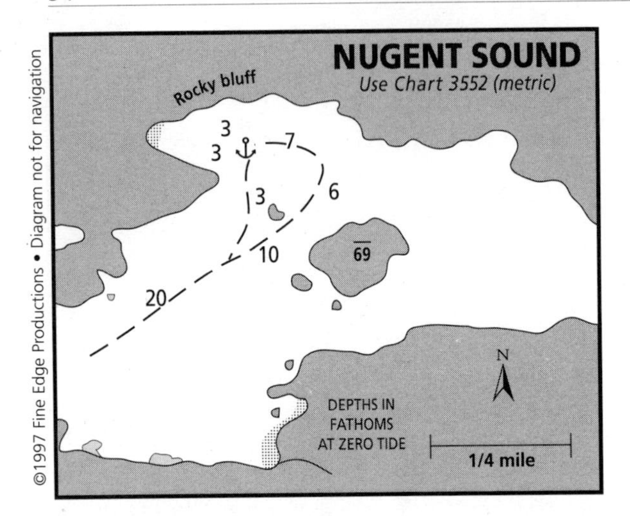

"Nugent Sound Cove"

Chart 3552 metric; anchor island (69):
51°05.56′ N, 127°23.28′ W (NAD 27)

> *Anchorage for small vessels can be obtained in the bay NW of the island in mid-channel 3 miles inside the entrance; depths are about 15 m (49 ft), sand. Anchorage can also be obtained in the bay at the head of Nugent Sound, on the north side, in a depth of about 25 m (82 ft), mud and sand.* (p. 266, SD, Vol. 1)

The second cove, 3 miles east of Holmes Point in Nugent Sound and northwest of island (69), is a better anchorage. This cove is perfectly calm when northwest winds blow on the outside, and it offers good protection from most winds. This cove and Westerman Bay in Belize Inlet are the better anchorages near Nakwakto Rapids.

The water is colored muskeg brown and tastes of a mixture of saltwater and fresh water. Summer water temperature hovers in the mid- to high 50s (F).

Notice an old steam boiler and a 4-foot steel gear on shore.

Anchor in 3 to 4 fathoms over a bottom of sand and small wood debris with good holding.

Schwartzenberg Lagoon

Chart 3552 metric; entrance:
51°05.00′ N, 127°11.75′ W (NAD 27)

> *Schwartzenberg Lagoon, at the head of Nugent Sound, has a very narrow entrance with depths of less than 1 m (3 ft) and several drying rocks. Inside depths range between 50 and 75 m (164 and 246 ft).* (p. 266, SD, Vol. 1)

We have not visited Schwartzenberg Lagoon, but it appears interesting despite some of the logging that's been going on in Nugent Sound for the last few years.

"Unnamed Inlet"

Chart 3552 metric; north entrance:
51°02.06′ N, 127°19.10′ W (NAD 27)

> *An unnamed inlet extends 2.5 miles SE from the south entrance point of Wawatle Bay and is separated from Seymour Inlet by Florence Range. . . . A narrows at the head of the unnamed inlet has depths of less than 1 m (3 ft) and several obstructions in it. It is not suitable for navigation. Tidal streams through the narrows are 6 kn on the ebb and 5.5 kn on the flood.* (p. 266, SD, Vol. 1)

This narrow channel, which we call Unnamed Inlet as does *Sailing Directions*, is a great place for serious exploring. While you are warned by *Sailing Directions* that the inlet is not suitable for navigation, we have found it to be a region that should seriously be considered by cruising boats that like a good challenge. Except for the sizeable logging operation which is clearcutting old-growth cedar, this area is pristine and primitive, a place that can become "spooky" when you're deep inside without reference to the outside world.

Just before the entrance to Woods Lagoon, the logging operation occupies the south shore. Beyond this point the Unnamed Inlet becomes narrower and shallow (3 to 4 fathoms). Boats can anchor here midchannel or nearer the constricted south narrows (in 4 fathoms in sticky mud) in order to reconnoiter the route ahead.

In the constricted south narrows of Unnamed Inlet, favor the north shore to avoid rocks awash that extend from the south shore and kelp that clogs the center of the channel. About 30 feet from the trees on the north shore we found a route 5 feet deep near low water.

Don't be surprised if the tides here and farther south are confusing and seem to reverse at will.

There appear to be strange tidal dynamics at work in this narrows and in Whelakis Lagoon suggesting that a kind of resonance or oscillation is present. Please share your observations with us.

Once you are past the constricted narrows, you arrive at what we call the Four Lagoon Intersection. Bamford, McKinnon, and Nenahlmai lagoons all offer good anchorage near their heads. Whelakis Lagoon, an offshoot of Nenahlmai Lagoon, is a wild place unto itself.

Woods Lagoon

Chart 3552 metric; entrance:
51°00.90′ N, 127°17.52′ W (NAD 27)

Woods Lagoon enters the south side of this [unnamed] inlet about 1.3 miles inside the entrance. The entrance to Woods Lagoon dries and has several boulders in it; inside depths are about 8 m (26 ft). (p. 266, SD, Vol. 1)

At last check, Woods Lagoon was a noisy place, its north side occupied by a logging operation.

Bamford Lagoon

Chart 3552 metric; entrance:
50°59.90′ N, 127°15.10′ W; anchor:
50°59.40′ N, 127°18.25′ W
(NAD 27)

Bamford Lagoon extends SW from it [above-mentioned narrows]. (p. 266, SD, Vol. 1)

The entrance to Bamford Lagoon has several obstacles: an uncharted 10-foot shoal about 150 feet off the northeast point and islets and rocks on its south side. You can avoid these islets and rocks by favoring island (40) which marks the south side of the first cove on the north shore.

In the first cove on the north side of Bamford Lagoon scars and debris from recent clear-cutting have left their mark along shore.

The head of Bamford Lagoon offers good anchorage with the added attraction of a creek that can be entered by dinghy for several hundred yards for a close look at this part of the rain forest. Part way up this creek are the wooden remains of an old dam, and on the south shore you can find the ribs of an old shipwreck.

Anchor in about 7 fathoms over a sand gravel bottom with fair-to-good holding.

McKinnon Lagoon

Chart 3552 metric; entrance:
50°59.88′ N, 127°13.95′ W (NAD 27)

McKinnon Lagoon extends NE . . . from it [above-mentioned narrows]. (p. 266, SD, Vol. 1)

McKinnon Lagoon has a large inner basin beyond its narrows. Although deep, this remote basin offers some anchor sites using stern ties, with little chance of crowding.

Nenahlmai Lagoon

Chart 3552 metric; entrance:
50°59.70′ N, 127°14.20′ W (NAD 27)

Nenahlmai Lagoon is entered through the above-mentioned narrows. (p. 266, SD, Vol. 1)

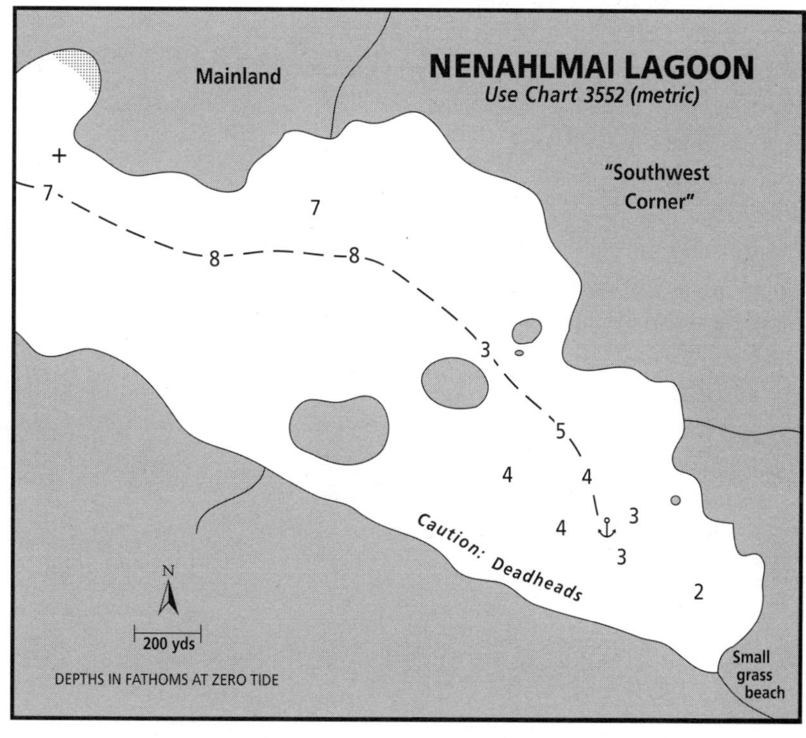

Nenahlmai Lagoon is fairly deep until you enter the basin at its southeast head. By keeping the two biggest islands to your starboard, you can enter a well-sheltered basin with excellent protection from all weather over a nearly flat 4 to 6 fathom bottom.

Anchor in 4 fathoms over a soft mud and sand bottom with good to very good holding.

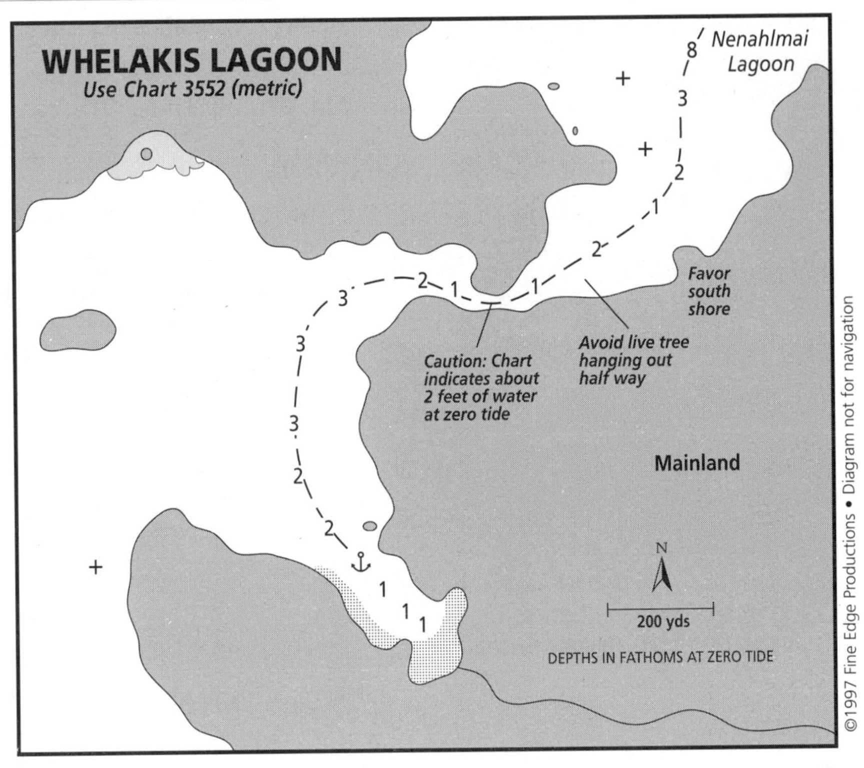

Whelakis Lagoon

Chart 3552 metric; entrance: 50°58.23′ N, 127°11.73′ W; anchor: 50°57.90′ N, 127°12.18′ W (NAD 27)

> *Whelakis Lagoon enters the south end of Nenahlmai Lagoon through a narrows with a depth of 0.8 m (3 ft) in its entrance.* (p. 266, SD, Vol. 1)

Whelakis Lagoon is an end in itself: cedar and muskeg rain forest where strange pollen patterns weave across the lagoon and around the point, as if they were lateral moraines on a frozen glacier. The water is so still we felt almost guilty disturbing it.

We recommend reconnoitering the narrows (or the lagoon itself!) by dinghy before you enter it. We did this on our first transit and were able to assure ourselves that, at high water, we had 10 feet of water in the shallowest spot on the east side of the narrows near the living horizontal tree.

You cannot see the entrance to Whelakis Lagoon from either the north or south when passing it in Nenahlmai Lagoon; GPS is useful to keep you headed in the right direction. As you approach the narrows, avoid two uncharted rocks off the west point which are just below the surface during high water. Favor the south shore in the narrows; however, avoid the live tree that extends about 30 feet into midchannel. We found minimum depth in the fairway to be about 10 feet on either side of the horizontal tree during high water, and current was weak at this time.

You can find good shelter in the first cove to the south side of the narrows or farther in at the head of the lagoon.

Anchor in 1 to 2 fathoms over a sticky mud with very good holding.

Belize Inlet

Chart 3552 metric (inset); entrance: 51°07.70′ N, 127°33.10′ W (NAD 27)

> *Belize Inlet is entered north of Mignon Point and extends 25 miles east. The sides of the inlet are steep and mountainous. Fraser Range, Nicholl Range and Tottenham Range are on its south side. The head of the inlet reaches within 1 mile of Maunsell Bay in Seymour Inlet.* (p. 267, SD, Vol. 1)

Belize Inlet, a beautiful fjord that extends 25 miles due east gradually becoming narrower and more precipitous, shows little evidence of man's travels.

As you enter the inlet, give Mignon Point a wide berth since several submerged rocks lie off its west and north sides. About a mile northeast

Overhanging "echo" rock, entrance to Belize Inlet

of Mignon Point, there is a sheer black granite cliff on the north side of Belize Inlet that we call "Echo Rock;" try your powers of echoing as you glide closely by. This remarkable overhanging rock which focuses the sound directly back to you is covered with bright white stains. Seals congregate on a 2-meter rock islet a half-mile east of Echo Rock, making themselves comfortable in its wide grooves. The seals here and in Seymour Inlet seem less concerned about passing boats than in other areas—perhaps they have not been shot at for their consumption of fish!

Westerman Bay

Chart 3552 metric; entrance:
51°08.25′ N, 127°28.00′ W; anchor:
51°09.18′ N, 127°27.17′ W (NAD 27)

> *Westerman Bay, on the north side of Belize Inlet, is entered west of Charles Point and has depths of about 45 m (148 ft), sand bottom. Depths shoal rapidly near its head. Small craft can find anchorage at the head of the bay in about 4 m (13 ft).*
> (p. 267; SD, Vol. 1)

Westerman Bay which offers very good protection from up- and downslope winds and chop has easy access and convenient depths.

Anchor in 4 fathoms, sand and mud with good holding.

Mereworth Sound

Chart 3552 metric; entrance:
51°08.10′ N, 127°25.00′ W (NAD 27)

> *Mereworth Sound, 2 miles east of Westerman Bay, extends 4.5 miles north then 6.5 miles east.*
> (p. 267, SD, Vol. 1)

Mereworth Sound has a large floating log camp operation (1996) and with clearcutting at the head

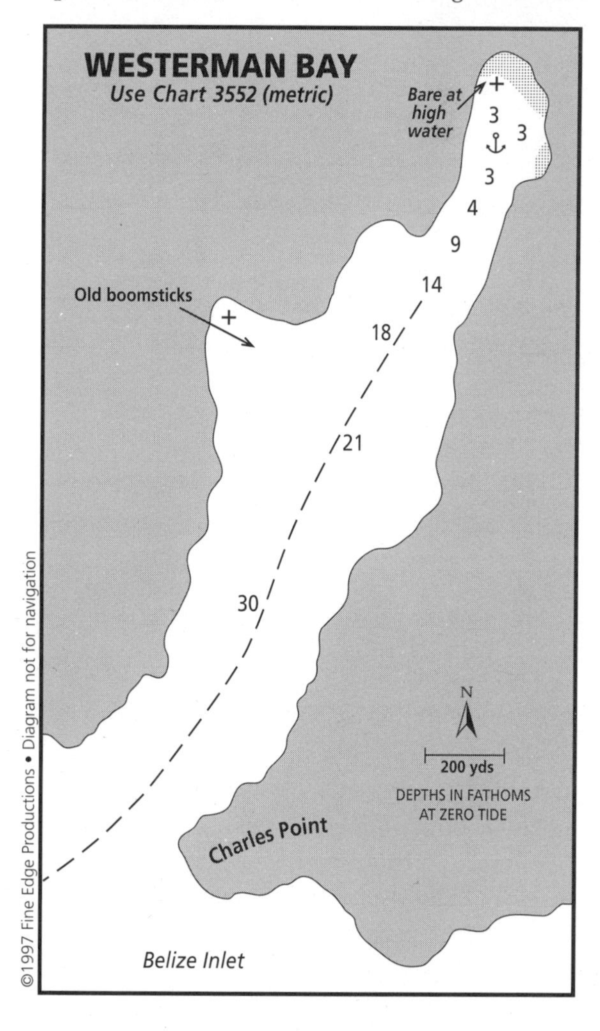

"Half-dome," north shore Belize Inlet

of the sound there is little reason to tour this region. There is reported to be anchorage behind Rock Island and in Village Cove.

Strachan Bay

Chart 3552 metric; entrance:
51°10.00′ N, 127°25.30′ W; anchor (cove):
51°09.58′ N, 127°28.43′ W (NAD 27)

> *Strachan Bay, on the west side of Mereworth Sound, affords anchorage in its SW part, mud bottom. A narrow channel at its NE end leads into Pack Lake. A small cove at the SW end of Strachan Bay has a narrow entrance with depths of 3 m (10 ft); it offers shelter and anchorage for small craft.* (p. 267, SD, Vol. 1)

Strachan Cove, the small cove mentioned in the quotation from *Sailing Directions,* is landlocked and almost perfectly sheltered from all weather. During outside southeast gales some wind sneaks across the isthmus from Belize Inlet; however, the fetch is minimal and the effect is small.

The entrance to Strachan Cove is about two hundred feet wide with a fairway depth of 4 fathoms at mid-tide. There is swinging room for several boats over a large flat bottom.

A float house and boomstick have appropriated the entrance to Pack Lake, and the trail mentioned in Hugo Anderson's book is no longer evident.

Anchor in 5 fathoms over a bottom of sticky brown mud with very good holding.

Village Cove

Chart 3552 metric; anchor:
51°10.49′ N, 127°24.65′ W (NAD 27)

> *Village Cove, on the east side of Mereworth Sound, offers anchorage which is well sheltered by two wooded islands in its entrance.* (p. 267, SD, Vol. 1)

Anchorage can be found west of the small grassy beach, north of the island in the center of the cove. Heavy Spanish moss droops from the trees above the beach.

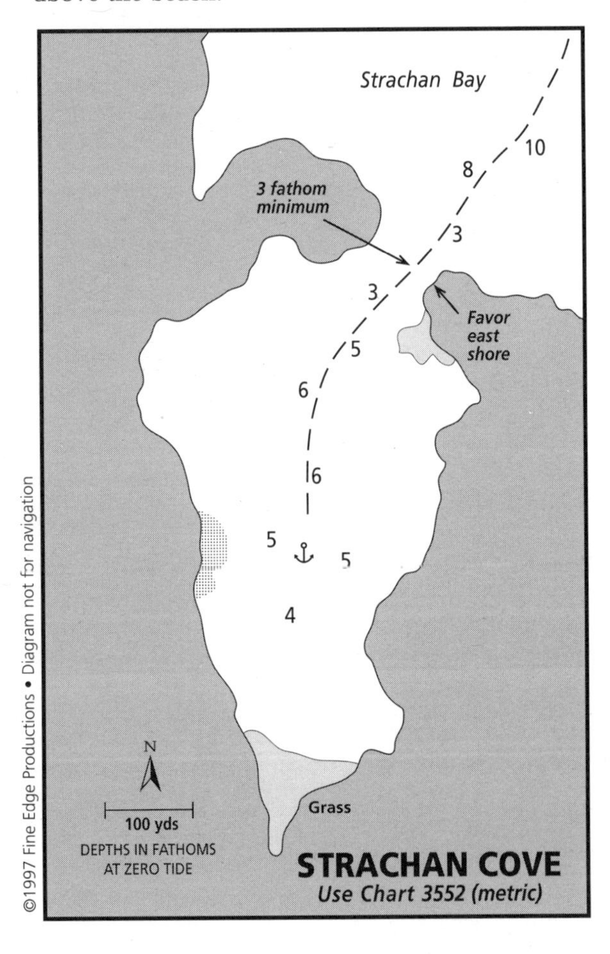

Anchor in 8 to 12 fathoms over an unrecorded bottom.

"Power Wash Waterfall"

Chart 3552 metric, position:
51°08.35′ N, 127°18.40′ W (NAD 27)

Power Wash is the name we gave to the spectacular waterfall on the north shore of Belize Inlet, 4 miles east of the turnoff to Mereworth Sound. This powerhouse of water falling directly into the saltwater could swamp your boat if you were forced in against the strong wind and outward flowing current.

"Half-Dome Waterfall"

Chart 3552 metric, position:
5l°08.00′ N, 127°11.25′ W (NAD 27)

Half-Dome Waterfall is our name for the lovely waterfall feeding out of the U-shaped valley that drains the north shore, 4.6 miles east of Power Wash Waterfall. This valley has some spectacular scenery including an almost-perfect half-dome-shaped vertical granite slab at least 1,000 feet high. Note the green "toupee" of evergreens growing along the very edge of the drop-off.

Alison Sound

Chart 3552 metric; entrance:
51°07.55′ N, 127°07.80′ W (NAD 27)

> *Alison Sound leads 3.5 miles NNE from Belize Inlet then 8 miles in an easterly direction. A sill, about 0.5 mile inside its entrance, has 31 m (102 ft) over it. A shoal with 3.4 m (11 ft) over it lies about 0.1 mile off the west shore, close south of the above-mentioned sill.* (p. 267, SD, Vol. 1)

A 3-fathom rock shoal, part of a submerged terminal moraine, crosses the entrance to Alison Sound.

Alison Sound is considered the most scenic of the inlets behind Nakwakto Rapids. Somewhat misnamed *sound* in the traditional sense, it is more similar to two freshwater lakes connected by a narrow bar which in turn is connected via a river gorge to Belize Inlet. The shores are steep with many granite slabs and overhanging cliffs. Evergreens attempt to grow on all the nearly vertical surfaces. As you proceed up the inlet, you have views of snow-covered peaks and ridges to the north and east. This lovely sound seems so remote from civilization and the Pacific Ocean, that you can hardly believe it's just miles away from Queen Charlotte Sound.

Entering Alison Sound

Unfortunately Alison Sound is losing some of its pristine quality as small clearcuts appear near Indian Reserves. Until now the narrows kept out the effects of both weather and man.

Obstruction Islet

Chart 3552 metric; position:
51°08.56′ N, 127°06.82′ W (NAD 27)

> *Obstruction Islet, 1.4 miles inside Alison Sound, is 30 m (98 ft) high and conspicuous. The channel on its west side is about 90 m (295 ft) wide with a depth of 9.9 m (32 ft); east of the islet the channel is narrower with a depth of 7 m (23 ft). Tidal streams through the narrows at Obstruction Islet attain 5 to 6 kn.* (pp. 267–268, SD, Vol. 1)

Pictographs, Belize Inlet

Obstruction Islet lies in the middle of beautiful Alison Narrows. Favor the west shore as you pass Obstruction Islet in a fairway about 100 yards wide and 5 fathoms deep. Current can reach 5 to 6 knots alongside Obstruction Islet but flow is generally laminar with minimum turbulence.

Pictographs

High on a vertical face in Belize Inlet near Alison Sound, a series of pictographs executed in ochre paint depict what appears to be the Native People's first encounter with White Man. (See photo.) The paintings are well preserved, due probably to their location below an overhanging cliff where they have escaped damage from rain. Belize Inlet was surveyed for the first time in 1865. In 1869, a government party in a warship was dispatched to this area to put down a skirmish between Natives and Whites. These pictographs may possibly date from that era or from an earlier encounter with White Man in Queen Charlotte Strait—perhaps even as early as Vancouver's time.

"No Name Bay"

Chart 3552 metric; position:
51°09.25′ N, 127°06.30′ W (NAD 27)

A bay on the north side of the peninsula, 0.7 mile north of Obstruction Islet, has depths of 44 m (144 ft), mud and sand; it offers sheltered anchorage. (p. 268, SD, Vol. 1)

No Name Bay appears to be well sheltered and to offer good protection from all winds at the north end of the narrows below a clear-cut area high on the mountainside. The bay is steep-to and you must look carefully to find an anchor site off the tiny grass beach at the outlet of the creek.

Chief Nollis Bay

Chart 3552 metric; position:
51°11.05′ N, 127°05.45′ W (NAD 27)

Chief Nollis Bay, 2 miles north of Obstruction Islet, has a steep-to drying flat at its head. Depths in the bay are 60 to 70 m (197 to 230 ft), mud bottom. A shoal with 2.2 m (7 ft) over it lies in its entrance, 0.2 mile off its east entrance point. (p. 268, SD, Vol. 1)

Chief Nollis Bay is the largest body of open water in Alison Sound. It has a long, grassy beach with many stumps and trees stranded along its shore. A sizeable creek that drains a large area enters the bay on the west end of the beach.

Chief Nollis Bay is reported to offer anchorage near its head in 10 to 15 fathoms, but it has little protection from the south

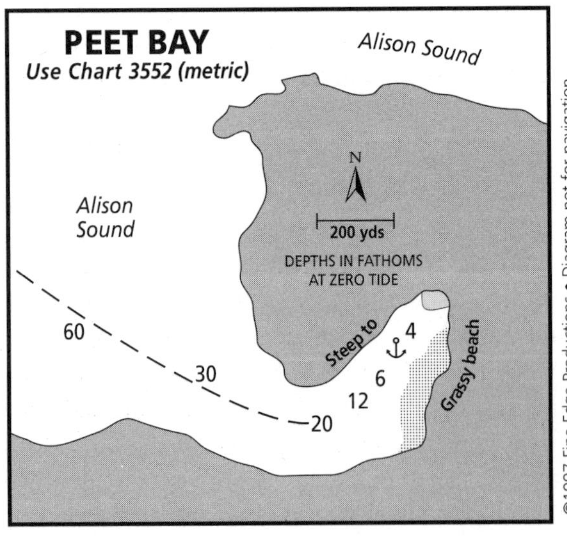

Peet Bay

**Chart 3552 metric; anchor:
51°09.83′ N, 127°04.23′ W (NAD 27)**

> *Peet Bay, on the south shore of Alison Sound, lies on the SW side of a small peninsula and has depths of 7 m (23 ft) near its head. Small craft can find sheltered anchorage in this bay.* (p. 268, SD, Vol. 1)

Peet Bay is a small, attractive anchorage that offers very good protection if you tuck deep in its north corner. This corner is completely landlocked and shows no signs of chop. As you head toward the bay, notice a beautiful waterfall along the south shore.

Anchorage for one vessel can be found north of the grassy beach in 4 to 5 fathoms. Swinging room is limited, so larger vessels should consider using a shore-tie.

Anchor in 4 to 5 fathoms over soft brown mud and sand with fair-to-good holding.

Summers Bay

**Chart 3552 metric; position:
51°10.20′ N, 127°01.50′ W (NAD 27)**

> *Summers Bay, on the north shore of Alison Sound, has quite steep slopes which level out at a depth of 70 m (230 ft), mud and sand bottom. Small craft can find anchorage close to shore.* (p. 268, SD, Vol. 1)

Summers Bay is a picturesque anchorage with very good protection from downslope winds.

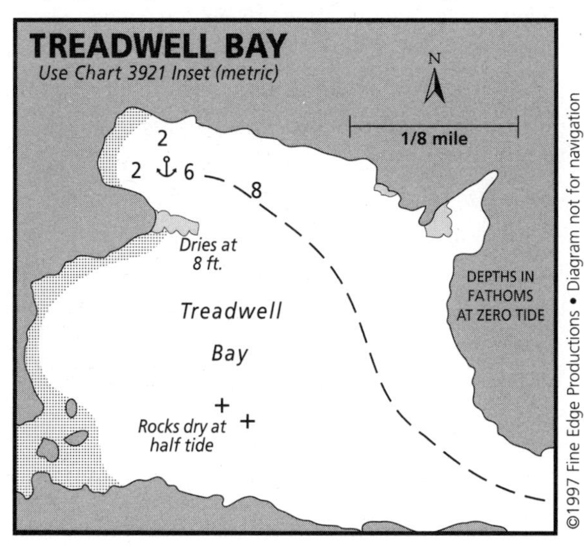

High snowy peaks tower above the bay. A white bluff rises above the cove's north side, a black bluff to its south.

Anchor off the grassy flat in about 12 fathoms over an unrecorded bottom.

Waump Creek

**Chart 3552 metric; position;
51°11.15′ N, 126°55.15′ W (NAD 27)**

> *Waump Creek flows into the head of Alison Sound across steep-to drying flats.* (p. 268, SD, Vol. 1)

Slingsby Channel

**Chart 3921 metric; east entrance (0.15 mile South Kitching Point): 51°05.50′ N, 127°31.30′ W (NAD 83); Chart 3551; west entrance:
51°05.00′ N, 127°39.05′ W (NAD 27)**

> *Slingsby Channel is the main channel leading from Queen Charlotte Strait to Seymour Inlet.* (p. 263, SD, Vol. 1)

Named for a now-obscure baron, we feel that Slingsby Channel would be more aptly named *Slingshot* Channel due to its strong currents that propel you either into or out of Seymour Inlet.

Treadwell Bay

**Chart 3921 metric (inset); entrance:
51°05.77′ N, 127°32.00′ W; anchor:
51°06.27′ N, 127°32.68′ W (NAD 83)**

> *Treadwell Bay . . . is entered between Quiet Point and the east side of Anchor Islands. The bay lies north of the larger Anchor Island and is well sheltered from tidal streams.*
>
> *Anchorage for small vessels, with good holding ground, can be obtained in Treadwell Bay. It is used by vessels awaiting slack water at Nakwakto Rapids or Outer Narrows.* (p. 264, SD, Vol. 1)

Treadwell Bay is another good place to spend the night if you want to be near Nakwakto Rapids. The far northwest corner of the bay is out of the current (2.5 knots ebb off Stream Point).

Favor the right shore upon entering to avoid two rocks in the main channel that dry at midtide. Anchor deep in the cove for good shelter from all winds. You may experience some chop

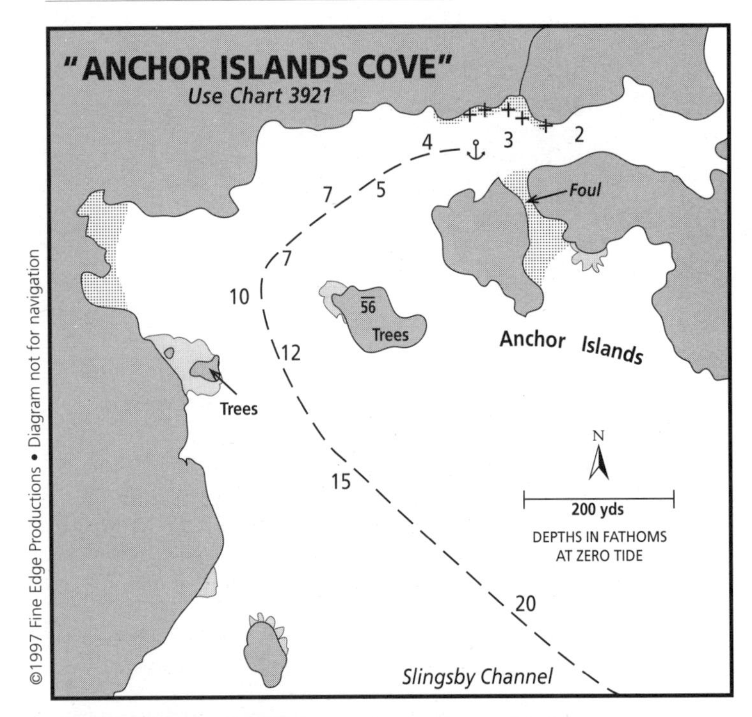

on strong southeast or Squamish winds.

Anchor in 5 to 6 fathoms over a mud bottom with fair-to-good holding.

"Anchor Islands Cove"

Chart 3550 metric; entrance:
51°05.80′ N, 127°33.30′ W; anchor:
51°05.97′ N, 127°33.11′ W (NAD 83)

Anchor Islands Cove, suitable for a number of small cruising boats, offers very good shelter from all weather. It is located immediately west of Treadwell Bay at the northwest extremity of Anchor Islands.

The water here which seldom turns over is full of small flotsam and Moon jellyfish; moss-covered cedars bend over the water, giving the cove an aspect of primeval times. The cove is effectively blocked from any major wind, and currents are a half-knot at most.

Anchor just west of a line between the drying spit—which nearly connects the main island with the island to its west—and the small creek on the north shore.

Anchor in 4 fathoms over a sand and mud bottom with good holding.

Overhanging garden, Belize Inlet

Fox Islands

Chart 3550 metric; east entrance:
51°05.08′ N, 127°35.40′ W; west entrance:
51°04.55′ N, 127°36.70′ W (NAD 83)

Note: If you wish to proceed west down Slingsby Channel and enter Miles Inlet, consider using the narrow channel between Fox Islands and Bramham Island. Contrary to the chart, we found a minimum depth of 5 fathoms in the fairway at the east end of the passage, and 8 fathoms in the fairway on the west, with a smooth ride on an ebb current. But vigilance is required for safe passage!

Outer Narrows, Slingsby Channel

Chart 3550 metric; position:
51°05.25′ N, 127°37.85′ W (NAD 83)

Outer Narrows, at the west end of Slingsby Channel south of Vigilance Point, is about 0.1 mile wide with depths of 21 fathoms (38 m). The narrows should be navigated only at or near slack water; small vessels should also await fine weather.

Tidal streams in Slingsby Channel flow east on the flood and west on the ebb. In Outer Narrows the flood attains 7 kn and the ebb 9 kn.

A west wind against a strong ebb tide forms a steep short swell which can be dangerous to small craft at the entrance to Outer Narrows. With a strong ebb during these conditions mariners should be careful not to be carried into the narrows as it is very difficult to reverse or turn in Outer Narrows. (p. 263, SD, Vol. 1)

The Outer Narrows is located between Fox Islands and Vigilance Point. Turbulence and breaking chop at the Outer Narrows can be both frightening and dangerous to small craft. Currents here may run at 5 knots or more on a spring ebb, with 3 to 4 knots on spring or neap floods. The west end of Slingsby Channel is notorious for rough seas when a strong spring ebb tide meets the westerly swells, and we have seen 15 foot seas build up a mile offshore. However, all chop and swells disappear a half-mile or so east of Vigilance Point.

Vigilance Cove

Chart 3551; entrance: 51°05.30′ N, 127°38.40′ W; anchor: 51°05.45′ N, 127°38.14′ W (NAD 83)

Vigilance Cove, on the north side and at the west end of Slingsby Channel, is too exposed to be of any value as an anchorage. (p. 263, SD, Vol. 1)

Vigilance Cove can serve as an emergency anchorage when very strong currents in Slingsby Channel meet the swell and chop in Queen Charlotte Strait creating threatening seas. When conditions off Vigilance Point are threatening, you may get marginal and temporary relief in Vigilance Cove; however, the only good shelter in the immediate area is Miles Inlet, 2 miles to the southeast.

The north shore of Vigilance Cove is steep-to and the bottom flat. A diminished swell enters the cove making it somewhat uncomfortable. Beware of an uncharted rock surrounded by kelp, awash on an 8-foot tide, just east of the knob on the south shore.

Marginal and temporary anchorage can be found in the middle of the cove in 6 fathoms over an unrecorded bottom.

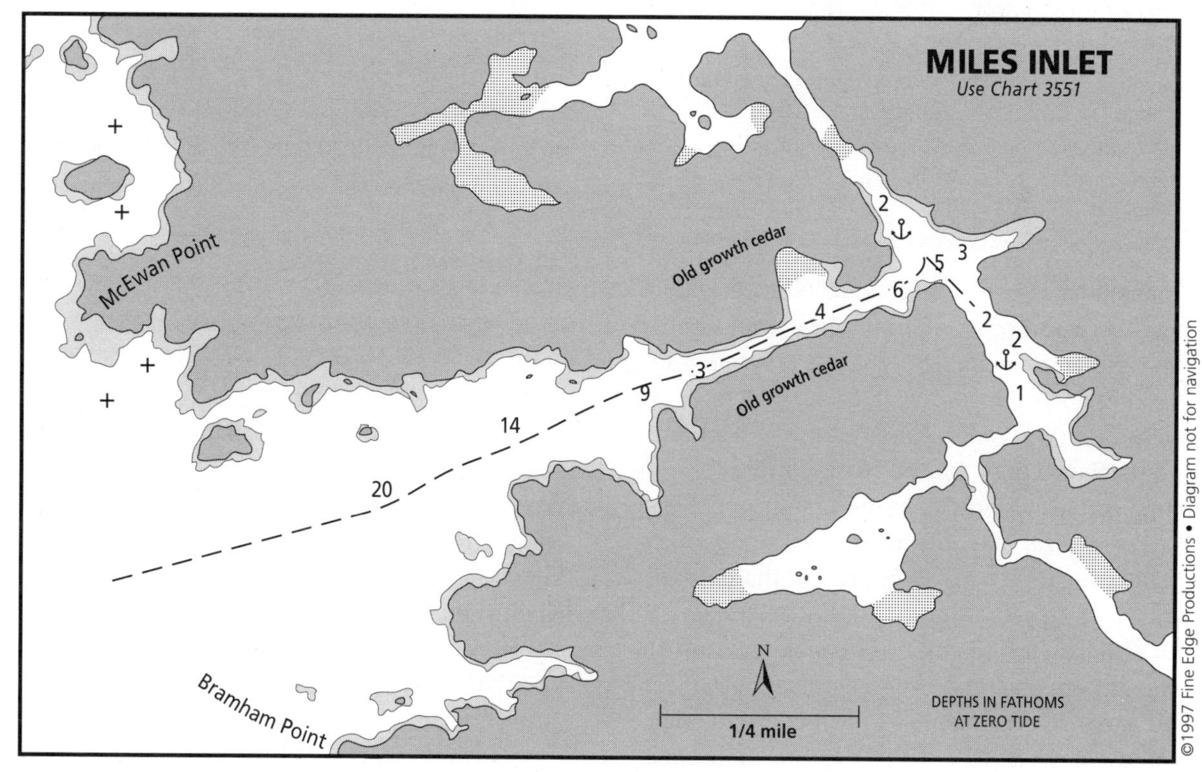

Elyxir *anchored in Miles Inlet at start of worldwide voyage*

Miles Inlet

Chart 3551; entrance: 51°03.58′ N, 127°36.31′ W; anchor (north arm): 51°04.03′ N, 127°34.82′ W (NAD 83)

> *Miles Inlet, entered between Bramham Point and McEwan Point, penetrates the west coast of Bramham Island and divides into two arms at its head. Anchorage for small craft can be obtained at the head of Miles Inlet, where it branches.* (p. 261, SD, Vol. 1)

Miles Inlet is one of the best small craft anchorages along this coast. Since it is near Cape Caution you can easily complete an early morning transit to Fitz Hugh Sound during calm weather. Since the entrance to Miles Islet is narrow it may cause you some anxiety if there is a following sea running and waves break over the entrance rocks.

On a clear day, the inlet lines up perfectly with a high snow-covered peak to the northeast (north of Nugent Sound). McEwan Rock or GPS can help you identify the opening and the straight channel that heads northeast. Beautiful, old-growth cedar line the 75-foot wide channel, a forest noteworthy for silver snags that point in all directions with a chaotic collection of organic material growing on them. A few hundred yards north of the intersection, the north arm of the inlet dries. The south arm has several shallow passages that can be explored by dinghy.

From 1/4 mile south of McEwan Rock, the course is approximately 043° magnetic. Use the light on McEwan Rock as your entrance mark and avoid the detached rocks on either side of the entrance to the inlet.

Miles Inlet is well protected from swell and chop. It is a quiet sanctuary, undisturbed by man. Several boats can anchor in here using short rodes, but in May and June when the fishing fleet heads north, it may be crowded.

Anchor in either arm in 2 to 3 fathoms over a mud bottom with good holding.

Burnett Bay

Chart 3550 metric; position (north end): 51°08.30′ N, 127°42.27′ W (NAD 83)

> *Burnett Bay, between Bremner Point and Wilkie Point, is fringed with a sandy shelving beach. Hayes Rock, 1 mile NW of Bremner Point, has less than 6 feet (1.8 m) over it.* (p. 261, SD, Vol. 1)

Burnett Bay is wide open and most of the time looks like a good surfing beach. Small boats will want to keep well offshore.

"Wilkie Point Cove"

Chart 3550 metric; north entrance: 51°08.30′ N, 127°44.00′ W; south entrance point: 51°08.15′ N, 127°43.70′ W; anchor: 51°08.44′ N, 127°43.47′ W (NAD 83)

Wilkie Point Cove is the small, rather well-protected cove between Burnett Bay and Silvester Bay, 2.75 miles southeast of Cape Caution. Its strategic location near Cape Caution make it useful as emergency shelter or as a good lunch stop where you can get relief from the perpetual westerly swells and southeast chop.

A sizeable ledge of rocks extends from the north shore, backed by large patches of bull kelp. This ledge, the kelp, and the treed islet to its immediate south cut prevailing westerly swells to almost nothing. The cove has a beautiful sandy beach where you can land a dinghy in fair weather in contrast to the larger, more exposed beaches to the north and south.

We have used the north entrance when a 2-meter swell was running outside. However, the entrance is very narrow and the whitewater can be quite intimidating. Favor the island side. Using the north entrance you must work your way through the kelp where minimum depths in the fairway are 3 to 4 fathoms. We found enough shelter under these conditions to land a dinghy on the beach (no more than a foot or two of breakers). The south entrance is free of kelp, easier to enter, and has 4 to 5 fathoms in the fairway.

Cape Caution

Anchorage can be found east of the unnamed island, anywhere along the beach, just inside a secondary line of kelp in about 1 to 2 fathoms at zero tide. If you anchor next to the rock in the south corner, the bluffs may provide some protection from southeast chop.

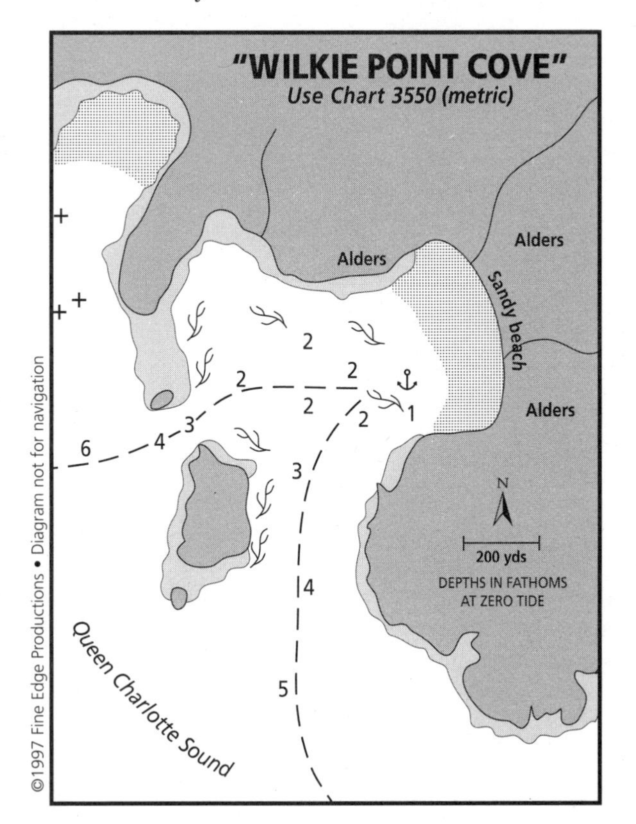

Anchor in 2 fathoms over a sand bottom with some kelp; fair-to-good holding.

Silvester Bay

Chart 3550 metric; position (north end): 51°09.45′ N, 127°45.30′ W (NAD 83)

> *Silvester Bay, between Raynor Point and Cape Caution, has shoals and drying rocks at its north end.* (p. 261, SD, Vol. 1)

Silvester Bay, along with Blunden Bay and Indian Cove 3 miles north, appears to have wonderful beaches and campsites for skilled kayakers. The surf tends to keep small boats well to windward.

Cape Caution

Chart 3551; position (10 fathom patch 1.3 miles SE of point): 51°09.27′ N, 127°48.93′ W (NAD 83)

> *Cape Caution is moderately high and level; the coast in the vicinity is granite and appears white. Cape Caution light (578) is shown at an elevation of 72 feet (22 m) from a tower, 25 feet (7.6 m) high.* (p. 261, SD, Vol. 1)

During strong southwest winds and/or conditions of high westerly swell, swells reflect off Cape Caution causing confused sea conditions for at least 1 mile to seaward. This condition is accentuated by shallow water directly off the cape.

Please note: From this point, all quotations from *Sailing Directions* are taken from Volume 2, north portion.

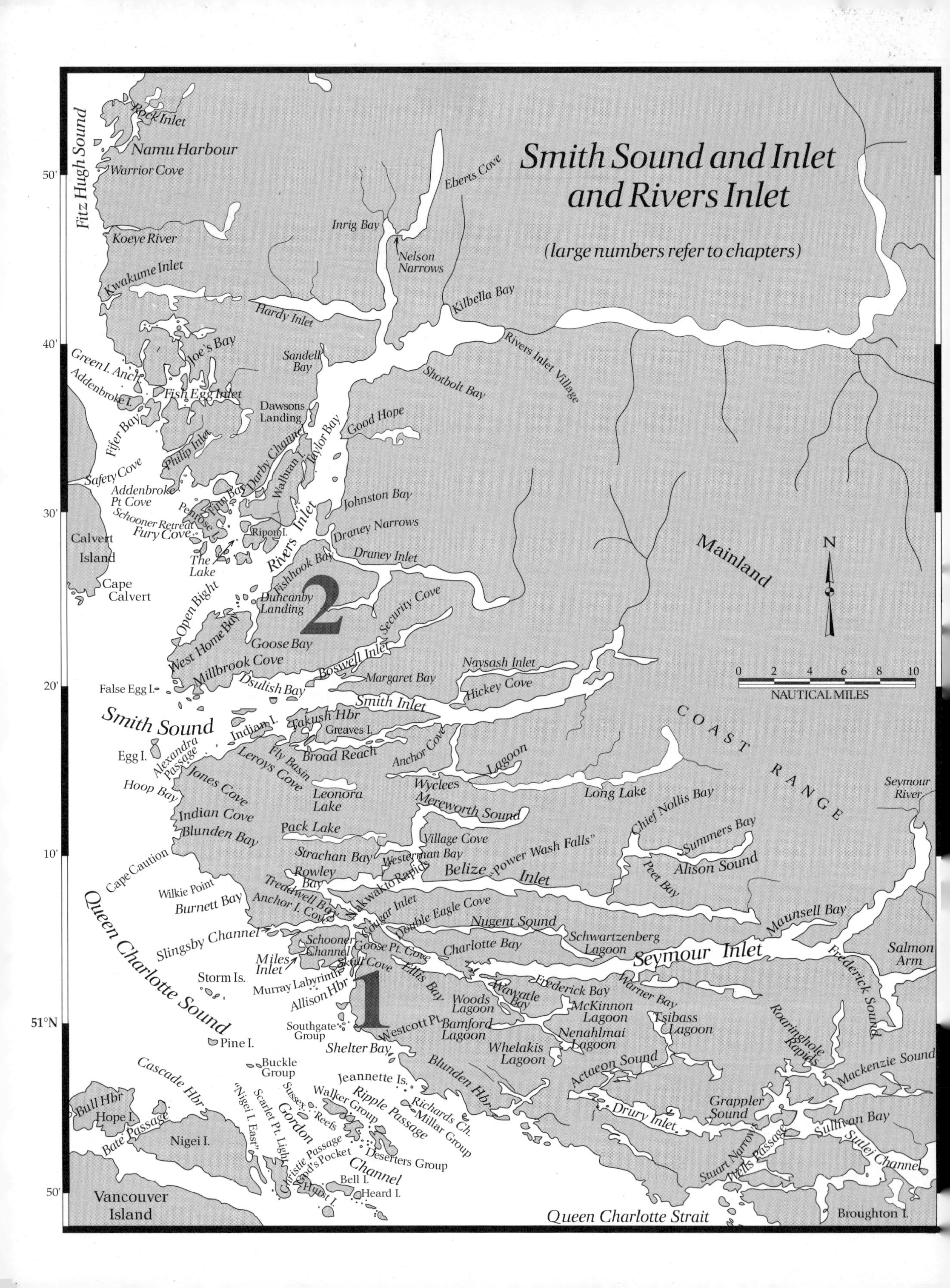

Smith Sound and Inlet
and Rivers Inlet
(large numbers refer to chapters)
Fitz Hugh Sound
Rock Inlet
Namu Harbour
Warrior Cove
Koeye River
Kwakume Inlet
Hardy Inlet
Joe's Bay
Green I. Anch.
Addenbroke I.
Fish Egg Inlet
Fifer Bay
Philip Inlet
Safety Cove
Addenbroke Pt Cove
Schooner Retreat
Fury Cove
Penrose I.
Finn Bay
Darby Channel
Walbran I.
Taylor Bay
Ripon I.
The Lake
Calvert Island
Cape Calvert
Open Bight
West Home Bay
Millbrook Cove
Goose Bay
Duncanby Landing
Fishhook Bay
Rivers Inlet
Dawsons Landing
Sandell Bay
Inrig Bay
Nelson Narrows
Eberts Cove
Kilbella Bay
Rivers Inlet Village
Shotbolt Bay
Good Hope
Johnston Bay
Draney Narrows
Draney Inlet
Security Cove
Boswell Inlet
Margaret Bay
Naysash Inlet
Hickey Cove
Mainland
N
0 2 4 6 8 10
NAUTICAL MILES
False Egg I.
Dsulish Bay
Smith Sound
Smith Inlet
Takush Hbr
Greaves I.
Indian I.
Egg I.
Alexandra Passage
Fly Basin
Broad Reach
Anchor Cove
Lagoon
COAST RANGE
Hoop Bay
Jones Cove
Leroys Cove
Leonora Lake
Wyclees
Long Lake
Chief Nollis Bay
Seymour River
Indian Cove
Blunden Bay
Pack Lake
Mereworth Sound
Village Cove
Summers Bay
Alison Sound
Peet Bay
Strachan Bay
Westerman Bay
"Power Wash Falls"
Belize Inlet
Cape Caution
Rowley Bay
Nakwakto Rapids
Wilkie Point
Treadwell Bay
Burnett Bay
Anchor I. Cove
Cougar Inlet
Double Eagle Cove
Nugent Sound
Maunsell Bay
Queen Charlotte Sound
Slingsby Channel
Schooner Channel
Goose Pt. Cove
Charlotte Bay
Schwartzenberg Lagoon
Seymour Inlet
Salmon Arm
Frederick Sound
Miles Inlet
Skull Cove
Storm Is.
Murray Labyrinth
Ellis Bay
Frederick Bay
Warner Bay
Allison Hbr
1
Woods Lagoon
Wawatle Bay
McKinnon Lagoon
Tsibass Lagoon
Roaringhole Rapids
Southgate Group
Westcott Pt.
Bamford Lagoon
Nenahlmai Lagoon
Pine I.
Shelter Bay
Whelakis Lagoon
Actaeon Sound
Mackenzie Sound
Buckle Group
Cascade Hbr
Blunden Hbr
Jeannette Is.
Bull Hbr
Hope I.
Bate Passage
Nigei I.
"Nigei I. East"
Scarlet Pt. Light
Gordon
Sussex Reefs
Walker Group
Ripple Passage
Richards Ch.
Millar Group
Drury Inlet
Grappler Sound
Sullivan Bay
Christie Passage
God's Pocket
Deserters Group
Channel
Bell I.
Heard I.
Hurst I.
Stuart Narrows
Wells Passage
Sutlej Channel
Vancouver Island
Queen Charlotte Strait
Broughton I.
2
50'
40'
30'
20'
10'
51°N
50'

2

Smith Sound and Inlet and Rivers Inlet

Smith Inlet, directly to the east of Egg Island, offers several sheltered anchorages along the shore facing Queen Charlotte Sound, and interesting but rarely-visited spots farther east. Takush Harbour and Village Island have some of the longest continuously inhabited native sites in this area. Dsulish Bay has a beautiful sandy beach marked only by bear and cougar tracks. Boswell Inlet and the inlets and lagoon to the east offer some excellent sportfishing in a seldom-visited environment. Because Smith Inlet trends east and west, you can cruise here when southeasters make it impractical to head south or north along the coast.

Rivers Inlet has a lovely archipelago centered around the marine park at Penrose Island and Klaquaek Channel. Rivers Inlet is busier than Smith Sound due to the numbers of posh fishing resorts recently converted from old canneries. Sportfishing boats in these areas zip around from dawn to dusk in search of the "big ones," and Channel 16 sounds like CB radio on Interstate 5. The interior of Rivers Inlet cuts forty miles into the mainland where you can find quiet, remote wilderness. A number of rivers culminate there, as the name suggests, and grizzlies abound.

Duncanby Landing and Dawsons Landing, once fuel and supply centers for commercial fishing boats, now cater primarily to sportfishing and cruising boaters.

All *Sailing Directions* from here north are from Volume 2, north portion.

Blunden Bay

Chart 3550 metric;
position: 51°11.05′ N, 127°46.70′ W (NAD 83)

> *Blunden Bay and Indian Cove lie between Cape Caution and Neck Ness.* (p. 63, SD)

Blunden Bay is a half-moon-shaped indentation into the mainland immediately north of Cape Caution. Its north and south points must have given protection to early canoeists as well as present-day sea-kayakers. This and the next three coves are useful for kayakers or small craft in calm weather only. Although the beautiful sandy beach looks inviting, cruising boats generally give the coast from Cape Caution to Alexandra Passage a wide berth due to the heaping and breaking swells along the rocks and reefs of the shore.

Photo courtesy Michael Woodward, CHS, Pacific Region

CHS's inflatable measuring speed of the rapids

Hoop Bay

Chart 3550 metric; position:
51°13.30′ N, 127°46.68′ W (NAD 83)

> *Hoop Bay . . . is encumbered with drying and sunken rocks and suitable only for small craft.* (p. 63, SD)

The bay behind the outlying rocks and reefs can appear calm and enticing, but it is best explored by high-speed inflatable from a mother ship safely anchored in Jones Cove.

Fishing boats rafted to piling, Jones Cove

Protection Cove

Chart 3550 metric; position:
51°14.06′ N, 127°47.00′ W (NAD 83)

> *Protection Cove, close east of Milthorp Point, dries at LW.* (p. 63, SD)

Protection Cove is too small and shallow to offer much protection from good-sized westerly swells. We once entered here under difficult conditions and got "spooked" by the solid white foam filling the cove, and strong surges from the crashing reefs close on our starboard hand. The cove clearly offers little protection except when small seas are running. Jones Cove, a mile north, offers superior protection and significantly more room to maneuver.

Alexandra Passage

Chart 3934 metric; south entrance (0.35 mile south Egg Rocks): 51°14.00′ N, 127°50.00′ W (NAD 83)

> *Alexandra Passage, the south entrance to Smith Sound, is deep but extreme care is necessary during thick weather as soundings will give little warning of the approach to dangers.* (p. 65, SD)

Boats crossing Queen Charlotte Sound bound directly for Fitz Hugh Sound pass roughly a mile west of Egg Island as do the ferries and cruise ships. Those wishing to enter Smith Sound can use Alexandra Passage by carefully passing between Egg Rocks and North Iron Rock, or closer to shore between South Iron Rock and Hoop Reef.

Generally the seas around both North and South Iron rocks break or heap up so you can spot them easily. If you take the inside route, monitor your position carefully. In rare calm weather, when the rocks aren't easily spotted, GPS is a good way to double-check your progress.

During southeast gales, Alexandra Passage and Browning Channel are somewhat protected by the lee of the mainland coast, and have less chop than Queen Charlotte Sound or the more exposed parts of Blackney Channel and Smith Inlet. Because the same lee effect takes place in Open Bight in Rivers Inlet, small southbound cruising boats sometimes take advantage of these conditions to move down to Millbrook Cove or Jones Cove, shortening their transit of Queen Charlotte Sound and Cape Caution.

Egg Island

Chart 3550 metric, 3934 metric; light:
51°14.90′ N, 127°49.93′ W; anchor (tiny east cove): 51°14.93′ N, 127°49.85′ W (NAD 83)

> *Egg Island is high, wooded, and makes a conspicuous landmark. Egg Island light (579) is shown from a lattice tower, 25.9 m (85 ft) high.* (p. 65, SD)

Egg Island Lightstation's timely weather reports are critical to the success and comfort of countless sailors and, for the past 25 years, veteran lightkeepers Judy and Stan Westhaver, have been helpful to cruising boats that cross Queen

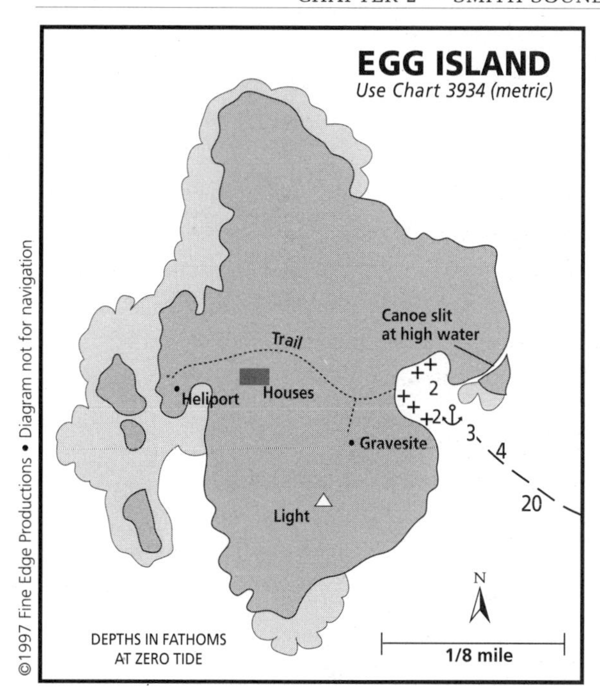

Charlotte Sound. Stan and Judy volunteer updated weather information on Channels 82A or 09 with the call sign "Egg Yolk." They welcome visitors for a tour of the station when weather and sea conditions permit landing in the small cove on the east side of the island.

In the fall of 1994, seas were so calm in Queen Charlotte Sound that our vessel was able to raft with the lighthouse supply ship, *Narwhal*, anchored a half-mile west of Egg Island. We toured the ship and watched the helicopter ferry supplies to the lightstation. This weather was highly unusual; it's seldom that conditions on the east side of Egg Island allow a skipper to leave his vessel alone.

The cove east of Egg Island is extremely small and subject to heavy 2- to 3-foot surge caused by the many ships passing a mile or so to the west. A small 4-fathom shelf, 75 feet wide, ringed with above- and below-water rocks, can be used as temporary anchorage in calm weather. We have used a stern line to shore here with good success. The boat should lie on a line from the canoe slit of the islet to the southern point, on about 160 feet of line to shore. The unpredictable surge and

Narwhal anchored off Egg Island on a rare, calm day

lack of swinging room make this shelf rather dangerous. *Caution:* Do not leave your boat alone or with a crew member who doesn't know how to move it if conditions deteriorate. The shore party should carry a hand-held VHF for communicating with the boat.

It is better to anchor off the shelf farther east in about 8 to 12 fathoms (rocky bottom, poor holding). Leave a crew member aboard as anchor

Egg Island, temporary anchorage in fair weather only

Stan & Judy Westhaver, Egg Island lightkeepers

Stan and Judy Westhaver tell the legendary story behind the man whose grave lies within the picket fence at Egg Island.

One of the previous lightkeepers lived on the island with a female companion who was separated from her husband. The lightkeeper lived in constant fear that his companion might leave him and return to her husband. One weekend she left the island to go to town, saying she would return the next day. The weather worsened, preventing her return as planned. She radioed to the lightkeeper that she wouldn't return until the day after, but the transmission was so bad, all he could hear was "won't return." Crazed with grief, he committed suicide.

watch, or drift or circle farther outside while your party is ashore. If you survive the challenge of landing on the rocky beach in surge, the 118 steps to the top of the island will be easy! An alternate, safer plan is to anchor in Jones Cove and shoot across in a fast inflatable.

Anchor (tiny east cove) in 4 to 6 fathoms over a mixed rocky bottom; fair holding if your anchor is well set. Larger boats can anchor farther out in 8 to 12 fathoms.

Jones Cove

Chart 3934 metric; entrance: 51°15.10′ N, 127°45.90′ W; anchor: 51°14.88′ N, 127°45.90′ W (NAD 83)

> *Jones Cove, close NE of Macnicol Point, affords shelter to small craft . . .* (p. 66, SD)

Jones Cove, 2.5 miles due east of Egg Island, offers good protection for small craft with somewhat limited swinging room. Ropes on a piling near the entrance can be used in conjunction with a second anchor or to tie up. Inside the piling there is room for two or three small boats to anchor. In the past this cove was used as a logboom storage area, but small craft and fishing boats now use it frequently. Millbrook Cove, on the north side of Smith Sound, has more swinging room and is more popular with larger pleasure craft.

Jones Cove is easy to enter but avoid the rocks

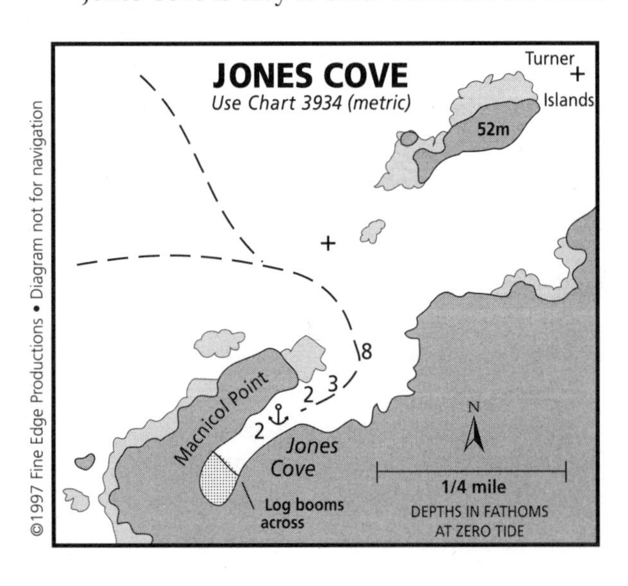

off the north point or those extending from Turner Islands. The pass inside Turner Islands has a fairway depth of about 20 fathoms and inside Chest Island about 6 fathoms. Avoid the rocks off Chest Island.

Anchor in 2 to 3 fathoms over a soft mud bottom with good holding.

Millbrook Cove

Chart 3934 metric; entrance: 51°19.14′ N, 127°43.96′ W; anchor: 51°19.67′ N, 127°44.20′ W (NAD 83)

> *Millbrook Cove is encumbered by several islets and rocks; Millbrook Rocks, off the entrance to the cove, are marked by starboard hand buoy "E6". The cove is used extensively by fishing vessels.* (p. 66, SD)

Millbrook Cove offers excellent protection with room for a number of good-sized vessels. Entering requires some careful navigation, but the calm, well-protected waters inside are worth the effort. We have taken refuge here more than once, and while the wind may howl here, the shallow water, good holding, and swinging room will make you happy. Once when we anchored here prior to crossing to Cape Scott, we were able to receive a radio wake-up call at 4 a.m. and a weather briefing from Stan at Egg Island.

Enter Millbrook Cove by using buoy "E6" to line you up for a direct course toward island (30) on Chart 3934 metric. Post a sharp bow lookout to avoid rocks and reefs. Just before island (30), turn right and circle around to the north side, anchoring where convenient.

We have entered Millbrook Cove on the west side of island (30) and have exited by staying to the far east side. However, both of these routes are subject to irregular bottoms and shallow depths. Sometimes there is a small fishing float here used for net repairs. Note that the back bay appears to have shallower depths than those indicated on the chart.

Anchor in 3 to 4 fathoms over a soft mud bottom with fair-to-good holding.

Dsulish Bay

Chart 3934 metric; anchor: 51°20.37′ N, 127°40.55′ W (NAD 83)

> *Dsulish Island is 2 miles ENE of Millbrook Cove in Dsulish Bay.* (p. 67, SD)

Dsulish Bay is known for its beautiful, wide sandy beach. We have seen over two dozen puffins, as well as tracks of cougar and deer on the beach. You can enjoy browsing among the driftwood on shore or taking long walks.

Dsulish Island provides protection from prevailing winds on its northeast side but is open to

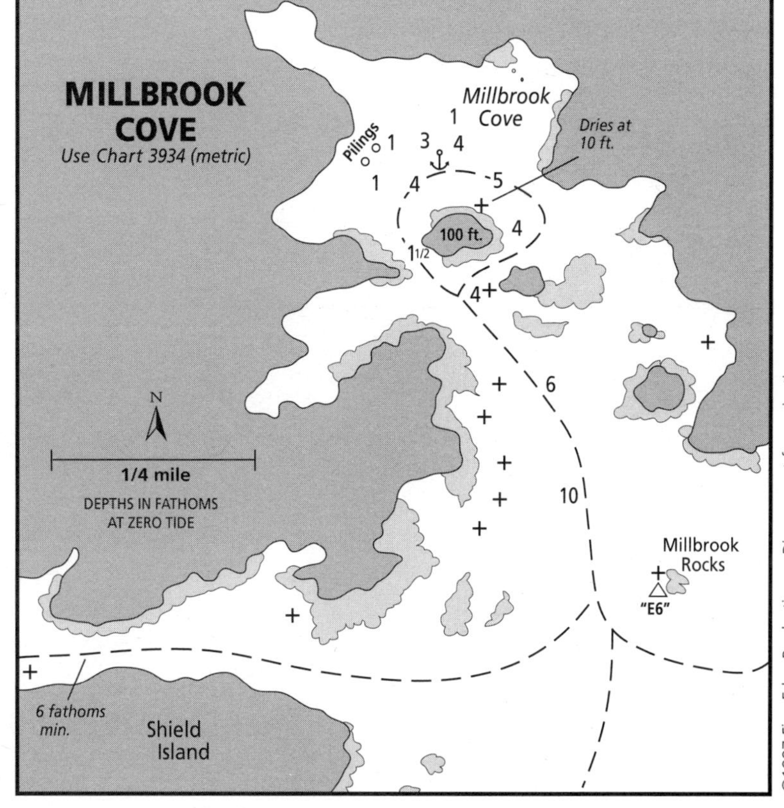

the southeast. Although we have spent the night here, we use it only in stable weather.

Anchor a short distance anywhere off the beach if you are stopping for lunch or beachcombing. (If you remain overnight, consider staying behind Dsulish Island, or in East Cove.)

Anchor in 2 to 3 fathoms over a sandy bottom with good holding.

Sandy Beach in Dsulish Bay

"East Cove," Dsulish Bay

Chart 3934 metric; anchor:
51°20.39′ N, 127°40.06′ W (NAD 83)

More protection from northwest winds can be found behind the small peninsula at the east side of Dsulish Bay. Avoid the rock that breaks on an 8-foot tide off the peninsula and another rock just north when entering. Anchor off the small creek at the head of the bay. Driftwood along shore here indicates that this bay is exposed to southerly winds.

Anchor in 1 to 2 fathoms over a sandy bottom with some grass; holding is fair to good.

Leroy Bay

Chart 3934 metric; position:
51°16.34′ N, 127°39.90′ W (NAD 83)

Leroy Bay, entered south of Leroy Rock, is protected on its north side by Leroy Island. A drying rock lies on the south side of the approach to the bay. A fishing resort float is reported to be on the south shore of the bay and some broken submerged piles are at the head. (p. 66, SD)

Leroy Bay, at last check, was filled with logbooms and there was no space to anchor. When Leroy Bay is vacant, there's fairly good protection deep in the bay. The outer bay, however, gets its share of westerly chop.

Cathcart Island, 2 miles due north of Leroy Bay, has a small nook on its south side which makes good temporary anchorage in prevailing west winds.

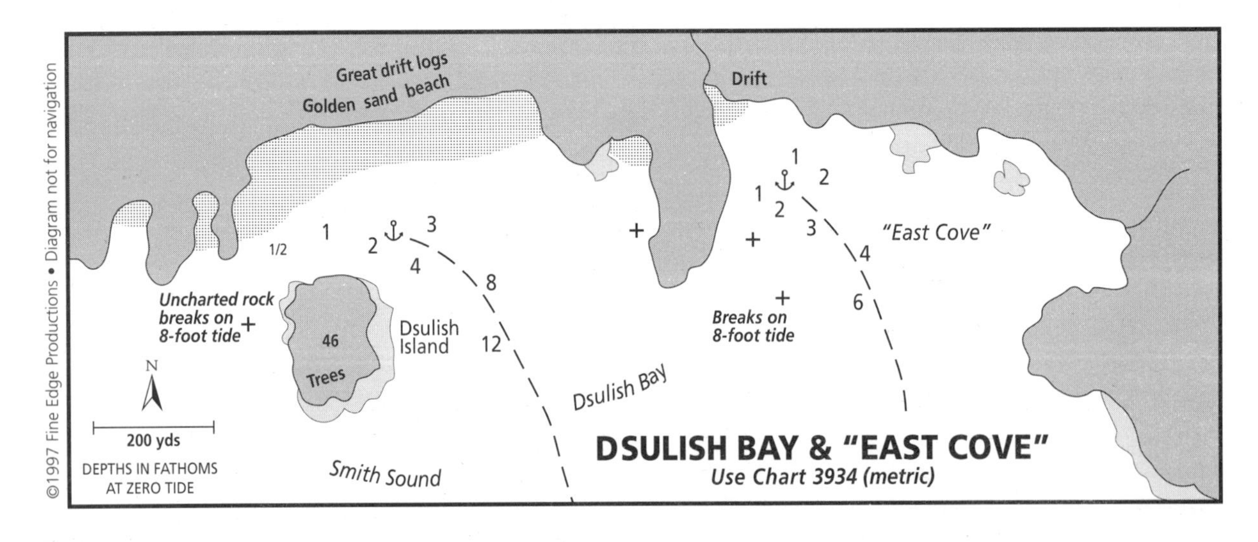

Takush Harbour

Charts 3934 metric, 3931 metric; entrance: 51°17.26′ N, 127°37.00′ W (NAD 83)

> *Takush Harbour is entered by way of Ship Passage. Gnarled Islets, on the west side and close within the entrance, extend 0.4 mile east of Bloxam Point.* (p. 66, SD)

Takush Harbour, a large indentation on the south side of Browning Channel, offers a choice of anchor sites for good protection from southeast storms; Bull Cove and Fly Basin are the more convenient sites. Ship Passage is the deep-water route between Gnarled Islets and Petrel Shoal on the west and Fish Rocks on the east. A private wooden beacon is mounted on the east tip of the easternmost of the Gnarled Islets. Once white, this beacon has faded.

There are many detached rocks and reefs in Takush Harbour and its bottom is uneven; careful piloting is required, especially in poor visibility. Takush Harbour is largely untouched by modern development and is a quiet, scenic anchorage. Perhaps the most interesting feature in Takush Harbour is Indian Island.

Photo by Ian Douglas

Anchored in a quiet cove

Anchor Bight

Charts 3934 metric, 3931 metric; anchor: 51°16.75′ N, 127°38.88′ W (NAD 83)

> *Anchor Bight, the west arm of Takush Harbour, is entered between Gnarled Islets and Anchor Islets. The fairway leading into this bight is reduced in width by a shoal extending north from the east Anchor Islet.*
>
> *Anchorage can be obtained in Anchor Bight in 16 m (9 fms), mud bottom, midway between Ship Rock and Abrupt Point.* (p. 66, SD)

Anchor Bight is located in the western section of Takush Harbour between Ship Rock and Indian Island. Protection can be found in shallow water close to the spit connecting the two. This is reported to be a fair-weather anchorage only. The recommended anchorage for smaller boats in a southeast gale or storm force winds would be Fly Basin. Large fishing boats frequently use the entrance west of the connecting spit to anchor at night.

Anchor in 4 to 7 fathoms over mud and sand bottom with good holding.

Indian Island

Charts 3934 metric, 3931 metric; anchor: 51°17.15′ N, 127°38.38′ W (NAD 83)

> *Indian Island lies close offshore on the south side of Browning Channel. Foul ground, with an islet on it, extends west from the island to Leroy Rock.* (p. 66, SD)

Indian Island is an Indian Reserve. Middens attest to its long history of habitation, and the island's integrity should be respected.

The cove on the east side of Indian Island offers good protection but has limited swinging room. The bottom is very soft and we had difficulty getting a good hold. We would recommend it as a lunch stop only; Fly Basin, 1.5 miles to the southeast, is preferable as an overnighter.

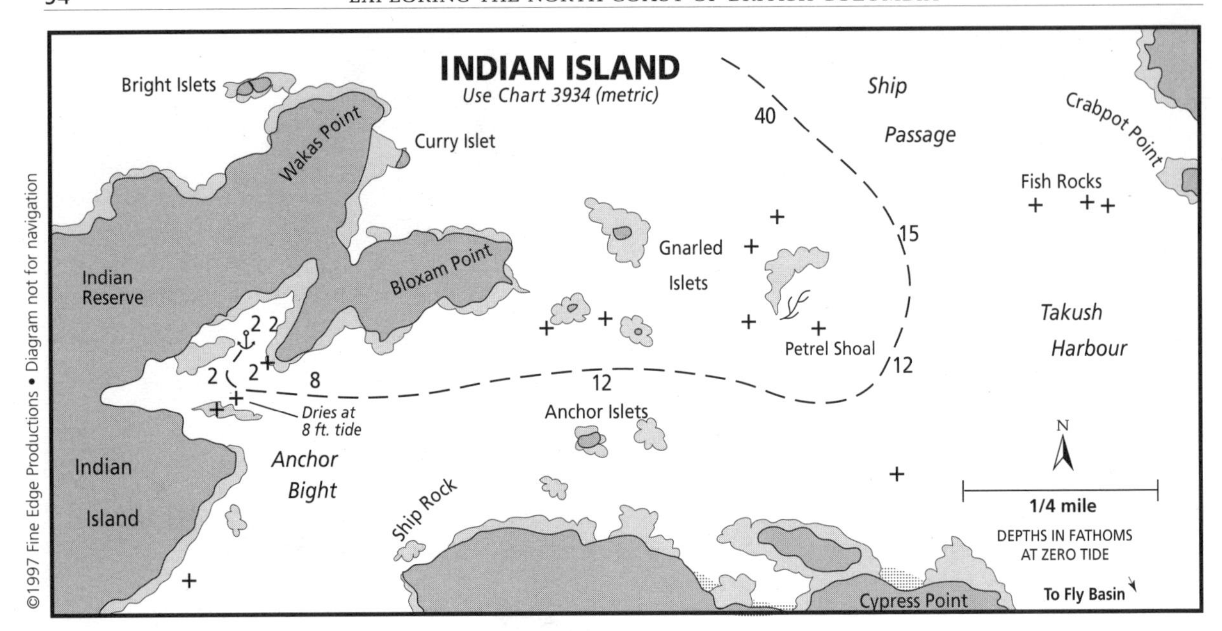

Enter Indian Island cove by favoring the north point and avoiding the reef and rocks off the south point.

Anchor in 2 fathoms over a soft and difficult bottom with only poor-to-fair holding.

Bull Cove

Charts 3934 metric, 3931 metric; position: 51°16.67′ N, 127°36.30′ W (NAD 83)

Bull Cove is a convenient, simple-to-enter anchorage, but the swinging room is minimal and protection is not as complete as that found in Fly Basin immediately south. The drying flat at the head of the basin is steep-to but a small boat can find an anchor site, avoiding the foul north shore, in 6 fathoms over mud bottom with good holding. But in general—forget it!

Fly Basin

Charts 3934 metric, 3931 metric; entrance: 51°16.65′ N, 127°36.60′ W; anchor: 51°16.30′ N, 127°36.00′ W (NAD 83)

Fly Basin, the south arm of Takush Harbour, has a narrow entrance encumbered by drying and sunken rocks. It is well sheltered but only suitable for small craft. (p. 66, SD)

Fly Basin is a wonderful landlocked shelter that feels bombproof. It has a large, flat shallow bottom and lots of swinging room. This tranquil place is disturbed only by the sounds of birds and inquisitive seals. Surrounded by old-growth cedar, you feel as though you're in a landlocked swimming pool. Underwater visibility in the basin is good to about 15 feet.

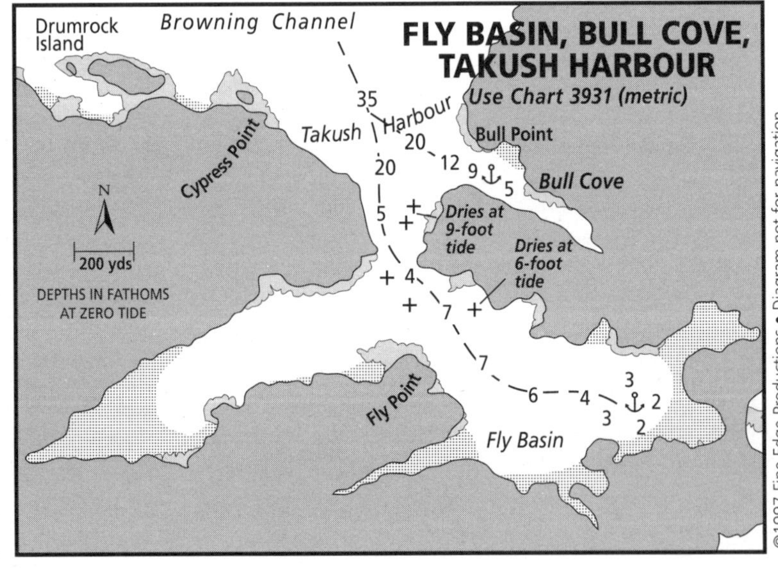

Entering Fly Basin, favor the west shore as you cross the 2-fathom bar to avoid a rock complex off the east entrance point. Then favor the east shore until you enter the 5-fathom basin proper. We prefer to anchor in the eastern section of the cove.

Anchor in 4 fathoms over a sticky grey mud bottom with worms; very good holding.

Broad Bay

Charts 3934 metric; 3931 metric; anchor:
51°17.28′ N, 127°35.74′ W (NAD 83)

Broad Bay, the east arm of Takush Harbour, has a narrow drying passage at its east end leading into Ahclakerho Channel. . . . (p. 66, SD)

Broad Bay, 0.5 mile due east of Crabpot Point, offers good shelter from all winds and is almost landlocked. It south side is the western high-water dinghy entrance to tortuous 10-mile-long Ahclakerho Channel that leads along Greaves Island's south side.

Anchor in the head of the bay in 7 to 9 fathoms, unrecorded bottom.

"Tom's Cove"

Charts 3934 metric, 3931 metric; anchor:
51°18.25′ N, 127°34.50′ W (NAD 83)

Tom's Cove is what we call the cove 0.7 mile east of Birkby Point on the north shore of Greaves Island. This cove has excellent views of the snowy peaks of the high country behind Boswell Inlet. The head of the bay is a large beach and drying flat with easy landing access. A very large stump sits in the middle of the beach. The islets across the north end keep out the westerly chop. This is a good anchorage in prevailing westerlies or fair weather; however, it is poor in easterlies. (In Smith Inlet and the north side of Smith Sound, southeast gales usually occur as easterlies.) "Gill Net Cove," east of Tom's Cove, offers more protection under east winds.

Anchor in 2 to 3 fathoms over a mud bottom with good holding.

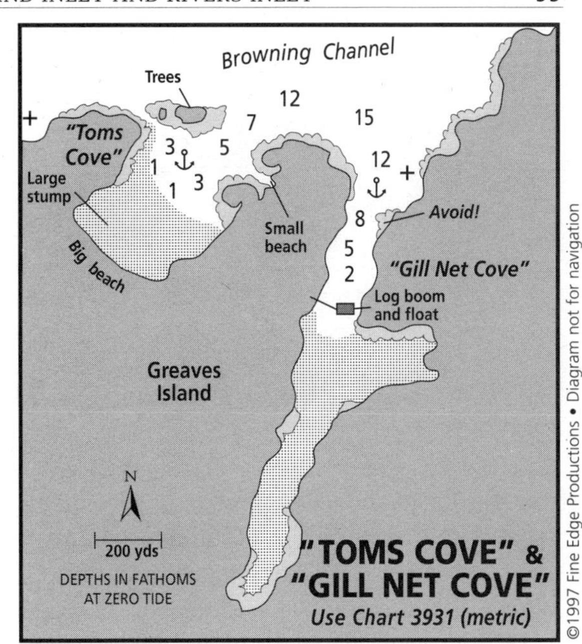

"Gill Net Cove"

Charts 3934 metric, 3931 metric; anchor:
51°18.05′ N, 127°34.17′ W (NAD 83)

Gill Net Cove is our name for the cove that nearly cuts Greaves Island in half at its western end. The fishing fleet keeps a small float anchored here for a place to unload and work on their nets. The float is attached to shore at the point where the mud flat dries at zero tide. Two or three boats can find room to anchor north of the Gill Net float. Upon entering, favor the west shore to avoid a detached rock on the east entrance. Larger vessels prefer to anchor in McBride Bay.

Anchor in 2 to 4 fathoms over a mud bottom with good holding.

McBride Bay

Chart 3931 metric; position:
51°18.47′ N, 127°32.30′ W (NAD 83)

McBride Bay, south of Ripon Point, affords anchorage in 18 to 37 m (10 to 20 fms). The fairway leading to the anchorage is between Oblong Island and Middle Patch. (p. 67, SD)

McBride Bay is a large, well-sheltered bay at the north end of Greaves Island; it is deep and the bottom irregular. There is plenty of swinging

Surge Rock *visits Smith Inlet*

room for boats with lots of anchor rode. Locals report that anchorage can be taken in 12 to 20 fathoms over an irregular bottom with fair-to-good holding; larger vessels anchor mid-bay, avoiding the rocky patch south of Middle Patch.

Margaret Bay

Chart 3931 metric; entrance:
51°19.89′ N, 127°31.29′ W; anchor:
51°20.00′ N, 127°29.62′ W (NAD 83)

> *Margaret Bay lies between Smith and Boswell Inlets. The site of an abandoned cannery lies at the east end of Margaret Bay. Few traces of the buildings remain and there are no facilities here. Approaching Margaret Bay vessels can pass on either side of Frank Rock. . . . When in the bay steer to pass in mid-channel, south of Chambers Island.* (p. 67, SD)

Margaret Bay lies at the west end of a peninsula that separates Smith Inlet from Boswell Inlet. At the far east end of the bay near the remains of an abandoned cannery and an old pier, small boats can find good protection in all but very strong westerlies.

When entering the bay, favor the north shore near Mills Point to avoid Camosun Rock which extends beyond midchannel from the south shore. Prevailing westerly chop dies out as you approach the head of the bay. When entering the inner basin, avoid the dangerous rock awash at 11 feet by favoring the south side of the channel. Use a stern tie to the islet just west of the cannery ruins for more security. One boat can tuck in behind the islet west of the pier ruins.

Anchor in 1 to 3 fathoms over a sand and mud bottom with good holding.

Ethel Cove

Chart 3931 metric; entrance:
51°20.06′ N, 127°31.66′ W; anchor:
51°20.26′ N, 127°31.32′ W (NAD 83)

> *Ethel Cove lie[s] close NW of Mills Point, the north entrance point of Margaret Bay.* (p. 67, SD)

Ethel Cove, immediately north of Margaret Bay, offers good protection in all but strong southwest weather. Anchor off a small, sandy beach. Larger boats will like the additional swinging room found here, in contrast to that of Margaret Bay.

Anchor in 3 to 6 fathoms over a sand and mud bottom with fair-to-good holding.

Smith Inlet

Chart 3931 metric; entrance:
51°18.90′ N, 127°32.30′ W (NAD 83)

Smith Inlet begins at McBride Bay on Greaves Island and continues 20 miles east, deep into the coast mountains where Nekite River meets the sea. Smith Inlet then divides into Naysash Inlet on its north side, and Ahclakerho Channel and Wyclees Lagoon on its south shore.

Ahclakerho Channel

Chart 3931 metric; east entrance
51°17.48′ N, 127°23.28′ W (NAD 83)

> *Ahclakerho Channel is a narrow, winding channel separating Greaves Island from the mainland. From Cape Anne to Ahclakerho Islands the channel is narrow, but with local knowledge, is navigable at all stages of the tide. The channel then opens into Broad Reach. At the head it turns north into a shallow lagoon which has a narrow passage leading to Broad Bay in Takush Harbour. This passage is navigable only at HW.* (p. 67, SD)

The entrance rapids are navigable only at very high-water slack. A rock ridge extends across the channel completely blocking access at moderate

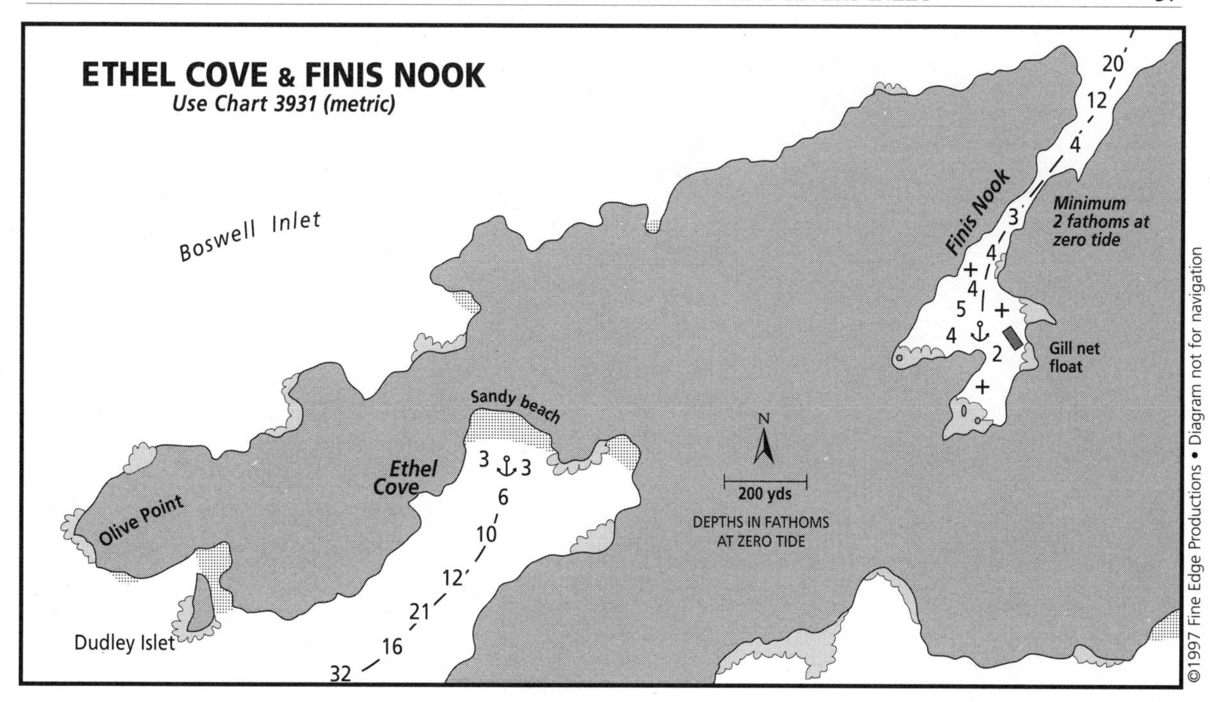

tidal heights. When the current is running across this ridge, there is significant overfall. Anchorage possibilities look interesting anywhere between Broad Reach and the drying spit east of Broad Bay. This part of the channel is shallow but access is difficult and requires careful piloting. We are told this section of Ahclakerho Channel is fun to explore with a skiff. Prawn fishermen report anchorage in the channel east of the narrows and in the bay just to the north.

Quascilla Bay

Chart 3931 metric; entrance:
51°17.65′ N, 127°22.20′ W (NAD 83)

> *Quascilla Bay, on the south side of Smith Inlet, is entered about 6 miles east of Ripon Point. A steep-to drying rock lies close east of Cape Anne, the west entrance point to the bay. Islets, drying rocks and shoals lie along the shore in the east approach.* (p. 67, SD)

Quascilla Bay has Anchor Cove in its southwest corner.

Anchor Cove

Chart 3931 metric; anchor:
51°17.23′ N, 127°22.68′ W (NAD 83)

> *Confined anchorage can be obtained by small vessels in 15 to 37 m (8 to 20 fms) in Anchor Cove on the south side of Quascilla Bay.* (p. 67, SD)

Anchor Cove is sometimes used by fishing boats, but it is a bit deep for convenient anchorage, and swinging room is said to be limited.

Anchor in about 10 fathoms over an unrecorded bottom.

Naysash Inlet

Chart 3931 metric; entrance:
51°18.37′ N, 127°22.10′ W (NAD 83)

> *Adelaide Point about 1 mile north of Quascilla Bay is at the entrance to Naysash Inlet. . . . Four miles within the entrance the inlet is narrowed by the delta of Naysash Creek. The inlet east of this delta is shallow but navigable, by small craft, to its head. The water in the inlet is discoloured and opaque.* (p. 67, SD)

Naysash Inlet is a long inlet with relatively shallow depths. The bitter end of the inlet opens into a large basin about 20 fathoms deep which is reported to be suitable for anchorage. This basin has an impressive landslide formed by a stream of rubble that jumped a cliff and extended down

A friendly visit by Fisheries & Oceans

into the inlet. The inlet waters, which have little exchange with outside waters, appear to serve as a breeding ground for plankton that discolor the water. At the outlet of Naysash Creek a large bar extends well into the inlet almost closing off the water to the east; favor the south shore here.

Hickey Cove

Chart 3931 metric; position:
51°18.45′ N, 127°20.55′ W (NAD 83)

> *Hickey Cove and Naysash Bay are on the east coast about 2 miles within [Naysash] inlet.* (p. 67, SD)

Hickey Cove, 1 mile inside Naysash Inlet, is reported to offer good protection from downslope or east winds close to the drying flat at the head of the cove.

Naysash Bay

Chart 3931 metric; position:
51°19.00′ N, 127°20.55′ W (NAD 83)

Wyclees Lagoon

Chart 3931 metric; entrance:
51°17.40′ N, 127°20.84′ W (NAD 83)

> *Wyclees Lagoon is entered 0.5 mile east of Quascilla Bay. A tidal rapids 0.5 mile within the entrance is narrow and shallow but clear of rocks and can be navigated at HW slack by craft drawing up to 1 m (3 ft). From the rapids the lagoon leads 2 miles south, then joins a basin from which arms extend 3.5 miles east and west. The daily variation in water level rarely exceeds 0.2 m (1 ft), however, during the course of a month the water level in Wyclees Lagoon fluctuates approximately 0.6 m (2 ft).* (p. 67, SD)

Wyclees Lagoon is an extraordinary example of the distance the Pacific Ocean reaches into the mainland coast, flooding steep-walled canyons. The bar at the entrance to Wyclees Lagoon can be very hazardous at spring tides with a 6-foot overfall reported over a distance of 50 yards. Within the lagoon, tidal level varies just 1 to 2 feet regardless of the level of the ocean tide. You can enter rather easily when the water in Smith Inlet is near the level inside the lagoon. At other times there can be very strong currents in the narrows.

The Docee River, which drains Long Lake, is considered one of the most important sockeye rivers between the Fraser and the Skeena. Department of Fisheries maintains a small float near the outlet to the river. Small and medium-size fishing vessels enter the lagoon during fishing season, anchoring in reasonable depths at the head of either arm of the lagoon. Anchorage can also be taken in the "Seine Hole," 0.3 miles inside the entrance and north of the rapids where depth on Chart 3931 is marked 7.4 meters. Boats that anchor here swing with the turn of the tide. The current in Seine Hole may run to 2 knots or more at spring tides. The drying rocks to the east and north of the Hole are reported to be treacherous.

Boswell Inlet

Chart 3931 metric; entrance:
51°20.00′ N, 127°34.70′ W (NAD 83)

> *Boswell Inlet is entered between Napier Island and Barb Point, on the north shore of Smith Sound.*

The passage between Denison Island and Olive Point leads from Margaret Bay into Boswell Inlet. (p. 67, SD)

Boswell Inlet has a major logging operation based in Security Bay. Otherwise, it is undeveloped with a very good cruising boat anchorage on the north side of the narrows.

Finis Nook

Chart 3931 metric; entrance:
51°20.85′ N, 127°30.07′ W; anchor:
51°20.47′ N, 127°30.41′ W (NAD 83)

Finis Nook, on the south shore of the inlet, about 1.3 miles ENE of Olive Point, is entered by a narrow passage with a least depth of 3.7 m (12 ft). The inner basin is only suitable for small craft. A private float house and floats are in Finis Nook (1982). (p. 67, SD)

Finis Nook is another "out-of-this-world" place, hidden from view and protected from outside weather. Anchorage can be taken in the center of the bay or, for small boats, closer to the southeast corner, avoiding the private gill-net floats, old pilings and shipwreck to the northeast.

The narrow entrance with its overhanging trees offers no particular problem. Midchannel fairway depth is about 2 fathoms minimum. The narrows has an irregular bottom; avoid the rock 10 feet from shore at the south side of the entrance.

Anchor in 2 to 4 fathoms over soft mud with good holding.

Security Bay

Chart 3931 metric; entrance:
51°22.02′ N, 127°28.33′ W (NAD 83)

Security Bay, 0.8 mile ENE of Twain Islands, is clear of dangers but too deep and confined for satisfactory anchorage. Small vessels may be able to anchor close to shore. A large logging camp with A-frame, oil tanks, floats and booming area are in the bay (1984). (p. 67, SD)

"Boswell Cove"

Chart 3931 metric; anchor:
51°22.53′ N, 127°26.47′ W (NAD 83)

Secure anchorage for small craft is obtainable in 7 m (23 ft), mud and shell, in a small cove, 0.4 mile NW of the narrows. The entrance is narrow with a least depth of 5.7 m (19 ft) in mid-channel. (p. 67, SD)

Boswell Cove, 0.7 mile northeast of Security Bay, is wonderfully quiet and secluded; it offers very good protection from all weather. Tucked into the north corner you are in a landlocked scenic old-growth forest environment.

Slightly favor the south shore when entering. Minimum depth in the fairway is 3 fathoms

Anchor in 2 to 3 fathoms over soft mud, sand and some grass; good to very good holding.

PASSAGES FROM SMITH SOUND TO RIVERS INLET

Chart 3934

Boats using Millbrook Cove or continuing north from Smith Sound can exit via Radar Passage or Irving Passage to rejoin the ferryboat route to Fitz Hugh Sound.

Edward and Wood rocks, 1½ miles northeast of Table Island, can be dangerous hazards upon leaving or entering Smith Sound. As an aid to identifying these hazards, Kevin Monahan has supplied this local knowledge:

"The old fathom-Chart 3776 had the accurate drying heights of 14 feet for Edward Rock and 7 feet for the easternmost of Wood Rocks. However when the new metric Chart 3934 was issued, the height of Edward Rock was shown as 2.1 meters, the same as Wood Rock. This is inaccurate. When tidal height is 3 meters, on a relatively calm day only Edward Rock shows. If Edward Rock is mistaken for Wood Rock, a skipper may find himself in trouble. The true height of Edward Rock is 4.3 meters. Any chart purchased after 1994 should have the proper corrections and should show the accurate height of Edward Rock. The older fathom-Chart 3776 was cancelled in 1994 and is now unobtainable. Skippers should check their charts and ensure that the proper drying height for Edward Rock is shown."

Boats wishing a challenge or those wanting to stay close to shore to avoid chop may find the passage north of Shield Island, around Ada Rock, inside False Egg Island and Dugout Rocks, a more comfortable route. Ada Rock is generally marked by kelp or breaking waves. While this route may be shorter, it can cause high anxiety unless a skipper is certain of his position at all times. GPS can be used to identify the proper turning points.

We have also gone inside Spur Rocks during a southeast blow. Because there are many breaking rocks off Kelp Head this route requires precise navigation.

Eliza Bay and Lucy Bay

Chart 3934 metric; east entrance:
51°19.05′ N, 127°44.25′ W (NAD 83)

> *Eliza Bay can be entered by small craft through the narrow passage between Shield Island and the mainland; local knowledge is recommended.* (p. 66, SD)

Both Eliza and Lucy bays are exposed to southwest swell and offer little or no protection for cruising boats.

Rivers Inlet

Chart 3934 metric; west entrance:
51°25.00′ N, 127°46.80′ W (NAD 83)

> *Rivers Inlet, on the east side of the entrance to Fitz Hugh Sound, is entered between Cranstown Point and Addenbroke Point, 8.7 miles north. The two entrance channels to Rivers Inlet are separated by a group of islands. The main entrance channel lies south of this group; Darby Channel, which is narrow, lies north of it.* (pp. 67, 69, SD)

Once you are past its choppy entrance, Rivers Inlet has protected waters and a reputation for some of the finest salmon fishing anywhere on the midcoast. There are a number of good anchor sites for cruising boats within Rivers Inlet, especially between Penrose and Walbran islands.

Open Bight

Chart 3934 metric; anchor:
51°22.17′ N, 127°46.44′ W (NAD 83)

> *Anchorage of a temporary nature can be obtained in Open Bight, which lies on the east side of Cranstown Point. . . .As it is exposed to north and there is usually a swell, it is only suitable for anchorage during moderate weather. The best position in which to anchor is about 0.3 mile ESE of Cranstown Point in depths of 18 to 24 m (10 to 13 fms).* (p. 69, SD)

Open Bight has a lovely, wide, white sand beach where you can take temporary shelter in all but northerly winds and chop. Outflow winds generate a bad chop against the beach here, setting you against a lee shore, but during a southerly, there is just a hint of swell here and the waters are nearly flat. Although there are several kelp patches in the bight they present little trouble in finding a clear anchor site.

Open Bight, looking out toward Queen Charlotte Sound

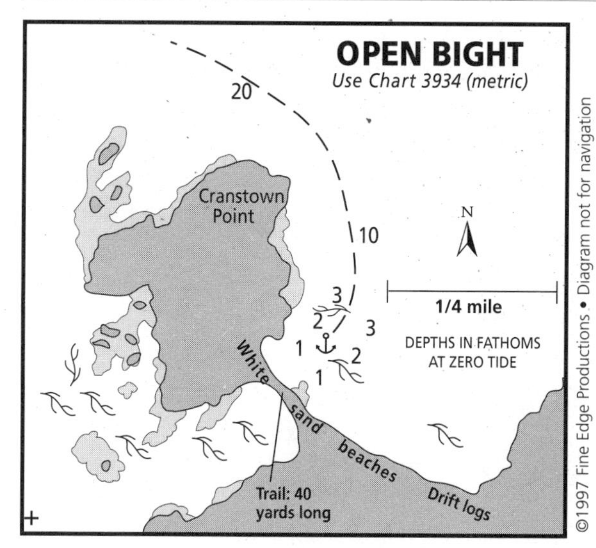

A 40-yard-long primitive trail heads south across the spit to a rugged, exposed beach facing southwest; the contrast is remarkable. This beach has white sand and the driftwood is worn and scattered. We call the trail "Cougar Trail" because of the tracks we've noticed. Make lots of noise when you hike or climb around here.

Anchor in 1 to 2 fathoms near shore over a sandy bottom with good holding.

"West Home Bay" (South Shore Rivers Inlet)

Chart 3934 metric; anchor:
51°23.88′ N, 127°43.26′ W
(NAD 83)

Uninhabited West Home Bay provides a quiet retreat and good shelter from all but down-inlet winds. Anchor between the two treed islets.

Anchor in 2 fathoms over a soft mud bottom with fair-to-good holding.

Home Bay

Chart 3934 metric; entrance:
51°23.88′ N, 127°42.48′ W (NAD 83)

> *A large floating fishing camp is at the head of Home Bay about 1 mile south of Sharbau Island.* (p. 69, SD)

Big Springs Resort, located in Home Bay, is built on a former ferry barge for rail cars. The resort provides all amenities, including a swimming pool and hot tub for its guests, many of whom fly in from overseas. It maintains a fleet of forty sportfishing boats for its guests who are reputed to be successful at catching spring Tyee. As you enter, avoid two rocks marked with a private buoy. Although you can anchor south of the resort, we prefer West Home Bay.

"Duncanby Cove"

Chart 3934 metric; anchor:
51°24.42′ N, 127°40.17′ W (NAD 83)

> *A snug anchorage for small craft is on the west side of the 44 m (145 ft) high island 0.8 mile west of Duncanby Landing.* (p. 70, SD)

Snug Duncanby Cove is a delightfully quiet anchorage when fast sportfishing boats are not active in the vicinity. Its south entrance is clear. However, if you use the north entrance, favor the east shore to avoid a dangerous rock awash on a 4.8-foot tide off the small north islet.

Anchor in the center of the bay in about 10 fathoms, or use a stern tie to shore farther north; the bottom is mixed with fair-to-good holding.

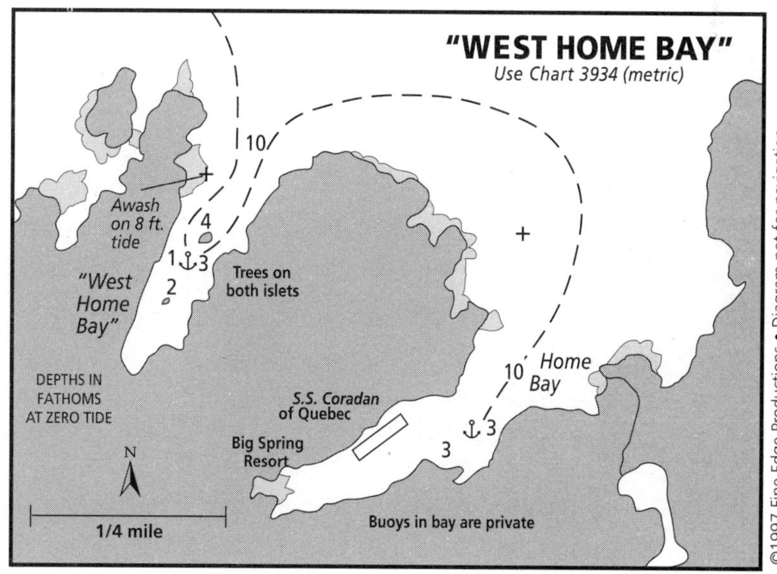

Duncanby Landing, fuel dock and store

Duncanby Landing

Chart 3934 metric; floats:
51°24.35′ N, 127°38.75′ W (NAD 83)

> *Duncanby Landing is on the east side of the entrance of Goose Bay. Floats. . .have a depth alongside of 4.3 m (14 ft). Gasoline, diesel fuel, fresh water and provisions are available . . .* (p. 70, SD)

Until 1992, Duncanby Landing was a B.C. Packers camp that supplied commercial fishing boats exclusively. Now owned and operated by Ken Gillis, Duncanby is open year-round and caters to all kinds of vessels. Its newly renovated facilities are especially convenient for cruising boats. In addition to fuel (gasoline, diesel, and propane) and water, showers, laundry, groceries and liquor are available. Future plans include additional new floats. Although there is no garbage disposal here, if you're in dire straits you may burn your "burnables" and bag up your bottles and aluminum cans for collection. Telephone is by satellite only. After riding the swells on Queen Charlotte Sound, the friendly, helpful service here makes you forget your few hours of misery. This is a welcome stop on the way north!

Goose Bay, looking north

Goose Bay

Chart 3934 metric; position:
51°22.47′ N, 127°40.09′ W (NAD 83)

> *Goose Bay is on the south side of Rivers Inlet. Cow Island, Calf Islet, and some drying rocks between them, encumber the entrance. Deep passages lie on the east and west sides of these dangers, both of which narrow to about 0.1 mile on either side of Cow Island. If entering east of Cow Island, the east shore should be favoured to avoid the shoal about 0.1 mile south of Cow Island. The best approach to the bay is east of Bull Island. A deep passage on the SW side of Bull Island is also available, but note the shoal rock on its south side.* (p. 69, SD)

Despite the discouraging comments about Goose Bay in *Sailing Directions,* we feel that small boats can find the best storm shelter in the vicinity anchored deep in Goose Bay, on either the north or southeast side of island (53). The water at this particular spot is shallow, the fetch minimal, and holding ground good. You can make your boat additionally secure if you use a stern tie to the south side of island (53), with your main anchor set well out in the mud flat.

South of the cannery, favor the island along the west shore staying about 80 feet off to avoid the first drying mud flat, as indicated in the diagram.

Examine the pilings of the old cannery at low water which display a gallery of stalked sea squirts. The water here in Goose Bay is muskeg color with visibility limited to 1 to 2 feet. The area is a major bird sanctuary where you can hear songbirds that live in the trees along shore or view eagles, blue herons, and gulls poking about the greenish mud flats. At low water, a pervasive musty odor fills the air.

Just south of Bilton Island north of Goose Bay we spent an hour watching a "herring ball" feeding frenzy—hundreds of screaming rhinoceros auklets, gulls, and bald eagles churned the water in search of their main meal.

Captain Kevin Monahan's experience in 50- and 60-foot boats differs from ours: "Goose Bay is not suitable for anchorage in southeast storms where furious gusts are experienced. In milder weather there is room for a number of boats, and it is a pleasant anchorage. I commonly use it for overnight stays. It is well protected from westerly summer winds."

Anchor in $1\frac{1}{2}$ fathoms south of island (53) over soft brown mud with very good holding.

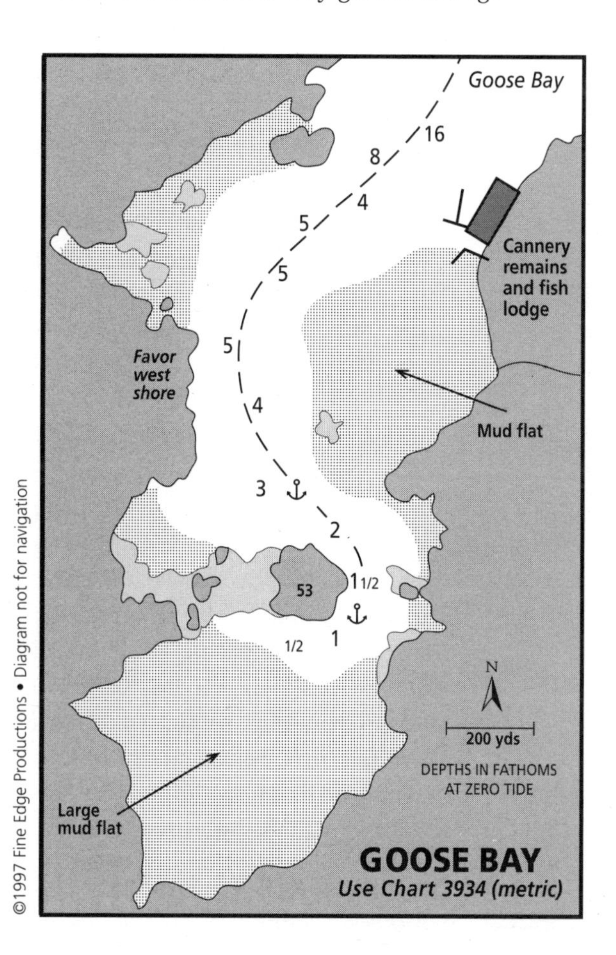

Old cannery, Goose Bay

Penrose Island and Walbran Island

Chart 3934 metric; position (Rouse Reef): 51°29.10′ N, 127°46.67′ W (NAD 83)

> *The three largest islands of the group in the entrance to Rivers Inlet are Penrose Island, Ripon Island and Walbran Island. Quoin Hill, near the centre of Penrose Island, rises to 253 m (830 ft).* (p. 69, SD)

Penrose Island was established as a British Columbia marine park in 1992. Its undeveloped 5000 acres are popular with kayakers. Penrose and Walbran islands form a unique archipelago of small coves and narrow channels best enjoyed by kayak or dinghy; a destination unto themselves.

"Fury Cove," Schooner Retreat

Chart 3934 metric; anchor: 51°29.25′ N, 127°45.65′ W (NAD 83)

> *Schooner Retreat is the group name given to several anchorages among the group of islands off the SW side of Penrose Island. Named anchorages of this group are Frigate Bay, Secure Anchorage and Exposed Anchorage; they afford secure anchorage for small vessels. During SE and SW gales the gusts are furious in these anchorages, but with good ground tackle and care there is no danger in Schooner Retreat. . . . The bay to the NE of Fury Island offers good anchorage and shelter for small craft. A private cabin and float are on the NW shore of Fury Island.* (p. 69, SD)

Fury Cove, located on the far west end of Penrose

Fury Cove, looking west

Island, is one of our favorite anchorages. On either a north- or southbound journey, its strategic location can provide relief from outside weather. From the spit at its west end you can watch conditions in the sound outside. Although winds and chop funnel across the spit at high tide, in our many visits, we've never found it to be uncomfortable. We enjoy poking about on shore and the views from the outer beach. This area is now included within the Penrose Marine Park boundaries, and Fury Cove makes a good base from which to explore the entire park by kayak or skiff.

Entering Schooner Retreat and Fury Cove for the first time can be a hair-raising experience. It's not easy to identify all the islands and openings, but with experience it becomes easier. The fairway is deep and we have not yet seen waves break across the entrance (unlike Breaker Pass, the next pass north, which can be used safely only in calm weather). However, if there is a big southwest swell running outside with wind blowing, white water and foam do blow across the outer entrance to Schooner Retreat, making it more difficult and dangerous to enter, and you should not attempt to do so in poor visibility. Although we don't recommend it, it's possible to enter using radar, with the help of GPS.

Cleve Island, with Fury Point on its south end, lies southwest of Fury Island. It has vertical walls on its northwest side as if it had been cleft from Fury Island. Stay east of Cleve, noting the white paint on the islet north of Folly Islet that marks the entrance.

In poor visibility avoid Rouse Reef, which is awash on about a 14-foot tide. The waves heaping and breaking on this reef show up on radar at high tide. Rouse Island is covered with trees. Rouse Point lies on its southern tip. When you are correctly lined up to enter Exposed Anchorage—the outer chamber for Fury Cove—your heading should be about 015° magnetic. On this heading you are directly in line with Dyer Islets at the north center end of Exposed Anchorage. When you are about 250 yards in front of Dyer Islets, execute a sharp left turn. The swell diminishes at once and you pass through the narrow opening to calm Fury Cove.

Anchor in 2 to 3 fathoms over a soft bottom with good holding.

"FURY COVE" & SCHOONER RETREAT

Use Chart 3934 (metric)

The western Penrose Island complex includes the following anchor sites:

Schooner Retreat entrance:
51°28.57′ N, 127°45.73′ W (NAD 83)

Frigate Bay entrance
(Safe Entrance): 51°27.78′ N, 127°45.00′ W;
anchor: 51°28.40′ N, 127°43.75′ W (NAD 83)

Secure Anchorage anchor:
51°28.48′ N, 127°44.42′ W (NAD 83)

Exposed Anchorage position (turn for Fury Cove):
51°28.90′ N, 127°45.15′ W (NAD 83)

Rocky Bay position:
51°28.83′ N, 127°44.26′ W (NAD 83)

Klaquaek Channel, "The Lake"

Chart 3934 metric; southwest entrance:
51°27.25′ N, 127°44.00′ W; northeast entrance:
51°30.60′ N, 127°40.82′ W (NAD 83)

Klaquaek Channel is entered from south between Dimsey Point and Bilton Island. Barry Rock, 1.3 miles ESE of Dimsey Point, lies in the south approach. The channel between Bilton Island and Ripon Island, to the NE, is narrow and tortuous. The north end of Klaquaek Channel leads into Darby Channel through two narrow boat passages. (p. 69, SD)

Klaquaek Channel separates Penrose Island from Walbran Island. Because both the north and south entrances to the channel are encumbered with small islands the channel is very well protected and is sometimes referred to as "The Lake." On either side of Klaquaek Channel there are a number of secure anchorages, namely Frypan, Big Frypan, Magee Channel, Five Window Cove and Sunshine Bay. These waters are fantastic exploring grounds for kayaks or dinghies.

As Monahan puts it, "The north entrance is known as "Slaughter Alley" as it is the site of a massacre of the local Owikeno natives by the Haida from Queen Charlotte Islands. As you approach the passage on a heading of 224° true, if the shoreline of the 96-foot island lines up, you are headed directly for the westernmost dangerous rock. However, if you stay to the east of this line by a small amount, approximately 100 meters, so that the whole length of the shoreline through the narrows is visible, then the approach can be made in safety. Be careful not to stray too far to the east, because there is another off-lying rock to the east. The western [northern] entrance to 'The Lake' should not be attempted."

The authors have found the western [northern] entrance to be useful for small boats. Approaching from Fitz Hugh Sound, make an S-shaped turn through the narrows. First favor the east shore island (96) staying within about 60 feet in 4 fathoms of water to avoid the rock awash in about 13 feet in the center of the channel. Then favor the west shore (Penrose Island) to avoid a long, narrow, bare islet that has a submerged shoal at its north end which lies along island (96). Minimum depth in the fairway is about 3 to 4 fathoms.

Frypan Bay

Chart 3934 metric; entrance:
51°29.64′ N, 127°42.02′ W; anchor:
51°29.65′ N, 127°42.40′ W (NAD 83)

Frypan Bay, a similar bay about 0.7 mile north, has the NE corner obstructed by boomsticks (1988). (p. 69, SD)

Frypan Bay, on the northeast corner of Penrose Island, offers very good anchorage over a generally flat 9-fathom bottom. Larger boats can anchor in the middle of the bay, while small boats may want to use the cove just inside the entrance. The northern nooks of Frypan Bay are full of boomsticks and net floats; the south shore offers good protection. Avoid several small rocks along the shore.

Anchor (south cove) in 3 fathoms over a mixed bottom of unrecorded holding.

Big Frypan Bay

Chart 3934 metric; entrance:
51°29.17′ N, 127°42.36′ W; anchor south cove:
51°28.87′ N, 127°42.82′ W; anchor 10-foot hole:
51°28.90′ N, 127°43.16′ W (NAD 83)

Big Frypan Bay, an almost landlocked bay, lies close east of Quoin Hill. (p. 69, SD)

Big Frypan Bay offers excellent protection from southerly weather along its south shore. Large

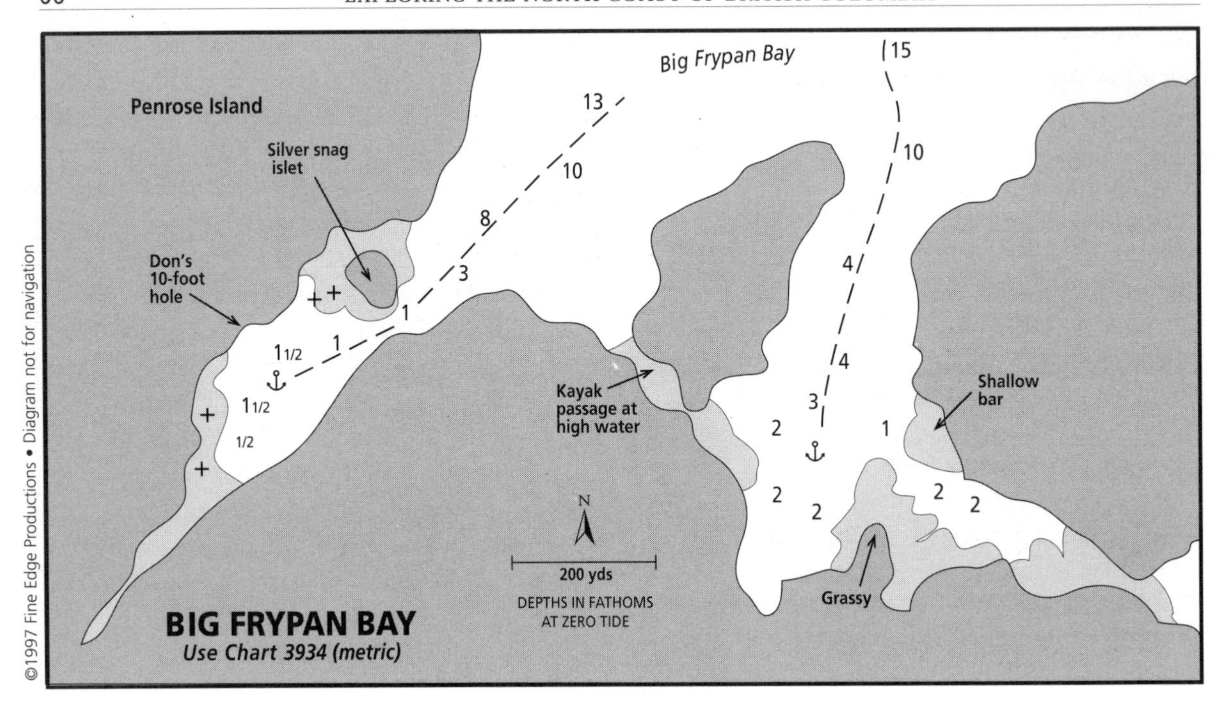

boats may find anchorage in the center of the bay in about 15 fathoms, while small boats have a choice of intimate anchor sites close to shore. The narrow entrance carries a minimum depth of 6 1/2 fathoms in its fairway.

Pleasant anchorage can be found off the entrance to the lagoon between a small grassy peninsula and a high-water kayak route south of the island to the west. Small boats may anchor in the lagoon entrance east of the grassy peninsula and the 1-fathom entrance bar.

A more secluded anchorage for one or two small boats can be found in the very southwest corner of Big Frypan Bay behind what we call Silver Snag Islet. There is a narrow passage on the east side of Silver Snag Islet with about 4 feet at zero tide. To the southwest of the islet is a small, flat bottom area which has a depth of 10 feet at zero tide. The *Baidarka* crew calls this "Don's 10-Foot Hole."

The sun seldom reaches this nook; tree branches overhang the water and there is no beach. But there are lots of eagles and lime-green moss, and it's a good place to sit out a storm. Avoid the foul area west of the islet and two large rocks on the southwest side of the nook. If more than one boat uses this nook, consider using a stern tie.

Anchor in 4 fathoms over a sand and mud bottom with good holding.

Sunshine Bay

Chart 3934 metric; entrance:
51°28.55′ N, 127°40.75′ W; anchor:
51°28.65′ N, 127°40.00′ W (NAD 83)

> *. . . Sunshine Bay penetrates Ripon Island. This bay provides excellent anchorage for small craft. Several private float houses are in the bay (1988).* (p. 69, SD)

Sunshine Bay has a narrow entrance with an irregular bottom and a minimum depth of about 2 fathoms. Inside Sunshine Bay there is plenty of swinging room for several boats over a flat 5-fathom bottom. The bay is very busy, however, and while it offers excellent protection, it no longer offers a wilderness experience. Those seeking such an experience can find it in the next bay north which we call Five Window Cove (see diagram).

Anchor in the center of the bay in 5 fathoms over soft sand with grass bottom with fair holding.

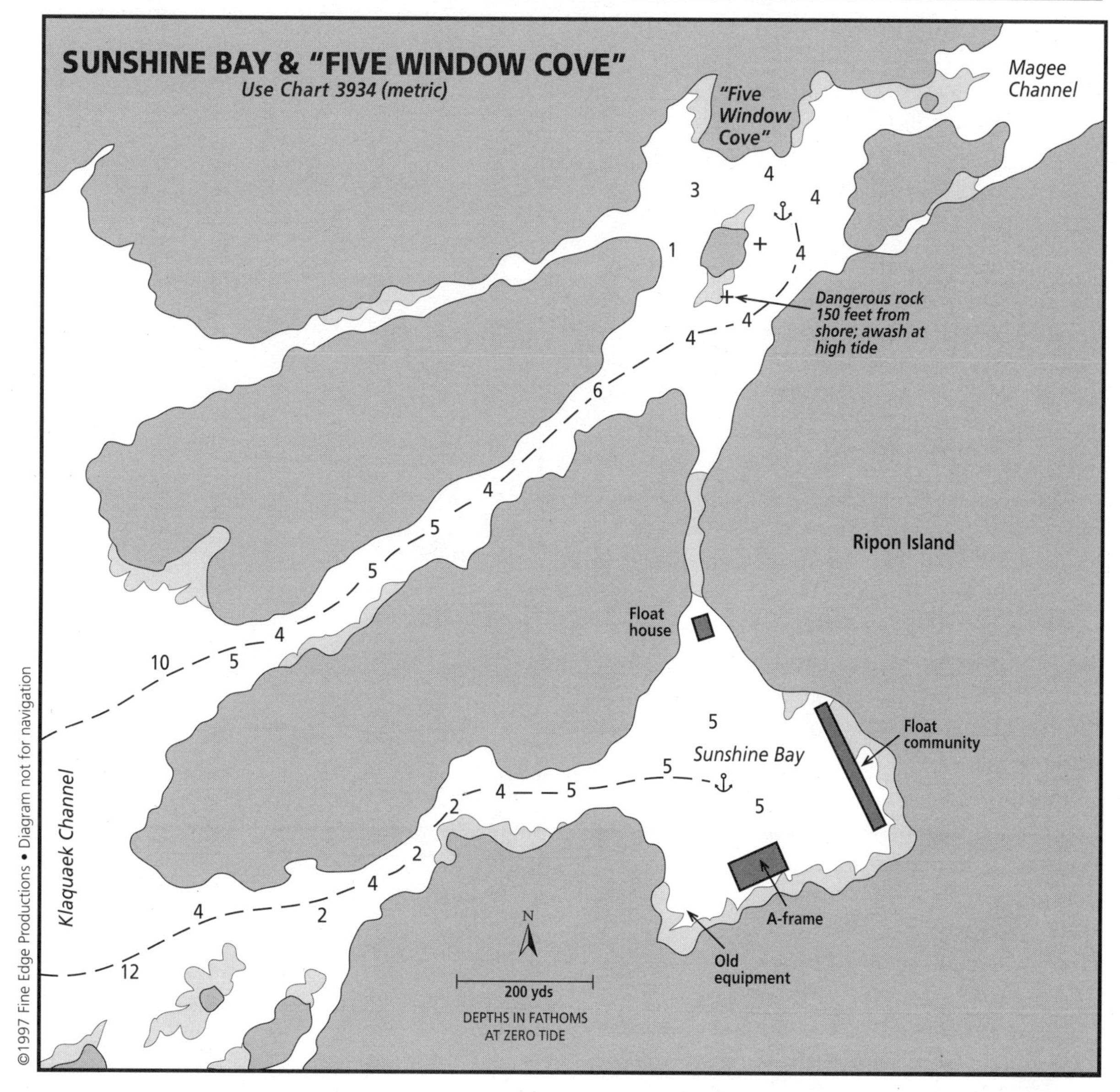

"Five Window Cove"

Chart 3934 metric; entrance:
51°28.73' N, 127°40.75' W; anchor:
51°29.08' N, 127°39.95' W (NAD 83)

Immediately north of Sunshine Bay there is a cove formed by the intersection of five islands. The windows represent the extremely narrow passages between the islands. Five Window Cove is quiet and offers a pristine wilderness experience.

The southwest passage indicated on the diagram is the only viable small-boat passage since the others can be used only at high water by kayaks. The water in Five Window Cove is calm with overhanging cedar, hemlock and alder branches along shore.

The best anchorage is on the east side of the center islet, avoiding its two rocks, especially the rock 150 feet from the south shore.

Anchor in 4 fathoms over a largely sand bottom with some grass with fair-to-good holding.

Magee Channel

Chart 3934 metric; west entrance:
51°29.52′ N, 127°40.95′ W; anchor:
51°29.36′ N, 127°38.72′ W (NAD 83)

> *Magee Channel is only suitable for small craft because of the rocks and shoals in it.* (p. 69, SD)

The western end of Magee Channel is easily navigable and well protected. The east end of the channel has foul ground and is suitable only for dinghies. Small boats can find another wilderness experience in the center portion of Magee Channel east of the second narrows and east of the mid-channel islet. Spruce, cedar and hemlock branches hang down into the saltwater at high tide.

The islet just east of the second narrows has a canoe pass on its south side which is blocked by limbs. Small boats can pass north of the islet in a passage about 50 feet wide between tree branches. Favor the north shore. Anchor between the islet and the rock at the east end of the basin which bares 1 foot above high water. Larger boats can anchor just west of the second narrows between the float houses at either side of the channel in 12 fathoms.

Anchor in about 6 fathoms over an unrecorded bottom.

Wilson Bay

Chart 3934 metric; entrance:
51°27.55′ N, 127°39.05′ W (NAD 83)

> *Wilson Bay, 4 miles north of Goose Bay, is too deep and exposed to have value as an anchorage.* (p. 70, SD)

Wilson Bay has a basin in its northwest corner which can be entered by small craft at high water.

Taylor Bay

Chart 3934 metric; anchor:
51°30.78′ N, 127°36.25′ W (NAD 83)

> *Taylor Bay and Hemasila Inlet, both north of Geetla Point and on the east side of Walbran Island, are unsuitable as anchorages, except for small craft, owing to insufficient swinging space.* (p. 70, SD)

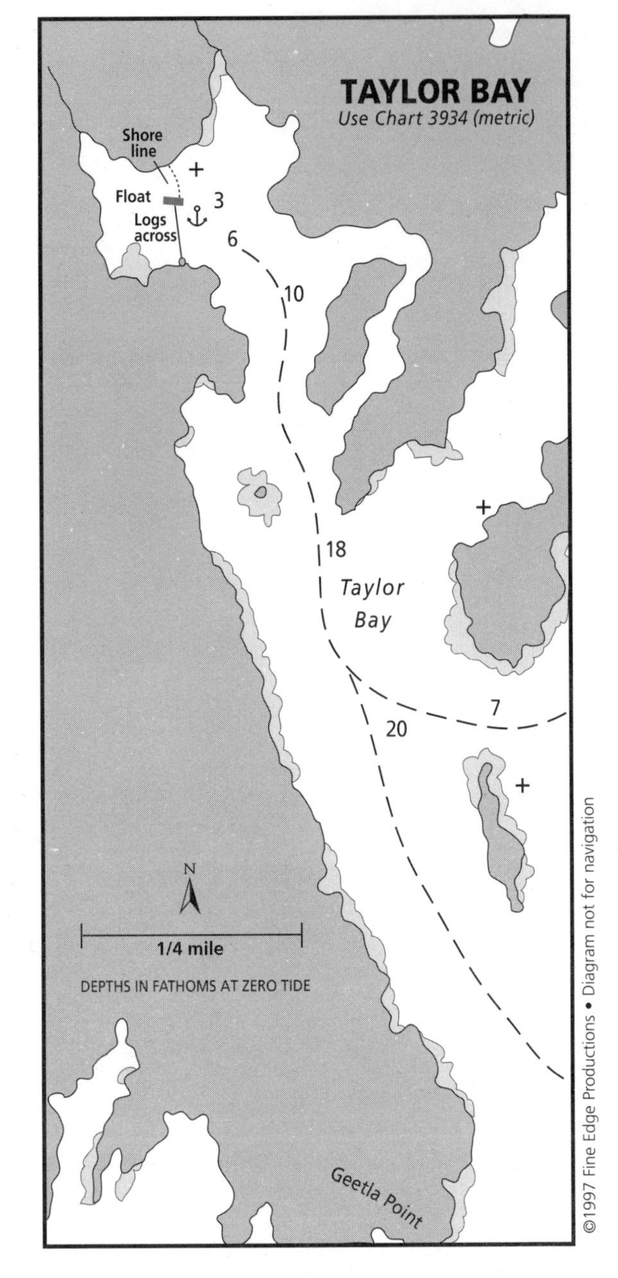

Taylor Bay, on the east side of Walbran Island, is typical of the myriad of small inlets, channels, and lagoons found in Rivers Inlet. From the east side of Walbran Island to the west side of Penrose Island, you can explore narrow, shallow channels by kayak or dinghy. If you do, don't be surprised by an outboard that occasionally whizzes by. There is a cemetery on the small island in Taylor Bay.

Good protection is afforded for small craft at

the far northwest end of Taylor Bay; although this area is sometimes used to store floats and boomsticks. Larger boats can find good protection and more swinging room in deeper water northwest of the island.

Anchor as far west as appropriate in 2 fathoms over a mud bottom of unrecorded holding power.

Hemasila Inlet

Chart 3934 metric; entrance:
51°31.30′ N, 127°35.15′ W (NAD 83)

> *Taylor Bay and Hemasila Inlet, both north of Geetla Point and on the east side of Walbran Island, are unsuitable as anchorages, except for small craft, owing to insufficient swinging space.* (p. 70, SD)

Darby Channel

Chart 3934 metric; west entrance:
51°30.80′ N, 127°45.40′ W; east entrance: 51°34.50′ N, 127°35.00′ W (NAD 83)

> *Darby Channel is entered between the north side of Penrose Island and Addenbroke Point.* (p. 70, SD)

Darby Channel is the northern route from Fitz Hugh Sound to Dawsons Landing in the upper part of Rivers Inlet. The narrows west of Pendleton Island offers little problem to cruising boats; consult the inset on Chart 3934 metric to help avoid Stevens Rocks and the rock marked with a daymark in the center of the narrows.

Pierce Bay

Chart 3934 metric; anchor (West Cove): 51°31.96′ N, 127°46.00′ W; anchor (East Cove): 51°32.23′ N, 127°45.00′ W (NAD 83)

> *Pierce Bay, on the north side of Darby Channel, is exposed and offers little shelter.* (p. 70, SD)

Pierce Bay, the first bay on the north shore east of Addenbroke Point, has a number of small islands in its western portion that form an isolated cove where you can get good protection from all weather. The bottom of Pierce Bay is not well charted, and since there are a number of isolated uncharted shoals in the bay you should not attempt to enter it during times of poor visibility or under radar. There is an active log dump at the north end of Pierce Bay.

The entrance to West Cove has an irregular bottom and an intricate passage that hugs the west shore. This passage is not for the faint-hearted, and it is important to identify and avoid each rock and kelp bed. Entry may be easiest at low tide to help identify the various hazards. Underwater visibility is poor due to the opaque water. Seagulls

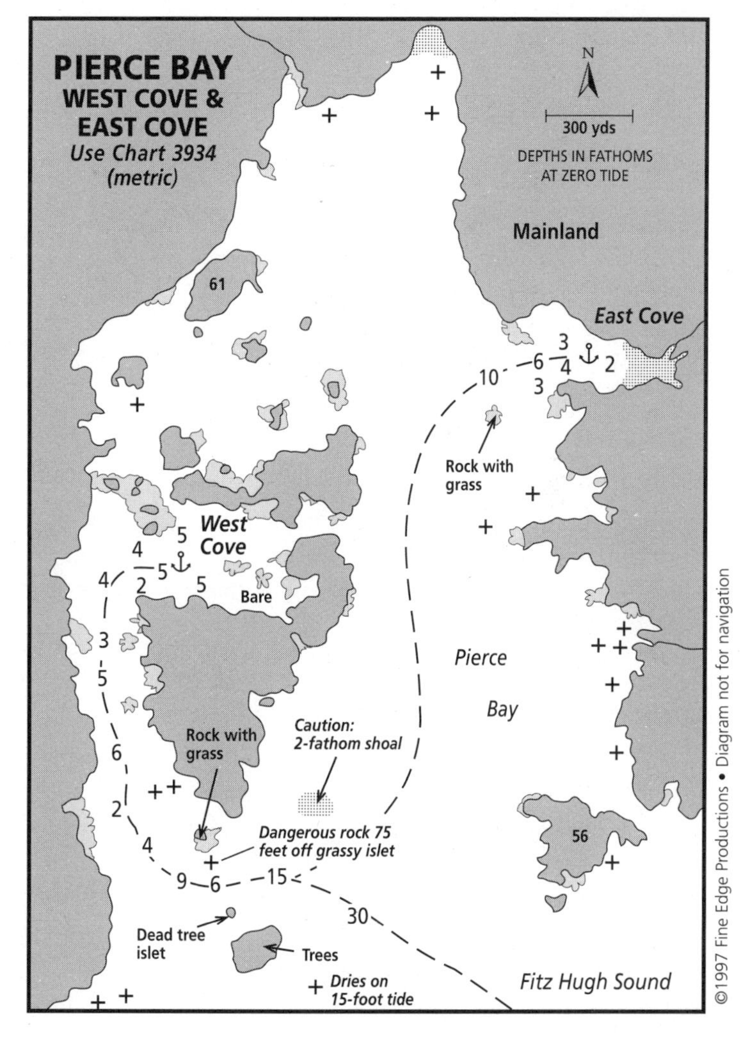

use this cove to sit out gales, and during quiet weather you can hear loons calling, so you know it must be a good place.

The bottom—extremely soft black mud—is the consistency of jello so be sure your anchor is well set, and consider using a stern tie to shore if strong winds prevail.

East Cove offers good protection in most weather, if you anchor just short of the drying flat, deep in the cove. Old-growth trees line the shore, and a stream from Elsie Lake comes in at the head of the cove.

Anchor (West Cove) in about 4 fathoms over a soft black mud bottom; holding is poor to fair.

Anchor (East Cove) in about 4 fathoms over an unrecorded bottom.

Morgan Bay

Chart 3934 metric; position:
51°31.96′ N, 127°40.90′ W (NAD 83)

A shoal lies 0.2 mile SW of the east entrance point of Morgan Bay. Shoals, with less than 2 m (6 ft) over them, lie in the approach and the entrance to the small cove 0.6 mile SE. (p. 70, SD)

"Float Camp Cove"

Chart 3934 metric; position:
51°31.52′ N, 127°40.28′ W (NAD 83)

A float camp is at the head of this cove (1988). (p. 70, SD)

Float Camp Cove, a half mile north of Fleming Point, is reported to offer good shelter for small craft in the center of the bay.

Finn Bay

Chart 3934 metric; entrance: 51°30.42′ N, 127°43.36′ W; position: 51°30.07′ N, 127°44.10′ W (NAD 83)

Finn Bay, on the north side of Penrose Island, provides shelter for small craft. Float houses and floats are moored in the bay and houses lie on the north shore, just within the entrance. A rock, with less than 2 m (6 ft) over it, lies off the north side of the bay, about 0.2 mile inside the entrance. (p. 70, SD)

The Discovery Coast ferry stopped here on its initial run in 1996, but we hear that this stop may have been cancelled. Numerous float camps and barges line the shore, and a log dump and fill ramp are located on the north side of the bay. Float plane and boat activity make this a noisy bay. However, if you get caught in Fitz Hugh Sound in a southeast storm, Finn Bay offers very good protection, and its floats and logbooms can provide emergency mooring.

Sleepy Bay

Chart 3934 metric; entrance:
51°30.48′ N, 127°40.13′ W; position:
51°30.14′ N, 127°39.23′ W (NAD 83)

Sleepy Bay penetrates the north shore of Walbran Island. (p. 70, SD)

Sleepy Bay, along with Finn Bay to the west, are good places to seek shelter from southeast storm winds, but both are full of float houses, fishing boats, and float planes, and we recommend their use only in an emergency.

Dawsons Landing

Chart 3934 metric; float:
51°34.48′ N, 127°35.50′ W (NAD 83)

Dawsons Landing is a small settlement. It has a public wharf 12 m (40 ft) long with a least depth of 4.6 m (15 ft) alongside, also a Department of Fisheries float 18 m (60 ft) long with depths of 1.5 to 6.7 m (5 to 22 ft) alongside. There is a post office (V0N 1M0), a liquor store, and a general store with about 244 m (800 ft) of floats for visiting craft and a good stock of food, hardware, fishing gear and dry goods. Charts, water, ice, gasoline, diesel fuel, stove oil, naphtha and lubrication products are available. A coastal supply vessel calls regularly and air service is available. Float houses line the shore north of the floats. (p. 70, SD)

Dawsons Landing is a resort and supply center for the sport and commercial fishing trade. The store is one of those old-fashioned general stores that stocks everything from soup to outboard motor parts. Both diesel and gasoline are now available with the installation of new storage tanks. A water hose is available on the float in front of the store. Dawsons monitors Channel 06 VHF.

Photo courtesy CHS, Pacific Region

Dawson's Landing

Draney Inlet

Chart 3931 metric; entrance:
51°28.50′ N, 127°34.00′ W (NAD 83)

> *Draney Narrows, the entrance to Draney Inlet, is 4 miles NE of Goose Bay.* (p. 70, SD)

Draney Inlet penetrates 14 miles into the mainland coastal mountains.

Draney Narrows

Chart 3931 metric (inset); position (shoal rock):
51°28.42′ N, 127°33.77′ W (NAD 83)

> *A shoal rock lies in the west entrance with deeper water around it and through the narrows.*
>
> *Tidal Streams through Draney Narrows have an estimated rate of 8 to 10 kn. With strong ebb streams a chute of white water develops around the rock mentioned above. Secondary current station Draney Narrows (Index No. 8508), referenced on Prince Rupert, is given in the Tide Tables, Volume 6.* (p. 70, SD)

The water in Draney Narrows is turbulent but not particularly dangerous for well-powered boats. At low current or near slack water the passage is quite easy. By approaching the narrows from the north during ebb flow, it is possible to stay out of the tidal stream and observe conditions before entering. Attention should be paid to the turbulence over the shoal and the shoal avoided. (See inset on Chart 3931.) Remember that turbulence occurs some distance down-current from the rock. It is not always easy to judge the conditions in the narrows from the west when the tide is flooding, due to the curves in the channel.

Fishhook Bay

Chart 3931 metric; anchor:
51°27.69′ N, 127°33.11′ W
(NAD 83)

> *. . . Fishhook Bay affords anchorage for small vessels in the cove on the south side of its entrance and anchorage with excellent shelter inside the bay.* (p. 70, SD)

Fishhook Bay offers landlocked shelter at its far west end. However, it is used as a base for logging operations.

Anchor in 3 fathoms over an unrecorded bottom.

Allard Bay

Chart 3931 metric; entrance:
51°26.40′ N, 127°19.20′ W; position:
51°27.75′ N, 127°19.07′ W (NAD 83)

> *Allard Bay, 9 miles within the inlet, is narrow, shallow and dries 0.4 mile within the entrance.* (p. 70, SD)

Allard Bay offers good protection from westerly winds. Although it may offer protection from other winds we have no knowledge of what happens in southeast storms.

Johnston Bay

Chart 3932 metric; position:
51°29.50′ N, 127°32.70′ W (NAD 83)

> *Johnston Bay, on the east side of the inlet and opposite the entrance to Hemasila Inlet, has a reef awash in the middle of its entrance.* (p. 70, SD)

Johnston Bay offers excellent anchorage in most weather. A fishing lodge reportedly will be located here in the near future.

Enter west of the reef in the middle of the

Heading north past False Egg Island

entrance. Favor the west shore as you approach the inner basin.

Anchor in 5 to 6 fathoms over a mud bottom with good holding.

Good Hope

Chart 3932 metric; position:
51°34.25′ N, 127°30.95′ W (NAD 83)

> *Ida Island lies close off a small bay in which is the former cannery of Good Hope. The Sandell River flows into the bay close south of the old settlement. Good Hope is now a private resort and during the fishing season a floating breakwater, constructed of logs, is placed south of the wharf and floats. The resort was not operating in 1983 but a caretaker was there. A narrow passage, on the NE side of Ida Island, has a least depth of 7.6 m (25 ft) and is usable by small craft.* (pp. 70-71, SD)

The resort located at Good Hope has been operating as Salmon King Lodge.

Sandell Bay

Chart 3932 metric; position:
51°39.60′ N, 127°32.87′ W (NAD 83)

> *Sandell Bay has Tseeiskay River at its head. Rutherford Creek enters the inlet at Brunswick. Only a few ruined piles remain at this former cannery site.* (p. 71, SD)

Sandell Bay is open to south and upslope winds which likely die off near the head of the bay.

Shotbolt Bay

Chart 3932 metric; position:
51°39.23′ N, 127°21.28′ W (NAD 83)

> *A logging camp is in . . . Shotbolt Bay. A floating sports fishing camp is moored 1.5 miles NE of Shotbolt Bay (1988).* (p. 71, SD)

King Salmon Resort operates a fishing camp located here in Shotbolt Bay. Sportfishing for fin fish is not permitted during summer periods near the mouth of the Wannock River. The boundary is marked by square markers just east of Shotbolt Bay on the south and east of Kilbella Bay on the north. Check the current edition of *Tidal Waters Sport Fishing Guide* for details of this famous fishing area.

Kilbella Bay

Chart 3932 metric; position:
51°42.20′ N, 127°20.40′ W (NAD 83)

> *Kilbella Bay is on the north side of Rivers Inlet about 3 miles from the head. The mud bank in the bay is steep-to and forms the delta to both Kilbella River and Chuckwalla River. A logging camp is in Kilbella Bay (1988). . . .* (p. 71, SD)

Kilbella Bay has a log dump and log booming facility on its east shore. Sportfishing is restricted in this area; consult the *Tidal Waters Sport Fishing Guide*. The Kilbella and Chuckwalla rivers flow into Kilbella Bay through a large U-shaped valley. This is good grizzly country and they are usually found feeding along the rivers.

Rivers Inlet

Chart 3932 metric; float:
51°41.10′ N, 127°15.75′ W (NAD 83)

> *Wannock River, which flows into the head of Rivers Inlet, drains Owikeno Lake, about 3 miles to the east. Steep-to sand banks have formed on both sides of the river. An Indian village, with wharf and float, is on the north side of the river mouth. A public wharf and float and an active logging operation (1988) are on the north side at the head of the inlet. A marine farm is on the north shore (1988) about 1 mile west of the public wharf.* (p. 71, SD)

Rivers Inlet is the name of the post office located at the outlet of Wannock River. There is a breakwater and small-boat harbor with public floats in front of Owikeno, a First Nation's village.

Hardy Inlet

Chart 3932 metric; entrance:
51°41.40′ N, 127°27.50′ W (NAD 83)

> *Hardy Inlet is very deep and the shores are steep-to the head.* (p. 72, SD)

The area from Hardy Inlet north is grizzly bear country, and in the fall, they are generally found fattening themselves along the streams or occasionally rummaging along the mud flats at low tide.

Moses Inlet

Chart 3932 metric; entrance:
51°39.50′ N, 127°27.50′ W (NAD 83)

> *Moses Inlet entered to the west of McAllister Point leads about 14 miles north.* (p. 72, SD)

Moses Inlet is a deep steep-sided fjord with many high bluffs along the shore. This is in the heart of grizzly country. Inrig Bay, Eberts Cove and the head of Moses Inlet have logging facilities.

Photo by Herb Nickles

Constant maintenance!

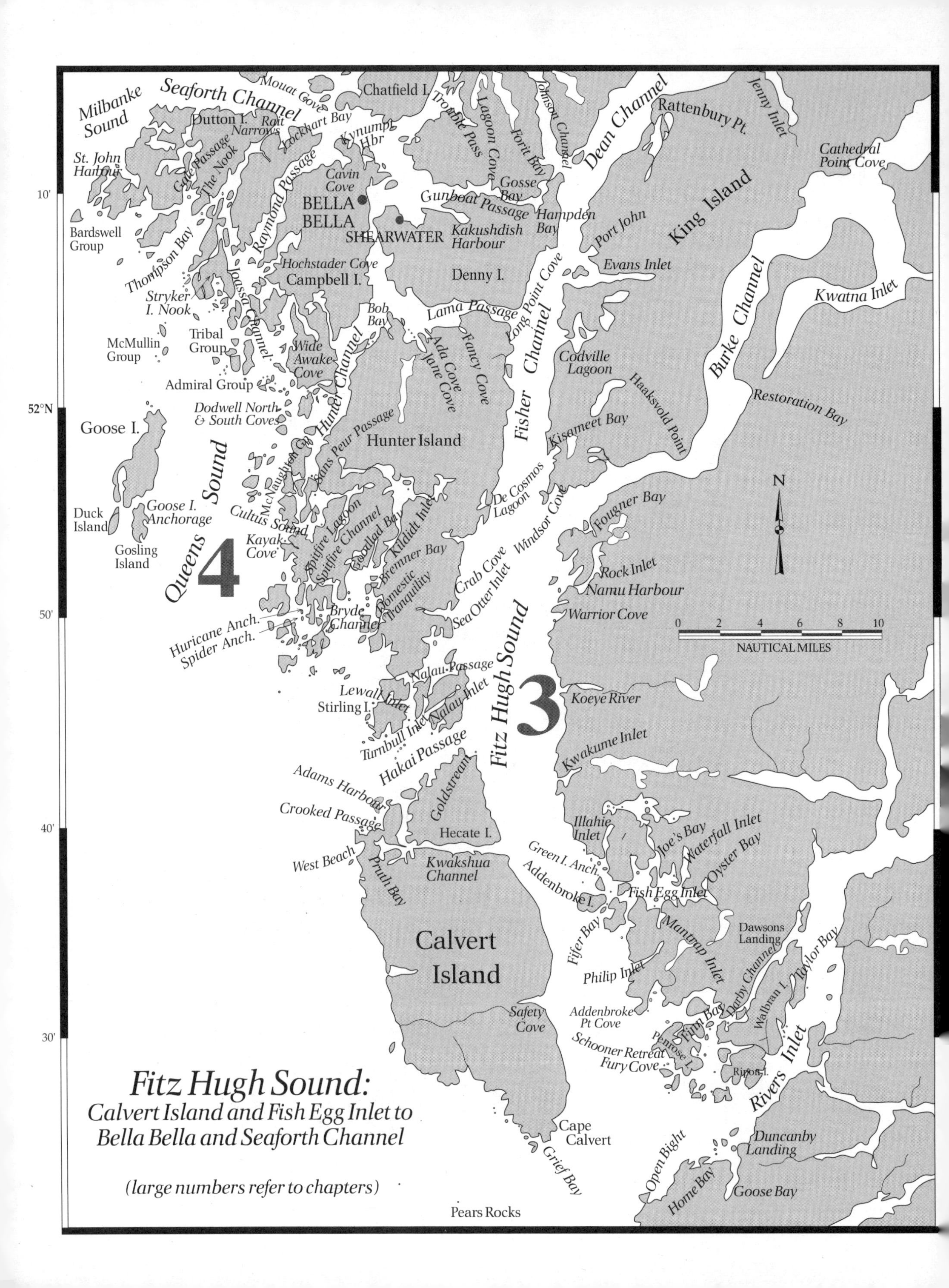

Fitz Hugh Sound:
Calvert Island and Fish Egg Inlet to Bella Bella and Seaforth Channel

(large numbers refer to chapters)

3

Fitz Hugh Sound: Calvert Island and Fish Egg Inlet to Bella Bella and Seaforth Channel

Fitz Hugh Sound, on the east side of Calvert Island, marks the continuation of the Inland Passage smooth-water route. There are a number of good anchorages along Fisher Sound and Fisher Channel that allow you to cruise at a leisurely pace before or after you cross Queen Charlotte Sound. For years Safety Cove, on the east side of Calvert Island, has been the most popular anchorage. More and more cruising boats, however, are finding favorable anchor sites in other locations, such as Fury Cove (noted in Chapter 2), Green Island Anchorage at the entrance to Fish Egg Inlet, or Goldstream Harbour at the north end of Calvert Island, all quieter and more scenic than Safety Cove; farther north, Codville Lagoon in Fisher Channel, is a favorite site.

Fitz Hugh Sound, Lama Passage, and Seaforth Channel have ferry, cruising ship and commercial traffic at all hours of the day and night, so you need to be on the alert at all times. Although Calvert Island has a radio repeater that repeats Comox radio transmissions on Channel 16 and weather channel 2, it has poor modulation and is difficult to understand. As you approach Bella Bella, you can pick up Prince Rupert Coast Guard radio on both Channel 16 and the weather channels, and reception is better.

Fitz Hugh Sound

Chart 3934 metric; south entrance: 51°23.50′ N, 127°50.00′ W; north entrance: 51°55.50′ N, 127°56.25′ W (NAD 83)

The entrance to Fitz Hugh Sound lies between Cranstown Point and Cape Calvert, about 5.5 miles NW. (p. 72, SD)

Grief Bay, Calvert Island

The westerly swells quickly die off as you proceed north of Cape Calvert in Fitz Hugh Sound. However, a nasty chop can be found southeast of Cape Calvert on westerlies or southwest winds when large ebb currents flow out of Rivers Inlet. Tidal streams in Fitz Hugh Sound and the channels north and east flow south at up to 2 knots. North/south winds enhance or retard this

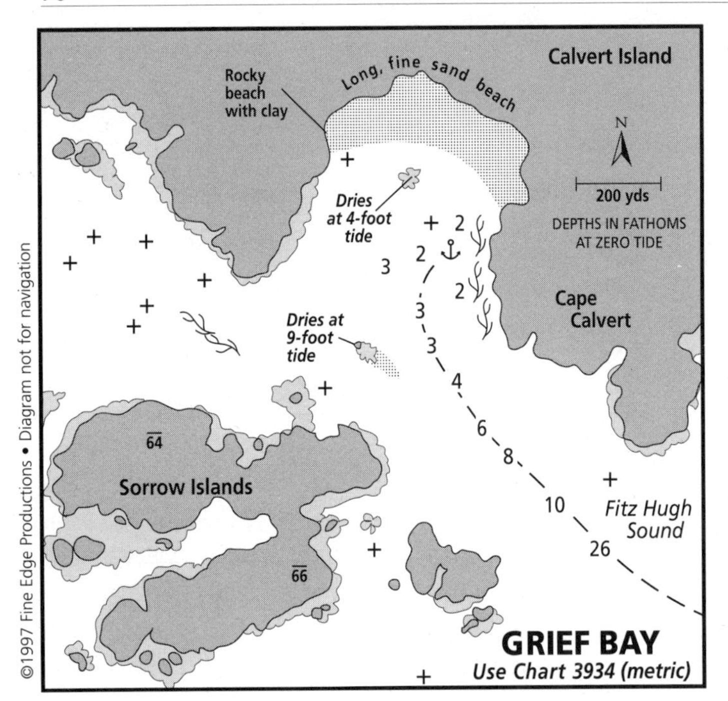

current, and during times of heavy runoff, the northbound flood all but disappears. When the current and wind are in opposition, a nasty chop can develop and a quick duck into one of the nearby coves is highly recommended.

Cape Calvert

Chart 3934 metric; Clark Point light:
51°25.80′ N, 127°53.20′ W (NAD 83)

> *Cape Calvert is about 300 feet (91m) high and densely wooded; it presents a broad face of rocky coast.* (p. 65, SD)

Cape Calvert, at the southern end of steep, high Calvert Island, marks the beginning of Fitz Hugh Sound and the smooth-water route to Prince Rupert. There is a weather repeater atop Calvert Island. As you head north, Safety Cove offers the first shelter.

Grief Bay

Chart 3934 metric; entrance:
51°24.90′ N, 127°54.40′ W; anchor:
51°25.31′ N, 127°54.68′ W (NAD 83)

> *Grief Bay, north of Sorrow Islands, offers fair shelter for small craft; however, during onshore gales the swell entering the bay makes landing both difficult and dangerous.* (p. 65, SD)

Grief Bay, at the southern tip of Calvert Island, offers an interesting temporary anchorage in the lee of Sorrow Islands, but this is not a good place to be caught in a southeast storm. While history suggests that the coast along the west shore of Calvert Island is foul and treacherous, we find Grief Bay a wonderful place to spend an afternoon. A large, sandy beach with a varied collection of driftwood, flotsam and jetsam surrounds the bay. Because of the large kelp beds between Sorrow Island and Calvert Island, westerly swells don't penetrate.

Monahan suggests that Grief Bay offers protection from winter outflow winds although the surge of northeast seas can make things uncomfortable.

Anchor in 2 to 3 fathoms over a sand bottom with fair holding.

Canoe Cove

Chart 3934 metric; position:
51°28.02′ N, 127°52.68′ W (NAD 83)

Canoe Cove is just that—a good place to haul out a canoe or a kayak, but too small for cruising boats, other than as a lunch stop.

Safety Cove

Chart 3934 metric; anchor:
51°31.85′ N, 127°55.90′ W (NAD 83)

> *Safety Cove, on the west side of Fitz Hugh Sound, is entered about 6 miles north of Clark Point. There is good anchorage, in a depth of 27 m (15 fms), mud, in the middle of Safety Cove. During SE or NE gales, strong gusts blow across the valley at the head of the bay. . . Public mooring buoys are in the cove.* (p. 72, SD)

Although Safety Cove is easy to enter and provides good protection in most weather, it isn't our favorite place. It is too deep for convenient anchorage, and because large vessels tend to choose this anchorage, smaller boats are subjected to the noise of generators and the glare of deck lights.

Photo by Ian Douglas

Anchored in popular Safety Cove

The public mooring buoys mentioned in *Sailing Directions* have not been seen for several years.

We prefer to anchor in the smaller, more scenic coves on the east side of Fitz Hugh Sound or in sites farther north.

Anchor in 10 fathoms at the steep-to head of the cove over a mud bottom with fair holding.

"Addenbroke Point Cove"

Chart 3934 metric; entrance:
51°31.50′ N, 127°47.50′ W; anchor:
51°31.58′ N, 127°45.69′ W (NAD 83)

> *The bay between this [Addenbroke] point and Arthur Point, about 0.8 mile NW, is too exposed for satisfactory anchorage. Two shoal areas lie in the outer part of the bay, and rocks, with less than 2 m (6 ft) over them, lie about 0.1 mile south and west of Arthur Point.* (p. 73, SD)

Addenbroke Point Cove, our name for the small bowl-shaped basin 0.6 mile north of Addenbroke Point, offers good protection from up- and down-channel wind and chop. The bowl has no beach

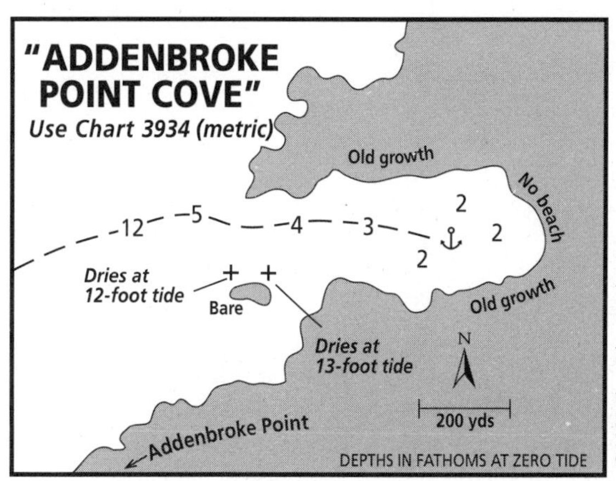

and is steep-to right up to the rocky shore where old-growth forest surrounds the cove. Entering the cove is easy but you must avoid the large bare rock and two additional small rocks awash on a 12 to 13-foot tide off the south entrance point.

Anchor in 2 fathoms over a hard mud bottom with fair-to-good holding.

Philip Inlet

Chart 3934 metric; entrance:
51°33.33′ N, 127°47.20′ W; anchor:
51°34.18′ N, 127°45.35′ W (NAD 83)

> *Philip Inlet is entered 1.5 miles north of Arthur Point. Just within the entrance is a narrow part encumbered with rocks, but small vessels could find shelter in 16 to 26 m (9 to 14 fms) east of the island in mid-channel.* (p. 73, SD)

Philip Inlet, 5 miles northeast of Safety Cove, is a narrow inlet cutting into the mainland coast that has an entrance largely hidden from Fitz Hugh Sound. Inside the inlet you have total protection

Entrance to Philip Inlet

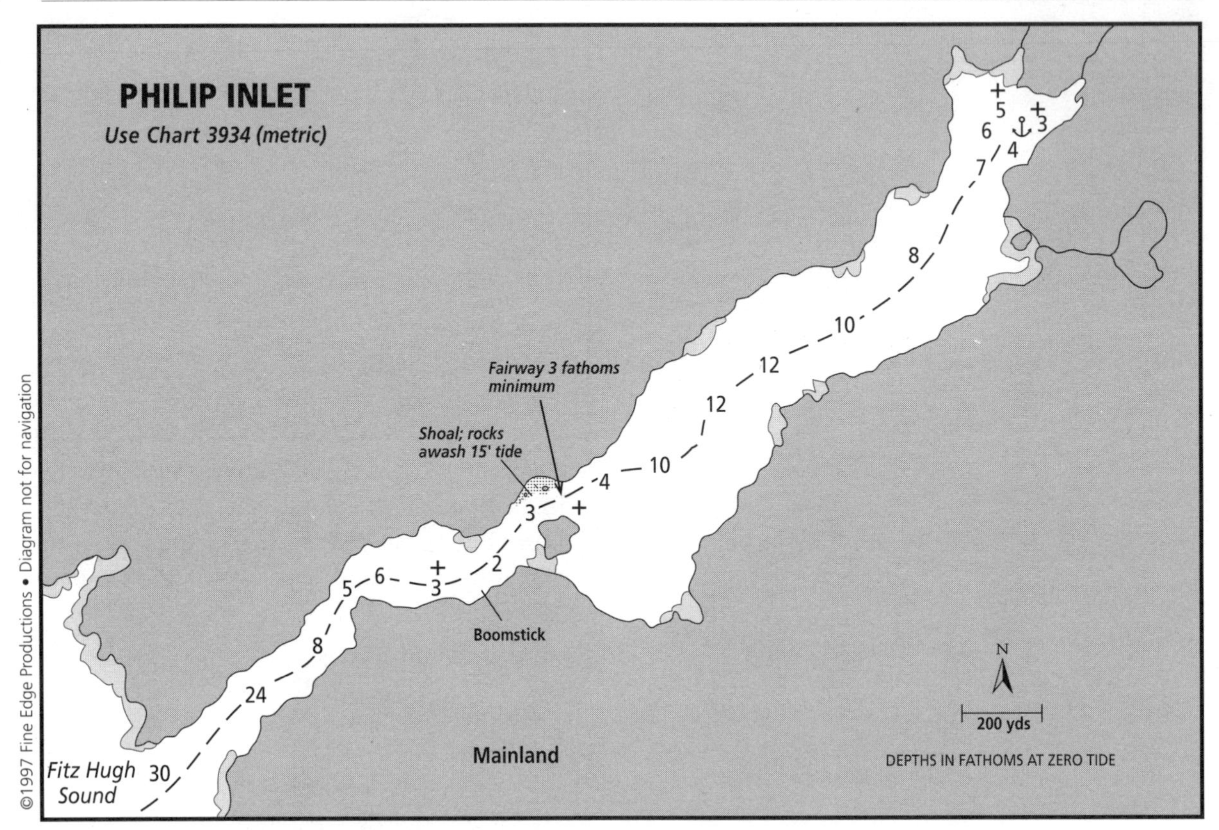

from all weather, and it's calm and quiet even when chop outside is heavy. The shores of the entire inlet are lined with overhanging trees.

The entrance to Philip inlet is straightforward, but the bottom is irregular as you approach the narrows. West of the narrows, favor the south shore to avoid a rock and a shoal that extends to midchannel from the north shore. The narrow fairway north of the islet has a minimum depth of 3 fathoms. To the south of the islet, there is a boomstick tied to shore which can be used for moorage. Or you can anchor anywhere in the inner basin or at the north end as indicated in the diagram.

Anchor in 3 to 6 fathoms over a mixed hard bottom with fair holding if your anchor is well set.

Fifer Bay

Chart 3921 metric, 3934 metric; entrance: 51°35.80′ N, 127°49.90′ W; anchor: 51°35.44′ N, 127°49.51′ W (NAD 83)

Fifer Bay has an islet and some rocks extending north from its south entrance point. A narrow inlet in the NE corner of the bay has its entrance obstructed by above- and below-water rocks. Anchorage for small vessels can be obtained in the south part of Fifer Bay in 20 m (11 fms); the bottom is uneven. (p. 73, SD)

We have found good shelter deep in the head of Fifer Bay where it is protected from all south winds and swells. Northerly winds and outflows from Fish Egg Inlet should not be a problem. It's so quiet here we once woke up to what sounded like machine-gun fire, only to discover it was a woodpecker pecking at a tree above us.

The western tip of Blair Island has a number of rocks and islets that you need to identify and clear. The bottom is quite uneven and gives no warning of approaching shoals. Set a course well off the point of Blair Island, steering directly for small No Tree Islet. Turn south about 100 yards out, but only after you have identified and avoided the easternmost rock that dries at 4 feet. Then, turn directly south for the end of the bay.

There's a good small-boat exit from Fifer Bay

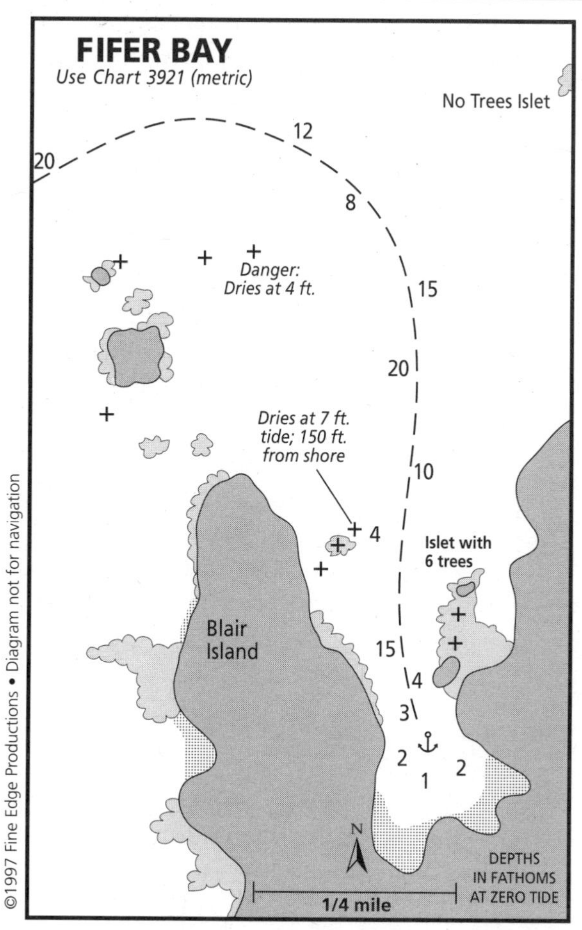

Moored to a boomstick in Philip Inlet

directly into Patrol Passage and Fish Egg Inlet that has a minimum of 6 fathoms in its fairway.

Anchor in 1$^1/_2$ fathoms over soft bottom with good holding.

Addenbroke Light Station

Charts 3921 metric, 3934 metric; position (light): 51°36.20′ N, 127°51.82′ W; anchor: 51°36.35′ N, 127°51.80′ W (NAD 83)

> *Addenbroke Island light (585), on the west extremity of Addenbroke Island, has an emergency light, a heliport and a fog signal consisting of one blast on a horn every 30 seconds.* (p. 73, SD)

The Addenbroke Lightstation, on the west side of Addenbroke Island, can be visited in fair weather by taking temporary anchorage in a tiny cove 300 yards north of the station. Make prior arrangements with the lightkeepers and they will meet you at the landing in the cove.

Fish Egg Inlet

Chart 3921 metric; note the entrance waypoints listed below (NAD 83)

> *Fish Egg Inlet is deep except for a shoal area about 0.8 mile east of Salvage Island.* (p. 73, SD)

Caution: This is a newly charted area, and we have found many soundings to be less than those shown on Chart 3921.

Convoy, Patrol, Fairmile, Souvenir and Sweeper Island Passages

Chart 3921 metric; south entrance (Convoy Passage): 51°34.80′ N, 127°48.90′ W; west entrance (Patrol Passage): 51°36.90′ N, 127°51.20′ W; west entrance (Fairmile Passage): 51°37.80′ N, 127°50.20′ W; east entrance (Souvenir Passage): 51°37.35′ N, 127°48.60′ W (NAD 83)

> *Convoy Passage is east of Blair Island. Patrol Passage is clear of mid-channel dangers. It lies*

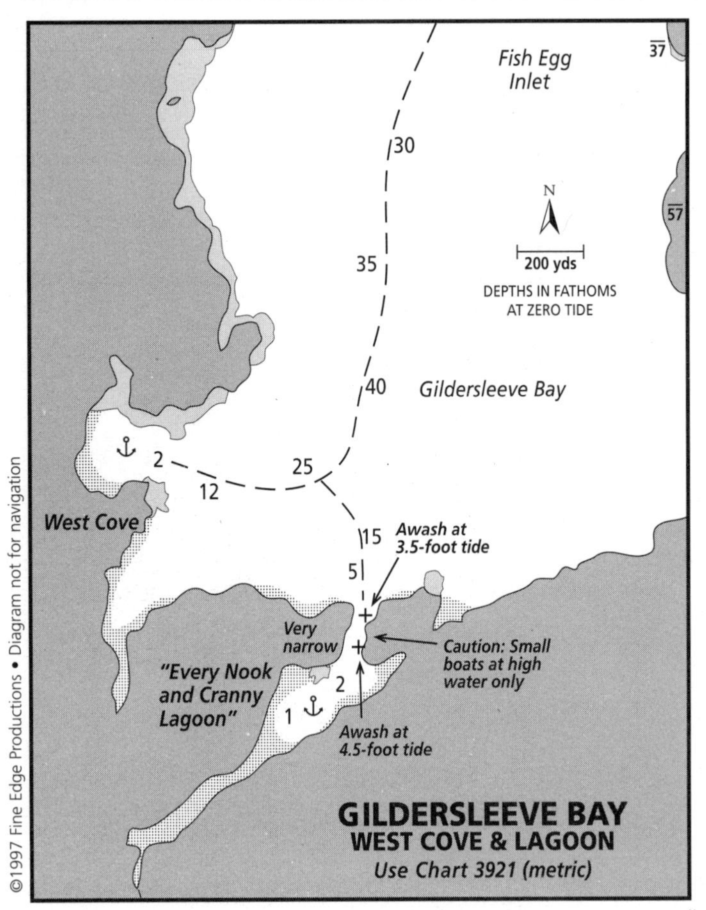

Gildersleeve Bay is the first bay inside Fish Egg Inlet on the south shore. It is too deep for convenient anchorage except in tiny "West Cove" where you can anchor in 2 fathoms when the cove isn't filled with log-booms, as it sometimes has been in the past.

The lagoon at the south end of Gildersleeve Bay, which we call "Every Nook and Cranny," has a very tight entrance suitable only for very small boats or dinghies at high water. Small boats with draft less than 4 feet can enter the lagoon at high water. On a 3-foot tide only a dinghy can make it through, and at zero tide only a kayak. One or two boats can find room to anchor inside the lagoon in 1 to 2 fathoms. The lagoon is the home to large sea cucumbers with dark centers and red and brown spots, as well as a number of small white and tan starfish.

south of Corvette Islands, which have several shoals within 0.2 mile west. Fairmile Passage has an islet, with rocks close south of it, at its SE end. Souvenir Passage, north of Salvage Island, is very narrow at the east end. (p. 73, SD)

Henderson Bay

Chart 3921 metric; position:
51°35.29′ N, 127°47.26′ W (NAD 83)

Henderson Bay, on the east side of the [Convoy] passage, has a shoal in the entrance and drying rocks at the head. (p. 73, SD)

Gildersleeve Bay, West Cove

Chart 3921 metric; position (west cove):
51°36.07′ N, 127°46.53′ W; entrance (lagoon):
51°35.98′ N, 127°46.24′ W (NAD 83)

A bay on the south side of Fish Egg Inlet has a group of islands and shoals in the centre with Gildersleeve Bay within the group. (p. 73, SD)

Mantrap Inlet

Chart 3921 metric; narrows entrance:
51°35.53′ N, 127°45.36′ W; anchor (north): 51°35.84′ N, 127°44.78′ W;
anchor (south):
51°35.04′ N, 127°45.41′ W (NAD 83)

Barracuda Rock lies in the middle of the approach to Mantrap Inlet. The eastern part of the inlet can be entered either north of a large island or by The Narrows south of this island. (p. 73, SD)

Mantrap Inlet, located one mile southeast of Gildersleeve Bay, is an isolated and primitive inlet suitable only for small craft. Because of uncharted rocks in the narrows, you can, in fact, be trapped inside the inlet at low water. The fairway is less than 20 feet wide and should be reconnoitered first by dinghy to determine suitability for entering. There is a 3-knot current on ebb tide.

Anchorage can be taken almost anywhere in the inlet, with the far north end the most secluded. You can carefully enter the lagoon at the south end of the inlet using the diagram as a guide but realizing that not all hazards are charted. We have not explored the large body of water to the southwest and were unable to tell whether

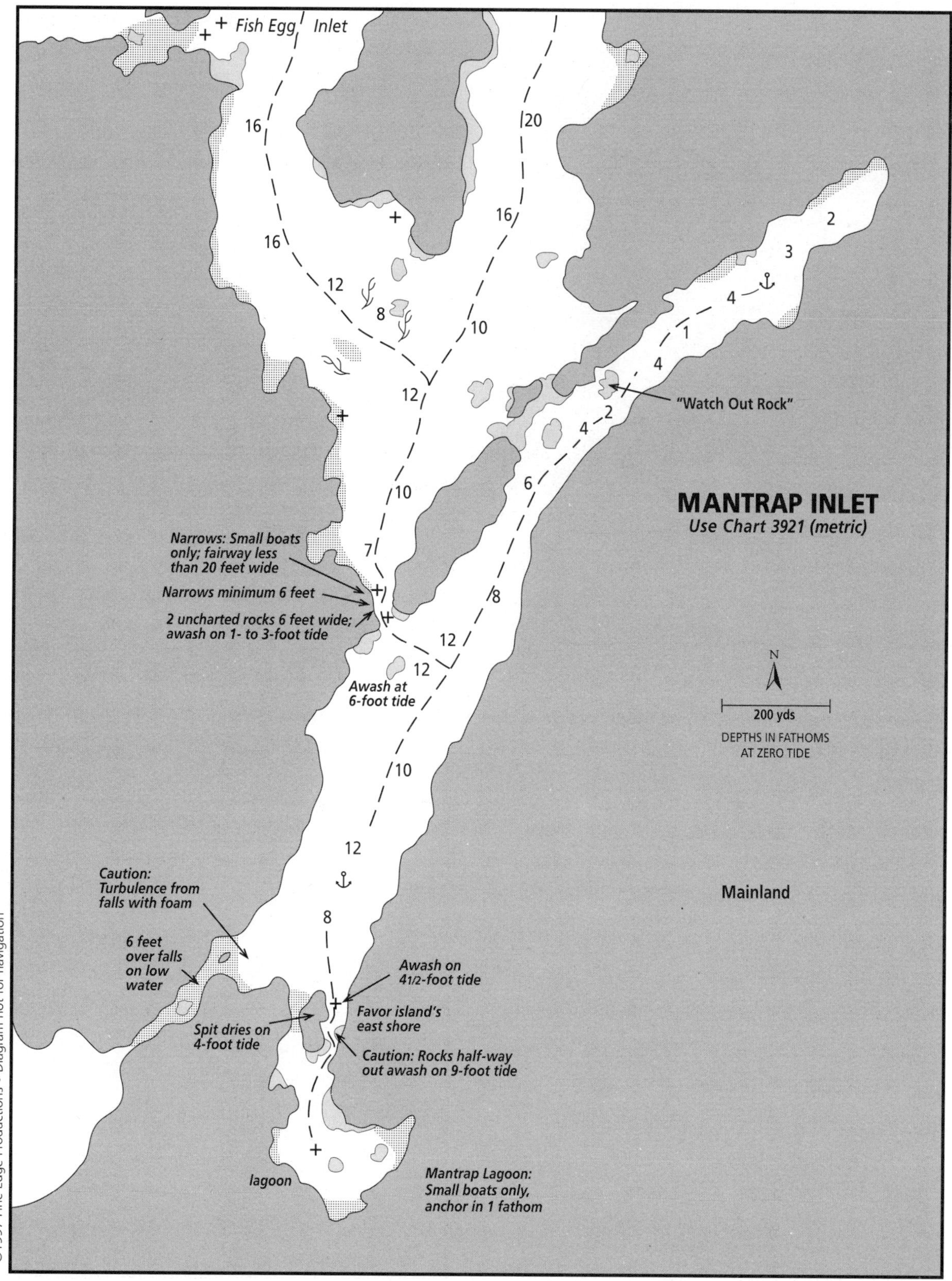
Fish Egg Inlet
16
20
16
16
2
3
12
8
4
10
1
4
12
"Watch Out Rock"
2
4
6
10
MANTRAP INLET
Use Chart 3921 (metric)
Narrows: Small boats only; fairway less than 20 feet wide
7
Narrows minimum 6 feet
8
2 uncharted rocks 6 feet wide; awash on 1- to 3-foot tide
12
12
N
Awash at 6-foot tide
200 yds
DEPTHS IN FATHOMS AT ZERO TIDE
10
12
Caution: Turbulence from falls with foam
Mainland
8
6 feet over falls on low water
Awash on 41/2-foot tide
Spit dries on 4-foot tide
Favor island's east shore
Caution: Rocks half-way out awash on 9-foot tide
lagoon
Mantrap Lagoon: Small boats only, anchor in 1 fathom

Mantrap Inlet, entrance to unexplored lagoon

it is a freshwater lake or a saltwater lagoon. We did, however, hike to the 6-foot overfalls to have a look; it appears to be a lagoon that can be entered at high water. Along the edge of the overfalls we saw a colorful display of small starfish—orange, blue, grey, red and purple—as well as sea anemones in all colors, green, white, beige, brown and orange. This inlet would be an excellent place for a boardwalk nature trail.

Anchor (north) in about 3 fathoms over soft mud with fair-to-good holding. A shore tie can be helpful.

Anchor (south) in about 9 fathoms over soft mud with fair-to-good holding.

McClusky Bay

Chart 3921 metric; anchor:
51°38.65′ N, 127°47.43′ W (NAD 83)

> *McClusky Bay, the NW bay in the inlet, has numerous islets, drying rocks and shoals on its east side.* (p. 73, SD)

McClusky Bay is exposed to the south and, except for temporary anchorage in the northeast corner, there is little protection available unless you anchor in the lagoon at the north end of the bay. This interesting double lagoon offers very good protection to small boats which can carefully enter its narrow, rock-strewn entrance.

The fairway to the lagoon, which is lined on both sides by reefs, has about 1 fathom at zero tide. The currents run at about 2 knots. The mid-channel rock at the north end of the entrance, awash on a 12-foot tide at Bella Bella, can be passed by favoring the west side of the channel, keeping the rock close to starboard. In the first lagoon, there is enough room for several boats in 1 to 3 fathoms. Some shallow-draft small boats could anchor in parts of the second lagoon since depths are greater than shown on Chart 3921.

If you enter the second lagoon, favor the west side of the fairway to avoid rocks on the north side. We recommend that you reconnoiter both lagoons by dinghy before entering to properly identify the fairway, its hazards, and the amount of current.

Anchor in 2 fathoms (inside the first lagoon) over a sand and shell bottom with good holding.

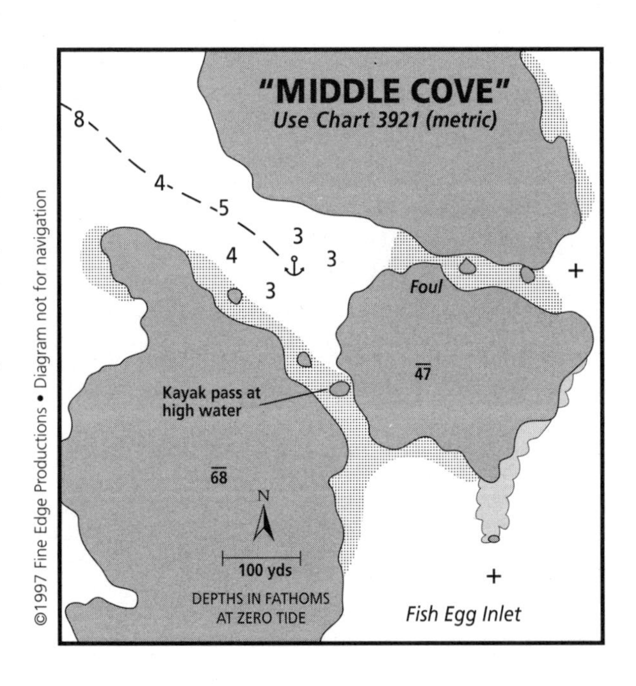

"Middle Cove"

Chart 3921 metric; anchor:
51°37.27′ N, 127°45.70′ W (NAD 83)

Middle Cove is our name for the small cove located almost in the middle of Fish Egg Inlet. The cove, formed by three islands, is located one mile northeast of Gildersleeve Bay. Although open to the northwest, it offers good shelter for one boat in stable weather.

Anchor in 3 fathoms over a bottom of soft brown mud with broken shells; fair-to-good holding.

Joe's Bay

Chart 3921 metric; anchor:
51°38.97′ N, 127°45.54′ W (NAD 83)

> *The bay east of McClusky Bay can be entered on either side of a large island in the approach. Joe's Bay, the basin at the head of this bay, affords good although tight anchorage for small vessels.* (p. 73, SD)

Joe's Bay is decidedly off the beaten path in an area of wild territory. You and your crew need to be alert at all times, because the hazards may not all be visible or even shown on the chart.

Entering Joe's Bay is straightforward; you can anchor farther north in shallow water between the islands and shoals. Because this north anchorage has several below-water rocks, you should approach it slowly and carefully. The waterfall at the entrance to Elizabeth Lagoon generates a tremendous amount of foam on spring tides, and you may want to anchor out of the current as noted on the diagram. Larger boats can anchor farther south for more swinging room.

Anchor in the north end of Joe's Bay in 2 to 3 fathoms over a mud bottom with fair-to-good holding.

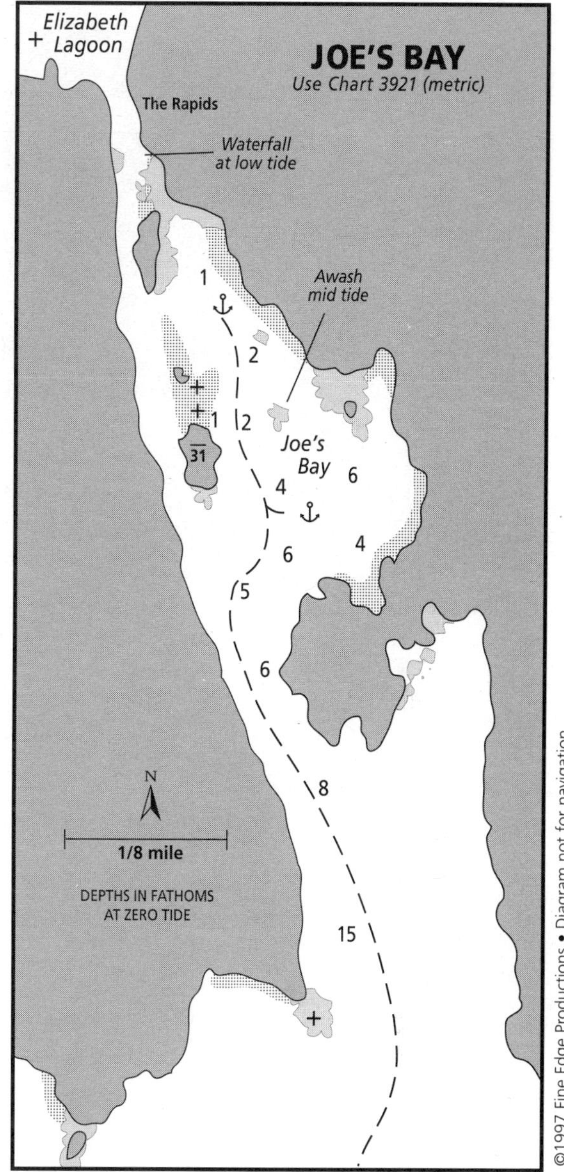

Elizabeth Lagoon

Chart 3921 metric; position (Rapids):
51°39.23′ N, 127°45.85′ W (NAD 83)

> *The Rapids can be navigated at HW slack, by shallow draught boats, through a narrow slot between the rocks. The Rapids leads to Elizabeth Lagoon which is deep in its central basin but numerous shoals and drying rocks lie along the shores and in Sulphur Arm, the east end of the lagoon. The water in the lagoon is discoloured and opaque making it impossible to see the dangers.* (p. 73, SD)

Elizabeth Lagoon is a major attraction if you want to visit truly pristine wilderness. A tree blaze on the south side of the rapids is the only sign of man that we observed for miles. Within the lagoon, there are at least 30 miles of shoreline—twice

Joe's Bay, entrance to Elizabeth Lagoon

what the 1962 charts showed as uncharted and estimated. We found no cut logs, no shell middens, no clearings or clearcuts inside. It was a thrill to visit an area that appears untouched.

The challenge to entering Elizabeth Lagoon is negotiating the rapids, which look like a major waterfall most of the time except at high water slack. At low tide, foam from the waterfall spreads out over the water for a half-mile, resembling "bergy-bits" from a glacier. Be patient—it took us four tries to make it over the rapids, and we nearly destroyed our outboard in 2 feet of water on the "lip." The dark, discolored water makes trying to avoid the rocks all the more challenging. But once we had passed beyond the entrance bar and shoal, within a mile north the water deepened and we felt free to travel at high speed.

In the bay to the northeast of Sulphur Arm, the mud is soft and boots are an absolute necessity for getting around. Water level in the lagoon appears to move up and down just a few inches with each tidal change.

Sulphur Arm

Chart 3921 metric; entrance:
51°40.50' N, 127°45.30' W (NAD 83)

Sulphur Arm is pristine wilderness that appears to be frozen in time; however, it is an interesting study in biological diversity. Its entrance is narrow with about 4 to 12 feet in the fairway. The shoreline bottom is so soft it will hardly support a person's weight; it acts like quicksand, but it is just very, very soft mud. You will find no evidence of human visitation; please help keep it that way.

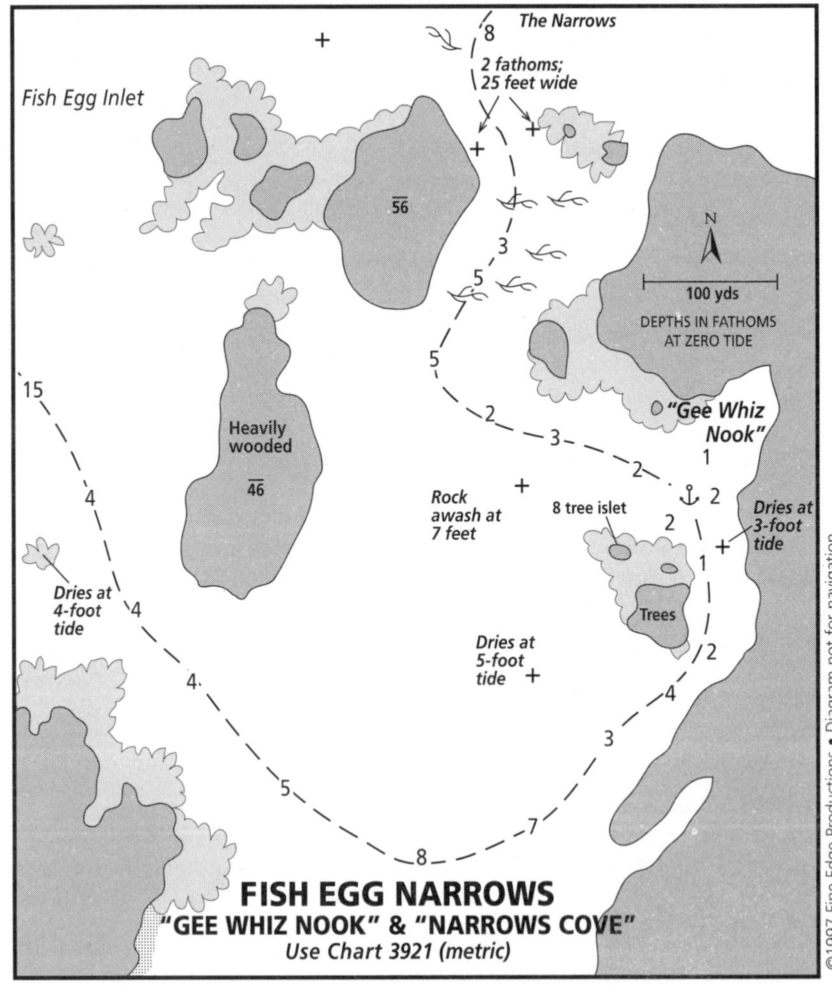

"Narrows Cove"

Chart 3921 metric; entrance:
51°36.38′ N, 127°44.16′ W (NAD 83)

The Narrows is the route to the eastern part of Fish Egg Inlet and Oyster Bay. The island at the east side of The Narrows can be passed on either side; however, avoid the uncharted rock off the southeast corner of the island awash on a 6-foot tide.

Good shelter from all weather can be found in the island complex directly south of The Narrows; choose the depth and proximity to shore you desire. The bottom is irregular with a number of rocks, so scout out your swinging room and make sure your anchor is well set.

Anchor in about 8 fathoms over a mixed bottom with fair-to-good holding.

"Gee Whiz Nook"

Chart 3921 metric; anchor:
51°36.37′ N, 127°43.82′ W (NAD 83)

Gee Whiz Nook is our name for the eastern end of Narrows Cove. Small boats can find very good shelter here with limited swinging room. A shore tie will make your boat steady as a rock. Enter slowly with an alert lookout on the bow, remembering that not all hazards are charted, and enjoy the pristine surroundings in this quiet, secure anchorage.

Anchor in about 2 fathoms over a soft mud bottom with good holding.

Waterfall Inlet

Chart 3921 metric; south entrance:
51°36.95′ N, 127°43.57′ W (NAD 83)

> *Waterfall Inlet, extending north from the islets that separate the central and east parts of Fish Egg Inlet, has three shallow, winding, entrance channels.* (p. 73, SD)

Landlocked Waterfall Inlet, north of The Narrows, is a beautiful place surrounded by old-growth forest. The muskeg water has restricted turnover and is almost without a ripple. There is little evidence that wind or chop enter here.

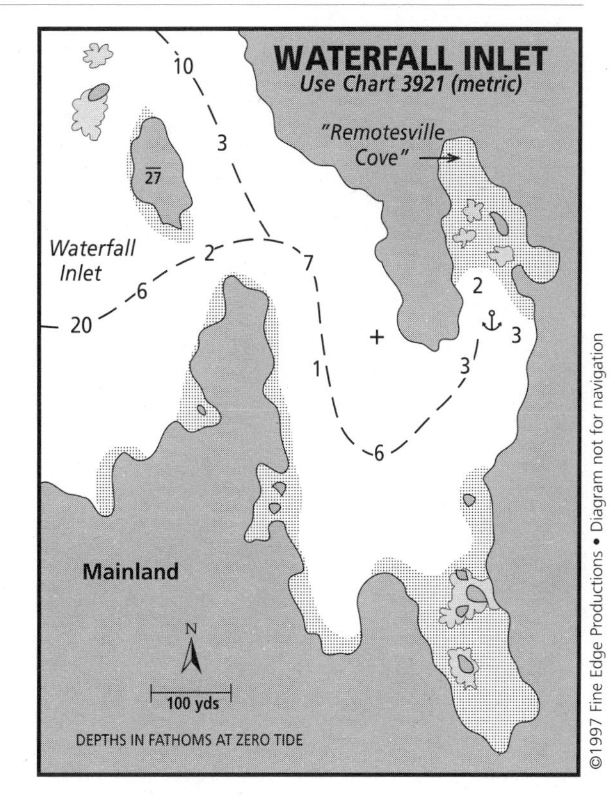

The main entrance is from the south in a fairway of about 1 fathom. (Note that the chart shows 4 fathoms!) Favor the west shore to avoid the midchannel rock awash on a 9-foot tide. Waterfall Inlet can also be entered from its west side with a fairway minimum of about 2 fathoms—not 1.5 meters as shown on the chart!—and with about a 2-knot current.

Waterfall Inlet is fairly deep, however you can use a shore tie almost anywhere you wish. We prefer the small cove in the southeast corner which we call Remotesville Cove.

"Remotesville Cove"

Chart 3921 metric; anchor:
51°37.54′ N, 127°42.94′ W (NAD 83)

This cove and Oyster Bay to the east are about as remote and intimate as you can find. The area is surrounded by the mainland coastal mountains, filled with innumerable lakes and thick rain forests. Remotesville Cove is a good place to explore by dinghy and to observe local flora and

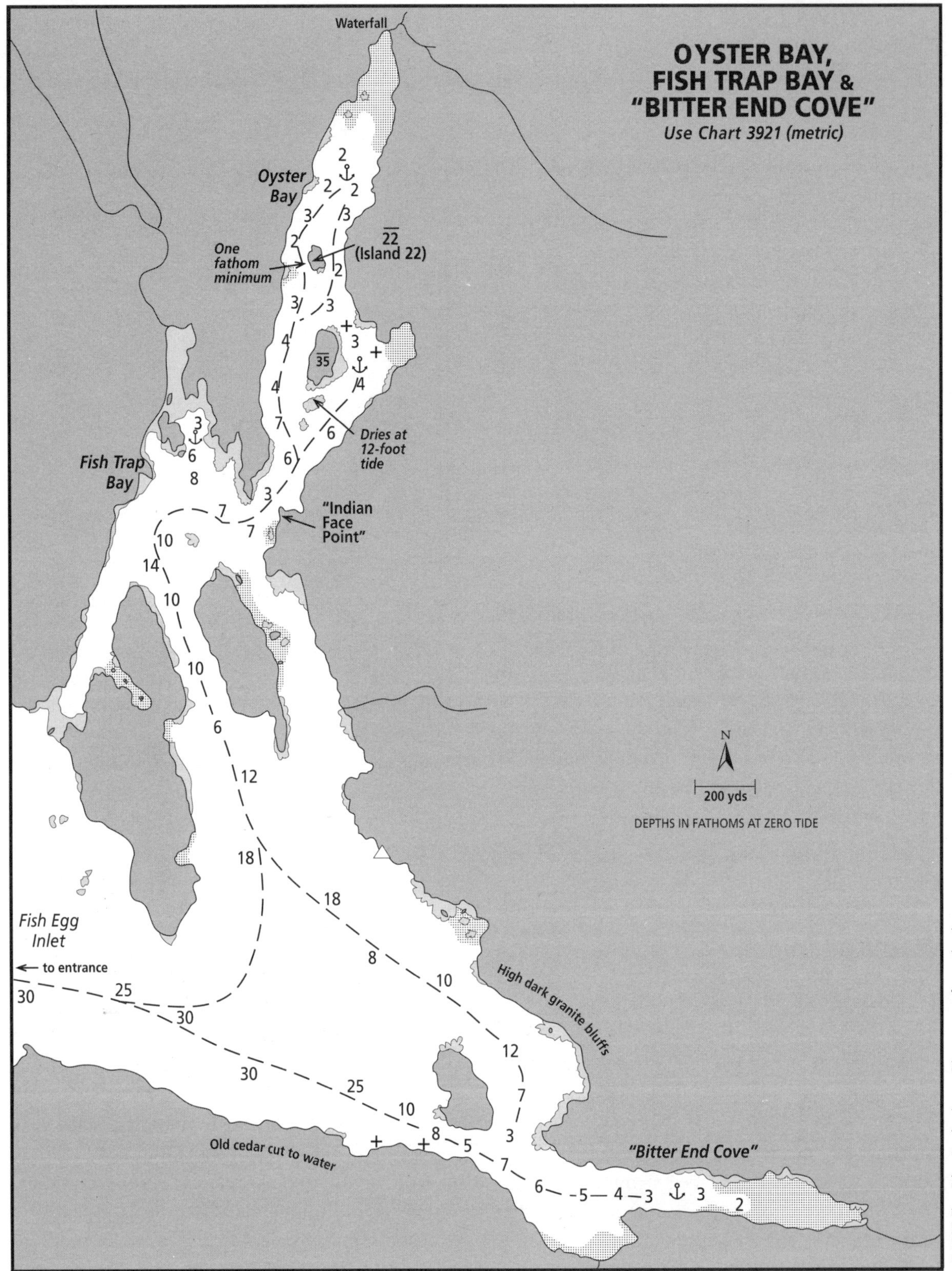

OYSTER BAY,
FISH TRAP BAY &
"BITTER END COVE"
Use Chart 3921 (metric)
Waterfall
Oyster Bay
One fathom minimum
22 (Island 22)
35
Dries at 12-foot tide
Fish Trap Bay
"Indian Face Point"
N
200 yds
DEPTHS IN FATHOMS AT ZERO TIDE
Fish Egg Inlet
to entrance
High dark granite bluffs
Old cedar cut to water
"Bitter End Cove"
©1997 Fine Edge Productions • Diagram not for navigation

fauna. We like to anchor in the east nook off the drying flat at the head of the creek, with a shore tie useful. Entry from either side of island (27) is possible; however, you should proceed slowly and maintain a sharp lookout.

Anchor in 3 fathoms over soft mud with broken shells; fair-to-good holding.

Fish Trap Bay

Chart 3921 metric; position:
51°37.45′ N, 127°41.74′ W (NAD 83)

Fish Trap Bay and Oyster Bay are in a narrow inlet leading north. (p. 73, SD)

Explore Fish Trap Bay and see if you can figure out how it got its name!

Oyster Bay

Chart 3921 metric; anchor (north):
51°37.85′ N, 127°41.34′ W; anchor (east):
51°37.55′ N, 127°41.28′ W (NAD 83)

Oyster Bay is well-sheltered and shallow and you can anchor almost anywhere. We prefer the cove east of island (35) or north of island (22) at the head of the bay where you have a view of the waterfall that descends from the lake above. Note that island (22) has about a 1-fathom shoal on its west side; its east side is deeper.

The water in Oyster Bay is calm and there are no indications that chop ever invades this quiet place. Note the lifelike "Face" reflection of the rock surface in still water at the entrance along the east shore.

Anchor (north) in 2 fathoms over a soft mud bottom with good holding.

Anchor (east) in 4 fathoms over a soft mud bottom with good holding.

"Bitter End Cove"

Chart 3921 metric; anchor:
51°36.17′ N, 127°40.40′ W (NAD 83)

Bitter End Cove is what we call the far east end of Fish Egg Inlet. This well-sheltered anchorage has granite bluffs on its north side, a long drying flat to the east, and a large stream that tumbles down from Doris Lake on the south. This is a quiet place where you have good viewing of flora and fauna. It is also a good base camp from which to explore the surrounding nooks and crannies by dinghy.

Anchor off the flat in 3 fathoms over mud with shells; good holding.

Illahie Inlet

Chart 3921 metric; entrance:
51°37.94′ N, 127°49.76′ W (NAD 83)

Illahie Inlet is best entered between the islands in its SE corner . . . Illahie Inlet is clear of mid-channel dangers except for Storm Rock, in the centre of the inlet, 0.3 mile NNE of Green Island. (p. 73, SD)

Good anchorage can be found at the head of Illahie Inlet not far from Fitz Hugh Sound; however, the area has been clearcut and noisy logging operations may be still be active.

Green Island Anchorage

Chart 3921 metric; anchor:
51°38.55′ N, 127°50.40′ W (NAD 83)

Good anchorage for small vessels can be obtained in Green Island Anchorage in 8 m (26 ft). (p. 73, SD)

Green Island Anchorage, close to Fitz Hugh Sound, is well protected from weather.

The first passage to the west is a canoe pass filled with foul rocks; the second passage has a flat bottom of about 3 fathoms (the chart says 3 meters); the south passage is clear and can be entered using radar. Avoid the rock with 5 feet over it at zero tide.

The small island covered with brambles on the east side of the anchorage is a midden. The north anchor site is slightly more protected and shallower than the roomier, deeper south site.

Anchor (south) in 4 fathoms over sand, mud, shells, and grass with good holding.

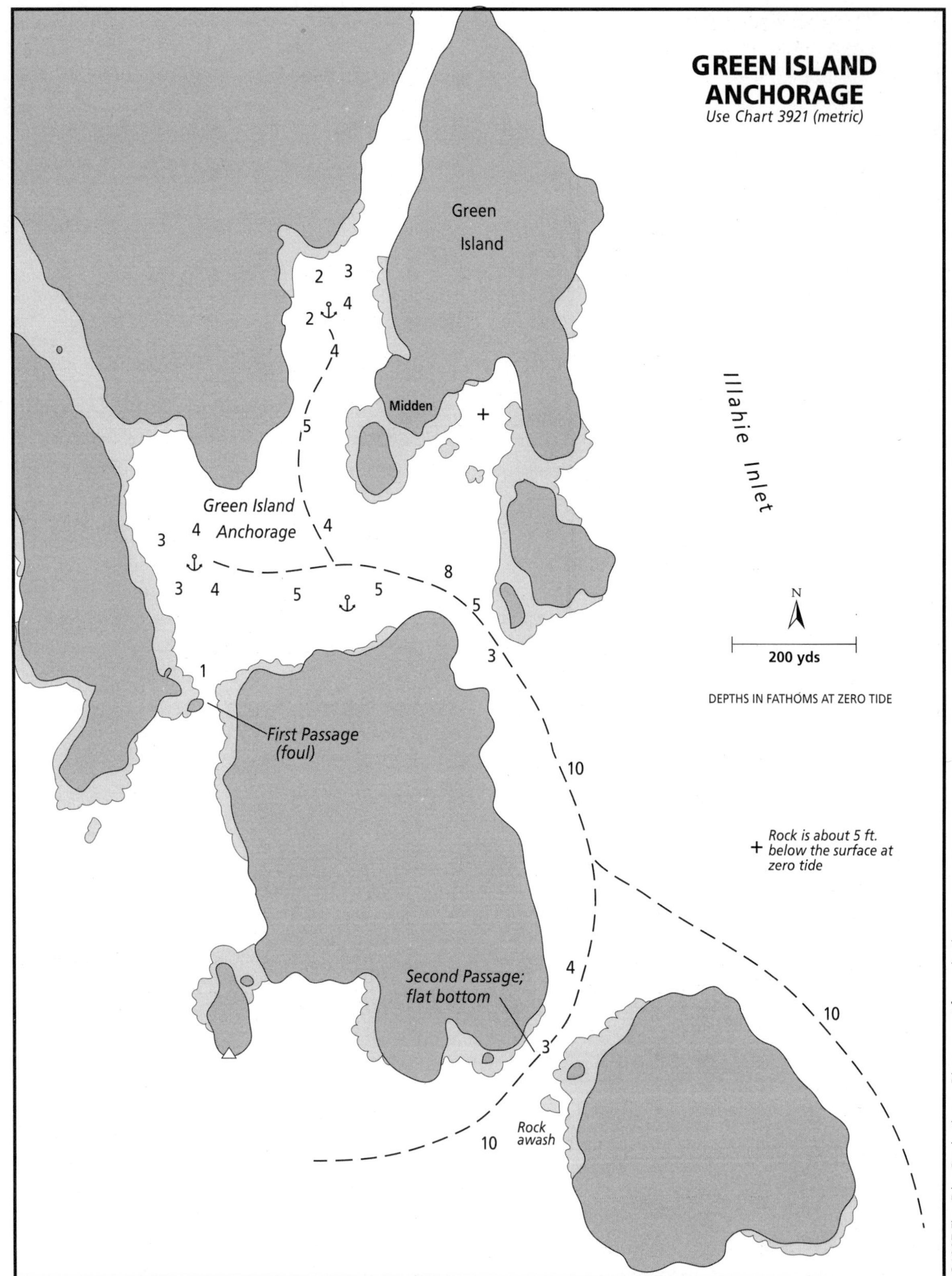
GREEN ISLAND ANCHORAGE
Use Chart 3921 (metric)
Green Island
Midden
Illahie Inlet
Green Island Anchorage
First Passage (foul)
Second Passage; flat bottom
Rock awash
200 yds
DEPTHS IN FATHOMS AT ZERO TIDE
+ Rock is about 5 ft. below the surface at zero tide
©1997 Fine Edge Productions • Diagram not for navigation

Goldstream Harbour

Chart 3784; anchor: 51°43.68′ N, 128°00.16′ W (NAD 27)

> *Goldstream Harbour, at the north extremity of Hecate Island, is entered between Umme Point and the NE point of Hecate Island . . . The fairway between Hat Island and Evening Rock is 300 feet (91 m) wide and intricate, with depths of 24 to 36 feet (7.3 to 11 m); favour the Hat Island side unless Evening Rock is clearly visible.*
>
> *Anchorage for small vessels can be obtained in Goldstream Harbour, sand and mud bottom.* (p. 73, SD)

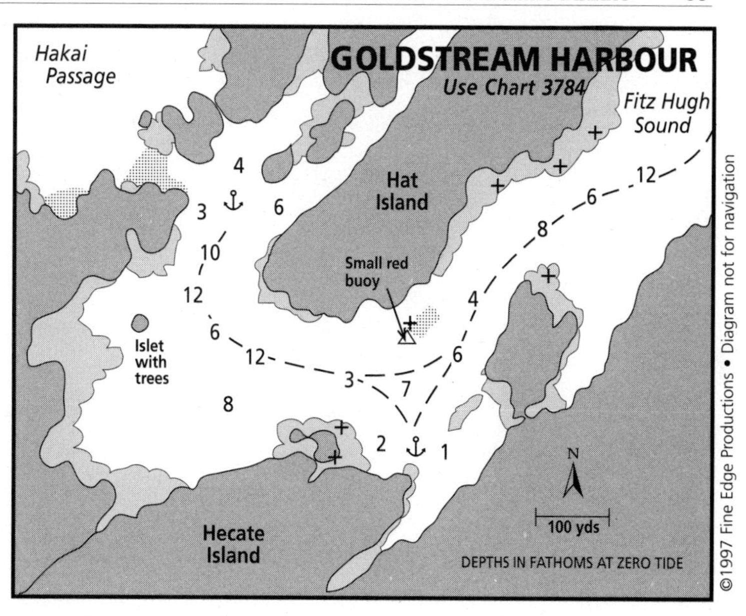

Well protected from all seas, Goldstream Harbour has rugged, beautiful surroundings. You can make this a good base-anchorage for exploring either Queens Sound to the northwest, or Koeye River to the east.

At the very northeast end of Hecate Island there is a small convoluted island appropriately called Hat Island. Hat and Hecate islands create an almost perfect anchorage for small craft. Be careful upon entering as noted above in *Sailing Directions;* inside there is room for several boats.

Anchor in 8 fathoms over sand and mud with some rocks; holding is good.

Kwakume Point

Chart 3784; point position: 51°41.57′ N, 127° 53.23′ W (NAD 27)

Kwakume Point, 4.6 miles southeast of Goldstream Harbour, has a flashing light (3) on its western extremity. Behind the point to the east, is a bay that offers good temporary protection from downslope northerly winds, but drift logs on shore indicate there is no shelter from southerly winds.

In fair weather, the northeast corner, close to the drying lagoon, makes a good lunch stop in 7 fathoms. Two treed islets, 0.7 mile south of Kwakume Point, are connected to shore by a white sandy beach. This is also an excellent kayak haul-out point. The cove behind the islets is too shallow for anything but a lunch stop near high water.

Anchor in $1/2$ fathom, over a mud and clamshell bottom.

Kwakume Inlet

Charts 3784 or 3727; entrance: 51°42.90′ N, 127°53.40 ′ W; anchor (south): 51°42.17′ N, 127°52.66′ W; anchor (inner cove): 51°42.73′ N, 127°51.57′ W (NAD 27)

> *Kwakume Inlet, entered about midway between Kwakume Point and Whidbey Point, has islets on the north and south sides of the entrance which reduce the fairway to a width of 250 feet (76 m). A rock awash lies about 0.1 mile west of the entrance. This inlet should be used only by small craft.* (p. 73, SD)

Kwakume Inlet is pretty and well protected. Entry is somewhat dicey due to the below-water rock shown on the chart and diagram which is difficult to locate since it can be seen only at low water. You can pass on either its north or south side. However, by favoring the north shore it may be easier to avoid this rock.

The extremely well-protected inner cove is quite narrow and shallow. Do not pass south of the islet with four trees—the passage is foul. Pass midway between the 4-treed islet and the larger island with many trees immediately north. The fairway has a minimum depth of about 3 fathoms;

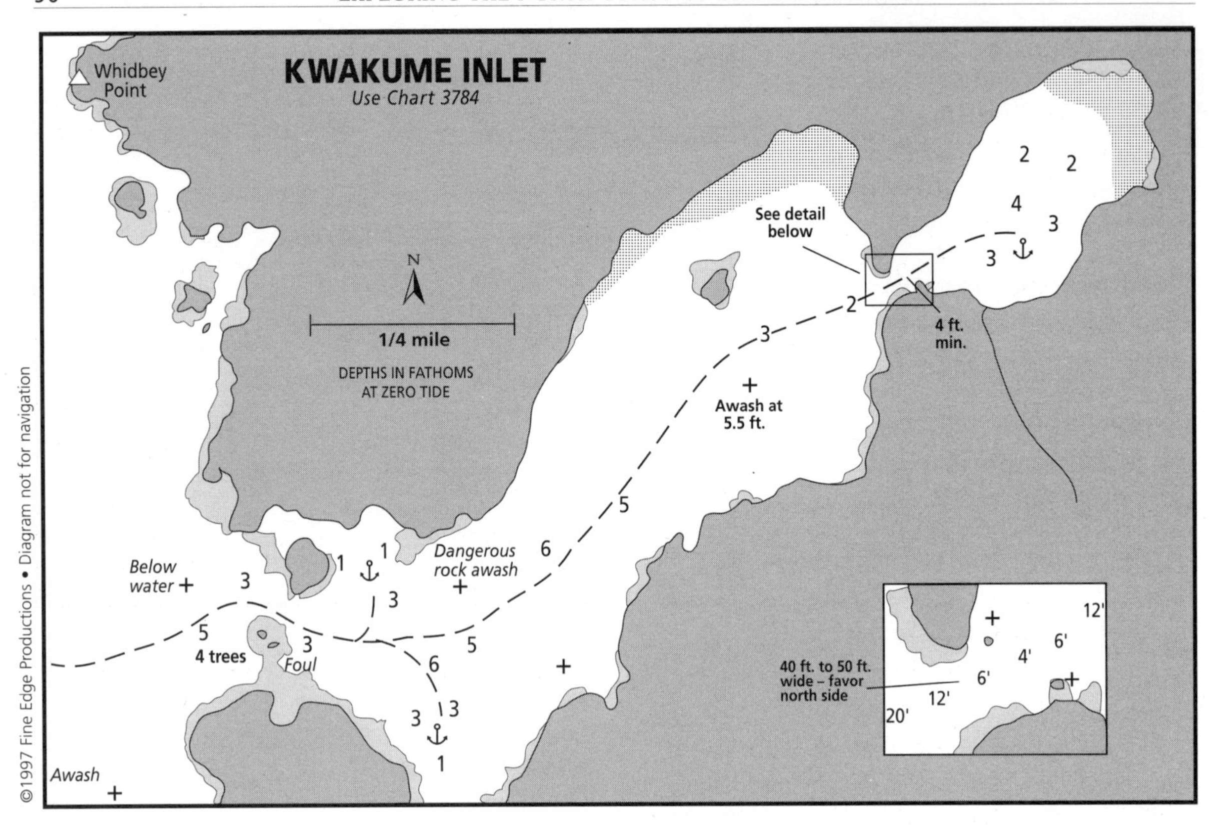

slightly favor the north side of midchannel. (The anchor site on the north, just inside the entrance, is quite shallow, and while the view of the channel is good, at low water you may find your keel kissing the mud bottom.)

If a major storm were approaching, we wouldn't hesitate to anchor against the south shore as indicated on the diagram, or inside the inner cove. What we show on the diagram as a dangerous rock awash (on about a 7-foot tide), sits on a reef that extends southward about 300 feet from shore.

Anchor (south) near shore in 2 to 3 fathoms over a mud bottom with good holding.

Anchor (inner cove) in 3 to 4 fathoms over a mud bottom with good holding.

Koeye River

Chart 3784; anchor: 51°46.42' N, 127°52.58' W (NAD 27)

Koeye River, nearly 5 miles north of Kwakume Point, is entered on the north side of a rock awash lying about 0.1 mile north of Koeye Point. The shallow bay east of Koeye Point is used by local fishermen. A narrow boat channel extends about 1 mile upstream to the site of a lime plant, now in ruins. It was reported (1975) that an uncharted rock lies in the entrance to the boat channel.
(pp. 73–74, SD)

Koeye River (pronounced Kwy) is a wonderful place for viewing animal and bird life. However, it's a marginal anchorage. We've anchored here twice overnight, and each time spent a rolly, uncomfortable night. It's far better to use as a temporary anchorage and take a kayak or inflatable upstream. We sighted our first snow goose at the far end of the inlet, and in our opinion, this little inlet would make an excellent wildlife sanctuary. It may be possible to take a small craft just beyond the old mill site at high water, but it is not recommended. There are several rocks awash off the shoal at the river's outlet. If Fitz Hugh Sound is kicking up, consider tucking just inside the south point, dropping the hook for a while, and having a look around. There is now a fishing lodge on the point at Koeye Bay.

Anchor in 1 to 2 fathoms over a sand bottom with fair-to-good holding.

Sea Otter Inlet

Chart 3784; entrance: 51°50.20′ N, 128°00.90′ W; anchor (west): 51°50.38′ N, 128°03.47′ W (NAD 27)

> *Sea Otter Inlet, in Hunter Island, offers confined shelter for small craft in its south arm.* (p. 73, SD)

Anchor (west) in 8 fathoms, unrecorded bottom.

"South Arm," Sea Otter Inlet

Chart 3784; anchor (South Arm): 51°49.54′ N, 128°01.59′ W (NAD 27)

Unfortunately the sea otters are nowhere to be seen in Sea Otter Inlet, but the south arm offers very good protection from all weather. You can anchor north of the high-water canoe pass to Target Bay. The "window" to the east allows you to determine conditions in Fitz Hugh Sound.

Anchor (South Arm) in 5 to 6 fathoms over a mud bottom with good holding.

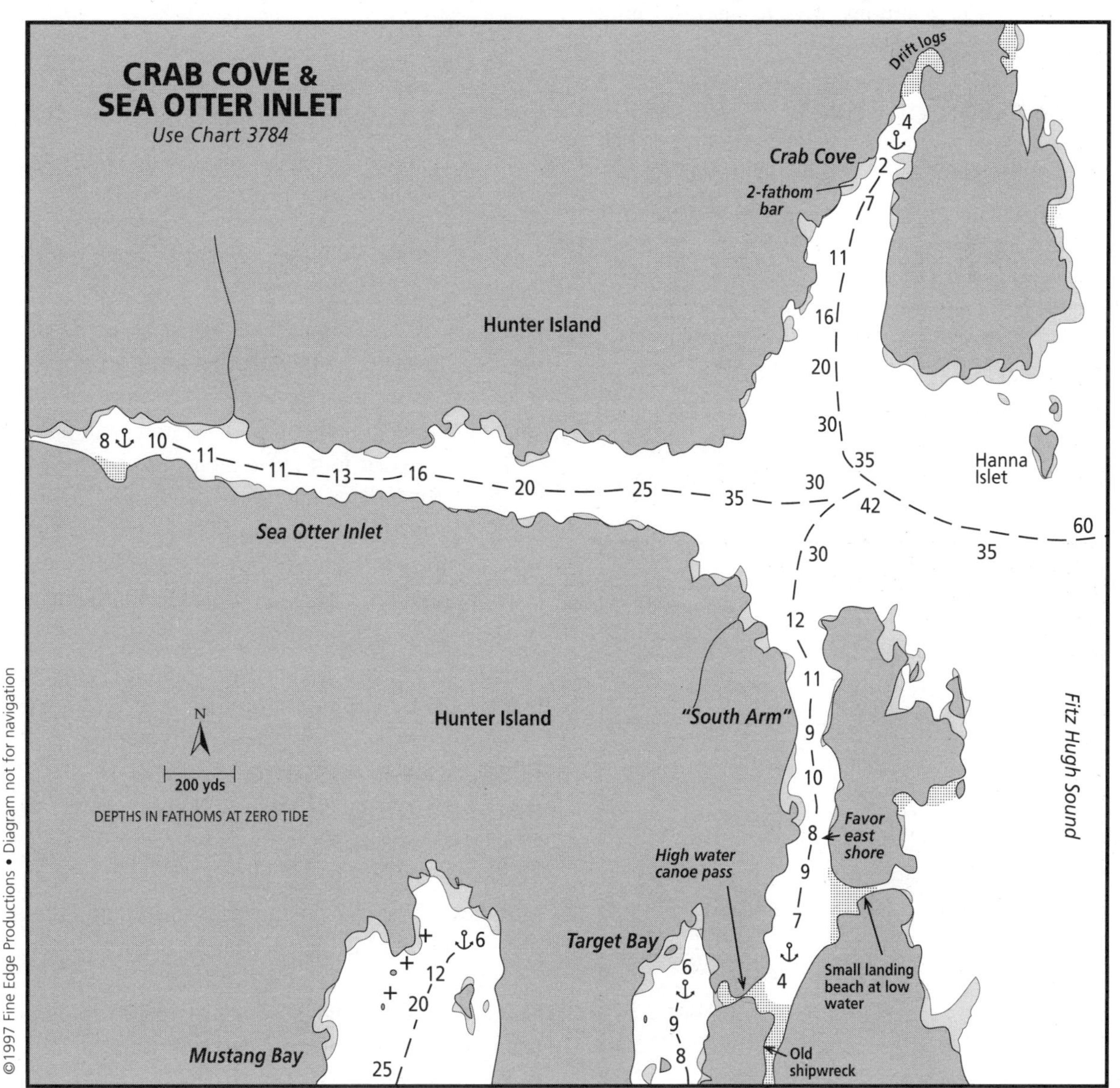

Crab Cove

Chart 3784; anchor (north):
51°50.87′ N, 128°01.28′ W (NAD 27)

> *Crab Cove is the north arm near the entrance of the [Sea Otter] inlet.* (p. 73, SD)

Crab Cove, opposite Sea Otter South Arm, is partially exposed to south winds as driftwood at the head of the cove suggests. It is a good anchorage for small boats in prevailing northwest winds. Anchor midchannel on the north side of the 2-fathom bar.

Anchor in 3 to 4 fathoms over a sand and mud bottom with good holding.

"Inner Warrior Cove"

Chart 3784; entrance: 51°49.90′ N, 127°53.50′ W, anchor: 51°50.45′ N, 127°52.49′ W (NAD 27)

> *Warrior Cove, about 1 mile north of Uganda Point, is separated from Kiwash Cove, by the peninsula with Ontario Point at its SW extremity; both coves are deep. An islet with drying rocks close north and south of it partially obstructs the entrance to Warrior Cove . . .* (p. 74, SD)

Inner Warrior Cove offers some surprisingly good protection from channel winds and seas. Entry is straightforward and can be made by radar if necessary. The fairway appears to have a flat bottom with no sign of rocks except at its outer entrance.

A 3-foot chop in the channel completely dies off once you pass island (270). Under stable conditions, anchor midchannel at the head of the bay. There are minimal drift logs ashore. Small boats can tuck into the little bight at the west wall and become almost landlocked.

Anchor as indicated in 3 fathoms over a mud and sand bottom with some kelp, with good holding if you set your anchor well.

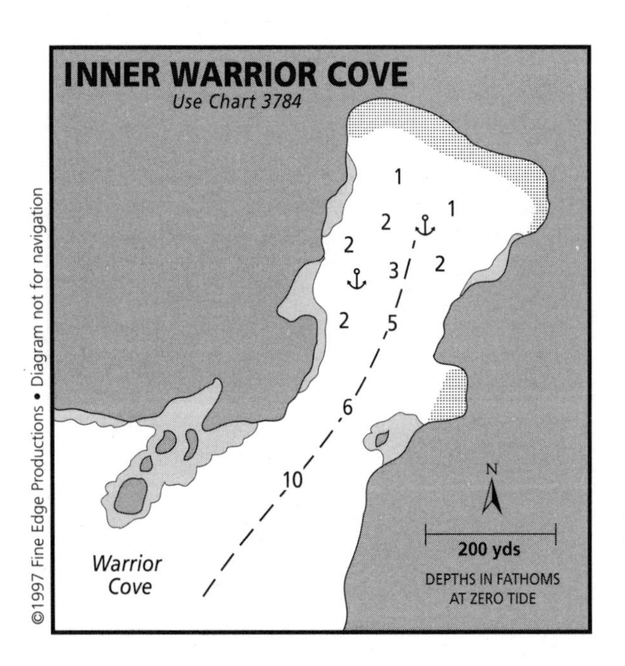

Kiwash Cove

Chart 3784; entrance: 51°50.70′ N, 127°53.30′ W; anchor (northwest corner):
51°50.98′ N, 127°52.91′ W (NAD 27)

> *. . . a rock, with less than 6 feet (2 m) over it, lies in the middle of the entrance to Kiwash Cove. The fairway into each of the . . . coves [Warrior, Kiwash] lies close to their SE sides, which are steep-to.* (p. 74, SD)

Kiwash Cove makes a good lunch stop in fair weather between the islands that form the northwest corner of the cove. This scenic spot, unfortunately, has a gravel and kelp bottom with poor holding. You can find protection from southeast winds in the eastern end of the cove, off a steep-to, drying gravel flat at the outlet of a little creek; it's easy to detect the shallows by the light-colored water. This is not a good spot to anchor in westerlies.

Anchor (northwest corner) in 2 fathoms, gravel, rock and kelp with poor holding.

Morehouse Passage and Lapwing Island

Chart 3785 (inset); Morehouse (south entrance):
51°51.30′ N, 127°53.50′ W (NAD 27)

Morehouse Passage is the route to Namu that passes south of Kiwash Island. From outside Kiwash Cove, you can head directly toward old Namu fuel dock by passing between Lapwing Island and the mainland. Least depth in the fairway is 4 fathoms.

Namu Harbour

Chart 3785 (inset), 3784; north float:
51°51.73′ N, 127°51.93′ W (NAD 27)

Namu Harbour can be entered by either Morehouse Passage or Cloverleaf Passage. (p. 74, SD)

Namu Harbour is the site of an old, formerly successful cannery now rapidly falling into ruin. The operation has been closed since 1993, and two revitalization projects in the 1990s failed. In 1996, the fuel dock float was missing; no one was permitted on shore by the watchmen, yellow danger tape was strung along the docks, and "neighborhood watch" signs were posted in prominent places. It is sad to see a once-thriving community with such attractive houses and gardens fall into ruin. Perhaps a future attempt to revive Namu as a resort will be successful.

The bay still teems with salmon that wait for mainland streams to swell and, if you want to fish this area, consider anchoring in Inner Warrior Cove or deep inside Rock Inlet. In heavy weather we recommend using Fougner Bay, 3 miles north in nearby Burke Channel, as a better storm anchorage. (see Chapter 5)

Namu, the old cannery

Whirlwind Bay

Chart 3785 (inset), 3784; position:
51°51.78′ N, 127°51.73′ W (NAD 27)

Whirlwind Bay, on the east side of Namu Harbour, is entered between Sunday Island and Clam Island, which is connected to the south shore of Whirlwind Bay by a drying bank on which there are several rocks. (p. 74, SD)

Photo by Herb Nickles

Cruise ship heading north, Seaforth Channel

Whirlwind Bay is aptly named—it's a poor place to anchor in southeast winds. Rock Inlet to the northeast offers better shelter.

Rock Inlet

Chart 3785 (inset); anchor:
51°52.42′ N, 127°51.28′ W (NAD 27)

Rock Inlet, entered east of Verdant Island, is fringed with islets and rocks and only suitable for small craft. The narrowest part of the inlet, with islets on both sides, has a least depth of 12 feet (3.7 m). (p. 74, SD)

Rock Inlet offers almost complete protection from weather and is close to good fishing grounds. Make a careful entry to identify and avoid the many islets and rocks. You can anchor almost anywhere in the inner basin avoiding the floats sometimes stored here. We like the notch on the north shore as shown in the diagram. For larger boats, the south side has more swinging room in 4 to 7 fathoms.

Anchor in 2 fathoms over a mud and gravel bottom with fair-to-good holding.

Harlequin Basin

Chart 3785 (inset); entrance:
51°52.40′ N, 127° 52.90′ W; position:
51°53.25′ N, 127°51.63′ W (NAD 27)

The preferred approach to Harlequin Basin is on the east side of Que Que Rocks. Rocks and shoal water extend from both sides of the entrance. (p. 74, SD)

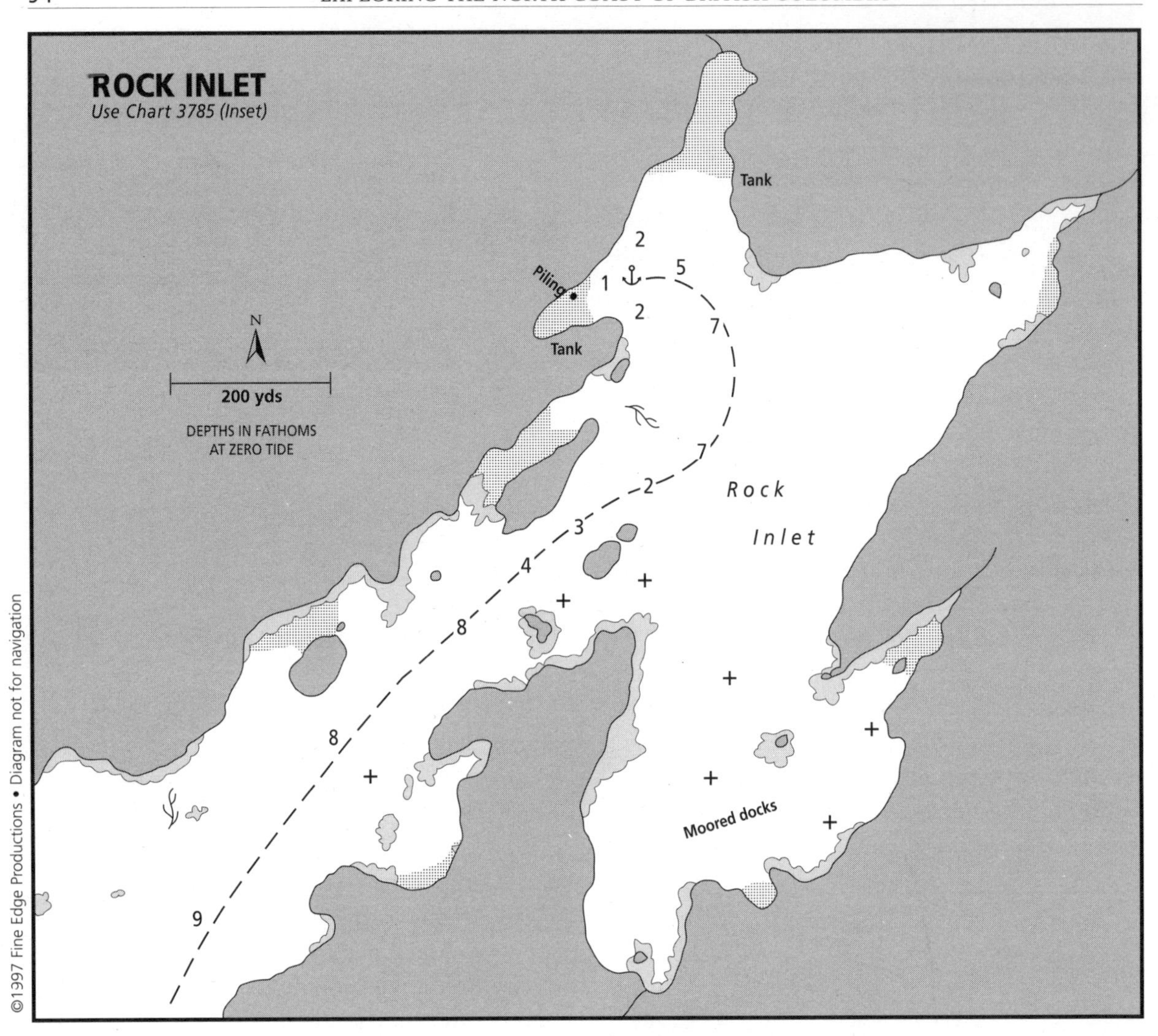

Harlequin Basin is protected from most weather, but most of it is too deep for small-craft anchoring. Also, old logs and branches that float round and round the basin, collecting at the north end, present a nuisance for anchoring.

The fairway in the entrance narrows has a least depth of 9 fathoms in its center. The bottom rises rapidly from 16 to 4 fathoms. There is a small 4-fathom bench near shore; the gravel and rock bottom has poor holding.

Kiltik Cove

Chart 3785; entrance: 51°53.80′ N, 128°00.00′ W; anchor (south cove): 51°53.71′ N, 128°00.63′ W (NAD 27)

Kiltik Cove has a drying flat extending 0.5 mile from its head. (p. 74, SD)

The southern arm of Kiltik Cove is well protected from all weather, and you can find good shelter in the south cove by anchoring west of the large rock that bares at high water; the cove dries just south of this rock. Kiltik is a snug anchorage when a south wind kicks up a good chop on ebb tide.

Anchor (south cove) in 5 fathoms over a soft bottom with fair-to-good holding.

De Cosmos Lagoon

Chart: 3785; position: 52°56.30′ N, 127 57.88′ W (NAD 27).

De Cosmos Lagoon is a landlocked lagoon where tree limbs nearly meet in the center of the narrows. Its entrance is choked with kelp and tidal currents are strong. The lagoon, a wildlife refuge, is also the site of a dredge used to remove clay reportedly used in manufacturing cosmetics. You can anchor outside the lagoon entrance in about 6 fathoms in fair weather (no protection) and enter by dinghy near slack water. Entry by boat is not advised.

Logging tug at work

Fisher Channel

Chart 3785; south entrance: 51°55.50′ N, 127°56.25′ W; north entrance: 52°15.70′ N, 127° 46.40′ W (NAD 27)

> *Fisher Channel . . . leads to Dean Channel and Cousins Inlet at its north end. Lama Passage, on its west side, is part of the main route of the Inner Passage leading west and north. Johnson Channel and Gunboat Passage, farther north, are alternative routes connecting with the main Inner Passage.* (p. 79, SD)

The south end of Fisher Channel also marks the entrance to Burke Channel and the route to Bella Coola. (See Chapter 5.)

Kisameet Bay

Chart 3785; entrance: 51°56.60′ N, 127°54.30′ W, anchor: 51°58.10′ N, 127°52.80′ W (NAD 27)

> *Kisameet Bay, east of Kisameet Islands, has several drying rocks in it.* (p. 79, SD)

Kisameet Bay offers good shelter tucked in on the northwest side of the easternmost Kisameet Island.

Anchor in 6 fathoms over a mud bottom with good holding.

Long Point Cove

Chart 3785; entrance: 55°03.25′ N, 127°56.90′ W; anchor: 52°02.80′ N, 127°57.03′ W (NAD 27)

> *Long Point Cove is an excellent anchorage for small craft. A drying rock lies in the entrance to the cove, about 0.2 mile north of Long Point.* (p. 79, SD)

Easy to miss, Long Point Cove is located one mile south of the old Pointer Island lighthouse where you turn west into Lama Passage. (The lighthouse was removed a few years ago—only a lighted marker and helicopter pad remain.) Long Point Cove affords good protection from southerly storms or chop, but because the head of the cove has been used from time to time to store float houses or commercial operations, it's not the most scenic anchorage. It is, however, a good place to hide if you're hit in the face coming out of Lama Passage heading southbound.

Entry is easy, but watch out for the small, mid-channel rock 300 yards north-northwest of Long Point; it dries on a 3-foot tide.

Anchor in 6 fathoms, well into the cove; unrecorded bottom.

Codville Lagoon

Chart 3785; entrance: 52°03.30′ N, 127°53.00′ W; anchor: 52°03.68′ N, 127°50.15′ W (NAD 27)

> *At the head of Lagoon Bay a narrow passage leads east into Codville Lagoon. A rock with less than 6 feet (2 m) over it lies in this passage, slightly north of mid-channel.*
>
> *Anchorage for small and medium sized vessels can be obtained in Codville Lagoon; it is well sheltered.* (p. 79, SD)

If there ever was a natural harbor, it's Codville Lagoon. This is a good place to head if a major

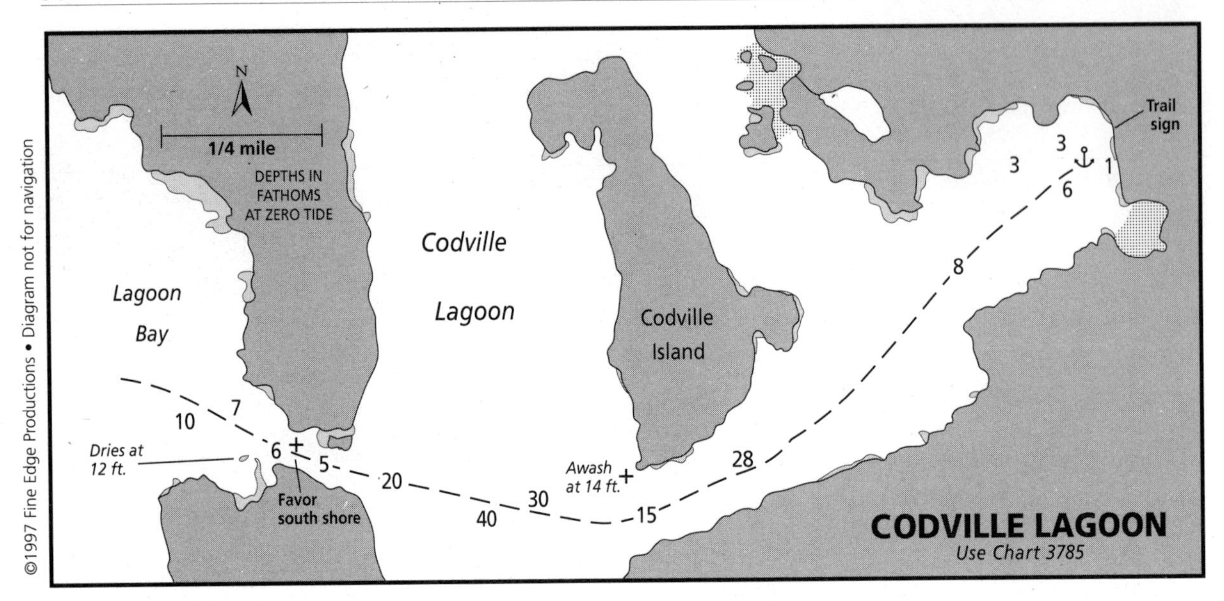

blow develops while you're in Fitz Hugh Sound, but it's easy to pass right by the entrance without realizing such a great anchorage is nearby. The lagoon is a large, saltwater lake, surrounded entirely by old-growth cedar (no clear-cut scars) and lots of silver snags. Wildlife viewing, especially birding, is a pastime here at the lagoon.

A signed trail leads from the lagoon to fresh-water Sagar Lake. The trail, the picnic facilities at the lake, and the small float in the bight were once maintained by the Ocean Falls Yacht Club as one of several outpost projects in that town's heyday.

Sagar Lake Trail

The trail to Sagar Lake begins at the sign as shown in the Codville Lagoon diagram. The trail is wet and muddy in places and requires boat boots, *not* running shoes. Elevation rise is plus or minus 300 vertical feet. At the lake, there's a wide, sandy beach about 200 yards long with a gently sloping sand bottom—a big treat and ideal for swimming. Fishing did not appear promising off the beach, but a small inflatable kayak could access the upper lake, narrows, and second lake (really the same lake); it almost touches Evans Inlet to the north and is unlogged.

The trail is a slow half-mile. You need an hour and a half for the full trip with time for a dip at the lake. This is a superb beach, rare in this part of the Northwest where the trees usually meet the water.

—*Rod Nash*

We would not trust the float with anything more than a dinghy now.

Entry to Codville Lagoon is through a narrow passage that has a minimum depth of about 5-fathoms. A rock underwater at zero tide on the north side of the narrows can be avoided by favoring the south shore. From the south, Codville Hill is a leading landmark, noticeable as a series of lumpy, bald rock knobs. Most of the lagoon is too deep for convenient anchoring, but the far east side has a shoal where you can find good anchorage and almost complete shelter. There is no driftwood or indication of weather in here; it's just peaceful, quiet, and pristine.

Anchor in 4 to 6 fathoms over a mud bottom with fair-to-good holding.

Evans Inlet

Chart 3785; entrance: 52°06.10' N, 127°52.70' W (NAD 27)

Evans Inlet, on the east side of Fisher Channel, is entered between Brend Point. . .and Bold Point. Luke Island and Matthew Island are in the entrance to Evans Inlet; a drying rock lies in the middle of the passage between them. Luke Passage is the best entrance to Evans Inlet. Matthew Passage is obstructed by islets and rocks at its SE end, by a drying rock off the NE part of

Matthew Island, and by Peril Rock which lies in mid-channel and is steep-to.

Anchorage suitable for vessels of moderate size can be obtained at the head of Evans Inlet in 15 to 17 fathoms (27 to 31 m). (p. 79, SD)

Evans Inlet, rather a long way off Fisher Channel (4.5 miles), is seldom used by cruising boats. Although its depths are too great for small boats, it's a good place for larger boats to find adequate swinging room. Well-sheltered anchorage is reported behind Boot Island near the head of the bay on its south side. The bottom is reported to be rocky with fair holding.

Port John

Chart 3785; entrance: 52°07.20′ N, 127°51.20′ W; anchor: 52°07.32′ N, 127°50.40′ W (NAD 27)

Port John. . .is entered between Salisbury Point and Exeter Point. A steep-to reef, about 0.2 mile from its head near the mouth of Hook Nose Creek, has Mark Rock at its SW end.

Anchorage of indifferent quality from small craft can be obtained close to shore in Port John. (p. 79, SD)

Port John can offer shelter in fair weather tucked close to shore between Hook Nose Creek and the south shore. This avoids the reef mentioned above; however, the water is deep and the shore steep-to. Small boats can use the piling in the southeast corner for a stern tie (the pilings are in just a few feet of water at zero tide) and set a main hook to the west.

Anchor in 4 to 10 fathoms over a sand/mud bottom with fair-to-good holding.

Lama Passage

Chart 3785; east entrance: 52°04.10′ N, 127°56.70′ W; north entrance: 52°11.20′ N, 128°06.00′ W (NAD 27)

Lama Passage is the main passage connecting Fisher Channel with Seaforth Channel and Milbanke Sound; its east entrance can be identified by a conical mountain 995 feet (303 m) high on the NE end of Hunter Island. It lies to the south and west of Denny Island. The north shore at the east end of the passage is bold. (p. 84, SD)

Lama Passage, largely free of chop, has several good anchorages for small boats. Since nearly all north- or southbound traffic uses this narrow passage, be on the lookout for vessels of all sizes transiting Lama Passage. Gunboat Passage, 8 miles north, is far less travelled, and is a scenic small-boat passage that comes out just east of Shearwater. (See Chapter 5.)

Fancy Cove

Chart 3785; entrance: 52°04.00′ N, 128°01.20′ W; anchor: 52°03.68′ N, 128°00.63′ W (NAD 27)

Fancy Cove is about 1 mile SW of Serpent Point. (p. 84, SD)

Sailing Directions does not do justice to this fine, scenic cove. Small craft can find good protection from southerly weather here, and most westerly

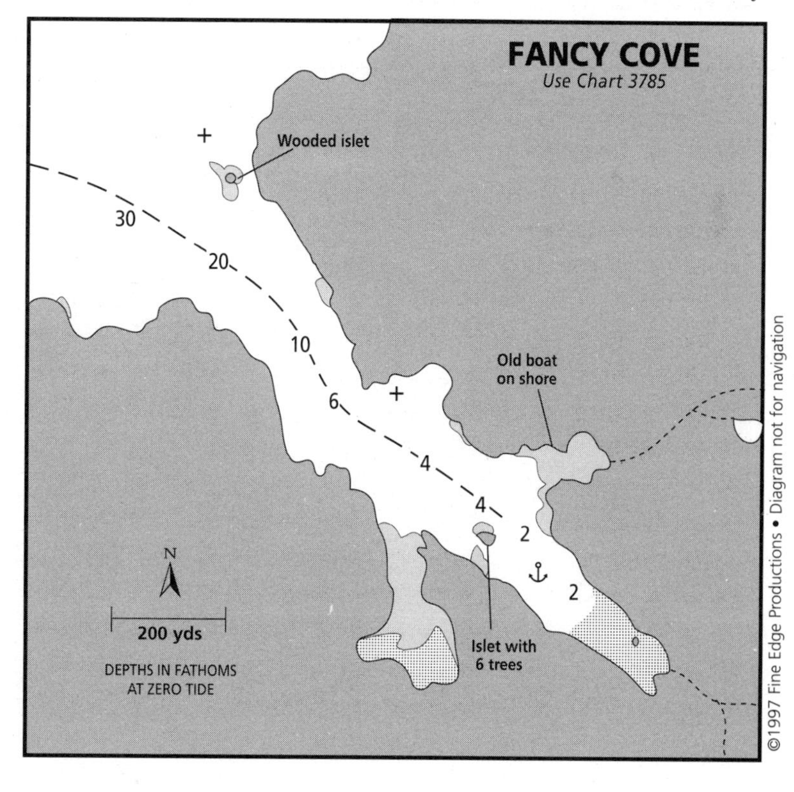

chop passes right by. At one time a large float house occupied the cove behind the islet, but this spot is now available for boats looking for solitude and a small landing beach.

Anchor in 2 fathoms over a sand and shell bottom with good holding.

Cooper Inlet

Chart 3785; entrance: 52°04.00′ N, 128°04.25′ W (NAD 27)

> *Cooper Inlet, entered between Harbourmaster Point and Westminster Point, about 1.6 miles WNW, has several islets and rocks across its entrance. It contains several coves which offer shelter.* (p. 84, SD)

Ada Cove

Chart 3785; entrance: 52°03.85′ N, 128°03.70′ W; anchor: 52°03.51′ N, 128°03.09′ W (NAD 27)

> *Ada Cove, between Harbourmaster Point and Strom Point, is entered on the SW side of two islets situated midway between the entrance points. Foul ground lies between the islets and Harbourmaster Point.* (p. 84, SD)

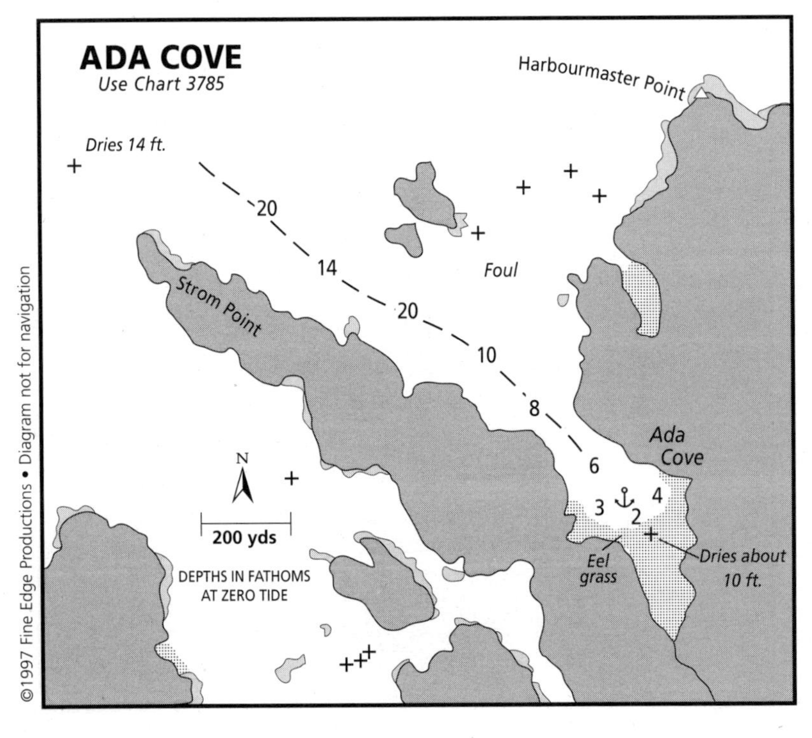

Ada Cove is another good anchorage that's calm when southerlies blow outside. The small anchor-hole just inside the narrows is adequate for several boats. The head of the cove which shoals rapidly, drying at about 10 feet, is marked by heavy eel grass.

Entry should be made as indicated, avoiding the rock off Strom Point and the foul ground between the cove and Harbourmaster Point. Harbourmaster Point is marked with a small white light as well as white paint on the rocks.

Anchor in 4 to 5 fathoms over a soft sand and shell bottom with fair-to-good holding.

Jane Cove

Chart 3785; entrance: 52°03.90′ N, 128°04.40′ W; anchor: 52°03.11′ N, 128°03.52′ W (NAD 27)

> *Jane Cove, entered between Strom Point and Gibson Point, is obstructed by a drying rock and shoals close within the entrance. The cove is suitable for small craft.* (p. 84, SD)

Jane Cove is the third of five coves located along the north side of Hunter Island. Like Ada and Fancy Coves, it too offers good shelter from southerly weather. Entry requires avoiding several shoals and rocks.

Favor the south shore and anchor near the head of the cove in about 8 fathoms over an unrecorded bottom.

Fannie Cove

Chart 3785; position: 52°02.92′ N, 128°04.02′ W (NAD 27)

> *Fannie Cove, on the west side of Gibson Point, and Lizzie Cove, the west arm of Cooper Inlet, are fronted by islets and rocks.* (p. 84, SD)

While Fannie and Lizzie, two of the five coves in this series, are recommended in some books for small craft, we *do not recommend* them as cruising anchorages, especially Lizzie Cove. While Lizzie looks good on paper, it is in fact very difficult to determine the position of the dangerous rocks at the entrance in order to avoid them. Furthermore, the bottom of both coves is rocky and uneven (not as charted!), and we could not get a satisfactory set on our anchor despite several serious tries.

Lizzie Cove

Chart 3785; entrance; 52°04.90′ N, 128°04.90′ W; position: 52°03.15′ N, 128°05.20′ W (NAD 27)

> *Small craft can obtain secure anchorage in 7 to 9 fathoms (13 to 17 m) in the middle of Lizzie Cove, but local knowledge is advised because of rocks in the entrance.* (p. 85, SD)

(See Fannie Cove above.)

Canal Bight

Chart 3785; entrance: 52°05.30′ N, 128°05.10′ W; anchor: 52°05.48′ N, 128°05.20′ W (NAD 27)

> *Start Point is on the north side of the east entrance of Lama Passage; White Point is 0.9 mile west. Cliff Bluff and Canal Bight lie 3 and 4.5 miles farther west.* (p. 84, SD)

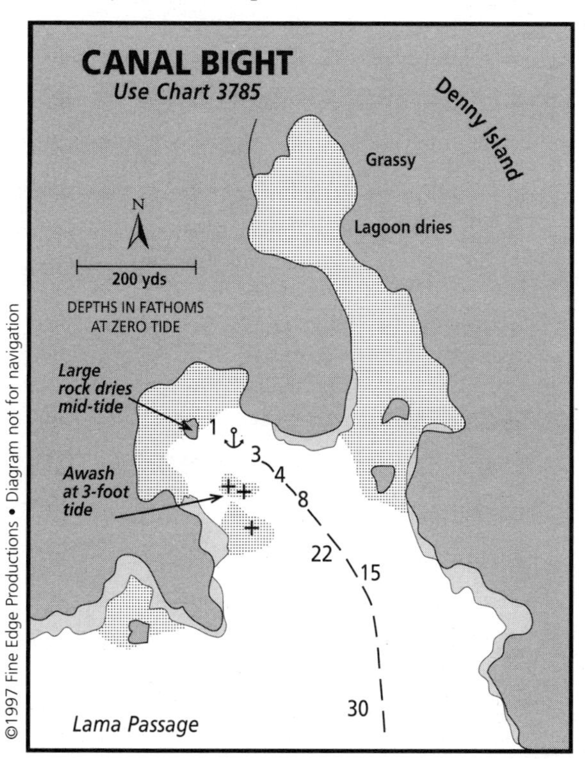

Canal Bight is exposed to south winds and has limited swinging room, but it's a delightful place to take a lunch stop and explore the nearby lagoon-like mud flats. Avoid the large rock deep in the cove as well as rocks on the south side. In fair weather you may find, as we do, that a 2-fathom spot on the northwest corner makes a nice rest stop.

Alarm Cove

Charts 3785, 3787; entrance: 52°07.10′ N, 128°07.10′ W; position: 52°07.04′ N, 128°06.83′ W (NAD 27)

> *Alarm Cove, on the east side of the passage, is entered north of Alert Island. The cove is encumbered by above- and below-water rocks.* (p. 85, SD)

Alarm Cove looks like a rock pile as you go by. It may offer some shelter northwest of Alert Island, but we surmise that its bottom is rocky.

McLoughlin Bay

Charts 3785, 3787; entrance: 52°08.40′ N, 128°08.20′ W; position: 52°08.28′ N, 128°08.47′ W (NAD 27)

> *McLoughlin Bay is on the west side of Lama Passage, a short distance NNW of Napier Point.* (p. 85, SD)

McLoughlin Bay, now a stop for the Discovery Coast ferry, is growing busier.

Although local fishermen have traditionally anchored north of the fish plant in 14 fathoms, it is exposed to southeast winds and swells from channel traffic. Avoid the pipeline in the bay that extends underwater northeast from the shore.

Bella Bella

Charts 3785, 3787; fuel dock: 52°09.77′ N, 128°08.37′ W (NAD 27)

> *New Bella Bella is a large Indian village on the west side of Lama Passage about 1 mile NNW of Story Point.* (p. 86, SD)

Bella Bella, known also by its native name Waglisla, has grown a great deal in the last several years. Now that the Discovery Coast Ferry makes frequent stops here, it will continue to serve as the main supply and communication

Photo by Herb Nickles

Provisioning at Bella Bella

center for the north-central coast of British Columbia. It boasts the first available land telephone on the Inside Passage north of Queen Charlotte Strait. Although in the past during periods of drought, we heard complaints about water quality at PetroCan fuel dock, a new water system seems to be greatly improved.

The public docks are quite busy and tend to be crowded, but we always look forward to stopping here. The Band store at the head of the wharf usually has a good selection of groceries, bakery bread, and general merchandise. The liquor store is open Tuesday through Saturday; the bank is open Tuesday afternoon and Wednesday morning. There is a RCMP detachment stationed here and a hospital. For serious marine repair work, good float space, and a less frantic pace, visit Shearwater, located 2 miles to the southeast.

Bella Bella—returning from trip to Queens Sound

Martins Cove

Charts 3785, 3787; floats:
52°10.32′ N, 128°08.38′ W (NAD 27)

> *Martins Cove . . . is protected on its east side by a rock breakwater and port hand buoy "E19" marks the drying rock at the entrance. Within the cove are three public floats with 1,762 feet (543 m) of berthing for small craft.* (p. 86, SD)

Martins Cove, where the Bella Bella fishing fleet moors, generally has little room and does not hold much interest for private cruising boats.

Cavin Cove

Charts 3785, 3787; entrance:
52°10.60′ N, 128°08.05′ W (NAD 27)

> *Cavin Cove, 0.8 mile north of New Bella Bella, has a bar 0.2 mile within its entrance with a depth of 6 feet (1.8 m). It is only suitable for small craft.* (p. 86, SD)

Cavin Cove, a storage area for floats, boomsticks and other equipment, is sometimes used as an anchorage for boats wishing to remain close to Bella Bella.

Whisky Cove

Charts 3785, 3787; position:
52°09.45′ N, 128°06.15′ W (NAD 27)

> *Whisky Cove lies south of Spirit Island.* (p. 86, SD)

Whisky Cove has a number of private homes, floats and buoys. Boats may find anchorage in the middle of the cove taking care to avoid the floats and buoys.

Kliktsoatli Harbour

Chart 3785 (inset); entrance:
52°09.70′ N, 128°05.60′ W; anchor:
52°08.67′ N, 128°04.48′ W (NAD 27)

> *Kliktsoatli Harbour is entered between Spirit Island and Robins Point, about 1 mile ESE.*
>
> *Anchorage, with good holding ground, can be obtained in 11 fathoms (20 m), mud bottom, about 0.3 mile SE of Shearwater Island.* (p. 86, SD)

Kliktsoatli Harbour provides good protection from southerly weather. Pleasure craft can anchor in the southeast corner, just inside the 10-fathom curve, avoiding private floats and buoys frequently found here. Additional small-boat protection from northerly winds can be found behind Klik Island in 5 fathoms. Public mooring buoys lie in the south end of the harbor. The large buoys just south of Shearwater are reserved for the Discovery Coast Ferry that calls here.

Anchor in 9 fathoms, mud bottom, good holding.

Photo courtesy Bryce Gillard

Bryce Gillard & Trevor Ruelle with two hours' catch near Bella Bella

Shearwater

Charts 3785 (inset), 3787; float: 52°08.82′ N, 128°05.20′ W (NAD 27)

> *The settlement of Shearwater is close north of Atli Point. It has a hardware store, laundromat and a resort hotel with restaurant and pub. Bella Bella post office is in Shearwater. Shearwater Marine Limited has 600 feet (183 m) of berthing for visiting craft, a 13.5 tonne hoist and a marine ways that can haul vessels up to 80 feet (24.4 m) long and 90 tonnes displacement. . . . Charts, water, ice, groceries, hardware and showers are available. Welding, electronic and engine repairs and hull and fiberglass repairs can be carried out.* (p. 86, SD)

Located on the west side of Kliktsoatli Harbour, Shearwater—the only serious repair and haul-out operation between Port Hardy and Prince Rupert—is a major resort with 1,500 feet of moorage at a new concrete float. *Note:* Haul-out capabilities for sailboats at Shearwater Marine may be limited by a vessel's depth or keel configuration.

Preparing the catch of the day

Water and some power are available on the floats, and there are showers and laundry (self-serve or wash and fold), ice, and propane on shore. There is also a marine store, restaurant, and pub. The resort suggests that if you wish moorage during summer, you phone ahead for reservations 604-270-6204, or from the U.S., 800-663-2370. (Both telephone numbers, located in the Vancouver area, are manned year-round. The direct number for the office at Shearwater is 250-957-2305.) Stryker Electronics, 250-957-2333, has replacement radar, GPS, sounders, etc. For electronic repairs contact Ron Sale at 250-957-2281.

A floating ferry dock for Discovery Coast ferry service was installed just south of Atli Point; two large orange anchor buoys, 150 yards off the terminal, are reserved for ferry use.

Kakushdish Harbour, "Gullchuck"

Chart 3785; entrance: 52°09.50′ N, 128°02.70′ W; anchor: 52°08.97′ N, 128°00.85′ W (NAD 27)

> *Kakushdish Harbour is approached from either south or east of Cypress Island. A shallow bar extends across the harbour about 0.3 mile within the entrance. A drying rock and a rock awash close NE, lie in the middle of the basin near the head of the harbour. Anchorage for small craft*

Photo by Herb Nickles

Bella Bella fuel dock

can be obtained in Kakushdish Harbour in 21 feet (6.4 m), mud. (p. 87, SD)

Kakushdish Harbour, located 3 miles east of Shearwater, is known locally as "Gullchuck" for the numbers of gulls that seek shelter here when strong winds are blowing on the west coast. The landlocked harbor offers good protection. Its entrance bar is shallow (about 7 feet minimum in the fairway at zero tide), with an irregular bottom. However, the basin has a nearly-flat bottom of 3 to 5 fathoms over a large area. There is plenty of swinging room for a number of boats. Avoid the mid-basin rock which dries at a 3-foot tide. With the exception of a few cabins on the east shore, there is no development here.

The cove in the entrance on the south shore largely dries. The east point of the cove has an old cabin fronted at low water by a rock wall which may be an old fish weir. Powerlines from Ocean Falls, with 83 feet (25 meters) of overhead clearance, cross the harbor at its entrance bar. We had difficulty setting our lunch hook, so be sure to set your anchor carefully.

Anchor in about 3 fathoms over a soft mud bottom with fair-to-good holding only if you set your anchor well.

Seaforth Channel

Charts 3720, 3787; Dryad Point light: 52°11.18′ N, 128°06.60′ W; turning point: 52°11.20 ′ N, 128°06.00′ W (NAD 27)

Seaforth Channel is part of the deep draught Inner Passage route . . . (p. 92, SD)

Seaforth Channel is a busy area where all north- or southbound boats converge. There are several isolated rocks and reefs in the channel, some of which are marked. Alert navigation is required as you pass through this channel.

Ormidale Harbour

Charts 3787, 3720; entrance: 52°12.40′ N, 128°09.00′ W(NAD 27)

Ormidale Harbour, NW of Ardmillan Bay, is protected from north and east by Thorburne Island and Nevay Island. The main entrance is west of Nevay Island; foul ground extends 450 feet (127 m) from the west shore of this entrance. The passage between Nevay and Thorburne Islands is encumbered by rocks.

Anchorage can be obtained in Ormidale Harbour in 17 fathoms (31 m), mud, about 0.2 mile south of Nevay Island. When approaching, take care to avoid Wellington Rock, 0.2 mile NNW of Nevay Island. (p. 92, SD)

Ormidale Harbour is only a "harbor" for large vessels which can anchor in mid-bay. The overall bottom is deep and irregular and appears to offer little comfort for cruising boats due to its rocky bottom. With the exception of the tiny lagoon area at its south end, where small boats might find limited anchorage, we couldn't find any reasonable anchorage along shore. Carefully pass the Waglisla Fuel Dock (for float planes only), located on the peninsula south of the lagoon, and proceed to a 1.5-fathom hole just east of the treed islet. Swinging room here is limited.

Kynumpt Harbour ("Strom Bay and Cove")

Charts 3787, 3720; anchor (Strom Bay):
52°12.44′ N, 128°09.79′ W; anchor (Strom Cove):
52°12.17′ N, 128°09.90′ W (NAD 27)

> *Kynumpt Harbour, known locally as Strom Bay, is entered between Defeat Point and Lay Point, which can be identified by Oland Islet, lying close off it. Shelf Point and two shoal rocks lie on the west side of the harbour. Active Islet lies close SW of Defeat Point. Green Neck is a narrow isthmus of formerly cultivated land.*
>
> *The best anchorage in Kynumpt Harbour is in 7 to 9 fathoms (13 to 16 m) about 0.1 mile west of Spratt Point, at the entrance to Strom Cove.*
> (p. 92, SD)

Strom Bay and Strom Cove in Kynumpt Harbour are well-protected anchorages with calm waters in most weather. Just an occasional wake of a cruise ship is felt in here.

Entry is easy, even by radar. Avoid Active Islet and its reef which form a natural breakwater for the outer Strom Bay anchorage. If you are headed deep into Strom Bay, give wide clearance to the rocks on the west shore.

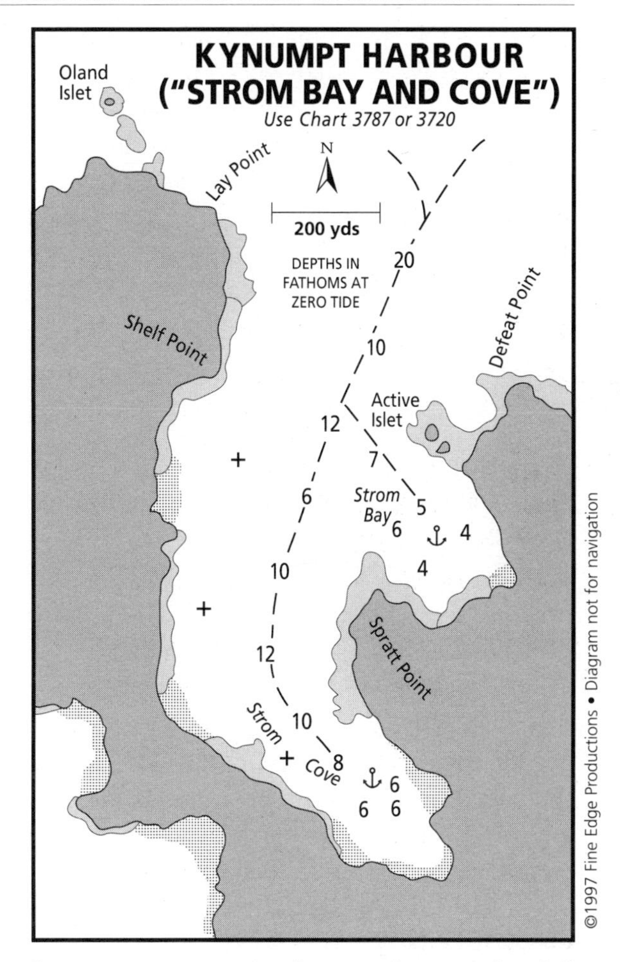

Anchor (Strom Bay) in 5 to 6 fathoms over a mud bottom with good holding.

Anchor (Strom Cove) in 6 to 8 fathoms over a mud bottom with good holding.

We met Scott Davis in Strom Cove on August 27, 1994, just as he'd passed the 2,000-mile rowing mark on his epic round-trip from Puget Sound to Glacier Bay. He accomplished this feat of seamanship by following the West Coast Outer Passage southbound all the way from Lisianski Strait to Bert Millar Cutoff, including Higgins Passage. His craft, *Crystal Vision*, is a handsome, custom-designed, 24-foot rowing machine. He completed his remarkable 6-month, 2,500-mile trip at Port Townsend on October 15, 1994.

Odin Cove

Chart 3787, 3720; entrance:
52°12.80′ N, 128°10.70′ W; anchor:
52°12.56′ N, 128°10.67′ W (NAD 27)

> *Odin Cove, close west of Kynumpt Harbour, has a rock with 3 feet (0.9 m) over it in its middle.*
> (p. 92, SD)

Odin Cove offers good protection in southerly weather and fair protection in strong westerlies. The chop in Seaforth Channel tends to flow right by Odin Cove, and although some wind penetrates the cove, it slowly dies off. The charted rock mentioned with 3 feet over it at zero tide presents little concern except on low tides. The bottom gradually shoals, and good anchorage can be found south of the treed islet in the center of the cove. The bottom of sand and shells has large areas of iridescent seaweed which can foul some anchors; verify that yours is well set.

Anchor in 3 fathoms over sand and shell with some seaweed; holding depends on set of anchor.

Dundivan Inlet

Chart 3787; entrance: 52°13.70′ N, 128°15.30′ W (NAD 27)

> *Dundivan Inlet, west of Mount Gowlland, is entered between McGown Point and the NE point of Dufferin Island. Depths within the inlet are too great for satisfactory anchorage.* (p. 92, SD)

Dundivan Inlet is the entrance to Rait Narrows and the route to Queens Sound. (See Chapter 4) Temporary anchorage can be found in the cove southwest of Penny Point where you can wait for proper tide conditions in Rait Narrows.

Lockhart Bay

Chart 3787; anchor: 52°12.28′ N, 128° 15.95′ W (NAD 27)

Temporary anchorage with good shelter from all weather can be found at the head of the cove southwest of Penny Point. Swinging room is limited and a stern tie is useful if you stay any length of time.

Anchor in 2 to 3 fathoms over sand and mud with good holding.

Berry Inlet

Chart 3728; entrance: 52°15.85′ N, 128°20.25′ W; anchor: 52°17.08′ N, 128°17.78′ W (NAD 27)

> *Berry Inlet is entered between Wootton Islet and Fisher Point then leads between Evening Islets and the islet 125 feet (38 m) high lying in the fairway 0.1 mile north. Berry Inlet is useless as an anchorage.* (p. 93, SD)

The head of Berry Inlet provides good anchorage since moderate wind and chop die off before you reach the far end. There is inadequate protection in a southeast or southwest storm and, if strong winds are expected, you can find additional shelter in Mouat Cove.

Anchor in 5 fathoms over a soft mud bottom (somewhat stinky) with good holding.

Mouat Cove

Chart 3728; anchor: 52°16.57′ N, 128°19.32′ W (NAD 27)

> *. . . small vessels can find shelter in Mouat Cove. Local knowledge is recommended.* (p. 93, SD)

Mouat Cove is a small labyrinth of islets, reefs and rocks worth exploring. The anchor site is not self-evident—the chart isn't even close. Anchoring here is sort of a find-it-yourself game, much like trying to find a place to lie down in a formal Japanese garden. In any case, Mouat Cove offers good shelter from all weather and it is *quiet*, except for the occasional moan of Ivory Island's foghorn. We once stopped here after a disagreeable all-night run from Cape Saint James, and it was a stable non-rocking paradise that we didn't leave for 24 hours!

Cruise slowly around Mouat Cove and pick your own flat spot. The bottom is uneven, with plenty of surprises here and there, especially just when

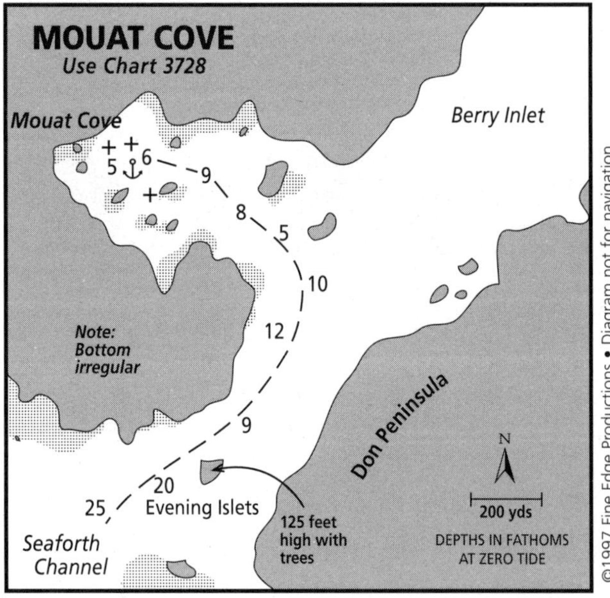

you think you've it figured out. You may also enjoy the islets which Iain Lawrence describes in *Far Away Places*: ". . . capped by twisted trees that sprout from a shag of bushes and lichen, crowding on the rock like shipwrecked sailors atop a raft."

Birds rule here, with kingfishers setting a staccato beat. Ravens chortle, Canada geese honk, loons cry and small deer graze on the grassy margins of the cove.

Anchor in about 4 to 6 fathoms over a mixed bottom; holding depends on finding the flat sand and mud spots.

"The Watchmen," Fisher Point

Chart 3787; position: 52°15.85′ N, 128°20.80′ W (NAD 27)

Fisher Point is the home of two totems known locally as the "The Watchmen." Located high up on the granite face of Fisher Point, they can be seen from your boat if you approach the point carefully.

Gale Passage

Chart 3787; entrance: 52°14.55′ N, 128°22.30′ W (NAD 27)

> *Gale Passage separates Dufferin Island from Athlone Island and leads from the north end of Thompson Bay to Seaforth Channel. This passage is only suitable for small craft and local knowledge is advised to navigate it safely. Tidal rapids are formed about 1.8 miles from its south entrance and again at about the same distance from its north entrance where the fairway dries.* (p. 161, SD)

Gale Passage is very narrow, fraught with hazards and suitable only for experienced kayakers at high-water slack. The passage leads to Queen Sound via Thompson Bay.

Note: St. Johns Harbour, 5 miles west of Gale Passage, and Ivory Island Lightstation are discussed in Chapter 7. Blair Inlet and Reid Passage are discussed in Chapter 6.

"Watchmen" on duty, Fisher Point

"Watchmen," detail

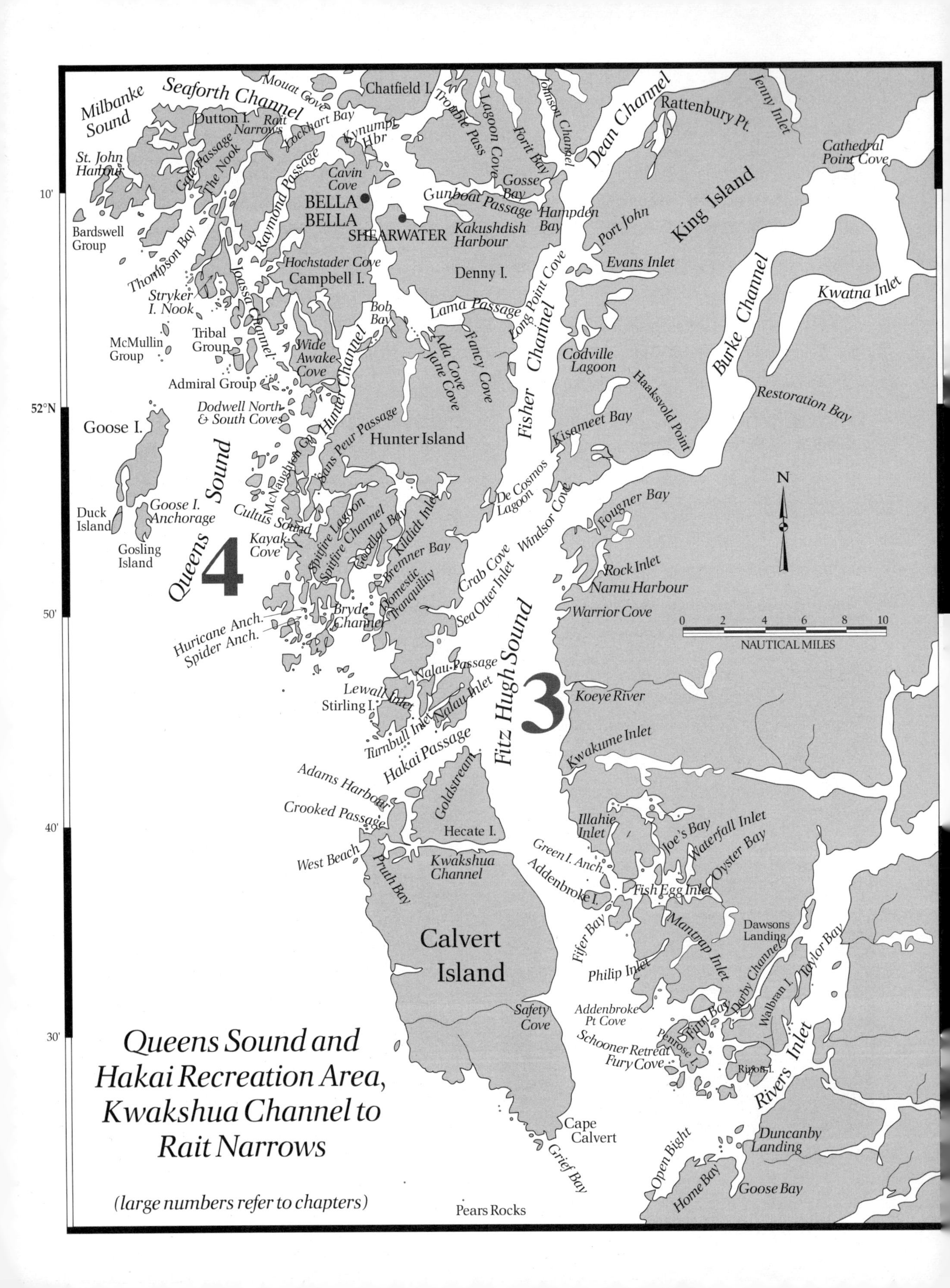

Queens Sound and Hakai Recreation Area, Kwakshua Channel to Rait Narrows

(large numbers refer to chapters)

4

Queens Sound and Hakai Recreation Area, Kwakshua Channel to Rait Narrows

Queens Sound comprises the outer coastal islands between Calvert Island and Seaforth Channel. Seldom described in cruising circles, this unique archipelago offers outstanding recreational opportunities for boaters, canoeists and kayakers. Untold passages, coves, and nooks are there to be discovered and enjoyed.

The southern half of Queens Sound, designated as the Hakai Recreation Area, encompasses over a quarter-million acres of land and sea. It is the largest provincial marine park on the coast of British Columbia and, with the exception of a ranger float moored in Pruth Bay, it is undeveloped.

Dramatic contrasts, from fully exposed shorelines to rolling, forested hills and 1,000-meter summits, create some of the most varied and scenic coastline in the province. Lagoons and reversing tidal rapids, beaches, all-weather anchorages and tombolos (sand spits) make this area an ideal cruising ground for boaters, anglers, kayakers, scuba divers and naturalists. Please be aware that the outer coast is subject to sudden and dramatic changes in weather; fog can roll in quickly and sea conditions can change dramatically within a few hours. *Caution:* Charts for Queens Sound, derived from old surveys, are small-scale, and the routes and coves shown are not well defined. The text that follows is a first and modest attempt at describing what this area has to offer.

Pruth Bay, looking east down Kwakshua Channel

Kwakshua Channel

Chart 3784; east entrance: 51°39.00′ N, 127°57.30′ W; north entrance: 51°42.30′ N, 128°04.00′ W (NAD 27)

Kwakshua Channel leads south and east from Hakai Passage into Fitz Hugh Sound. (p. 154, SD)

Kwakshua Channel, on the west side of Fitz Hugh Sound, is the east-west channel between Calvert and Hecate Islands. It marks the southern end of the Outer Passage for those following the west coast route to Prince Rupert. Out of the current and chop found in Fitz Hugh Sound, the west end of the channel gives excellent protection for cruising boats.

"Unnamed Cove"

Chart 3784; anchor: 51°38.92′ N, 128°04.51′ W (NAD 27)

A small cove, 0.2 mile east of Keith Anchorage, has a wooded islet in its entrance. (p. 154, SD)

Unnamed Cove, immediately west of Keith

Pruth Bay, trail to west beach

Photo courtesy CHS, Pacific Region

Pruth Bay, west arm

Anchor in 2 to 5 fathoms over sand and mud bottom with fair holding.

Pruth Bay

Chart 3784, 3727; anchor:
51°39.27′ N, 128°07.52′ W (NAD 27)

> *Pruth Bay, a popular small craft anchorage, has three arms at its head. The south arm has an islet close off its west entrance point that is joined to shore by a drying ledge; a reef extends 0.1 mile east from this islet terminating in a drying rock. An uncharted shoal with a depth of 9 feet (2.7 m) is close off the north shore just inside the entrance to the bay.* (p. 154, SD)

Pruth Bay has always been a popular anchorage for cruising boats, as well as a favorite sportfishing area. Shelter in the bay is very good and there is adequate swinging room for a number of boats. The earlier, wild charm of this place was lost when the private inholding at the west end of the bay was

Anchorage, is a small indentation in Calvert Island that offers more solitude for small boats than the anchorages farther west. During southeast storms, it may be subject to gusts that deflect off the high peak on Calvert Island.

Anchor in 4 fathoms over sand and mud with eel grass bottom with good holding.

Keith Anchorage

Chart 3784; entrance:
51°39.05′ N, 128°05.25′ W (NAD 27)

> *Anchorage can be obtained midway between the entrance points of Keith Anchorage in 11 fathoms (20 m). This anchorage is reported to be unsafe in SE gales because of heavy squalls that funnel down the valleys at its head.* (p. 154, SD)

Keith Anchorage offers good protection in most summer weather, especially in its western portion.

Pruth Bay, west beach looking south

developed and much of the cedar forest behind the beach was cut. The outer exposed white sand beach is still accessible by a modified trail that weaves through the Hakai Beach Resort.

The resort welcomes visitors, and you can purchase ice and sundries in their small general store, or have dinner in the lodge (best to reserve ahead of time). If you'd like to spend the night, or arrange for a fishing charter, the resort will gladly accommodate. (Call 604-990-9198 in Vancouver.) No fuel is available at the resort.

Pruth Bay, west beach at low tide

Boaters are invited to stop at the park float moored in Pruth Bay, when the park ranger is in residence, to obtain information about recreational possibilities in the greater Hakai Recreation Area and Queens Sound. The inner bay on the north shore, part of the recreational area, is interesting to explore by dinghy or kayak at high water; at low water the bay becomes a drying mud flat.

Anchor midchannel in 5 fathoms over a mud bottom with good holding.

Hakai Passage

Chart 3784; east entrance: 51°44.60' N, 128°00.00' W; west entrance: 51°42.30' N, 128°08.00' W (NAD 27)

Hakai Passage leads east from Queen Charlotte Sound into Fitz Hugh Sound. Several dangers lie in the west approach and numerous islets and dangers are on both sides of the fairway.

Tidal streams in Hakai Passage attain 4 kn at springs, with strong eddies along the shores, on both the flood and ebb. The flood stream sets east past Adams Harbour thence NE through the fairway. (p. 153, SD)

Hakai Passage is renowned for its salmon fishing, particularly Chinook (Spring). The Recreation Area accommodates a number of commercial floating fish camps and resorts. Popular fishing spots are Odlum Point, The Gap, Foster Rocks and Barney Point. Salmon are commonly caught on cut-plug herring. The area also has good fishing for halibut, Ling cod, and rock fish.

The outer portion of Hakai Passage can be extremely dangerous on large ebb tides when strong

Travelling with the *Hakai Ranger*

I join *Hakai Ranger*'s crew on her inaugural trip up the coast from the builder's yard in Campbell River.

Park ranger Andy MacDonald points to a small tug towing a single log and signals fellow ranger Nelson Tallio to get his camera ready. B.C. Parks patrol vessel *Hakai Ranger* slows and pulls alongside. MacDonald and Tallio hop aboard to talk to the two crew members, leaving me to wonder if a bust is going down. But everything checks out; it seems they're log salvors collecting beach logs. Waving good-bye, we continue the evening patrol.

Hakai Ranger was built by Daigle Welding and Marine Limited. Equipped with radar, GPS, VHF and an Autotel, it has a top speed of 31 kts and cruises at 27. The aluminum vessel is a quantum leap from the open river-boat previously used by rangers at Hakai. Then, bad weather meant blasting through waves in survival suits and sometimes having to wait to make the 73-mile run from Bella Coola to the floathouse in Pruth Bay. Now, the wheelhouse with a Dickinson heater has increased the ranger's safety margin and comfort in rough weather.

Enforcing the Park Act, protecting wildlife, logging sightings of marine mammals for a current survey, coordinating commercial operators in the rec area (the sportfishing lodges and three kayak companies)—it's all part of the job.

—Excerpted by permission of Ian Douglas,
from *Pacific Yachting,* September 1995

southwest winds and westerly swells oppose the 4-knot current. Captain Kevin Monahan has experienced 20-foot breaking seas midchannel north of Odlum Point.

Hakai Passage leads to Choked Passage where wonderful fair-weather cruising and anchoring opportunities exist.

Choked Passage, northwest tip Calvert Island

Choked Passage

Chart 3784; north entrance:
51°41.55′ N, 128°05.80′ W (NAD 27)

> *Choked Passage, extending south from Adams Harbour, is encumbered with rocks and shoals.*
>
> *Exposed anchorage for vessels up to 200 feet (61 m) long can be obtained at the south end of Choked Passage, about 0.1 mile north of an unnamed point on Calvert Island; depths here are 7 to 9 fathoms (13 to 16 m).* (p. 153, SD)

Choked Passage is a popular sportfishing area offering great opportunities for exploration by dinghy or kayak—there are beautiful beaches along the Calvert Island shore at the south end of the passage.

The best reported anchorage lies in a nook between Starfish and Odlum Islands on the Choked Passage side.

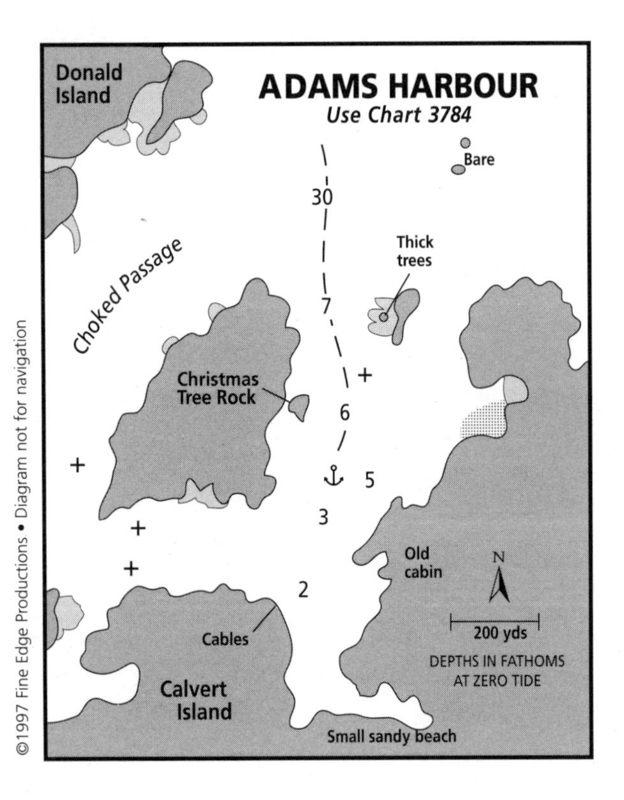

Adams Harbour

Chart 3784; anchor: 51°41.15′ N, 128°06.17′ W (NAD 27)

> *Adams Harbour, on the south side and near the west end of Hakai Passage, lies between the chain of islands consisting of Lower, Starfish and Odlum Islands and the peninsula that forms the NW part of Calvert Island. It is known locally as Welcome Harbour. Though confined, this harbour affords sheltered anchorage for small vessels from all but strong west winds, which send a swell into the harbour. Local knowledge is advised for entering the harbour.* (p. 153, SD)

Adams Harbour, southeast of Donald Island, offers good protection close to the fishing and recreation area of Choked Passage. Fishing resorts sometimes moor in the very southern end of the bay, and at times it may be plugged with fishing boats. When you anchor be careful to avoid old steel cables that may litter the bottom. The two private mooring buoys in the harbor should not be used by cruising boats.

Anchor in 3 to 5 fathoms over a sand bottom with fair-to-good holding.

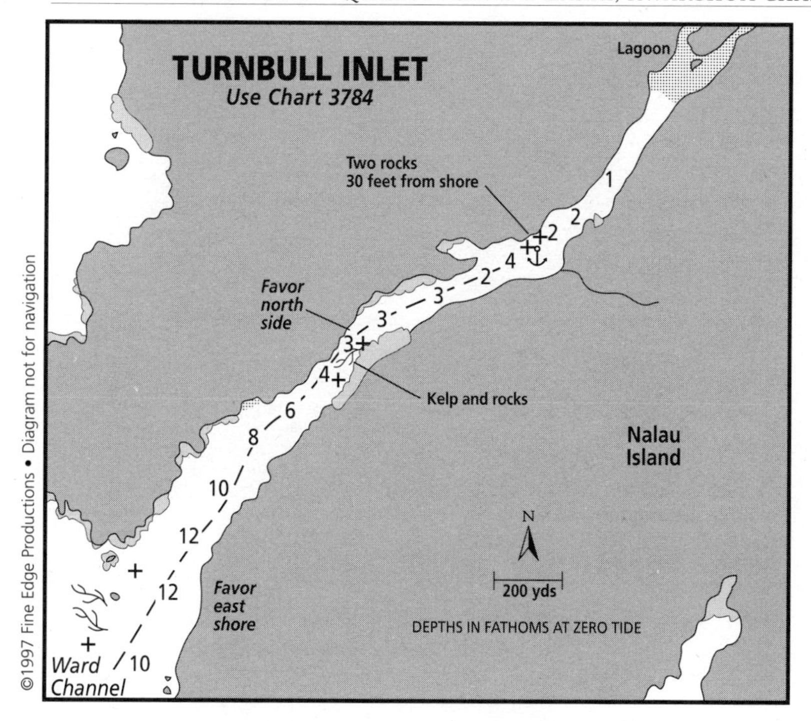

shore; larger boats in the middle of the inlet in 8 fathoms over an unrecorded bottom.

Turnbull Inlet

Chart 3784; entrance: 51°45.25′ N, 128°03.20′ W; anchor: 51°45.83′ N, 128°02.28′ W (NAD 27)

Turnbull Inlet, NE of the Planet Group, penetrates the SW side of Nalau Island. A reef extends 0.2 mile SSW from the north entrance point of the inlet. (p. 154, SD)

River-like and remote, Turnbull Inlet is lined with a variety of trees where songbirds make their summer home. The inlet and the lagoon at its head almost cut Nalau Island in two. This is a good temporary lunch stop or overnighter in fair weather. Some southwest puffs might enter but there is very little chop, as the lack of drift logs indicates.

Upon entering Turnbull Inlet, favor the east shore to avoid rocks and kelp off the north shore. At the narrows, favor the north shore to avoid kelp and rocks at the bend in the inlet. Flood currents run from 1 to 2 knots in the narrows. Anchor in the basin and explore the lagoon to the north by dinghy for an adventure that will bring to mind the African Queen.

Anchor in 2 fathoms over a bottom of mud and decaying vegetation; good holding.

"Northwest Hecate Island Cove"

Chart 3784; position: 51°42.18′ N, 128°03.22′ W (NAD 27)

Northwest Hecate Island Cove is located one mile northeast of Rattenbury Island at the north end of Kwakshua Channel. Anchorage deep in the cove is excellent, but avoid the fish camp located here during the summer.

Anchor in 4 to 5 fathoms over a sand and mud bottom with fair-to-good holding.

"Nalau Inlet"

Chart 3784; entrance: 51°44.58′ N, 128°02.74′ W (NAD 27)

An unnamed inlet, 0.8 mile south of Turnbull Inlet, has its entrance encumbered with drying and below-water rocks. (p. 154, SD)

Nalau Inlet is what we call the indentation on the southwest end of Nalau Island. During the summer two signs at the entrance point to Joe's Salmon Lodge. The inlet provides excellent anchorage in all weather. Use the narrow east entrance where 3-fathom depths are found in the fairway.

Small boats can anchor in 4 fathoms close to

Ward Channel

Chart 3784; south entrance:
51°45.38′ N, 128°03.47′ W; north entrance:
51°47.00′ N, 128°02.60′ W (NAD 27)

Ward Channel, between Underhill and Nalau Islands, is less than 300 feet (91 m) wide but has a good depth in the fairway. A rock awash, 0.4 mile south from the north entrance, is close to the east shore of the channel. (p. 154, SD)

Ward Channel is the easy way to get from Hakai Passage to Nalau Passage. The bight on the east

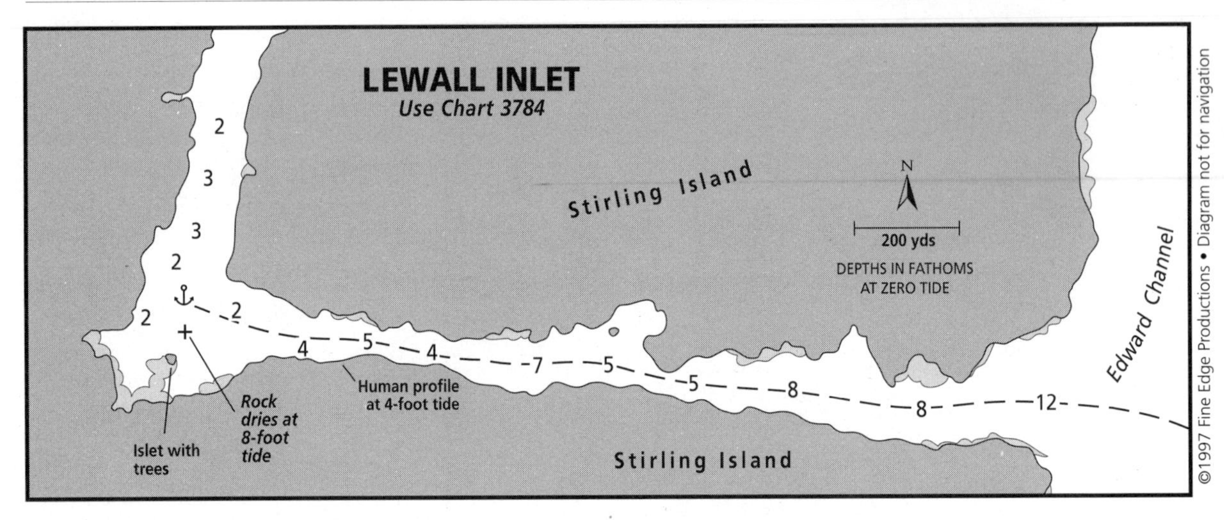

side of the channel should be well suited as an anchorage for small boats.

"Underhill Island Coves"

Chart 3784; entrance: 51°46.16′ N, 128°03.42′ W (NAD 27)

Underhill Island Coves is our name for the narrow protected coves along the east shore of Underhill Island. While we don't know how far into the basins you can go, the outer part of these coves is reported to offer good protection. If you do anchor in the area, using a shore tie is recommended to prevent your hitting the rocks and reefs.

Edward Channel

Chart 3784; south entrance:
51°45.00′ N, 128°04.77′ W; north entrance:
51°47.03′ N, 128°04.40′ W (NAD 27)

> *Edward Channel, between Stirling Island and Underhill Island, is restricted to less than 0.1 mile wide by islands abreast the entrance to Lewall Inlet and by islets and rocks in its south entrance. A recent survey found a depth of 10 feet (3 m) in mid-channel between the islets and rocks at the south entrance. Local knowledge is advised. Sheltered anchorage for small craft can be found in the small cove at the NE end of Edward Channel.* (p. 154, SD)

Edward Channel is entered a half-mile northwest of the Planet Group of islands, with the simplest entrance utilizing the channel with the 10-foot depth mentioned above.

The small cove at the northeast end of Edward Channel is well sheltered; however, we found the bottom is rocky with poor holding. Lewall Inlet, however, offers very good protection without this problem.

Lewall Inlet

Chart 3784; entrance: 51°45.98′ N, 128°04.74′ W; anchor: 51°46.11′ N, 128°06.19′ W (NAD 27)

> *Lewall Inlet, on the west side of Edward Channel, is shallow and less than 300 feet (91 m) wide at its narrowest part.* (p. 154, SD)

Lewall Inlet is extremely well sheltered from all chop, and because its waters are so calm you get wonderful reflections along the rocky shore. A human profile is evident in the rocks on the south shore as you approach the basin with tide level near 4 feet. Excellent anchorage can be found anywhere in the inner basin.

Anchor in 2 to 3 fathoms over a soft mud bottom with very good holding.

Nalau Passage

Chart 3784; west entrance:
51°47.10′ N, 128°07.30′ W; east entrance:
51°48.40′ N, 128°00.70′ W (NAD 27)

> *Nalau Passage connects Kildidt Sound to Fitz Hugh Sound and is joined to Hakai Passage by Edward and Ward Channels. It should not be attempted without the aid of local knowledge.*
>
> *Several drying reefs and below-water rocks lie*

in Kildidt Sound off the west entrance of Nalau Passage. The outer danger is a drying rock 0.8 mile west of the SW entrance point. Drying rocks are on the north side of the west entrance. (pp. 154–155, SD)

Nalau Passage offers no difficulty to cruising boats unless it is open-season for gill-netters. In this case, the boats and their nets nearly close off the passage north of Edward Channel.

Mustang Bay

Chart 3784; position: 51°49.54′ N, 128°02.50′ W (NAD 27)

Mustang Bay is at the east end and on the north side of Nalau Passage. A number of islands, drying reefs and rocks extend 1 mile south from the entrance of Mustang Bay. (p. 155, SD)

Mustang Bay is not suitable for anchorage in southerly winds.

Target Bay

Chart 3784; position: 51°49.47′ N, 128°01.87′ W (NAD 27)

Target Bay lies 0.3 mile east of Mustang Bay. Several shoals are within 0.5 mile south of the entrance to this bay. (p. 155, SD)

Target Bay, like Mustang, is open to southerly winds but should offer very good protection in northeasterlies. Anchorage from southeast gales can be found between Tomahawk Island and the islands to its south where holding is reported to be fair.

Kildidt Sound

Chart 3784; southwest entrance:
51°47.00′ N, 128°12.00′ W (NAD 27)

Kildidt Sound penetrates the SW side of Hunter Island, leading through Kildidt Narrows into Kildidt Inlet. The sound is too deep for anchorage and is exposed to SW winds, however, small craft can find shelter in Bremner Bay or in some of the numerous bays at the head of the sound. The land on both sides of the sound is relatively low; the mountains on Hunter Island line its east coast.

The approach to Kildidt Sound from Queen Charlotte Sound is between Stirling Island, on the north side of Hakai Passage, and Blenheim Island, about 4.5 miles NW. Alternative approaches are from Fitz Hugh Sound by way of Nalau Passage . . . or from Queens Sound by way of Spider Channel or Fulton Passage, thence through Brydon Channel into Kildidt Sound. Spitfire Channel is an alternative approach for small craft. These alternative approaches are intricate and local knowledge is advised. (p. 155, SD)

Kildidt Sound is the beginning of the fascinating Queens Sound archipelago. The primary cruising route for small to medium boats leads through Spitfire Channel on the north side of Hurricane Island. Large boats must pass outside to the west.

"Leckie Bay Cove"

Chart 3784; position: 51°48.50′ N, 128°06.50′ W (NAD 27)

Leckie Bay, at the SW end of Hunter Island, is too deep and exposed to have any value as an anchorage. The shores of the bay have several indentations and are fringed with rocks. (p. 156, SD)

Leckie Bay Cove is the small inlet at the north end of Leckie Bay. Open to south winds and any storm swells from the southwest, it is a marginal anchorage. In fair weather, you can use it as a good lunch stop or temporary anchorage. It's best to enter at low tide so you can see the rocks that lie in the eastern basin and along the channel to the south.

Anchorage can be taken in the west basin over a soft mud bottom on a 4-fathom shelf or in deeper water over a rocky bottom with fair holding.

"Rupert Island Passage"

Chart 3784; south entrance:
51°48.84′ N, 128°08.07′ W; north entrance:
51°49.95′ N, 128°07.00′ W (NAD 27)

Camel Island and Clare Island, with Rupert Island east of the latter, are separated from each other and from Hunter Island by narrow boat passages. The west sides of Camel and Clare Islands are steep-to. (p. 156, SD)

Rupert Island Passage is an interesting L-shaped

passage whose waters are well protected. The passage is an easy way to get to Watt Bay. A rocky patch, not well shown on the chart, lies midway through the north leg. Favor the east shore with about 2 fathoms minimum in the fairway.

Watt Bay

Chart 3784; southwest entrance:
51°50.32′ N, 128°08.23′ W (NAD 27)

Watt Bay is entered between Clare Island and Seafire Island, about 1 mile north; its entrance is encumbered by three islands and a rock awash. A deep, clear channel into the bay is between Clare Island and the two islands north of it. An islet, 80 feet (24 m) high, almost in the middle of the bay, has a shoal 0.1 mile ENE of it. Several islets and rocks are close off the south and east shores of Watt Bay. (p. 156, SD)

Watt Bay is well sheltered from southerly swells, with good anchorage available in what we call Domestic Tranquility Cove or in Bremner Bay on its north side.

"NFG" Cove

Chart 3784; entrance: 51°50.31′ N, 128°06.62′ W (NAD 27)

The lagoon in the far east end of Watt Bay appears to offer bombproof protection in all weather, but its entrance is so tricky and dangerous that few people will have the patience to enter it. The entrance is almost completely encumbered by reefs. There is a very narrow entrance slot along the north shore. However, until the lagoon is adequately charted, you may have to use reverse gear and back out as we did.

"Domestic Tranquility Cove"

Chart 3784; entrance: 51°50.29′ N, 128°06.71′ W, anchor: 51°50.41′ N, 128°06.70′ W (NAD 27)

The first time we went through Spitfire Channel we were on the return leg of a trip to Alaska. Don, busily shooting video from atop the pilothouse, told Réanne to head for the extremely narrow western entrance of Spitfire Channel. She thought Don had gone mad with his filming since his

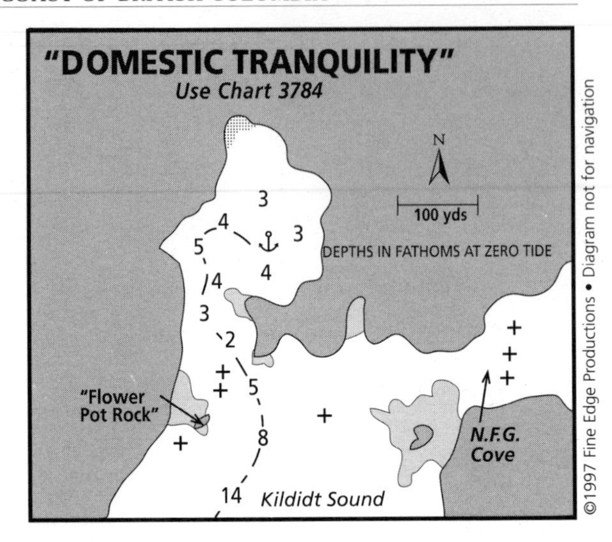

directions seemed to lead straight to a rock pile. She worked her way through with flying colors but had a few unkind words to say to the nonchalant captain. An hour later, well anchored in what we now call Domestic Tranquility Cove, after a bottle of Dubonnet, peace and quiet returned to *Baidarka*.

Domestic Tranquility Cove is the scenic indentation a half-mile north of Rupert Island Passage, at the east end of Watt Bay. You enter the cove by staying east of the bare, grassy rock we call Flower Pot Rock, favoring the east shore to avoid rocks off its north side. As you approach the basin, avoid rocks off the rocky spit on the east shore. The basin itself has a flat bottom of 3 to 4 fathoms and anchorage can be taken anywhere in the east side behind the rocky spit. Larger boats or those seeking more swinging room may stay in Bremner Bay a half-mile to the north.

Anchor in 3 fathoms over a sand and mud bottom with good holding.

Bremner Bay

Chart 3784; entrance: 51°50.87′ N, 128°07.14′ W, anchor: 51°50.85′ N, 128°06.75′ W (NAD 27)

Bremner Bay, in the NE part of Watt Bay, affords good sheltered anchorage for small vessels in 7 to 14 fathoms (13 to 26 m). The entrance is narrow and lies between a rock with less than 6 feet (2 m) over it close north of the south entrance point and

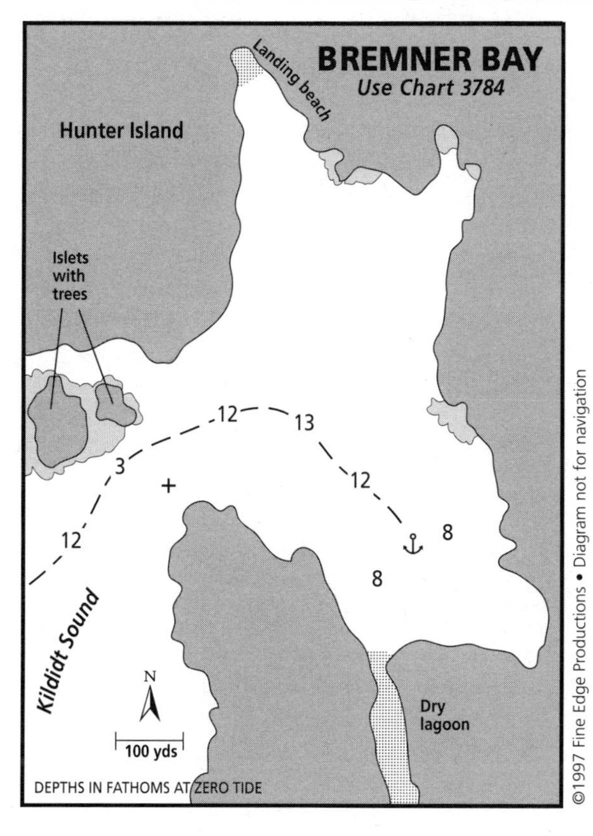

two islets on the north side. Local knowledge is advised. (p. 156, SD)

Bremner Bay offers good protection over a large swinging area. Favor the entrance islets to avoid the rock on the south side of the bay. The entrance fairway carries about 5 fathoms. For best protection, anchor in the south portion of the bay.

Anchor in 9 to 12 fathoms over a mud bottom with good holding.

Kildidt Inlet and Lagoon

Chart 3786; inlet south entrance: 51°52.32′ N, 128°06.78′ W (NAD 27)

Kildidt Inlet extends north from Kildidt Narrows and branches into two arms in the vicinity of Gnat Islets.

The east arm of Kildidt Inlet has a narrow, winding entrance channel that leads to a wide basin.

Kildidt Lagoon extending NW from Gnat Islets is the wider and deeper of the two arms of Kildidt Inlet. (pp. 156–157, SD)

Kildidt Inlet and Lagoon appear to be interesting cruising destinations; unfortunately, they are too deep for anchoring and are exposed to northwest and southeast winds. This is a wonderful place for bird watching and nature viewing; you may even spot a wolf or a black bear along shore.

Kildidt Narrows

Chart 3786

Kildidt Narrows has a least depth of 30 feet (9.1 m) in the fairway but is only suitable for small craft at HW slack. Tidal streams are strong and islets and below-water rocks are on both sides of the fairway. Local knowledge is advised. (p. 156, SD)

Currents as high as 8 to 10 knots on spring tides, and at other times, are reported in the narrows; overfalls form on both flood and ebb tides.

Stewart Inlet

Chart 3786; entrance: 51°52.50′ N, 128°07.68′ W (NAD 27)

Stewart Inlet, 1 mile NE of Goodlad Bay, has a minimum navigable width of 300 feet (91 m). Several islets and rocks are on both sides of the fairway. (p. 156, SD)

Goodlad Bay

Chart 3786; entrance: 51°52.30′ N, 128°09.20′ W; anchor: 51°52.65′ N, 128°09.62′ W (NAD 27)

Goodlad Bay is at the NW end of Kildidt Sound. An islet, about 0.3 mile inside the entrance and in the centre of the bay, has a rock awash close south of it. A rock islet is 0.2 mile ESE of the east entrance

Kildidt Narrows, south entrance

point of Goodlad Bay, and 0.1 mile offshore.

Anchorage for small craft can be obtained in 6 to 10 fathoms (11 to 18 m) in the SW part of Goodlad Bay; swinging room is limited. (p. 156, SD)

Goodlad Bay is reported to be a good place to wait for slack water in Kildidt Narrows, but swinging room is limited to one or two boats.

Anchor in the southwest corner in 6 to 10 fathoms over an unrecorded bottom.

Brydon Channel

Chart 3784; east entrance:
51°50.08′ N, 128°10.61′ W; west entrance:
51°49.83′ N, 128°10.60′ W (NAD 27)

Brydon Channel, between the Kittyhawk Group and Hurricane Island is a winding passage encumbered with islets, drying reefs and below-water rocks; it connects Kildidt Sound with Spider Anchorage . . . (p. 156, SD)

Brydon Channel is navigable by vessels of all sizes. But use caution if you enter; trying to avoid the 8- and 10-foot drying rocks in the channel makes this a particularly interesting experience at high tides. If you are nervous about using the channel, enter it only when the tide levels are below 8 feet—then it's a relative piece-of-cake.

Brydon Channel is the main protected (east) entrance into Spider Anchorage, and Fulton Passage is the west entrance. The area around Breadner Point on the west side of Spider Island has confused wave patterns, even on a calm day. Stay either well out to sea or transit through Spider Channel. This is dinghy and kayak country, and the routes for shallow-draft small craft are endless. It's also a favorite place of scuba divers.

Brydon Anchorage

Chart 3784; entrance: 51°50.25′ N, 128°12.15′ W;
anchor: 51°50.54′ N, 128°12.05′ W (NAD 27)

Brydon Anchorage is the local name for the nearly-enclosed bay north of Brydon Channel just before it turns south into Spider Anchorage. The anchorage is well protected and has a deep sticky mud bottom—be prepared to wash off your foredeck after hoisting anchor.

Anchor in 15 fathoms over a deep mud bottom with very good holding.

"Kittyhawk Cove"

Chart 3784; anchor: 51°49.80′ N, 128°11.20′ W
(NAD 27)

Kittyhawk Cove is the well-sheltered cove in the center of the Kittyhawk Group, one mile west of Mosquito Islets. It is best to enter Kittyhawk Cove from the northwest channel leading to and from Brydon Channel

Anchor in 8 to 10 fathoms over an unrecorded bottom.

Spider Anchorage

Chart 3784; Edna Island anchor:
51°49.52′ N, 128°14.38′ W (NAD 27)

Spider Anchorage has uneven depths ranging from 8 to 40 fathoms (15 to 73 m). A rock islet is 0.2 mile NNE of the north end of Anne Islands. Brydon Channel . . . leads east from Spider Anchorage into Kildidt Sound.

Anchorage can be obtained about 0.3 mile west of the south extremity of Hurricane Island in 34 fathoms (62 m). Small vessels can obtain anchorage about 0.1 mile NNE of the north extremity of Manley Island in 16 to 19 fathoms (29 t o 35 m) or between Edna Island and Anne Islands in about 15 fathoms (27 m). (p. 157, SD)

Of the three anchor sites mentioned above, the bay between Edna Islands and Anne Islands is reported to be the best. There is plenty of anchoring room for several boats here. On a nice day, you

World War II Names

Have you noticed the number of islands on the west side of Kildidt Sound with names of famous World War II aircraft? During the early years of the war when these islands were still unnamed, Canadian and U.S. pilots were based at Shearwater east of Bella Bella. As the pilots began flight patrols over the coast they gave names to each island to help identify coastal checkpoints—Airacobra, Spider, Spitfire, Mosquito, Lancaster, Kittyhawk, Typhoon, etc., all legendary airplanes used in the Battle of Britain.

can carry your dinghy across the tombolo between the Edna Islands and row out to weather-beaten Typhoon Island.

Anchor in about 15 fathoms over a sandy bottom with fair holding.

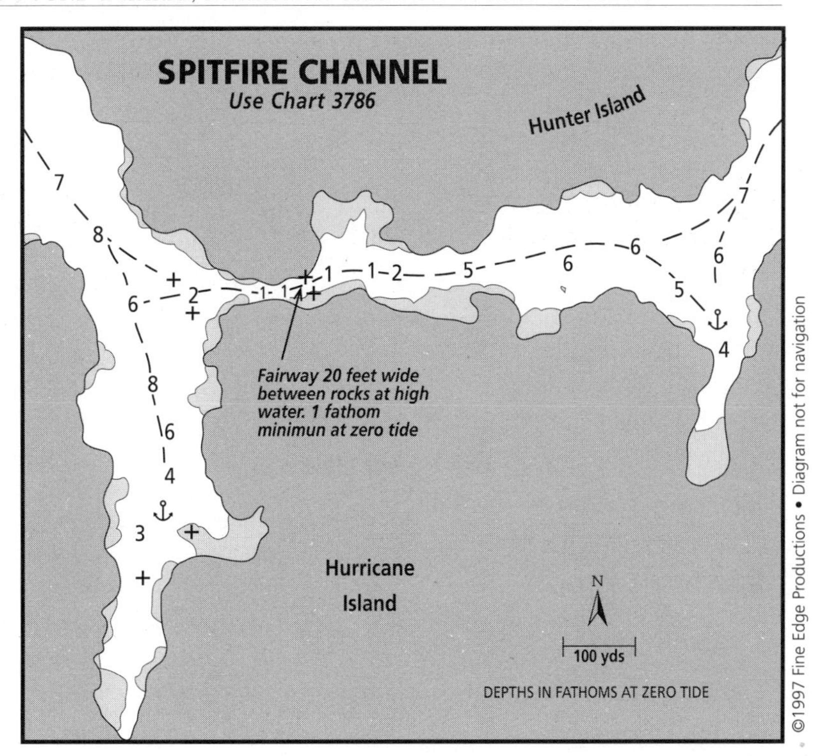

"Hurricane Anchorage"

Chart 3784; anchor:
51°50.21′ N, 128°12.62′ W
(NAD 27)

Very good shelter from all weather can be found in the cove created by the hook at the very southern tip of Hurricane Island, presumably named after the famous British fighter plane. While the easiest entrance lies north of the islets, it is reported that entry can also be made directly east of island (90).

Anchor in 10 to 12 fathoms over a mud bottom with good holding.

Spitfire Channel

Charts 3784, 3786; east entrance:
51°50.69′ N, 128°10.07′ W; west entrance:
51°51.64′ N, 128°13.78′ W (NAD 27)

> *Spitfire Channel, which separates Spitfire Island and Hurricane Island from Hunter Island, is a very narrow boat passage leading from Spider Channel into Kildidt Sound. It has a least depth of 9 feet (2.7 m) at its narrowest part. The east end is encumbered with islets, drying rocks and below-water rocks. Local knowledge is advised.* (p. 158, SD)

Spitfire Channel is the smooth-water route from central Kildidt Sound to Spider Channel and around Superstition Point into Cultus Sound. It is suitable only for small craft and should be attempted only at slack water so that you can proceed at dead-slow speed. We have heard that the biggest vessel to make the transit was a 50-footer whose skipper claimed he made it only because the underwater configuration of his hull happened to correspond exactly to the shape of the rocks on either side of the narrows!

The key to transiting is to identify visually the rock on the north shore at the east end of the narrow portion and stay close, halfway to the rock ledge on the south shore. The depth of 9 feet occurs only in the center of the V-shaped channel. At low water the narrowest part is perhaps 15 feet wide at the top of the V-channel and about 25-feet wide at highwater. Once you are safely past this rock, the rest is a straight shot and not particularly difficult.

"Spitfire East Cove"

Charts 3784, 3786; anchor:
51°51.59′ N, 128°11.47′ W (NAD 27)

Spitfire East Cove is the name we've given the tiny cove east of the narrows on the south shore. This is a good place to anchor and wait for the correct tide conditions in Spitfire Channel; it is a well-sheltered anchorage. Swinging room is restricted and a stern tie to shore is advisable if you plan to stay long. Current in this channel, usually moderate, does not present a problem.

Anchor in 3 fathoms over a mud and sand bottom with good holding.

"Spitfire West Cove"

Chart 3784; anchor: 51°51.44′ N, 128°12.21′ W (NAD 27)

Spitfire West Cove is the small cove on the south shore of Spitfire Channel's west side. This is a good place to reconnoiter the narrows or to wait for proper tidal conditions before proceeding.

Anchor in 4 to 6 fathoms over a gravel and rocky bottom with poor to fair holding.

"Spitfire Lagoon"

Chart 3786; entrance: 51°51.92′ N, 128°12.59′ W; anchor: 51°52.10′ N, 128°12.66′ W (NAD 27)

Spitfire Lagoon is a great place for exploring, viewing wildlife, rowing or paddling, or poking about on shore. Its entrance is narrow and a bit tricky, and current can flow swiftly here, especially on a spring ebb tide, but that's half the fun of it!

Favor the islet on your starboard side until you can identify the shoal on the west side, then split the difference as you proceed. At high-water slack entry is easy for most cruising boats of moderate size. Once you're inside the narrows, depths are a nearly-constant 3 fathoms, and you can anchor anywhere over a large area.

Anchor in 3 fathoms over a sandy bottom with fair holding.

Swordfish Bay

Chart 3786; entrance: 51°52.56′ N, 128°14.23′ W (NAD 27)

Swordfish Bay, 1 mile SE of Superstition Point, has a shoal spit extending 0.1 mile south from its north entrance point; a drying reef is at the south end of this shoal spit. The bay has three shallow arms but the outer part has depths up to 10 fathoms (18 m). (p. 158, SD)

Swordfish Bay is an interesting place to explore. However, since it is open to prevailing southwest swells, it is not to be trusted. During periods of southeast or southwest gales the seas are reported to break right into the entrance.

Superstition Point

Chart 3786; turning point (0.2 mile WNW of Superstition Point): 51°53.47′ N, 128°15.56′ W (NAD 27)

Superstition Point is the NW extremity of a group of islets which are connected to Hunter Island by a narrow drying ledge. Superstition Ledge, 0.2 mile SSW of Superstition Point, consists of a group of drying and below-water rocks. The sea breaks heavily at times on this ledge and there are strong tide-rips in the vicinity. (p. 158, SD)

"Superstition Point Cove"

Chart 3786; entrance: 51°53.67′ N, 128°14.79′ W (NAD 27)

The intricate cove and lagoon just north of Superstition Point is another place that appears to offer good exploring in fair weather. It has a remarkable beach, but it is open to the west and large swells, chop, or surge can easily enter the cove. Although we have had no experience here, it's on our "to-do" list. The low hills around this cove would make it of doubtful value in heavy weather.

Queens Sound

Chart 3786; south entrance: 51°50.00′ N, 128°22.00′ W; entrance (Golby Passage): 52°01.50′ N, 128°26.00′ W (NAD 27)

Queens Sound is entered from south between the Breadner Group and Gosling Rocks, 8 miles WNW. From the west it is entered from Golby Passage, which lies between Goose Group and McMullin Group. The east side and the head of the sound are encumbered by a maze of islands through which navigable channels lead to Hunter Channel and Raymond Passage. Fulton Passage, north of Breadner Group, leads to Spider Anchorage and then by way of Brydon Channel into Kildidt Sound. Spider Channel, 2 miles north of Fulton Passage, leads east through Spitfire Channel into Kildidt Sound. Islands on the east and west sides of Queens Sound are relatively low and featureless. Mount Merritt, at the north end of Kildidt Inlet, has an elevation of 2,960 feet (902 m) and is the highest land in the vicinity.

Tidal streams attain 2 to 3 kn about 2 miles NW of Purple Bluff. Strong tide-rips are encountered over and around Gosling Rocks and in the vicinity of Superstition Ledge. (p. 157, SD)

In calm weather, Queens Sound can be benign, and under such conditions many kayaks, inflatables, and small boats cross over to the Goose Group. However, the weather can change quickly, becoming a nightmare if a southerly kicks up. Trying to return to protected waters on the east side of the sound under poor conditions is dangerous because of the many off-lying rocks and reefs, which with a southwest swell and wind create an ugly lee shore; it can be particularly hazardous coming from Cultus Sound into Queens Sound.

Goose Group

Chart 3786; entrance (Goose Island Anchorage): 51°56.25′ N, 128°25.00′ W (NAD 27)

Goose Group consist of Goose, Swan, Duck, Gosling and Gull Islands, all connected by drying ledges, and Gosling Rocks, which lie south of the main group. Drying and below-water rocks fringe the west and north coasts of Goose Group.
(p. 157, SD)

The Goose Islands, the westernmost islands within the Hakai Recreation Area, receive the brunt of the storms that blow through Queens Sound. Windswept trees, polished silver snags, glistening beaches—some piled high with drift logs—show the effects of strong storm winds. The low-lying topography of the Goose Group is perfect for getting around by small boat and the area is particularly popular amongst kayakers.

Watch the weather carefully, and monitor the weather channels for any sign of change in stable conditions. There is no safe storm anchorage for small craft in the Goose Group. Kayakers or people travelling in inflatables can carry their craft up to high, dry turf and make the best of it. The north side of Snipe Island has a lovely sand beach where kayakers can camp. The north tip of Goose Island has a beautiful sandy beach, as well, but kayakers are asked to camp on the other side of the island because the Heiltsuk band runs a rediscovery camp here.

The only confirmed sea otter colony on the north coast has taken up residence around the Goose Group in recent years. Please do not disturb these wonderful, amusing mammals.

Goose Island Anchorage

Chart 3786; anchor: 51°55.87′ N, 128°25.92′ W (NAD 27)

Goose Island Anchorage is on the east side of Goose Group. Snipe Island lies between Gosling Island and Gull Island on the south side of the anchorage. Drying rocks and rocks with less than 6 feet (2 m) over them extend 0.3 mile east and NE from Gull Island.

Anchorage can be obtained about 0.3 mile north of Gull Island in about 12 fathoms (22 m).
(p. 157, SD)

A visit to Goose Island Anchorage can be a rather lonely, sobering experience when blue skies turn to grey or fog rolls in. The stunted trees and gentle but ominous surge are a constant reminder that you really are exposed to the forces of the Pacific Ocean. It's particularly unnerving when the tide rises and you watch the beach you've just walked on disappear under water. Although the captain of the *Baidarka* likes this type of seascape, it's not the first mate's favorite destination.

You can anchor deep in the southwest corner of Goose Island Anchorage over a flat shallow bottom during prevailing northwesterlies when seas are flat calm. However, this site is poor in any other weather and can be extremely bumpy.

Small boats can anchor about 0.2 mile northwest of Gull Island; larger ones north of Gull Island.

Anchor in 3 to 4 fathoms over sand and mud, with occasional kelp; fair-to-good holding in calm weather.

Island Roamer *in Cultus Sound*

Cultus Sound

Chart 3786; southwest entrance:
51°54.08′ N, 128°14.31′ W (NAD 27)

> *Cultus Sound leads NE, then north, through Sans Peur Passage into the south part of Hunter Channel.*
>
> *Anchorage can be obtained in an emergency about 0.2 mile north of Goolden Islands in 34 fathoms (62 m). Emergency anchorage can also be obtained 0.2 mile NE of the same islands in 9 to 20 fathoms (16 to 37 m). Swell is encountered in these anchorages.* (p. 158, SD)

The turn into Cultus Sound (when you're northbound) brings welcome calm water again and the choice of several fine anchor sites. One of the more popular, which we refer to as Kayak Cove, is just inside the sound on the south shore.

"Kayak Cove"

Chart 3786; anchor: 51°53.91′ N, 128°13.88′ W (NAD 27)

Kayak Cove is well known to kayakers as a great haul-out place and campsite, and it probably has been used as a kayak and canoe base camp for centuries. The beach is large, easy to land on, and well protected. Although some swell and surge can be felt here, especially in a strong Norwester, it is a safe place to anchor in any summer weather. The cove can accommodate several boats including a few big ones.

Anchor in 4 to 5 fathoms over a sand bottom with fair holding.

"McNaughton Group Anchorage"

Chart 3786; entrance: 51°54.60′ N, 128°13.45′ W (NAD 27)

> *McNaughton Group . . . lie[s] northward of Superstition Point.* (p. 158, SD)

McNaughton Group Anchorage is a maze of narrow passages, many of which are great anchorages for cruising boats. You can choose a depth and swinging room from the diagram to suit your purpose. All anchorages have good holding if your anchor is well set.

We rank the anchorages as follows—let us know what you think.

1. **Bombproof Anchorage:**
   Anchor in 5 fathoms,
   51°55.46' N, 128°14.29' W
2. **Great Salt Lake Anchorage:**
   Anchor in 7 fathoms,
   51°56.29' N, 128°13.77' W
3. **Back Door Anchorage:**
   Anchor in 10 fathoms,
   51°55.97' N, 128°12.98' W
4. **Intersection Anchorage:**
   Anchor in 14 fathoms,
   51°55.98' N, 128°13.60' W
5. **Deep Anchorage:**
   Anchor in 24 fathoms,
   51°55.50' N, 128°13.20' W

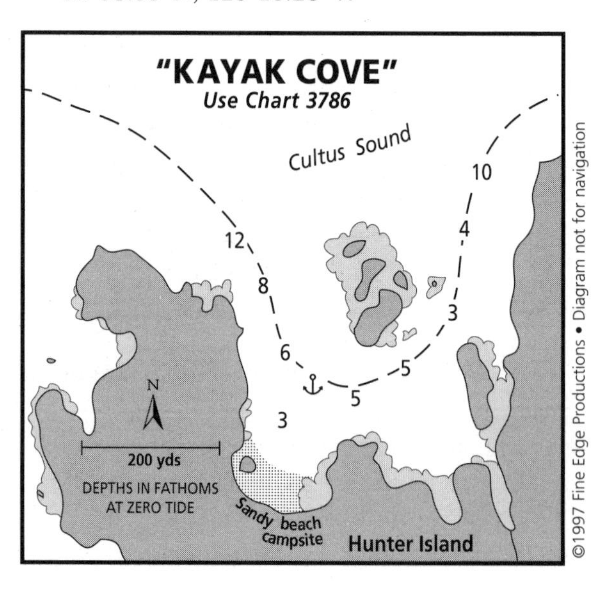

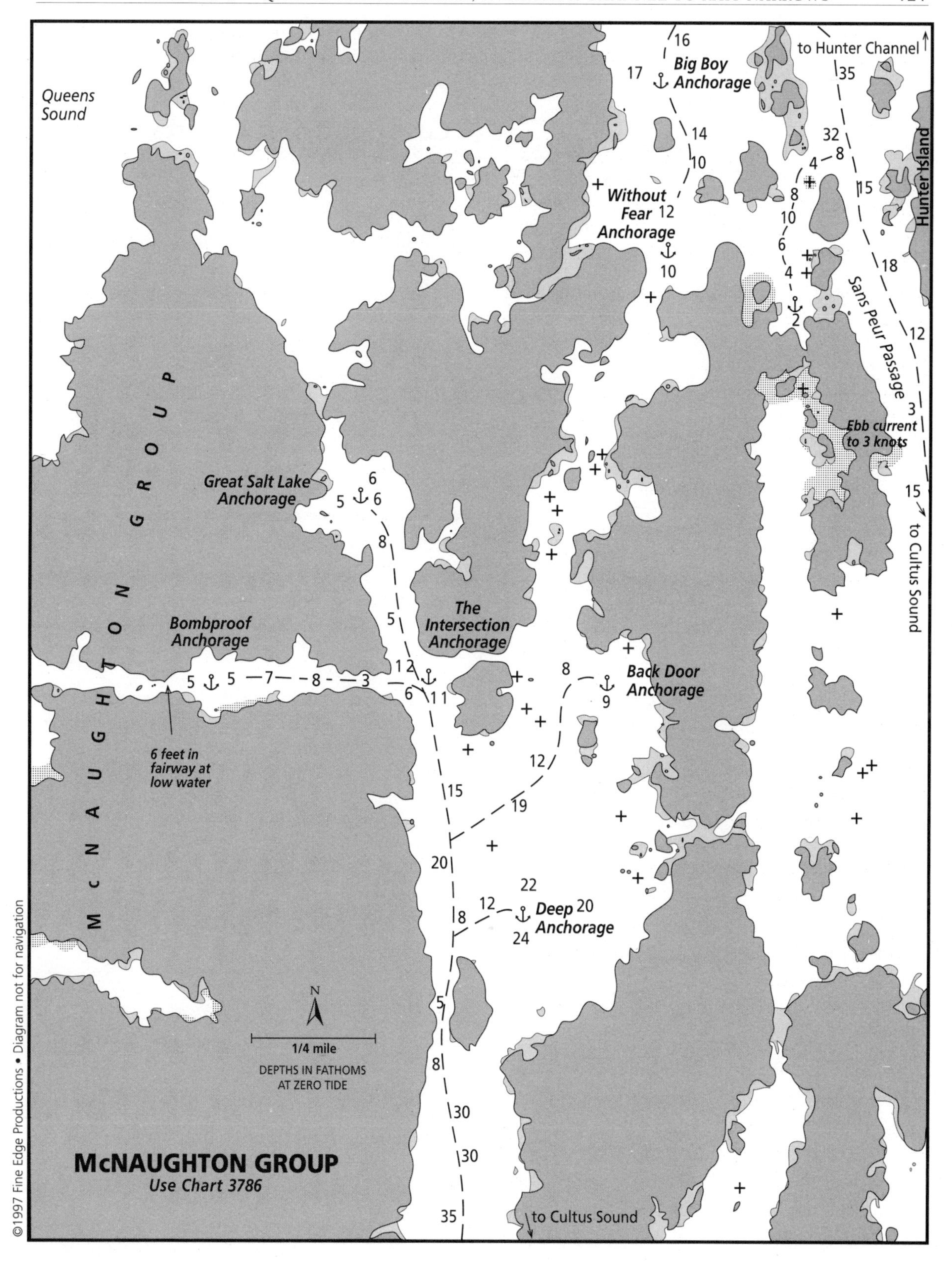
Queens Sound
to Hunter Channel
Big Boy Anchorage
Without Fear Anchorage
Hunter Island
Sans Peur Passage
Ebb current to 3 knots
to Cultus Sound
Great Salt Lake Anchorage
McNAUGHTON GROUP
Bombproof Anchorage
The Intersection Anchorage
Back Door Anchorage
6 feet in fairway at low water
Deep Anchorage
1/4 mile
DEPTHS IN FATHOMS AT ZERO TIDE
to Cultus Sound
McNAUGHTON GROUP
Use Chart 3786

"Cultus Bay"

Chart 3786; anchor: 51°54.44′ N, 128°11.56′ W (NAD 27)

Cultus Bay, frequently used by fishing boats, offers very good protection from southerly weather and is considered a safe place to stay during the summer. A large lagoon to the east with several islets and an entrance that dries at 10 feet looks like an interesting place to explore.

Anchor in 6 fathoms mud bottom with good holding.

Kinsman Inlet

Chart 3786; entrance: 51°55.88′ N, 128°11.33′ W (NAD 27)

> *Kinsman Inlet is entered 1 mile north of Lane Rock. Rocks are on both sides of the entrance and in mid-channel 0.4 mile within the entrance, and a depth of 6 feet (1.8 m) lies in the narrow section about 1 mile within the entrance. The south arm of the inlet has many dangers and a narrow shoal section where tidal streams reach 10 kn.* (p. 158, SD)

Kinsman Inlet is surrounded by low-lying land, and the water within the inlet is a typical muskeg brown. It is perhaps best explored by a high speed inflatable with due caution for its many rocks and shoals.

Sans Peur Passage

Chart 3786; south entrance: 51°56.14′ N, 128°11.95′ W; anchor: 51°56.75′ N, 128°12.46′ W (NAD 27)

> *Sans Peur Passage, 1.5 miles north of Lane Rock, is less than 0.1 mile wide at its narrowest part with shoals lying near mid-channel.* (p. 158, SD)

Sans Peur Passage has moderately strong current and turbulence, but it can generally be transited on any stage of the tide. (See McNaughton Group diagram.) There is a small cove immediately west of the passage which is out of the current and can be used by small craft tucked deep in the south end, as indicated in the diagram. The bottom is irregular with marginal holding, so set your anchor well or use a shore tie. Larger boats might want to check out the more roomy anchorages called Without Fear and Big Boy, in the basin to the west, as indicated on the McNaughton Group diagram.

"Cove Southeast of Latta Island"

Chart 3786; entrance: 51°58.60′ N, 128°11.75′ W (NAD 27)

The cove southeast of Latta Island has an irregular rocky bottom and we had difficulty finding enough mud or sand to label it an anchorage. It is out of the current and most of the weather, however.

Hunter Channel

Charts 3787, 3786; north entrance: 52°04.80′ N, 128°07.30′ W; south entrance: 51°59.80′ N, 128°11.00′ W (NAD 27)

> *Hunter Channel, between the NW side of Hunter Island and Campbell Island, connects Queens*

The Little People

We call them the Little People. They travel by day, close to the land. At night they haul their frail little boats up on the beach and light fires of driftwood and bark. For years we knew they were there. We stumbled on their campsites, on those magical circles of stones in the moss. On sandy beaches we found their mysterious markings still not erased by the tide, as though they had fled at our coming.

And then one morning they rounded the point in a steamy calm, emerging from the morning mist. Their boats were long and sleek, open to the sun and the rain, driven by oars in delicate frames.

Kayakers and rowers, the sailors of very small boats, travel in an intimate way, learning each indent and point, every outcropping, rock, and overhung tree. Those marks in the sand are the tracks of their keels. The beaten-down patches of moss were their beds for the night.

They're friendly folk, the Little People. They'll gladly let you look inside their small boats. They'll spend hours telling of their travels and adventures. If they seem elusive and shy, it's because they're not used to being seen. Two of them in a boat like a peashell told us they used to wave at everyone they saw. But the only people who ever waved back were lost and needed rescuing.

Now we don't pass them at sea without waving. We never meet them on shore without stopping to talk. And we've learned a bit of the lore, a bit of the wisdom of the Little People.

—by Iain Lawrence, author of *Far Away Places*

Sound to Lama Passage. . . . The fairway is deep throughout and there are no dangers more than 0.2 mile offshore. (p. 160, SD)

You can proceed north of Latta Island into Hunter Channel and directly to Bella Bella, turn west and continue along the east side of Prince Group Islands, heading northwest using Brown Narrows; or for an intimate, highly sheltered route, pass east of Dodwell Island and island (165) on its east shore and follow an intricate route west along the north shore of Dodwell Island.

Hunter Channel is the main channel connecting Queens Sound with Lama Passage and Bella Bella. Good protection can be found in Bob Bay and in the unnamed inlet on Campbell Island. At the south end of the channel there are moderate tide rips with collected flotsam as well as the first hint of the Pacific swell which pervades Queens Sound.

"Dodwell South Cove"

Chart 3786; position: 51°59.88′ N, 128°13.06′ W (NAD 27)

Anchorage for small craft, out of the main tidal stream, can be obtained in the cove on the south side of Dodwell Island, west of Stubbs Point. (p. 160, SD)

Scenic but indifferent anchorage can be taken in Dodwell South Cove although it does offer moderate protection from southerly weather. The first entrance west of Stubbs Point is choked with kelp and floating logs; the west entrance is the preferred approach. Since this entrance is narrow and fringed with rocks and kelp on its south side, stay close to the southwest point of Dodwell Island and its south shore all the way in. The center of the cove is deep, with a depth of about 14 fathoms. Small boats using shore ties can find temporary anchorage in either the north-northwest nook or in the tiny notch in the island on the south side. Avoid all kelp patches which mark submerged rocks.

Anchor between 3 and 14 fathoms over a mixed bottom of sand, mud and rocks. A stern tie near shore may be preferred.

"Dodwell North Cove"

Chart 3786; position: 52°00.40′ N, 128°13.35′ W (NAD 27)

The channel north and east of Dodwell Island has several islands and below-water rocks in it. (p. 160, SD)

There appears to be a well-protected cove in the northwest corner of Dodwell Island that could provide shelter from any southerly weather; however, it's open to the prevailing northwest winds. We have not used this cove and have no local knowledge to share. We have used the cove formed in the center of the maze of islets 0.6 mile to the northwest and found it well protected.

"Maze Cove"

Chart 3786; anchor: 52°00.97′ N, 128°12.73′ W (NAD 27)

The maze of islets north and east of Dodwell Island form an intricate, smooth-water route from Hunter Channel to Queens Sound to the north. Depths are sometimes less than those indicated on the chart, but a safe passage can be made with alert bow lookouts and by approaching at slow speeds. We have anchored in what we call Maze Cove in the shallow, flat-bottom area to the northwest of the island on the south side of Campbell Island.

You can enter on either side of the treed islet but stay south of the rock which dries on about a 16-foot tide. When passing the northern tip of Dodwell Island, favor the south side of the channel to avoid the large underwater rock on the north side.

Anchor in 4 to 6 fathoms over a mud bottom with good holding.

"Campbell Island Inlet"

Chart 3787; entrance: 52°02.93′ N, 128°10.92′ W; anchor (Wendy Cove): 52°05.36′ N, 128°12.59′ W (NAD 27)

The west side of Hunter Channel has a major inlet that leads 3-miles deep into Campbell Island, terminating in a lagoon. This inlet nearly divides the island in two. We refer to this anchorage as Campbell Island Inlet.

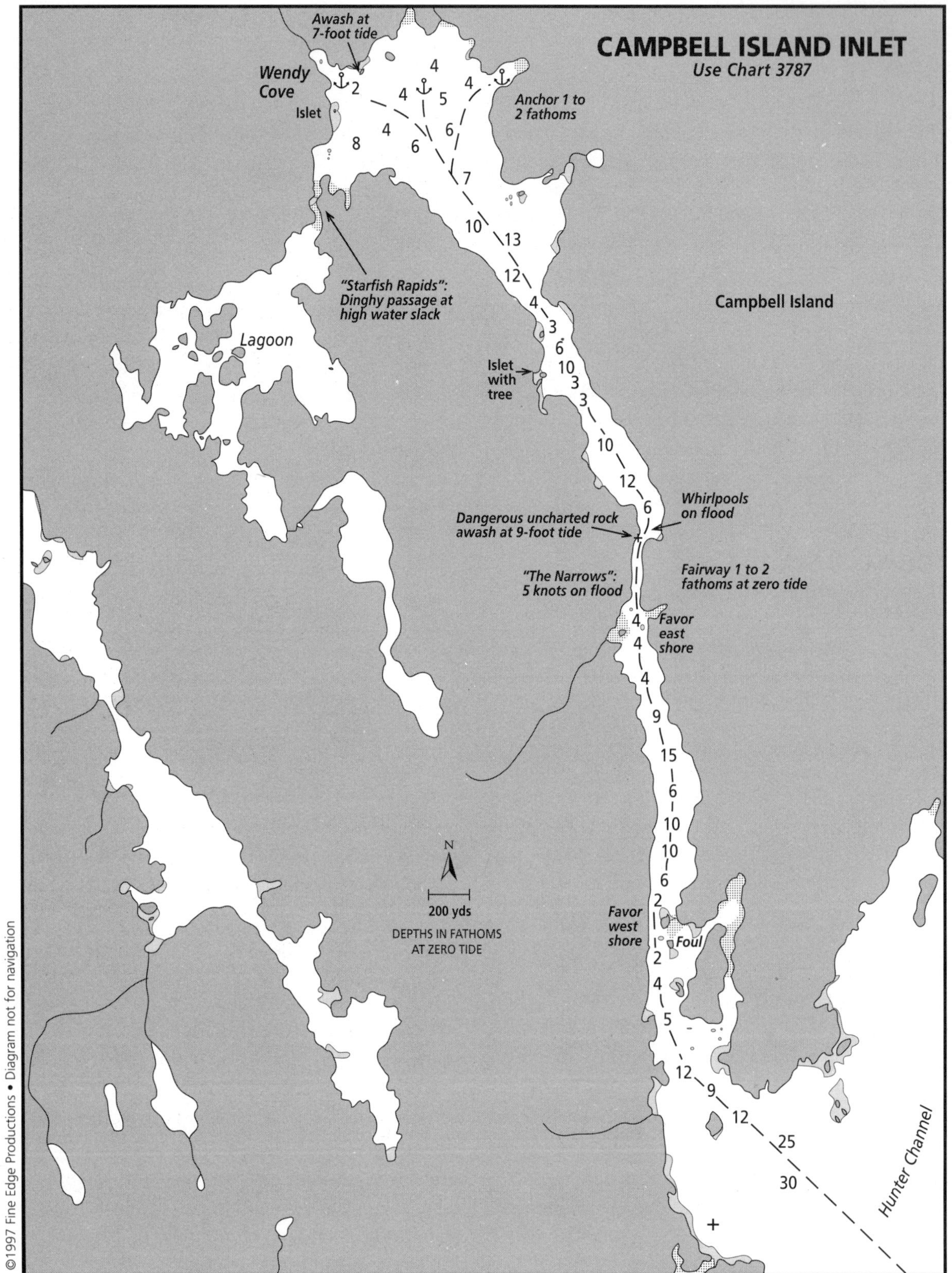
CAMPBELL ISLAND INLET
Use Chart 3787
Awash at 7-foot tide
Wendy Cove
Islet
Anchor 1 to 2 fathoms
"Starfish Rapids": Dinghy passage at high water slack
Lagoon
Campbell Island
Islet with tree
Whirlpools on flood
Dangerous uncharted rock awash at 9-foot tide
"The Narrows": 5 knots on flood
Fairway 1 to 2 fathoms at zero tide
Favor east shore
N
200 yds
DEPTHS IN FATHOMS AT ZERO TIDE
Favor west shore
Foul
Hunter Channel

Seldom, if ever, visited the inlet provides excellent protection from all weather deep in its labyrinth and is a rare find for cruising boats that want solitude and wilderness. We found no sign of man here—no stumps, middens, cables, or pollution of any kind. There are signs of deer but no bear, and ravens and eagles abound. You can hike over the rocky shore about 200 yards to the large lagoon and view a starfish "rookery" that feeds upon millions of small mussels attached to the rocks along the tidal waterfall. The lagoon receives saltwater on spring tides only.

Photo by Herb Nickles

Campbell Island Inlet

Because the south end of Campbell Island is so low and flat, it is easy to miss the entrance to the inlet. You can enter from either side of the island located in the entrance, avoiding the reefs along the Hunter Channel side. The inlet narrows rapidly, and you should favor the west shore until you've passed the chain of treed islets which, while scenic, have foul water behind them. The bottom is irregular but deep until you reach the narrows, recognizable by the small islet on its west shore, with a big tree and rocks alongside. The narrows have strong currents, and if you don't want to enter, you can anchor south of the islet in 4 fathoms.

The narrows is a picturesque channel with minimum depths of 3 to 6 feet at zero tide. A rock, about 10 feet in length, awash on a 9-foot tide, lies crosswise to the channel on the west side at the north end of the narrows. This rock—dangerous because it extends about a third of the way into the narrow channel—is dark-colored and hard to see. During flood currents, the current glancing off the rock could easily set a boat toward the east shore.

Safe passage through the narrows is possible at or near high-water slack when there is less current and you can go dead-slow. We have traversed the narrows during the middle of a 10-foot tidal range and found 4 knots of flood in the narrows, with a stronger current adjacent to the north-end rock.

North of the narrows, the bottom continues to be irregular, but it is fairly deep until you reach the large basin at the head of the inlet. This basin offers fine anchorage over a large area in 5 to 10 fathoms and is big enough to take the flotilla of the Vancouver Yacht Club. (Avoid the charted reefs along shore.)

Small boats may want to use either the northwest cove we call Wendy Cove (after our intrepid bow watch), or the east cove. Sunflower stars inhabit the shallows of the east cove; be sure to take a look, they're impressive.

Boats using Wendy Cove should anchor on a line between the tall-treed islet and the east point to avoid a steep-to shelf; at low water, this shelf is a living aquarium, and a great place to study the interaction of Dungeness crabs, fingerlings, flounders, sea anemones, and eel grass.

Anchor (Wendy Cove) in 4 to 5 fathoms over a brownish-black, primordial, stinky mud that's thick with clamshells and debris; holding is very good.

Hunter Channel Complex

Chart 3787; anchor: 52°03.06′ N, 128°07.93′ W (NAD 27)

At the north end of Hunter Channel, due east of the entrance to Campbell Inlet, lies a complex of islands that creates sheltered waters. Southwest

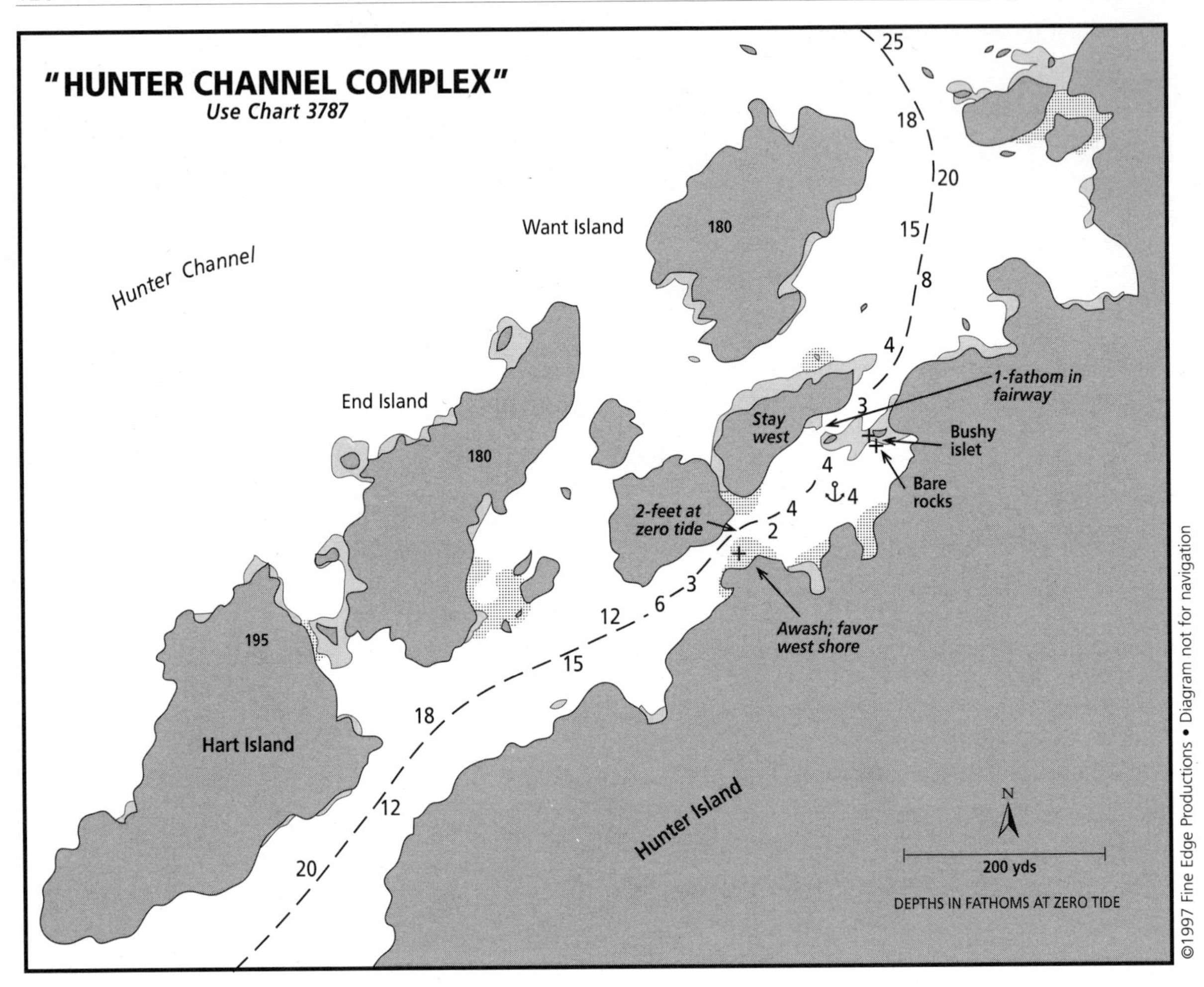

winds in Hunter Channel sometimes blow through this complex, but no chop enters. The innermost basin, formed by Hunter Island and two small unnamed islands, can provide good anchorage for two or three boats in a 4-fathom hole. This is a good area for sportfishing or exploring by dinghy or kayak.

The south entrance can be entered keeping Hart Island to port and favoring the Hunter Island shore until you reach the southernmost unnamed island east of End Island. Hug the east shore of this unnamed island to avoid a midchannel-rock awash. The fairway is about 2 feet deep at zero tide—not the 2 fathoms shown on the chart!

For the north entrance, pass Want Island to starboard and close the Hunter Island shore. (The basin east of Want Island has an irregular bottom.) Approach the northernmost unnamed island, avoiding rocks that bare on a 2-foot tide off its north end. Enter the narrow channel, favoring the northernmost unnamed island on your starboard. The fairway has a minimum of about one fathom west of the bushy islet and the rocks on its west side.

Anchor in 4 fathoms over a sand and mud bottom with some rocks with fair-to-good holding.

Bob Bay

Chart 3787; entrance: 52°03.90′ N, 128°06.90′ W; anchor: 52°02.24′ N, 128°06.39′ W (NAD 27)

Bob Bay, entered SE of Mouse Island, has Spire Point on the east side of its entrance.

Anchorage about 0.2 mile from the head of Bob Bay is well sheltered though swinging room is

limited; depths are about 18 fathoms (33 m).
(p. 160, SD)

Bob Bay is a long narrow bay offering good protection from southerly weather; the prevailing winds die out before reaching the head of the bay. Spindly cedars, thick with moss, overhang the rocky shore—scenery typical of the flat land and thick forests found in Queens Sound to the west.

Small boats can find temporary shelter on the north side of the island north of Spire Point in 2 fathoms with limited swinging room. Larger boats and those wanting more protection will proceed to the head of the bay and anchor on or near the shoal off the east shore. Avoid the cluster of rocks near the small peninsula.

Anchor in 2 fathoms (south end of Bob Bay) over a gravel and small rock bottom with iridescent seaweed and poor-to-good holding depending on set.

Admiral Group

Chart 3786; position (east turn at Admiral Group): 52°01.30′ N, 128°15.20′ W (NAD 27)

Proceeding northwest from Dodwell Island you can proceed more or less directly toward the upper end of Athabaskan Island headed for Brown Narrows, or turn northeast and work your way toward Redford Point, or you can follow the smooth-water route which turns north a half-mile northwest of Dodwell Island and proceed along the west Campbell Island shore.

"Wide Awake Cove"

Chart 3787, 3786; entrance:
52°03.00′ N, 128°14.16′ W; anchor:
52°02.76′ N, 128°14.38′ W (NAD 27)

Wide Awake Cove is located on the Campbell Island shore, 1.2 miles southeast of Piddington Island and 2.2 miles east of the north end of Athabaskan Island.

We have found good shelter here from gale-force winds blowing down the coast on a clear day, when thermal heating over the mainland was sucking cooler marine air eastward. The cove should be equally as good in southeast or southwest gales.

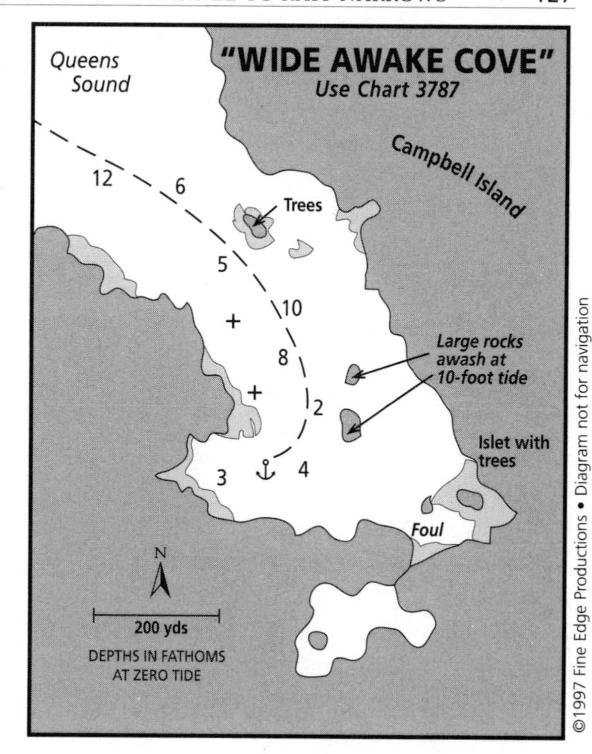

As indicated on the chart, the entrance to the cove is intricate and dangerous unless the rocks are carefully identified and avoided. Upon entering, first favor the islet with trees located on the east side of the entrance and continue southeast until you sight the large, light-colored, underwater rock that dries at about 9 feet. Turn west into the cove, avoiding the rocky ledge that extends east about 100 feet from the trees, and tuck in behind the point. You may want to use a stern tie to assure a bombproof anchorage in this landlocked cove. Avoid the tiny lagoon at the south end of the cove—it is foul.

Loons, eagles, and seals will entertain you as the gusts of wind blow by outside.

Anchor in 5 fathoms over a sand bottom with small rocks with good holding.

"Pictograph Passage"

Chart 3787

The channel east of Piddington Island is encumbered with islands and rocks at its south end.
(p. 159, SD)

You can continue north from Wide Awake Cove, working your way carefully through the islets and reefs along Campbell Island shore. At the north end of these islands and reefs you can see some rock paintings of faces and hands executed in red ochre—hence the name Pictograph Passage. These paintings are located above waterline approximately 1 mile south of Redford Point on Campbell Island.

"End of the World Inlet"

Chart 3787; entrance: 52°05.00′ N, 128°14.25′ W (NAD 27)

From Redford Point, a narrow, 2.5-mile long inlet proceeds southeast deep into Campbell Island. We call this End of the World Inlet due to its remoteness and windswept appearance. Except for four narrows with shallow bars, the inlet is deep. At the first narrows avoid the "unicorn" tree, a silver snag projecting from the east shore at a 45° angle. Cedar trees extend over the water, adding an eerie quality as you penetrate this world of stillness and mystery.

Peter Bay

Chart 3787; northeast entrance: 52°05.75′ N, 128°16.50′ W; anchor: 52°04.50′ N, 128°16.95′ W (NAD 27)

> *Peter Bay, on the north side of Piddington Island, has Gow Island and two unnamed islands in its entrance. The passage NE of Gow Island is only about 300 feet (91 m) wide but provides the easiest access; a rock awash lies in this passage, close off the NE shore.*
>
> *Anchorage for small vessels can be obtained in the south part of Peter Bay in 15 fathoms (27 m). When entering Peter Bay, round the north end of Gow Island and keep close to the NE shore of that island until clear of the rock awash.* (p. 159, SD)

Peter Bay is reported to offer good protection from southeast winds deep in the south end of the bay. Its northwest entrance is easy to use if you favor the west shore, avoiding a string of rocks and reefs that extend south from island (210).

Anchor in about 12 fathoms over a mud bottom with very good holding.

Hochstader Basin

Chart 3787; entrance: 52°06.35′ N, 128°16.90′ W (NAD 27)

> *Hochstader Basin is entered 0.5 mile NE of Gow Island through a channel encumbered with numerous islands, drying and below-water rocks. Local knowledge is advised.* (p. 160, SD)

Hochstader Basin penetrates deep into Campbell Island. It is too deep for convenient anchoring except along its margins, and its entrance is confusing and very shallow. This basin needs a good large-scale chart. For secure anchorage use Hochstader Cove.

"Hochstader Cove"

Chart 3787; entrance: 52°06.96′ N, 128°15.80′ W; anchor: 52°06.79′ N, 128°15.68′ W (NAD 27)

Hochstader Cove, the small, landlocked cove on the east shore of the channel that leads into Hochstader Basin, provides very good shelter from all weather. (The cove is 0.9 mile northeast of the entrance to Hochstader Channel, which is 0.2 mile northeast of Gow Island.)

The route into the outermost entrance follows the east shore of island (200) in a fairway of 9 fathoms minimum. Continue north, favoring the west shore to avoid a rock pile in the center of the channel. To the west of the rock pile, the fairway carries

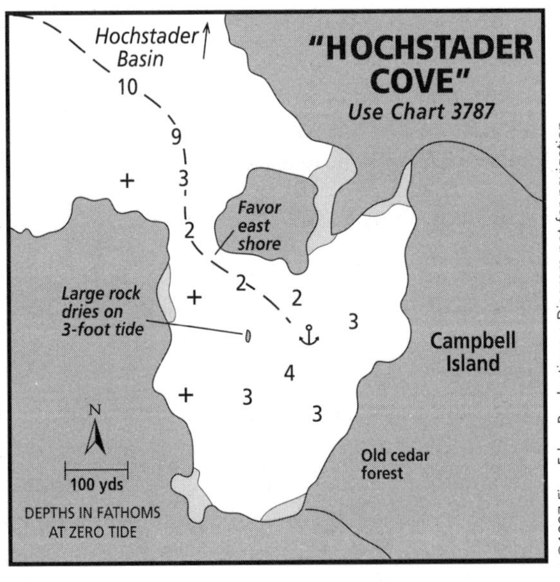

a minimum of 6 fathoms. Before entering the basin narrows, turn east. The entrance to the cove lies 0.4 mile northeast of the rock pile and is 50 to 60 feet wide, with a minimum depth of 2 fathoms in its fairway. Turn south into the cove and anchor over a 2- to 3-fathom bottom, avoiding a large flat rock in the western part of the cove which dries on a 3-foot tide—the rock is covered with purple and ochre sea stars. Three or four boats can anchor here; however, there isn't any good landing beach.

Anchor in 2 to 3 fathoms over brown mud and clamshells with very good holding.

Raymond Passage
Chart 3787

Raymond Passage connects Queens Sound to Seaforth Channel. The south approach is by way of Codfish Passage or Safe Passage. (p. 160, SD)

Raymond Passage (via Codfish Passage) is the easiest and quickest way to get to the Bella Bella area from the north end of Queens Sound. If you're looking for shelter from northwest winds, consider the two coves just north of Kingsley Point; in south winds, the cove east of the north end of Matilda Island.

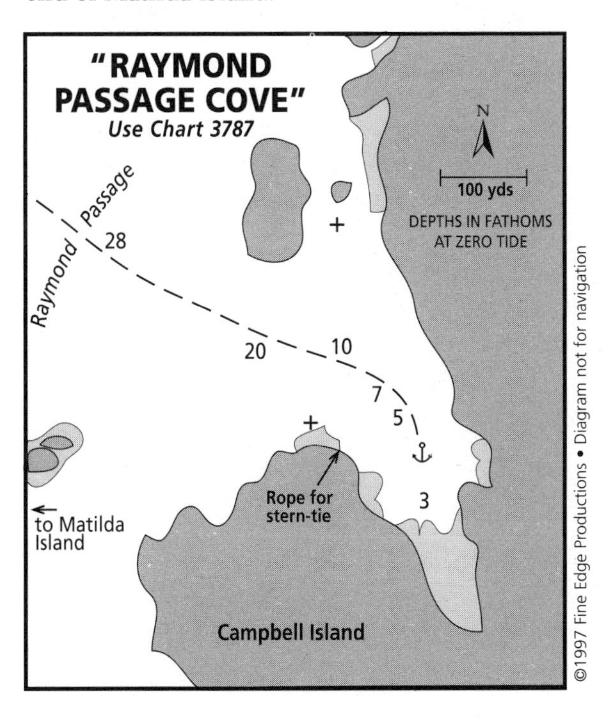

"Raymond Passage Cove"
Chart 3787; anchor: 52°07.11' N, 128°17.06' W (NAD 27)

Raymond Passage Cove, located 0.3 mile east of the north end of Matilda Island, provides very good protection in southeast weather—no drift logs on its shore indicate its safety. The cove is small with limited swinging room but ropes hanging on the west shore can sometimes be used for a stern tie. If strong westerlies pose a problem, consider Kingsley Point Coves on the west side of Raymond Passage.

Anchor in about 4 fathoms over a sand and shell bottom with fair-to-good holding.

Kingsley Point Coves
Chart 3787; entrance: 52°07.60' N, 128°18.35' W; anchor (south cove): 52°07.64' N, 128°18.68' W; anchor (north cove): 52°07.78' N, 128°18.57' W (NAD 27)

The first small cove north of Kingsley Point (south cove) is essentially landlocked, affording very good protection in most weather. Entering it can be difficult and dangerous, however, due to several drying rocks. Only small boats should attempt it and then, preferably near low water, when the entrance reefs can be clearly identified. Larger boats can easily find protection from northwest winds in Cundall Bay, 1.9 miles north, where the water is deeper (3 to 4 fathoms).We have no information about the holding power in Cundall Bay, but it has swinging room for two or three boats. (In the south cove, avoid the rock close to the west shore that dries near 12 feet, a zero-tide reef in the southeast corner of the bay, and a reef south of the entrance reef.)

The fairway leads through a narrow channel, 35 feet wide, between the large light-colored reef that dries on about a 4- or 5-foot tide, and the rock that projects from the southwest corner of the island at the north side of the entrance. Minimum depth in the fairway is about 10 feet at zero tide.

Anchor (south cove) in 3 fathoms over a bottom of brown mud and shells with small rocks; good holding.

The second cove north of Kingsley Point (north cove) is much easier to enter and affords good protection for small boats when northwest winds are howling. Avoid a rocky complex along the north shore by favoring the south shore until you're well inside the cove. This cove is easy to enter and exit and affords good protection from northwest winds. We have used both of these small coves when gales were blowing outside in Milbanke Sound and found them quite comfortable

Anchor (north cove) in 3 fathoms over a sand and shell bottom with fair-to-good holding.

Norman Morrison Bay

Chart 3787; entrance: 52°12.10′ N, 128°11.60′ W; anchor: 52°11.47′ N, 128°10.54′ W (NAD 27)

> *Anchorage, sheltered from SE winds, can be obtained in 25 to 28 fathoms (46 to 51 m) about 0.3 mile off the south shore of the outer part of Norman Morrison Bay; in this anchorage Kintail Point in line with the west extremity of Christiansen Point bears 008°. Small vessels can find anchorage closer to the head of Norman Morrison Bay.* (p. 160, SD)

Norman Morrison Bay is located at the north entrance of Raymond Passage just south of Seaforth Channel. The southernmost arm of the bay is reported to offer good anchorage, especially in southeast storms, but small boats may be more comfortable at the head of Kynumpt Harbour, one mile to the north.

Anchor in 12 to 15 fathoms over a mud, gravel and shell bottom with good holding.

Joassa Channel

Chart 3787; south entrance:
52°07.20′ N, 128°18.70′ W (NAD 27)

> *Joassa Channel is entered from Raymond Channel between Clarie Island and Kingsley Point. Horsfall Island forms the east shore. It is only suitable for small craft. Local knowledge is advised.* (p. 160, SD)

Joassa Channel is a scenic, smooth-water route that leads from upper Queens Sound to Seaforth Channel. Rait Narrows, lying at the upper end of Joassa, while not particularly difficult, should not be attempted by larger boats with limited maneuvering or by skippers who lack experience transiting narrows or fast-moving waters.

Boddy Narrows

Chart 3787; south entrance:
52°07.20′ N, 128°18.75′ W (NAD 27)

> *Boddy Narrows, at the south end of Joassa Channel, has Isabel Point on its east side. The fairway as far north as Reba Point is deep and free of dangers. Between Reba Point and Quinoot Point, 0.8 mile north, a group of drying rocks lie on the east side of the fairway.* (p. 160, SD)

Boddy Narrows is the south entrance to Joassa Channel, and the rocks at the turning point, 0.5 mile north of Reba Point are a frequent haul-out place for seals. Southeast winds funneling through Boddy Narrows have sometimes been recorded at over 100 knots, while just a few miles away, reported velocity was 60 knots. Protection can be found in the cove just west of Reba Point.

"Potts Island Hideaway"

Chart 3787; entrance: 52°08.50′ N, 128°19.90′ W; anchor: 52°08.65′ N, 128°20.43′ W (NAD 27)

Potts Island Hideaway, a cove in Louise Channel North to the west of Boddy Narrows, makes a good lunch stop, or an overnight stay in fair weather—it is partially exposed to the south. As you leave Boddy Narrows, you must work your way carefully though a rocky patch in order to enter this cove. Despite its trickiness, the cove is centrally located. It has a small beach and campsite, and can be quite comfortable in prevailing northwesterlies.

Louise Channel narrows is blocked to all but skiffs at high water.

Anchor in 2 fathoms over a bottom of sand and mud with good holding.

Reba Point Cove

Chart 3787; entrance: 52°09.25′ N, 128°20.30′ W; anchor: 52°09.04′ N, 128°20.35′ W (NAD 27)

Reba Point Cove, immediately west of Reba

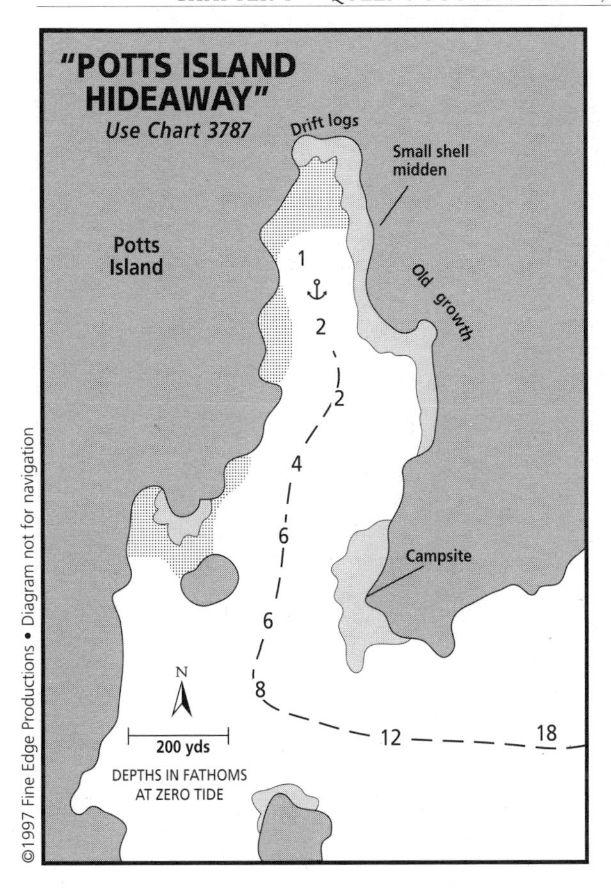

Point, is an indentation in Potts Island's east shore reported to offer protection from southeast winds. Seals haul out on the various reefs and rocks in the vicinity of Reba Point.

A quarter-mile north of Quinoot Point, there is a large, rusty, steel buoy which could be used for emergency moorage.

Anchor in 12 fathoms over a good bottom.

"Rait Narrows, South Cove"

Chart 3787; entrance: 52°12.38′ N, 128°17.33′ W; anchor (central cove):52°12.02′ N, 128° 16.85′ W; anchor (small nook): 52°12.00′ N, 128°16.80′ W (NAD 27)

Immediately southeast of Rait Narrows there is a deep cove that offers very good protection in all weather. Avoid several rocks on the south shore awash on a 14- to 15-foot tide.

Small boats can tuck into a nook on the north side of this cove and anchor with a stern tie to

Rait Narrows

shore in a calm, quiet setting. The entrance into the nook carries a depth of about 3 feet at zero tide with a little over 6 feet in its center. Eel grass growing in the channel makes entering appear more difficult than it really is.

Anchor (central cove) over a relatively flat bottom in 5 to 7 fathoms, mixed bottom with fair holding.

Anchor (small nook) in 1 fathom over sand, mud, and eel grass with fair holding.

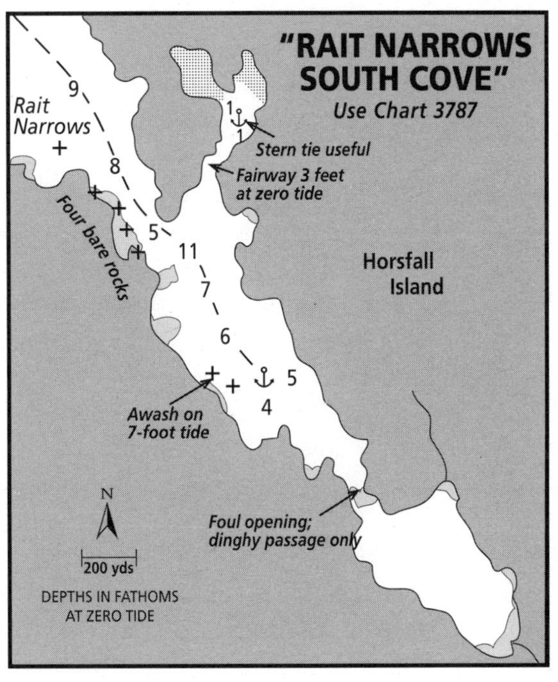

Photo courtesy CHS, Pacific Region

Rait Narrows, north entrance with rock showing

Rait Narrows

Chart 3787; south entrance:
52°12.45′ N, 128°17.30′ W; north entrance:
52°13.10′ N, 128°16.35′ W (NAD 27)

> *Rait Narrows, at the north end of Joassa Channel, is only 150 feet (46 m) wide and has a least depth of 18 feet (5.5 m).* (p. 160, SD)

Rait Narrows is a picturesque passage which can serve as either the finale or the overture for a cruise through beautiful Queens Sound. Moderate currents through Rait Narrows appear to flow in a direction determined as much by outside wind as by the tide. (We've seen the current reverse one or two hours after high or low water.)

Before you enter the narrows, determine the direction and strength of the current in order to gauge its impact on your maneuverability. You may want to sound a horn or announce your presence on Channel 16 before entering Rait Narrows since there is little passing room. Avoid the submerged rocks on the southwest side of the channel south of the south entrance.

The fairway in Rait Narrows has a minimum depth of about 3 fathoms just south of the small dog-leg near the north end of the narrows where a bushy islet and large rock extend to near mid-channel from the west shore. This rock dries at about 14 feet so it is easy to identify. Overhanging trees line much of the narrows, and there is seldom any chop through here.

Lockhart Bay

Lockhart Bay, at the north end of Rait Narrows, offers good shelter for boats waiting to enter the narrows. It is described in Chapter 3.

Thompson Bay

Chart 3787; south entrance:
52°06.20′ N, 128°24.60′ W (NAD 27)

The name Thompson Bay is sometimes used by locals to indicate the area south of the Bardswell Group of islands and west of Codfish Passage and the Tribal Group. This area, at the north end of Queens Sound, has a fearsome appearance during strong northwesterlies or southerlies when surf breaks over the thousands of rocks and reefs.

Tribal Group

Chart 3787; north entrance:
52°03.40′ N, 128°18.60′ W (NAD 27)

> *Tribal Group consists of Athabaskan Island, Iroquois Island, Huron Island and several smaller islands.*
>
> *Tide Rip Passage, on the SE side of Athabaskan Island, is not recommended without the aid of local knowledge. Drying and below-water rocks extend 0.4 mile south from the south end of Athabaskan Island.* (p. 159, SD)

The Tribal Group, a good jumping off point for boats wishing to head to Goose Islands, is interesting in its own right. The waters are largely sheltered although strong currents and concentrated patches of logs and driftwood can be encountered. The small cove at the north side of Iroquois Island makes a good anchorage from which to explore the region.

"Iroquois Cove"

Chart 3787; anchor: 52°02.53′ N, 128°19.18′ W (NAD 27)

There are two unnamed islands off the north side of Iroquois Island that form a well-sheltered cove in the basin between the three islands. The east entrance to the cove, contrary to the chart, is choked with kelp and may be foul. The north entrance, however, is clear, but you must avoid the rocks and reefs upon entering. The bottom is irregular, and a shore tie can be effectively used on the west side of the basin. Anchor in the cove just north of the high-water kayak passage to the west.

Anchor in about 8 fathoms over a mixed bottom with fair holding if your anchor is well set.

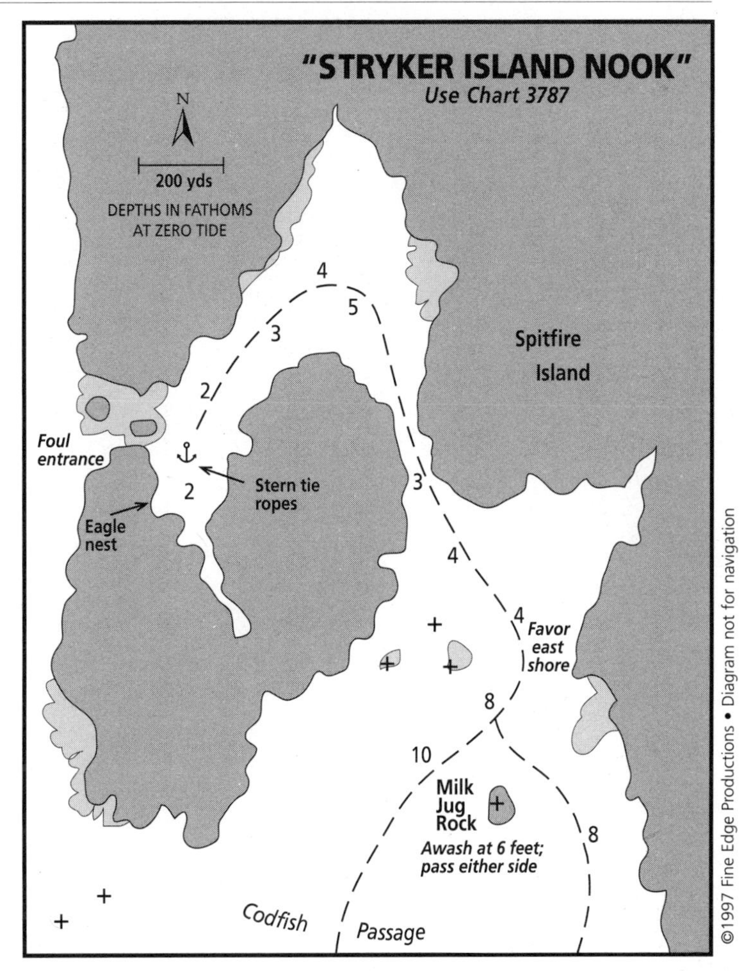

"Stryker Island Nook"

Chart 3787; entrance: 52°04.50′ N, 128°20.40′ W; anchor: 52°06.02′ N, 128°20.54′ W (NAD 27)

Stryker Island is on the west side of the entrance to Raymond Passage.
(p. 159, SD)

Stryker Island Nook, 1.5 miles north of Alleyne Island, is the small, well-protected cove off the bottom of Stryker Island. (It is located behind the island that on the chart looks like water wings.) Kevin Monahan first told us about this fisherman's nook. Although the cove is somewhat difficult to enter, its security and scenic views through the "windows" to the west make it one of our favorites.

Hakai Passage looking north

From Alleyne Island, turn north along its west shore and continue generally true north for 1.6 miles. Avoid the dangerous isolated rock 300 yards southeast of the water-wing island. (We call this rock Milk Jug Rock because some fishermen marked it with a plastic milk jug.)

Favor the east shore until you reach the top of "water wings" island, then turn southwest toward the islets which form the "windows." Minimum depth in the narrows north of Milk Jug Rock is about 3 fathoms. Anchor as depth and swinging room allow. Small boats can anchor off the head of the cove and use a stern tie for a happy, bomb-proof sleep.

Anchor in 2 fathoms over a mud and shell bottom with good holding.

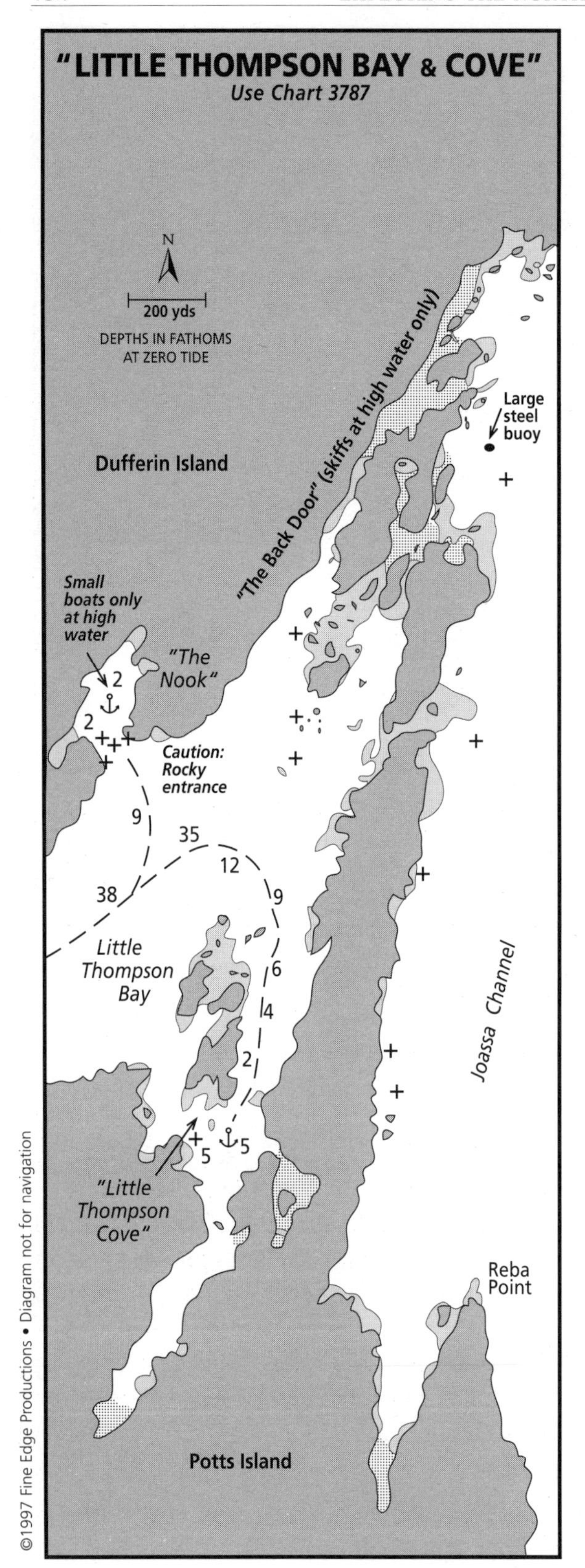

"Louise Channel South"

Chart 3787; entrance: 52°05.50′ N, 128°22.80′ W; anchor: 52°06.58′ N, 128°22.23′ W (NAD 27)

A well-protected anchorage used by fishing boats is reported in the southern part of Louise Channel. It is close to fishing activity in greater Thompson Bay.

Louise Channel is blocked in its narrows to all but skiffs at high water.

Anchor in 2 fathoms, unrecorded bottom

"Little Thompson Bay and Cove"

Chart 3787; entrance:
52°09.00′ N, 128°22.40′ W; anchor (Little Thompson Cove): 52°09.36′ N, 128°20.77′ W; anchor ("The Nook"):
52°10.00′ N, 128°21.03′ W (NAD 27)

Little Thompson Bay and Cove, located at the north end of Thompson Bay, provide sheltered anchorage for large and small craft respectively. Little Thompson is the local name for the area north of the three islands in the northeast corner of Thompson Bay, deep in the labyrinth at the northwest corner of Potts Island. The entrance to both starts at the north end of Thompson Bay, avoiding the midchannel rock east of Cree Point and entering Little Thompson. Large vessels can find anchorage here in mostly very deep water. Small boats will find more suitable anchorage by continuing northeast before turning east, then circling south into the indent in Potts Island. As you turn south, avoid the islets and rocks by favoring the east shore and then avoid the rocks on the east shore as you enter the inner basin. Little Thompson Cove is secure from most weather.

Another small craft anchorage can be found in the small cove at the north end of Little Thompson which indents Dufferin Island shore. The entrance to this small nook is littered with rocks and requires a careful approach near high water. This cove has a 2- to 3-fathom depth. The far north channel into Joassa Channel is known as "The Back Door" and can only be traversed by dinghies, kayaks and power skiffs at high water. This channel is choked with rocks and kelp.

Fishing lodge, Hakai Passage

Large boats anchor in Little Thompson in 35 fathoms over an unknown bottom.

Anchor in Little Thompson Cove in 5 fathoms over sand and mud with good holding.

Anchor in Little Thompson Nook in 2 fathoms over an unrecorded bottom.

Gale Passage

Chart 3787; north entrance:
52°14.50′ N, 128°22.30′ W (NAD 27)

> *Gale Passage separates Dufferin Island from Athlone Island and leads from the north end of Thompson Bay to Seaforth Channel. This passage is only suitable for small craft and local knowledge is advised to navigate it safely. Tidal rapids are formed about 1.8 miles from its south entrance and again at about the same distance from its north entrance where the fairway dries.* (p. 161, SD)

Gale Passage should be avoided unless you are an experienced wilderness kayaker with a lot of time to reconnoiter both the north and south rapids and to wait for proper conditions before attempting a transit. A steep tidal fall 6 feet high is reported at the rapids during spring tides.

"Gale Passage Landlocked South Cove"

Chart 3787; position: 52°10.95′ N, 128°23.00′ W (NAD 27)

A well-sheltered anchor site, reported to lie just south of the south rapids in Gale Passage, is a good place for small craft to observe the rapids and explore the inner basin. There may also be such an anchor site at the north entrance. At this time, we have no local knowledge to offer. Caution is required; fast water flows among the islets and rocks and a large-scale chart is not currently available.

Note: Saint Johns Harbour, on the west side of Athlone Island, fronts Milbanke Sound and is discussed in Chapter 7.

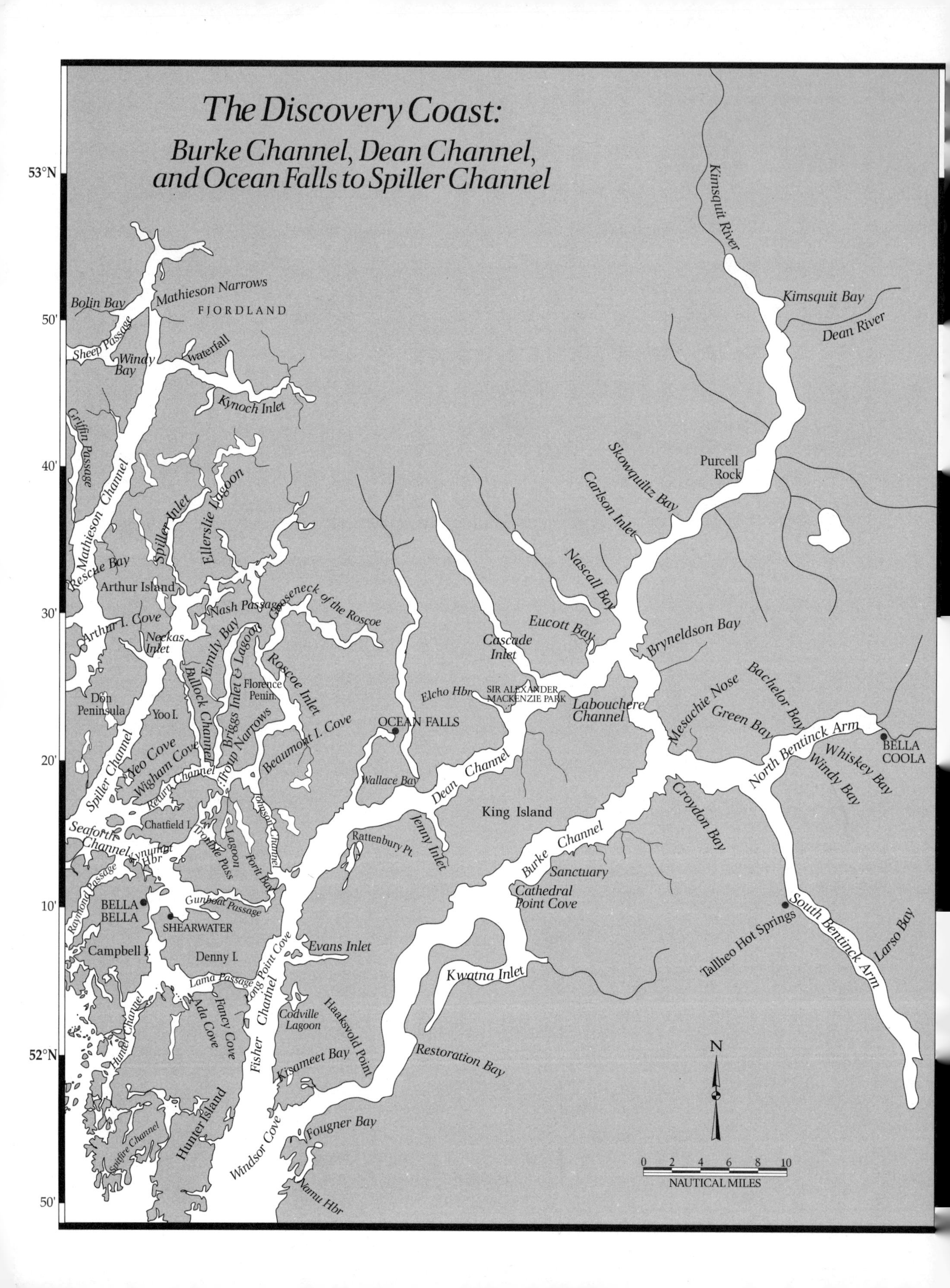

The Discovery Coast:
Burke Channel, Dean Channel, and Ocean Falls to Spiller Channel
53°N
50'
40'
30'
20'
10'
52°N
50'
Kimsquit River
Kimsquit Bay
Dean River
Bolin Bay
Mathieson Narrows
FJORDLAND
Sheep Passage
Windy Bay
Waterfall
Kynoch Inlet
Griffin Passage
Mathieson Channel
Spiller Inlet
Ellerslie Lagoon
Rescue Bay
Arthur Island
Nash Passage
Gooseneck of the Roscoe
Arthur I. Cove
Neekas Inlet
Emily Bay
Briggs Inlet & Lagoon
Roscoe Inlet
Florence Penin.
Don Peninsula
Yoo I.
Bullock Channel
Troup Narrows
Beaumont I. Cove
Neo Cove
Wigham Cove
Spiller Channel
Return Channel
Chatfield I.
Johnson Channel
Seaforth Channel
Kynumpt Hbr
Lagoon
Troup Passage
Forit Bay
Raymond Passage
BELLA BELLA
SHEARWATER
Gunboat Passage
Campbell I.
Denny I.
Lama Passage
Hunter Channel
Ada Cove
Fancy Cove
Long Point Cove
Fisher Channel
Codville Lagoon
Haaksvold Point
Kisameet Bay
Hunter Island
Spitfire Channel
Windsor Cove
Fougner Bay
Namu Hbr
Evans Inlet
OCEAN FALLS
Wallace Bay
Rattenbury Pt.
Jenny Inlet
Dean Channel
Elcho Hbr
SIR ALEXANDER MACKENZIE PARK
Cascade Inlet
Eucott Bay
Labouchere Channel
King Island
Burke Channel
Sanctuary
Cathedral Point Cove
Kwatna Inlet
Restoration Bay
Skowquiltz Bay
Carlson Inlet
Nascall Bay
Purcell Rock
Bryneldson Bay
Mesachie Nose
Bachelor Bay
Green Bay
North Bentinck Arm
BELLA COOLA
Whiskey Bay
Windy Bay
Croydon Bay
Tallheo Hot Springs
South Bentinck Arm
Larso Bay
N
0 2 4 6 8 10
NAUTICAL MILES

5

Discovery Coast: Burke Channel, Dean Channel, and Ocean Falls to Spiller Channel

The Discovery Coast, formerly known as the undiscovered coast, is in the process of being discovered! With the inauguration of the summer ferry service covering the area from Fitz Hugh Sound to Bella Coola, Bella Bella, Ocean Falls, and Klemtu, recreational opportunities for trailerable boats, inflatables, kayaks, and those wishing to cruise the central coast have been greatly expanded.

From Hakai Recreational Area, with its innumerable rugged islets, to the deep fjords and inlets penetrating deep into the mainland coastal range, the Discovery Coast encompasses some of the best cruising grounds found along the British Columbia coast. Many boaters familiar with the entire Inside Passage consider this area to be their first cruising choice.

Every mile a surprise, Burke Channel

The region around Spiller Channel remained, until in April 1996, the largest uncharted portion of the British Columbia coast. Following the publication of Chart 3940, more than 300 square miles of wilderness have been added to the list of cruising possibilities. Any boater planning to travel in this newly-charted area should exercise caution in using the information on Chart 3940, as well as the local knowledge present in this chapter, since not all hazards to navigation are correctly or completely identified. Time will increase and improve upon the information about this beautiful wilderness.

Burke Channel

Charts 3729, 3730

Burke Channel leads 38 miles along the SE side of King Island. High precipitous snow-capped mountains, with sides covered with stunted trees, lie on each side of the channel.

On warm summer days the sea breeze blowing across Fitz Hugh Sound is led up the inlet, as through a funnel, following the directions of the different bends. The breeze generally sets in at about 1000 hours and blows fresh until sunset, when it usually becomes calm.

Tidal streams from Edmund Point to Restoration Bay are strong and heavy tide-rips are encountered, particularly off Hvidsten Point. (p. 75, SD)

Burke Channel is a beautiful, glacier-cut inlet between the mainland and King Island. Its outlet at Fitz Hugh Sound has an entrance bar between 20 and 70 fathoms. Once you are north of Haaksvold Point, the water deepens gradually to 300 fathoms. The shores on either side of the channel are steep-to, with depths of 50 to 100 fathoms frequently just 50 yards offshore. Strong westerly winds tend to build up on summer

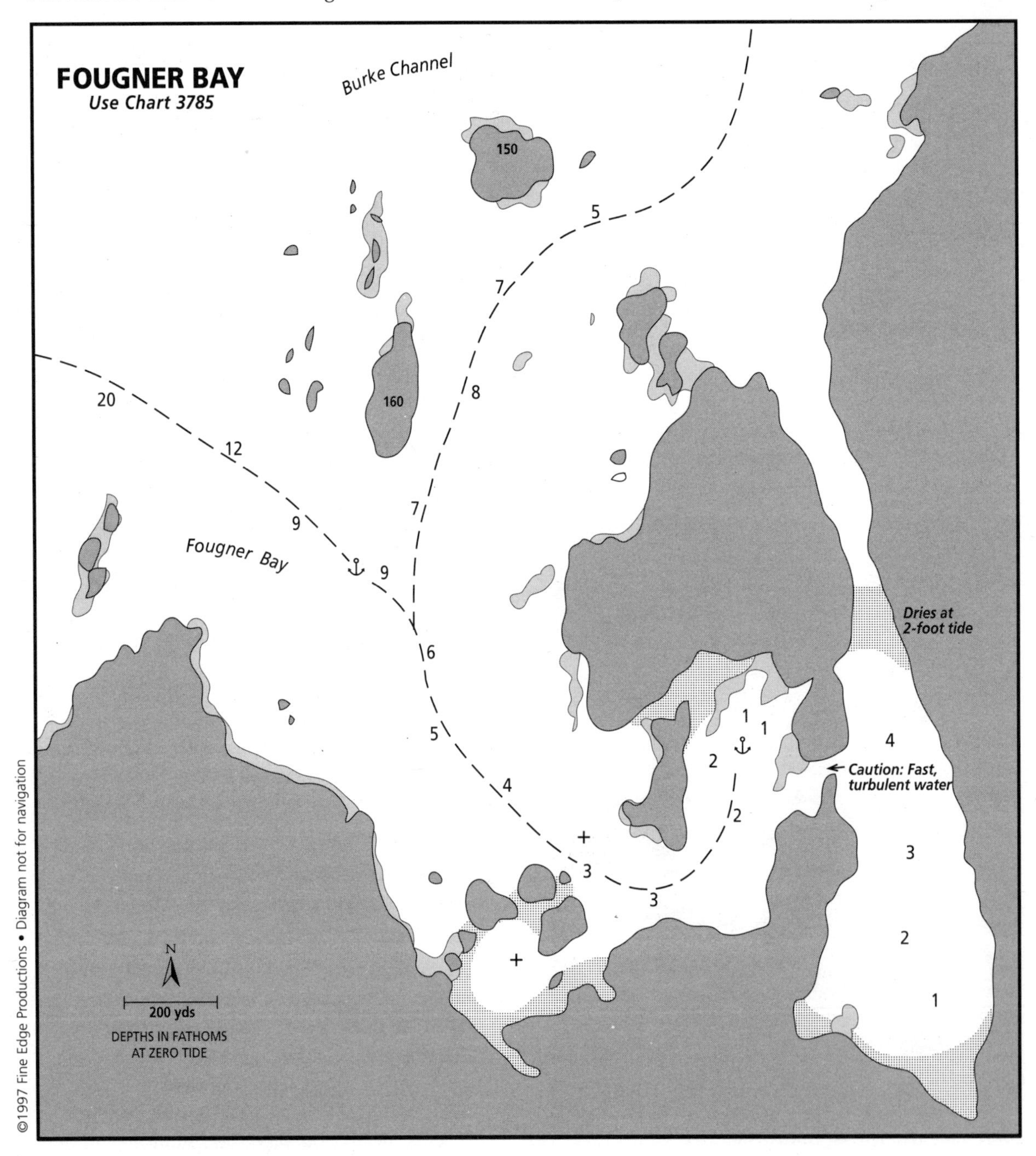

afternoons; during such conditions, it's a good idea to get an early morning start. Squamish outflow winds are gale force winds occuring when high pressure over the interior flows through the channels to a low pressure area offshore. These winds are most prevalent in winter. However, they can occur in summer, and in such conditions, it's better to wait, seek shelter and wait until they die down, usually in the afternoon.

You can escape prevailing strong ebb currents by playing the back eddies and lesser ebb current along the steep shores. Kelkpa Point, 19 miles from Fitz Hugh Sound, marks the beginning of the rougher waters for which Burke Channel is known. The S-shaped curve of the channel creates turbulence and back eddies—appreciated by any river runner—that result in a confused surface full of whitecaps, even though up-inlet wind may be light. Kwatna Inlet, entered just east of Mapalaklenk Point, offers quick relief from these confused seas. Monitor VHF channels for information on the latest weather conditions at Cathedral Point .

Fougner Bay

Charts 3785 or 3729; entrance: 51°54.60′ N, 127°51.60′ W; anchor (outer anchorage): 51°54.40′ N, 127°51.20′ W; anchor (inner cove): 51°54.28′ N, 127°50.60′ W (NAD 27)

> *Fougner Bay, entered 0.5 mile NE of Edmund Point, is encumbered with islets and shoals. Drying rocks are the outermost danger in the approach. Small craft can obtain anchorage in Fougner Bay.* (p. 75, SD)

Fougner Bay, on the south shore of the entrance to Burke Channel, contains an intricate group of islands, islets and rocks and is one of the more well-protected anchorages along this part of the coast. Heads-up navigation and an alert bow lookout are required to enter the bay since no adequate large-scale chart is available.

Large boats can anchor in the outer anchorage in 9 fathoms northeast of a 12-foot drying rock where holding power is unrecorded; however, local reports say there's good holding in southeasterly winds. The bottom is a flat 5 to 9 fathoms over a large area with good protection from southerly weather, but with moderate exposure to downslope and westerly winds.

A very scenic and secluded anchor site can be found in the south portion of Fougner Bay west of the mainland peninsula, east of the small unnamed island, and south of the large unnamed island. The inner cove is landlocked, with cedar, hemlock, and old silver cedar snags over 6 feet in diameter. Anchor just south of a line from the south end of the tiny tree-filled rock islet in the head of the cove west of a 30-foot white granite wall. The anchor site is out of the current flowing through the passage. We heard loon calls and those of other birds echoing off the trees.

Anchor (outer anchorage) in 9 fathoms over an unrecorded bottom, with fair-to-good holding.

Anchor (inner cove) in 1 to 2 fathoms over a brown sand bottom covered with extensive lettuce kelp. Holding is poor to good depending on how you set your anchor.

Windsor Cove

Chart 3729; position (head of cove): 51°56 31′ N, 127°52.96′ W (NAD 27)

> *Windsor Cove, 2 miles north of Edmund Point, affords temporary anchorage in 16 fathoms (29 m) but little shelter. Sagen Islet lies on the west side of the approach.* (p. 75, SD)

Protection from strong westerlies can be found in Windsor Cove deep in the head of the cove. A temporary anchorage and good lunch stop can be taken north of Sagen Islet between the rocks and the southern tip of King Island.

Haaksvold Point

Chart 3729; position (light): 51°57.60′ N, 127°42.10′ W (NAD 27)

At Haaksvold Point we have observed a tidal bore occurring on spring tides. The fast flood current meets the strong freshwater outflow on top coming down the channel, creating small standing waves and whirlpools across the channel. Below the bore, the flood moves northeast about 1 to 1.5 knots; on top the fresh water flows southwest about 2 knots.

This strong, almost constant ebb current in Burke Channel causes an uncomfortable chop when the afternoon up-inlet winds pick up.

Restoration Bay

Chart 3729; entrance: 52°01.00′ N, 127°38.90′ W; anchor (southeast of yellow triangle): 52°01.50′ N, 127°38.00′ W (NAD 27)

> *Restoration Bay is on the east side of Burke Channel, about 4 miles NE of Haaksvold Point. Sharp Cone, close north of the bay, rises steeply. Several streams flow into the head of the bay through a sandy beach.*
>
> *Anchorage can be obtained in Restoration Bay in 17 fathoms (31 m) about 0.15 mile from the LW mark; the shore should be approached slowly when coming to anchor as the coastal bank is steep-to.* (p. 75, SD)

Restoration Bay was named by George Vancouver during his explorations along the coast here in 1793. He happened to anchor here on May 29, the 133rd anniversary of the restoration of Charles II—hence the name.

Restoration Bay is a fair-weather stop, since it is exposed to winds that blow up the inlet. Tuck close into the northeast corner where you can find protection from downslope gales. The shoreline of the bay is steep-to with high granite cliffs that rise about a thousand feet vertically to Sharp Cone—the 2,970-foot peak on the north side of Restoration Bay. Trees grow out of nearly every crack along these ramparts. The east side of the bay is less precipitous and falls more gently to the shore of Kwatna Inlet. During times of heavy rain or runoff, Quatlena River, one mile east of Restoration Bay, comes charging out of a saddle between 2,000- to 3,000-foot peaks and cascades down the face in a series of waterfalls on its way to sea level in Kwatna Inlet.

Anchor southeast of the yellow triangle on a sloping bottom, or close-in to the 1½-fathom shelf, just below the outlet of the creek where holding is reported to be good.

Anchor in 4 to 8 fathoms over an unrecorded bottom.

Kwatna Inlet

Chart 3729; entrance: 52°04.50′ N, 127°28.00′ W (NAD 27)

> *Kwatna Inlet is free of dangers and deep except toward the head where depths gradually shoal; for the last mile the bottom is irregular.*
>
> *Good anchorage can be obtained in 15 fathoms (27 m), mud and sand, 0.3 mile from the edge of the drying flat at the head of Kwatna Inlet.* (p. 75, SD)

The entrance to Kwatna Inlet is just above Mapalaklenk Point, where Burke Channel follows an S-shaped curve. As you approach Mapalaklenk Point, stay well out from Odegaard Rocks that extend 400 yards northwest of the point.

The inlet curves south, then west and southwest to a large, drying mud flat at the base of Quatlena River. The inlet is 13 miles long, with steep sides that rise to 3,000-foot peaks less than a mile from the saltwater. Until you reach the far southwest end, depths are too great for anchoring.

Kwatna Bay

Chart 3729

> *Kwatna Bay is on the east shore of Kwatna Inlet 4 miles within the entrance.*
>
> *Kwatna Bay is deep but indifferent anchorage can be obtained about 0.2 mile from the edge of the drying flat, in about 32 fathoms (59 m), mud bottom. Approach this anchorage with caution because the mud flat is steep-to.* (p. 75, SD)

Photo courtesy CHS, Pacific Region

Kwatna Bay

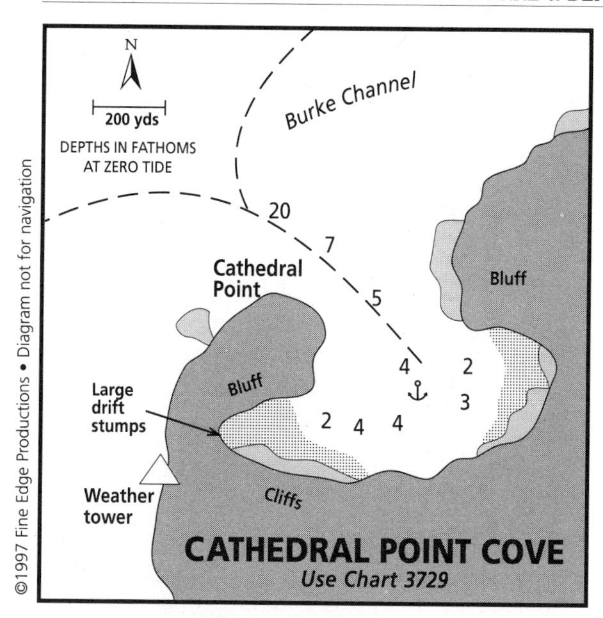

"Cathedral Point Cove"

Chart 3729; anchor: 52°11.24' N, 127°28.00' W (NAD 27)

Cathedral Point, on the north side of the entrance to Kwatna Inlet, is indented by a small bay which has a drying rock on the west side of its narrow entrance and drying flats around its shore. (p. 75, SD)

Cathedral Point is a landmark remarkable for its rosy-orange cliffs that face southwest; Cathedral Point Cove is also a remarkable topographic feature. The cove is surrounded by granite walls and a stand of old-growth hemlock and spruce. Just west of the point, the bold cliffs give way to a circular bay which provides welcome relief from the channel chop and good protection from both up- and downslope summer weather. The cove has a large, flat 4-fathom bottom with swinging room for two or three small boats. The south end of the cove gives the best protection from up-inlet winds. Notice, however, the large tree roots collected on the south beach, and low windswept trees hugging bend southward, attesting to terrific Arctic outflow winds in winter. If downslope winds are anticipated during the nighttime, the east center of the cove is a better place to anchor.

Winds in the vicinity of the point swirl into the cove periodically and some rocking can be expected. During inflow gales this anchorage

Cathedral Point Cove, north end

may be uncomfortable. However, chop largely blows by and you should have a fine view of the channel and the pink granite and tree-covered mountains on the western shore. To minimize rocking, consider a stern anchor to keep your bow pointed toward the opening. All in all, Cathedral Point Cove is a welcome respite in an otherwise steep and deep fjord.

Anchor in 4 fathoms over a mud bottom with some rocks with good holding.

Glacier-carved rock, upper Burke Channel

Upper Burke Channel (above Cathedral Point)

Chart 3729; position ("The Crack"): 52°13.40′ N, 127°22.80′ W (NAD 27)

North of Cathedral Point, the east side of Burke Channel has some of the most spectacular scenery we've encountered.

In the rain, light granite rock turns grey, small streams develop and race down rounded slabs of boulder—formations so smooth and rounded that soil cannot develop, and the tiny plants and trees frequently found in crevices along vertical faces have no chance along this two-mile stretch. The rock cliffs are paintings in themselves—some mauve, some ochre or violet-hued; some heavily glaciated with white and grey striations. Then, 0.7 mile east of Gibraltar Point, the first of many beautiful surprises—a waterfall we call "The Crack" drops out of a narrow fissure 70 feet above; sometimes in mid-summer, snow still remains wedged in the fissure, just 200 feet from the water.

The scenery is so magnificent we're loathe to attempt describing it. Instead, we'd like you to take pleasure in your own discovery of upper Burke Channel. Stay within 50 to 100 yards from the east shore for the full impact of the peaks and overhanging cliffs.

Avalanche chute, The Sanctuary

"The Sanctuary"

Chart 3729; position: 52°13.50′ N, 127°21.40′ W (NAD 27)

The Sanctuary is our name for the small indentation 1.5 miles east of Gibraltar Point on the south shore of Burke Channel. Approximately 300 yards deep by 75 yards wide and carved out of high granite cliffs and conglomerate, there is a large avalanche chute where a stream flows underneath snowbridges that descend to within 200 feet of the water. The head of the bay at the foot of the chute is choked with chunks of yellow granite that contrast dramatically with grey granite slabs, brilliant green trees and bushes, and patches of pure white snow.

Five miles east of Gibraltar Point, the stunning scenery you've grown accustomed to disappears—the slopes are clearcut and, although new growth is taking hold, it's a disappointment after the splendor of the past few miles. Then as you approach Kwaspala Point, the water becomes greener, announcing glacier run-off from North Bentinck and South Bentinck arms, and a promise of grandiose scenery again.

Immediately south of Kwaspala Point, there is a small nook that may offer protection from downslope winds. The head of the nook is a gently-sloping mud flat.

Croyden Bay

Charts 3730, 3729; anchor: 52°18.68′ N, 127°09.56′ W (NAD 27)

> *Croyden Bay and Jacobsen Bay lie close NE of Kwaspala Point. Both bays are too deep for anchorage except for small craft close inshore. A cliff rises almost vertically from shore on the east side of Kwaspala Point.* (pp. 75, 77, SD)

Croyden Bay is a wide, deep bay which offers

some relief from outside weather and chop. There are two beaches at the head of the bay. The western beach is steep-to and has a rocky bottom, 5 fathoms deep, 60 feet from shore. The eastern beach has small grassy patches and is the outlet of a small creek. A temporary stop can be found in favorable weather in 4 fathoms, about 100 feet from the beach. Old steel cables on the east shore indicate shore ties were made here at one time. The islet off the east point provides fair protection on the east side of the bay from downslope chop.

Anchor in 4 fathoms over mud, gravel and rocks with some grass and wood debris, with poor-to-fair holding.

Jacobsen Bay

Charts 3730, 3729; position: 52°18.88′ N, 127°09.23′ W (NAD 27)

Jacobsen Bay provides less protection than Croyden Bay and is equally steep-to. Depths 60 feet from shore are about 60 feet, indicating a 45-degree slope. A major creek empties into the head of the bay, flowing between two patches of green grass and some driftwood.

A temporary stop can be found in calm weather with your bow headed into the outflow of the creek.

Anchor in about 12 fathoms over mixed bottom of gravel and rock with poor holding.

North Bentinck Arm

Chart 3730; entrance: 52°19.50′ N, 126°18.50′ W (NAD 27)

> *North Bentinck Arm is entered between Tallheo Point and Loiyentsi Point. It is deep throughout with no off-lying dangers, and its shores are moderately steep-to. At the head of the arm a steep-to mud and sand flat extends from low, swampy ground which is submerged at HW. The Bella Coola River, a stream of considerable size and velocity, flows through the flat which, from recent surveys, shows indications of extending west. The Necleetsconnay River flows into the NE side of the head of the inlet.* (p. 77, SD)

Bella Coola lies at the head of North Bentinck Arm.

Green Bay

Chart 3730; position: 52°20.53′ N, 126°58.70′ W (NAD 27)

> *Green Bay lies close NE of Loiyentsi Point, with Big Bay farther NE. Green Bay has an extensive sand and gravel bank within it, and a ruined wharf and several cabins on its north side.*
>
> *Small craft can obtain anchorage in the vicinity of the ruined wharf in Green Bay.* (p. 77, SD)

Green Bay lies at the bottom of a classic U-shaped, glacier-carved valley which is the outlet of the Nooseseck River. The river outlet is at the far west side of the bay and we could not find the 6-fathom shoal shown on the chart. Instead we found depths of 20 fathoms up to the very edge of the rapidly flowing river. A house is located on the east side of the bay 100 yards from the beach.

Loiyentsi Point offers some protection from west winds blowing up Burke Channel. We would consider this a temporary anchorage only. A small 4- to 6-fathom shelf, 50 yards west of the end of the old pier pilings, extends to the front of the pier and can be used for temporary anchorage in fair weather. The saltwater is milky green with poor underwater visibility.

Anchor in 4 to 6 fathoms over rocky bottom with poor holding.

Windy Bay

Chart 3730; position: 52°20.70′ N, 126° 54.90′ W (NAD 27)

> *Windy Bay is on the east side of Flagpole Point.* (p. 77, SD)

Windy Bay, named for its openness to downslope winds, affords some protection from upslope winds, but the shore is steep-to and appears to offer no anchorage unless a shore tie is used to the steep rocks.

Bachelor Bay

Chart 3730; position: 52°22.05′ N, 126°54.60′ W (NAD 27)

Bachelor Bay, the name given to the small bight directly across from Windy Bay, is east of a peninsula on the north side of North Bentinck Arm. It has a gravel and rock beach which can serve as a kayak haul-out and campsite. Drift logs blow down the channel onto this beach, but it offers fair-to-good protection in up-channel winds. The beach is steep-to.

We have no information about anchoring in Bachelor Bay.

Whiskey Bay

Chart 3730; position: 52°21.74′ N, 126°52.52′ W (NAD 27)

> *Whiskey Bay, a short distance NE, affords temporary anchorage for small craft, close inshore. An old log dump and gin pole are in the bay. Logbooms lie along the shore for 1.5 miles to the east.* (p. 77, SD)

Whiskey Bay is slowly healing itself. The log dump, gin pole and pier shown on the chart are all gone. A large log dump is presently located 2 miles east, just west of Sutlej Point. The rocky beach has a gravel section on its west side which can offer temporary anchorage, preferably with a stern tie to the sheer bluff on the west side. It is 4 fathoms deep 40 feet from shore, and very deep farther out.

Anchor in 20 fathoms over an unrecorded bottom or use a stern tie to the sheer bluff on the west shore.

Bella Coola

Chart 3730 (inset); harbour entrance: 52°22.60′ N, 126°47.60′ W (NAD 27)

> *Bella Coola is a settlement on the south shore of the river of the same name, about 0.8 mile inland from the head of North Bentinck Arm.*
>
> *Public floats east of the wharf have 3,058 feet (932 m) of berthing space and are protected by floating breakwaters. Power (110V/15 amp) and fresh water are laid on the floats. A 4.5 tonne crane and a public telephone are on the wharfhead leading to the floats, and a launching ramp is nearby. A tidal grid is at the shoreline close east of the wharfhead.* (pp. 77, 78, SD)

The harbor for Bella Coola lies outside the delta of the river of the same name. Its entrance is protected by a rock breakwater marked by a quick-flashing red light. The public floats are located east of the ferry dock and wharf. The harbormaster's office lies at the head of the gangway (closed during the noon lunch hour). Two pay phones (land phones), located just behind the office, were functioning in the summer of 1996. The fuel dock, on a small float at the foot of the wharf, is also closed during lunch.

The Discovery Coast ferry calls at Bella Coola several times a week from the end of May to the latter part of September. The road to Williams Lake, 452 kilometer away, leads up the beautiful Bella Coola valley, and passes through Tweedsmuir Park, the largest provincial park in British Columbia. (The first 100 kilometers of this road from Bella Coola remained unpaved in 1996). Hagensborg, 15 kilometers east of Bella Coola, is home to the central coast Ministry of Forestry office.

Ice can be purchased at the ice plant located on the Bella Coola Harbour wharf. Groceries, hardware and liquor are available at the co-op in town, a mile from the harbor. The co-op will deliver free to the dock groceries of over $70 (Canadian), and Visa and Mastercard are accepted. Repair shops, motels, guides, credit union,

Photo courtesy Bella Coola Harbourmaster

Bella Coola Harbour

Bella Coola public floats

hospital and laundromat are all found in town; both B.C. Parks and Conservation Service have offices in town where you can obtain information on recreational possibilties in the region. Bella Coola Valley Museum, located at the west entrance to town is worth visiting.

Good-tasting water is available on the landing zone float and along some of the other floats; some power is available as well. There is no water at the fuel dock. A tidal grid and launching ramp are also provided.

While the majority of boats in the harbor are fishing vessels, the Harbormaster has seen a dramatic increase in visits from pleasure boats in the 1990s. A few even winter over. (The bay has no ice in the winter, we were told.)

South Bentinck Arm

Chart 3730; entrance: 52°18.50′ N, 126°59.00′ W (NAD 27)

> *South Bentinck Arm leads 25 miles SE between high mountains.*
>
> *Anchorage, suitable for vessels of moderate size, can be obtained in the basin between Taleomey Narrows and Bentinck Narrows; there are depths of 33 fathoms (60 m) in this basin but the anchorage is well sheltered during summer months.* (p. 78, SD)

South Bentinck Arm is the continuation of Burke Channel. Upslope winds which blow northeast in lower Burke Channel frequently turn and fol-

Hanging glacier, South Bentinck Arm

low South Bentinck Arm to the southeast.

Snow-capped mountains rise to 7,000 feet on both sides of the arm, providing a continuation of the spectacular scenery found in Burke Channel. There are reported to be well over a dozen glaciers visible from the water on a rare clear day. Until mid-summer, the entire arm has snowy peaks that nearly overhang the channel, and you feel you could reach out and grab a handful of snow. Like Burke Channel, there is little evidence of mankind except for clear-cut scars (some fresh and ugly; others well into developing second-growth) that attest to the importance of logging to this area.

The only reasonable anchorage for small boats in the entire arm is 10 miles within the inlet on the east shore of Larso Bay. It is strange to see the strong west wind blow northeast in Burke Channel, then turn and blow southeast in South Bentinck Arm.

One of the dangers of traversing Burke Channel and Bentinck Arms in times of spring tide is that the 16-foot tide lifts many logs, branches, and tree stumps off beaches and river flats and fills the channels with debris. You could easily damage your propeller if you take your eyes off-course for a minute. In the channel chop, the drift is hidden from view 90 percent of the time.

South Bentinck Arm is seldom visited by cruising boats and its outstanding scenery and solitude are well worth the effort and risks.

Lunch break at Larso Bay

Tallheo Hot Springs

Chart 3730; position:
52°12.10′ N, 126°56.05′ W (NAD 27)

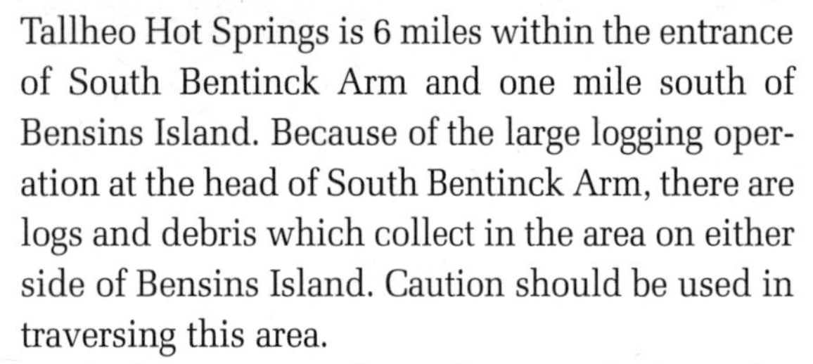

Tallheo Hot Springs is 6 miles within the entrance of South Bentinck Arm and one mile south of Bensins Island. Because of the large logging operation at the head of South Bentinck Arm, there are logs and debris which collect in the area on either side of Bensins Island. Caution should be used in traversing this area.

The hot springs is located just inside the outlet of Hot Springs Creek. There is a cabin on shore at the outlet; however, there is no dock or easy access since the water is relatively deep, and there is no protection from up- or downslope winds.

Temporary anchorage in fair weather may be found in about 14 fathoms immediately off the creek over an unrecorded bottom.

Larso Bay

Chart 3730; anchor: 52°10.85′ N, 126°51.58′ W (NAD 27)

> *Larso Bay affords anchorage for vessels up to 150 feet (46 m) long in about 18 fathoms (33 m). The pilings of an old wharf and a logging camp and log dump are in the bay.* (p. 78, SD)

Larso Bay, 15 miles from the head of the arm, gives welcome relief from up-channel wind and chop. There is a 30-foot-square float used by the logging boats in the northwest corner of the bay. Logging-crew boats normally land on its south side, and a new section for float planes lies on its east side. A logging maintenance shed is located 100 yards to the northwest on shore. Pleasure boats can use the float when it's not occupied by work boats. Anchoring is also possible in 8 fathoms between the float and the shoal at the outlet of the creek.

On shore, wild strawberry, salmonberry, clover, daisies, and salal grow amidst the hemlock, cedar, spruce and alder. High on the ridge are clear-cut scars. On the west shore there is a remarkable waterfall that cascades from the snowfield on a 4,200-foot peak above.

Larso Bay is the best place in the south arm for small boats to anchor. It has very good protection from upslope winds, which in this area flow from the northwest. Only moderate protection from downslope winds is offered by the point and the logbooms on the southeast side of the bay.

Anchorage can be found in 5 to 10 fathoms between the float and the shoal from the small creek at the head of the bay. The bottom is sand, mud and gravel with fair holding.

Labouchere Channel

Chart 3730; south entrance:
52°21.00′ N, 127°10.90′ W; north entrance:
52°26.80′ N, 127°15.10′ W (NAD 27)

> *Labouchere Channel connects Dean Channel to Burke Channel.*
>
> *Labouchere Channel is usually calm in summer, no matter how strong the winds may be in Burke and Dean Channels. During the winter very*

strong north or NE winds can be experienced. (p. 82, SD)

The calm waters of Labouchere Channel offer welcome relief from Burke Channel chop as soon as you pass Mesachie Nose—a spectacular cliff—on the east side of the south entrance. Southeast and southwest winds blowing up Burke Channel strike the cliff and the waves rebound, causing a confused sea in the immediate vicinity. Look closely and you will see a picture of a Fisheries officer painted on the cliff to warn local commercial fishermen not to stray over the fishing boundary of Mesachie Nose.

Geza and Don input info on Burke Channel

"Bryneldson Bay"

Charts 3729, 3730; entrance:
52°26.60′ N, 127°13.00′ W; anchor:
52°26.83′ N, 127°13.27′ W (NAD 27)

. . . about 1 mile SE of Ram Bluff, is a small cove known locally as Bryneldson Bay.

Anchorage for small craft can be obtained in Bryneldson Bay in 18 feet (5.5 m), but there is only 7 feet (2.1 m) in the entrance. (p. 82, SD)

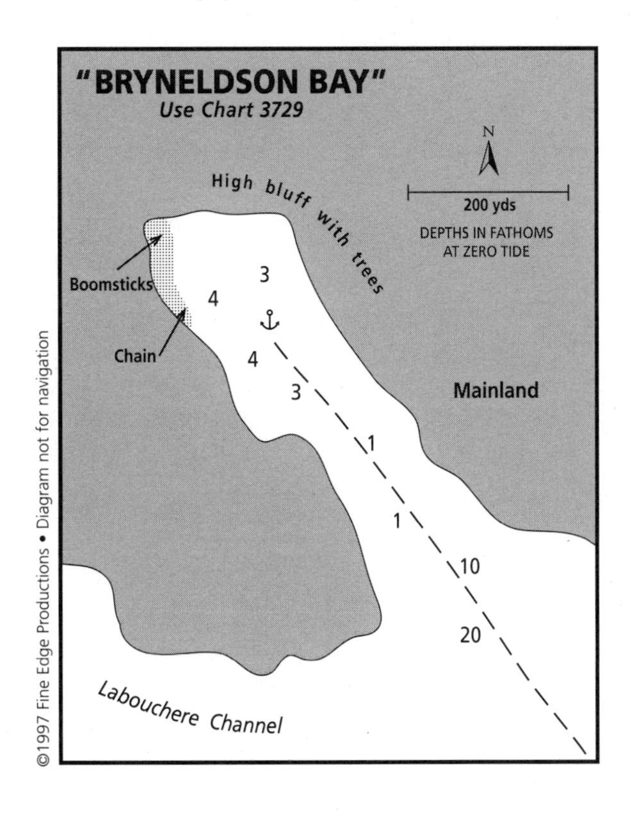

Bryneldson Bay offers very good protection deep in the small cove located one mile southeast of Ram Bluff. There are very few drift logs in the bay and the grassy margins show no signs of chop. This is a tranquil anchorage with lovely trees and striking granite bluffs.

The west shore is sometimes used as a log storage area; you may find boomsticks tied along shore. A sand bar lies approximately one-third of the way into the bay. Minimum depth is about 7 feet across the bar. North of the bar the bay has an almost flat bottom of 3 to 5 fathoms.

Anchor near the head of the bay in 4 fathoms over mud bottom and some wood debris with good-to-very-good holding.

Dean Channel

Chart 3781; west entrance:
52°15.00′ N, 127°46.00′ W (NAD 27)

Dean Channel, 53 miles long, lies between high, often precipitous mountains. Depths in the fairway are great and the shores are, for the most part, steep-to. Dean Channel can be entered from Fisher Channel, north of Rattenbury Point, or from Burke Channel by way of Labouchere Channel.

The prevailing wind in Dean Channel in

summer is from the SW, being led up the channel as through a funnel, following the direction of the channel. The breeze usually sets in about 1000 hours and reaches a maximum in early afternoon; it continues blowing fresh until sunset when it usually falls calm . . .

Tidal streams between Rattenbury Point and Carlson Inlet, about 30 miles to the NE, attain 1 to 2 kn. . . In summer, tidal streams become masked by the effect of the freshet from the rivers and creeks, and an overlay of fresh water is quite marked; in these circumstances the current is mostly an ebb . . . (pp. 80, 82, SD)

Dean Channel begins east of Rattenbury Point in rugged, scenic cruising grounds. In the channel, during periods of strong runoff, the ebb currents completely override the flooding currents on the surface, and it is not uncommon to have a 1/4- to 3/4-knot down-channel current the entire time the tide is rising! The saltwater temperature runs around 50° F, a good 10° colder than Seaforth Channel a few miles west! Upslope winds, which start about 10 a.m. and usually blow fresh all afternoon, can cause a nasty chop on a strong ebb current.

The color of the water in upper Dean Channel is not as light-colored or opaque as the water in the Bentinck Arms, indicating less glacier activity.

You will not see much traffic in Dean Channel, where logging and fishing are the commercial attractions. The route from Bella Bella to the town of Bella Coola, and the deep channels to the east, follows Dean Channel. Bella Coola, a major settlement at the head of Burke Channel and North Bentinck Arm, on the river of the same name, is connected to the British Columbia highway system at Williams Lake, 479 kilometers inland.

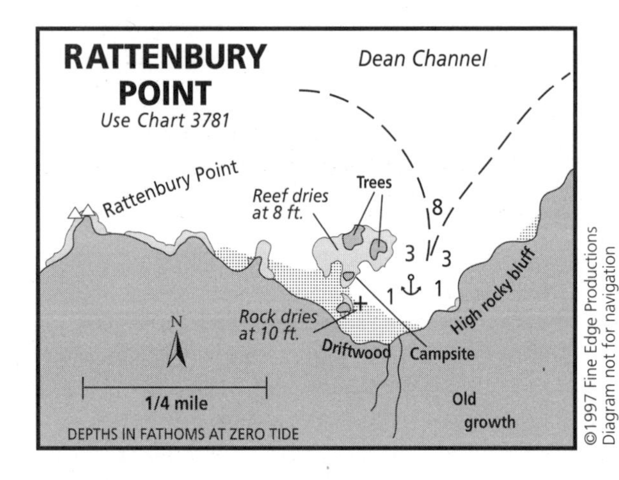

Cousins Inlet, 1 mile north of Rattenbury Point, is known as a sportfishing area, and Ocean Falls is a cruising destination with modest facilities and a Discovery Coast ferry stop.

Rattenbury Point

Charts 3781; anchor: 52°14.70′ N, 127°45.12′ W (NAD 27)

We have found temporary shelter on the east side of Rattenbury Point. Since the winds and seas can change dramatically in this area, it's a good place to take a break.

One-half mile east of Rattenbury Point, a small collection of islets makes a lee for small craft during southerly and westerly weather. The inside islet has a pleasant sandy beach that serves as a campsite for fishing and hunting parties. Old-growth hemlock, cedar, and alder that grow on the point show the effects of the strong winter outflow winds. The peaks to the east are high and steep. In this remote area we have seen dolphins, orcas, seals, and numerous species of birds, including puffins.

Avoid the small rock that dries at about 10 feet and anchor on the 2- to 4-fathom shelf just southeast of the islets. You may be able to find some protection from downslope winds on the west side of the islets, but we found foul ground there and would recommend a run into Cousins Inlet, Wallace Bay, or Ocean Falls if these conditions develop.

Anchor in 2 fathoms over a hard, rocky bottom with some kelp and poor-to-fair holding.

Cousins Inlet

Charts 3781, 3720, 3729; entrance position: 52°16.10′ N, 127°46.20′ W (NAD 27)

Cousins Inlet is entered between Boscowitz Point, which is steep-to and prominent, and Barba Point. The port facilities of Ocean Falls are at the head of the inlet. High, precipitous hills lie on both sides of the inlet. (p. 80, SD)

The entrance to Cousins Inlet is located 1.5 miles north of Rattenbury Point. Up- or downslope chop in Dean Channel quickly dies down as you pass north of Wallace Bay.

Ocean Falls

Wallace Bay

Charts 3781, 3720, 3729; anchor: 52°17.50' N, 127°44.95' W (NAD 27)

> *Anchorage in 22 fathoms (40 m) can be obtained in Wallace Bay. This anchorage is generally used as an overnight anchorage by vessels arriving at Ocean Falls after dark.* (p. 80, SD)

Wallace Bay is a shallow bight on the east shore, just inside the entrance to Cousins Inlet. A number of old cabins on shore formerly served as summer and weekend homesites for the residents of Ocean Falls. Wallace Bay affords moderate protection close inshore from southerly winds. You can find a good lunch stop at the head of the bight, south of the large green patch of alder trees. Avoid the Guns Rock at the north end of the bight when heading north.

Anchor in 12 fathoms, unrecorded bottom.

Ocean Falls

Chart 3781; floats: 52°21.14' N, 127°41.76' W (NAD 27)

> *Ocean Falls is at the head of the Cousins Inlet, on the north side of Link River. A paper mill, owned by the Province of British Columbia, but closed in 1982, is opposite the townsite. Precipitous hills rise immediately north of the townsite and south of the mill.* (p. 80, SD)

Discovery Coast *visiting Ocean Falls*

Cousins Inlet, at the head of Fisher Channel where Dean Channel begins, leads north to the site of Ocean Falls, where visiting boats can take moorage at good floats. Once a mighty industrial complex and a regular stop of Princess ships and cargo vessels, Ocean Falls is presently a quiet settlement that runs on its own rhythm. The paper mill and support infrastructure is largely decaying into a ghost town. The outpouring of a giant lake immediately behind the old paper mill's cement dam is as impressive as ever.

Ocean Falls has a post office, city hall, and pleasure boat dock with 20-amp power, good water (let the hoses run a while to clean them out), and reasonable docking fees. The Discovery Coast ferry service, initiated in 1996, calls at Ocean Falls, and perhaps the increase in tourist visits will stimulate local business.

The Ocean Falls Lodge, nicely renovated, has showers and laundry facilities as well as a cafe open for lunch about five days a week. Ocean Falls Fishing Lodge provides accommodations for sportfishing enthusiasts. The general store in Martin River (hours 9 a.m. to 4 p.m.) will deliver your groceries to the dock in the evening. Old roads around town, and the trail to Link Lake above the falls, offer the best opportunity for exercise for miles around. The lake, itself, is quite extensive but the dam site is choked with stumps, slash, and debris left from some former commercial operation.

Jenny Inlet

Chart 3781; entrance: 52°16.00′ N, 127°37.50′ W; anchor: 52°13.75′ N, 127°35.60′ W (NAD 27)

> *Jenny Inlet is entered between Neavold Point and Fosbak Point. Several streams empty into the head of the inlet and drying banks extend off the mouths of these streams.* (p. 82, SD)

Jenny Inlet is undergoing a large clear-cutting operation with a log dump located on the east shore.

Anchorage is reported in 11 fathoms at the head of the inlet over an unrecorded bottom.

Elcho Harbour

Chart 3781; entrance: 52°22.40′ N, 127°28.90′ W; anchor: 52°23.83′ N, 127°31.8′ W (NAD 27)

> *Elcho Harbour is entered 1 mile north of Hokonson Point; Elcho Creek, at its head, has an extensive flat at its mouth. A booming ground is on the south shore (1989).* (p. 82, SD)

Elcho Harbour is a scenic fjord which affords good protection from up- and downslope wind and chop. The head of the harbor is a good place to anchor while visiting Mackenzie Park. The harbor has depths of 10 to 20 fathoms. A barge anchored off the head of the inlet in 1993 was resting high on the beach in 1996. The valley behind the head is V-shaped with very steep sides.

Anchor in about 12 fathoms over a mud bottom with very good holding.

Mackenzie Rock

Sir Alexander Mackenzie Rock Provincial Park

Chart 3781; anchor: 52°22.69′ N, 127°28.22′ W (NAD 27)

> *Sir Alexander Mackenzie Park extends NE from Elcho Point. A cairn marks the place where Sir Alexander Mackenzie landed on July 21, 1793, at the end of his cross country journey. Mackenzie's Rock lies close off this cairn.* (p. 82, SD)

This small park, commemorating the first recorded walk across the North American continent, is the place where Alexander Mackenzie became convinced that the Bella Coola River did in fact flow into the Pacific Ocean. Interestingly, Mackenzie just missed sighting George Vancouver who was on his first sailing expedition to this area in July 1793.

When you're approaching the park, the obelisk monument makes a good landmark. The shoreline off Mackenzie Rock is steep-to and, in calm weather, you can anchor off the small beach, climb the rocks to the monument, then scramble down to look at the message. However, if you prefer not to anchor and go ashore, the inscription on Mackenzie Rock can easily be seen from your boat. Mackenzie wrote on the rock: "Alex Mackenzie from Canada by land 22 July 1793." The message, originally written in vermilion grease, has been chiseled into the stone.

The anchor site off the beach, while good in calm weather, affords little shelter in any winds. If you anchor here, be prepared to leave at any moment. Were an outflow wind to come up, you might find your boat carried around the corner. Better protection can be found nearby at the head of Elcho Harbour.

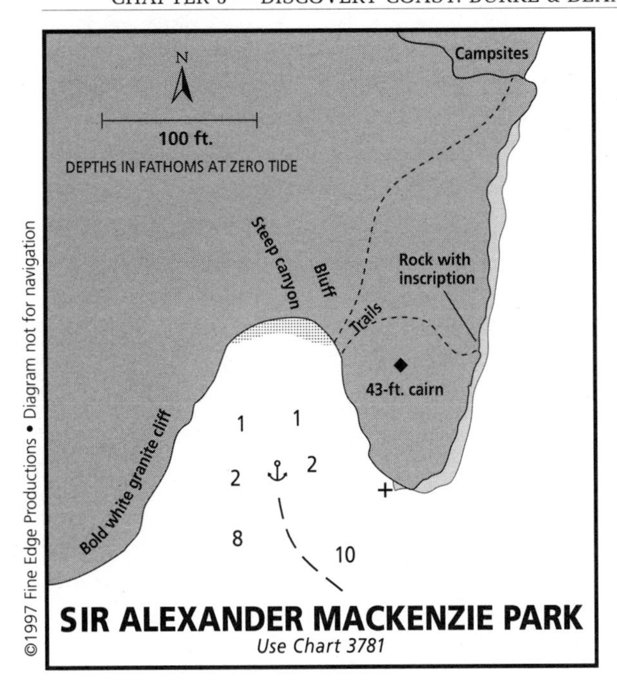

SIR ALEXANDER MACKENZIE PARK
Use Chart 3781

From the beach, you have a wonderful panorama of snow-clad peaks that rim the nearby fjords. A high waterfall across Elcho Harbour on the west shore breaks the perfect silence, a silence otherwise so profound that you can hear the sound of bird wings and the swoop of hawks between the trees. This is a nice place to contemplate the heroic feats accomplished by the area's native peoples and early explorers.

There are attractive campsites on a small stream just to the east. Notice how the hemlock roots on the west side of the bight cling like large spider webs to the granite walls.

Anchor temporarily in 2 to 3 fathoms over a gravel and rock bottom with fair holding if your anchor is well set; swinging room is limited.

McKay Bay

Charts 3781, 3729; entrance: 52°24.10′ N, 127°26.40′ W; position: 52°24.77′ N, 127°26.05′ W (NAD 27)

McKay Bay is out of the current and downslope winds of Dean Channel. Temporary shelter may be obtained in the small nook at the head of the bay, avoiding the drift logs which indicate exposure to southerly winds.

Cascade Inlet

Chart 3729; entrance: 52°24.60′ N, 127°24.60′ W; anchor: 52°36.40′ N, 127°37.20′ W (NAD 27)

> *The fairway is deep and the inlet is free of dangers. At the head of the inlet there is a mud and grass flat but this flat is steep-to and depths off it are too great for anchorage.* (p. 82, SD)

Cascade Inlet has majestic scenery similar to that of upper Dean Channel and South Bentinck Arm. The inlet is only half the width of Dean or Burke channels so the steep slopes, some of which exceed 45-degree angles, appear all the more impressive. Roughly every half-mile of its 13-mile length there is a spectacular cascade or waterfall. Some of the crevasses or canyons are seldom touched by sunlight and reveal patches of snow lasting into late summer when the peaks are bare.

Cascade Inlet can provide welcome escape from the afternoon upslope winds and chop in Dean Channel. The inlet was named by George Vancouver, for obvious reasons, and he considered it one of the loveliest he had seen.

Anchorage is reported to be found at the head of the inlet on the east shore in 10 fathoms, soft bottom.

Eucott Bay

Chart 3729; anchor: 52°27.25′ N, 127°18.95′ W (NAD 27)

> *Eucott Bay is 3 miles NE of Fougner Point. A drying mud bank extends a short distance off the NW side of the bay and from its head. . .*
>
> *Anchorage with good shelter can be obtained by small craft in 8 to 12 feet (2.4 to 3.7 m) in Eucott Bay.* (p. 82, SD)

Eucott Bay is the best-protected anchorage in these parts. Green grass rings the high-tide line and spindly trees cling tenaciously to vertical cracks along the steep granite cliffs. On the south shore, a remarkable stream cascades a thousand feet down from snowy peaks, emptying directly into the saltwater. The unnamed 4,665-foot peak to the southwest has a cirque on its eastern side which holds snow patches until late summer.

Hot springs, Eucott Bay

The 2,000-foot vertical grey monolith on the northeast side of the bay rises from a talus and treed slope in a bold face reminiscent of Yosemite's Half Dome, while the rugged, jagged volcanic ridge of the 3,780-foot peak to the northwest plays hide-and-seek with scudding clouds. The grassy meadows echo with bird calls while a seal scans the bay waiting for the incoming tide to bring fresh fish. Giant mussels grow at the bottom of the bay in great clusters. But wait! If you think we're getting too gushy, paradise has its blemishes—two clear-cut patches along the west shore catch your view across Eucott Bay.

In the crater-like basin, the hot springs emerge from a rock wall below the southwest base of "Half Dome." The hot pool, formed of natural rock augmented with some concrete slabs, is large enough for about six people, and sadly in need of care. Porcelain pipe carries the water to the pools. There is a wading pool and a "kiddie" pool below, not far from the high-tide line. The location of the pools is in line with the old pilings at the northeast corner of the bay. Since the bay is quite flat, it may be best to visit the pools at high water and carry your dinghy back to the water, or tie it to one of the pilings, so you can retrieve it after your soak.

The view from the hot tub and the upper end of the bay looks out onto the beautiful valley and peaks to the northwest. Eucott Bay and Hot Springs should be preserved for public use in its present form—it is too valuable to squander.

Unfortunately, there are pieces of 6-inch aluminum irrigation pipe scattered about in the water, indicating that someone tried to harness the hot springs at one time and move the water farther south.

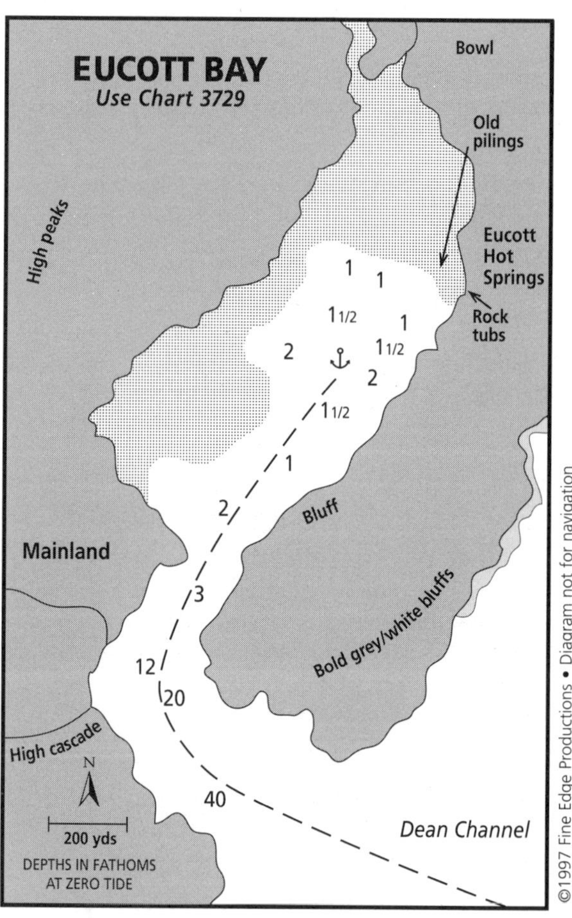

The bay is too shallow to anchor off the upper end. The inner bay is reported to be nearly calm when a 40-knot westerly is blowing in the outside channel. The inner bay largely dries at zero tide; however, there is a large flat-bottomed area of 1.5 fathoms (we measured it on a 1.8-foot tide) where you can find very good holding in a mud bottom.

Anchor in 1.5 fathoms over brown sand and soft mud with very good holding. There is enough swinging room for a number of boats, even at zero tide.

Nascall Bay

Charts 3729, 3730; anchor:
52°29.63′ N, 127°16.43′ W (NAD 27)

> *Nascall Bay is 3 miles NNW of Ram Bluff. . .*
> *Anchorage for small craft can be obtained in Nascall Bay but it is exposed to SE winds. A steady current flows out of the bay from the Nascall River.* (p. 82, SD)

Nascall Bay, on the west shore of Upper Dean Channel, lies 2.8 miles northwest of Ram Bluff. The outer bay is deep, but the inner bay which is the delta of the Nascall River, is quite shallow. When entering the inner bay, avoid the mid-bay rock on the drying spit by staying close to the north shore. The current here can be quite strong, making maneuvering difficult. Good anchorage can be obtained, out of the current, on the south side of the drying spit in 7 fathoms. At high water you can ease your bow up to a small waterfall on the south side of the bay and fill your water jugs.

Nascall Hotsprings Resort under construction

Nascall Bay, anchorage behind spit

The land around Nascall Bay, an original land grant dating back to 1906, is now owned by Frank Tracey who is in the process of constructing a large resort with hot tubs that will capture the waters of Nascall Hot Springs. The old bathhouse with two tubs has been razed, and plans are to have the new bathhouse, including changing rooms, a lounge and bar, open by spring of 1997. Future plans include construction of a 20-room lodge on the north point that will cater to charter outfits, as well as a marina in deep water on the south side of the bay with 1,600 feet of dock space. Six docks are scheduled to be in place by summer 1997, including the main dock and a ramp in front of the lodge.

The lodge will eventually have fresh water available for pleasure boats, and a nominal fee will be charged for taking a hot bath. Temperature of the water, which has few minerals and is drinkable, is around 113°F.

A new trail leads from the bath lodge to the point above Dean Channel where there is a lovely view. The trail passes muskeg ponds, mossy "gardens" covered with ground dogwood, ferns, blueberries and other plants, and forests of hemlock and cedar.

Pleasure boaters wishing to anchor are advised to do so on the south side of the bay protected from the river stream by the rock and gravel peninsula—the site of the eventual marina. Boats unfamiliar with the area should inquire on-site.

Anchor in 7 fathoms over a sand and gravel bottom with unknown holding.

Helicopter logging in Dean Channel

Helicopter Logging

Helicopter logging is increasingly seen along the British Columbia coast. This involves transporting the logs from where they are felled (perhaps high on a mountainside) to a log-booming area in the saltwater directly below by means of cables attached to a large helicopter. In some cases, the logs are deposited directly onto a log-carrying barge. This particular method avoids the need for extensive logging roads, and erosion is thus minimized or eliminated.

In Dean Channel, recently, we watched the operation of *Helioforester*, a large support ship for a helicopter operation. Trees were logged out of view high on a 1,500-foot bench, two miles east of Cascade Point. The helicopter picked up the logs and deposited them in the channel with a round-trip time of well under ten minutes. An old whaler, *David Frederick*, took part in the log-booming operation on the opposite side of the channel, east of Fougner Point.

Helicopter logging is a dangerous, high-performance operation—maintain a safe distance since tree limbs frequently fall off in flight!

Nascall Island and Rocks

Charts 3729, 3730; position: 52°30.60′ N, 127°14.70′ W (NAD 27)

Nascall Rocks are a major haul-out place for seals. The small trees on the rocks bend upslope, indicating the direction of prevailing winds.

The passage between Nascall Island and the mainland has 4 fathoms minimum. The bight on the west shore, northwest of Nascall Island, can be used as a temporary stop in fair weather. The bight dries almost completely at low water and has several rocks on either side. There is an attractive grassy meadow on the south side of the creek which makes a good kayak haul-out and campsite.

When you're returning from the north, you can see a waterfall high up on the crest that falls into the valley north of the bight.

Carlson Inlet

Chart 3730; entrance: 52°33.80′ N, 127°13.00′ W; head of inlet: 52°34.80′ N, 127°24.30′ W (NAD 27)

> *Carlson Inlet, on the NW side of the channel, does not provide anchorage except for small craft off the drying flat at the head.* (p. 82, SD)

Carlson Inlet is the most sheltered spot in upper Dean Channel, out of both up- and downslope winds and the current. The head of the inlet stretches back into a series of V-shaped valleys where waterfalls cascade down on both sides. This is a scenic, quiet and serene place. The south entrance point has bright white rock cliffs. North of here, the rocks are darker in color.

Upper Dean Channel has high mountains on either side which, as in South Bentinck Arm, reach to over 7,000 feet. The peaks have perpetual snow patches, and some of the gullies are filled with snow well into the summer. There are fewer signs of logging in upper Dean Channel than in

South Bentinck Arm. It is deep and steep-to, and we were only able to get one good set out of nearly a dozen tries in 4 to 10 fathoms just off and across the drying flat. We could not get a bottom sample, but it was consistent with soft sand.

A small 6-fathom shelf is just west of the charted 15-foot rock on the south shore. A small creek comes to the west side of the rock, and there is a very small bench of 6 fathoms, brown sand and mud, that gives fair holding. It would be appropriate, as well as convenient and easy, to use a stern tie to one of the vertical tree snags along shore, since the shore is so steep-to.

Anchor in 4 to 10 fathoms over a soft bottom. Holding depends on how well the anchor is set.

Skowquiltz Bay

Chart 3730; position: 52°35.80′ N, 127°09.20′ W (NAD 27)

Skowquiltz Bay is 2.5 miles NE of Carlson Inlet …
Anchorage for small craft can be obtained in the NE corner of Skowquiltz Bay, in about 12 fathoms (22 m), close to the edge of the drying flat. A drying rock lies close off Skowquiltz Point. (pp. 82, 83, SD)

Skowquiltz River cuts a deep V-shaped valley on the west shore of Dean Channel. As it is exposed to the south, Skowquiltz Bay can be used as a temporary anchorage in fair weather only.

Purcell Rock and Ironbound Islet

Chart 3730; position: 52°39.40′ N, 127°01.00′ W (NAD 27)

Purcell Rock and Ironbound Islet lie in the bay between Sylvester and Engerbrightson Points. This bay offers no anchorage due to its depths and mariners are advised to give it a wide berth to clear Purcell Rock. (p. 83, SD)

Kimsquit Bay

Chart 3730; position: 52°50.20′ N, 126°58.00′ W (NAD 27)

Anchorage can be obtained near the head of Kimsquit Bay, about 0.1 mile offshore, but the water is deep. (p. 84, SD)

Kimsquit Bay lies on the north side of the Dean River outlet immediately north of the old village site of the same name. The water here and near the outlet of the Kimsquit River at the head of Dean Channel is reportedly too deep for convenient anchorage. However, this area is extremely remote and picturesque and is worth a day trip from the more protected anchorages in Carlson Inlet and Nascall Bay. In Kimsquit Bay, a shore tie may be the solution to anchoring along the steep-to shore.

Gunboat Passage

Chart 3720 (inset); east entrance: 52°09.64′ N, 127°55.00′ W; west entrance: 52°10.20′ N, 127°58.50′ W (NAD)

Gunboat Passage leads east from the east end of Seaforth Channel, between Denny Island and Cunningham Island, to the south end of Johnson Channel close to the junction with Fisher Channel. This passage, narrow, intricate and with numerous rocks and kelp patches, is recommended only for small vessels.
Tidal streams in Gunboat Passage are not strong and generally set west. (p. 87, SD)

While Lama Passage is used by all cruise ships and ferries, Gunboat Passage is far more scenic and interesting. We do not recommend entering it without consulting Chart 3720 (inset). Gunboat Passage is protected from the effects of most weather. The range markers are the key to the western part of the passage, while careful judgment of the position of the notch in the bar just south of Maria Island is the key to the eastern entrance. Be sure to use the inset on chart 3720 for navigating intricate Gunboat Passage. *Caution:* Chart 3729 indicates that there is a 4-fathom passage north of Maria Island—this is not the case. It is closed by a string of islands to the shore of Cunningham Island, as shown in the large-scale inset on Chart 3720.

At Draney Point the power lines from the Ocean Falls power station cross under Gunboat Passage.

On the east side of Gunboat Passage, consider anchoring at Forit Bay.

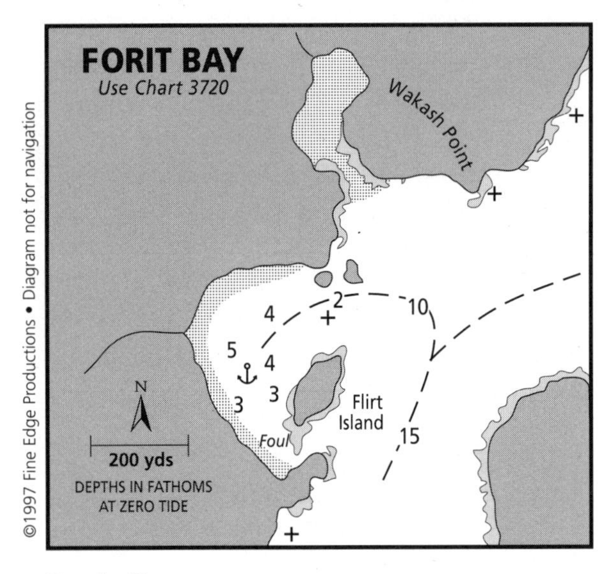

Forit Bay

Chart 3720; anchor: 52°10.38′ N, 127°54.63′ W (NAD 27)

> *Forit Bay is entered between a rock which dries 11 feet (3.4 m) and a rock awash lying close north of Flirt Island. This narrow passage has a least depth of 3 fathoms (5.5 m). Good sheltered anchorage for small craft can be obtained in about 5 fathoms (9 m), mud, close west of Flirt Island.* (p. 87, SD)

Forit Bay is a well-protected anchorage with excellent shelter from southerlies. While it may get some downslope katabatic gusts, it receives little chop. It is quiet and secluded and, if not for the power lines on the west shore, the setting would be pristine.

To enter, stay well north of Flirt Island, passing between the large 75-foot-long rock, 200 feet off the north shore, and an underwater rock to the south. We stay within about 50 feet of the large rock and have no problems with a 2-fathom minimum in the fairway. The bottom of the bay is flat and is 3 to 5 fathoms deep.

Anchor west of Flirt Island in 3 to 4 fathoms over a mud-and-pebble bottom with good holding.

Hampden Bay

Chart 3720; anchor: 52°09.12′ N, 127°54.70′ W (NAD 27)

> *Anchorage can be obtained in Hampden Bay in 20 fathoms (37 m), mud bottom, about 0.1 mile from its head.* (p. 87, SD)

Hampden Bay, on the south side of the east entrance to Gunboat Passage, affords excellent protection in southerly weather and good protection in all other weather. It's a good place to anchor while you wait for proper tides and currents in Gunboat Passage. The foreshore is steep-to off the gravel beach, with eel grass lining the one-fathom curve. The head of the beach is grassy and is a good kayak haul-out spot.

When traversing Gunboat Passage, favor a midchannel course between Denny Point and Maria Island, passing south of the rock which dries on a one-foot tide.

Anchor in 10 fathoms off the head of the easternmost creek draining into the bay. Mud bottom, good holding.

Gosse Bay

Chart 3720; anchor: 52°09.94′ N, 127°55.68′ W (NAD 27)

> *Anchorage for small vessels can be obtained in Gosse Bay in 8 fathoms (15 m), mud.* (p. 87, SD)

Gosse Bay, off the west shore in the middle of Gunboat Passage, is a safe anchorage. It is out of the current, in 7 fathoms over a fairly large area. Anchor in a well-protected cove about 200 yards northeast of Algerine Island, avoiding the large grass-covered rock east of the island.

Anchor in 7 fathoms, brown mud, shells, and some kelp with fair-to-good holding.

Dunn Bay

Chart 3720; position: 52°10.35′ N, 127°58.10′ W (NAD 27)

Dunn Bay is steep-to, rather rocky, and a marginal anchorage. The next anchorage west is the preferred site with more convenient depths and bombproof protection.

"Gunboat Lagoon Cove"

Chart 3720 (inset); entrance: 52°10.40′ N, 127°58.75′ W; anchor: 52°10.59′ N, 127°58.55′ W (NAD 27)

Two bays, fronted by islets and drying ledges, are on the north side of the passage, about 1 mile east of Manson Point. The east bay, which has an islet 6 feet (1.8 m) high in its entrance, provides good shelter for small vessels. (p. 87, SD)

The best-protected anchorage in Gunboat Passage can be found in what we call Lagoon Cove. The cove is located a half-mile northwest of Dunn Point and one mile east of Manson Point on the north shore of Gunboat Passage. It offers excellent shelter from all winds and seas. To enter the cove, pass east of an islet that has one short tree and a snag at its summit. The fairway has 2 to 3 fathoms minimum midway between the islet and the eastern shore. Avoid the two submerged rocks, awash on about a 10-foot tide, that extend 75 yards from the west shore at the entrance to the lagoon rapids. You can explore the rapids and the lagoon at slack water only. We have been unable to locate the trail marked on the chart.

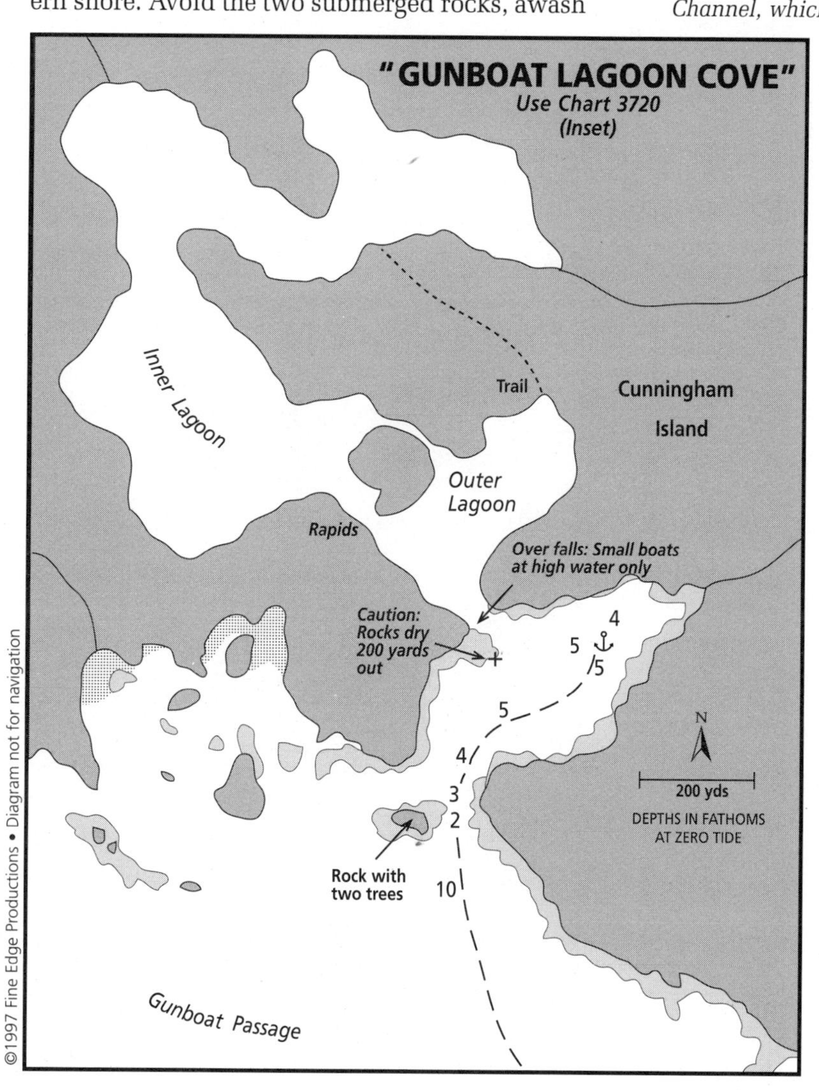

Anchor in 5 fathoms slightly east of the lagoon entrance. The bottom is stiff brown mud with very good holding.

Johnson Channel

Chart 3720; south entrance:
52°11.70′ N, 127°53.20′ W; north entrance:
52°18.20′ N, 127°56.50′ W (NAD 27)

Georgie Point is the SE entrance point of Johnson Channel, which is free of dangers in the fairway. (p. 87, SD)

Johnson Channel connects Fisher Channel to scenic Roscoe Inlet and Bullock Channel for those headed toward Spiller Channel.

Bainbridge Cove

Chart 3720; entrance:
52°11.70′ N, 127°59.00′ W
(NAD 27)

Bainbridge Cove, 0.5 mile NW of Madigan Point, is only suitable for small craft as it is shallow and encumbered by rocks and islets. (p. 88, SD)

Bainbridge Cove has a foul entrance and can be safely entered only by sportfishing boats using extra caution.

"Beaumont Island"

Chart 3720; entrance (east):
52°17.45′ N, 127°56.40′ W;
anchor (south end):
52°17.40′ N, 127°56.68′ W
(NAD 27)

Anchorage for small craft can be obtained west of Beaumont Island. (p. 88, SD)

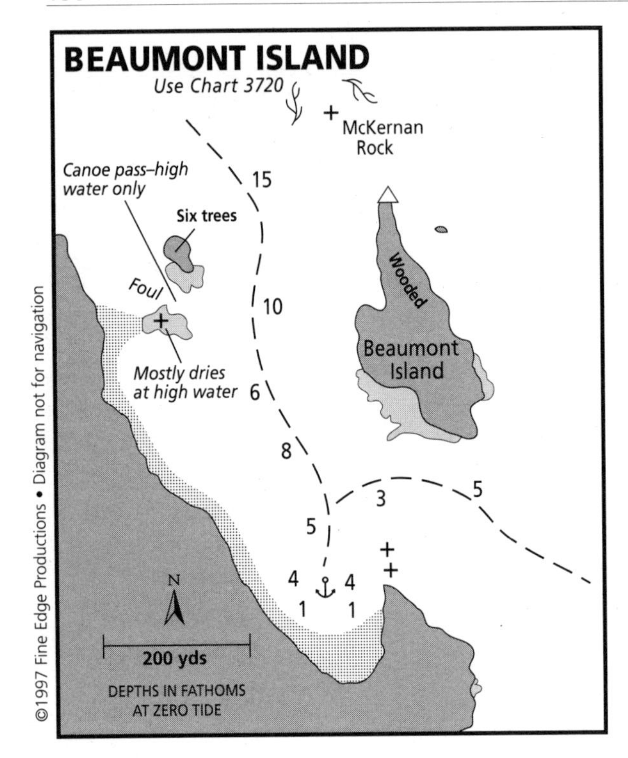

On the northwest corner of Johnson Channel, Beaumont Island Cove offers good protection from southerly storms. It is well sheltered from all weather except strong williwaws sweeping down the 3,000- to 4,000-foot peaks to the north.

Chart 3720 is not too accurate in its portrait of this cove. The rocks off the southeast point extend about 100 yards beyond the trees. The spit at the north end provides more shelter than indicated, and you can anchor off its southern side. All-in-all, this cove provides welcome shelter and a comfortable anchorage in an impressive setting.

Anchor (south end) in 4 fathoms over a sandy bottom with good holding.

Roscoe Inlet

Chart 3940 metric; entrance: 52°19.40′ N, 127°56.30′ W (NAD 83)

Roscoe Inlet extends 21 miles north and east in a winding manner. The shores are very rugged and, for the most part, the inlet is free of mid-channel dangers. Tidal streams in Roscoe Inlet are negligible. (p. 88, SD)

Photo by Herb Nickles

Time for a swim, head of Roscoe Inlet

Roscoe Inlet has some of the most scenic and striking granite faces and domes that you can find along the entire Inside Passage. With publication of the new Chart 3940 in 1996, the magnificent scenery and park-like setting in Roscoe Inlet is becoming known to cruising boats. Except for some logging just inside the narrows, the entire inlet is pristine and worthy of park status.

Strong summer westerlies rarely have much

Photo by Herb Nickles

Rock wall, east side Florence Peninsula, Roscoe Inlet

effect past Clatse Bay and definitely not past the narrows. The head of Roscoe Inlet receives little tidal flow and swimming off your boat is a real joy when the fresh surface-water reaches depths of 3-4 feet with a water temperature of 75°F during long summer days.

Clatse Bay

Chart 3940 metric; entrance:
52°21.80′ N, 127°51.40′ W; anchor:
52°20.53′ N, 127°50.54′ W (NAD 83)

The shores of the bay are fringed with drying shingle ledges on which there are above-water rocks. Clatse Creek flows into the head of the bay over a drying flat. (p. 88, SD)

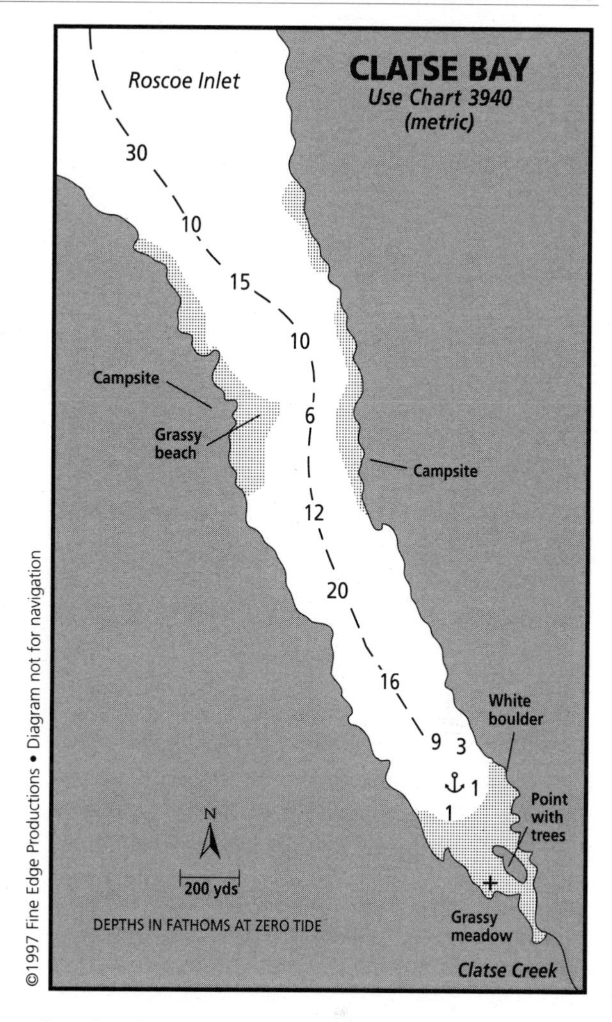

Clatse Bay, on the south shore of Roscoe Inlet, offers good anchorage in all weather except strong outflow gales. The bay is a small classic fjord with high snowy peaks to the southeast. Loons, seagulls and honkers find the bay and the flat off Clatse Creek most desirable. An earthslide six-tenths of a mile inside the bay reaches to mid-channel and you should favor the east shore. This spit provides a kayak haul-out and campsite with anchorage possible in 1 or 2 fathoms off the grassy point. The most secure anchorage can be found off the drying flat near the east shore not far from a bare white boulder. The mud flat is steep-to and largely dries. The point with trees in the center of the flat is a good place to leave your dinghy while you explore the meadows and creek to the south.

Anchor in 3 fathoms over mud and some wood debris with good holding.

Shack Bay

Chart 3940 metric; anchor:
52°23.34′ N, 127°51.62′ W (NAD 83)

Shack Bay, 1 mile north of Clatse Bay, is fringed with drying shingle ledges on which there are some above-water rocks.

Anchorage for small vessels can be obtained in the north portion of Shack Bay in about 10 fathoms (18 m). (p. 88, SD)

Shack Bay offers good protection from northwest winds at the north end of the bay off a small grassy beach. This place has an excellent view of the snow cornices on 4,010-foot Mount Keys four miles to the south and the perpendicular grey granite wall just east of Shack Bay. Avoid the natural rock breakwater which extends about 300 feet out from the grassy point on the northwest corner of the bay.

Anchor in 6 fathoms, mud bottom with good holding.

Ripley Bay

Chart 3940 metric; entrance:
52°24.70′ N, 127°53.30′ W; anchor:
52°25.38′ N, 127°53.30′ W (NAD 83)

Ripley Bay, 2 miles north of Shack Bay, is too deep for convenient anchorage.

A rock, with less than 6 feet (2 m) over it, lies about 0.1 mile from the east shore and 0.8 mile

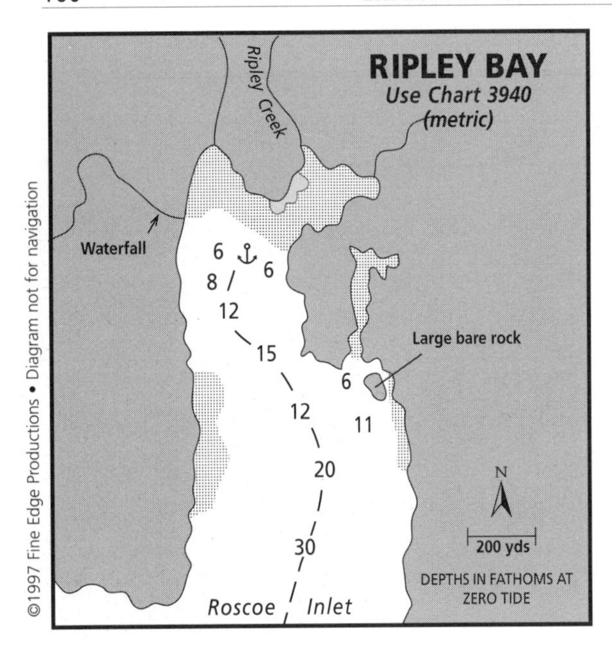

NW of the west entrance point of Ripley Bay. (p. 88, SD)

Ripley offers temporary anchorage off the steep-to drying flat at the northeast corner of the bay. There is a waterfall on the west side of the bay as well as a large creek at the head.

Anchor in about 6 fathoms, smooth mud bottom with fair holding. Consider using a stern anchor on the flat to maintain a good bite on the steep-to face.

Boukind Bay

Chart 3940 metric; entrance:
52°27.00′ N, 127°56.30′ W; anchor:
52°27.75′ N, 127°56.25′ W (NAD 83)

> *Boukind Bay, 5 miles NNW of Roscoe Point, has shores fringed by ledges but is free of dangers outside a distance of 150 feet (46 m).*
>
> *Anchorage for small vessels can be obtained off a bight on the east shore of Boukind Bay in 17 fathoms (31 m). More confined anchorage can be obtained in 18 feet (5.5 m) near the head of the bay.* (p. 88, SD)

Boukind Bay, one mile north of Roscoe Narrows, provides very good anchorage in most weather. The anchor site is on a flat shelf which starts approximately 300 yards off the shore and gently tapers to a small creek outlet.

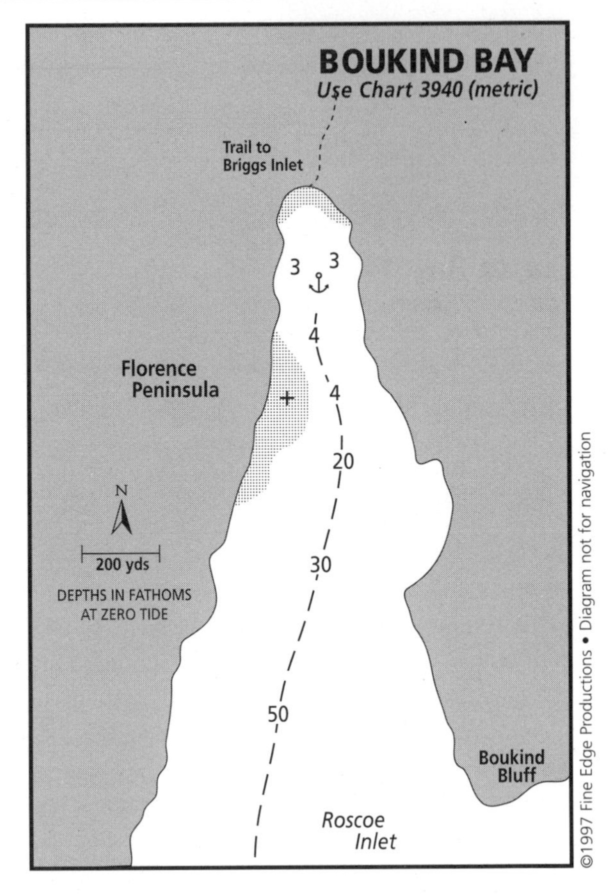

There is a primitive animal trail which extends a quarter-mile due north to Briggs Lagoon. This is a scenic and interesting hike through the rain forest, and you should carry a whistle or noisemaker to alert the bears that frequent this trail. Boots are advised because of the muskeg terrain.

Kevin Monahan writes, "In 1980 I awoke here one morning to a serenade of wolves howling. They called and called for over an hour and were answered by more howls, some probably from several miles away. By the time this song reached a crescendo, there must have been hundreds of wolves howling."

Anchor in 5 fathoms over a mud and sand bottom with very good holding.

Roscoe Narrows

Chart 3940 metric; position:
52°26.85′ N, 127°55.70′ W (NAD 83)

Roscoe Narrows is the quarter-mile-wide channel

between Boukind Bluff and Home Point leading east into what we call the "Goosenecks of the Roscoe."

Kevin Monahan states, "In some freezing weather, I have seen the inlet choke with ice several inches thick from Roscoe Narrows to the head."

"Goosenecks of the Roscoe"

Chart 3940 metric

The upper end of Roscoe Inlet, starting with Roscoe Narrows, could easily be mistaken for one of the world's finest alpine freshwater lakes. The serpentine route up Roscoe Inlet flows between granite domes which disappear vertically into the ocean below. Water streams down the cracks and slab faces and snow patches linger on mountain tops and in gullies into late summer. The granite ridges attempt to close the inlet east of Quartcha Bay and divert the currents the way "goosenecks" do in a giant river. Overhanging granite "chimneys," amphitheaters and arches dot the landscape. Nothing manmade is in sight. With no icefields to cool the inlet, summer saltwater temperatures exceed 70°F. The farther we go into the Goosenecks, the slower we go and the less we say.

Surely this place begs for long-term protection for its superior natural environment.

Quartcha Bay

Chart 3940 metric; entrance:
52°30.10′ N, 127°50.60′ W; anchor:
52°30.74′ N, 127°50.18′ W (NAD 83)

> *Quartcha Bay has depths too great for anchorage except for small craft close off the drying flat near the head; caution should be exercised as the edge of the flat is steep-to.* (p. 88, SD)

Quartcha Bay is a beautiful cul-de-sac with high granite mountains on each side and two main U-shaped valleys emptying into its head. The western valley follows Quartcha Creek, winding in a broad turn to the north. A large grassy flat hides the creek behind a small peninsula. The northeast canyon is a classic glacier-carved shape with a high cascade falling directly down 2,000 feet from an alpine lake high in a granite bowl above. The creek is unnamed and has a cabin and very good campsite in the trees at its outlet behind the grass shore.

If you enjoy alpine mountains, Quartcha Bay is one of the most spectacular anchorages in the world. Bold dark grey granite walls overhang the bay while evergreens cling on vertical ledges, filling the valleys and spreading their branches over saltwater in a perfectly horizontal line. There are no drift logs or evidence of chop. On a sunny day serenity rules. The saltwater is 68°F (near the surface!) and swimming is in order. There are some pesky deer flies, but luckily, they can easily be captured or driven off.

Temporary anchorage can be found along the steep margins of the drying flat along a 2- fathom shelf. Watch the tide level and signs of upslope winds.

Anchor in 2 to 4 fathoms on the steep-to shore over a sand and mud bottom with fair-to-good holding.

Roscoe Creek

Chart 3940 metric; position:
52°28.14′ N, 127°44.45′ W (NAD 83)

> *Roscoe Creek, 1.6 miles NE of Latch Point, flows into a drying bay.* (p. 88, SD)

Roscoe Creek flows from another beautiful 5-mile-long U-shaped valley. The shore is steep-to and extends farther into the bay on its west margin than is indicated on the chart.

The fairway between treed Latch Island and the grassy delta on the south side of the narrow channel is 12 fathoms.

"Bitter End of Roscoe Inlet"

Chart 3940 metric, position:
52°27.02′ N, 127°42.94′ W (NAD 83)

> *Anchorage can be obtained about 0.5 mile from the head of Roscoe Inlet in depths of 14 to 20 fathoms (26 to 37 m).* (p. 88, SD)

At its head, the finale of Roscoe Inlet features a crescendo of snow-covered ridge to the east, large grassy meadow on the valley delta to the southwest, high peaks, and silence. Bears roam the high meadows. With a water temperature as high as 75°F, swimming is refreshing in the fresh- and saltwater bay. There are no signs of serious weather reaching the far end of the inlet and winds largely die out along the way. There is seldom any wind here. The old log dump ramp on the delta shows fresh signs of caterpillar tractor tracks even as alders fill in the old clear-cut scars in the beautiful unnamed valley.

Anchorage can be found at the bitter end of the bay or temporarily, for bear watching, off the steep-to creek delta to the west.

Anchor in 8 to 10 fathoms at the head of the inlet over a bottom of brown sand and mud with occasional rocks and wood debris, with generally very good holding.

Return Channel

Charts 3940 metric, 3720; east entrance: 52°18.20′ N, 127°58.20′ W; west entrance: 52°16.90′ N, 128°12.60′ W (NAD 83)

> *Return Channel connects the north end of Johnson Channel to Seaforth Channel.*
>
> *Eddies that can be troublesome to small craft sometimes occur off Donald Point in the vicinity of Lorne Islet. Disturbed water can also be encountered in the vicinity of the 10 fathom (18.3 m) shoal lying 0.6 mile WNW of Jagers Point.* (p. 88, SD)

Return Channel connects Roscoe Inlet, Briggs Inlet, Bullock Channel and Spiller Channels. There are several good anchorages along the way (east to west), namely Beaumont Island, Troup Narrows, Morehouse Bay, Wigham Cove and Raven Cove.

Except for turbulence noted in *Sailing Directions*, Return Channel has protected waters and is usually very calm.

Morehouse Bay

Chart 3940 metric; entrance: 52°17.40′ N, 128°06.25′ W; anchor: 52°16.28′ N, 128°05.10′ W, (NAD 83)

> *Morehouse Bay has several islands and drying and submerged rocks within it.*
>
> *Anchorage, suitable for small craft, can be obtained in Morehouse Bay over mud and sand bottom in the cove in the SW part of the bay. When approaching this anchorage take care to avoid the dangers on both sides of the approach.* (p. 90, SD)

Morehouse Bay, 4 miles within the west entrance of Return Channel, has good protection from all weather deep at the head of the bay. The southwest cove in Morehouse Bay is easy to enter and provides good shelter in 12 to 15 fathoms. The cove in the southeast portion of the bay has very good shelter in 7 to 9 fathoms, but you must cross or avoid the two shoal areas shown on Chart 3940 which are covered with about 4 feet at zero tide.

Anchor in 8 fathoms over mud and sand bottom with very good holding.

Raven Cove

Chart 3720; anchor: 52°14.93′ N, 128°08.97′ W (NAD 27)

> *Raven Cove, near the west end of Chatfield Island, is useless as an anchorage except for small craft. Beak Island and drying rocks lie in the entrance*

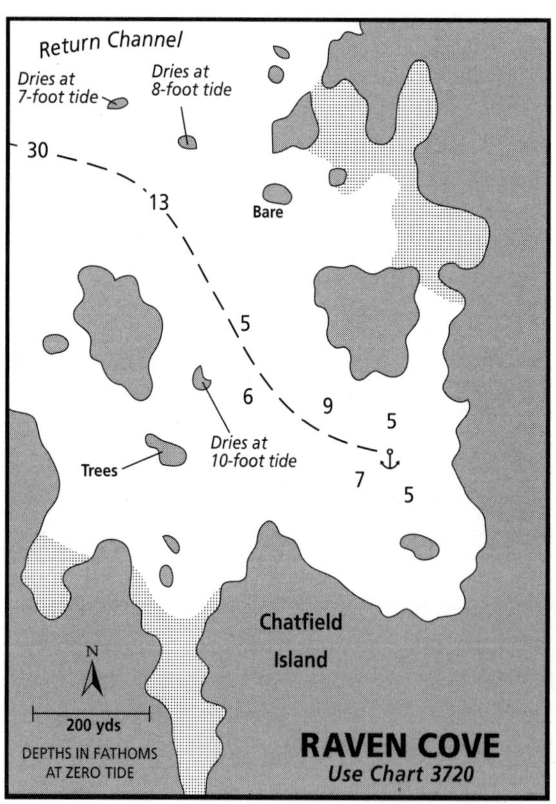

to the cove and drying rocks extend up to 300 feet (91 m) offshore between Beak Island and Noon Point, 0.8 mile west. (p. 90, SD)

Raven Cove offers good shelter deep in the southeast corner of the bay. The bottom is somewhat irregular and you need to avoid the rocks in the approach.

Anchor in 6 to 7 fathoms over a mixed bottom with good holding if well set.

"Dearth Island Cove"

Chart 3720; anchor (south):
52°14.98′ N, 127°56.58′ W (NAD 27)

The south side of Dearth Island has a small cove which, while open to the west and not generally considered a viable anchorage, is in fact an intimate scenic cove in calm weather, offering good protection from everything except the prevailing westerlies. The cove is almost landlocked and shows little evidence of exposure to anything except southwest chop. This is one of the few anchor sites along Seaforth Channel where you will not feel the wake of passing cruise ships or large commercial craft.

Anchorage can be found on the north side of island (140) opposite a canoe passage and a small peninsula on the south side of Dearth Island, just north of Beazley Island. Approach from the west only as the area north of Beazley Island is foul.

Anchor in 7 fathoms over a mud bottom with good holding.

Wigham Cove

Charts 3940 metric, 3720; entrance:
52°16.50′ N, 128°10.60′ W; anchor (east end):
52°16.94′ N, 128°10.00′ W (NAD 83)

Wigham Cove, at the south end of Yeo Island, has a drying rock in its entrance; the fairway is west of this rock and about 300 feet (91 m) wide. Two rock islets and a rock awash lie in the middle of the cove.

Anchorage for small craft can be obtained at the NE end of Wigham Cove; the holding ground is

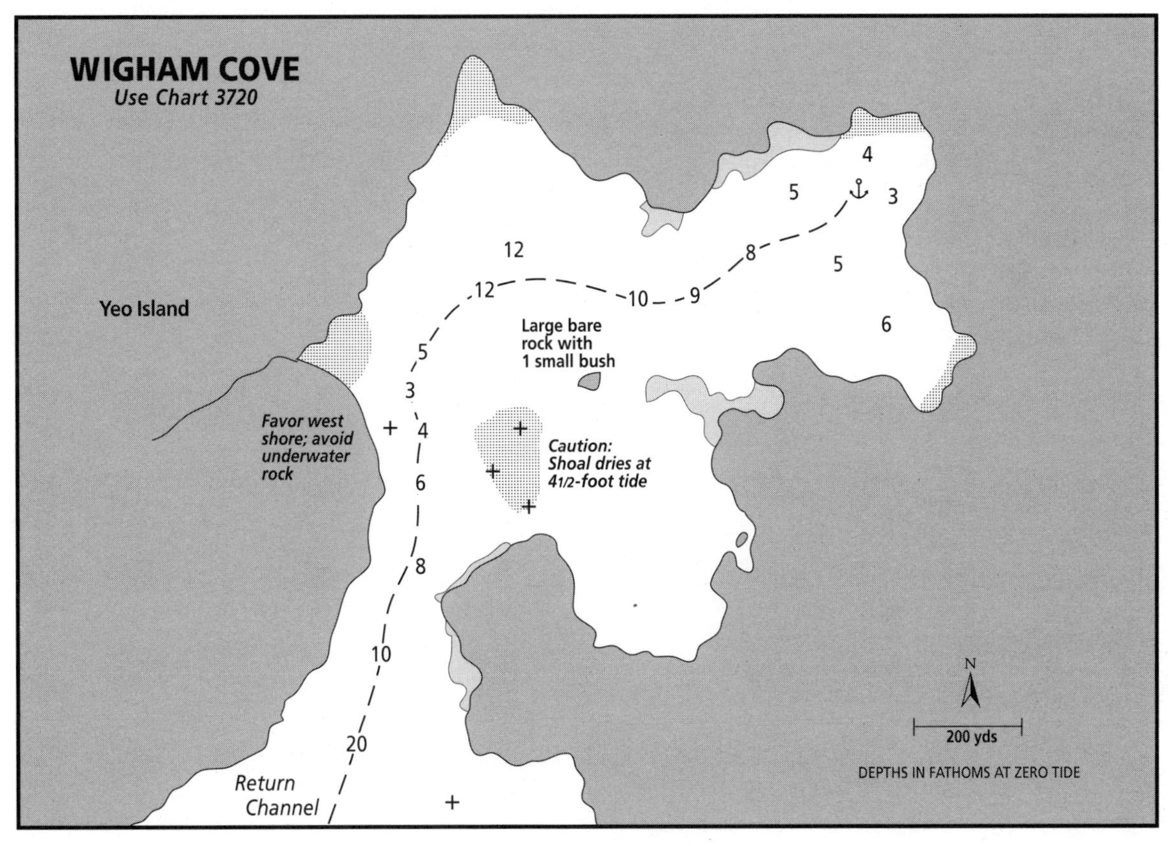

good. When entering Wigham Cove keep to the west side of the channel until the islets in the middle of the cove are abeam, then pass to the north of them. (p. 90, SD)

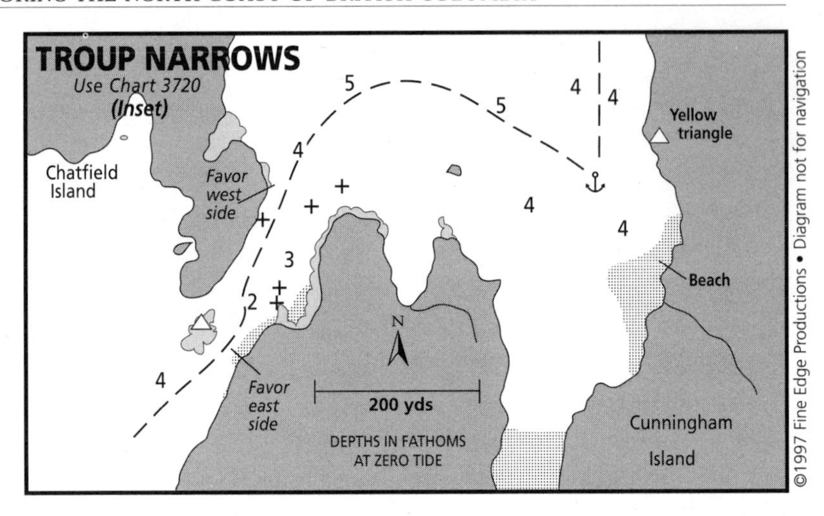

Wigham Cove offers perhaps the most secure and easy-access anchorage in the area. The entrance channel is narrow and you must favor the west shore to avoid the large shoal extending well into midchannel. Commercial and larger boats find anchorage in the north end of the cove while smaller boats find a little more shelter in the east end of the cove. The bottom in Wigham Cove is a flat 10 to 15 fathoms, and there is room for a number of boats. This is a popular place when the west end of Seaforth Channel is fog-bound.

Anchor (east end) in 5 fathoms over stinky mud known locally as "loon shit" with very good holding.

Troup Narrows ("Deer Passage")

Charts 3720 (inset), 3940 metric; position: 52°06.00′ N, 128°00.00′ W (NAD 27)

Troup Passage, known locally as Deer Passage, leads SW from Return Channel to Seaforth Channel. The north entrance, north of Troup Narrows, has islands, shoal rocks and rocks awash in it, and should not be attempted without local knowledge.

Anchorage for small craft can be obtained in the east part of the north entrance to Troup Passage, but local knowledge is advised to enter between the islands.

Troup Narrows has a drying rock and rocks awash lying up to 200 feet (61 m) off the Cunningham Island side, a drying reef near the south end, and depths of 2 to 3 fathoms (3.7 to 5.4 m) in mid-channel. Tidal streams in the narrows are about 2 kn. (pp. 91–92, SD)

Troup Narrows (Deer Passage) is a calm, well-sheltered destination that makes a good overnight stop or an extended base camp for further exploration. The beautiful bay is landlocked and has a mostly flat, sandy bottom that is 5 fathoms deep with plenty of swinging room. On the west side of the narrows, you may find pictographs suggesting large human and animal shapes. We transit the north end, keeping close to the east shore of Cunningham Island all the way. We prefer to anchor on the north side of the narrows in a cove to the east, safe from all southerly storms.

Caution: There are many small underwater rocks and obstructions in this area, so until an up-to-date large-scale chart is available, move slowly with good bow lookouts and scout out your projected swinging area. The current is moderate and the narrows are not difficult to transit, but the fairway is narrow and an alert crew is essential. Favor the west shore on the north side, and the east shore on the south, but beware of rocks close off both shores. We have found the water to be clear to about 3 fathoms, so you can see most of the bottom as you transit the center of the passage.

"Troup Narrows Cove"

Charts 3940 metric, 3720; anchor: 52°16.98′ N, 127°59.59′ W (NAD 83)

We call the first cove east of Troup Narrows on the north side Troup Narrows Cove and find it offers excellent protection in all weather. When approaching from the narrows, enter north of the

19-foot island (shown as 17 meters on Chart 3940) because the area south of it is foul. Avoid the shoaling flat off the creek on the east side of the bay.

Anchor in 4 fathoms, brown sand, shells, small rocks and kelp. Fair-to-good holding.

"Discovery Cove"

Chart 3720; entrance: 52°14.20′ N, 128°01.10′ W; anchor: 52°13.78′ N, 128°00.32′ W (NAD 27)

Discovery Cove is our name for the unnamed and undocumented cove on the west side of Cunningham Island, 5.5 miles due northeast from Shearwater. This overlooked and seldom-visited cove is centrally located in the middle of the Discovery Coast and provides very good shelter in all weather. This scenic place is surrounded by high peaks and granite ridges forming a landlocked bowl with a pristine environment. The entrance bar has irregular depths and, in keeping with the spirit of exploration, we recommend you enter slowly with alert lookouts on the bow. Anchorage can be found almost anywhere in the bay. We prefer to anchor in either of the two nooks on the north side of the cove. This is a good, quiet place to explore by dinghy or kayak and it's only 8 miles from bustling Bella Bella.

Anchor (north nook) in 4 fathoms over a sand and mud bottom with good holding.

Briggs Inlet

Chart 3940 metric; entrance: 52°19.15′ N, 128°00.85′ W (NAD 83)

> *Briggs Inlet is entered east of Coldwell Point, the south end of Coldwell Peninsula.* (p. 90, SD)

From its entrance, Briggs Inlet appears to be a deep bay 2.5 miles long. In reality, you can see only the first quarter of the inlet because the first narrows makes a jog to the west, then resumes its northward path. It forms a fjord that ends less than 3/4 mile from the south end of Ellerslie Lake and 300 yards from Roscoe Inlet at Boukind Bay. The inlet has high angular mountains with exposed granite walls. Briggs Inlet, because of its position, is not subject to strong inflow or outflow winds. Drift trees collect on the beach on the west shore at Lat 52°21.04' N. Some protection from northerly winds may be found here.

"First Narrows Cove"

Chart 3940 metric, anchor: 52°21.78′ N, 128°00.28′ W (NAD 83)

First Narrows Cove is what we call the cove directly east of First Narrows in Briggs Inlet. This is a good place to wait for proper tide conditions and is out of the current and any westerly or northerly winds. It is exposed to southerly winds as shown by the thick collection of derelict trees, stumps and drift wood.

Temporary anchorage can be found 100 yards off the beach.

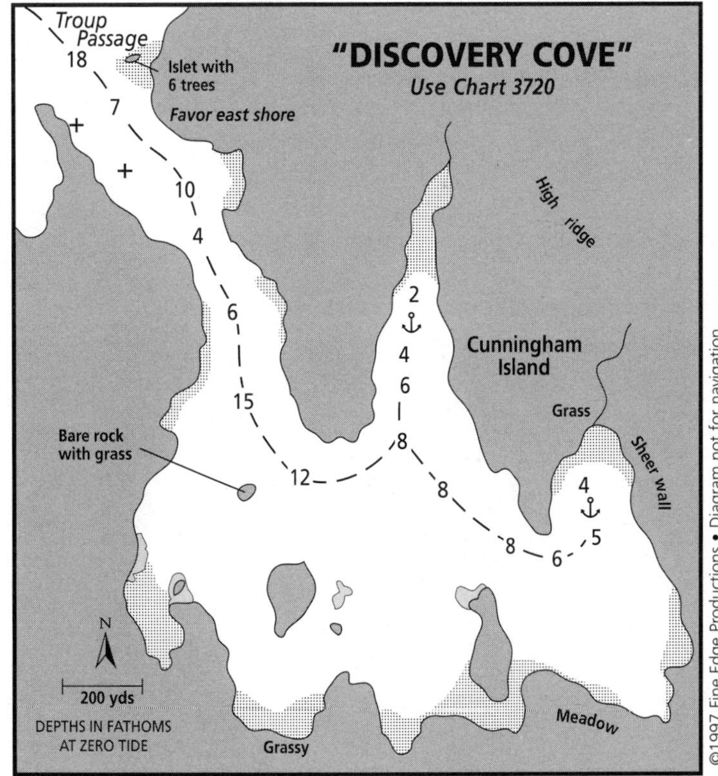

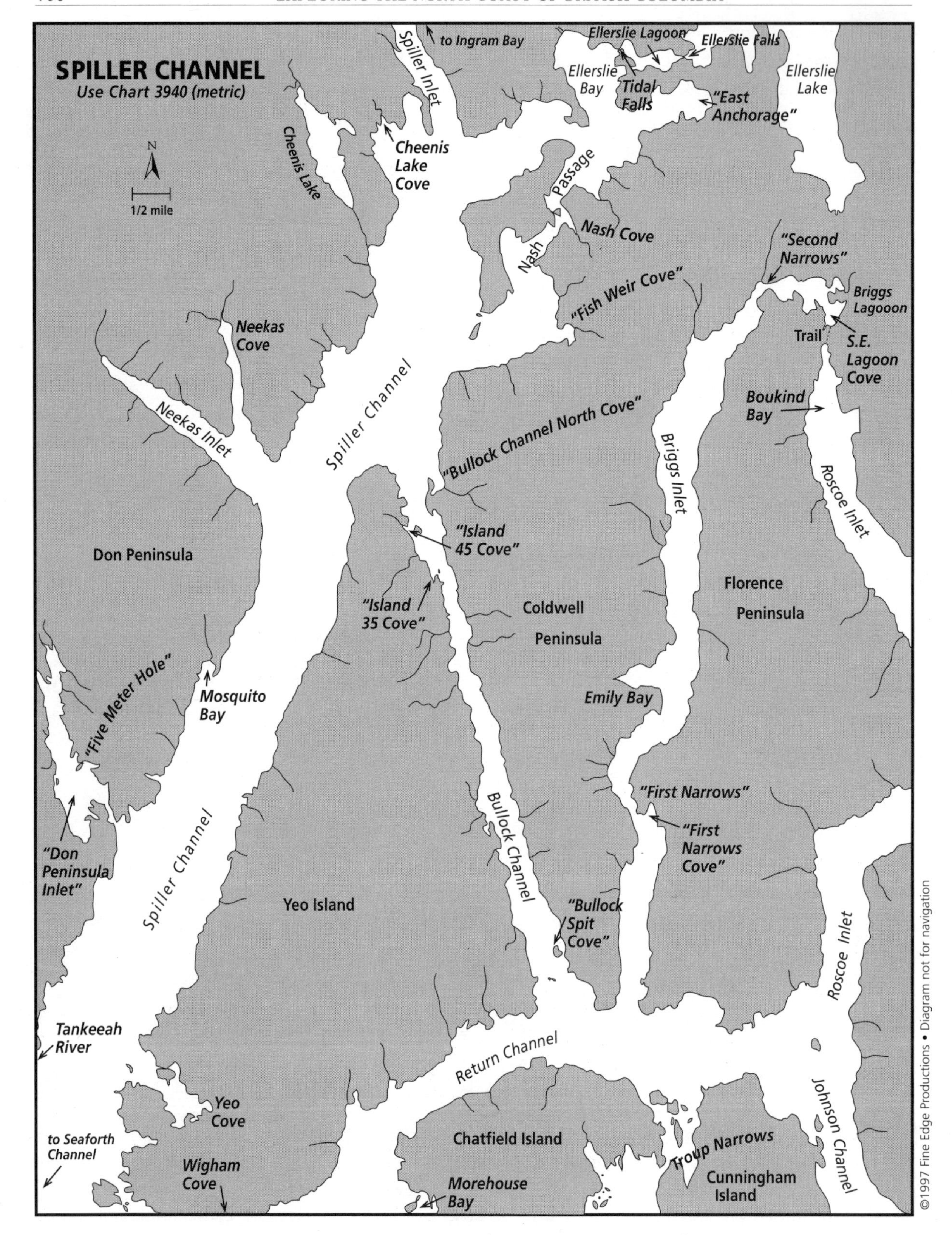
SPILLER CHANNEL
Use Chart 3940 (metric)
N
1/2 mile
to Ingram Bay
Spiller Inlet
Ellerslie Lagoon
Ellerslie Falls
Ellerslie Bay
Tidal Falls
"East Anchorage"
Ellerslie Lake
Cheenis Lake
Cheenis Lake Cove
Passage
Nash
Nash Cove
"Second Narrows"
Briggs Lagooon
"Fish Weir Cove"
Trail
S.E. Lagoon Cove
Neekas Cove
Neekas Inlet
Spiller Channel
Boukind Bay
"Bullock Channel North Cove"
Briggs Inlet
Roscoe Inlet
"Island 45 Cove"
Don Peninsula
Florence
Peninsula
"Island 35 Cove"
Coldwell
Peninsula
"Five Meter Hole"
Mosquito Bay
Emily Bay
"First Narrows"
"First Narrows Cove"
Bullock Channel
"Don Peninsula Inlet"
Spiller Channel
Yeo Island
"Bullock Spit Cove"
Roscoe Inlet
Tankeeah River
Return Channel
Johnson Channel
Yeo Cove
to Seaforth Channel
Wigham Cove
Chatfield Island
Troup Narrows
Cunningham Island
Morehouse Bay
©1997 Fine Edge Productions • Diagram not for navigation

Anchor in 6 fathoms over a sand and gravel bottom with fair holding.

"Briggs First Narrows"

Chart 3940 metric; position:
52°21.68′ N, 128°00.61′ W (NAD 83)

> *The channel through the narrows has depths in the fairway of 5 to 7 fathoms (10 to 13 m) and leads west of a drying rock lying near mid-channel in the south part of the narrows. Tidal currents in the narrows reach 3 kn. Within 0.5 mile north of the narrows, rocks with 2 fathoms (3.7 m) over them extend 0.1 mile from the east shore.* (p. 90, SD)

Favor the west shore to avoid the rocks off the southern end of the small peninsula. Water flow is laminar on a moderate flood with no apparent motion unless you look along the shore and see how fast the trees are flying by. With a 3-knot flood current, there is a large area of turbulent water starting just north of the narrows and lasting for the next half-mile or so with upwellings and small whirlpools; nothing dangerous, but enough to require a positive response from the helmsman. *Caution*: We have measured 4.1 knots through the narrows on an 8-foot tidal range which would suggest perhaps 5 or so knots on spring tidal range of 16 feet. There were small waves on the east side of the fairway with a current of 4 knots. We found a minimum depth of 3.5 fathoms in the fairway rather than the 5 or more fathoms indicated on the chart.

The shores grow steep north of the first narrows with treeless slabs of dark granite climbing high up the steep ridges.

Emily Bay

Chart 3940 metric; entrance:
52°23.50′ N, 128°00.00′ W; anchor:
52°23.53′ N, 128°00.83′ W (NAD 83)

> *Emily Bay, which extends 0.6 mile west from Briggs Inlet, has mid-bay depths of 10 fathoms (18 m), several drying rocks across its entrance and a rock with 7 feet (2.1 m) over it 0.2 mile within the entrance and 0.1 mile off the north shore.*
>
> *Anchorage in Emily is good over a bottom of sand and shell.* (p. 90, SD)

Emily Bay offers good protection from any weather and is a very scenic anchorage with high mountains surrounding it. Ravens, crows, bald eagles and songbirds fill the air with calls and songs while seals cruise in the bay. A sharp-pointed peak lies directly behind the long lake which feeds the creek a short distance inland.

A primitive trail leads to the lake behind Emily Bay. Land your dinghy below the cabin out of the creek outflow and tie to a line connected to a beach log. Note the number of scurrying tiny crabs

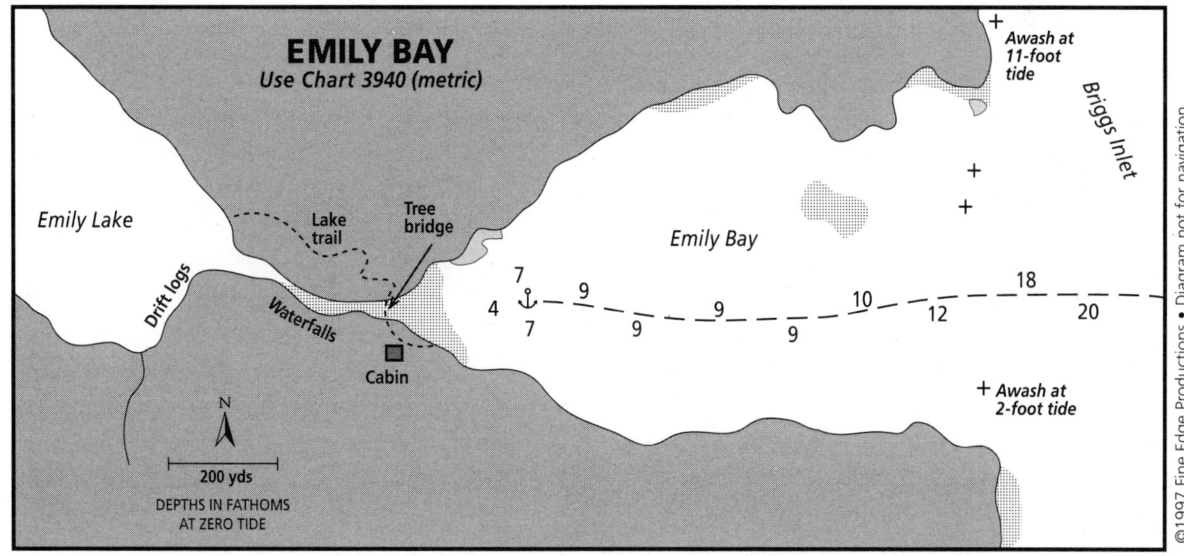

which inhabit the logs. A challenging trail starts on the west side of a small cabin on the south side of the creek with the word "hatchery" written on it. A black plastic pipe brings water down from the lake above for what appears to have been an old research project. The trail crosses the stream on a double-log bridge, then climbs 100 feet or so north of the waterfalls through the brush to the lake outlet. The trail follows the black plastic water pipe the entire way through soggy, muddy terrain with some log rounds for steps. It is slippery in places so use caution. Old asphalt roof shingles nailed to fallen trees mark the trail, reducing some of the otherwise slippery surfaces.

In the bay, avoid the rock off the south entrance which bares on a 2.5-foot tide and the two rocks on the north entrance which dry on an 11-foot tide. The fairway between the rocks has a depth of 12 fathoms and lies about 40 percent of the distance from the south shore to the north. Emily Bay has an almost flat bottom of 9 fathoms, sand and shell. We found no signs of isolated rocks in our research other than a one-fathom shoal on the north side of the bay near the entrance. Where the bottom slopes upward at the head of the bay off the creek, small boats can find anchorage. The creek has substantial flow and will keep your boat tethered in, even on a flood tide. An occasional back eddy may cause your boat to drift in toward the two rocky patches (with many small sharp barnacles) on either side of the creek exit or the mud flat with eel grass on the south shore. For this reason you may not want to anchor in less than 6 or 7 fathoms.

Anchor in 7 fathoms over a sand and shell bottom with good-to-very-good holding.

"Briggs Second Narrows"

Chart 3940 metric; west entrance: 52°28.67′ N, 127°57.60′ W (NAD 83)

The lagoon at the head of the inlet has an entrance passage about 50 feet (15 m) wide with a depth of less than 7 feet (2.1 m) which leads south of two drying rocks. Tidal currents in the entrance reach 5 kn or more. The tidal range inside the lagoon is one-half the range outside. (p. 90, SD)

Photo by Herb Nickles

Trail to Emily Lake

The Second Narrows are tidal rapids of very fast-moving water on large tides and care must be taken not to be swept into the rock attached to the north shore at the entrance or the more dangerous rock farther east and almost exactly mid-channel. *Note*: The isolated rock is not a continuation of the rock attached to shore.

Entry should be made at or near high-water slack only. The water is quite brown and opaque so visual sighting of the midchannel rock cannot be counted upon. We have exited Briggs Lagoon at low-water slack with the midchannel rock showing 2 inches just one hour and 20 minutes after a low tide of 3.9 feet at Bella Bella. We passed between the isolated rock and the south shore having only 10 feet between us and the rock to starboard and 10 feet to the south shore to port. Slack water at low tide lasts for only a few minutes and the current builds quickly. The foam generated on the lee of

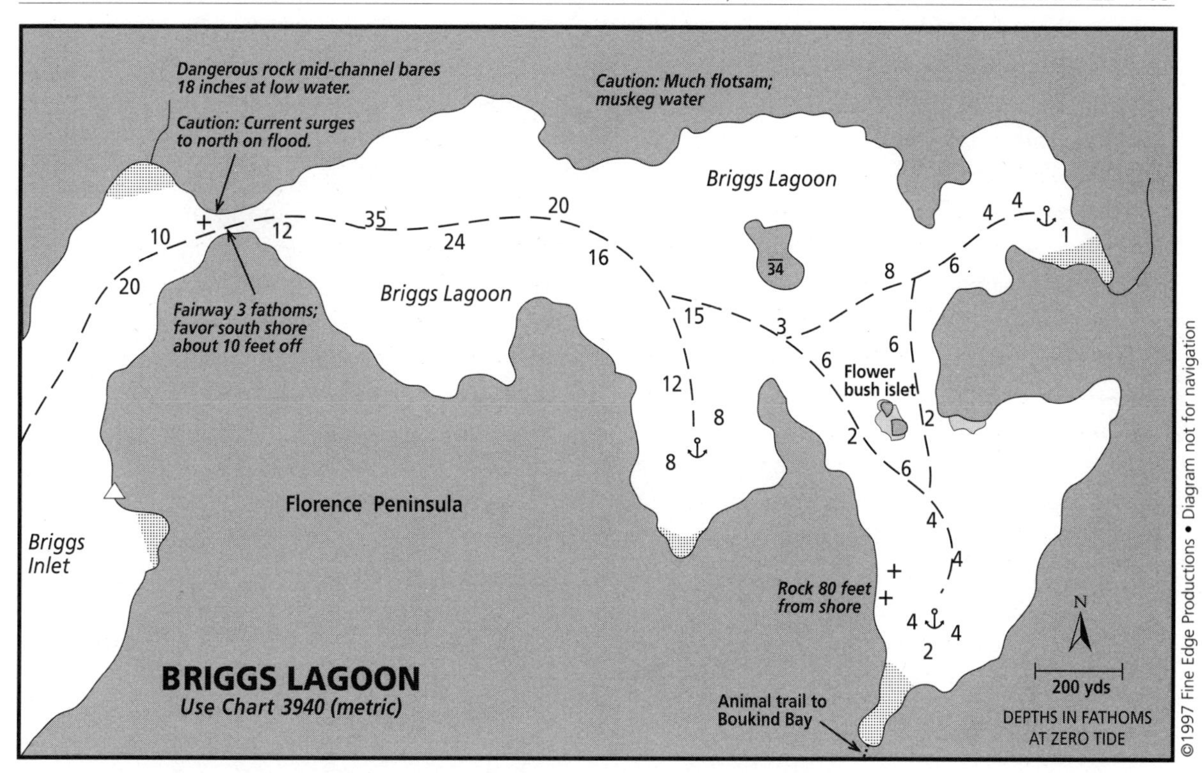

the rock on the last of the ebb will stop moving and then start moving east indicating slack water. The flood current makes a sweeping turn tending to set you over the midchannel rock—so beware! Minimum depth in the fairway at low water was about 8 feet, *not* the 6 meters (19 feet) indicated on the chart. Second Narrows is short and brief and you soon encounter deep water again.

Fisheries boats sometimes anchor overnight west of the narrows and report calm anchorage even when a southeast gale is blowing in the outer channels.

Briggs Lagoon

Chart 3940 metric; Second Narrows, east entrance: 52°28.71′ N, 127°57.49′ W (NAD 83)

The lagoon has general mid-channel depths of 11 to 27 fathoms (20 to 50 m) in its west part and 3 to 5 fathoms (5 to 10 m) in its east part. A shoal rock lies in mid-channel NE of the only island, and a drying reef and a shoal rock lie in the entrance to the bay at the SE end of the lagoon. The tidal range inside the lagoon is one-half the range outside. (p. 90 SD)

Briggs Lagoon is entered through Second Narrows at the head of Briggs Inlet at the east side. This is a true "hole-in-the-wall" experience. You can only see high granite ridges in all directions until you are directly in front of the narrow opening. The lagoon has very poor water exchange with the inlet since there is no freshwater creek to provide an outflow current. Once inside, the water becomes deep and you find trees, limbs, rockweed and other flotsam which are caught in the lagoon and never leave. Briggs Lagoon has plenty of protected anchorage space.

There are a number of places where you can anchor, such as the southeast lagoon cove, the northeast cove, or in the central south portion which is used occasionally by fishing boats.

"Southeast Lagoon Cove"

Chart 3940 metric; anchor: 52°28.24′ N, 127°56.22′ W (NAD 83)

The southeast corner of Briggs Lagoon offers very good protection off the drying flat. Enter on the south side of island (34) over a shoal of about 2 fathoms. Once past either side of "Flower Rock," the bottom is a flat 4 to 5 fathoms There is extensive flotsam throughout Briggs Lagoon—trees, branches and small patches of floating rockweed—and careful helmsmanship is required. This is a quiet place where ravens chortle, crows cahh-cahh, loons croon their forlorn cry, kingfishers issue staccato alarms, woodpeckers hammer, and songbirds sing, while man-o-war pulse by, small jellyfish wander in all directions, and all is well with Mother Nature.

Boukind Bay lies only 300 yards due south across a small low spit. While there is no trail as such, a route can be found through the wet rain forest. Boots are required since you have to climb over some slippery logs and wade through bogs. There is an elevation gain of about 60 feet or so to the saddle. If you find yourself climbing more, you are off-route. Favor the west side of the very small creek on the Briggs Lagoon side and the east side of a small creek on the Roscoe Inlet side. The only annoying thing about this lovely, quiet place is the small black flies which find the boat when the wind stops—they love to bite.

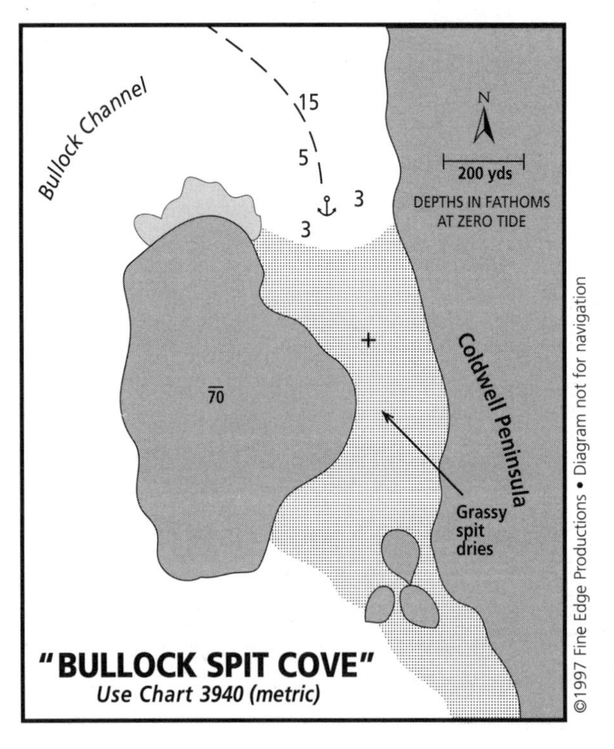

Anchoring can be found almost anywhere in the eastern part of Briggs Lagoon in moderate depths. Larger boats may want to use the cove south southwest of island (34) where anchorage can be found in 8 fathoms off the small gravel beach.

The best anchorage is in the far southeast corner near where the short hike to Boukind Bay begins. In Southeast Lagoon Cove, an uncharted rock extends about 80 feet from the west shore and a bare rock extends from the east shore at the head. An orange sign on the tree immediately behind this rock indicates a logging boundary.

Anchor (southeast corner) in 4 fathoms over a soft black mud bottom with very good holding.

Bullock Channel

Chart 3940 metric; south entrance: 52°19.20′ N, 128°02.30′ W; north entrance: 52°26.40′ N, 128°05.50′ W (NAD 83)

Bullock Channel is entered east of Ettershank Point. Mid-channel depths for 4 miles north of the islets 0.5 mile within the entrance are generally 27 to 44 fathoms (50 to 80 m) with a few areas of 15 to 18 fathoms (27 to 33 m). Farther north, in the narrowest section, mid-channel depths decrease to 11 to 16 fathoms (20 to 30 m) then increase to 22 to 44 fathoms (40 to 80 m) in the north mile of the channel. . . . In several places through Bullock Channel shoal water extends up to 0.15 mile from shore. (p. 90, SD)

Bullock Channel, on the east side of Yeo Island, is the quickest way to reach the upper reaches of Spiller Channel from the Bella Bella region. The currents are moderate, there is less wind and chop than Spiller Channel, and a midchannel course is free of dangers. We have found a north-flowing ebb on occasions.

There are several places which make good temporary stops along the way.

"Bullock Spit Cove"

Chart: 3940 metric ; anchor: 52°20.00′ N, 128°02.27′ W (NAD 83)

Bullock Spit Cove is our name for the small nook on the north side of island (70), on the east side of

Bullock Channel, $^3/_4$ mile from its entrance. The spit gives good protection from southerly weather.

There is a grassy spit between the island and the peninsula, navigable only by kayak on 14-foot spring tides.

Anchor in 5 fathoms, over brown sand, small rocks, and mud with good holding.

"Mouth of Bay," Bullock Channel

Chart 3940 metric; anchor:
52°23.68′ N, 128°04.54′ W (NAD 83)

> *Small craft can obtain fair anchorage in 5 fathoms (10 m) in the mouth of a bay on the west side of Bullock Channel 2.8 miles south of the north entrance, but there are drying rocks in the bay.* (p. 90, SD)

There is a small bay two-thirds of the way up Bullock Channel on the west shore which can offer anchorage in fair weather and makes a good lunch stop. The bay is one-half mile north of a small grass-covered rock which dries at 14 feet close along the west shore. The beach of the bay is fairly steep-to and has eel grass marking the low-tide line. You'll probably see a seal cruising the bay.

Tuck in close to the south point, avoiding a rock about 75 feet northwest of the south point. Underwater visibility is limited to about six feet due to the muskeg water.

Anchor in 4 fathoms, sand and gravel bottom with good holding.

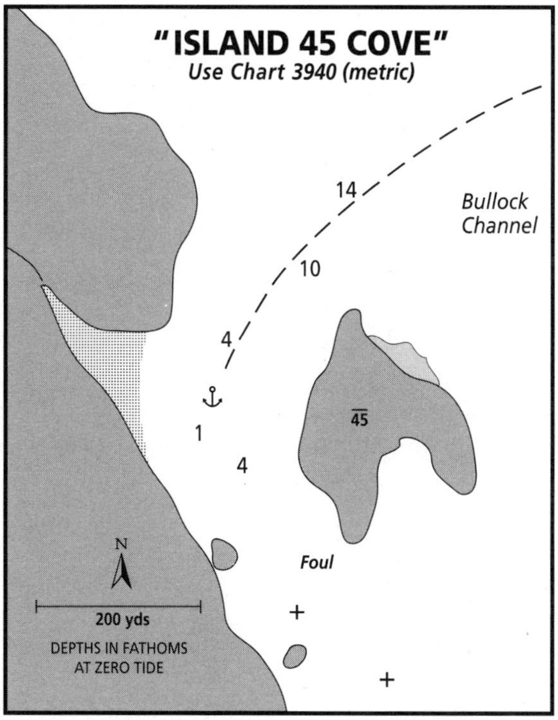

"Island (35) Cove," Bullock Channel

Chart 3940 metric; anchor:
52°24.94′ N, 128°04.99′ W (NAD 83)

The cove on the west side of island (35) can be used for protection against southerlies, but it is open to the north. This cove has a nice view and makes a good lunch stop.

Anchor on a shelf at 3 fathoms off the southwest shore. The bottom is sand with worm casings. Holding is fair.

"Island (45) Cove," Bullock Channel

Chart 3940 metric; anchor:
52°25.48′ N, 128°05.53′ W (NAD 83)

Island (45) Cove is located one mile southeast of Gerald Point and provides moderate protection from southerly weather due to its extensive drying reefs and rocks between island (45) and the shore. It is open to downslope winds from the north. The preferred entry is from the north side of island (45).

Anchor in $4^1/_2$ fathoms, sand bottom with eel grass marking the low-tide line; fair holding.

"Bullock Channel North Cove"

Chart 3940 metric; anchor:
52°26.14′ N, 128°04.89′ W (NAD 83)

> *Good anchorage can be found in the bay behind a small peninsula on the east side of the north entrance to Bullock Channel in 8 fathoms (15 m), sand bottom. A rock awash lies almost mid-way between the peninsula and an island, 128 feet (39 m) high, 0.1 mile north.* (p. 91, SD)

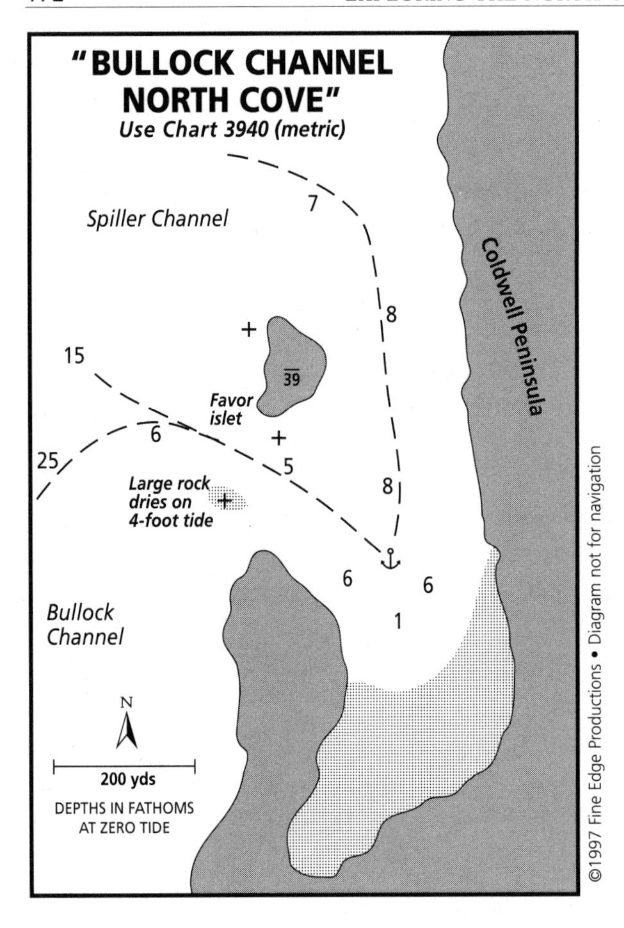

Enter west of island (39) by staying north of a line extending west from the south tip of island (39) until you are close aboard the island, then head southeast into the cove, avoiding the rock on the south tip of the island. There is very good protection from southerlies and moderate protection from downslope northerly winds. Anchor anywhere in the cove over a relatively flat 6- to 7-fathom bottom. The south end of the cove dries, so do not anchor south of the line between the point of the peninsula and the creek on the east shore.

Caution: The midchannel entrance rock extends well west of a line between the peninsula and island (39) and can be dangerous in poor visibility.

Anchor in 6 fathoms over a sand and shell bottom with good holding.

Spiller Channel

Chart 3940 metric; south entrance:
52°17.00′ N, 128°14.20′ W (NAD 83)

The entrance to Spiller Channel lies between Early Point and Shingle Rock, close off Don Peninsula, to the west.

Grief Island and Mid Island form the SW side of Early Passage, which is suitable only for small craft. (p. 91, SD)

Spiller Channel and the surrounding hundreds of square miles between Don Peninsula and Roscoe Inlet were the largest uncharted area of the British Columbia coast before Chart 3940 was released in early 1996. Spiller Channel is wide and very deep. It has a strong ebb flow which can quickly kick up a chop when moderate south upslope winds prevail. Spiller Channel leads to some fine cruising in the area of Ellerslie Bay and in the Ingram Arm of Spiller Inlet.

Tankeeah River

Chart 3940 metric; anchor:
52°17.74′ N, 128°15.70′ W (NAD 83)

Tankeeah River, known locally as "Tinkey," is 2 miles due west of Grief Island. It is a shallow river flowing out of the low, flat, south end of Don Peninsula 4 miles south of Lake Mountain. Cruising boats can anchor temporarily off a small gravel beach on the west shore a quarter of a mile inside the entrance. This anchorage is well out of the chop frequently found in this part of Spiller Channel.

On entering Tankeeah River, avoid the rocks near shore and the silver snags which have fallen and point directly out into the river. You can explore the upper reaches of the river at high water by dinghy, paddling through a narrow channel with cedar branches nearly filling the route. This is not mountainous like the area to the north, but a swampy muskeg environment of thick cedar rain forest with dark brown water. Eagles and seals patrol the river.

Anchor in 3 fathoms over a gravel bottom with fair holding.

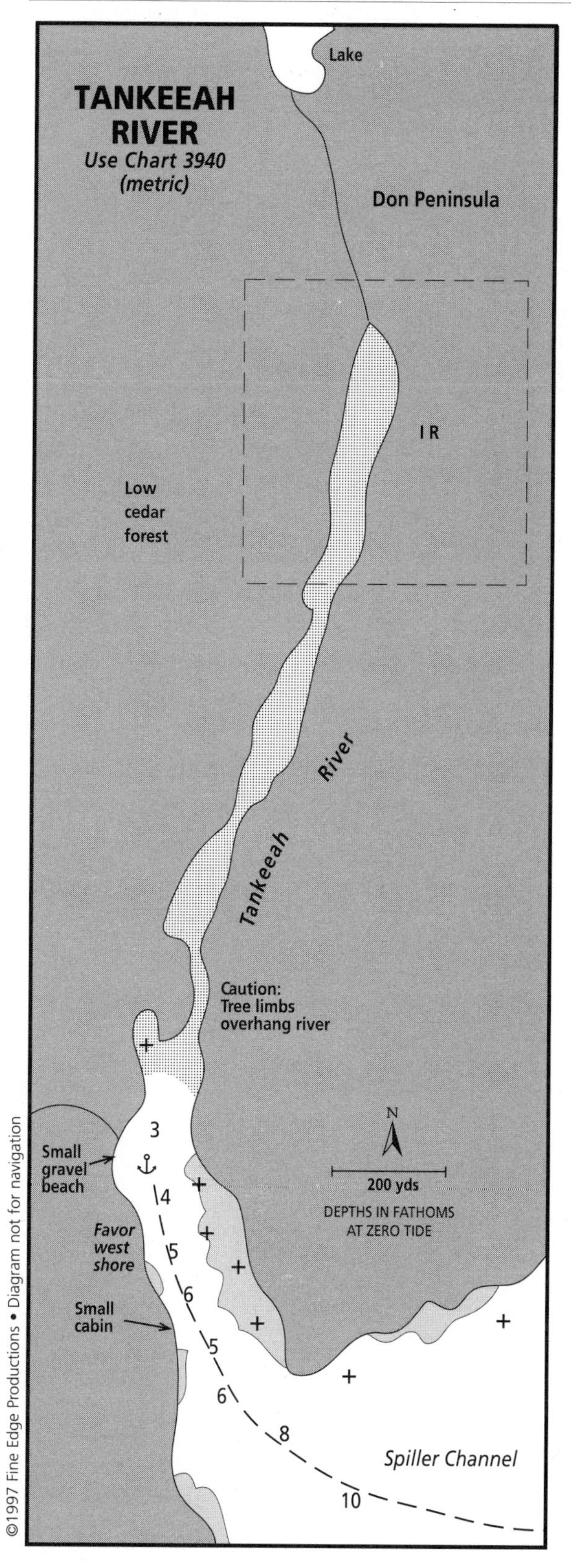

Yeo Cove

Chart 3940 metric; anchor:
52°17.78′ N, 128°10.98′ W (NAD 83)

> *Yeo Cove, entered south of Dove Point, has drying rocks in its entrance and should not be entered without local knowledge.* (p. 91, SD)

Very good protection can be found in the far end of Yeo Cove tucked in behind the small island in the southwest corner. Yeo Cove has been a major log processing and shipping area and is quite noisy, hence we try to get as far from the action as possible. The approach is on the west side of island (72). The fairway is located between the rocks alongside island (72) and the rock and reef complex which extends north from the south shore. A slow, cautious approach is prudent.

The small secluded nook behind the island in the southwest corner of the cove is hidden from the logging activity. Swinging room is limited and a stern tie to the island can be useful.

Anchor in 2 to 3 fathoms over a mud bottom with very good holding.

"Don Peninsula Inlet"

Chart 3940 metric; entrance:
52°21.68′ N, 128°12.10′ W (NAD 83)

> *The unnamed inlet on the west side of Spiller Channel has depths under 7 feet (2.1 m), many drying rocks and much kelp in its entrance channel. Inside, a trough running a little west of the centre-line of the inlet has general depths of 16 to 33 fathoms (30 to 60 m), but shoals with 5 and 7 fathoms (10 and 13 m) over them lie up to 0.3 mile off the east and west shores. About 1 mile north of the south end of the inlet, a large area of drying rocks extends from the east side to near mid-channel. The NE arm of the inlet has depths ranging from 11 fathoms (20 m) in the south to 3 fathoms (5 m) in the north but rocks with as little as 7 feet (2.1 m) over them lie in mid-channel.* (p. 91, SD)

Don Peninsula Inlet, a 3-mile deep penetration of Don Peninsula, is what we call the waterway on the west shore of Spiller Channel, 3.5 miles due north of Yeo Cove. This was probably a freshwater lake until recent geologic time. It has

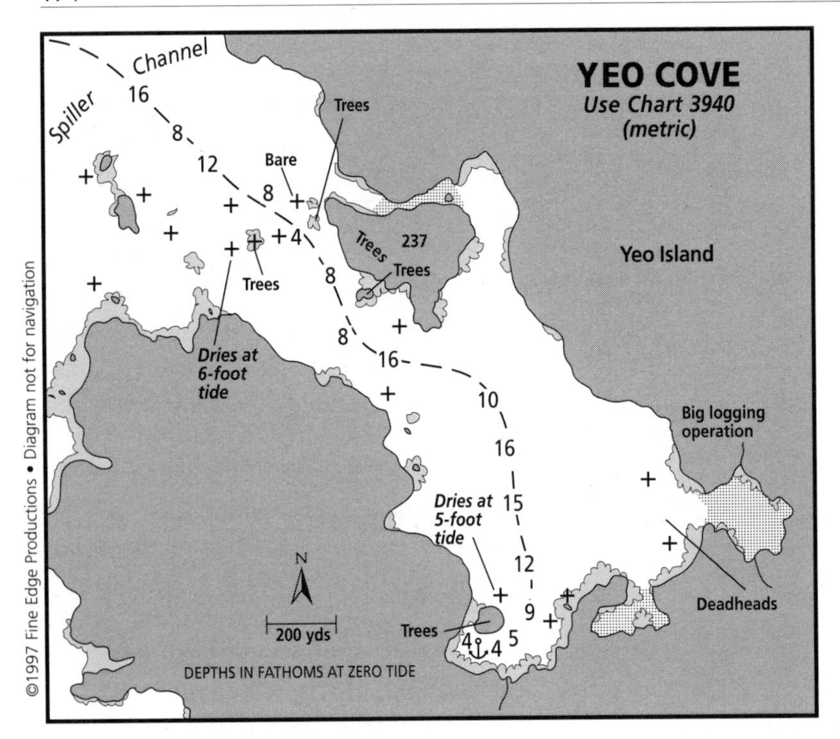

a difficult and dangerous entrance and we do not recommend it to general cruising boats. The current is quite strong in the entrance and it's a good idea to reconnoiter first by dinghy before entering. Rocks and reefs fill the narrow and shallow entrance to the inlet, and currents on flood and ebb run 2 to 3 knots, pulling the thick kelp under and interfering with steerage. At high water, many of the key rocks are submerged and are particularly dangerous. At low water, the rocks are generally visible but do not seem to be in their relative position on the chart because of the chart scale. Because of these difficulties, there has been no commercial exploitation and the inlet is filled with more than its share of seals, eagles, loons and other fauna.

Favor the west shore at the entrance until the large drying rock system clogging the midchannel is passed, then immediately favor the east shore to avoid the rock sticking out from the south shore. The route requires a significant left turn prior to reaching island (21) and its shallow bar, and staying between two rocks which submerge at about 10 feet on the south side and 13 feet on the north side. The bar has a minimum depth of about 6 feet at zero tide. A strong flood current will quickly carry you into foul ground between the dangerous dry reef, which dries at about 13 feet, and the small island directly east. Both of these rocks are part of a larger shoal complex which is marked with substantial bull kelp patches, visible when the current is minimum but pulled under and invisible on spring tides. Anchorage can be taken at the deep south end of the inlet or in either of the two shallow coves at the north end of the inlet. Five Meter Hole, a half-mile north of the shallow bar, is centrally located for convenient anchorage while exploring the inlet by dinghy.

"Five Meter Hole"

Chart 3940 metric; entrance:
52°22.35′ N, 128°12.83′ W; anchor:
52°22.53′ N, 128°12.81′ W (NAD 83)

There is a shallow gunk hole on the north shore of Don Peninsula Inlet which provides good protection in stable weather. It is sheltered by a number of rocks and reefs which must be carefully negotiated. Enter from the south avoiding the charted rocks as well as an uncharted rock near the southeast corner of the hole off the peninsula.

Because the inlet has been uncharted and lacks a commercial interest, it is pristine and has an abundance of fauna. Seals, loons, eagles and ducks find refuge here.

Five Meter Hole is a good base camp for exploring the inlet. Additional anchor sites can be found in both the north and south end of the inlet.

Anchor in 2 fathoms over a mud bottom with good holding

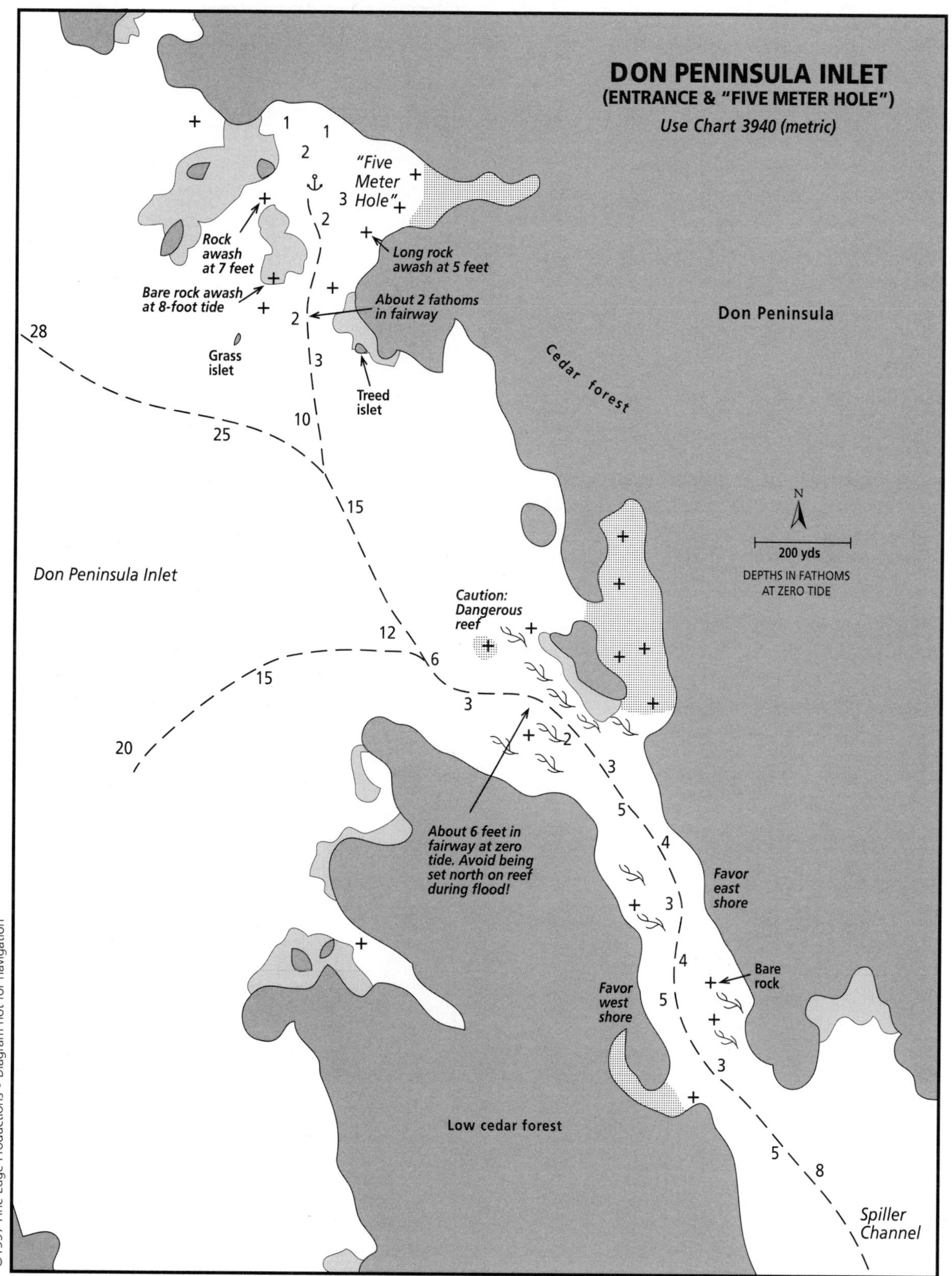
DON PENINSULA INLET
(ENTRANCE & "FIVE METER HOLE")
Use Chart 3940 (metric)
"Five Meter Hole"
Rock awash at 7 feet
Bare rock awash at 8-foot tide
Long rock awash at 5 feet
About 2 fathoms in fairway
Grass islet
Treed islet
Don Peninsula
Cedar forest
N
200 yds
DEPTHS IN FATHOMS AT ZERO TIDE
Don Peninsula Inlet
Caution: Dangerous reef
About 6 feet in fairway at zero tide. Avoid being set north on reef during flood!
Favor east shore
Favor west shore
Bare rock
Low cedar forest
Spiller Channel

Mosquito Bay

Chart 3940 metric; position: 52°23.70′ N, 128°10.10′ W (NAD 83)

Mosquito Bay, 2.5 miles south of Neekas Inlet, offers no protection from southerly weather, but it does make a good lunch stop in prevailing northwest winds if you anchor close to the rocky beach. The shore is steep-to, rising dramatically from a depth of 16 fathoms to one fathom. Avoid the two rocks due south of Mosquito Bay which dry at about 2 feet at zero tide.

Neekas Inlet

Chart 3940 metric; entrance: 52°26.10′ N, 128°08.70′ W; anchor: 52°27.77′ N, 128°12.32′ W (NAD 83)

> *Neekas Inlet has general mid-channel depths in its entrance and west arm ranging from 82 fathoms (150 m) in the entrance to 7 fathoms (13 m) near the head.* (p. 91, SD)

Neekas Inlet is easy to enter and provides fair protection for all but southeast winds. Anchorage is reported at the head of the inlet. We prefer to anchor in nearby Neekas Cove for its better protection and more scenic surroundings.

Anchor (head of inlet) in 7 fathoms over a mud and gravel bottom with unrecorded holding.

Neekas Cove

Chart 3940 metric; entrance: 52°26.75′ N, 128°09.30′ W; anchor: 52°27.99′ N, 128°09.57′ W (NAD 83)

> *Neekas Cove, the NE arm, mid-channel depths are 16 to 33 fathoms (30 to 60 m) near the entrance and 7 to 16 fathoms (12 to 30 m) within the cove. A reef with 5 fathoms (9 m) over it projects 0.5 mile SE from the point between the arms.* (p. 91, SD)

Neekas Cove offers surprisingly good protection, even when Spiller Channel is kicking up a nasty up-channel chop. Southerly winds die down as you proceed up the cove and there is little driftwood or indication of exposure common to south-facing coves. Local knowledge, however,

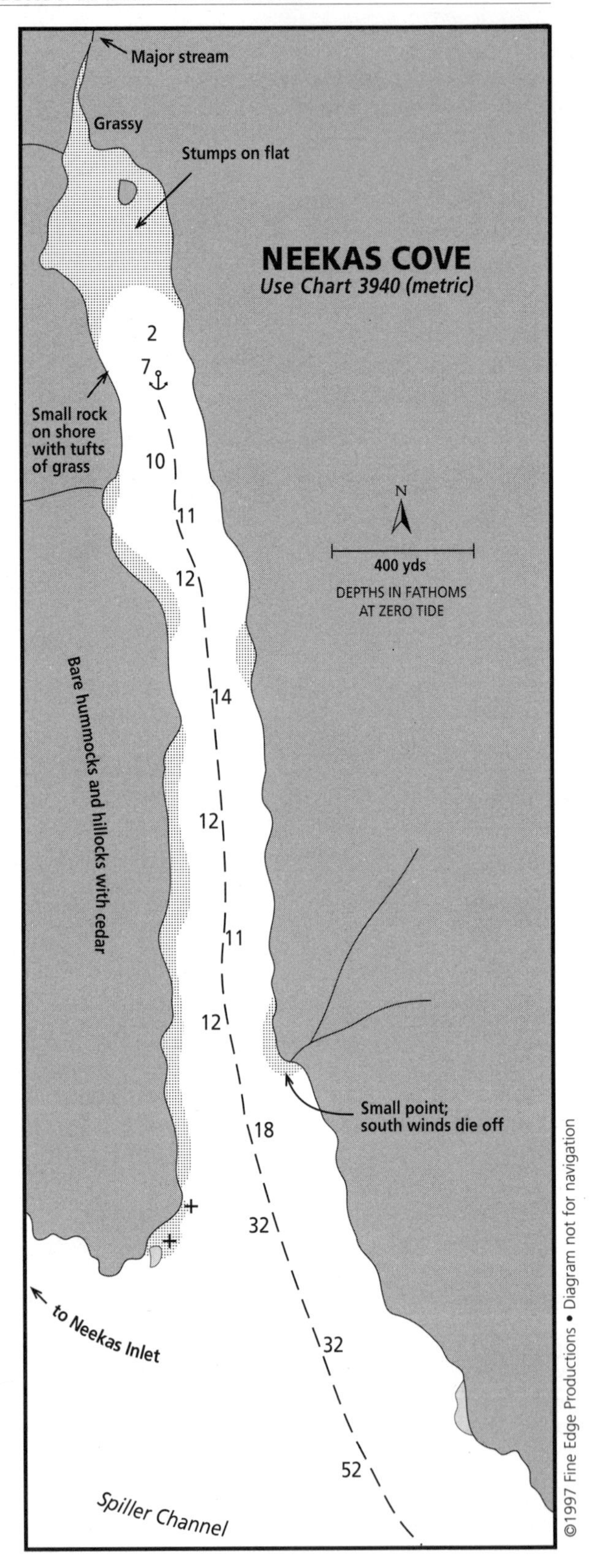

relates that this is not a good place to be in a southeast gale.

The head of the cove is a large drying flat with a few stumps, rocks, and lots of flat grassy areas. This is a scenic and quiet place and is easy to enter. A shoaling area is half-way up the cove but is of no concern when keeping a midchannel route.

Anchor in 4 fathoms over a sand and mud bottom with good holding.

"Nash Passage"

Chart 3940 metric; south entrance:
52°27.90′ N, 128°04.00′ W; north entrance:
52°30.40′ N, 128°01.60′ W (NAD 83)

There is a small, well-sheltered passage east of the large unnamed island at the head of Spiller Channel which we call Nash Passage. Professor Roderick Frazier Nash, environmental historian, Harvard graduate, and author of *Wilderness and the American Mind*, provided an inspiring education to thousands of students at the University of California at Santa Barbara over a period of 30 years. He is a descendent of Simon Fraser—the Canadian pioneer who discovered and explored Fraser River. He is a veteran of many British Columbia and Alaska boating explorations and a professional Grand Canyon River guide. Rod and his wife Honeydew, aboard their 26-foot trawler *Forevergreen*, helped us document Ellerslie Lagoon (see *Pacific Yachting*, October 1996).

Nash Passage is entered from the south between two rocky projections and appears to be a dead-end in the bay. After 0.6 miles, a number of large rocks are encountered. Turn east and pass the rocks on your port side. When abeam the deep valley to the south ("Nash Narrows Cove"), turn hard left at the "elbow" and proceed up the channel. The east shore is a bold overhanging granite bluff. *Caution:* We have found an uncharted one-fathom shoal on the north side of the easternmost rock near the east shore. There are several rocks close ashore beneath the overhanging bluff. Minimum depth in the passage, except for the shoal noted above, is about 3 fathoms. A scenic and safe anchorage can be found off the drying flat at the elbow turning point.

"Fish Weir Cove," Spiller Channel

Chart 3940 metric; entrance:
52°28.05′ N, 128°02.20′ W; anchor (north side):
52°28.15′ N, 128°01.98′ W (NAD 83)

Fish Weir Cove, at the south end of a large, unnamed bay off the northwest side of Coldwell Peninsula, offers good protection from almost all winds. A large avalanche scar lies to the east, along the north-facing granite slope. We've given the cove this name because of the prehistoric fish weir located off the north point of the cove. It is one of the best preserved we've seen.

A one-fathom, sandy shoal extends into the cove for about 100 feet midway between two large stumps on the beach. You can see to depths

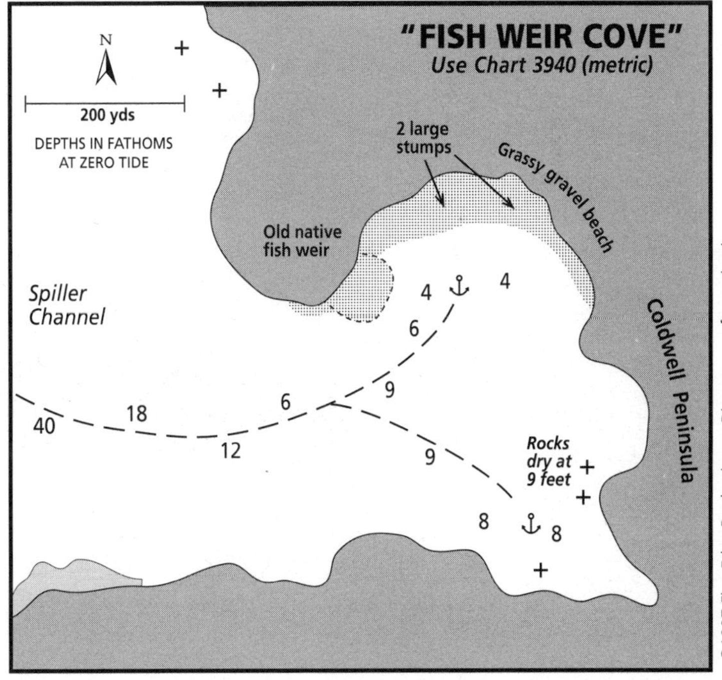

of about 12 feet in the brown water; the temperature—at 67°F—was the warmest we encountered in the Spiller Channel area.

Anchor in 3 to 4 fathoms on a shelf on the north side, or in 8 fathoms on the south side. The bottom is brown mud, with very good holding.

"Nash Narrows Cove," Spiller Channel

Chart 3940 metric; anchor:
52°30.45′ N, 128°01.96′ W (NAD 83)

The cove at the narrows between Coldwell Peninsula and the large unnamed island provides good anchorage in almost all weather. We call this Nash Narrows Cove and find it scenic with a lot of interesting flora and fauna. Water temperature reaches a balmy 67°F in the summertime and masses of small fish live in the eel grasses off the steep-to beach.

Anchor in 2 to 5 fathoms off the creek delta over brown sand with shells; fair-to-good holding.

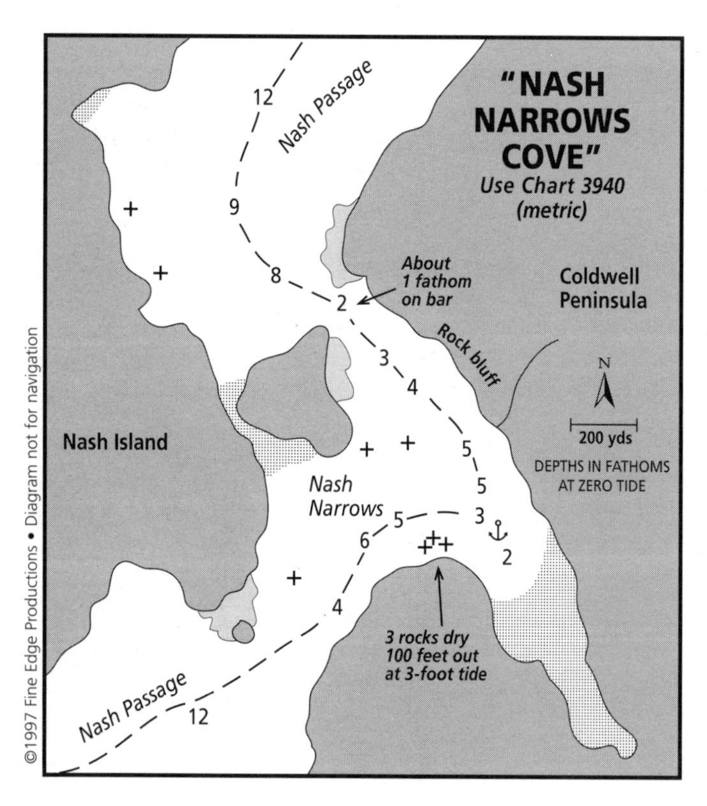

"Ellerslie Bay, East Anchorage"

Chart 3940 metric; entrance:
52°30.85′ N, 128°00.50′ W; anchor (north shore):
52°39.30′ N, 127°59.45′ W (NAD 83)

> *The bay lying south of Ellerslie Lagoon, separated from it by a peninsula, has general depths of 7 to 19 fathoms (12 to 35 m) and a reef projecting from its south side toward an islet, 75 feet (23 m) high, in its centre.* (p. 91, SD)

"Ellerslie Bay, East Anchorage," known locally as Ellerslie, is a well-protected anchorage and a convenient place to stay while you reconnoiter Ellerslie Lagoon or wait for favorable tidal conditions to enter the narrows. You can enter on either side of the small treed islet; however, close to the south side, the channel is deeper.

Anchorage can be taken either along the north shore, if fair weather is expected, or along the south shore, if winds are expected from that quarter. There is ample swinging room for several boats in East Anchorage and this is one of the most popular anchor sites in Spiller Channel.

Anchor (north shore) in 7 fathoms over sand, mud and shell bottom with good to very good holding.

Ellerslie Bay

Chart 3940 metric; south entrance:
52°31.00′ N, 128°01.00′ W (NAD 83)

> *Ellerslie Bay, the approach to Ellerslie Lagoon, has mid-channel depths of 33 to 55 fathoms (60 to 100 m). Shoal ledges with depths of 9 to 10 fathoms (16 to 19 m) project 0.2 mile south from the point on the east side of the entrance to Spiller Inlet. . . .* (p. 91, SD)

Ellerslie Bay is surrounded by high peaks with a wooded dome on the east side, the end of a peninsula forming the south shore of Ellerslie Lagoon. The dome has a 200-foot granite slab wall on its northwest corner, a half-mile south of the entrance to the narrows of Ellerslie Lagoon.

The entrance to Ellerslie Lagoon, via a narrow tidal rapids, is on the east shore of

Ellerslie Bay. The bay is generally too deep for anchorage; however, temporary anchorage, while reconnoitering the lagoon entrance, can be taken directly off the entrance. Avoid the rocks on the south side of the narrows which extend almost 100 yards into Ellerslie Bay.

Ellerslie Lagoon, First Narrows

Chart 3940 metric; entrance: 52°31.78′ N, 128°00.96′ W; anchor (northwest of the falls): 52°31.71′ N, 127°59.75′ W (NAD 83)

Ellerslie Lagoon, at the entrance to Ellerslie Lake, has an entrance channel about 100 feet (30 m) wide with a depth of 3 feet (0.9 m). Tidal streams ebb at 5 kn or more. Inside the lagoon depths are generally 2 to 23 feet (0.6 to 7 m). About 0.2 mile inside the entrance, a drying spit projects from the SW shore to within 100 feet (30 m) of the NE shore. A large waterfall is at the head of the lagoon. Tidal range inside the lagoon is one-half the range outside. (p. 91, SD)

Ellerslie Lagoon and Ellerslie Falls have all the makings of classic cruising destinations: outstanding scenery—the falls are about the best on the entire British Columbia coast—and the major challenge of navigating two sets of narrows. Until

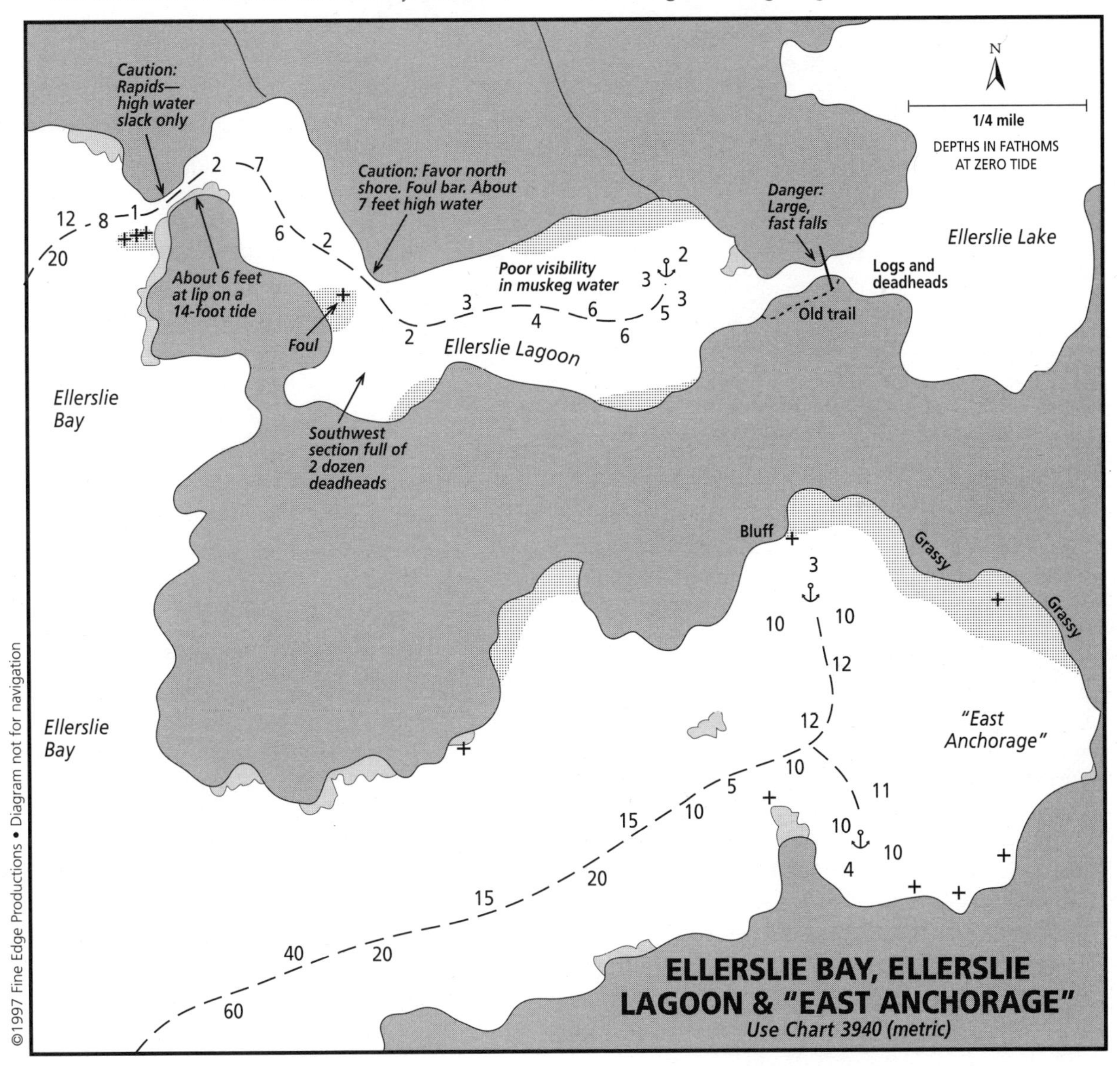

Ellerslie Lagoon Narrows at low tide

Ellerslie Lagoon—"Seabird Rock" turbulence, first narrows upper lip, ebb tide

Ellerslie Lagoon Entrance

Our only mishap was with the new Spiller Channel chart. Both the chart and *Sailing Directions* were wrong for the entrance to Ellerslie Lagoon. It is a beautiful place and I can foresee a lot of boats having the same trouble we did. We took our 45-foot powerboat with 16-foot beam into the lagoon at an 11-foot tide (slack). It is a minefield of rocks. The water in the lagoon is about 6 feet higher than that outside the lagoon, so you can see that even with an 11-foot tide, if there were no rocks you'd have 5 feet maximum water depth half-way in the entrance channel. But the place abounds with menacing rocks. I videotaped it at low tide. The clear channel is about 15 or 16 feet wide and zigzags with rocks lurking on both sides. Current is present even at slack. With a lookout on the bow, the current moved our stern enough to ding our prop on the largest of the rocks we were trying to miss.

The lagoon, itself, is fouled with deadheads and logs, at and past the spit, but there is a fantastic waterfall from Ellerslie Lake just above the lagoon. We had hoped to anchor in front of the waterfall which we visited by dinghy. Instead, we anchored in 30 feet just inside the lagoon in nice sand and mud; it was very pleasant.

I wonder how many others will read *Sailing Directions* (it describes a 100-foot channel with a shelf on the right upon entering the lagoon). The chart shows the same thing. In reality, the channel may be 50 feet at most from shore to shore, but the whole thing is rock-infested and there is now a rock with *our name on it* right in the middle. We have a single engine and barely managed to limp back to Shearwater at 750 rpms. Fortunately, we had a spare prop with which to replace the bent one.

—Bob and Anne Reeves,
Seabird, Port Townsend, Washington

the narrows have been better charted, and depths and hazards are understood, all boaters should approach the narrows with healthy skepticism.

First Narrows is a waterfall and rapids at all times except at high-water slack.

Caution: Ellerslie Lagoon is not advised for any vessel other than a small, easily maneuverable boat. We recommend that, before *any* boat enters the narrows, a careful reconnoitering by dinghy be made. Due to the muskeg water, underwater visibility within the lagoon is poor, and the rocks are difficult to see. Boats with limited maneuvering ability, larger boats (around 40 feet or more), those with vulnerable twin screws, or those drawing 4 feet or more should anchor in East Anchorage and visit the lagoon and falls by dinghy.

To enter the lagoon at high-water slack, favor the north shore at the west entrance since all the rocks are on the south shore. Pass through the channel slightly south of midchannel, then favor the south shore as you pass into the lagoon to avoid a rock that projects from the north shore. You should not attempt to enter the narrows when there are any barnacles visible on the shore rocks.

Because the water in Ellerslie Lagoon is generally higher than that west of the tidal rapids, there are two slack water periods in the narrows that differ from high and low water in Ellerslie Bay or from the Bella Bella tide predictions. The incoming flood reaches the level of the lagoon a couple of hours after the time of low water in Bella Bella and starts filling the lagoon. Due to the narrow restriction at the entrance, the lagoon water level is seldom the same as outside water, and the flood current flows into the lagoon well after high water is reached in Ellerslie Bay. There is a second slack current for a few minutes after high water is passed and the outside level drops to the new higher lagoon level. This is the time of maximum depth in the narrows fairway. At this time the fairway depth on spring tides is on the order of 7 feet; it can be as little as 4 feet or less if the outside tide has not raised the inside lagoon level sufficiently. This is precisely why we recommend a careful reconnoitering before entry—we expect that a lot of bottom paint will be left on the rocks at the lip of the narrows in the next few years due to the complex nature of the tidal patterns.

Entering Ellerslie Lagoon, high-water slack tide

There is a second "narrows" and a shallow area 0.25 mile inside the lagoon with about the same depth in the fairway as the lip of the falls. The fairway passes between two submerged rocks near the point on the north shore. Favor the north shore and approach dead slow since the rocks and shoal water are not visible. The entire area, from just off this point to the south shore, is shallow and fouled with dozens of deadheads.

Past the second narrows, the lagoon appears to be clear. Some boats may want to anchor in the outflow of stunning Ellerslie Falls, but the bottom is shallow and rocky at that point; we suggest anchoring north of the current in about 2 fathoms over a mud bottom. Ellerslie Lagoon is well sheltered.

About 200 yards south of the falls, there's a small beach where you can haul-out your dinghy, and hike uphill on an old primitive logging trail that leads to Ellerslie Lake. Much of the trail is muddy and slippery, so boots are recommended. If you take children or pets on the trail supervise them closely. It's possible to walk to the water's edge at several places along the falls and a slip or fall could be fatal.

Ellerslie Lake is 10 miles long and the outlet of the lake is clogged with logs. Good swimming is reported south of the head of the falls—but, again be careful of slippery logs. Avoid any current which could carry you over the falls.

Anchor (northwest of the falls) in 2 to 3 fathoms over soft mud with good holding.

Photo by Herb Nickles

Forevergreen *and friends exploring Ellerslie Lagoon*

"Cove East of Cheenis Lake"

Chart 3940 metric; anchor:
52°30.88′ N, 128°06.07′ W (NAD 83)

Temporary anchorage can be found with shelter from northwest winds in the cove east of Cheenis Lake. The pebble beach is strewn with drift logs indicating serious exposure to southeast and up-channel winds. The shore is fairly steep-to but it has a good bottom that will hold you against prevailing northwest winds.

Anchor in 4 fathoms over a mud, gravel, eel grass and clamshell bottom with fair-to-good holding.

Spiller Inlet

Chart 3940 metric; entrance:
52°30.70′ N, 128°04.60′ W; anchor:
52°38.92′ N, 128°03.03′ W (NAD 83)

> *Spiller Inlet has general mid-channel depths of 55 to 109 fathoms (100 to 200 m), decreasing to 14 to 27 fathoms (25 to 50 m) in the northernmost arm. Banks with 39 and 22 fathoms (71 and 40 m) over them lie respectively in mid-channel and on the east side of the channel 2.5 miles within the entrance. A reef with 5 to 7 fathoms (10 to 12 m) over it extends from the east shore to mid-channel 0.3 mile south of the entrance to the northernmost arm.* (p. 91, SD)

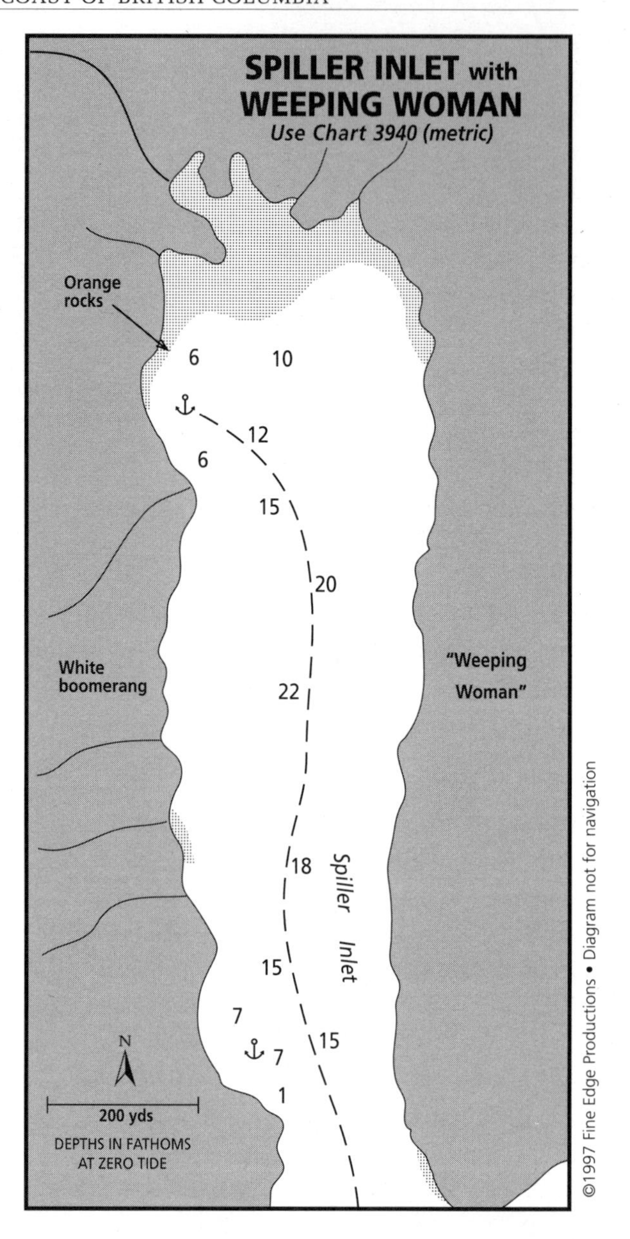

Spiller Inlet is the continuation of Spiller Channel north of the large unnamed island and heading due north for 10 miles. Nine miles inside the inlet is a large cove to the east at the outlet of Ingram Creek.

As you enter the narrow tip of Spiller Inlet, watch for the overhanging granite slabs high up on the east shore. You will see a large granite shelf which appears to be the sculptured face of a weeping woman, Picasso style. The weeping woman is quite striking when observed from midchannel. The mixed forest on shore appears to be old growth. On the hill above the west side of the bay, a large, white granite slab in the shape of a boomerang about 200 feet long also makes a good landmark.

The very head of Spiller Inlet is steep-to; 100 yards from the shore a shelf rises from 10 fathoms to just one! A grassy margin lines the shore, and the bay has very little driftwood, indicating that the anchorage is fairly safe in most weather and offers moderate protection in southerly weather. Anchorage can be found on the west side of the head of the inlet, south of the orange-colored rocks, in the lee of a small point.

Anchor in 7 fathoms, soft brown mud and large clam shells; holding is very good.

Lucky Girl *in Ellerslie Bay, East Anchorage*

"Ingram Bay"

Chart 3940 metric; entrance: 52°37.80′ N, 128°02.20′ W; anchor: 52°37.63′ N, 128°01.72′ W (NAD 83)

Ingram Bay is what we call the sheltered anchorage 350 yards north of a spectacular waterfall. The waterfall is a two-stage affair; the upper part falls 15 feet and the lower part 9 feet before plunging directly into Ingram Bay. Ingram Lake, several miles long, is immediately behind the falls and is said to be colder than the bay (about 66°F in the summer). A ruined log cabin is 1.75 miles southwest on a small creek. In 1996 a commercial vessel was tied to shore off the creek and a helicopter was parked on the point.

Good protection can be found from stable weather. Anchorage close off the small gravel and grass beach offers a good view of the falls with easy access to the beach. Avoid the large 3-meter shoal in the center of Ingram Bay. The inner cove, south and east of the this 3-meter shoal, is considerably more shallow in general than shown on the chart. Use caution as the water is opaque brown muskeg and the bottom difficult to discern even in less than 10 feet. The small beach at the outlet of Ingram Creek is used by locals as a campsite and has a fire ring and improvised bench.

Anchor in 2 to 3 fathoms over a gravel and sand bottom with fair-to-good holding.

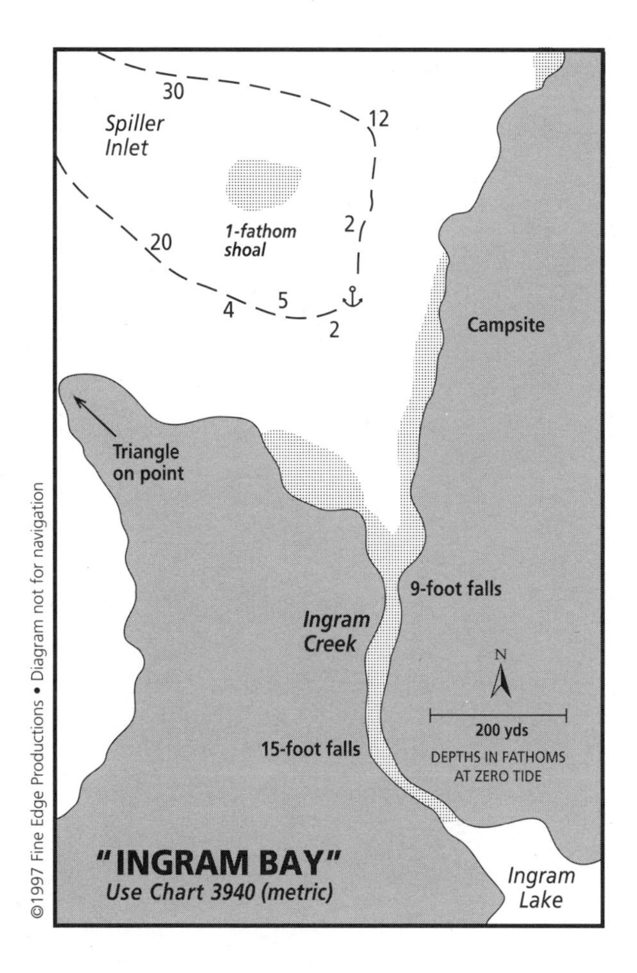

Tug pulling West Coast Lodge to its winter anchorage

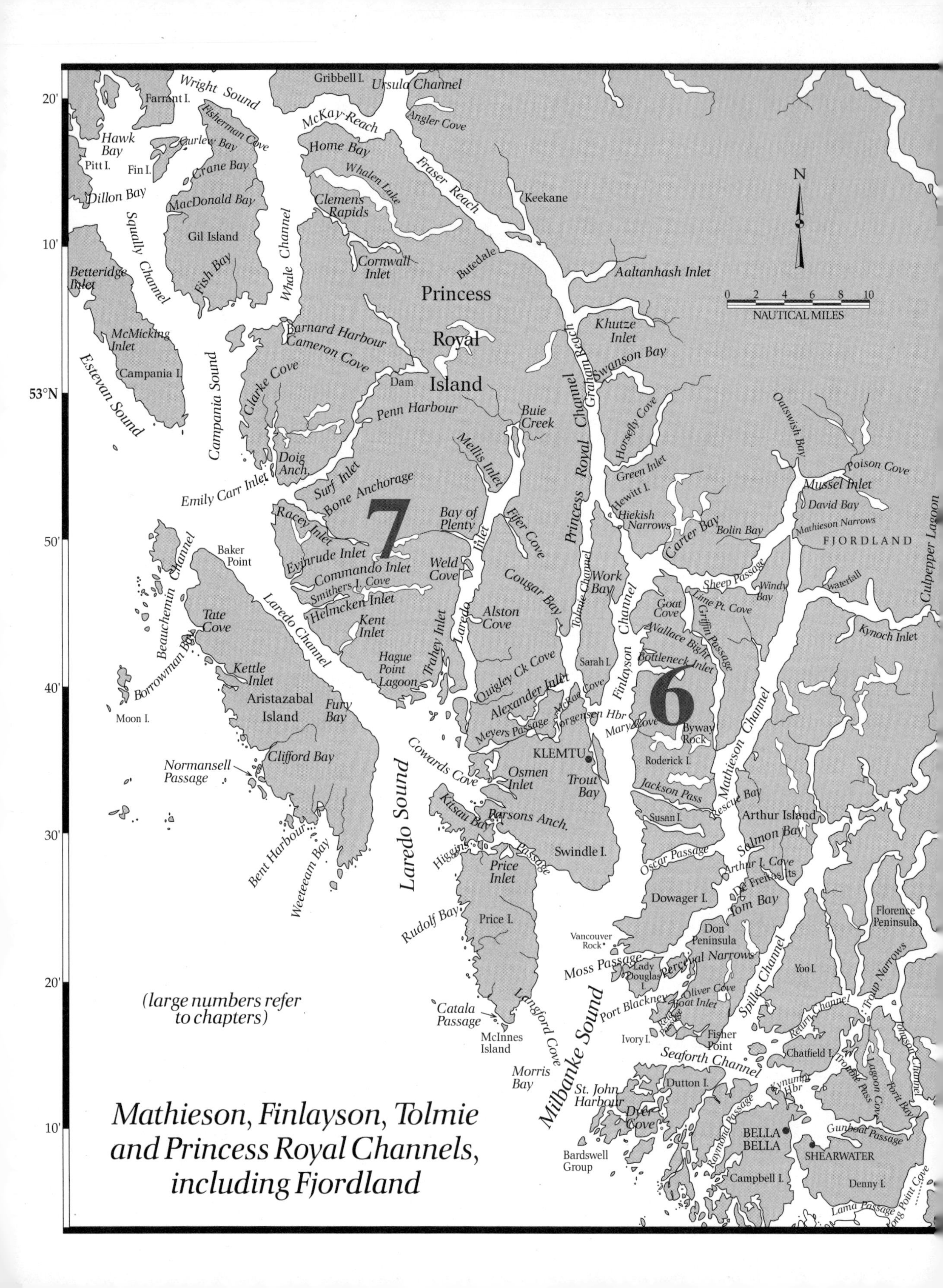
Mathieson, Finlayson, Tolmie and Princess Royal Channels, including Fjordland
(large numbers refer to chapters)
7
6
NAUTICAL MILES
0 2 4 6 8 10
N
20'
10'
53°N
50'
40'
30'
20'
10'
Wright Sound
Gribbell I.
Ursula Channel
Farrant I.
Fisherman Cove
Curlew Bay
Hawk Bay
Pitt I.
Fin I.
Crane Bay
Dillon Bay
MacDonald Bay
Squally Channel
Gil Island
Whale Channel
Fish Bay
Betteridge Inlet
McMicking Inlet
Campania I.
Estevan Sound
Campania Sound
McKay Reach
Angler Cove
Home Bay
Whalen Lake
Fraser Reach
Clemens Rapids
Keekane
Cornwall Inlet
Butedale
Aaltanhash Inlet
Princess Royal Island
Barnard Harbour
Cameron Cove
Clarke Cove
Dam
Penn Harbour
Khutze Inlet
Swanson Bay
Graham Reach
Princess Royal Channel
Buie Creek
Mellis Inlet
Doig Anch.
Emily Carr Inlet
Surf Inlet
Bone Anchorage
Racey Inlet
Bay of Plenty
Fifer Cove
Evinrude Inlet
Commando Inlet
Smithers I. Cove
Weld Cove
Helmcken Inlet
Kent Inlet
Laredo Inlet
Trahey Inlet
Hague Point Lagoon
Alston Cove
Cougar Bay
Quigley Ck Cove
Alexander Inlet
Meyers Passage
McRae Cove
Jorgensen Hbr
KLEMTU
Horsefly Cove
Green Inlet
Hewitt I.
Hiekish Narrows
Carter Bay
Bolin Bay
Tolmie Channel
Work Bay
Sarah I.
Finlayson Channel
Mary Cove
Oatswish Bay
Poison Cove
Mussel Inlet
David Bay
Mathieson Narrows
FJORDLAND
Culpepper Lagoon
Sheep Passage
Windy Bay
Waterfall
Lime Pt. Cove
Goat Cove
Griffin Passage
Wallace Bight
Bottleneck Inlet
Kynoch Inlet
Byway Rock
Roderick I.
Jackson Pass
Susan I.
Rescue Bay
Mathieson Channel
Arthur Island
Salmon Bay
Oscar Passage
Arthur I. Cove
De Freitas Its
Dowager I.
Tom Bay
Florence Peninsula
Baker Point
Beauchemin Channel
Borrowman Bay
Tate Cove
Laredo Channel
Kettle Inlet
Aristazabal Island
Fury Bay
Moon I.
Clifford Bay
Normansell Passage
Bent Harbour
Weeteeam Bay
Laredo Sound
Cowards Cove
Osmen Inlet
Trout Bay
Kitsau Bay
Parsons Anch.
Swindle I.
Higgins Passage
Price Inlet
Price I.
Rudolf Bay
Vancouver Rock
Don Peninsula
Moss Passage
Lady Douglas I.
Perceval Narrows
Yoo I.
Spiller Channel
Troup Narrows
Catala Passage
McInnes Island
Langford Cove
Milbanke Sound
Port Blackney
Oliver Cove
Boat Inlet
Reid Passage
Ivory I.
Fisher Point
Return Channel
Seaforth Channel
Chatfield I.
Morris Bay
St. John Harbour
Dutton I.
Kynumpt Hbr
Lagoon Cove
Troupe Pass
Johnson Channel
Forit Bay
Dyer Cove
Raymond Passage
BELLA BELLA
Gunboat Passage
SHEARWATER
Bardswell Group
Campbell I.
Denny I.
Lama Passage
Long Point Cove

6

Mathieson, Finlayson, Tolmie and Princess Royal Channels, including Fjordland

Mathieson Channel is a beautiful smooth-water route that leads all the way to the magnificent Fjordland Park. During the summer, channel waters are frequently calm, and since Mathieson sits away from the ferry-boat route, you seldom encounter traffic. Dolphins and puffins like this environment, and you probably will see more of them than you do people.

Fjordland Park and Princess Royal Channel have some outstanding waterfalls, and where the granite walls of Mathieson overhang the channel, you can take the bow of your boat right up to the side without concern.

There is even more to explore in this part of the coast: Lombard Inlet and Lady Trutch Passage are still uncharted as is the mysterious 13-mile-long Griffin Passage.

Klemtu, the home of the Kitasoo Band, is the only settlement in this area, and its telephone, store, and fuel dock can be a welcome sight.

In addition, there are a number of great coves offering outstanding shelter along the route north to Princess Royal Channel and you are invited to take some side trips and find a few for yourself.

Reid Passage

Charts 3710 (inset), 3728; south entrance: 52°15.90′ N, 128°23.28′ W; north entrance: 52°19.45′ N, 128°20.90′ W; Carne Rock light: 52°18.12′ N, 128°21.80′ W (NAD 27)

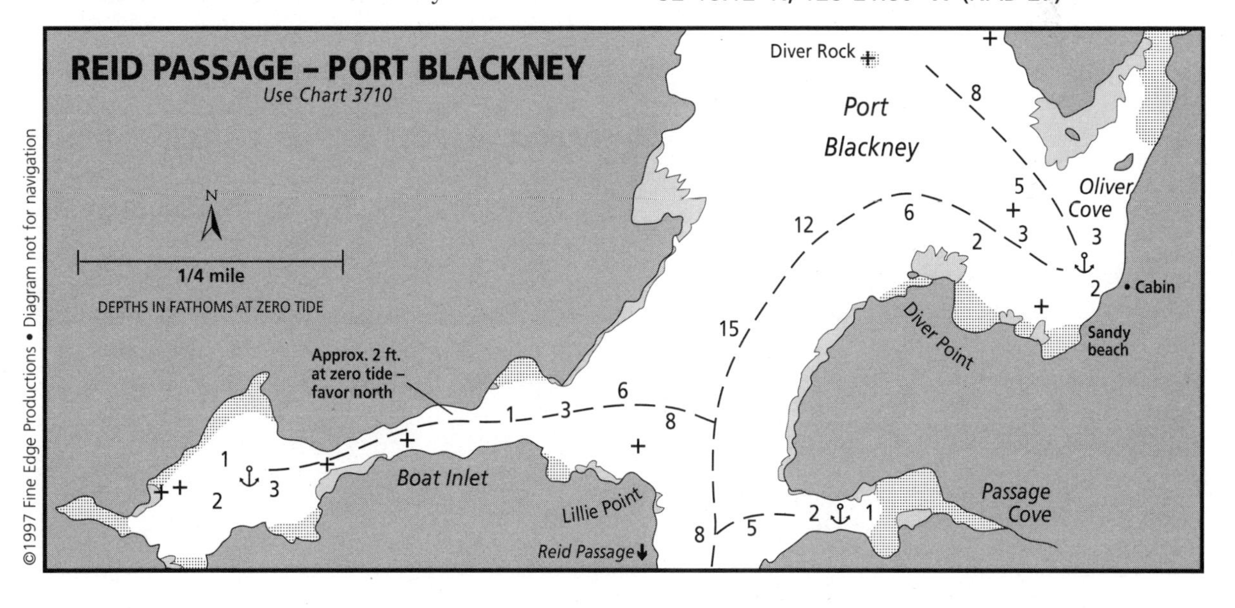

Reid Passage leads south from Port Blackney into Powell Anchorage; it provides a route for small craft following the Inner Passage that avoids the exposed waters of Milbanke Sound. Local knowledge is advised to navigate this passage.

Tidal streams in Reid Passage generally set north on both the flood and ebb. The maximum is about 2 kn. (p. 97, SD)

Hobbit *heading through Reid Passage*

The smooth waters of Reid Passage allow you to avoid the swells occasionally found near Ivory Island Lighthouse and in Milbanke Sound. While most commercial fishing boats round Ivory Island and cross Milbanke Sound directly, cruising boats usually take the scenic route north through Reid Passage, then up through Mathieson Channel. Numerous reefs at the south entrance to Reid Passage make entering it a bit dicey, and you should first study the large-scale inset on Chart 3710 before transiting. We have seen waves heap up and break on these reefs and spew sea-foam clear across the entrance. At such times (luckily they're rare) you risk raising the ire of your crew, if not threatening the survival of your boat by surfing the entrance and it's better to wait in Kynumpt Harbour (northbound) or in Oliver Cove (southbound).

Approaching Reid Passage from Seaforth Channel, continue west until you are due south of red buoy "E50." Turn north, passing the buoy to starboard. In this manner, and in most sea conditions, you can run with the swells on your port quarter making a more comfortable ride. Once you have passed the red buoy, travelling is fine even in 30 knots of wind or more. Most of the many reefs and rocks in this area are marked by breaking or heaping swells even on calm days, and they do a good job of dissipating the southerly swells. Once you are in Reid Passage proper, the seas calm and there are no swells north of Carne Rock. Favor the east shore in Reid Passage when passing Carne Rock. Both ebb and flood currents seem to flow north through Reid Passage—hydraulic effects that can make you scratch your head.

Southbound from Perceval Narrows, be sure to identify Promise Point at the north end of Cecilia Island; it is easy to confuse the rock piles north of there at the north entrance into Reid Passage.

Passage Cove

Charts 3710 (inset), 3728; entrance:
52°18.48′ N, 128°21.44′ W (NAD 27)

Passage Cove is a nifty little cove 0.3 mile south of Oliver Cove that nearly dries on low water, but you can find pleasant anchorage here by using a stern tie to shore just inside the entrance.

Oliver Cove

Charts 3710 (inset) , 3728; entrance:
52°18.75′ N, 128°21.18′ W; anchor:
52°18.69′ N, 128°21.05′ W (NAD 27)

Oliver Cove, on the east side of Port Blackney, has drying ledges extending from its north and south shores. . . . A rock, with 2 feet (0.6 m) over it, lies in the centre of the entrance to Oliver Cove. . . . Small craft can obtain anchorage sheltered from all winds in the middle of Oliver Cove in 6 fathoms (11 m), mud bottom. (p. 97, SD)

Oliver Cove is a popular, well-protected layover for both north- and southbound cruising boats. It has a small, sandy beach backed by woods, where you can see many deer and find evidence of early habitation.

Enter Oliver Cove by passing Carne Rock to your port side. Avoid Diver Rock (marked by kelp) and a small, underwater rock in Oliver Cove itself. Logs and debris find their way into Oliver Cove and seldom escape.

While you can anchor over a fairly wide area, some boaters tie a line to the spike-shaped rock on shore in front of the cabin site.

Some locals prefer to pass Boat Inlet and Oliver Cove and continue north for 2 miles into uncharted Lombard Inlet where the mud is said to be "deep and stinky" but holding is good. Only the southern portion of Lombard Inlet is charted and there is no reference to it in *Sailing Directions.*

Anchor in 3 to 4 fathoms over a gravel bottom with fair holding.

Boat Inlet

Charts 3710 (inset), 3728; entrance: 52°18.57′ N, 128°21.70′ W; anchor: 52°18.51′ N, 128°22.24′ W (NAD 27)

> *Boat Inlet, on the west side of Port Blackney, is entered north of Lillie Point, which has a rock with less than 6 feet (2 m) over it lying about 300 feet (91 m) north. The entrance to this inlet is narrow and has rocks with less than 6 feet (2 m) over them at its west end.* (p. 97, SD)

Boat Inlet is one of those quiet places where you feel you're the only people left on the planet. There is never a ripple here, but during a storm you can hear the surf crashing on the outside. The entrance is quite shallow (about 2 feet at zero tide!) and a bit tricky. Favor the north shore the entire route. We once had to remain inside for several hours waiting for the tide to rise so we could exit. The bottom through the passage is visible the entire way and, since the current is slight, you can enter slowly. Inside, there is ample swinging room over a flat bottom.

We have sighted sandhill cranes here and "Penpoint Gunnels," a blue eel-like fish that swims along the surface scooping up its food. There were also *thousands* of fingerlings that left an expanding V-shaped wake on the calm surface. A small group of four or five sandhill cranes summers in the region around Seaforth Channel, and we have spotted them in various coves between Boat Inlet and Ardmillan Bay. Please do not disturb these beautiful rare birds.

Anchor in 2 fathoms over a sand and mud bottom with good holding.

Mathieson Channel

Charts 3728, 3734, 3962; south entrance: 52°18.20′ N, 128°25.40′ W; north entrance: 52°50.70′ N, 128°08.60′ W (NAD 27)

> *Mathieson Channel, entered from Milbanke Sound between Lady Douglas and Cecilia Islands, leads 36 miles north. The fairway through the channel is deep and wide except at Perceval Narrows, which is near the south end between Lady Douglas and Lake Islands, and at Mathieson Narrows, which is at the north end.* (p. 97, SD)

Mathieson Channel is a well-protected, smooth-water route that you can use all the way to its end. Or you can bail out part way and head to Klemtu using Jackson Passage.

Perceval Narrows

Chart 3728; south entrance: 52°19.85′ N, 128°22.55′ W; north entrance: 52°20.17′ N, 128°22.47′ W (NAD 27)

> *Perceval Narrows, the main route leading north through Mathieson Channel, lies between Grautoff Point, the south extremity of Lake Island, and Martha Island. The navigable channel through the narrows is 0.1 mile wide and deep.*
>
> *Tidal streams in Perceval Narrows flood north and ebb south with a maximum of 5 kn.* (p. 97, SD)

From Reid Passage to Perceval Narrows, you cross the southern part of Mathieson Channel which is exposed to southwest and southeasterly weather, conditions that will put your boat broadside to the waves and in their trough for a short distance. When southwest swells are running in lower Mathieson Channel, with opposing strong ebb currents in Perceval Narrows, large standing waves that form off Martha Island can be extremely dangerous to small craft. During times like this, it is a good idea for small boats to wait out the weather in Port Blackney.

Cockle Bay

Chart 3728; anchor: 52°20.75′ N, 128°23.25′ W (NAD 27)

> *Cockle Bay, north of Alec Islet, has a broad expanse of sandy beach at its head.*
>
> *Small vessels can obtain good anchorage in Cockle Bay, about 0.2 mile NNW of Alec Islet, in about 16 fathoms (29 m). Caution is required in approaching this anchorage as the depths decrease rapidly toward shore.* (p. 98, SD)

Cockle Bay, on the east side of Lady Douglas Island, offers protection close to its long, sandy beach and makes a good lunch stop. This is an excellent kayak haul-out and camping spot. It is also a good place to stretch your legs and enjoy the unusually fine, large beach with a collection of drift logs and stumps blown south from Fjordland by winter storm winds. Cockle Bay is out of the major current of Perceval Narrows and also benefits somewhat from the lee effect of Alec Islet. Note that Alec Island is thickly wooded while Lady Douglas has been clearcut.

Anchor in 4 fathoms over a sand and shell bottom with fair holding.

Moss Passage, Sloop Narrows

Charts 3710, 3728; east entrance: 52°21.68′ N, 128°22.70′ W; west entrance: 52°21.30′ N, 128°28.60′ W (NAD 27)

> *Moss Passage connects Milbanke Sound to Mathieson Channel. Sloop Narrows is its narrowest part. Local knowledge is recommended for navigating this passage. Oscar Passage . . . offers a better route.*
>
> *Tidal streams in Moss Passage flood east and ebb west; both streams attain 2 to 4 kn at springs.* (p. 96, SD)

Moss Passage, although not usually found on anyone's route to anywhere, has a charm of its own. Small Sloop Narrows on the south side of Squaw Island is choked with a patch of large bull kelp that weaves an almost hypnotic pattern in the moderately turbulent water. The fairway in Moss Passage is about 50 yards wide and about 6 fathoms deep. It is protected from major winds and chop and, along with Merilia Passage on its northwest corner, can offer a semi-protected route for those headed north to Higgins Passage. There are several small, sandy kayak haul-out beaches in Moss Passage.

Morris Bay

Chart 3728; entrance:
52°21.15′ N, 128°26.85′ W;
anchor: 52°20.89′ N, 128°26.74′ W (NAD 27)

> *Anchorage can be obtained in Morris Bay, about 0.1 mile from its west shore, in 13 fathoms (24 m), sand bottom.* (p. 96, SD)

Morris Bay is a small scenic bay on the south shore of Moss Passage, 2 miles east of Vancouver Rock. Some say it is good only in moderate weather, and that perhaps the pass between Salal Island and Lady Douglas is a better anchorage. For a small boat, we like Morris Bay tucked in at its southern end, perhaps using a stern tie for an overnight stay. Morris Bay is a good lunch stop and a place to observe and gauge the conditions in Milbanke Sound. There are no drift logs on the beach, and while it's true that at either anchorage you receive gusts and surge, Morris Bay has a good feel. It should provide very good protection in southeast weather and fair-to-good protection in strong westerlies. We find only gusts in Morris Bay when whitecaps are rolling up Moss Passage.

Avoid the large, dark rock complex awash on 14 feet on the southeast side of the bay.

Anchor in 3 to 5 fathoms over a sand and mud bottom with good holding.

Lady Trutch Passage

Chart 3728; north entrance:
52°20.96′ N, 128°20.69′ W; anchor:
52°21.80′ N, 128°20.50′ W (NAD 27)

. . . its north end has not been surveyed and should not be entered without local knowledge. (p. 97, SD)

We have anchored in the north end of Lady Trutch Passage on the west side of Nathan Island and found it well sheltered. There is also shelter in the islets on the north side of Nathan Island. Lady Trutch Passage may be a less exposed alternative to Perceval Narrows; however, its south end is choked with large rocks and a number of reefs which make navigation difficult. The passage should be attempted only by small boats at slack tide and in good weather conditions. Lady Trutch Passage is uncharted and those entering must locate and identify any and all hazards on their own.

Anchor in 6 to 8 fathoms over an unrecorded bottom.

Tom Bay

Chart 3728; entrance:
52°24.30′ N, 128°16.10′ W;
anchor: 52°23.97′ N, 128°15.95′ W (NAD 27)

Tom Bay, SE of Jermaine Point, extends south from Symonds Point and is free of off-lying dangers. A small bay at the NE entrance is filled with logbooms (1988).

Anchorage for vessels to about 130 feet (40 m) long can be obtained in Tom Bay about 0.5 mile south of Symonds Point in about 11 fathoms (20 m). (p. 98, SD)

Tom Bay is reported to offer good shelter from southeast storms; however, it is subject to down drafts from the high peaks along its shores.

Anchor in 8 to 10 fathoms over an unrecorded bottom.

"Cove Northwest of Arthur Island"

Chart 3734; east entrance:
52°27.32′ N, 128°15.80′ W;
anchor: 52°27.49′ N, 128°16.37′ W (NAD 27)

Arthur Island is on the west side of the fairway. A narrow but deep passage on its north and west sides separates the island from Dowager Island.

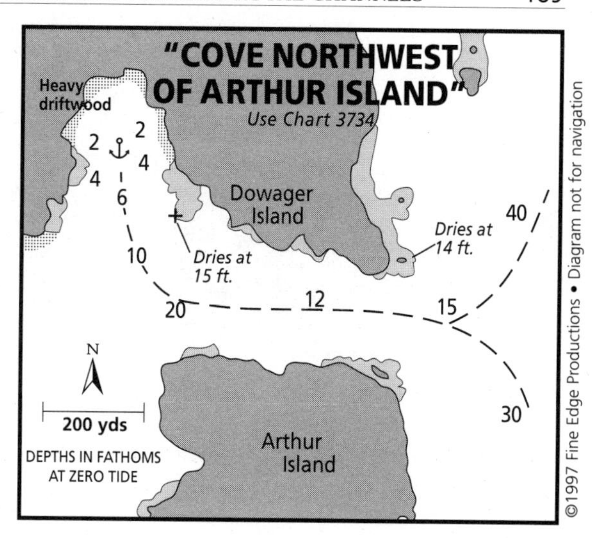

Anchorage for small craft can be obtained in either of the two small bays NW of Arthur Island. (p. 98, SD)

Cove Northwest of Arthur Island, the first of two small coves northwest of Arthur Island, can be used by small boats for protection from heavy northwest winds or chop. Heavy driftwood on the shore of both coves indicates that these would not be good anchorages in a southerly gale. In such weather, you should head quickly to Rescue Bay.

Entry to Cove Northwest of Arthur Island is over a deep, uneven bottom, indicative of a rocky surface. Be sure to avoid the rocks off Dowager Island.

Anchor in 4 fathoms over a mixed bottom of sand, rock, grass, and shells with good holding if your anchor is well set.

De Freitas Islets

Chart 3734; entrance: 52°27.15′ N, 128°14.00′ W;
anchor: 52°26.85′ N, 128°14.90′ W (NAD 27)

Anchorage, suitable for small vessels, can be obtained between De Freitas Islets and the east shore in about 12 fathoms (22 m). (p. 98, SD)

De Freitas Islets form a natural breakwater from westerly winds and chop, and anchorage is reported deep in the head of the bay.

Anchor in 7 to 10 fathoms over an unrecorded bottom.

Klemtu fuel dock

Bulley Bay

Chart 3734; position:
52°28.20′ N, 128°19.10′ W
(NAD 27)

> *Anchorage for small vessels can be obtained in Bulley Bay, about 0.1 mile offshore, in about 15 fathoms (27 m); local knowledge is advised.* (p. 103, SD)

Rescue Bay

Charts 3711 (inset), 3734;
entrance:
52°31.23′ N, 128°17.19′ W;
anchor: 52°30.92′ N, 128°17.17′ W
(NAD 27)

> *Rescue Bay, on the west side of Spaniel Point, affords good sheltered anchorage for small vessels about 0.2 mile from its head in about 9 fathoms (16 m).* (p. 98, SD)

As its name indicates, Rescue Bay provides the best protection you can find from stormy weather in Mathieson Channel. It can accommodate a lot of boats, and you usually find all sorts of vessels here in any weather. Entry requires care to avoid the reefs off the islets and shoal areas around the bay, but you can enter at night with radar if necessary.

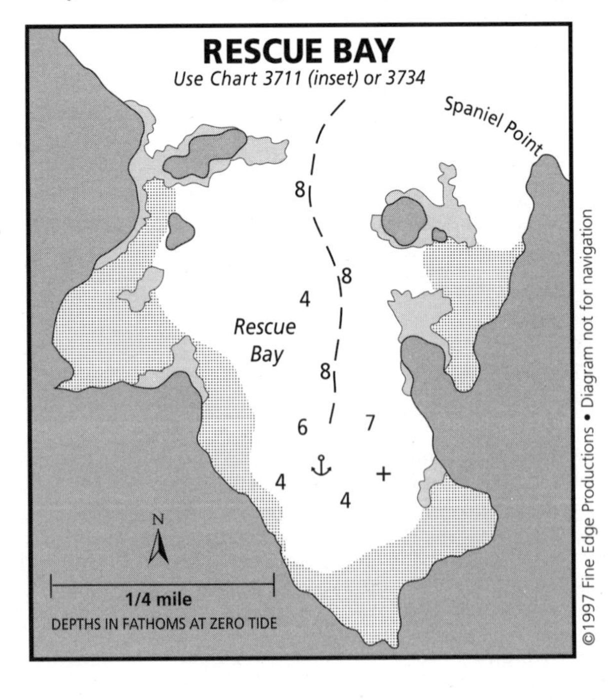

Salmon Bay

Chart 3734; entrance:
52°28.90′ N, 128°13.20′ W;
anchor: 52°29.12′ N, 128°12.95′ W (NAD 27)

> *Salmon Bay, 2 miles north of De Freitas Islets, is entered between Carmichael Point and Ursus Point. There is a drying flat at the head of the bay.*
>
> *Anchorage for small vessels can be obtained about 0.1 mile from the head of Salmon Bay in about 10 fathoms (18 m).* (p. 98, SD)

Anchor in 10 fathoms over an unrecorded bottom.

Oscar Passage to Klemtu

Chart 3734; east entrance:
52°29.00′ N, 128°16.00′ W; west entrance:
52°27.50′ N, 128°25.00′ W (NAD 27)

> *Oscar Passage is deep except at its east end where a ridge, on which there are some shoals, connects Buckley Head to Miall Point.*
>
> *Anchorage for small vessels can be obtained in Bulley Bay, about 0.1 mile offshore, in about 15 fathoms (27 m); local knowledge is advised.* (p. 103, SD)

Oscar Passage is an easy way to cross from Mathieson to Finlayson Channel and Klemtu, especially in east winds or with limited visibility. During heavy weather from the south, the west entrance of Oscar Passage receives heavy swells. Jackson Passage (3 miles north) generally provides a better and shorter route (you will still be in the trough of the swells however).

Since Rescue Bay shoals rapidly, stay in the middle towards the east side.

Anchor in 4 fathoms over a mixed mud bottom with good holding.

Jackson Passage to Klemtu

Charts 3711, 3734; narrows east entrance: 52°31.35′ N, 128°16.80′ W; west entrance: 52°32.75′ N, 128°26.50′ W (NAD 27)

Jackson Passage is very narrow and shallow near its east end, in Jackson Narrows. (p. 103, SD)

Jackson Passage offers a shorter and more scenic route to Klemtu than Oscar Passage does. The west end of Jackson Passage can put you in beam seas coming up Finlayson Channel, and while the distance across is short, you may want to turn north for the comfort of your crew or boat and run with the seas to Jane Passage and return south to Klemtu.

Jackson Narrows

Charts 3711 (inset), 3734 (inset); east narrows entrance: 52°31.33′ N, 128°17.60′ W; west narrows entrance: 52°31.47′ N, 128°18.25′ W (NAD 27)

Jackson Narrows, near the east end of Jackson Passage, is obstructed by rocks and drying reefs. A navigable passage through the narrows, suitable for small craft, is close to the Susan Island shore and should only be attempted near HW slack. (p. 103)

Jackson Narrows requires some tight maneuvering—especially when current is running and a local sportfishing boat from Klemtu happens to come screaming through at 20 knots!

Study the inset on Chart 3734 for the narrows, or the wider inset on Chart 3711. The width of the fairway in the narrows is not as great as has been reported in some publications—we would guess no more than 65 feet. The fairway through the narrows favors the south shore avoiding midchannel reefs and rocks. Minimum depth in the fairway is just over 2 fathoms. When you're westbound, at the narrowest point be sure to execute a turn to the left and favor the south shore in order to safely pass the last reef and rock to your starboard.

When transiting the narrows, watch for opposing traffic. Very fast, small commercial fishing boats often roar through at top speed, passing just a few yards away!

Griffin Passage (South Entrance)

Chart 3962; south entrance: 52°35.14′ N, 128°17.33′ W; south rapids (unsurveyed): 52°36.74′ N, 128°17.60′ W (NAD 27)

Griffin Passage is entered west of Charles Head at its south end and leads 12 miles north between Pooley Island and Roderick Island to Sheep Passage. The passage divides into two very narrow channels on either side of an unnamed island about 7 miles north of Charles Head. Strong tidal streams occur in both channels.

MAYDAY—Griffin Passage

At the upper end of the south tidal rapids in Griffin Passage, there's a rock we call "Byway Rock." At 1500 hours on July 16, 1996, while we were in Higgins Passage, we heard a MAYDAY sent by the *Byway*, a 42-foot fishing boat with two persons aboard, which had hit a rock located at 52°37.13′ N, 128°17.53′ W. (This was the same uncharted rock that alarmed my crew and me the previous summer when we were at the same spot!) The vessel *Byway* reported that it was listing at a 45-degree angle and Prince Rupert Coast Guard Radio sent the *Kitasu Responder* to their rescue. Later, we talked with Joe Tobacco, skipper of the *Byway*, in a call from Victoria. He told us that a small, log-salvage tug from Bella Bella, operated by Jim Darwin, did a marvelous job pulling the boat off the rock in the midnight darkness, and towing it to Shearwater where the boat was repaired.

Byway arrived in the area at low water and Joe had checked out the narrows through his binoculars. He thought the rock was far away, but it was lurking about 18 inches below the surface (awash on about an 11-foot tide) right in the center of the channel at the edge of the narrows. Joe struck the rock on the last of the flood and with power on. In future attempts, he suggests staying on the west side of "Byway Rock." Until there is definite information to confirm these observations, beware!

—DCD

Griffin Passage is unsurveyed and should not be entered without local knowledge. (p. 98, SD)

As you continue north in Mathieson Channel, 4 miles north of Jackson Narrows, you pass the south entrance to Griffin Passage, probably the largest area of the B.C. coast still uncharted.

Thirteen miles long, Griffin Passage connects Mathieson Channel to Sheep Channel four miles southeast of the entrance to Hiekish Narrows. Cruising boats have long speculated whether Griffin Passage could be used as a cruising route. However, we don't know anyone who has used it.

Griffin Passage, south entrance on beginning of ebb

Griffin Passage, south entrance rapids

South entrance at low tide, "Byway Rock" showing in center

Although long on the agenda for *Baidarka*, we did not try a transit until two years ago. At that time, we were on the very lip of the south narrows when Gloria Burke, our sharp-eyed bow lookout, went "ballistic," pointing straight into the water. We were able to stop just inches from hitting a large uncharted rock we now call "Byway Rock" (see sidebar). Since the ebb was quickly turning into a fast-moving river, we backed down to the basin and anchored. Don made the transit by inflatable to the north narrows and back. Between the two narrows lies a remote and deep saltwater lake whose shores have not been logged. This "lake," 6 miles long, varies slightly from tide to tide. Anchor sites south of the north falls look promising and there is little sign of chop or strong weather in this basin.

While we believe that a safe transit can be made, there are three major obstacles: 1) The narrows becomes a roaring tidal rapids (waterfall) at anything less than high water; 2) the rapids at the north end becomes a cataract less than 20 yards wide; and 3) north of the tidal rapids there is a shoal area choked with bull kelp and grass. Until Griffin Passage is surveyed and its tidal mechanisms well understood, it cannot be recommended as a cruising boat route.

At present, there is a large, active logging operation in the north end of Griffin Passage, and we hope that the next time we visit it we will still see trees along its slopes.

James Bay

Chart 3962; entrance: 52°41.45′ N, 128°12.15′ W; anchor: 52°42.68′ N, 128°12.65′ W (NAD 27)

James Bay, 7.5 miles north of Hird Point, and entered west of Pooley Point, is free of off-lying dangers.

Anchorage for vessels up to 200 feet (61 m) long can be obtained about 0.2 mile south of the drying flat in James Bay in 16 fathoms (29 m), mud and shell bottom. (p. 98, SD)

James Bay is exposed to southwest weather but protected from westerlies or downslope winds. Anchorage is reported off the drying mud flat.

Anchor in 13 fathoms over a mud and sand bottom with good holding.

Kynoch Inlet

Chart 3962; entrance: 52°45. 80′ N, 128°07.15′ W (NAD 27)

Kynoch Inlet, entered between Garvey Point and Kynoch Point, has shores which are generally bold and steep-to; a conspicuous waterfall is on the north shore, about 1.5 miles east of Garvey Point. (p. 99, SD)

Kynoch Inlet, part of the Fjordland Park, contains wild and magnificent scenery. High snow-covered peaks and ridges with vertical granite ramparts rise above its shores. You can approach the stunningly beautiful waterfall on the north shore of Kynoch Inlet, but be careful not to swamp your boat!

There is no shallow anchorage within Kynoch Inlet except what can be found along the shore in Culpepper Lagoon.

Desbrisay Bay, "Big Bay"

Chart 3962; entrance: 52°45. 50′ N, 127°59.50′ W (NAD 27)

Desbrisay Bay, known locally as Big Bay, extends north from Kynoch Inlet and terminates in a steep-to mud flat. Depths are too great for satisfactory anchorage. (p. 99, SD)

Culpepper Lagoon

Chart 3962 (inset); entrance: 52°45.16′ N, 127°52.97′ W; anchor (lagoon head): 52°43.95′ N, 127°49.75′ W (NAD 27)

Culpepper Lagoon, at the head of Kynoch Inlet, is entered through a narrow, shallow passage. Riot Creek and Lard Creek flow into Culpepper Lagoon. A small cabin is at the mouth of Riot Creek. (p. 99, SD)

Culpepper Lagoon, one of the most beautiful places on B.C.'s North Coast, is infrequently visited. Unfavorable reports in cruising literature frighten most boaters away and, for this reason, you may find you have this place all to yourself.

Rod Nash writes: "We entered the lagoon on a 6.3-foot tide (Bella Bella) and found no less than 17 feet of water in the fairway. There were no rocks or kelp in midchannel. Although current tends to draw boats toward the cliff on the south side, it appears mild in the entrance, and there is not as big an inflow here as there is in Ellerslie Lagoon.

Once you are inside Culpepper Lagoon, use Chart 3962 to find a 4- to 6-fathom shelf and consider using a stern-tie to shore. The flat off the river dries and has only 4 to 6 feet on it at higher tides. You can explore the river by dinghy for quite a distance admiring the glacier and snowfields above. There is a cabin on the south side half-way into Culpepper at the mouth of Riot Creek."

Kevin Monahan has this additional first-hand experience to offer: "Anchor in 14 fathoms (mud bottom) off the drying flat of Kainet Creek, northwest of the entrance to Culpepper Lagoon in Kynoch Inlet. This spot is not subject to southeast weather, but summer westerlies can be a bit of a problem. The scenery is some of the most spectacular in the central coast."

Heathorn Bay

Chart 3962; beach: 52°50.39′ N, 128°08.02′ W (NAD 27)

Heathorn Bay . . . is too deep for satisfactory anchorage. (p. 98, SD)

Crystal-clear Heathorn Bay, at the north end of Mathieson Channel, can provide protection from northerly winds if necessary, but the beach is steep-to, and it's difficult to find anchorage. In calm weather you can literally run your bow to the beach and hold it there, because there is absolutely no wave action. You can drift around and just enjoy the scenery.

It may be possible to get a line ashore and put a stern anchor into deep water if the situation requires it, but it's easier to pass through Mathieson Narrows and head into Windy Bay for shelter.

Mathieson Narrows

Chart 3962; position: 52°50.70′ N, 128°08.60′ W (NAD 27)

Mathieson Narrows is free of dangers. Mathieson Point, at the north end of the narrows, is the NE extremity of Pooley Island. . . . The flood tidal stream that flows north through Mathieson Channel and the flood that flows east through Sheep Passage meet in the vicinity of Mathieson Narrows and cause some turbulence. (pp. 98–99, SD)

We have seen a flock of at least 500, if not 1,000, puffins in the narrows here, frolicking in the slight turbulence, carrying on a mighty conversation!

Finlayson Channel

Charts 3728, 3734

Finlayson Channel leads 24 miles north from Milbanke Sound. The islands on both sides of the channel rise precipitously from the water's edge to elevations of 1,500 to 2,600 feet (457 to 793 m). The south part of Finlayson Channel, as far north as Sarah Passage and Tolmie Channel, is part of the main Inner Passage leading north toward Alaska.

Tidal streams flood north through Finlayson Channel and ebb south. The north-going stream is stronger in Finlayson Channel than in Tolmie Channel. The south-going stream, however, is stronger in Tolmie Channel and runs for 1 h.30 min. after the same stream has ceased in Finlayson Channel. In the narrow parts of these channels both streams attain 3 kn at springs but in the broader parts only 1 kn. (pp. 99, 101, SD)

Red tides, commonly encountered in Finlayson Channel from May to August, look like bright red paint poured on the water. Although not all red tides are toxic, it is unwise to eat clams taken from areas that are not regularly tested (i.e., the entire North Coast).

Nowish Cove

Chart 3734; north entrance: 52°31.60′ N, 128°26.20′ W; anchor: 52°31.33′ N, 128°25.64′ W (NAD 27)

Nowish Cove, on the west side of Susan Island, is sheltered by Nowish Island; it is approached from north and tidal streams are relatively weak in the fairway. Fell Point is the north entrance point to Nowish Cove.

Anchorage for small craft can be obtained in Nowish Cove in coarse sand in 12 to 15 fathoms (22 to 27 m). (p. 101, SD)

Nowish Cove has fair shelter, although eddies from current in the channel may cause your vessel to swing and risk fouling your anchor.

Anchor in about 12 fathoms over a rocky bottom with fair holding.

Klemtu Passage

Charts 3711 (inset), 3734; south entrance: 52°33.15′ N, 128°29.60′ W; north entrance: 52°36.65′ N, 128°31.25′ W (NAD 27)

Klemtu Passage has a least mid-channel depth of 49 feet (14.9 m), encountered about midway through the passage. The passage is safe, provided a mid-channel course is kept.

In order to avoid damage to vessels secured alongside the wharf and floats at Klemtu, mariners are advised to reduce speed to a minimum consistent with safe navigation when passing the settlement.

Tidal streams in Klemtu Passage are comparatively weak. (p. 101, SD)

Klemtu Anchorage, Clothes Bay

Charts 3711 (inset), 3734; anchor (Clothes Bay): 52°34.42′ N, 128°30.92′ W (NAD 27)

Klemtu Anchorage, abreast the entrance to Clothes Bay, is not recommended because it is in the middle of the fairway for Klemtu Passage which is used extensively by fish boats. The depth in the anchorage is about 12 fathoms (22 m), sand and shell bottom. It is suitable for vessels up to about 150 feet (46 m) long.

Anchorage for small craft can be obtained in Clothes Bay in 30 feet (9.1 m) or west of Star Island or Stockade Islets. (p. 101, SD)

Trout Bay

Charts 3711 (inset), 3734; public dock: 52°35.44′ N, 128°30.92′ W; fuel dock: 52°35.65′ N, 128°31.18′ W (NAD 27)

Trout Bay, 1 mile north of Base Point, is entered north of Klemtu Point. The settlement of Klemtu is on the north side and the Indian village is on the south side of Trout Bay. (p. 101, SD)

Klemtu (Trout Bay), although well sheltered from all weather, is such a busy place that cruising boats generally choose not to anchor here. Although the fuel dock on the north side of the village has a new, larger float, you may occasionally have trouble making contact for fuel; a telephone number is listed in case of emergencies. The public wharf has a pay telephone at its gangway.

Don't be surprised to see a ferryboat or cruise ship in narrow Klemtu Passage and be sure to give them as much clearance as possible. Courtesy requires a no-wake speed when you pass Trout Bay or the facilities on the north side.

Although Klemtu had a poor reputation among cruising boats in the past, this appears to have changed, and the Band now encourages pleasure boats to stop. There is a well-stocked store at the head of the fuel dock, a second public pay phone, and a cafe. The water at the dock is reported to be excellent.

Mary Cove

Chart 3734; entrance: 52°36.60′ N, 128°26.65′ W; anchor: 52°36.87′ N, 128°26.16′ W (NAD 27)

Mary Cove, 3.8 miles north of Begg Point, has a bar across it about 0.2 mile within the entrance with 18 feet (5.5 m) over it. Toward the head of the cove depths increase to nearly 60 feet (18.3 m). A sand beach is at the head of the cove.

Anchorage for small craft can be obtained near the head of Mary Cove; the holding ground is good. (p. 102, SD)

Mary Cove, on the west shore of Roderick Island 3.5 miles southeast of Boat Bluff, offers good shelter and is close for a run into Klemtu. Most weather seems to blow by outside while inside you're snug. If a storm were expected, we would head for Bottleneck Inlet, 4 miles north.

In Mary Cove, once you've crossed the shallow bar, you can anchor anywhere near a 9-fathom hole or on the north side off the beach.

Anchor in 7 to 9 fathoms over a sand and mud bottom with good holding.

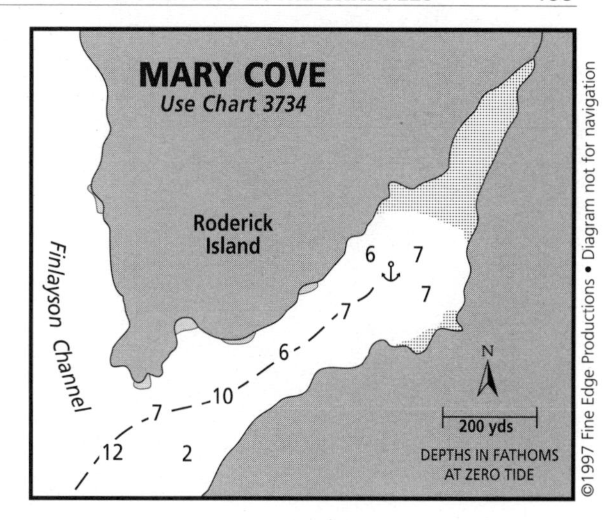

Watson Bay

Chart 3734; entrance: 52°41.20′ N, 128°25.95′ W (NAD 27)

Watson Bay, 4 miles north of Mary Cove, is entered between Bancroft Point and Howay Point. (p. 102, SD)

Roderick Cove

Chart 3734; entrance: 52°40.60′ N, 128°21.45′ W (NAD 27)

Roderick Cove lies east of Bolt Point and forms the head of Watson Bay. Depths in Watson Bay and Roderick Cove are too great for convenient anchorage. (p. 102, SD)

Although small boats may be able to find good shelter in the south nook of Roderick Cove using a stern tie, Bottleneck Inlet, one mile to the north, offers better protection.

Bottleneck Inlet

Chart 3734; entrance: 52°42.80′ N, 128°25.50′ W; anchor: 52°42.58′ N, 128°24.05′ W (NAD 27)

Bottleneck Inlet, 1.2 miles north of Howay Point, has an entrance only 300 feet (91 m) wide with a least depth of 10 feet (3 m) through it.

Anchorage for small craft, with good shelter, can be obtained anywhere within Bottleneck Inlet. (p. 102, SD)

Bottleneck Inlet, one of the more sheltered and peaceful anchorages in this area, is easy to enter. While depth over the entrance bar is only one

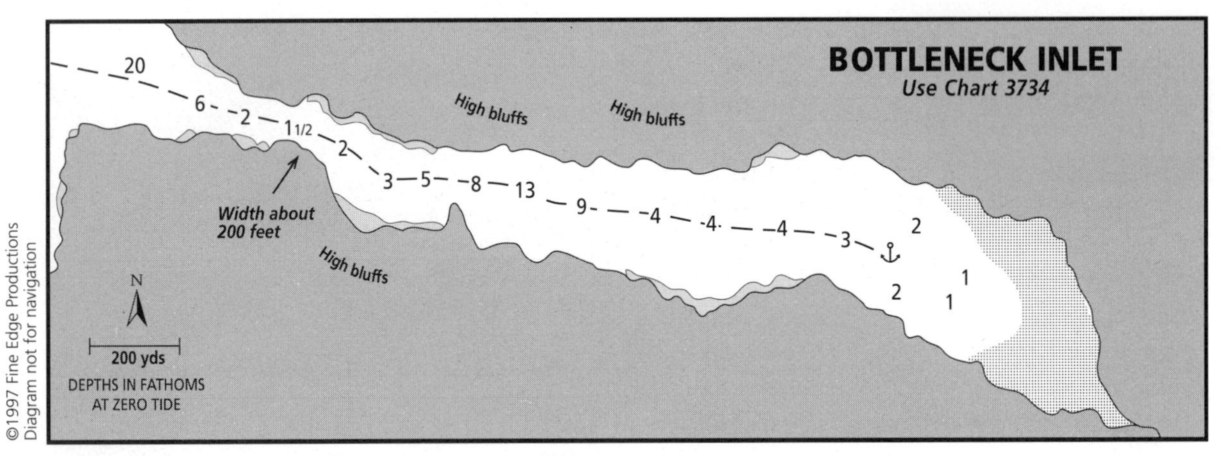

fathom or so at zero tide, it is not difficult to cross it, and you can enter under radar if necessary. The mud flat at the head of the inlet is quite large but because depths shoal slowly, you can find very good anchorage at any depth you please. There is plenty of room for several boats to swing and only radio reception suffers here.

Anchor in 3 to 4 fathoms over a mud bottom with very good holding.

Wallace Bight

Chart 3734; entrance: 52°43.80′ N, 128°25.90′ W; anchor: 52°43.64′ N, 128°23.90′ W (NAD 27)

Wallace Bight, 1 mile north of Bottleneck Inlet, is entered between Golder Point and Denton Point. Depths in the bight are too great for anchoring; the cove at the north end is exposed and not recommended as an anchorage. A narrow channel on the east side of Wallace Bight leads into a lagoon in which there are depths of 24 to 90 feet (7.3 to 27.4 m). The narrow entrance channel to this lagoon has a least depth of 1 foot (0.3 m) through it and is only suitable for small craft at or near HW. (p. 102, SD)

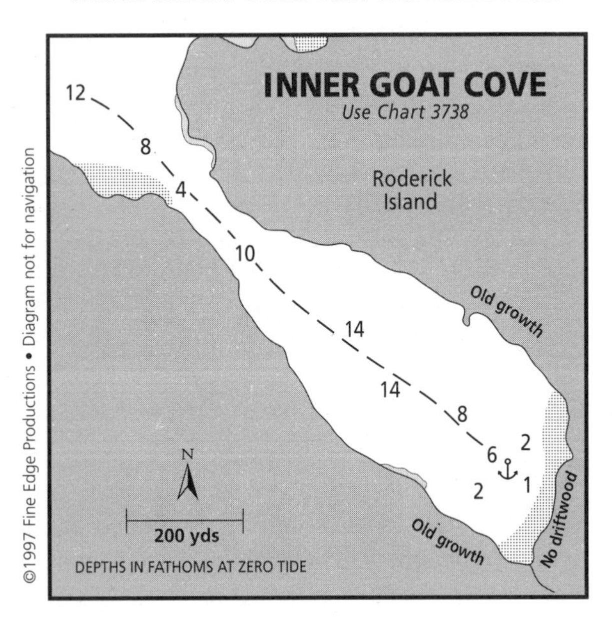

Wallace Bight may not be recommended as an anchorage but the lagoon on the east end of the bight appears to offer excellent shelter in its south end. Other than the shoal in the narrows we know of no other special hazards.

Anchor in 4 fathoms over an unrecorded bottom.

Work Bay

Chart 3738; entrance: 52°45. 95′ N, 128°28.90′ W; anchor: 52°47.05′ N, 128°28.80′ W (NAD 27)

Anchorage for small craft can be obtained in a small cove at the NE end of Work Bay. This is a good anchorage in about 7 fathoms (12.8 m). (p. 102, SD)

Work Bay is largely ignored by the cruising public as it appears to be exposed to the south but, in fact, it may offer good shelter as indicated above.

Goat Cove

Chart 3738; entrance: 52°47.10′ N, 128°24.60′ W; anchor (inner cove): 52°46.32′ N, 128°23.34′ W (NAD 27)

Goat Cove has a passage at its SE end less than 300 feet (91 m) wide with a least depth of 31 feet

(9.4 m) leading into a sheltered basin.

Anchorage for small vessels can be obtained in the basin in about 17 fathoms (31 m).

Goat Bluff, 2 miles ENE of Adze Point, a steep-to and precipitous cliff, is conspicuous. (p. 102, SD)

Griffin Passage, north narrows

Goat Cove is easy to enter and its inner cove is very well protected from any serious weather. The narrows has 4 to 5 fathoms in the fairway, and while depths in the basin are a little deep for convenient anchoring, we have been able to stay off the steep-to flat in the south end off the creek entrance.

Anchor in 4 to 8 fathoms over a sloping mud bottom with fair-to-good holding if you set your anchor well.

Kid Bay

Chart 3738; entrance: 52°48.00′ N, 128°23.70′ W (NAD 27)

Kid Bay, about 1 mile NNE of Goat Cove, is free of off-lying dangers but too deep for satisfactory anchorage. (p. 102, SD)

Sheep Passage

Charts 3962, 3738; west entrance: 52°48.60′ N, 128°24.60′ W; east entrance: 52°51.00′ N, 128°09.20′ W (NAD 27)

Sheep Passage is deep throughout with no off-lying dangers. At its west end a sill extends from Fawn Point to Finlayson Head, and near its east end another sill crosses the passage. The shores of the passage are moderately steep-to and the land rises steeply from the water's edge; the mountain peaks have elevations of about 3,000 feet (914 m). The slopes are thickly wooded except where landslides have removed the vegetation.

Tidal streams flood east through Sheep Passage and meet the flood flowing north through Mathieson Channel in the vicinity of Mathieson Narrows. (p. 103, SD)

Sheep Passage is the northern entrance to scenic Fjordland and the upper end of Mathieson Channel.

Carter Bay

Chart 3738; entrance: 52°49.35′ N, 128°23.80′ W; anchor: 52°49.82′ N, 128°23.35′ W (NAD 27)

Carter Bay, 1.3 miles ENE of Finlayson Head, is easily identified by the high cliffs on its west shore. Carter Point is its east entrance point. A shoal rock about 0.2 mile north of Carter Point is usually marked by kelp. Carter River flows into the head of the bay across an extensive sand flat. The remains of a wreck lie on the edge of the sand flat.

Temporary anchorage, which is exposed, can be obtained about 0.2 mile from the edge of the sand flat at the head of Carter Bay; depths are 14 to 15 fathoms (26 to 27 m), mud bottom. (p. 103, SD)

Griffin Passage (North Entrance)

Chart 3738; entrance: 52°46.92′ N, 128°20.82′ W (NAD 27)

You can take shelter from downslope winds or strong westerlies within the north entrance to Griffin Passage in what we call "Lime Point Cove."

"Lime Point Cove"

Chart 3738; anchor: 52°46.68′ N, 128°20.10′ W (NAD 27)

Lime Point, 2.3 miles SE of Fawn Point, is at the north end of Griffin Passage, which is unsurveyed and should not be entered without local knowledge. (p. 103, SD)

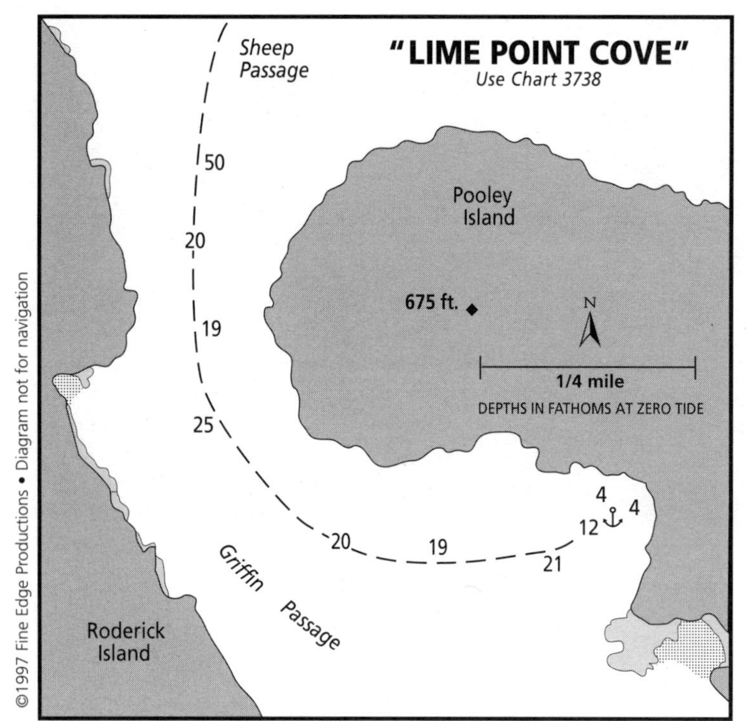

By tucking inside the very northwest tip of Pooley Island in Sheep Passage, you can find shelter in Lime Point Cove from all but southerly winds.

The water in this part of Griffin Passage is quite deep, and you can find convenient anchoring only by tucking in close to shore, as indicated in the diagram. Two disadvantages of this spot are the constant roar of loggers' chainsaws and the view of clearcuts down to the water's edge!

The shore is steep-to (4 fathoms, 60 feet from shore) and covered with large sea stars and sea cucumbers. A stern tie to shore is recommended.

Anchor in 4 to 12 fathoms over a sand, shell, rock, and kelp bottom with fair holding if your anchor is well set.

Windy Bay

Chart 3962; entrance:
52°47.30′ N, 128°13.60′ W;
anchor: 52°47.07′ N, 128°12.60′ W
(NAD 27)

> *Windy Bay is free of off-lying dangers. An islet close off the east entrance point is separated from shore by a very narrow passage encumbered by several drying rocks. A steep-to drying flat of stones and gravel is at the head of the bay.*
>
> *Anchorage can be obtained about 0.3 mile off the drying flat at the head of Windy Bay in about 12 fathoms (22 m).* (p. 103, SD)

Windy Bay is the easiest, most accessible place to anchor in this area. It offers good protection in almost all weather and, despite its name, it's our choice of anchorages when the wind picks up.

Anchor east of the islet in 10 fathoms over an unrecorded bottom.

Bolin Bay

Chart 3962; entrance:
52°50.25′ N, 128°11.90′ W; anchor:
52°50.13′ N, 128°12.93′ W (NAD 27)

> *Bolin Bay is 3 miles north of Windy Bay*
>
> *Anchorage can be obtained in Bolin Bay in about 25 fathoms (46 m) or for small craft, near the head of the bay, in 11 fathoms (20 m), mud bottom.* (p. 103, SD)

Mussel Inlet

Chart 3962; entrance: 52°51.00′ N, 128°09.20′ W (NAD 27)

> *Mussel Inlet is entered east of Crosson Point and the only dangers in it are close to shore. Mountains on both sides of the inlet are high.* (p. 103, SD)

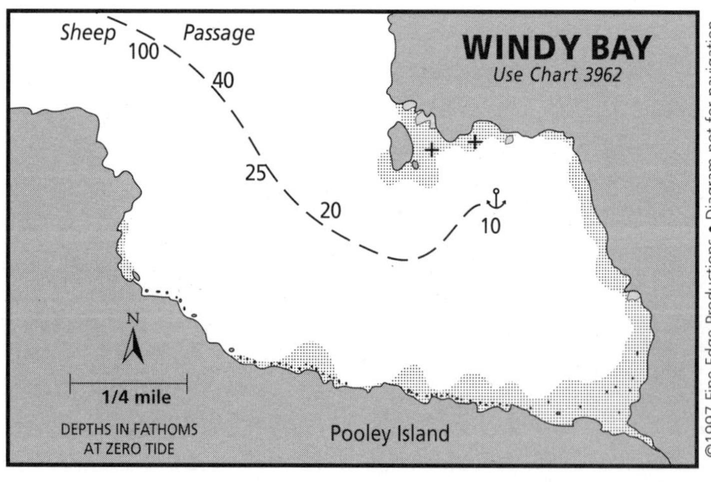

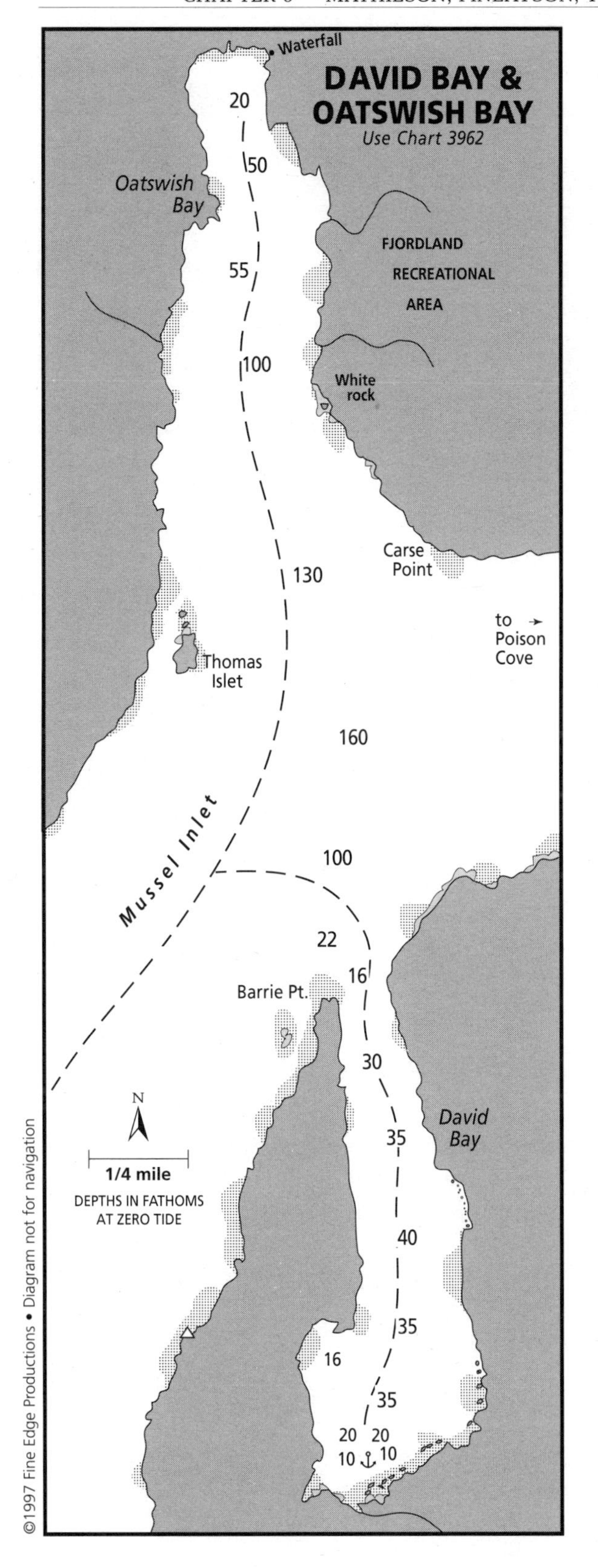

David Bay

Chart 3962; entrance: 52°53.60′ N, 128°07.30′ W; anchor: 52°52.50′ N, 128°07.20′ W (NAD 27)

> *David Bay has no off-lying dangers.*
>
> *Anchorage for small vessels is available in the SW part of David Bay, 0.4 mile from the head, in 7 to 12 fathoms (13 to 22 m).* (p. 103, SD)

David Bay, an attractive inlet on the south side of Mussel Inlet, offers good southerly protection. However, we've never been able to locate the 7 to 12 fathoms described in *Sailing Directions*. The head of the bay shoals so rapidly that the anchorage is marginal, unless you like to anchor in 100- to 200-foot-deep water. We anchored off the outlet to the creek in 10 fathoms, and with 90 feet of rode out, we found *Baidarka* swinging around and around with our stern alternately in 14 feet of water or 100 feet. While this worked all right in the calm weather we were experiencing, it would not be safe in windy conditions. Fifty feet from shore in the first bight on the west side of David Bay, there's an 8-fathom "hole" where you might be able to tie a stern line to the trees.

The granite rock along the shoreline of the bay has several parallel white lines that appear to have been incised by winter ice. This is spectacular country and well worth the short detour!

Oatswish Bay

Chart 3962; entrance: 52°54.50′ N, 128°07.60′ W; beach: 52°55.70′ N, 128°07.80′ W (NAD 27)

> *Oatswish Bay, entered between Thomas Islet and Carse Point, is deep and provides only fair weather anchorage, for small craft, close off the drying flat at its head in about 10 fathoms (18 m).* (p. 103, SD)

Oatswish Bay is both scenic and remote. It has a beach that you can explore and snow-covered peaks that tower above. Depths of the small gravel flat off the creek and its small waterfall are extensive, and we were unable to find the 10-fathom anchorage noted in *Sailing Directions*.

What we did find was this: On a 2.5-foot tide we measured exactly 2 feet of water under the bow where the lip of the gravel flat begins its 45-degree descent. The water is clear, and with the bow touching the beach (once again zero wave action), the stern of our 32-foot boat was in 5 to 6 fathoms of water! Our echo sounder indicated that this angle continues all the way to 50 fathoms!

We cannot, then, report any safe anchorage here. Oatswish Bay is fun to visit for a short time; you can let your boat drift around while a shore party explores the beach, but be sure to leave a responsible person aboard and beware of getting caught on the flat in a falling tide.

Tolmie Channel, looking north

The northwest corner of Thomas Islet, just south of the foul rocks and islets, is covered with seals, and here we found a 4-fathom patch of gravel that offers a temporary anchorage in fair weather only.

Mussel Bay

Chart 3962; position: 52°54.80′ N, 128°02.10′ W (NAD 27)

> *Mussel Bay, 3 miles east of Carse Point, is filled with drying flats which are moderately steep-to, and forms the mouth of the Mussel River.* (p. 103, SD)

Mussel Bay and Poison Cove are the far reaches of the Fjordland Park. This is wild scenery and as the tree tops on shore indicate here and farther south near Crosson Point, wild and woolly downslope winds blow hard during winter storms.

Mussel Inlet and Poison Cove were named by Captain George Vancouver when several of his crew became ill and one died after eating mussels contaminated with red tide (paralytic shellfish poisoning—PSP) obtained in Poison Cove.

Poison Cove

Chart 3962; entrance: 52°54.60′ N, 128°02.30′ W (NAD 27)

> *Poison Cove, close south of Mussel Bay, terminates in a steep-to drying flat of mud, sand and stones. Depths in the cove are too deep for satisfactory anchorage.* (p. 103, SD)

Tolmie Channel

Charts 3734, 3738; south entrance: 52°38.60′ N, 128°31.75′ W (NAD 27)

> *Tolmie Channel, which separates Sarah Island from Swindle Island and Princess Royal Island, forms part of the main Inner Passage route. Jane and Sarah Passages are the south approach channels.*
>
> *Tidal streams flood north through Tolmie Channel and ebb south. The north-going (flood) stream is stronger in Finlayson Channel than in Tolmie Channel. The south-going (ebb) stream, however, is stronger in Tolmie Channel and runs for 1h.30 min. after the same stream has ceased in Finlayson Channel. In the narrow parts of these channels both streams attain 3 kn at springs but in the broader parts only 1 kn.* (p. 104, SD)

Most cruise ships and commercial boats use Tolmie Channel, and traffic may be encountered at all hours of the day or night.

Split Head (Separation Point)

Chart 3734; anchor: 52°40.38′ N, 128°33.18′ W (NAD 27)

> *Split Head, locally known as Separation Point, lies 2.2 miles NNW of Boat Bluff.* (p. 104, SD)

If you want a lunch stop, consider either of the two nooks just west of Separation Point. Anchor close to shore in 4 to 5 fathoms.

Fjordland

Alexander Inlet

Chart 3734; entrance: 52°40.40′ N, 128°34.50′ W; anchor: 52°38.33′ N, 128°40.36′ W (NAD 27)

> *Errigal Point is the south entrance point to Alexander Inlet. Between Tunis Point, on the north side of the inlet, and Bingham Narrows, about 2.3 miles SW, several islets and drying reefs encumber the fairway. Bingham Narrows is contracted to a width of about 200 feet (61 m) by a drying ledge on the east side.* (p. 104, SD)

Alexander Inlet is another one of those seldom-visited inlets. It has some well-sheltered waters which are reported to offer good anchorage near it head, 1.5 miles west of Bingham Narrows.

Anchor in 8 fathoms over an unrecorded bottom.

Brown Cove

Chart 3734; entrance: 52°40.95′ N, 128°34.40′ W (NAD 27)

> *Brown Cove, on the west side of Nash Point, is too deep for convenient anchorage.* (p. 104, SD)

Cougar Bay

Charts 3738, 3734; entrance: 52°43.75′ N, 128°34.70′ W; anchor: 52°44.52′ N, 128°34.60′ W (NAD 27)

> *Cougar Bay, 2.6 miles north of Nash Point, is entered west of Ditmars Point.*
>
> *Anchorage for small craft can be obtained in the cove on the east side of Cougar Bay in 10 fathoms (18.3 m). Holding ground is reported to be poor.* (p. 104, SD)

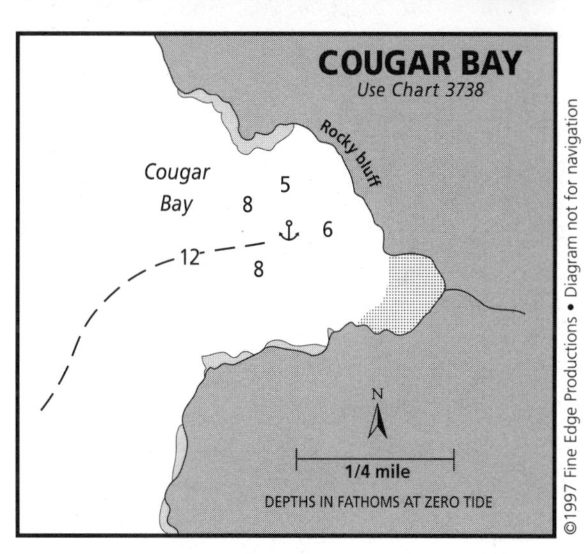

Cougar Bay is often used as an overnight anchorage, but we can't figure out why. We've seen a large commercial boat drag its heavy hook and chain all over the east side of the bay before it finally gave up and left. We agree with *Sailing Directions* that the holding ground is poor—hard rock as far as we can tell.

If you want to give it a try, anchor in the east part of Cougar Bay in 10 fathoms over a hard bottom with *poor* holding.

Hiekish Narrows

Chart 3738 (inset); south entrance: 52°48.75′ N, 128°26.35′ W; north entrance: 52°53.10′ N, 128°30.10′ W; Hewitt Rock light: 52°52.14′ N, 128°29.24′ W (NAD 27)

> *Hiekish Narrows connects Finlayson Channel to*

the junction of Tolmie Channel and Graham Reach of Princess Royal Channel

Predictions of time and rates of maximum current and the time of slack water when the direction of the current turns are given for Hiekish Narrows (Index No. 7500) in the Tide Tables, Volume 6. The maximum flood is 4 kn the ebb is 4.5 kn, the flood setting north and the ebb south. (p. 105, SD)

Hiekish Narrows is a deep-water passage to Princess Royal Channel; Hewitt Rock, midchannel, can be avoided by passing it on either side. Since there is minimum turbulence, you can transit Hiekish Narrows on all tides with sufficient power. The small channel behind Hewitt Island offers a convenient rest stop (enter from the north side).

Graham Reach, waterfall

Hewitt Island

Chart 3738 (inset); anchor:
52°52.48′ N, 128°30.15′ W (NAD 27)

Hewitt Island, 1 mile NW of the (Hiekish Narrows) beacon, is separated from Sarah Island by a narrow, shallow passage. (p. 105)

The narrow, shallow passage behind Hewitt Island offers good temporary protection if there's a storm front moving through, or if you just want to take a rest. Although the current is strong, its flow is linear, so if you set your anchor well, your boat should tether very nicely without budging. The water here is clear, so you can see the bottom and check your anchor easily. Be careful if you go out in your dinghy—the current is deceiving, and you might not be able to row back against it!

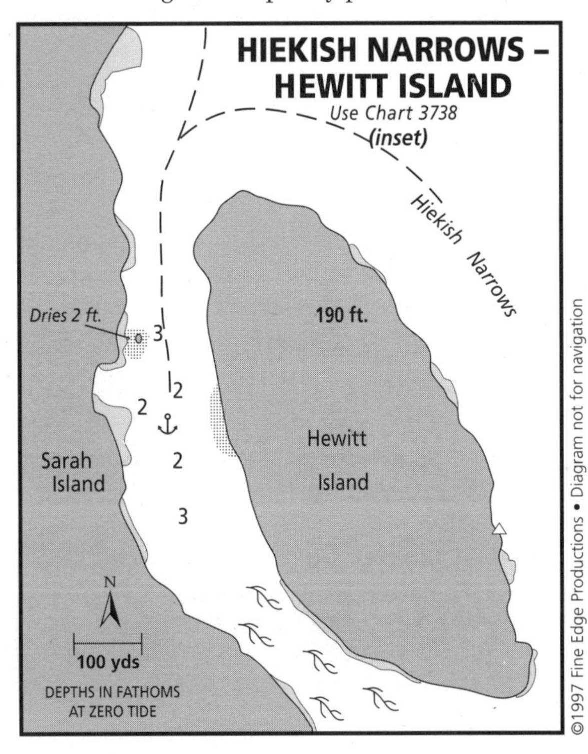

Enter via the north end of Hewitt Island; the south entrance is clogged with kelp.

Anchor midchannel in 2 fathoms over a bottom of sand and grass; holding is good if your anchor is well set.

Princess Royal Channel

Charts 3738, 3739; south entrance Graham Reach: 52°53.75′ N, 128°30.60′ W (NAD 27)

Princess Royal Channel, entered from Tolmie Channel or Hiekish Narrows at its south end, extends 38 miles NW to Whale Channel. Princess

Royal Channel is divided into four parts consisting of Graham Reach, Butedale and Malcolm Passages, Fraser Reach and McKay Reach.

Tidal streams in Princess Royal Channel come from north and south and meet in Graham Reach in the vicinity of Aaltanhash Inlet. In Graham Reach, between the north end of Sarah Island and Aaltanhash Inlet, the flood sets north and the ebb south. In Butedale Passage, Fraser Reach and McKay Reach the flood sets toward the SE and the ebb NW. Tidal streams in McKay Reach, at the NW end of Princess Royal Channel, are complicated. . . . (p. 105, SD)

Green Inlet

Chart 3738; entrance: 52°55.45' N, 128°29.90' W (NAD 27)

Green Inlet, 1.5 miles NNE of Quarry Point. . . . Horsefly Cove is on the north side of the inlet, 0.6 mile inside the entrance. . . . The tidal rapids at Baffle Point and the remainder of Green Inlet NE of them, are unnavigable. (p. 107, SD)

Green Inlet is another Cougar Bay as far as we can tell. Horsefly Cove proved too deep and difficult, so we visited the shoal just south of Baffle Point where we enjoyed the view of the ebb current at the rapids—it was like watching a jet fighter with its after-burner ignited. The roostertails of the waterfall pulsate for perhaps 100 yards on a good low tide. For the life of us, we couldn't get our trusty CQR to hold on the shoal close south, so we gave up and spent the night poorly secured to a spit that extends from the stream on the south shore across from Horsefly Cove.

Horsefly Cove

Chart 3738; anchor: 52°55.28' N, 128°28.95' W (NAD 27)

Anchorage for small craft can be obtained in Horsefly Cove in about 13 fathoms (24 m). (p. 107, SD)

Anchor, if you have lots of chain, in Horsefly Cove in 13 to 15 fathoms over a hard bottom of questionable holding.

Swanson Bay

Charts 3738, 3739; entrance: 53°00.60' N, 128°30.90' W; anchor (south): 53°00.82' N, 128°30.28' W; anchor (north): 53°01.93' N, 128°30.77' W (NAD 27)

Swanson Bay . . . does not afford satisfactory anchorage, except for small craft close inshore. (p. 107, SD)

You can find moderate protection from channel winds and chop at either of the two indicated sites in Swanson Bay. There is a large shoal off the beach, and caution is advised. The southern anchorage seems to be the better because the creek has created a small area with a sandy bottom. Both sites have limited swinging room. The ruins of a cannery smokestack can be found behind the brush on shore.

Anchor (south) in 3 to 4 fathoms over sand and grass with good holding.

Anchor (north) in 6 to 8 fathoms over sand and gravel with fair holding.

Khutze Inlet

Chart 3739; entrance: 53°04.90; N, 128°32.80' W; anchor (east side of spit): 53°05.42' N, 128°30.95' W (NAD 27)

Boat Bluff light station, Sarah Island

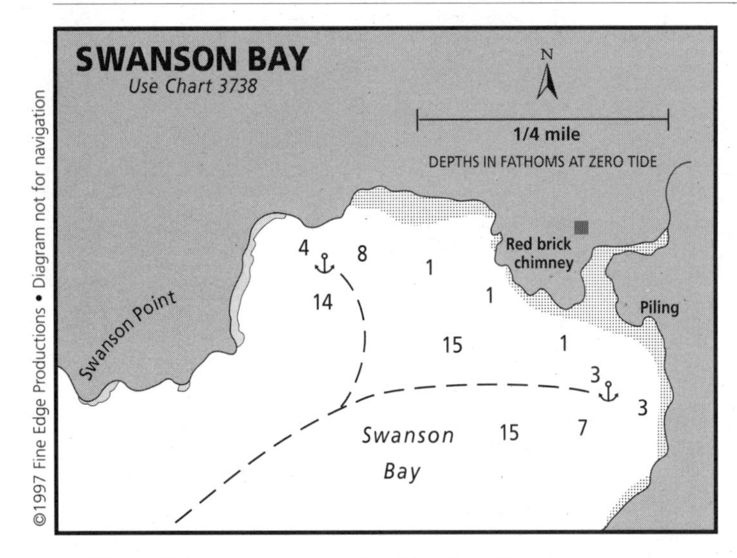

Khutze Inlet, on the east side of Graham Reach . . . Depths in Khutze Inlet are generally too great for satisfactory anchorage. Small vessels can obtain temporary anchorage about 0.1 mile from either side of Green Spit in depths of 10 to 20 fathoms (18 to 37 m). (p. 107, SD)

Locals report that one of the best anchorages in Graham Reach can be found in Khutze Inlet (pronounced Kootz) on the east side of Green Spit. Be careful not to anchor too deep (over 10 fathoms) or the length of your anchor line will allow you to swing onto the spit. If you have an anchor winch, it is best to anchor in 10 to 15 fathoms north of the spit in the fairway where it's protected from most winds.

Anchorage can also be found just off the river mouth, but the mud flats are steep-to and there is danger that the river's current may cause you to drag anchor. Some boaters report that anchorage is available off the waterfall 5 miles within Khutze Inlet, and that there is great crabbing at this site.

Anchor east of spit in about 6 to 8 fathoms over a mud, shell and kelp bottom with fair holding.

Fjordland waterfalls

Aaltanhash Inlet

Chart 3739; entrance: 53°07.50′ N, 128°34.10′ W (NAD 27)

> *Aaltanhash Inlet, 2.5 miles north of Khutze Inlet, is entered south of Heddington Point and extends 4 miles east. . . . The depths in this inlet are too great for satisfactory anchorage.*
> (p. 107, SD)

If you want to turn off your engine and just drift a while for respite from chop or traffic in the channel, Aaltanhash Inlet is not a bad place to do

Photo courtesy CHS, Pacific Region

Butedale

Photo by Robin Hill-Ward

Butedale, looking out over Fraser Reach

so. You might even find a "big one" lurking here in the deep waters, but it's too deep for an overnight stay.

Butedale

Chart 3739 (inset); entrance:
53°09.60′ N, 128°41.50′ W; light, west end Work Island: 53°10.72′ N, 128°41.55′ W (NAD 27)

> *Butedale, in a bay on the south side of Butedale Passage, is the site of a former cannery. The buildings are in ruins and the wharf is in bad repair. No fuel or supplies are available....* (p. 107)

Butedale, like Namu, was a going concern and a convenient fuel stop in days gone by. The facilities have been badly vandalized over the years, but currently there is an attempt to resurrect it. (See Sidebar.)

The Butedale waterfall is an inspiring sight at full rush, and big halibut can sometimes be caught just offshore. Should a southerly develop in Princess Royal Channel, you could try anchoring in the bight off the cannery, but we suggest it only as an emergency. Some people have used the pilings east of the cannery for moorage. Be cautious if you do anchor here; there may be old cables along the bottom in certain areas.

Anchor near the south bight pilings in 5 to 10 fathoms over a mud bottom with fair holding.

Butedale Restoration Project

Warren Miller, producer of ski movies and author of humorous books, recently notified us that a group which calls itself the Butedale Founders Corporation is soliciting support (financial or otherwise) to restore some of the old cannery structures and make them into a lodge. During the summer an alternating group of caretakers welcomes cruising boaters with a hot cup of coffee, a muffin, and a tour of the site. In 1996, the group stockpiled barrels of gasoline to make it available to cruising boats. If they get enough support, they hope to be able to dispense both gasoline and diesel in the future. You can contact the group in Deer Island, Oregon at 503-397-5392.

Klekane Inlet, Marmot Cove and Scow Bay

Chart 3739; entrance:
53°10.95′ N, 128°38.80′ W (NAD 27)

> *The drying sand and mud flats at the head of Klekane Inlet are steep-to.... Marmot Cove, close north, is filled with a drying flat.... Depths within Klekane Inlet are too great for satisfactory anchorage, except for small craft in Scow Bay, close to the edge of a drying flat.* (p. 107, SD)

Scow Bay and Marmot Cove within Klekane Inlet have drying flats with steep-to shores. Neither offers serious anchoring opportunities other than as a lunch stop. Some boats have used the pilings in Marmot Cove for moorage; however, it is not considered trustworthy protection.

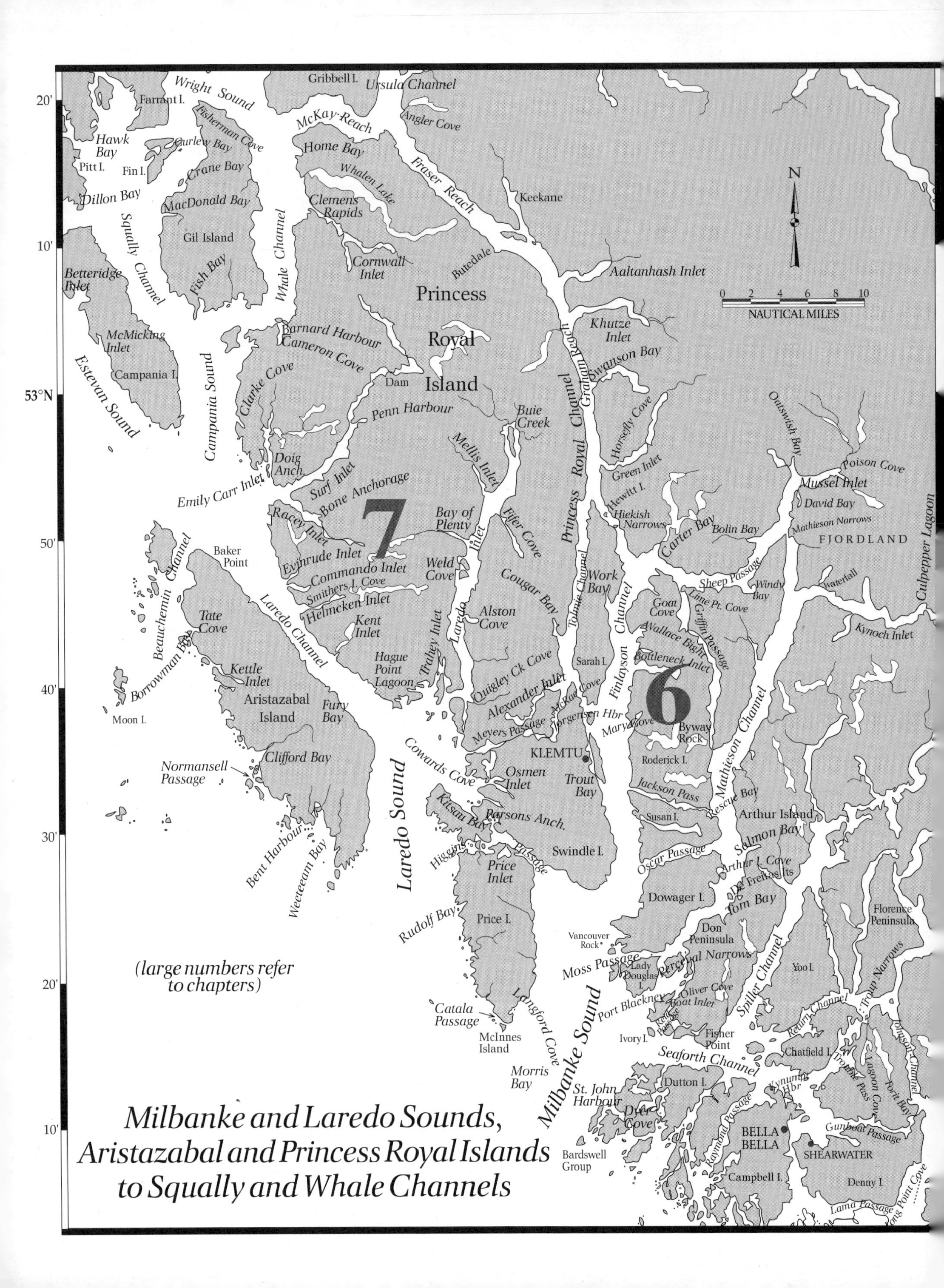

Milbanke and Laredo Sounds, Aristazabal and Princess Royal Islands to Squally and Whale Channels

7

Milbanke and Laredo Sounds, Aristazabal and Princess Royal Islands to Squally and Whale Channels

Crossing Milbanke and Laredo Sounds gives cruising boats a good introduction to the wild west coast. The finest inlets on Princess Royal Island all lie on its west side. For boats that want a taste of Hecate Strait, the west coast of Aristazabal (pronounced A-*ris*-ta-bal) Island offers well-protected inlets along the western edge of British Columbia's north coast.

The most direct route, and the one used by larger commercial boats, crosses south of Price Island and is exposed to southerly swells and chop. Catala Passage can minimize this exposure, but is best used by small boats in fair weather only.

The most scenic and interesting way to enter Laredo Sound leads through Higgins Passage. The narrows in the center of the passage dries on a 5-foot tide, so transit must be carefully timed. Higgins Passage, useful only for small or medium-sized cruising boats, should not be attempted without noting the cautions listed in this chapter. Meyers Passage, entered north of Klemtu, can be transited by most cruising boats at mid-tide and above.

Known for its population of bears, Princess Royal Island is reported to have the largest concentration of Kermodei bears (*ursus kermodei*)—a cream-colored black bear known in native lore as the spirit bear. The island could provide the keystone to a wilderness corridor connecting Tweedsmuir Park and the Kitlope to the east, with Gwaii Haanas National Park Reserve (South Moresby Island) directly to the west across Hecate Strait.

The outer coast from Dundas Island to Principe and Laredo Channels, along with the

St. John Harbour, West Coast Fishing Resort

Queen Charlotte Islands, is a major flyway for wild birds. Infrequently visited by cruising boats, the area sustains the highest concentration of flora and fauna along the Inside Passage.

The western coasts of both Aristazabal and Price Islands have a multitude of small islands, islets, and reefs where you can find nooks and crannies to explore by kayak or inflatable. Outstanding opportunities for beachcombing, scuba diving or observing nature can also be found. Weeteeam Bay and Borrowman Bay make well-protected base camps from which you can explore the marvels of the outer coast.

Note: Charts 3726 and 3737 were drawn prior to the adoption of NAD 27, thus all latitudes and longitudes derived from these charts should be used with caution, and allowance made for an adequate margin of safety.

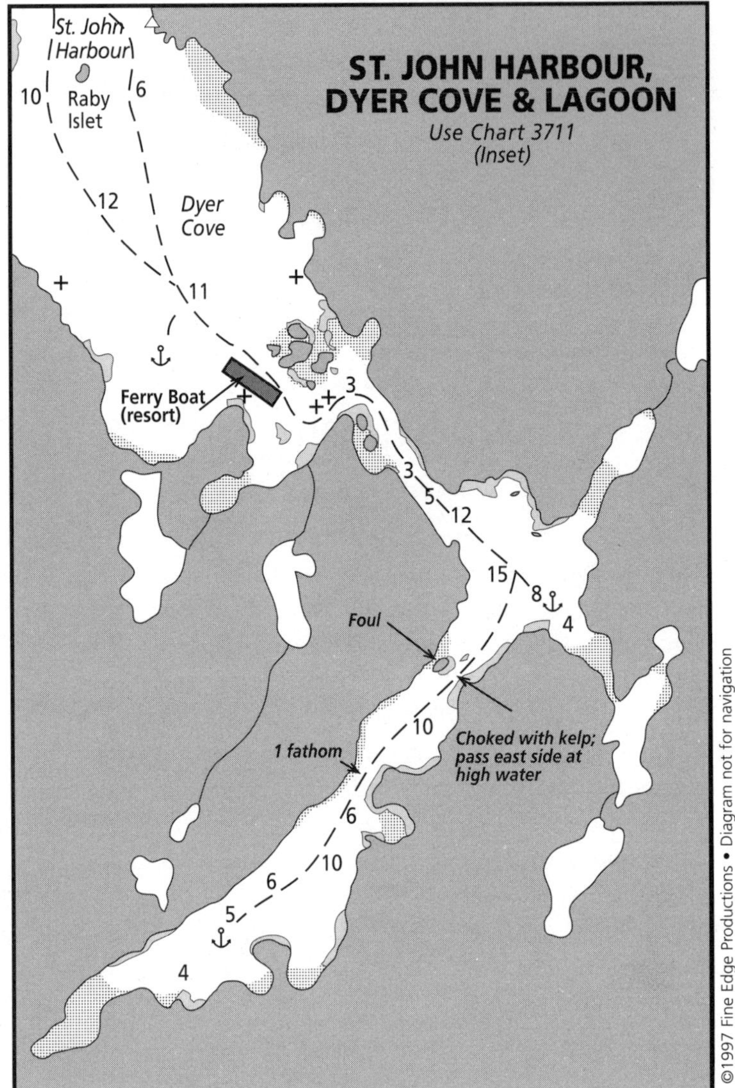

Milbanke Sound

Chart 3728; south entrance: 52°12.00′ N, 128°38.00′ W; north entrance: 52°25.00′ N, 128°29.00′ W (NAD 27)

> *Milbanke Sound is the main opening from seaward leading to Seaforth, Mathieson and Finlayson Channels. It is entered from seaward between Cape Mark, the SW extremity of Bardswell Group, and the group of islands and reefs extending SW from the south end of Price Island.* (p. 94, SD)

Milbanke Sound is exposed to southeast weather or remnant swells from that direction. In fair weather, it's a rather easy 10-mile run from Seaforth Channel across to Catala Passage and up into Laredo Sound. If you're headed for Higgins Passage, you can cross Milbanke Sound keeping Vancouver Rock to starboard. Or, if you want more protection, you can take Reid Passage to Moss Passage or Oscar Passage, then west through Higgins Passage. If you're heading to Klemtu and Meyers Passage, Milbanke Sound is the most direct route. However, the most protected route leads through Mathieson Channel and Jackson Narrows.

If you are southbound from Higgins Passage and a southerly swell or chop develops in Milbanke Sound, you can follow a smooth-water route east that hugs the Swindle Island shore, passing inside Pidwell Reef and around Jorkins Point into Finlayson Channel. From there you can cross Oscar Passage or Moss Passage, heading south in Mathieson Channel and Reid Passage to Seaforth Channel.

St. John Harbour

Chart 3711 (inset), 3787; entrance:
52°12.30′ N, 128°28.50′ W (NAD 27)

St. John Harbour is confined but affords anchorage for small vessels. The harbour is fairly well protected at its entrance by Rage Reefs, which extend 0.7 mile NNE of Townsend Point and are marked by starboard hand buoy "E46" at the NE end. Lenz Islet lies about midway along the reefs.

At HW, when Rage Reefs are covered, it is difficult to distinguish the entrance to St. John Harbour. At half tide, and at LW, the north end of Rage Reefs and also the drying ledges along the east side of the channel are visible and no undue difficulties should be encountered. (p. 95, SD)

St. John Harbour, 5 miles southwest of Ivory Island on the west shore of Athlone Island, offers very good protection in all weather. GPS should be used to identify the entrance since red buoy "E46" is not visible until you are close to Rage Reefs. The prevailing southwest swells that break so vigorously on the reefs die off as soon as you are abeam of "E46." Within St. John Harbour, the basin to the southwest is Louisa Cove; the one to the southeast is Dyer Cove. Two major fishing resorts are located here. St. John Lagoon lies to the south of Dyer Cove.

Dyer Cove

Chart 3711 (inset); entrance:
52°11.60′ N, 128°28.42′ W; anchor:
52°11.08′ N, 128°28.16′ W (NAD 27)

Anchorage, suitable for small vessels, can be obtained in 11 to 14 fathoms (20 to 26 m) in Dyer Cove; this is the usual anchorage for St. John Harbour. (p. 95, SD)

St. John Lodge, Dyer Cove

Dyer Cove can be entered on either side of Raby Islet, with the west side being the deeper of the two. Good anchorage can be taken anywhere in Dyer Cove; avoid the congestion around the fishing resorts. *Queen of the Islands*, formerly a B.C. ferry, is moored on the east side of the cove.

Anchor in about 12 fathoms over sand and mud with some rocks; fair-to-good holding.

Louisa Cove

Chart 3711 (inset); entrance:
52°11.60′ N, 128°28.80′ W; anchor:
52°10.92′ N, 128°29.12′ W (NAD 27)

The channel west of Reginald Island leads into Louisa Cove. (p. 95, SD)

Louisa Cove, less busy than Dyer Cove, holds more attraction for many boaters, although it does receive more wind and chop under northeast conditions. Inside Wurtele Island, there is a small high-water route choked with kelp which can be used by skiffs coming from or going to Queens Sound.

Anchor in 5 fathoms over sand and gravel bottom with fair-to-good holding.

St. John Lagoon

Chart 3711 (inset); entrance:
52°11.02′ N, 128°27.90′ W; anchor (first basin):
52°10.64′ N, 128°27.28′ W (NAD 27)

St. John Lagoon has two very well-protected basins which are entered just east of *Queen of the Islands* through a small channel, as noted on Chart 3711 (inset); both basins are removed from the noise and bustle of the sportfishing boats. The narrows has about 7 feet minimum in the fairway. The shores of the lagoon are surrounded by small cedars, typical of the west coast, making landing by dinghy difficult. Anchorage can be taken anywhere in the first basin. We prefer the entrance to the nook on the southeast corner of the first basin. Since swinging room is limited, a stern tie to shore can be effective.

St. John Lagoon entrance

The entrance to the second basin to the southeast, contains an islet and is choked with kelp. Small boats can pass to the south side of the islet near high water.

Anchor (first basin) in 4 fathoms over sand, mud, and grass bottom with good-to-very-good holding.

Ivory Island

Chart 3710 (inset); light: 52°16.17′ N, 128°24.30′ W; anchor: 52°16.67′ N, 128°23.49′ W (NAD 27)

Ivory Island, at the west entrance of Seaforth Channel, is the home of a classic red and white lighthouse, located on Robb Point, with a clear view of Milbanke Sound. The current lightkeepers, Rene and Sherrill Kitson, welcome visitors when time permits. To contact the lightkeepers for a possible tour, call Prince Rupert Coast Guard on Channel 16; they can connect you to the lightstation when the keepers are free from their weather-reporting duties.

Ivory Island, fair-weather anchorage

Small boats can anchor in fair weather only in a tiny cove on the northeast corner of Ivory Island. On the shore of this cove, a dilapidated cedar-planked walkway leads 0.6 mile to the lighthouse where you get a spectacular 270°-view.

Ivory Island Lightstation, looking toward Reid Passage

Anchor in about 3 fathoms over a mixed bottom with fair holding. Swinging room is limited and is subject to surge or swell.

Blair Inlet

Charts 3710 (inset), 3728; Ivory Island (light station): 52°16.18′ N, 128°24.30′ W (NAD 27)

The outer part of Blair Inlet, between Ivory and Cecilia Islands, is encumbered by numerous islands and rocks.

The preferred entrance is from Seaforth Channel by way of the passage, only suitable for small vessels, between Ivory and Watch Islands. (p. 93, SD)

The eastern part of Blair Inlet, which is uncharted, may have some protected anchorages at its far east end.

McInnes Island Light Station

Chart 3728; light: 52°15.70′ N, 128°43.22′ W (NAD 27)

McInnes Island is situated among a group of islands and reefs extending about 2.5 miles SW from the south end of Price Island. (p. 94, SD)

McInnes Island, strategically located between Milbanke and Laredo sounds, is a manned lightstation, and it is important to monitor their timely weather reports before attempting to round the south end of Price Island. The seas around McInnes Island frequently contain a lot of drift logs and flotsam, especially on spring tides, and you should use caution when transiting this area. Catala Passage, on the north side of McInnes Island, is a smooth-water connection between Milbanke and Laredo sounds.

Catala Passage

Charts 3733A, 3728; west entrance: 52°16.25′ N, 128°44.20′ W; east entrance: 52°15.65′ N, 128°40.90′ W (NAD 27)

Catala Passage leads through the islets and rocks and provides a safe and easy channel for small vessels travelling from Laredo Sound to Milbanke Sound. (p. 178, SD)

Catala Passage gives valuable relief from southwest swells when crossing from Milbanke to Laredo Sound. In a strong southerly, this area can be covered with sheets of white foam and small craft should not attempt a crossing during these times. From Catala Passage to Higgins Passage, the area is a maze of islets, rocks and reefs. If you want to explore the regions by kayak or inflatable, the anchorage at Rudolf Bay can be used as a base camp in fair weather. Higgins Passage is a viable alternative for small craft.

The south end of Price Island is another place where ebbing tidal currents interact with southerly seas and create nasty conditions off McInnes Island. The worst of these conditions can be avoided by using Catala Passage. Though large seas may be running in Milbanke and Laredo sounds, the waters of Catala Pass are relatively quiet. To the north of the pass, and along the southwest shore of Price Island, a series of reefs

High Waves on Ivory Island: April 25, 1996

Rene and I were alone on station that day and I was on morning shift. At 0340 (PST), we reported winds blowing east at 18 knots, with gusts to 23 knots. By 0600 the wind had turned to southeast, 18-20 knots. By 0940 we were recording southeast winds at 25 knots, with gusts of 31. The swell started building and I reported a low/moderate. At 1010 I had to file a special weather report: southeast 34 knots, gusting to 46 knots. For the following 8 hours, the winds never dropped below 30 knots, with steady gusts in the 40s, and occasional 50-55 knots. Around 1500, the wind was blowing from the south and swell was moderate. By 1800 hours, swells had built to heavy level. About 1830, swells started coming over the sea wall. The water went over our satellite dish and slammed into the living room windows; spray blew clear over the roof of our house. The back steps were covered in ebbing sea water, and Rene narrowly missed being hit by a wave while doing his 1840 hours observations! We have been on Ivory since June 22, 1992, and we have never seen such a swell.

The "system" was mostly cumulonimbus clouds—the most dangerous of clouds. We'd had hail during the day, but no thunderstorms. Normally I go to bed around 1900 when I'm on morning shift, but Rene and I sat at our kitchen table until just after 2100, when the tide turned. We knew that if nothing happened by high tide, we'd be all right (no wave through the house)!

Weather remained unsettled for the next two days, with southwest and south winds. On the 28th at 0640, we recorded winds southeast at 25 knots with 36-knot gusts, and 46 knots by noon. Swells were back up to moderate, but fortunately the wind eased off later in the day. By the 30th we were reporting rippled, one-foot chop seas with a low swell. During all our years on a light station, I'd never before felt frightened. But I certainly did on April 25!

—Sherrill Kitson, Ivory Island

enclose a large area of quiet water. We have been in this area when a large uncomfortable swell was running in Laredo Sound and high surf was breaking on the reefs, but the inner waters where we were anchored were quite placid. Only the brave should enter here since it is poorly charted and there are numerous isolated rocks.

Just to the northeast of Day Point lies Day Point Anchorage, between a triangular-shaped island and the southern point of Price Island. Though the swell does penetrate this anchorage somewhat, there is at best moderate holding in 8 fathoms; this is reported to be an ideal place to stay if you wish to get the flavor of the wild marine environment. Two rocks bracket the entrance, one drying at one foot, but since there is usually a swell running, the waves breaking over the top of the rocks will identify them during the lower half of the tide. The passage from the anchorage to the southwest side of Price island dries at low tide. Take your dinghy and pass into the area protected by the reef—there's enough exploring and beachcombing to keep you busy for several days. On one of the large rocks south of McInnes Island, you can observe a colony of sea lions.

Muir Cove

Charts 3728, 3726; position:
52°17.75′ N, 128°39.50′ W (NAD 27)

> *The east coast of Price Island between Day Point and Aldrich Point, 4.3 miles NE, is indented by Muir Cove and other small bays exposed to the sea.* (p. 95, SD)

Muir Cove appears to be little more than a kayak haul-out or place to beach a boat in an emergency. It is exposed to conditions in Milbanke Sound. Langford Cove, 3.25 miles north, should be considered if shelter is needed.

Langford Cove

Chart 3728; entrance: 52° 20.52′ N, 128°36.90′ W; anchor (south nook): 52°20.29′ N, 128°37.21′ W (NAD 27)

> *Langford Cove, close north of Aldrich Point, provides shelter for small craft.* (p. 95, SD)

Langford Cove can be used as an emergency anchorage if you are caught on the west side of Milbanke Sound. Protection from strong northwest winds can be found in the small northwest bight close to the rocky shore (favor the south side). Anchor in 4 fathoms over an irregular and rocky bottom with poor-to-fair holding. For protection from southeast through west winds and chop, tuck tightly into the small nook on the southwest side. Avoid the bare rocks at the north entrance and a large patch of kelp. At the south entrance, there is a rock awash on a 12-foot tide. Both nooks have many drift logs, so we would rate this site as a temporary anchorage only.

Anchor (south nook) in 2 fathoms over a mixed bottom of brown sand, stones, kelp, and eel grass with fair-to-good holding.

Higgins Passage

Charts 3710 (inset), 3728, 3726, 3737;
east entrance: 52°27.60′ N, 128°36.75′ W;
anchor (east side of narrows):
52°28.88′ N, 128°43.50′ W; anchor (west side of narrows): 52°28.50′ N, 128°41.10′ W;
west entrance (0.4 mile SW of Kipp Islet):
52°28.47′ N, 128°47.27′ W (NAD 27)

> *Higgins Passage separates the north end of Price Island from Swindle Island.* (p. 95, SD)
>
> *Higgins Passage leads from Laredo Sound into Milbanke Sound. Its shoalest part, west of Lohbrunner Island, dries 5 feet (1.5 m) and is only suitable for small craft near HW on a rising tide; local knowledge is advised. . . . The fairway leads north along the west side of Lohbrunner Island, where a bar dries 5 feet (1.5 m), then SE through a narrow rock infested passage which is full of kelp. The fairway then leads south along the east side of Lohbrunner Island to a wide basin.* (p. 178, SD)
>
> *The north-going tidal streams from Milbanke and Laredo Sounds meet near the middle of Higgins Passage. In the narrowest part of Higgins Passage, north of Lohbrunner Island, the tidal streams attain 4 to 5 kn.* (p. 179, SD)

The east side of Laredo Sound, between Price and Swindle islands, is a labyrinth of islands, islets and rocks that offers scenic, well-protected cruising waters known for excellent sportfishing. Scott Davis, who rowed from Port Townsend to Alaska and back in the summer of 1994, passed through Higgins Passage, both north- and southbound. On each occasion, he spotted sandhill cranes and heard wolves near the narrows.

Higgins Passage, view of the narrows from west anchor site

Photo courtesy CHS, Pacific Region

The narrows has a land bridge that dries at 5 feet at zero tide, and you can pass through only at an adequate tide level. Thick kelp grows in the area of this land bridge. We suggest that you anchor, then reconnoiter to get the lay of the area. Proceed when the tide is sufficiently high. Good, sheltered anchor sites, where you can wait for the tide to rise, lie at both the east and west sides of the narrows.

Swells breaking on the outer rocks of Laredo Sound obstruct the view of the intricate western entrance to Higgins Passage. GPS can help you locate your turning points to the entrance; however, CHS says *charted positions may be in error up to 150 meters.* Swells quickly die down inside the first islets.

Higgins Passage is an explorer's dream or a

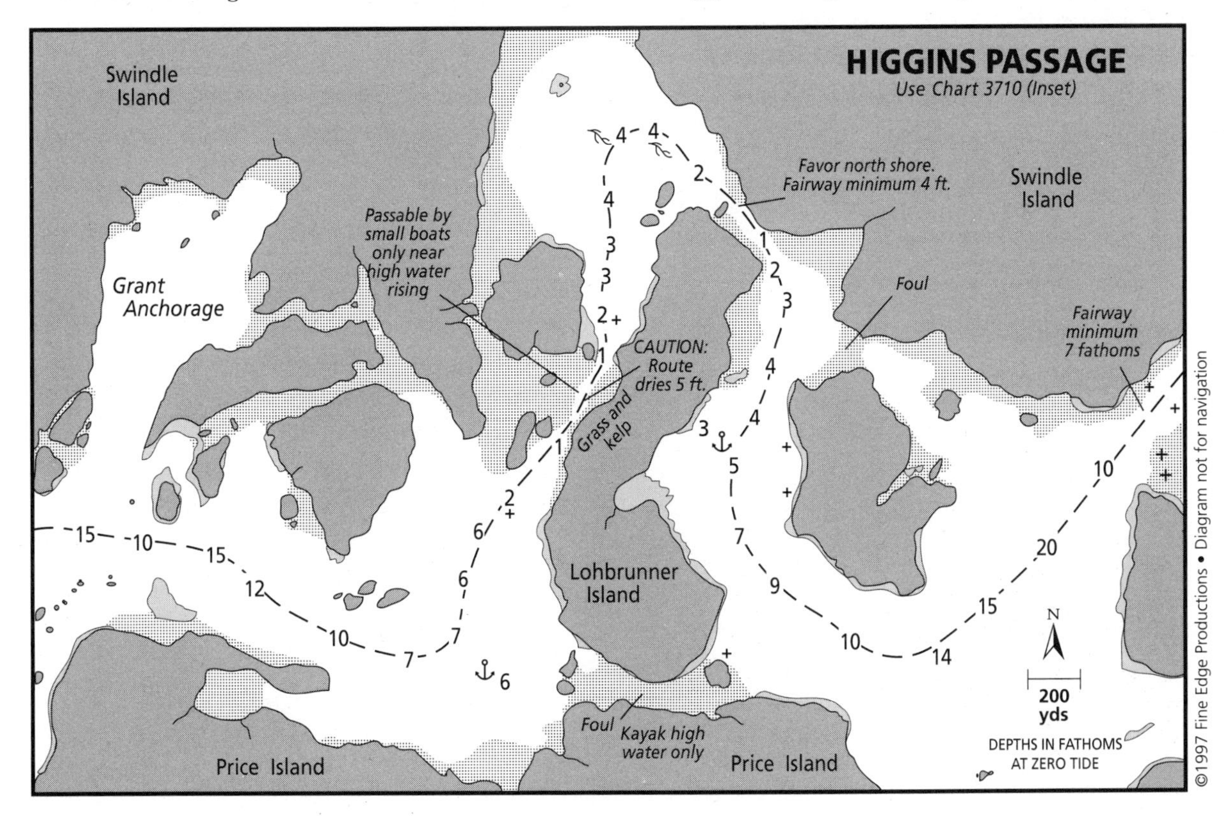

marginal navigator's nightmare. Approaching Higgins Passage from the east is straightforward. However, from Laredo Sound it is a challenge—the small scale of Chart 3737 (1:77,000) makes precise navigation difficult.

The west entrance is a maze of islets and reefs that requires careful plotting of your exact position, and the key to entering is to *unequivocally* identify Kipp Islet.

The *approximate* route we follow starts at the Higgins Passage entrance point, 0.4 mile southwest of Kipp Islet at 52°28.47' N, 128°47.25' W. From here, it proceeds at 026°M for 0.51 nautical mile, avoiding the rocks close south of Kipp Islet, to a position 0.25 mile east of Kipp Islet. From this point, the course changes to 335°M for 0.30 nautical mile, then turns east to 065°M for a distance of 0.30 nautical mile. It heads southeast at 011°M, passing close to the peninsula that forms the western side of Grant Anchorage. From this point, you can use the small-scale inset on Chart 3710 and head easterly until you reach Lohbrunner Island.

A shorter but narrower route starts from 1.0 mile northwest of Kipp Islet and passes east through an intricate passage, taking many of the small rocks and islets on their north side. The position for entering this route is: 52°29.28' N, 128°48.10' W. (The large-scale map MTS 01-95 by Shipwrite Productions, which shows both entry routes, is the best source for detailed observations of this area. Please see Appendix.)

Heading through the narrows, Higgins Passage

Tidal rapids in Higgins Passage, at the north end of Lohbrunner Island, create a lot of foam. An hour before high water, flood tide flows west here, and has a drop of about one foot over its 300-yard length. Since current is substantial, it's difficult to turn around inside the narrows.

Anchor (west side of narrows) in 6 fathoms over a sand and gravel bottom with good holding.

Anchor (east side of narrows) in 4 fathoms over mud with good holding.

Higgins Lagoon

Charts 3737, 3728, 3726; entrance: 52°29.80′ N, 128°41.90′ W (NAD 27)

Tidal rapids, rocks and kelp lie across the entrance to Higgins Lagoon. (p. 95, SD)

Higgins Lagoon is unsurveyed but, on a southeaster, it appears to catch everything blowing along the south end of Swindle Island and Milbanke Sound. Although we have not entered the lagoon because of poor visibility, the uncharted inlet across the way on Price Island is a place to explore.

"Price Inlet"

Chart 3728 (uncharted); entrance (uncharted inlet): 52°29.10′ N, 128°40.30′ W (NAD 27)

The uncharted inlet on the north corner of Price Island, which we call Price Inlet, is a charming area and the only secure anchorage on the west side of Milbanke Sound. It is easy to enter, has reasonable depths, and offers good shelter; unlike Higgins Lagoon to the north, it doesn't have a kelp-choked tidal rapids.

Central depths are about 8 fathoms over a large area. Because of unknown risks there has been little exploitation of this remote area. The shore is covered with mature old-growth forest and lots of moss and muskeg. The geometry of the inlet is more interesting than the dashed lines of the chart indicate, and we can hardly wait to give it a proper sounding. There are several arms and a couple of wooded islands. The tree limbs grow in a normal horizontal line, indicating that little chop ever develops here. It was late in the day when we pulled into Price Inlet and we were running out of time, so we checked the bottom not far from the entrance on the west shore, where a tiny stream had caught our eye. The bottom had good holding and we swung all night on our lunch hook.

Anchor in 5 fathoms over a mud bottom with good holding.

Grant Anchorage

Charts 3710, 3728, 3737; (uncharted) entrance: 52°28.83′ N, 128°45.17′ W (NAD 27)

> *Grant Anchorage, east of the island 0.5 mile ENE of Kipp Islet, is in the west entrance of Higgins Passage and affords anchorage to small vessels in 20 fathoms (37 m), mud bottom.* (p. 178, SD)

Grant Anchorage is the uncharted basin to the northwest of Higgins Passage. We find it best to anchor in front of the rapids where you can view the narrows.

Meyers Passage

Charts 3734, 3710 (inset); east entrance (Tolmie Channel): 52°40.20′ N, 128°34.00′ W; west entrance: 52°35.88′ N, 128°45.30′ W; anchor (elbow): 52°36.15′ N, 128°35.22′ W (NAD 27)

> *Meyers Passage, which leads from Laredo Sound into Tolmie Channel, is suitable for small vessels but local knowledge is advised. The least depth through the fairway is encountered in Meyers Narrows.* (p. 179, SD)
>
> *Tidal streams flood from Laredo Sound toward Tolmie Channel and the ebb flows in the opposite direction; the maximum rate for both is 3 kn.* (p. 180, SD)

Meyers Passage is the preferred smooth-water route when a southerly wind is blowing in Laredo Sound. Passage between Princess Royal Island and Swindle Island is easy, with the exception of a one-mile, shallow, kelp-filled shoal at Meyers Narrows. The shallowest point, in the vicinity of Buoy "E70," is approximately one fathom at zero tide. Although the kelp bed may cause some anxiety, the bottom in the narrows is fairly flat and you can easily guide between the patches.

Considerably easier to traverse than Higgins Passage, Meyers Passage demands less tedious navigation. Most cruising boats can pass through at moderate tide levels by holding a midchannel course and slowly passing buoy "E70." You can find excellent shelter in the center of Meyers Narrows in what we call "Meyers Narrows Cove."

Larger boats can find protection in all weather, except northerlies, at the elbow of Meyers Passage, one mile east of buoy "E70."

Anchor (elbow) in 5 to 10 fathoms over a rocky bottom.

McRae Cove

Chart 3734; anchor: 52° 38.92′ N, 128° 34.80′ W (NAD 27)

> *McRae Cove is 0.3 mile north of Jorgensen Harbour.* (p. 180, SD)

McRae Cove is a small indentation that offers some protection from northerlies for only one cruising boat. Tuck up against the shallow shore for maximum shelter.

Anchor in 2 to 5 fathoms near shore over an unrecorded bottom.

Jorgensen Harbour

Chart 3734; entrance: 52°38.50′ N, 128°35.05′ W; anchor: 52° 38.66′ N, 128° 34.94′ W (NAD 27)

> *Jorgensen Harbour, 2.3 miles north of Saunders Point and on the west side of Meyers Passage, is sheltered by an island off its north entrance point. Anchorage for small craft can be obtained in 13 fathoms (24 m) in Jorgensen Harbour.* (p. 180, SD)

Jorgensen Harbour is too deep and open for convenient small-craft anchorage. However, the flat, shallow bar between the island to the northeast and Princess Royal Island makes a great anchor site.

Anchor in 4 fathoms over a sand and mud bottom with good holding.

Meyers Narrows

Chart 3710 (inset); east entrance: 52°36.22′ N, 128°35.72′ W; west entrance: 52°36.56′ N, 128°37.88′ W (NAD 27)

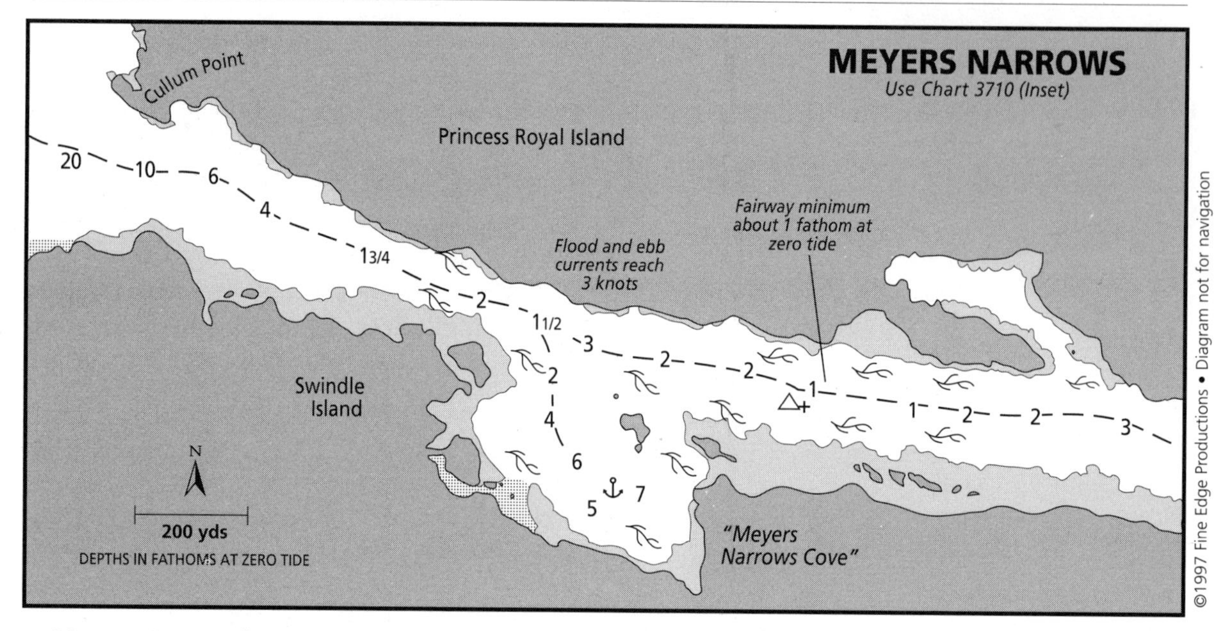

Meyers Narrows, between Cullum Point and Saunders Point, is less than 0.1 mile wide in its narrowest part and has a least depth of 4 feet (1.2 m) in the fairway. A drying rock on the south side of the fairway, about halfway through the narrows has starboard hand buoy "E70" close NW. A rock awash is on the north side of the fairway, about 300 feet (91 m) NE of the drying rock. During summer and autumn months kelp grows thickly in the shoal water on both sides of the narrows.

Small craft can obtain anchorage at the west end of Meyers Narrows in 10 fathoms (18 m), mud, about 0.25 mile SW of Cullum Point and 0.1 mile from the south shore. At the east end they can obtain anchorage west of the drying spit that is close west of Saunders Point. (p. 180, SD)

Cruising boats can transit Meyers Narrows at most tidal levels due to moderate current and a relatively flat bottom. Late in the summer, you can easily pass through patches of intimidating-looking bull kelp by keeping your speed low. Use Chart 3710 (inset) as a guide and pass close north of red buoy "E70."

"Meyers Narrows Cove"

Chart 3710 (inset); anchor:
52°36.27′ N, 128°37.00′ W (NAD 27)

Small craft can find complete shelter from all weather in the center of Meyers Narrows, just west of buoy "E70," on the south shore. The bottom is largely flat with depths of 6 to 7 fathoms, and there is adequate swinging room for several boats. Enter west of islet (58); the east side is foul. The entrance fairway carries 2 fathoms, with kelp patches on either side and, at times, in the center. If you are eastbound, this cove is a good place to wait for a favorable tide for passing over the shoal just east of buoy "E 70."

Anchor in 6 fathoms, over brown mud with good holding.

Corney Cove

Chart 3710 (inset); entrance:
52°36.50′ N, 128°42.60′ W; anchor:
52°36.93′ N, 128°42.68′ W (NAD 27)

Corney Cove, located on the north side of Meyers Passage inside its west entrance, is a well-sheltered and scenic anchorage for one or two boats. Boats with deep draft can wait for the proper tide before continuing their eastward transit. A small creek drains into the head of the cove, and no driftwood on shore indicates good shelter. Avoid a rock near shore off the creek.

Anchor in 8 to 10 to fathoms over an unrecorded bottom

Laredo Sound

Charts 3726, 3728, 3737; south entrance:
52°20.00′ N, 128°50.00′ W (NAD 27)

The west coast of Price Island is fringed by numerous islets and rocks extending up to 2 miles offshore. The east coast of Aristazabal Island is comparatively steep-to; islands and rocks extend 4 miles south from this island.

Tide-rips, dangerous to small craft, occur with the ebb stream on Moody Banks, especially during south winds, and south of McInnes Island at the junction of the streams from Laredo and Milbanke Sounds. (p. 174, SD)

Laredo Sound is subject to southerly swells which can keep up on an ebb tide when the wind is blowing from the south. Crossing Laredo Sound can be uncomfortable, but you can find coves on either side of the sound in which to await better conditions.

Rudolf Bay

Charts 3728, 3726; entrance:
52°24.45′ N, 128°45.10′ W; anchor:
52° 24.95′ N, 128°45.25′ W (NAD 27)

Rudolf Bay, 9 miles north of McInnes Island, has several rocks off its narrow entrance but is well sheltered and suitable for small craft. A detached shoal rock is 1.5 miles west of Rudolf Bay. (p. 178, SD)

If you want to explore the west coast of Price Island by kayak and dinghy, Rudolf Bay offers moderately good shelter. Pass the midchannel island on its north side and anchor in the inner basin. While the rocks and reefs to the south of Rudolf Bay may offer fascinating opportunities for exploration, we advise caution since the area is poorly charted.

Anchor in 2 to 3 fathoms at the head of the bay, unrecorded bottom.

"Larkin Point Basin"

Charts 3726, 3737 (uncharted); entrance:
52°29.80′ N, 128°48.75′ W; anchor:
52°31.00′ N, 128°48.80′ W (NAD 27)

Larkin Point Basin is strategically located in the center of Laredo Sound, west of Higgins Passage. This highly-protected basin, due east of Larkin Point on the east shore of Laredo Sound, provides good shelter in most summer weather. Larkin Point Basin is an uncharted area with an exposed southerly entrance, so caution is advised. A fairway can be found leading north into the basin. Keep most of the islets to port. The fairway has depths of about 12 fathoms. Anchor on the northeast side of the islet in the center of the basin. The large-scale map by Shipwrite Productions is the best source for detailed observations of this area.

Anchor in 9 fathoms over a mixed bottom with reported good holding.

Kitasu Bay

Charts 3737, 3726; entrance:
52°33.50′ N, 128°47.00′ W (NAD 27)

Kitasu (Kitasoo) Bay is entered between Wilby Point and Jamieson Point, 2 miles east. Kwakwa Creek, Cann Inlet and Osment Inlet, on the east side of Kitasu Bay, have not been surveyed and local knowledge is advised. Several islets lie in the common entrance of Kwakwa Creek and Cann Inlet; drying rocks encumber the entrance of Osment Inlet. (p. 179, SD)

Kitasu Bay provides protection from southerly swells, and you can find anchorage in Cowards Cove, Parsons Anchorage, Osment Inlet or Cann Inlet. There are also numerous nooks and crannies in Kitasu Bay. It's a major herring spawning area in late March and grey whales are a common sight. The large-scale map by Shipwrite Productions is the best source for detailed observations of this area.

"Cowards Cove"

Charts 3737, 3726; entrance:
52°33.60′ N, 128°44.65′ W; anchor (east of lagoon): 52°34.00′ N, 128°44.34′ W (NAD 27)

Cowards Cove is a tiny inlet immediately east of Jamieson Point on the north side of Kitasu Bay. The cove is well sheltered from basically all weather. Over the years fishing boats exiting Meyers Passage have found comfortable shelter here when they want to avoid crossing Laredo

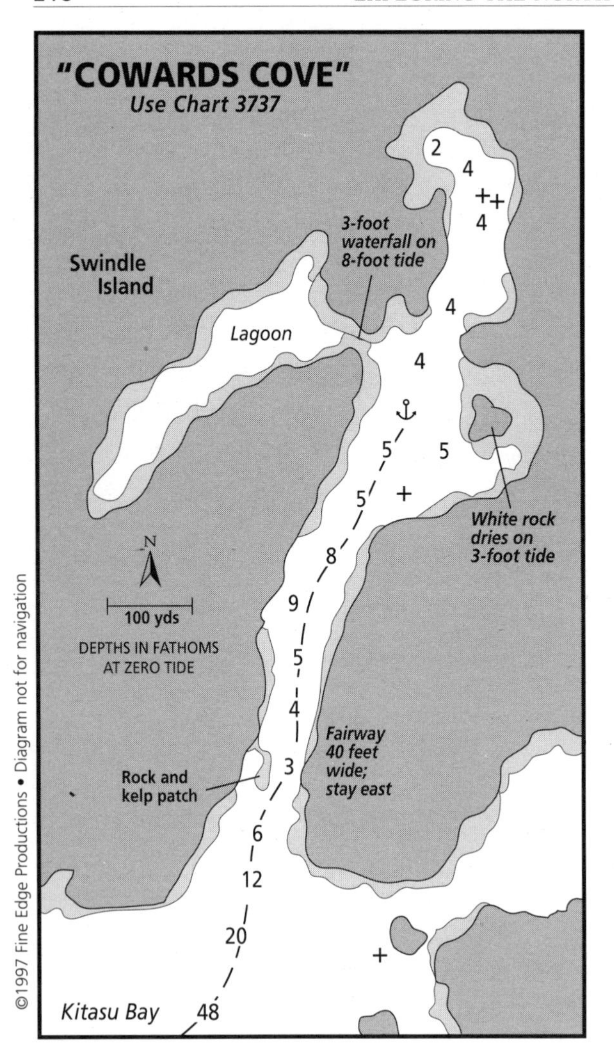

Sound with large beam seas. The entrance is narrow with about 3 fathoms in the 40-foot wide fairway. Avoid the kelp and a rock on the west shore by favoring the east shore in the narrows.

Anchorage can be found for moderate-sized boats east of the tidal rapids of the lagoon on the west shore. Avoid the white rock awash on a 3-foot tide in the east nook. Small cruising boats can anchor deep in the head of the cove where it is quiet and scenic. The lagoon can be entered on high water by dinghy only. See the large-scale map by Shipwrite Productions for the best observations of this area.

Anchor (head of cove) in 2 fathoms over a rocky bottom with poor-to-fair holding.

Anchor (east of lagoon) in 5 fathoms over soft mud bottom with good holding.

Parsons Anchorage

Chart 3737; anchor: 52° 31.00′ N, 128° 44.30′ W (NAD 27)

> *Parsons Anchorage, at the head of Kitasu Bay and south of Marvin Islands, affords good shelter to small vessels during SE winds. The anchorage is in 15 to 20 fathoms (27 to 37 m), sand and gravel. A rock which dries 3 feet (0.9 m) is 0.1 mile north, a rock with less than 6 feet (2 m) over it is 0.1 mile south and two cabins are on the west side of the easternmost Marvin Island.* (p. 179, SD)

Parsons Anchorage, deep in Kitasu Bay, offers very good shelter in heavy southerly weather, but it is open to strong westerlies. There is good holding with lots of swinging room. The large-scale map by Shipwrite Productions is the best source for this area.

Anchor deep in the cove in 7 to 10 fathoms, over a sand and gravel bottom with good holding.

Osment Inlet

Chart 3737 (inner basin uncharted); entrance: 52°32.30′ N, 128°43.50′ W; anchor (approximately): 52°31.88′ N, 128°41.87′ W (NAD 27)

> *. . . drying rocks encumber the entrance of Osment Inlet.* (p. 179, SD)

Well-sheltered anchorage is reported in the inner basin of Osment Inlet. The bottom of the inlet has irregular depths. Fishing boats anchor near the two midchannel islets in about 6 fathoms, while small boats anchor in the north nook farther east in 3 fathoms. The large-scale map by Shipwrite Productions is the best source of detailed observations of this area.

Monk Bay

Chart 3737 uncharted; entrance: 52°33.90′ N, 128°52.10′ W (NAD 27)

> *Monk Bay, between Dallain Point and Hague Point, is too deep for anchorage.* (p. 180, SD)

"Hague Point Lagoon"

Chart 3737; entrance: 52°40.05′ N, 128°50.92′ W; anchor: 52°40.19′ N, 128°51.87′ W (NAD 27)

Hague Point Lagoon, the small landlocked basin one mile northwest of Hague Point, offers excellent protection for small boats in all weather.

If Cowards Cove in Kitasu Bay is the place where northbound skippers head to avoid the seas in Laredo Sound, Hague Point Lagoon (aka "Chicken Cove") is the equivalent for southbound chickens who've had it with the sound.

Entering the lagoon, however, requires a measure of courage. It is extremely narrow with less than 20 feet between the rocks on a 9-foot tide, and it has a depth of less than one fathom at zero tide. An S-turn is required to avoid the initial rock on the south side of the channel, followed by two rocks on the north side. Current in the narrows is moderate, but underwater visibility is good to 25 feet. The lagoon has a large, flat bottom which permits swinging room for several vessels. Large concentrations of sea nettles are sometimes found in the lagoon.

Anchor in 6 to 9 fathoms over a bottom of soft mud, sand, kelp and some wood debris. Holding is fair to very good.

Laredo Inlet

Chart 3737; entrance: 52°37.40′ N, 129°48.90′ W (NAD 27)

Laredo Inlet, entered between Laidlaw and Jessop Islands on the west and Aitken and Croft Islands on the east, has high mountain ranges on both sides.

Laredo Inlet is generally deep in the middle; Burr Rock, about 16 miles inside the entrance, is the only danger in mid-channel. (p. 180, SD)

Laredo Inlet, at the south end of Princess Royal Island, is a deep fjord with high peaks and ridges on both sides. Southerly swell diminishes quickly as you enter the inlet. The river outlets and grassy meadows of Princess Royal Island are good places for bear observation. The cream-colored Kermodei bear is more common here than any-

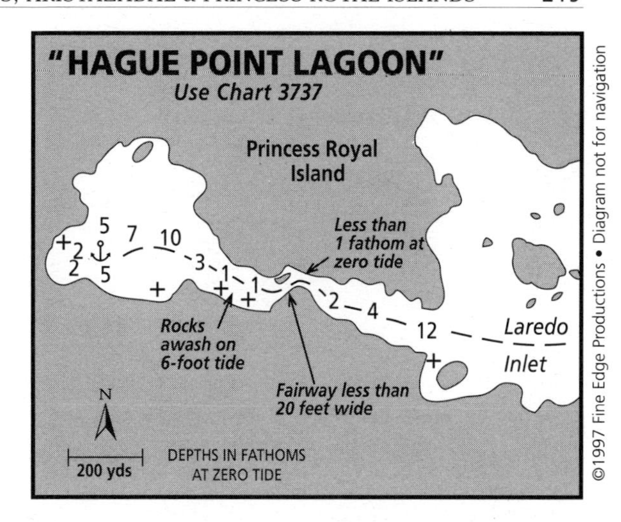

where else in the world. Laredo Inlet has several attractive anchor sites, the most popular being Alston Cove and Bay of Plenty.

Thistle Passage

Chart 3737; entrance (south): 52°36.20′ N, 128°45.85′ W; entrance (north): 52°39.50′ N, 128°45.30′ W (NAD 27)

Thistle Passage, east of Hastings Island, has several islands and rocks in it; north of Palmer Anchorage it is only suitable for small craft. (p. 180, SD)

Thistle Passage can be used as a smooth-water route for entering Laredo Inlet from Meyers Passage when Laredo Sound kicks up. Minimum depth of the fairway at the south end of the narrows is $4^1/_2$ fathoms. Avoid the rock awash at 4-foot tide, 30 feet off the east shore. Just north of this rock is another near the west shore, awash at 12 feet, that extends out about 90 feet from the trees. The north end of the narrows has about 3 fathoms in the fairway, which is less than the depth indicated on the chart.

Palmer Anchorage

Chart 3737; position: 52°37.30′ N, 128°45.50′ W (NAD 27)

Palmer Anchorage, in the south part of Thistle Passage, affords anchorage for small vessels in 19 fathoms (35 m), shell bottom. (p. 180, SD)

Palmer Anchorage is well protected from Laredo

Sound swell and chop; however, it is too deep for convenient cruising boat anchorage. Quigley Creek Cove, 2 miles north, is a better shelter.

"Quigley Creek Cove"

Chart 3737; entrance position:
52°39.44′ N, 128°45.20′ W; anchor:
52°39.37′ N, 128°44.66′ W (NAD 27)

> *Quigley Creek, on the east side and at the north end of Thistle Passage, has several islets in its entrance.* (p. 180, SD)

Quigley Creek has a group of small islets near its outlet that provides good shelter to cruising boats. The islets are more extensive than indicated on the chart and offer better protection than you might guess from studying the chart; the cove is essentially landlocked.

From Thistle Passage, enter the cove, passing north of the westernmost islet that lies close to the point on Princess Royal Island. The entrance is irregular with many isolated underwater rocks. "Elephant Rock" lies off the northeast corner of the westernmost islet and extends approximately a third of the way into the channel. Depths are considerably less than those indicated on the chart. The bottom is irregular until you have passed all the islets.

A large, drying flat lies off the north shore of Quigley Creek, and the bottom is steep-to. Anchor off the flat in the center of the cove. There is swinging room for two or three boats. Local fishing boats frequently use the cove.

Anchor in 8 fathoms, brown sand with shells, good holding.

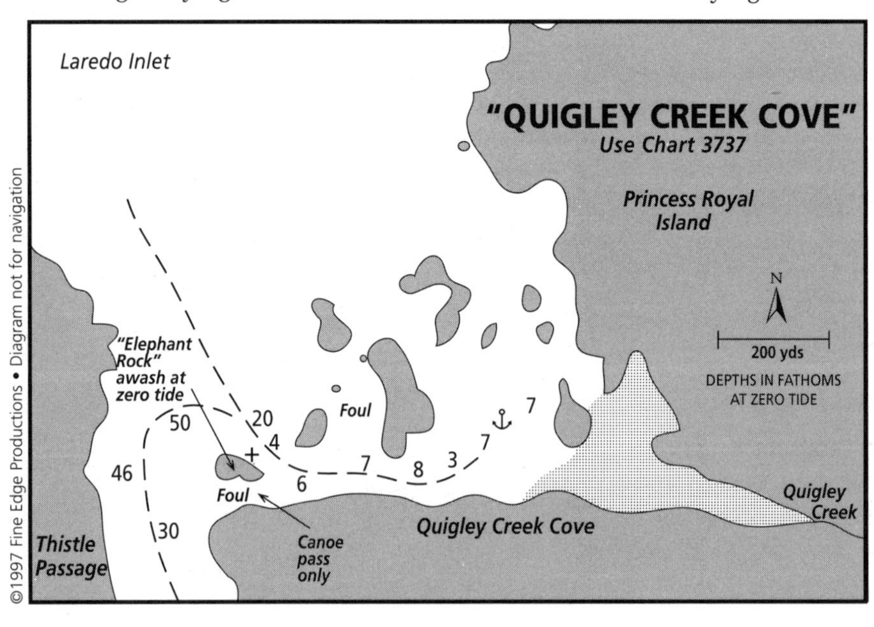

Trahey Inlet

Chart 3737; entrance (east):
52°39.90′ N, 128°47.55′ W (NAD 27)

> *Trahey Inlet, NE of Hague Point, can be entered on either side of Jessop Island; it is only suitable for small craft. Drying and above-water rocks lie in the approach and passage on the west side of Jessop Island.* (p. 180, SD)

Trahey Inlet is generally deep and exposed to southerly winds; we have not found good anchorage here except in the northeast corner as a temporary anchorage in fair weather.

"Unnamed Cove," Laredo Inlet

Chart 3737; entrance: 52°43.83′ N, 128°46.90′ W;
anchor: 52°43.52′ N, 128°47.09′ W (NAD 27)

> *The rock charted in the centre of the entrance to the unnamed cove is a very small treed islet. Pass to the east of this islet.* (p. 182, SD)

Unnamed Cove, located between two treed islets lying on the west side of the cove and the peninsula to the east, provides excellent protection from southerly weather with good views north up Laredo Inlet. Although the cove is open to downslope winds, there is little evidence of drift logs on shore.

A large rock, awash at 12 feet, extends about 100 feet from the trees on the east shore of the peninsula. South of this rock, the bottom is a flat 5 fathoms.

Anchor in 6 fathoms over a grey mud bottom with very good holding.

Alston Cove

Chart 3737; entrance: 52°45.10′ N, 128°45.60′ W; anchor: 52°44.83′ N, 128°44.58′ W (NAD 27)

Alston Cove, 3 miles north of Powles Creek, has a narrow entrance with a depth of 21 feet (6.4 m). Blee Creek empties into the head of the cove over a drying flat. Hards Creek is on the west shore opposite Alston Cove.

Anchorage for small craft can be obtained in Alston Cove and in the cove 1.5 miles SW of Alston Cove. The rock charted in the centre of the entrance to the unnamed cove is a very small treed islet. Pass to the east of this islet. (p. 182, SD)

Alston Cove is a beautiful cove, well protected from all weather. High peaks and deep valleys make this site particularly scenic. A rock slide extends from the north shore at the entrance, and a bar of 3.5 fathoms crosses the opening. Near the head of the cove, the bottom is steep-to where the drying mud flat comes out of Blee Creek. There is swinging room for a large number of boats.

Anchor in about 6 fathoms over sand and mud bottom with good-to-very-good holding.

Weld Cove

Chart 3737; entrance (between Kohl and Pocock islands): 52°48.15′ N, 128°45.10′ W; anchor: 52°49.10′ N, 128°46.00′ W (NAD 27)

Weld Cove is west of Pocock Island. (p. 182, SD)

Weld Cove is well protected in all weather.

You can enter Weld Cove from either the west side of Kohl Island or the passage between Kohl and Pocock Islands. Passing between the two islands is easier, and the fairway carries a minimum depth of 3½ fathoms. Care must be taken to avoid two dangerous charted rocks awash on about a 7-foot tide located about 400 yards northwest of Kohl Island. You can pass between the charted rocks and Pocock Island in 5 fathoms by favoring the Pocock shore. Once you're inside, you can anchor anywhere in the northern end of

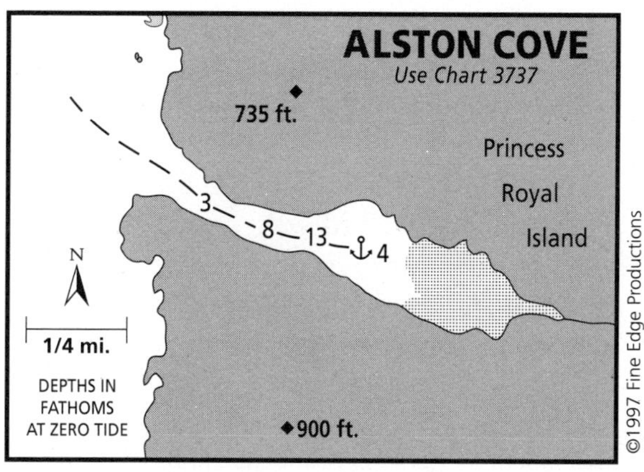

Weld Cove, where there's room for a number of boats along an 11-fathom bottom.

Entrance west of Kohl, contrary to Chart 3737, is more intricate and carries less water than indicated. Entering from the south, stay close to the Princess Royal shore on your port hand to avoid a rock that dries on 2 feet off Busey Creek; continue to favor this shore until you're about to enter the small cove formed by a short peninsula directly ahead. You will notice a large rock-reef complex that nearly connects to the peninsula from Kohl Island. The slot between this rock complex and the peninsula is only about 25 feet wide and has a midchannel depth of about 2 fathoms. You must turn due east and pass within about 15 feet of the peninsula to avoid the rock extending from the unnamed island, before turning north again to enter Weld Cove.

Anchor in 10 fathoms over a mud bottom with good holding.

Fifer Cove

Chart 3737; entrance: 52°52.30′ N, 128°41.60′ W; anchor: 52°51.67′ N, 128°40.77′ W (NAD 27)

Fifer Cove, east of Burr Rock, is entered between Tuite Point and the islands in its entrance. The fairway between Tuite Point and these islands is about 450 feet (137 m) wide with a depth of dark grey 24 feet (7.3 m). The outlet of Bloomfield Lake is at the south end of the cove.

Anchorage for small craft can be obtained in Fifer Cove. (p. 182, SD)

Picturesque Fifer Cove, on the east shore of Laredo Inlet, is surrounded by high peaks, characteristic of Laredo Inlet. The inlet between Tuite Point and the islands has a minimum depth of about 4 fathoms. The cove itself is fairly deep and its shores steep-to and well protected with no indications of driftwood or chop. Reported to be breezy in westerly winds, Fifer Cove may not offer adequate shelter in storms.

The creek from Bloomfield Lake has created a large drying flat on the southwest shore. The grassy shore here, and the flat-bottomed creek, are known as good bear habitat.

Small boats can anchor in about 8 fathoms in the southeast corner with limited swinging room, while larger boats can anchor anywhere in the middle of the cove.

Anchor in the southeast corner in 8 fathoms over a dark-grey mud bottom with very good holding.

Buie Creek

Chart 3737; anchor (northwest corner): 52°58.20′ N, 128°40.00′ W (NAD 27)

Buie Creek, at the head of Laredo Inlet, is an indifferent anchorage, useful only for bear-watching or for entering the creek in calm weather. The head of the bay is steep-to, but there is a small 4-fathom shoal at the northwest corner of the inlet, due north of Brew Island. The water temperature here can reach 70°F in the summer, higher than elsewhere in Laredo Inlet.

Anchor (northwest corner) in 4 fathoms over sand and gravel bottom with poor-to-fair holding.

Westbound, north of Brew Island, there is a shoal-route of not much more than one fathom. Avoid the two large rocks off the north side of Brew Island.

The cove at the head of Arnoup Creek has a large shallow bar on its east side. If you wish to anchor there, consider using a stern-tie to a tree on the west shore in 7 fathoms. Poor underwater visibility and a dark bottom make anchoring here difficult. It is recommended only as a lunch stop or for investigating the drying flat off the creek.

Mellis Inlet

Chart 3737; entrance: 52°53.45′ N, 128°43.00′ W (NAD 27)

Mellis Inlet is entered 1.5 miles north of Burr Rock. Nias Creek and Packe Creek drain into the head of the inlet. (p. 182, SD)

Mellis Inlet, a 2.2-mile-long inlet on the west shore of Laredo Inlet, has remarkable high peaks with exposed grey granite slabs on either side. Mellis Inlet appears too deep for convenient anchorage, and we have no further local knowledge to add.

Bay of Plenty

Chart 3737; entrance: 52°49.90′ N, 128°45.00′ W; anchor: 52°50.50′ N, 128°46.10′ W (NAD 27)

Bay of Plenty, 1 mile north of Pocock Island, is encumbered with islets and rocks. (p. 182, SD)

The Bay of Plenty is a favorite among cruising boats for its good protection and extended area of shallow water. Several boats can anchor in the bay with adequate swinging room. Among other things, the bay is known for plenty of crabs. As you enter the Bay of Plenty, favor the south shore, taking the first island (120) inside the entrance on your starboard, and the small treed islet in the center of the bay to port by favoring the north shore. The area between the small center islet and the south shore is foul on low water.

You can explore Pyne Creek by dinghy for over a mile—a good place to observe wildlife—or you can sit in your stern and admire the steep bluffs on the north side of the creek.

Anchor in 6 to 8 fathoms over soft brown mud with very good holding.

Laredo Channel

Charts 3737; southeast entrance: 52°38.50′ N, 128°53.80′ W; northwest entrance: 52°51.00′ N, 129°12.00′ W (NAD 27)

Laredo Channel connects Laredo Sound with Caamano Sound. The banks in mid-channel between Wilson Rock and Ramsbotham Islands, 3 miles NW, have several shoals on them which rise steeply from the bottom; soundings will give little warning of these shoals.

The coast of Princess Royal Island, between Dallain Point and Kent Inlet, 5.5 miles NW, is fringed by drying reefs and below-water rocks which extend 0.3 mile offshore. (p. 182, SD)

The eastern shores of Aristazabal Island, along Laredo Channel, have very few significant indentations where you can find shelter.

The Princess Royal Island shore does not offer easy anchorage until you reach the vicinity of Surf Inlet. Smithers Island Cove, on the east shore of Laredo Channel, is the most accessible anchor site in this area.

Walsh Rock

Chart 3737; anchor position:
52°38.20′ N, 128°47.67′ W (NAD 27)

Walsh Rock is steep-to on its east side. Fernie Point, 1.6 miles NW of Walsh Rock, is steep-to.

Anchorage for small vessels can be obtained west of Walsh Rock in about 60 feet (18.3 m), sand and shell bottom; this anchorage is about 0.1 mile off the coast of Aristazabal Island. (p. 182, SD)

Although there are few places to anchor in Laredo Channel, we would not put Walsh Rock on our list. The south-flowing ebb current is particularly strong in Laredo Channel and we've seen chop build very quickly inside both Ramsbotham Island and Walsh Rock, when there was just a moderate easterly blowing up the channel.

"Fury Bay"

Chart 3737; position: 52°40.02′ N, 129°00.75′ W (NAD 27)

Fury Bay, the local name for a small indentation on Aristazabal Island, 2 miles southeast of Ramsbotham Islands, is reported to offer moderate protection; it is out of the prevailing southeast or northwest chop in the main channel.

Anchor in 5 to 10 fathoms over an unrecorded bottom.

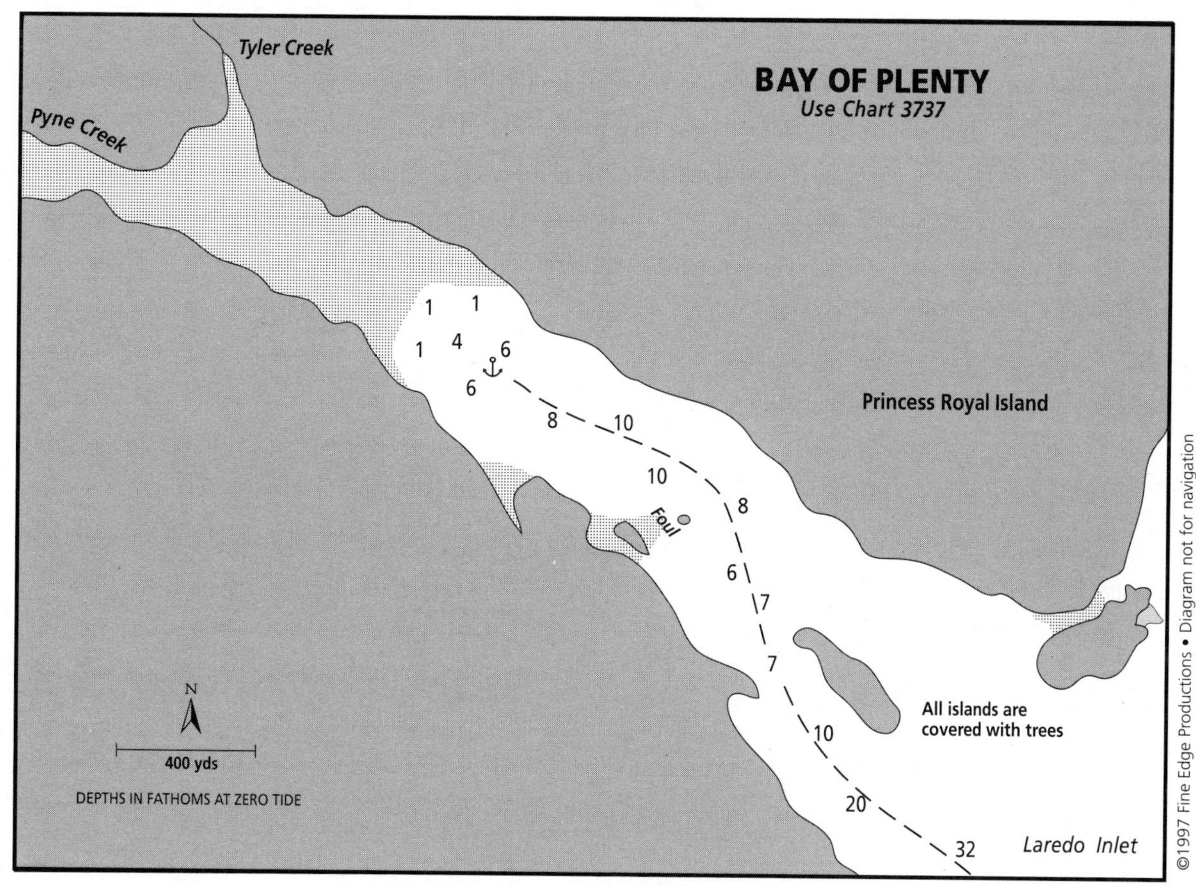

Ramsbotham Islands

Chart 3737; light: 52°41.92′ N, 129°02.10′ W (NAD 27)

> *Ramsbotham Islands, on the SW side of the channel and about 3 miles NW of Wilson Rock, consist of three islands and several islets. Foul ground extends 0.4 mile SE from the SE end of the islands.*
>
> *Anchorage can be obtained in 15 fathoms (27 m), rock and shell bottom, about 0.2 mile NE of the limestone quarry.* (p. 182–183, SD)

Photo courtesy CHS, Pacific Region

Philip Narrows, looking south

In addition to the anchorage noted above in *Sailing Direction*, anchorage is reported to be found on the west side of the two northernmost Ramsbotham Islands, tucked in between. Anchor east of the rock patch. This place is not recommended in southeast storms.

Kent Inlet

Chart 3719; entrance: 52°42.36′ N, 129°00.74′ W; anchor (inner basin): 52°43.24′ N, 128°58.78′ W (NAD 27)

> *Kent, Helmcken, Commando and Evinrude Inlets, which indent the NE side of Laredo Channel, are only suitable for small craft. Local knowledge is advised.*
>
> *Kent Inlet is entered south of Loap Point. Drying reefs and below-water rocks extend slightly more than 0.1 mile west of Loap Point. A rock awash, 0.1 mile south of Loap Point, lies in the middle of the entrance to the inlet.* (p. 183, SD)

Kent Inlet is located on the east shore of Laredo Channel, opposite Ramsbotham Island. It is a picturesque inlet where deer are often spotted along the shore. The inlet has an intricate entrance and two additional narrows that require careful navigation (see Philip Narrows below). The entrance is narrow, with several drying rocks, and the inset on Chart 3719 should be consulted carefully. Avoid the rock marked by kelp on the south side of the entrance and the dangerous rock midchannel that dries at 8 feet, 200 yards east of Loap Point. This midchannel rock should be passed on the east side with about 5 fathoms of water.

The second narrows, 0.3 mile north of Philip Narrows, has 3.5 fathoms minimum. Favor the west shore, avoiding the islets. Good protection can be found in the inner basin at the head of the inlet by favoring the north shore to avoid the midchannel rocks.

Anchor (inner basin) in 6 to 10 fathoms over an unrecorded bottom.

Philip Narrows

Chart 3737; fairway position: 52°42.68′ N, 129°00.24′ W (NAD 27)

> *Philip Narrows, a short distance within the entrance, is less than 150 feet (46 m) wide and has a depth of 7 feet (2.1 m). Tidal streams in the narrows attain 6 to 8 kn at springs. A drying rock and a rock with less than 6 feet (2 m) over it close SW are nearly in the middle of the south entrance to Philip Narrows; pass to the east of these rocks. Small craft should only enter at or near slack water.* (p. 183, SD)

Philip Narrows, an extremely narrow passage about 100 yards in length, is probably best transited at low-water slack so that you can see the rocks or at least the turbulence. The midchannel fairway is only about 30 feet wide and has a minimum depth of about 7 feet at zero tide. (We found 1.5 fathoms on a 2.2-foot tide with slack water 30 min-

Photo courtesy CHS, Pacific Region

Helmcken Inlet, entrance to lagoon

utes after Bella Bella.) Strong currents through the narrows make navigation hazardous at any time other than *at* or *near* slack water. Boats up to 100 feet have been known to navigate the entrance.

The small bay on the south side of the narrows has a floating line extending diagonally across, precluding easy anchoring. A small cove just west of Philip Narrows offers temporary sanctuary in 4 fathoms off a tiny drying beach.

Helmcken Inlet

Chart 3719 (inset); entrance: 52°45.31′ N, 129°04.52′ W; anchor (lagoon entrance): 52°45.88′ N, 128°01.72′ W (NAD 27)

> *Helmcken Inlet has Smithers Island in its entrance. The entrance channel north of Smithers Island is obstructed by drying rocks and dense kelp. The channel south of Smithers Island is only 150 feet (46 m) wide and has a least depth of 12 feet (3.7 m). A salt water lagoon is connected to the head of Helmcken Inlet by a narrow passage in which there are rapids.* (p. 183, SD)

Helmcken Inlet is entered through a narrows on the south side of Smithers Island. Favor the north shore of the narrows for the deepest water. The shallowest part is in the east end of the narrows. Kelp lines both shores of the narrows. Minimum depth through the narrows on the north side is 4 fathoms at zero tide, 30 feet or so off Smithers Island. Current in the narrows appears to be moderate.

The large lagoon at the head of the inlet can be entered by cruising boats at high-water slack. Caution is advised because currents at springs attain 6 to 8 knots through the narrows. The lagoon is uncharted and may provide some interesting sheltered anchorage. Although we have not entered the lagoon, we have observed a large tree-covered island inside.

Temporary anchorage can be found on the 2.5-fathom flat off the entrance to the lagoon. Due to the current into the lagoon, you must be sure your anchor is well set.

Anchor in 2.5 fathoms over sand and gravel bottom with some grass; fair-to-good holding.

"Smithers Island Cove"

Chart 3719 (inset); entrance: 52°45.37′ N, 129°04.68′ W; anchor: 52°45.53′ N, 129°04.14′ W (NAD 27)

> *Anchorage and shelter for small craft can be obtained in a small bight in the south shore of*

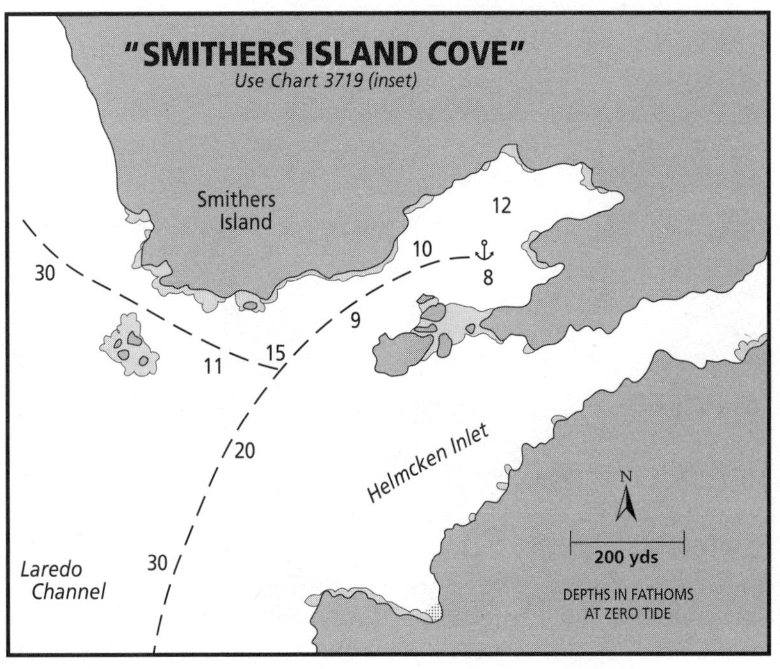

©1997 Fine Edge Productions • Diagram not for navigation

Smithers Island in 8 fathoms (15 m). (p. 183, SD)

Smithers Island Cove is fairly easy to enter and is rather well sheltered. However, the bottom is rocky, and it's difficult to get a good bite with your anchor. In moderate weather, there is not much strain on your anchor. In a blow we'd look elsewhere, such as Hague Point Lagoon, Meyers Passage or Racey Inlet.

Anchor in 8 to 10 fathoms over a rocky bottom with poor holding, unless your anchor is well set.

Commando Inlet

Chart 3719 (inset); entrance:
52°47.14′ N, 129°06.14′ W; anchor (reported at east end): 52°48.07′ N, 129°04.37′ W (NAD 27)

> *Commando Inlet is entered south of Hawkins Point through a narrow boat passage. At the east end of the boat passage, an islet is connected to the south shore by a drying ridge; depths north of the islet are 6 feet (1.8 m). Tidal streams in the narrow part of the entrance attain 8 to 10 kn at springs. Small craft should only enter at or near HW slack.* (p. 183, SD)

Commando Inlet is difficult to enter unless conditions are nearly optimum. One to 2-foot overfalls at the midchannel islet create a lot of foam and turbulence in the entrance. In addition, there is inadequate turning room in the entrance, and the channel on the north side of the islet is very narrow. A slow approach with bow lookouts is required since there is an underwater rock off the west end of the islet; you need to favor the north shore, avoiding overhanging branches. During spring tides there are overfalls on either side of the islet and passage should only be attempted very close to slack water. Good shelter is reported at the extreme eastern end of Commando Inlet; however, we have no additional local knowledge.

Photo courtesy CHS, Pacific Region

Commando Inlet, entrance east end

Evinrude Inlet

Chart 3719 (inset); entrance:
52°47.45′ N, 129°06.20′ W; log tie-up:
52°48.17′ N, 129°04.85′ W (NAD 27)

> *Evinrude Inlet is entered north of Hawkins Point and its entrance is less than 450 feet (137 m) wide at its narrowest part. A shoal with 10 feet (3 m) over it is on the north side of the fairway just within the entrance.* (p. 183, SD)

Evinrude Inlet provides good shelter from northwest and southeast gales since the outside chop rolls by the entrance. Silver snags covering the granite outcroppings of the inlet give it a wild look. On the north shore, near the outlet of the creek, there is a rusty donkey with a V-8 engine, remains of past logging days. Near this donkey, a black PVC pipe brings water from a small creek above.

Evinrude Inlet can be entered at all tide levels because there is minimal current. Favor the south shore at the second narrows to avoid a 3-fathom shoal.

A log tied to shore can be used for moorage as there is approximately one fathom or more of water along the steep-to rock. Depths elsewhere are too deep for convenient anchorage, unless you use a stern-tie to shore. The bottom is reported to be sticky mud with very good holding.

"Evinrude Inlet Bight"

Chart 3719 (inset); anchor:
52°47.32′ N, 129°05.87′ W (NAD 27)

The small bight 0.2 mile northeast of Hawkins Point can be used as temporary anchorage when strong ebb tides and southerly winds combine to create disagreeable chop in Laredo Channel. There is no swinging room here; however, in southeast winds you can drop your hook just off the small rocky beach and tether into the wind. The bight is open to westerly wind and chop.

Anchor in 2 fathoms, mixed bottom of small rocks, sand, eel grass and kelp. Holding is fair to good.

Baker Point

Chart 3737; light: 52°48.20′ N, 129°12.82′ W (NAD 27)

Baker Point, 5.3 miles NW of Shotbolt Point, is a low sandy point. (p. 183, SD)

Baker Point is an open roadstead where you can obtain temporary anchorage in 2 fathoms off the long and lovely stretch of sandy beach, in fair weather only. It is not much more than a lunch stop and a place to stretch your legs.

Anchor, as convenient, on either side of the light in 3 fathoms over a sand bottom with fair holding.

Aristazabal Island, West Coast

Charts 3726, 3737

Aristazabal Island faces Hecate Strait but is surprisingly well protected by innumerable islets, reefs and rocks. A favorite destination of fishermen and intrepid kayakers, this coast offers great fishing, wildlife viewing and exploring the rugged inner tidal zone by kayak or inflatable.

Weeteeam Bay

Chart 3710 (inset); entrance: 52°29.70′ N, 129°02.20′ W (NAD 27)

Weeteeam Bay is entered between Ede Island, which is wooded except for a bare rock ledge at the SE end, and Colston Islet, which has some bushes on it. Thistleton Islands are north of Ede Island and offer some protection from west winds. Bruce Islet is close east of this group. (p. 164, SD)

Weeteeam Bay, on the south tip of Aristazabal Island, offers sheltered water behind its many islands and islets. The bay should not be entered without consulting Chart 3710 (inset). Anchorage can be found in Weeteeam Bay at the entrance to Noble Lagoon and in Bent Harbour.

Endymion *in Bent Harbour, Weeteeam Bay*

Exploring the West Coast

After leaving the security of Clark Cove in early September and encountering brisk southerly weather, Réanne and I dropped our plan to explore the west coast of Aristazabal Island and decided to explore the Estevan group instead. That night we took secure refuge in Gillen Harbour. The next morning was misty and foggy so we crossed Campania Sound by radar and GPS and found our way into Barkley Passage amongst the biggest flock of loons we have ever seen.

We then resumed our original plan and continued south along the west coast of Aristazabal Island, keeping as many islands to windward as possible to avoid southerly chop. We found the smooth-water route on the north side of Thistleton Islands and, after a tricky passage, worked our way into Weeteeam Bay. We found the small gaff-headed ketch *Endymion* anchored securely in Bent Harbor. The *Endymion* was the first boat we had seen in three days.

Its owners were canoeing in the rain, combing the remote beaches for jetsam and flotsam, as they have been doing for 10 years. We invited Don and Gwen Burton aboard for tea. They said that, when they saw *Baidarka* through one of the "windows" in the maze of islands, they had to fight the urge to paddle out and tell us we were crazy fools and should head out to sea as quickly as possible. They confessed that they had second thoughts as their heads filled with visions of the jetsam they could pick up if we grounded!

The weather eased after tea and Réanne and I sailed across Laredo Sound to the west side of Higgins Passage where we became stormbound for 24 hours.

—DCD

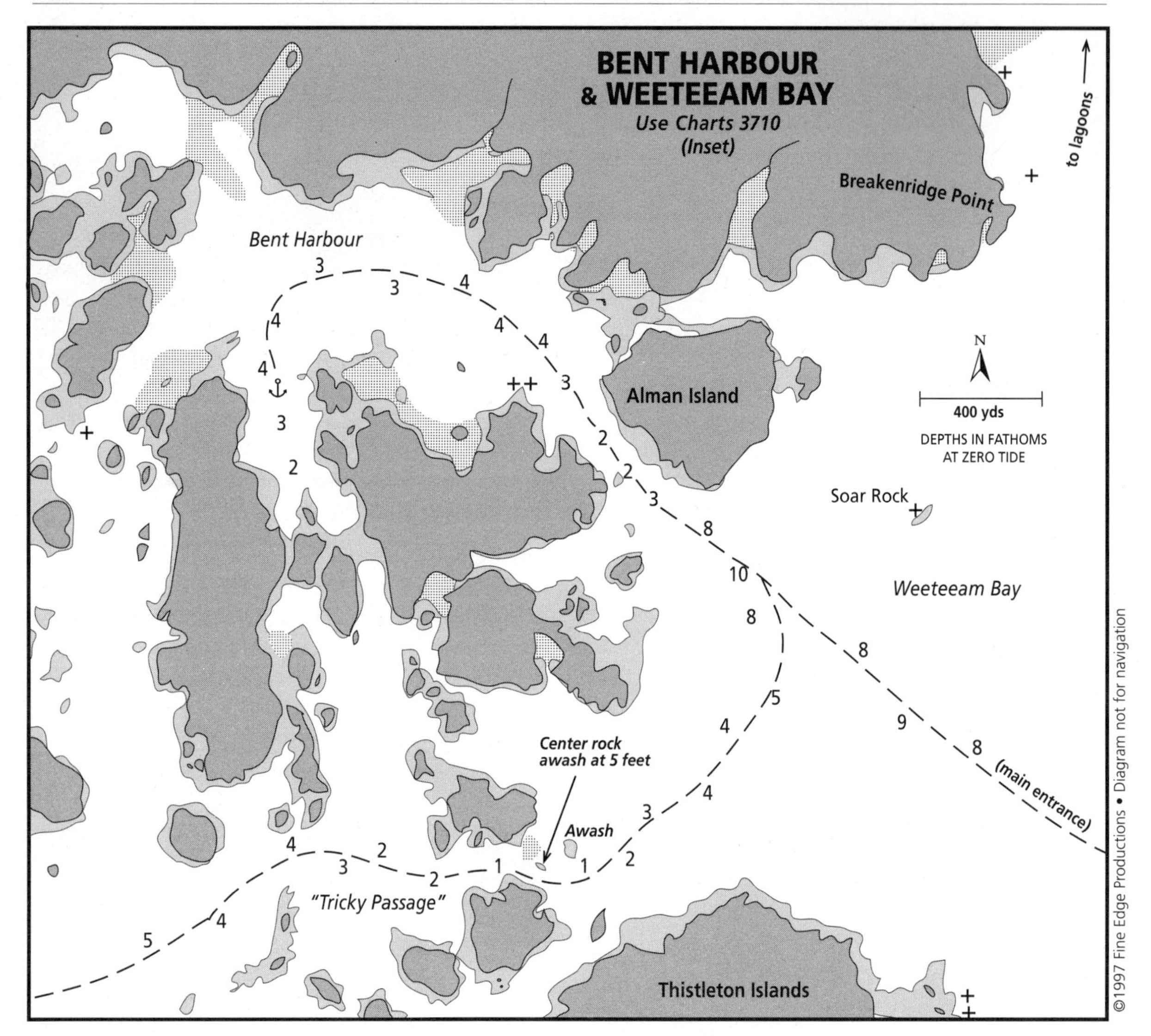

Bent Harbour

Chart 3710 (inset); entrance:
52°30.18′ N, 129°02.57′ W; anchor:
52°30.89′ N, 129°03.13′ W (NAD 27)

> *Bent Harbour, on the west side of Weeteeam Bay and north of Thistleton Islands, is entered SW of Alman Island through a narrow channel; it is only suitable for small craft.* (p. 164, SD)

Bent Harbour is the basin between Thistleton Islands and Aristazabal Island at the west side of Weeteeam Bay. While no swell or chop enters Bent Harbour, it is exposed to southeast winds. A shore tie can make this an almost bombproof anchorage.

Small boats can use the smooth-water passage north of the big Thistleton Island as noted by the soundings on Chart 3710 (inset); however, the narrows is highly restricted by underwater rocks and kelp, requiring adroit navigation.

Anchor in 4 fathoms over mud bottom with good holding.

Noble Lagoon

Chart 3710 (inset); anchor (0.25 mile northwest Archer Islets): 52°31.53′ N, 129°02.22′ W (NAD 27)

A good anchor site is located at the entrance to Noble Lagoon and Kdalmishan Creek near Archer Islets. Small boats can enter the lagoon near high-water slack.

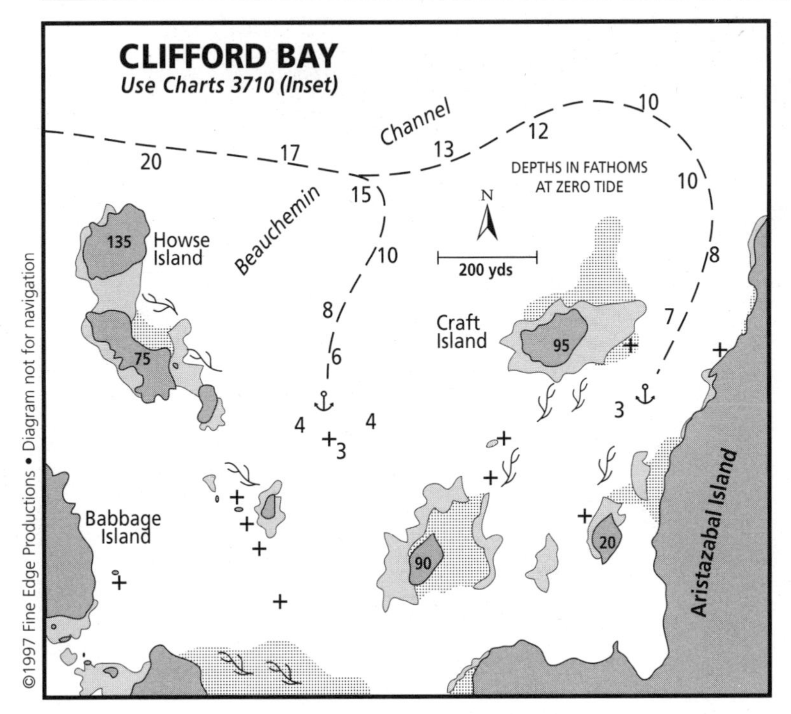

Anchor in 5 fathoms over mud bottom with good holding.

Clifford Bay

Chart 3710 (inset); entrance:
52°35.65′ N, 129°09.55′ W; anchor (west side of Craft Island): 52°35.36′ N, 129°08.98′ W (NAD 27)

Clifford Bay is entered between Dobbs Islets and Howse Island. The fairway through the entrance is about 0.15 mile wide and free of dangers.

Good anchorage can be obtained in 15 to 17 fathoms (27 to 31 m), mud, about 0.3 mile NE of the north extremity of Howse Island. Small craft can obtain anchorage in 3 to 6 fathoms (5.5 to 11 m) about 0.2 mile west of Craft Island. (p. 165, SD)

Clifford Bay is a large, sheltered bay offering anchorage to both large and small vessels. There is good protection from swells and chop although the wind may howl through the islets to the west and south. You can frequently spot loons in the area.

On the west side of Craft Island, the recommended anchorage has plenty of swinging room over a flat shallow bottom. Small boats may find more protection southeast of Craft Island; however, we have found the sand and gravel bottom to be covered with newspaper kelp with poor holding and a fouled anchor.

The Normansell Islands offer a sheltered route for boats heading to or from Clifford Bay. The passage inside Normansell Islands is protected from southerly swells and, within this network, you can find several possible anchor sites with good exploring. Notice, however, the disfigured tree limbs that indicate the strength of southeast storms!

Anchor (west side of Craft Island) in 5 fathoms over sand and kelp with fair-to-good holding.

Kettle Inlet

Charts 3737, 3724; entrance:
52°42.80′ N, 129°17.30′ W; anchor (east shore): 52°41.88′ N, 129°13.91′ W (NAD 27)

Kettle Inlet is encumbered in its entrance with numerous islets and rocks. A rock awash lies in the middle of the fairway, about 1 mile from the head of the inlet, with shoal depths SE of it. The passage between the large island and the peninsula forming the SW shore of Kettle Inlet is filled with drying rocks; the highest dries about 15 feet (4.6 m). (p. 165, SD)

Normansell Passage, Normansell Islands

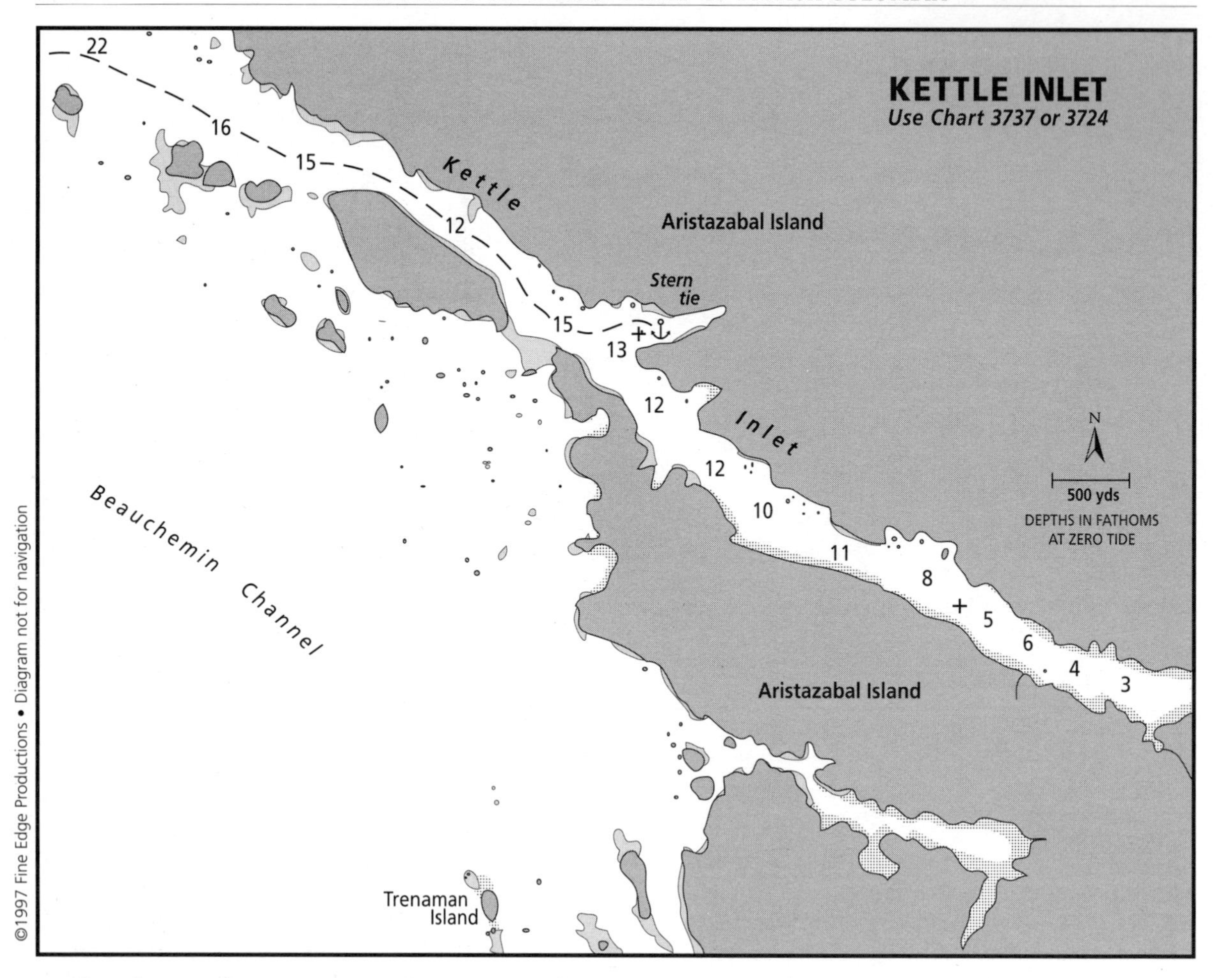

Kettle Inlet is a long, narrow indentation in the west coast of Aristazabal Island. Though the inlet is exposed to winds from the northwest or southeast, there is no swell. Captain Monahan writes: "I was anchored in Kettle Inlet experiencing 60+ knots, southeasterlies. In five minutes, the wind switched to 60 knots from the northwest. Though the anchor did drag somewhat, there was plenty of dragging room since the wind blew directly up and down the inlet."

When entering Kettle Inlet, take a midchannel course and anchor west of longitude 129°12.50' W in 8 to 10 fathoms. The best anchorage in Kettle Inlet is located in the nook on the east shore, just east of the tip of the peninsula which forms the south shore of the inlet. Tuck in behind a small islet on the south shore of the nook. A stern tie to the south shore makes it almost bombproof.

Anchor (east shore) in 6 fathoms over an unrecorded bottom with good holding.

Borrowman Bay, Turtish Harbour

Charts 3723 (inset), 3724; entrance (Morison Passage): 52°44.56′ N, 129°18.30′ W (NAD 27)

Borrowman Bay, between Wriglesworth Point and Pearse Point, 1.5 miles north, can be entered by Morison or Meiss Passages.

Small vessels can obtain anchorage south of Sere Rock, in Turtish Harbour, in 10 fathoms (18 m), mud. (pp. 165, 166, SD)

Borrowman Bay has the best protection for small craft, in Tate Cove, on the entire west coast of Aristazabal Island. When you approach the bay from the southwest, Trickey Island fades into the

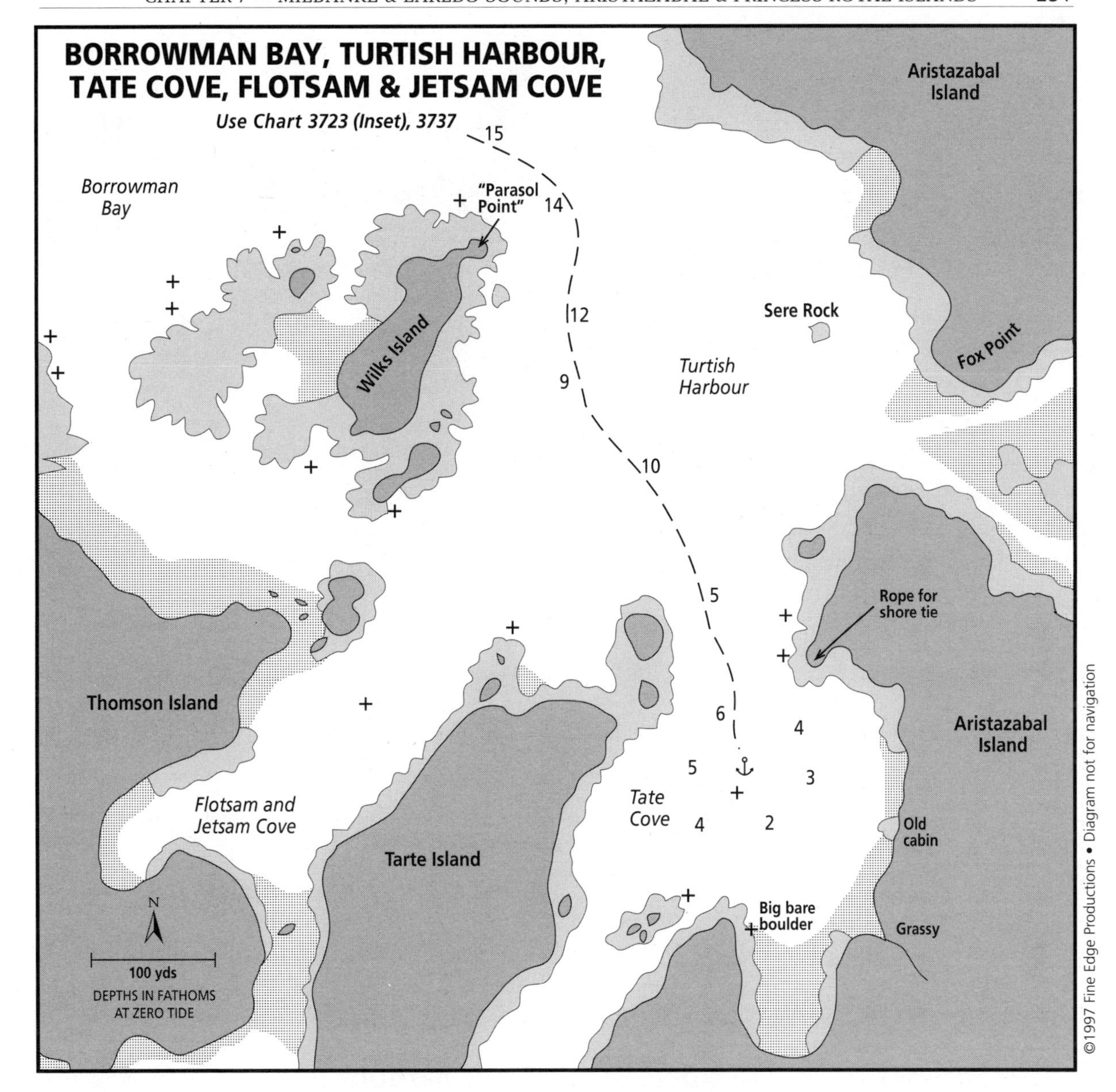

shore and is almost invisible. Wall Islets and the reef to Mesher Rock are also difficult to identify clearly; use caution when entering Morison Passage or Meiss Passage. GPS is useful for identifying the route.

In Turtish Harbour, wind shifts can cause vessels to swing so avoid anchoring near Sere Rock or the 3-fathom patch to its west. Otherwise holding is good in 8 to 10 fathoms over a mud bottom. Small boats can find more protection in Tate Cove immediately south.

Tate Cove

Chart 3723 (inset); entrance (Turtish Harbour): 52°44.27′ N, 129°16.68′ W; anchor: 52°44.02′ N, 129°16.53′ W (NAD 27)

> *Tate Cove is on the south side of Turtish Harbour east of Tarte Island.*
>
> *Tate Cove offers anchorage for small vessels in 6 fathoms (11 m).* (p. 166, SD)

Tate Cove offers virtually bombproof shelter for small boats. Wilks Island has a tree on its north point shaped like a Chinese parasol (we call this

"Parasol Point," entrance to Tate Cove

Parasol Point) that provides a landmark. Just beyond this point, you turn southeast into Tate Cove. There is a kayak haul-out beach at the head of the cove, and the east point has ropes that can be used for shore ties. The water here has better than 10-foot visibility. This is a good place to observe bald eagles, grebes, and gulls.

Anchor in 3 to 5 fathoms over a bottom of brown mud, with shells and sea lettuce; very good holding.

The cove on the west side of Tarte Island has been decorated by the Beaver family of Kitimat with jetsam and flotsam they've found on nearby beaches. Ropes and various plastic floats and buoys resemble Chinese lanterns suspended from the trees.

Surf Inlet

Chart 3737; entrance: 52°53.00′ N, 129°08.50′ W (NAD 27)

> *Surf Inlet extends from the east end of Caamaño Sound. Racey Inlet extends SE and Chapple Inlet and Emily Carr Inlet extend north from the entrance of Surf Inlet . . .* (p. 183, SD)

You will consider Surf Inlet aptly named if you enter when a strong westerly is blowing in against an ebb tide, but it is known principally for its scenic, narrow fjord with steep peaks that tower above its shores. Favor slack water for entering. Bears are known to inhabit this side of Princess Royal Island and this is a favorite place to look for them.

Tate Cove head

Surf Inlet extends about 13 miles northeastward from its entrance point off Johnstone Point to its head. Penn Harbour, 8 miles northeast of the entrance to Surf Inlet, provides excellent anchorage.

Argyh Cove

Chart 3737; position: 52°54.48′ N, 129°01.85′ W (NAD 27)

> *Argyh Cove, 2.5 miles ENE of Bryant Point, has a drying rock in its entrance.* (p.183, SD)

Argyh Cove makes a nice overnight stop in relatively good weather. Its bottom, however, is rocky and should not be trusted in a storm.

Penn Harbour

Chart 3737; entrance: 52°58.05′ N, 128°58.25′ W; anchor: 52°58.47′ N, 128°57.12′ W (NAD 27)

> *Penn Harbour, 1.5 miles NNE of Adams Point and on the east side of Surf Inlet, has a narrow entrance, about 180 feet (55 m) wide, with a least depth of 36 feet (11 m) through it. It is well sheltered from all winds.*
>
> *Penn Harbour affords good anchorage for small vessels in 11 to 12 fathoms (20 to 22 m), mud. Keep in mid-channel when entering and, when through the narrowest part, keep toward the NW side of the channel and anchor in the middle of*

the basin that forms the head of the harbour. (p. 183, SD)

Penn Harbour, 7.5 miles northeast of the entrance to Surf Inlet, provides excellent anchorage and is the safest anchorage in Surf Inlet. Its narrow entrance is clear on all tides, and inside you can find protection in all weather. While gales or storms blow outside in Hecate Strait, flags barely flutter inside Penn Harbour.

The harbor is landlocked. There is a lovely falls at its head that you can explore by dinghy. Or you can run 4 miles up to the head of Surf Inlet to explore an abandoned hydro-dam.

Anchor in 10 fathoms over an unrecorded bottom with good holding.

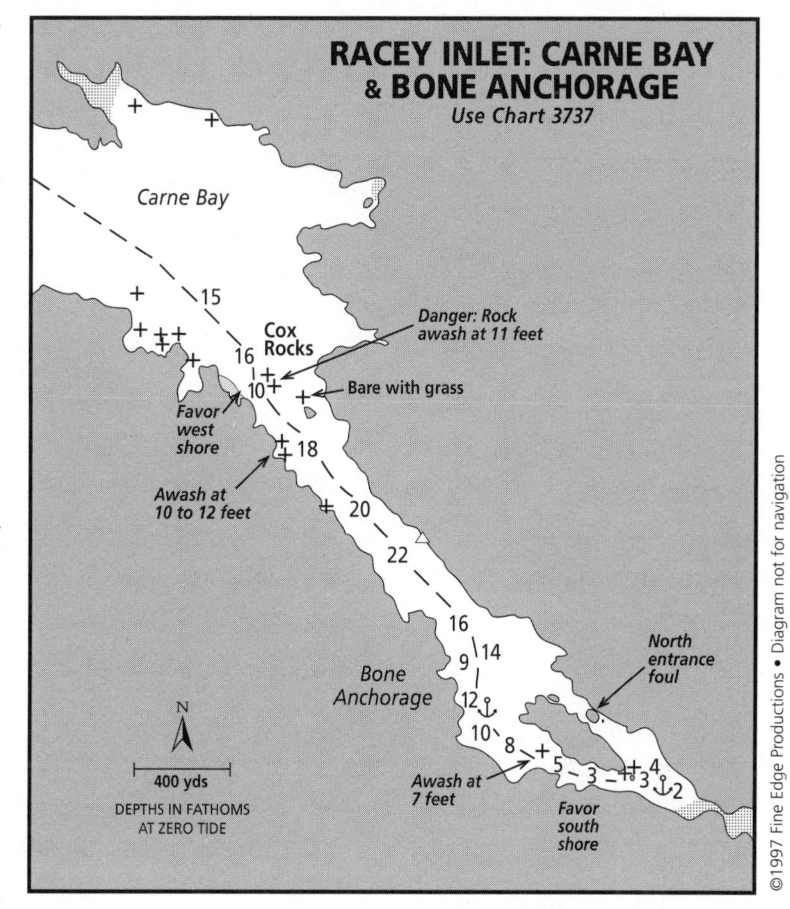

"Surf Inlet Head"

Chart 3737; position: 53°01.75′ N, 128°59.20′ W (NAD 27)

At the head of Surf Inlet, 4.5 miles NNE of Penn Harbour, are the ruined wharf and buildings of a former mining operation. A small creek at the head of Surf Inlet, is the overflow from a dam that separates Bear Lake from Surf Inlet.

Indifferent anchorage, with limited swinging space, can be obtained at the head of Surf Inlet in about 17 fathoms (31 m), mud, about 0.2 mile north of the creek; caution is necessary as the bottom drops steeply to depths over 40 fathoms (73 m). (pp. 183–184, SD)

The dam at the head of Surf Inlet creates Bear Lake. The dam and powerhouse make for good exploring as does the old mine at the end of Bear Lake.

Racey Inlet

Chart 3737; entrance: 52°53.12′ N, 129°06.64′ W (NAD 27)

Racey Inlet is entered between Johnstone and Bryant Points. Hallet Rock, in the middle of the entrance, has 2 feet (0.6 m) over it.

One of the Worst Nights in My Life

I knew a storm was coming, so I tucked *Babine Post* into the southeast corner of Carne Bay in about 15 fathoms. The wind rapidly peaked and kept up for 36 hours. (Bonilla Island reported gusts to 94 knots that night!) Carne Bay was abominable. The gusts in the bay came from northeast to southwest, straight down out of the hills. The boat horsed around so much she swung through more than 240°. She received such violent squalls and heeled so far that galley lockers burst open, spewing everything across the cabin sole. I maintained an anchor watch for 36 hours, regularly refitting the chafing guard and letting out anchor line. During those two days we lost two antennas and a canoe. None of us got much sleep, and we had some bruises, but I can report that the anchor held throughout, and that the bottom is rich dense mud with excellent holding power.

—Captain Kevin Monahan

Do not attempt to enter Racey Inlet at night or in thick weather. Entrance can be made on either side of Hallet Rock, then keep in mid-channel and pass NE of the rock awash opposite Carne Bay and SW of Cox Rocks, then to the anchorage 0.15 mile NW of Wale Island. (p. 185, SD)

Racey Inlet is strategically positioned to offer shelter when Campania Sound and Laredo Channel start kicking up or when entering Emily Carr Inlet is risky. (Penn Harbour, 7.5 miles up Surf Inlet, offers the best all-weather protection in this immediate area.) Deep in the head of Racey Inlet, Bone Anchorage offers shelter in moderate depths.

Bone Anchorage

Chart 3737; anchor: 52°50.49′ N, 129°00.60′ W (NAD 27)

Bone Anchorage, NW of Wale Island, is suitable for small vessels and anchorage can be obtained in 18 fathoms (33 m), mud. (p. 185, SD)

Bone Anchorage, located at the very head of Racey Inlet, has swinging room for several boats to anchor between the bare rock just southeast of Wale Island and the drying flat in front of the creek. This is a quiet, secluded anchorage that offers very good protection in all weather.

As you pass Carne Bay, Racey Inlet necks down; at this point you must avoid Cox Rocks to safely enter Bone Anchorage. Cox Rocks lie mid-channel, perhaps the most dangerous one being the northerly rock, awash on about an 11-foot tide. Once you have passed the bare 5-foot-high rock with grass, the channel appears clear. Favor the south shore but avoid the rocks close along shore.

Captain Monahan has observed a Seiche (water surge or oscillation) near Bone Anchorage during strong south winds that caused the water level in Racey Inlet to rise and fall slowly—18 inches within a 20-minute period.

When we anchored here (without a Seiche), we shared the spot with a flock of 18 surf scoters; northwest of Wale Island we found hundreds of large orange sea nettles.

Anchor in 3 fathoms, soft brown mud with worms, good holding.

Chapple Inlet, Doig Anchorage

Charts 3719 (inset), 3737; entrance: 52°54.00′ N, 129°07.90′ W; anchor: 52°55.28′ N, 129°07.80′ W (NAD 27)

Chapple Inlet is entered between Holler Rock and Mallandaine Point. About 0.8 mile north of Mallandaine Point the fairway is contracted to a width of about 450 feet (137 m) by islands on the west side. (p. 185, SD)

Chapple Inlet provides surprisingly smooth water and protection from weather as soon as you pass through the narrow entrance a half-mile north of Mallandaine Point.

Chapple Inlet will slowly regain its natural beauty now that the large clear-cut logging operation has ceased operation. Doig Anchorage, the small bight just inside the entrance to Chapple Inlet, off the beach of the east shore, is a convenient place to stage an exploration of the back-country bear areas or upper Surf Inlet. You can anchor with good protection from southerlies just inside Doig Anchorage.

Anchor in about 9 fathoms, sand and mud bottom with good holding

"Chettleburgh Point Cove"

Charts 3719 (inset), 3737; anchor: 52°56.58′ N, 129°08.57′ W (NAD 27)

Anchorage for small craft can be obtained in 7 fathoms (12.8 m) in the bay west of Chettleburgh Point. (p. 185, SD)

Chettleburgh Point Cove offers protection from southerlies for only one boat with limited swinging room. You can tuck into the tiny notch in the south corner behind the point. A shore tie is advised, or anchor farther out in the bay. Avoid the rock off the tiny treed islet as you round the point. The west shore of the cove has ugly clear-cut scars.

Anchor in 6 fathoms, brown sand, shells and wood debris, with good holding.

Kiln Bay, Chapple Inlet

Charts 3719 (inset), 3737; anchor: 52°57.95′ N, 129°08.83′ W (NAD 27)

> *Kiln Bay has two islands on its west side. A rock, with less than 6 feet (2 m) over it, about 300 feet (91 m) NE of these islands is on the west side of the approach to Kiln Bay.*
>
> *Anchorage for small craft can be obtained north of the islands in Kiln Bay in 11 fathoms (20 m); it is exposed to SE gales.* (p. 185, SD)

Kiln Bay offers anchorage where you can weather plenty of southerlies tucked in behind the north side of the island in 6 fathoms. The shore west of Baile Island has a large, filled area that was an active log dump in summer 1994; in 1996 it was inactive. A large, white steel anchor buoy used for log booms remains in Kiln Bay between the unnamed island and the log dump.

Anchor in 10 fathoms in the center of the bay, or tuck in close to the island in about 5 fathoms; the bottom is brown mud with good holding.

Photo by Ron Thiele

Admiring a totem on Princess Royal Island

"Chapple Inlet Lagoon"

Charts 3719 (inset), 3737; narrows fairway: approximately 52°57.78′ N, 129°08.08′ W (NAD 27)

Chapple Inlet Lagoon, our name for the basin at the head of the inlet, technically is not a lagoon, but gives that feeling with its narrow entrance and labyrinth of islands and nooks. There is no sign of recent logging inside; there is beautiful old-growth and granite bluffs on the east shore. The head of the bay is a large, drying flat with grassy margins, and there is no evidence that chop or driftwood enters the lagoon. We feel it is one of the most protected anchorages on this part of the coast.

It is imperative to use the inset on Chart 3719 if you wish to enter the lagoon and avoid the obstacles. Entrance is made east of Baile Island, favoring the east shore, in 2 fathoms minimum. There is a narrows east of McKechnie Point with a minimum of 4 fathoms in the fairway.

Anchor in 5 fathoms, brown mud with clam shells, very good holding. There is plenty of swinging room for a number of boats over a flat 5-fathom bottom.

Emily Carr Inlet

Charts 3719 (inset), 3737; entrance (lagoon): 52°55.65′N, 129°08.84′ W; cove (east entrance): 52°55.375′ N, 129°08.835′ W; anchor (northwest cove): 52°55.39′ N, 129°09.38′ W (NAD 27)

> *Emily Car [sic] Inlet, west of Webber Island, is encumbered by rocks and only suitable for small craft. Local knowledge is advised. Holgate Passage, north of Webber Island, is obstructed at its east end by a drying reef projecting from Webber Island.* (p. 185, SD)

Emily Carr Inlet, named after British Columbia's famous artist, is formed by a complex group of islands, islets and rocks. It offers cruising boats both a well-sheltered anchorage and an explorer's challenge, since the area has been inadequately charted. Use extra caution in traversing this area; it is easy to become confused, and turning room in the channel is very limited. You will need to use both the

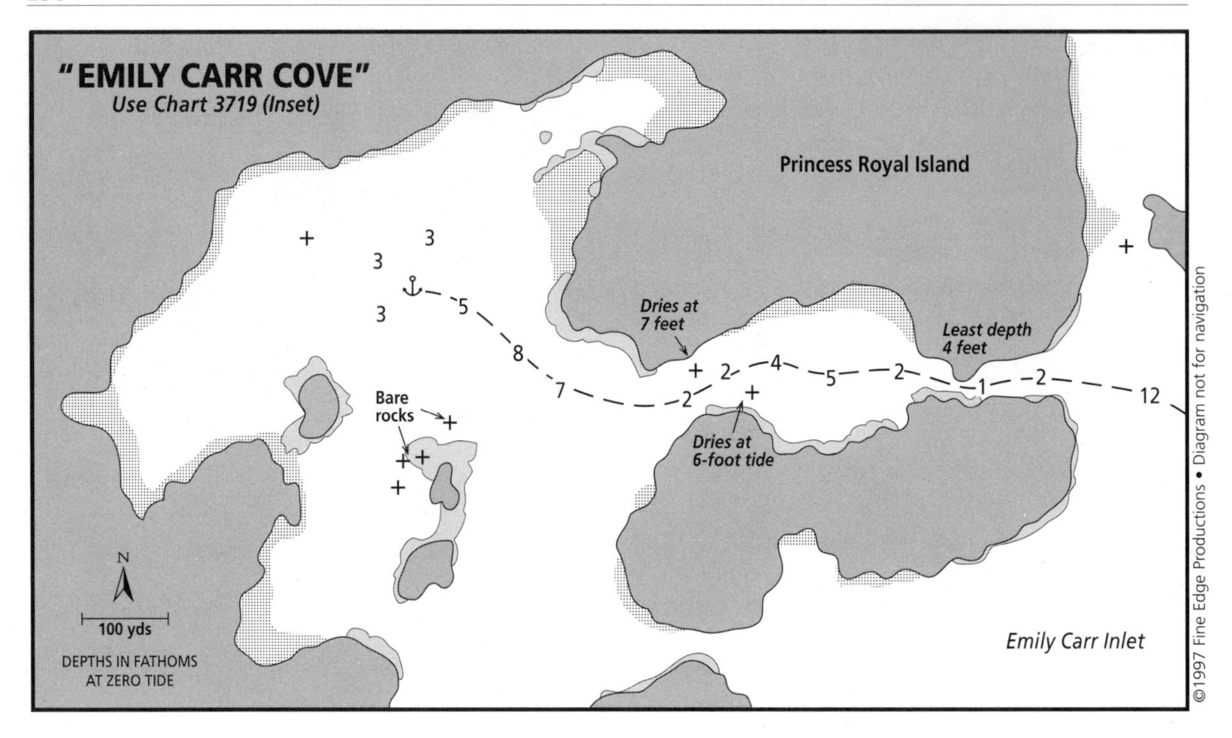

inset in 3719 and Chart 3737 to piece it all together.

The lagoon at the head of the inlet offers excellent protection from all weather. Its entrance is intricate, with about one fathom in the fairway; mid-lagoon rocks need to be avoided and the anchor site has limited swinging room. The east shore has an ugly clearcut to the water's edge.

We prefer the cove in the northwest corner of Emily Carr Inlet. It too has a very narrow, intricate entrance with less than one fathom in the fairway and very limited turning room. The cove is equally well protected from all weather. The northwest cove has more swinging room than the lagoon and old-growth trees line its shores.

Anchor (northwest cove) in 4 fathoms over sticky mud bottom with very good holding

Campania Sound

Charts 3737, 3724; position:
52°58.00′ N, 129°15.00′ W (NAD 27)

> *Campania Sound leads north from Caamaño Sound to Squally Channel and Whale Channel.*
>
> *The north-going flood stream enters Campania Sound from Caamaño Sound and runs from 5 to 2 hours before HW at Prince Rupert; for the most part it is weak and variable. The main ebb flows north of Ashdown Island into Campania Sound.* (p. 285, SD)

There is a strong ebb current on the order of 3 knots flowing south in Campania Sound. This can raise havoc causing a nasty chop on south winds or a confused sea during westerlies. The southwest swell sometimes felt in Caamaño Sound dies off as you head north toward Ashdown Island. Campania Sound has outstanding Clarke Cove on the Princess Royal Island coast.

Clarke Cove

Charts 3737, 3724; entrance:
52°58.48′ N, 129°11.80′ W; anchor:
52°58.00′ N, 129°10.88′ W (NAD 27)

> *Clarke Cove, 2.3 miles north of Duckers Islands, has a narrow entrance with a depth of 3 feet (0.9 m) in it. A strong tidal stream sets through the entrance which is only suitable for small craft at slack water.* (p. 185, SD)

Clarke Cove, along with MacDonald Bay on Gil Island, may be the best-kept secret for cruising boats on the entire coast. Tucked behind the three-islet-and-rock complex just inside the narrows,

Entrance to Clarke Cove

Clarke Cove, looking out from inside

this landlocked cove offers perfect protection from all weather. Its entrance is so small you need GPS or very careful navigation to find it because, when you're 100 yards off the shore, you still can't tell there's an opening.

On spring tides, the current in the narrows runs 2 to 3 knots and can be turbulent. The fairway is about 25 feet wide or less with underwater rocks evident on both sides. There is about 3 feet of water in the fairway at zero tide but only in the narrow center. Favor the north shore at the inside of the narrows because there are several square rocks off the south shore. Once inside, pass south of the islets in the middle of the cove.

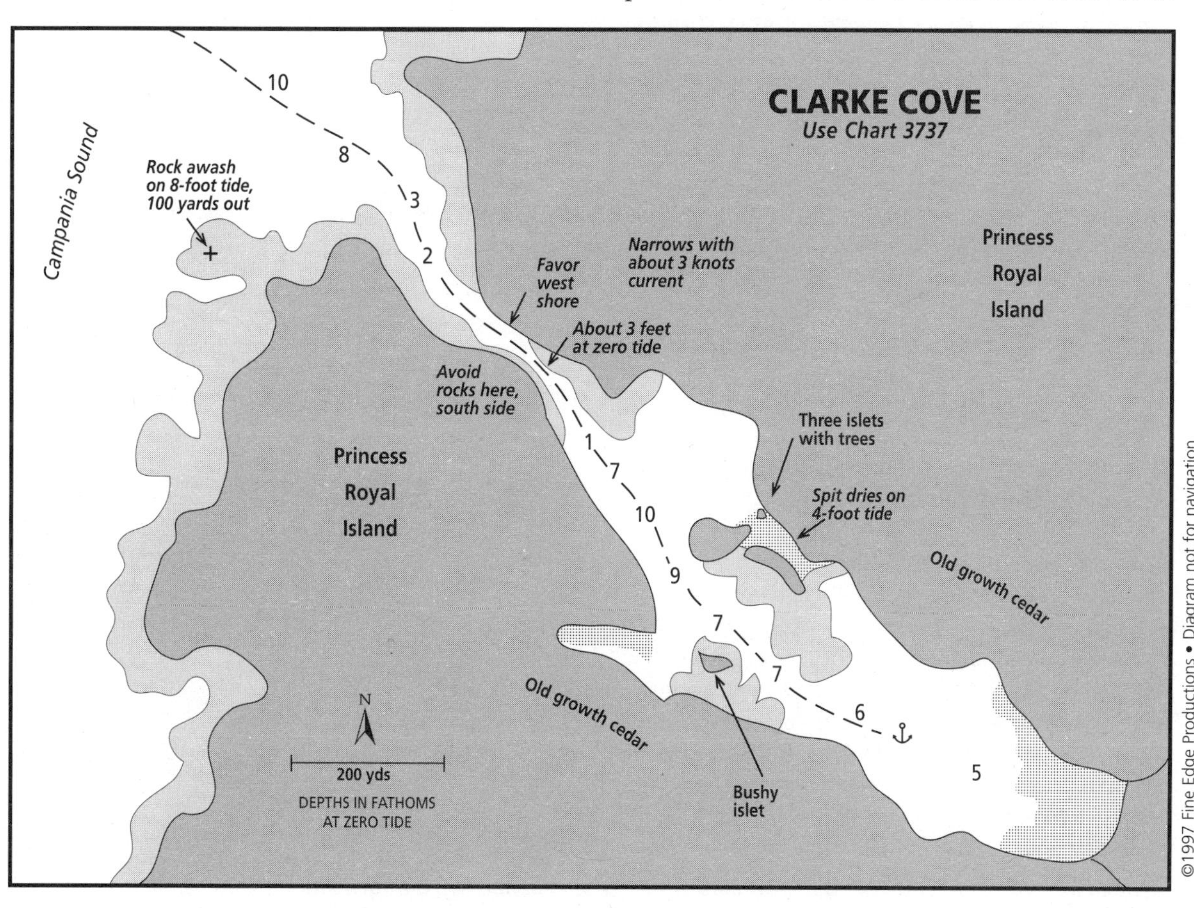

The cove is surrounded by old-growth forest where tree branches curve out over the water in a horizontal line. Chop appears never to enter the cove. During gales, the wind inside is probably felt only as gusts along the surface while overhead it howls.

There is plenty of swinging room for three or four small boats. The bottom, initially 12 fathoms, bounces between 10 and 6 near the islets, then slopes upward to a nearly flat 7 fathoms well east of the islets. There is no landing beach other than a small rocky shoal where two small creeks empty into the head of the cove. Radio reception inside the cove is nil.

Anchor in 6 to 7 fathoms at the head of the cove over a mud bottom with good holding.

Around the Next Point

I imagine people travel for hundreds of miles saying to each other, "Let's just see what's around that next point."

Sometimes there's a house in the woods, a lonely homestead left abandoned. Sometimes there's a fish camp or lodge, a bustle of people and noise. But often, at first glance, there's nothing. You pass the point and a cove appears, a sheltered place where every tree and rock is doubled on the water. It spreads before you like a pushed-open door. So you go in and anchor, and you wonder if it's possible that no one has been here before.

We've passed that next point and found a family of wolves so unaccustomed to people that they lounged on the beach like cats on a windowsill. We found ravens who mimicked the strange sounds of the anchor chain, a sea lion that came right to the boat, songbirds that perched like pilots by the tiller. In this sort of place the trees still grow to a monstrous size. The rocks at low tide are covered by incredible things. The water's so clear that you can watch the anchor dig in fathoms and fathoms below.

For thousands of years the forest has grown and died and grown again, untouched and maybe unseen. The cliffs and the beaches have only slightly given way to the sea. For all this time nothing has changed. Night falls, and the light at your masthead adds one more star to the hundreds of others that have filled this place every night through the centuries.

It's not empty at all.

by Iain Lawrence, author of *Far Away Places*

Whale Channel

Chart 3742; SW entrance:
53°04.20′ N, 129°15.00′ W; northeast entrance:
53°17.10′ N, 129°07.90′ W (NAD 27)

> *Whale Channel leads NE and north from Campania Sound into Wright Sound. . . . At the south end the main stream flows north of Ashdown Island into Campania Sound and attains its maximum of 3 to 4 kn in this part.* (p. 186, SD)

Whale Channel is fairly well protected and has considerably less chop than Squally Channel. Cameron Cove on its south shore provides good protection with easy access.

Barnard Harbour

Chart 3723 (inset); Aikman Passage entrance:
53°04.77′ N, 129°07.38′ W; Burnes Passage entrance: 53°05.08′ N, 129°06.60′ W;
anchor (extreme east): 53°04.16′ N, 129°05.76′ W (NAD 27)

> *Enter Barnard Harbour by either Aikman or Burnes Passages keeping in the centre of the fairway. The greater part of Barnard Harbour is too deep for convenient anchorage. Approaching Cameron Cove give Leighton Point a wide berth and keep in the middle of the fairway of the cove when approaching the anchorage.* (p. 187, SD)

Barnard Harbour with its Cameron Cove lies on the northwest corner of Princess Royal Island off Whale Channel and provides excellent anchorage for cruising boats.

You can enter the harbor on either side of Borde Island. In 1996 there were floating fish

Derelict tug, Barnard Harbour

Entrance to Clement Rapids, Cornwall Inlet

resorts at three different locations in the harbor, and their skiffs buzzed in and out with clients.

A resort that welcomes cruising boats at its docks generally ties to the east side of Cameron Cove, but you must clear out when the sportfishing fleet returns. The resort sells beer and soda, and gasoline may occasionally be available at one of the floating lodges. During the last week of August, the resorts pack up, clear out, and head south for winter storage; then everything in Barnard Harbour is restored to its natural condition.

Although depths in most of Barnard Harbour are too great for convenient small-boat anchoring, you can find good spots on the west side of Cameron Cove (the western lobe of the harbor) near the head of the cove. Be aware, however, of the rapidly shoaling bottom. In southeast storms, large boats are advised to anchor at the extreme east of Barnard Harbour close to shore.

Anchor (extreme east) in about 20 fathoms unrecorded bottom.

Cameron Cove

Chart 3723 (inset); anchor:
53°03.80′ N, 129°06.98′ W (NAD 27)

Cameron Cove is entered between Leighton Point and Goodfellow Point. Two wooded islets, connected to shore by drying ledges, are close off the west shore of the cove. Barnard Creek flows into the head of Cameron Cove, east of Uren Point.

Good anchorage can be obtained in the middle of Cameron Cove in 18 fathoms (33 m), sand and mud bottom. (p. 186, SD)

Strong southerly winds are known to blow down Barnard Creek into Barnard Harbour and Cameron Cove. To reduce the fetch and the effects of the gusty wind during southeast storms, anchor just outside of a line between the treed island and Uren Point in 3 to 4 fathoms.

Anchor in 3 to 4 fathoms, mud, sand, shells and eel grass with fair-to-good holding. Larger boats can anchor in the middle of the bay in 15 fathoms.

Cornwall Inlet and Drake Inlet

Chart 3742; entrance: 53°12.83′ N, 129°03.21′ W (NAD 27)

Cornwall Inlet extends SE from Clement Rapids. Drake Inlet extends south from Cornwall Inlet. (p. 186, SD)

Cornwall and Drake inlets offer beautiful and well-protected cruising, although Clement Rapids is wicked. The inlets are surrounded by 3,000-foot peaks and high ridges and are quiet and scenic places to visit. This is Princess Royal Island bear country with anchor sites reported to be near the heads of both inlets in about 10 to 15 fathoms.

Clement Rapids

Chart 3742; anchor (near Salmon Point):
53°12.63′ N, 129°03.02′ W (NAD 27)

Clement Rapids, SE of Salmon Point, connects River Bight to Cornwall Inlet.

In Clement Rapids the time of HW slack varies from 1h.30min. to 2h.10min. after HW at Prince Rupert; the time of LW slack varies from 1h.55min. to 3h.20min. after LW at Prince Rupert. (p. 186, SD)

Clement Rapids has been the site of nasty surprises for small boats trying to enter. The rapids are 8 feet high with 6- to 8-foot standing waves at the bottom on spring tides. The surprise comes because, approaching on a flood tide, you can see nothing except the laminar flow disappearing into a very narrow tree-lined passage. The waterfall and its heavy foam and turbulence are out of sight until it's too late! Enter Clement Rapids at high-water slack only.

It is possible to anchor temporarily at the small basin immediately southeast of Salmon Point. If you anchor against the south shore you are out of most of the current and can wait for slack water or reconnoiter the rapids ahead of time.

Anchor in 4 to 6 fathoms over a sand, gravel and mud bottom with fair-to-good holding.

Home Bay

Chart 3742; entrance: 53°16.60 ' N, 129°05.40' W (NAD 27)

> *Home Bay, in the SE part of Wright Sound, is entered between Swirl Point and Transit Point. A sand flat extends from the head of the bay and a rocky ledge, with above-water heads on it, fringes the south shore. Anchorage for small vessels can be obtained in Home Bay in about 14 fathoms, sand and mud. . . .* (p. 112, SD)

Primordial Wolf Calls

I stood naked on the foredeck at 0400, shivering with excitement and cold. Somewhere in the dense brush 50 yards away on the shore of MacDonald Bay was an alpha-male wolf howling in the dark late August night. The stars were as clear as I had ever seen them. Orion was rising in the east and Cassiopeia and the Pleiades were overhead. Ursa minor and Polaris defied identification because of the abundant lower magnitude stars that filled the cold, clear northern sky.

As I waited on deck, there came another long burst, a four-pitch howl not unlike an air-driven lighthouse foghorn needing maintenance. A quick shiver shot through me from head to toe. This wild animal, only yards from me, was a descendant of those who freely roamed the entire North American continent two centuries ago. I was glad I was in my small boat surrounded by a saltwater moat and not camped in a thin nylon tent on shore.

Long howls of slightly varying pitch and duration echoed through the hills, then silence as the wolf listened for a reply. Sometimes he gave a few short yelps; sometimes a series of mournful calls, powerful and long-lasting. Was he lonely and longing for the company of the pack or was he broadcasting his position, alerting them to an upcoming feast? His was a 30-minute performance that I shall long remember, a highlight of sailing the waters of northern British Columbia.

—DCD

MacDonald Bay entrance

Home Bay can provide some shelter from westerlies through southerlies; it is exposed to downslope winds and large drift logs line the shore. It does make a good lunch stop and trolling is reported to be good off Nelly Point.

Anchor in about 8 fathoms close to the south shore over a sand, mud, gravel and kelp bottom with fair holding.

Squally Channel

Chart 3742; south entrance: 53°04.10' N, 129°18.10' W (NAD 27)

> *Squally Channel is the NW continuation of Campania Sound. Violent squalls are often experienced in Squally Channel; they descend from the high land of Campania Island. At the same time calms or light winds are often experienced in Whale Channel.* (p. 187, SD)

MacDonald Bay

Chart 3742; entrance: 53°11.82' N, 129°20.64' W; anchor (east end): 53°11.82' N, 129°19.45' W (NAD 27)

> *MacDonald Bay, 6 miles north of Skinner Islands, has a very narrow entrance which dries.* (p. 187, SD)

MacDonald Bay, the small bay a half-mile south of Blackrock Point on Gil Island, is a bombproof anchorage once you're inside. Totally landlocked, it offers excellent protection from all weather, and moderate-sized cruising boats can

MacDonald Bay, looking out toward entrance

enter on the upper half of the tide. The entire world could be blowing away outside the bay and you'd never know it.

You can anchor temporarily in the outer bay in 7-8 fathoms while you're waiting for a favorable tide level to pass through the narrows, but the bottom is rocky; be sure to set your anchor well.

Minimum depth in the narrows has consistently measured 2 feet at zero tide and does not dry as indicated on Chart 3742. The shallowest spots are located just inside the west entrance, and again at the east end of the 500-yard-long narrows. Due to the dark rocks and muskeg water, underwater visibility is limited to about one foot. The bottom along the narrows is composed of basketball-sized rocks; however, we could detect no sign of isolated rocks when the tide level was at 3.5 feet in Bella Bella. Currents through the narrows are relatively moderate with laminar flow.

Large boats wanting maximum swinging room can anchor in the widest part of the bay in 10 fathoms. Smaller boats can anchor farther east on the 3-fathom flat in front of the drying flat that fills the eastern portion of the bay. Old-growth forest lines the shores, and there is a grassy beach at the head of the bay where you can land a dinghy or kayak. We saw Canada geese and grebes, kingfishers, and seagulls diving for their food, and heard wolves howling in the early morning hours.

Anchor (east end) in 3 fathoms over a sticky mud bottom with very good holding.

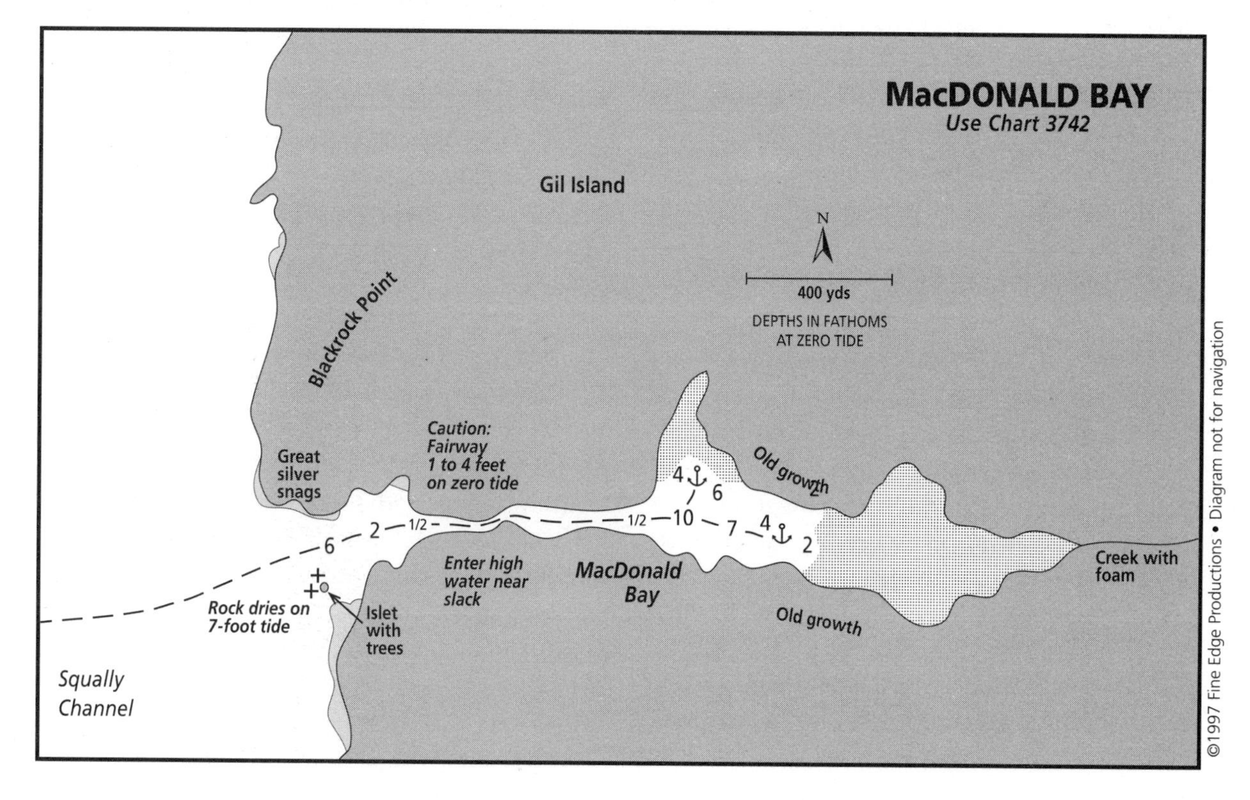

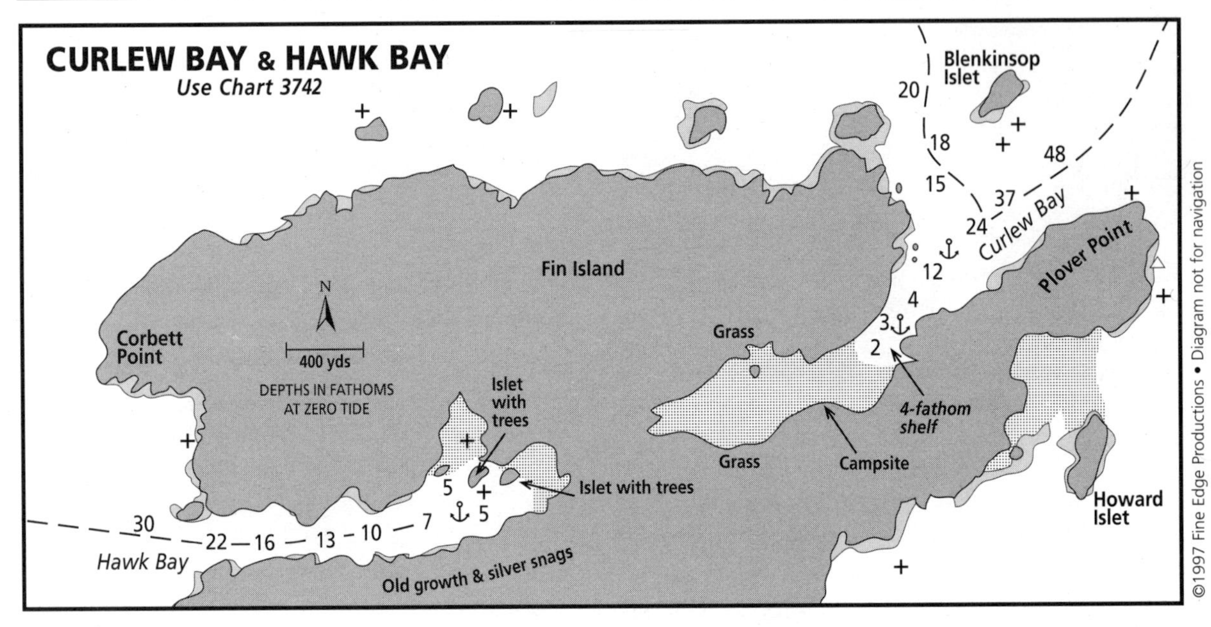

Dillon Bay

Chart 3742; entrance: 53°12.07′ N, 129°29.69′ W (NAD 27)

Dillon Bay has an islet close off its north entrance point. (p. 187, SD)

Dillon Bay, located at the east end of Otter Channel, in the lee of McCreight Point, can provide good temporary protection at its head from strong northwest winds and southwest swells. It is open to the southeast, however, and not considered secure in such conditions.

Crane Bay

Chart 3742; entrance: 53°13.75′ N, 129°18.50′ W (NAD 27)

Crane Bay, in the SE part of Lewis Passage, is too deep for anchorage. (p. 187, SD)

Crane Bay, located three miles north of MacDonald Bay on the south shore of Lewis Passage, offers some protection from northwest and outflow winds and chop. However, fishermen report that winds blow through the pass and that Crane Bay receives swells from inflow and outflow winds, making the anchorage rolly.

We found that the bay is too deep and steep-to for convenient anchorage. In calm weather, anchorage can be taken between Williams Islet and Gil Island over a large 3-fathom flat. Avoid the dangerous rock lying about 100 yards south of the rock islet near the south center of the pass which dries on a 10-foot tide.

Note: The 1987 reprint of Chart 3742 (corrected to 21 August 1992) does not show the flashing red light located on an islet 0.25 mile south of Blackrock Point, nor does it show that the flashing white light previously located on Fin Island at Plover Point was moved 200 yards southeast onto the charted reef.

Curlew Bay

Chart 3742; entrance: 53°17.10′ N, 129°18.53′ W; anchor (west side): 53°16.71′ N, 129°19.32′ W (NAD 27)

Anchorage for small craft can be found in the entrance to Curlew Bay, SW of Blenkinsop Islet. (p. 187, SD)

Curlew Bay provides welcome relief from southerly storms or inflow winds, although it is open to the northeast and susceptible to outflow chop.

Large boats can anchor at the entrance to the bay in 10 fathoms with plenty of swinging room. Smaller boats anchor at the west side of the narrows in 3 fathoms with limited swinging room. Two grassy beaches on shore can be used

Curlew Bay, looking north

as kayaker haul-out campsites or for landing a dinghy.

Anchor (west side) in 3 fathoms over a stony, gravel bottom, with fair-to-good holding depending on the set of your anchor.

Brant Bay

Chart 3742; entrance: 53°15.30′ N, 129°22.42′ W (NAD 27)

> *Brant Bay is to the south . . . of Buckle Point.* (p. 187, SD)

Brant Bay, on the southwest side of Fin Island, offers good shelter and easy access from northerly or outflow winds. The very head of the bay has a 5-fathom flat where it's possible to find anchorage with limited swinging room.

The bay, however, is open to the southwest and westerly chop enters it. Hawk Bay, immediately to the north, and Curlew Bay on the northeast corner of the island, provide better anchorages in most conditions.

Anchor in 5 fathoms, over a bottom where our test anchor was unable to get a good set, so we classify the bottom as poor holding.

Hawk Bay

Chart 3742; entrance: 53°16.23′ N, 129°22.30′ W; anchor (east): 53°16.27′ N, 128°29.98′ W (NAD 27)

> *. . . Hawk Bay to the north, of Buckle Point.* (p. 187, SD)

Hawk Bay is a small, picturesque inlet on the west side of Fin Island, 0.7 mile north of Buckle Point. The bay is surrounded by old-growth cedar and silver snags, with some spruce and hemlock. The bay is open to strong westerlies, although moderate westerlies die off before they penetrate the inner basin. The inner basin breaks into two coves: the north cove largely dries, but small boats can find protection from westerlies behind the treed islet, or south of the islets in the eastern cove.

Larger boats, or those wishing more swinging room, can anchor over a flat bottom in the widest part of the bay in 8 fathoms, unrecorded bottom.

Anchor (east) in 4 fathoms, mixed bottom of stones, sand, and kelp.

Tuwartz Inlet

Chart 3722 (inset); entrance: 53°16.70′ N, 129°29.40′ W (NAD 27)

> *Tuwartz Inlet is entered between Wilman Point and Leggeat Point. Detached drying reefs are 0.2 mile east of Wilman Point. Drying rocks are 0.1 mile south and 0.1 mile WSW of Leggeat Point. A bushy islet, 0.2 mile SSW of Leggeat Point, lies in the entrance of Tuwartz Inlet.* (p. 187, SD)

Tuwartz Inlet is an interesting, seldom-visited inlet in the southwest corner of Pitt Island. The best cruising boat anchor sites are located north of Tuwartz Narrows. Anchorage can also be found just north of Wilman Point with good protection in southeast gales.

Tuwartz Narrows

Chart 3722; south entrance: 53°18.38′ N, 129°31.31′ W (NAD 27)

> *Tuwartz Narrows, 1.7 miles NNW of Leggeat Point, is about 150 feet (46 m) wide at its south end. The passage through the narrows is only suitable for small craft at or near slack water. A drying rock is just within the south entrance, near the east shore. Three treed islets, on a common drying reef, are at the north end of Tuwartz Narrows; there is a narrow passage on either side of this reef.* (p. 187, SD)

When entering Tuwartz Narrows from the south,

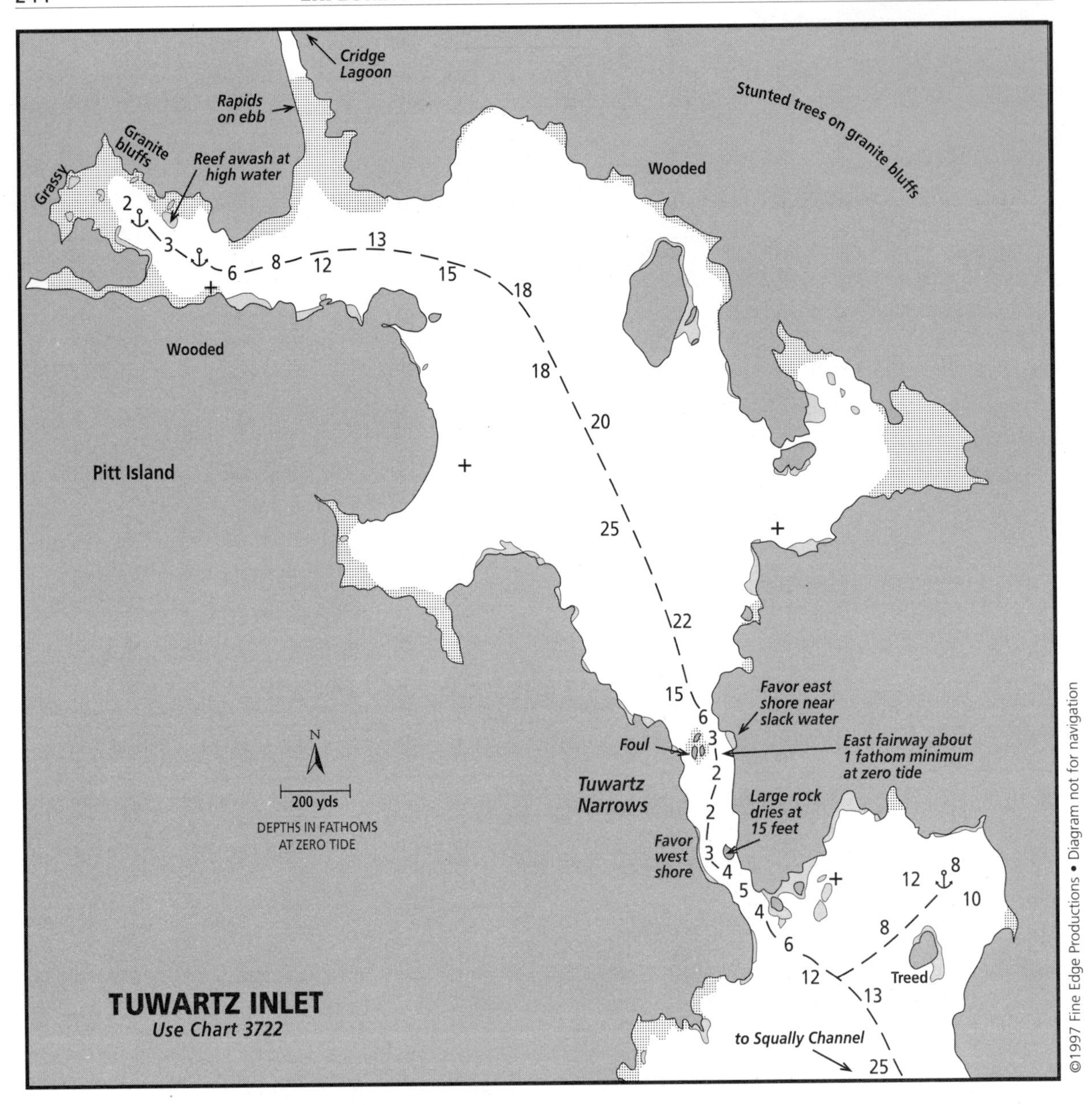

favor the west shore to avoid the large midchannel rock that dries at 15 feet. When you have passed the rock, favor the east shore and keep the three-treed islet at the north end of the entrance on your port hand passing to the east of the islet. Although the channel on the west side of the three islets is wider, the depths there are one fathom or less and it appears to be foul. Current is about 3 knots in the narrows.

"Tuwartz Lagoon Cove"

Chart 3722; anchor 3 fathoms (rock pile): 53°19.34′ N, 129°32.72′ W; anchor 7 fathoms: 53°19.26′ N, 128°32.41′ W (NAD 27)

Cridge Lagoon, at the north end of Tuwartz Inlet, is obstructed by a drying flat at its entrance. (p. 187, SD)

Tuwartz Lagoon Cove is what we call the well-sheltered cove on the west side of the entrance to

Photo courtesy CHS, Pacific Region

Tuwartz Narrows, looking north

Minnis Bay

Chart 3722; entrance:
53°19.30′ N, 129°27.27′ W;
anchor: 53°25.52′ N,
129°27.78′ W (NAD 27)

Minnis Bay penetrates the south side of Hinton Island. Hale Point, the west entrance point to Minnis Bay, has an islet, some drying reefs, and a below-water rock, extending 0.3 mile SSE from it. (p. 187, SD)

Minnis Bay is exposed to southerlies which moderate or die off as they approach the head of the bay.

Cridge Lagoon. Totally landlocked and calm when gales are blowing in Squally Channel, the cove has the appearance of an alpine lake near timberline. Bold granite bluffs with stunted trees cover the nearby peaks. At low water, the cove is considerably reduced in size by a number of glaciated rocks covered with golden rockweed. There is no driftwood along the grassy margins of the shore—an added indication of its good protection and remoteness.

Cridge Lagoon is fed by a series of lakes four miles away in the interior of Pitt Island, and the terrain to the north looks like good exploring. The entrance to the lagoon, foul with rocks, can be entered by dinghy or very small boats at high-water slack. The water in Tuwartz Lagoon Cove is shallower than that shown on Chart 3722, and the chart does not detail the extent of the rocks well so reconnoiter your own anchor spot.

Small boats only can anchor in the center of the "rock pile" in 3 fathoms, mixed bottom, with good holding if your anchor is well set.

Larger boats can anchor in the outer bay just west of the lagoon entrance in 7 fathoms, mixed bottom with mud and rocks; good holding when your anchor is well set.

Mitchell Cove

Chart 3722; entrance:
53°21.76′ N, 129°28.14′ W; anchor (two-snag island):
53°21.79′ N, 129°28.39′ W (NAD 27)

Mitchell Cove is at the north end of Payne Channel. (p. 187, SD)

Mitchell Cove, at the head of Payne Channel, offers protection from all winds except southerlies. Small boats can find some protection from southerlies by tucking in behind the "two-snag islet" avoiding the rock on the west side of the cove that dries at 6 feet. Larger boats should anchor farther out in 8 fathoms.

Those seeking storm shelter would do well to use the cove on the north side of Peters Narrows or the lagoon immediately north which has a large and shallow swinging area with excellent holding. (See Chapter 9, Union Passage area.)

Anchor (two-snag island) in about 6 fathoms over a mixed bottom with fair-to-good holding.

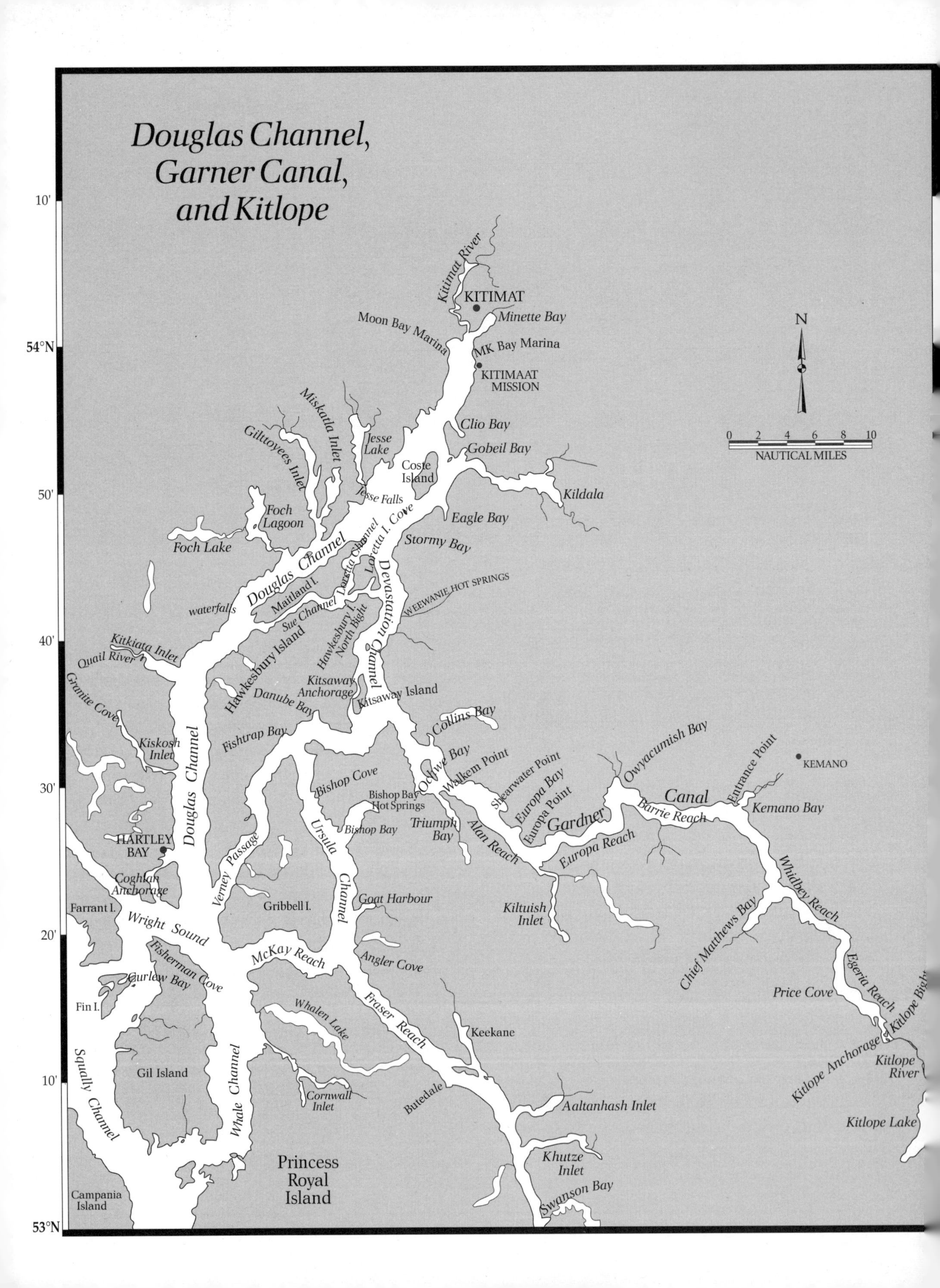

Douglas Channel,
Garner Canal,
and Kitlope
10'
54°N
50'
40'
30'
20'
10'
53°N
N
0 2 4 6 8 10
NAUTICAL MILES
Kitimat River
KITIMAT
Minette Bay
Moon Bay Marina
MK Bay Marina
KITIMAAT
MISSION
Miskatla Inlet
Gilttoyees Inlet
Jesse
Lake
Clio Bay
Gobeil Bay
Coste
Island
Kildala
Jesse Falls
Foch
Lagoon
Loretta I. Cove
Eagle Bay
Foch Lake
Stormy Bay
Douglas Channel
Loretta Channel
Devastation Channel
Maitland I.
WEEWANIE HOT SPRINGS
waterfalls
Sue Channel
Hawkesbury I.
North Bight
Kitkiata Inlet
Quail River
Hawkesbury Island
Granite Cove
Kitsaway
Anchorage
Kitsaway Island
Danube Bay
Collins Bay
Kiskosh
Inlet
Fishtrap Bay
Owyacumish Bay
Entrance Point
KEMANO
Douglas Channel
Bishop Cove
Oriwe Bay
Walkem Point
Shearwater Point
Europa Bay
Europa Point
Canal
Gardner
Kemano Bay
Barrie Reach
Bishop Bay
Hot Springs
Triumph
Bay
Bishop Bay
Alan Reach
Europa Reach
HARTLEY
BAY
Verney Passage
Ursula
Channel
Coghlan
Anchorage
Whidbey Reach
Farrant I.
Gribbell I.
Goat Harbour
Kiltuish
Inlet
Chief Matthews Bay
Wright Sound
Fisherman Cove
McKay Reach
Angler Cove
Egeria Reach
Curlew Bay
Price Cove
Fin I.
Whalen Lake
Fraser Reach
Kitlope Bight
Keekane
Kitlope Anchorage
Kitlope
River
Squally Channel
Gil Island
Whale Channel
Cornwall
Inlet
Butedale
Aaltanhash Inlet
Kitlope Lake
Princess
Royal
Island
Khutze
Inlet
Swanson Bay
Campania
Island

8

Douglas Channel, Gardner Canal and Kitlope

Some of the most stunning scenery along the north coast of British Columbia lies just miles off the Inside Passage to the northeast. Cruising boats that haven't yet explored the area are in for some wonderful surprises: spectacular waterfalls, granite domes and vertical faces, hanging glaciers, turquoise glacial melt, and miniature plants, brilliant green against dark granite fissures. The area also hosts three of the best hot springs on the coast—Bishop Bay, Weewanie, and Europa.

Douglas Channel, stretching 60 miles from its south end to Kitimat at its head, is one of the longest fjords along the coast; Gardner Canal runs east then southeast to its head at Kitlope, over a hundred miles from the ocean.

Cruising boaters who have shied away from this area as too remote will be happy to find that Hartley Bay, at the south end of Douglas Channel, has been designated as a stop along the Discovery Coast ferry route, and its fueling facilities are being expanded. Kitimat, at the north end of the channel, has two marinas.

Inland from the head of Gardner Channel (Whidbey Reach) lies the gem of North American forests—the Kitlope Valley, considered to be the world's largest undeveloped coastal temperate rain forest. In 1994, nearly 700,000 acres of this valley, which contains stands of trees over 800 years old, were set aside to protect it against future logging. This is the ancestral home of the Haisla People who welcome outsiders to participate in their rediscovery camps. (Please see Appendix.)

McKay Reach

Chart 3742; east entrance:
53°18.60′ N, 128°55.00′ W; west entrance:
53°18.10′ N, 129°06.30′ W (NAD 27)

McKay Reach separates the north end of Princess Royal Island from Gribbell Island. (p. 108, SD)

McKay Reach, out of the major up- and down-slope wind patterns, is generally much calmer than the south end of Douglas or Ursula channels. Because of this, it frequently has large patches of drift wood so keep a sharp lookout when you transit the area.

Ursula Channel

Charts 3740, 3742; south entrance:
53°18.60′ N, 128°54.00′ W (NAD 27)

Ursula Channel connects Princess Royal Channel to Verney Passage. The mountains on both sides of the channel rise abruptly from the coast.

Baidarka *visits* Poplar II, *Europa Bay*

Due to the amount of fresh water drainage into this channel the subsurface current can, at times, flow in an opposite direction to the surface current. (p. 108, SD)

At Ursula Channel the ferry boat route is left behind as you head north into outstanding territory.

Angler Cove

Charts 3740 or 3742; position: 53°18.90′ N, 128°53.10′ W (NAD 27)

Angler Cove has a small island off its south entrance point. The drying flat at the head of the cove is steep-to and a small stream enters the cove over it. (p. 108, SD)

Angler Cove, with its small sandy beach, is a favorite campsite for kayakers visiting the area. It offers marginal respite from strong southerly winds blowing in Princess Royal Channel. Angler Cove is incorrectly called Fisherman Cove in some publications. (Fisherman Cove is actually 15 miles west on the north tip of Gil Island. See Chapter 9.)

Temporary anchorage can be taken in fair weather off the sandy beach or the flat to the east, but the water is deep. Depth, bottom, and holding are unrecorded.

Goat Harbour

Chart 3740, 3742; entrance:
53°21.20′ N, 128°53.10′ W; head of bay:
53°21.68′ N, 128°51.24′ W (NAD)

Goat Harbour, 2.5 miles north of Angler Cove, is entered south of Kid Point; depths are too great for convenient anchorage. The drying flat at the head of the harbour is steep-to. There are hot springs here. (p. 108, SD)

We have tried to find the hot springs mentioned in *Sailing Directions,* but we have not yet located a spring. The best we could do was to locate some spots of warmer-than-average water along the north shore.

The drying flat is steep-to with little opportunity for anchoring. If you tie to logbooms here, be prepared to move in the middle of the night—tugs might tow the boom away.

Bishop Bay, Hot Springs

Charts 3742, 3743; entrance:
53°26.25′ N, 128°54.50′ W; float:
53°28.20′ N, 128°50.10′ W (NAD 27)

Bishop Bay is entered between Tomkinson Point and Riordan Point; its shores are steep-to and depths in it are for the most part great. . . . Bishop Bay Hot Springs, at the head of Bishop Bay, have been developed by the Kitimat Yacht Club. A small float is near the springs. (p. 108, SD)

Bishop Bay Hot Springs sits in a beautiful bowl at the head of Bishop Bay. It has become a well-known attraction in the Inside Passage and the toll is beginning to show. On the plus side, a new wooden float and aluminum gangway were installed in April 1994, replacing the one damaged in the storm of September 1992. The float is rather small, so thoughtful boaters should pull

Bishop Bay Hot Springs: soaking in outer tub during a storm; old dock in background

off and anchor nearby after having had their soak to allow access for other users.

Years ago, the Kitimat Yacht Club and other private groups built a cement bathhouse against the cliff, just above the high tide line. A small outside tub, which drains the inner pool, can be plugged; this is where guests soap up and rinse off before entering the inside pool. A path from the bathhouse leads uphill, past a covered picnic area with table and fire grate and an outhouse. The natural hot spring, located just beyond that, issues forth an unending flow of hot water which is tasteless, colorless, and odorless.

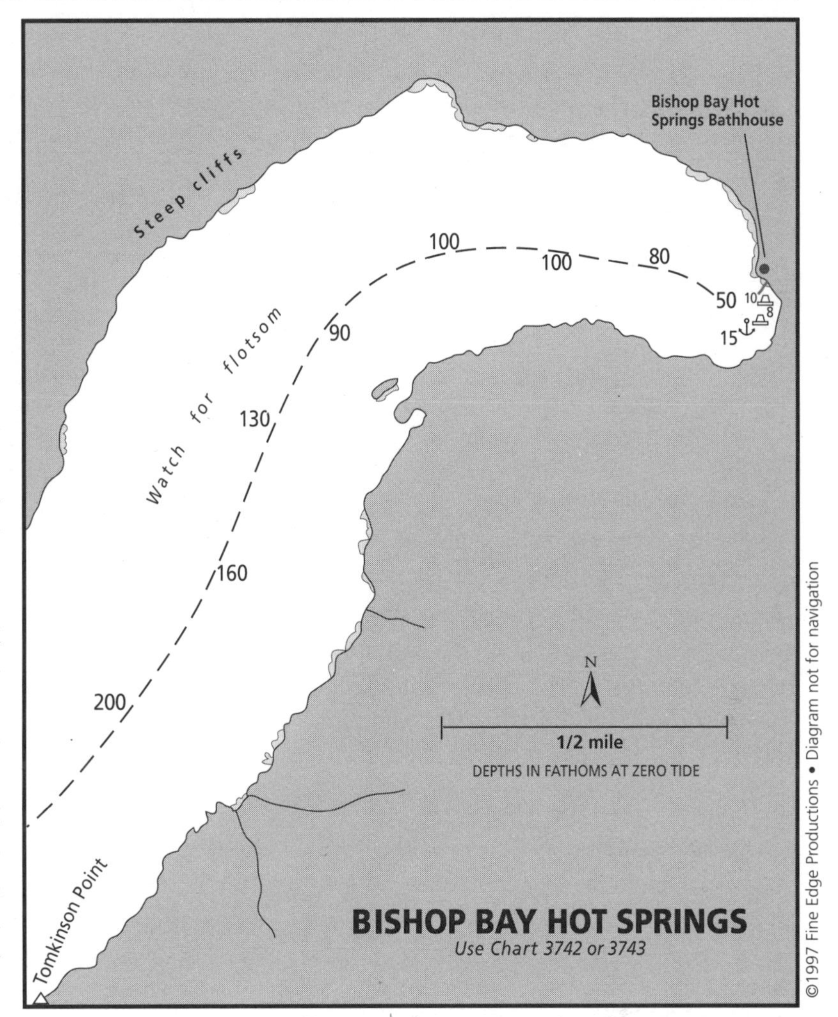

The hot springs flow as steadily as ever and are just as hot, but the sign in the changing room enumerating the hazards of using the hot springs seems out of keeping in this beautiful bay. Concern with legal liabilities has reached the far north!

We would like to think that Bishop Bay Hot Springs will always be a welcome stop on the Inside Passage, but were dismayed and embarrassed by the graffiti and trash left by Seattle-based fishing vessels in May 1994. Since there is no trash disposal, each boat must pack out its own refuse and respect other boaters' right of access to the hot springs. We urge everyone who stops here to help keep the area clean and to pass the word to others to prevent further deterioration.

On occasion, after a major storm front has passed, strong westerly winds penetrate Bishop Bay, rendering the anchorage untenable. This does not happen very often. Only occasionally do such gale force southwesterly winds follow a deep depression and, even then, the wind direction has to be exactly right and must blow from that direction for a considerable time.

Anchor in 8 to 15 fathoms southeast of the float over a mixed bottom with fair holding. Watch out for shoal water extending from shore about 100 feet east of the float ramp.

Verney Passage

Chart 3743; south entrance:
53°22.10′ N, 129°09.50′ W; north entrance:
53°34.90′ N, 128°50.50′ W (NAD 27)

Verney Passage leads 20 miles NE from Wright Sound to the junction of Devastation Channel and Gardner Canal. The shores in Verney Passage are generally steep-to; depths in the fairway are for the most part great. A sill, with relatively shoal depths over it, crosses Verney Passage near the mouth of Ursula Channel. (p. 112, SD)

The sill referred to above is considered by Kitimat sport fishermen to be the center of a very productive salmon area. There can be significant turbulence in this area on spring tides.

Fishtrap Bay

Chart 3743; position: 53°33.06′ N, 129°01.24′ W (NAD 27)

Fishtrap Bay is filled with drying flats. A drying spit extends 0.2 mile south into Verney Passage from its east entrance point.

Exposed anchorage can be obtained off the centre of the entrance to Fishtrap Bay, west of the drying spit, in 14 fathoms (26 m). In this anchorage Mary Point light bears 088° and Amy Point 153°. (p. 113, SD)

Use caution when approaching Fishtrap Bay from the north; the shoal on its east side which extends a long way into the channel should be given wide berth. Only the upper end is marked by a collection of stumps and trees.

Overnight anchorage in Fishtrap Bay is taken by small sportfishing boats in fair weather, tucked in behind the stumps, or close to shore in Danube Bay, 3 miles north; or on the southwest side of Kitsaway Island.

Gardner Canal

Charts 3743, 3745; entrance: 53°34.50′ N, 128°48.00′ W (NAD 27)

Gardner Canal, entered north of Staniforth Point, is an inlet which trends about 45 miles SE. The shores are very steep and rise to high mountains on which there are some spectacular glaciers. Kemano Bay port facilities are 30 miles inside the entrance. (p. 113, SD)

Gardner Canal is a major fjord of the British Columbia coast and, with the exception of clear-cut patches at its west entrance, is perhaps the most pristine and scenic in North America. As soon as you enter Gardner Canal, the chop in Devastation Channel dies off and the east-west-lying waterway is still; the water becomes a clear, greenish-blue, glacial melt from the mountains towering above. There is a constant overlay of fresh water

Storm in Bishop Bay

Leaving Juneau in late September 1992, *Baidarka* was one of the last pleasure boats to head south. When we reached Grenville Channel on the morning of September 28, the barometer which had reached a high of 1021.3 millibars, began to fall. The sky was overcast and we had moderate rain with little wind. Marine weather forecasts warned that the first winter storm with a center pressure of 956 millibars was headed for B.C.'s north coast from the Gulf of Alaska. We ducked into Bishop Bay and headed toward the hot springs, a comfortable spot but not one with a reputation for storm shelter. In the deep inlet, we quickly lost all VHF reception, including weather forecasts.

The next morning, the pressure had dropped to 1008 millibars and it was raining heavily. During the day, the barometer continued to fall until it bottomed out at 999 millibars, a 22-millibar drop in 36 hours—enough to cause a major disturbance! Rain continued without letup; noisy, heavy drops fell with an intensity we'd never seen before. Our deck bucket filled twice to overflowing—more than 20 inches in 24 hours!

In Bishop Bay, we witnessed such a surge in the tide that the water level reached well into the trees and completely covered the outside wash tub at the hot springs. The clouds scudded overhead continuously from south to north. Except for occasional gusts, we had little wind and the seas were completely calm. The log float at the foot of the trail broke up and, with the help of *Coast Ranger* (Ministry of Forestry vessel) and her skipper Tom Fraser, along with another fishing boat, we could manage only to secure the loose pieces and prevent them from floating away, becoming hazards to navigation. After that, all three boats sat out the storm and enjoyed a lazy layover. When at last we could weigh anchor and were back within VHF radio range, we heard that major flooding had occurred on the Skeena River and in the Prince Rupert area. —DCD

Captain Kevin Monahan responds: "I remember the storm you are talking about. Two days later, walking up Crane Bay Creek on the west side of Gil Island, I found salmon carcasses in the trees, 8 feet above the normal high-flood mark alongside the creek. It must have been a spectacular torrent!"

in the canal which ebbs continuously, reaching 2 knots or more. VHF weather channels die out quickly as you enter Gardner Canal, but it is possible to contact Prince Rupert Coast Guard on VHF Channels 16 and 22A throughout most of Alan Reach. East of Europa Point there is no radio reception and anchorages become marginal; mariners should be self-sufficient with fuel and supplies and use caution at all times.

Alan Reach is the first part of Gardner Canal that tends to the southeast. The high peaks with snow and icefields, seen directly ahead, are the 5,000-foot peaks standing immediately behind the entrance to Kiltuish Inlet. These icefields are remnants of the same glaciers that helped carve this great fjord.

At Europa Point, where the canal narrows and starts some majestic gooseneck turns, the saltwater becomes decidedly more milky in color. Deep grooves in the granite cliffs just east of Europa Point give evidence of the power of the moving glacier that cut this channel. The walls of the canal become more sheer with vertical slabs that, in places, reach all the way to bare ridges above. Europa Point also marks the end of the severe clearcutting in the western part of the canal. Water temperature drops to 52°F.

We call the beautiful area between Europa and Icy points the "Goosenecks to the Kitlope." There is a continuous ebb of surface current in the goosenecks regardless of the tide, and we have seen it flow as high as 2.5 knots on springs.

Collins Bay

Chart 3743; position: 53°33.20′ N, 128°44.20′ W (NAD 27)

> *Collins Bay is entered east of Collins Point. The bay is deep but anchorage for small craft can be obtained near the drying flat at the head of the bay; approach this anchorage with caution, especially at HW, because the drying flat is steep-to. A floating logging camp is in this bay (1988).* (p. 113, SD)

Due to its depths, Collins Bay is a marginal anchorage. Driftwood lines the beach, and an inactive log boom with a rundown floathouse lies on the northwest corner. We found that the small bight between the creek and the little point on the east side of the bay, where it is slightly less steep-to, could provide temporary anchorage in about 10 fathoms. Although the logboom could provide emergency moorage, it swings around with the current and wind.

The cove off Crab River to the north is sometimes used by locals for temporary anchorage. Its shores are equally steep-to, but fewer drift logs along shore indicate that the cove receives less severe weather.

Ochwe Bay

Chart 3743; position (Boulder Creek): 53°29.25′ N, 128°45.28′ W (NAD 27)

> *Ochwe Bay, SW of Rix Island, is too deep for anchorage. The Paril River flows into Ochwe Bay over an extensive drying flat.* (p. 113, SD)

In 1996, both Ochwe Bay and Triumph Bay were involved in large-scale logging operations that included helicopters, barges, float camps, and roads—an indication that operations may continue several years into the future. The entire area is filled with equipment and log booms. Because of the intense activity, noise, and floating debris, neither Ochwe nor Triumph bays provides an attractive anchoring site for pleasure craft.

Prior to this activity, locals preferred to anchor in the cove east of Paril River, known as Boulder Creek for the 16-foot-high boulder that lies on shore just east of the creek. Anchorage is reported to be good in about 12 fathoms.

The Paril River is known for its water which is wine-red from heavy muskeg. The river is tidal up to the falls at 2 kilometers, and offers an excellent canoeing or kayaking experience on high water.

Triumph Bay

Chart 3743; entrance: 53°29.40′ N, 129°43.50′ W; position: 53°27.20′ N, 128°41.10′ W (NAD 27)

> *Anchorage can be obtained in the wide part of Triumph Bay in depths of 22 fathoms (40 m). Small craft can find anchorage closer to the drying*

A relaxing soak! Europa Hot Springs

flat at the head of the bay but caution should be exercised as this drying flat is steep-to. (p. 113, SD)

Triumph Bay can offer good protection at its head on a line between the treed island which marks the drying flat and the western shore. In 1996, a log boom extended completely across the head of the bay, preventing access to depths less than 16 fathoms for small boats. The east shore holds a float camp and log booms; the southwest corner has a two-story float building and major log dump.

Large boats may want to anchor in the east side of the bay in 20 fathoms. Temporary anchorage can also be found on an entrance bar, 1/4 mile south of Walkem Point, in 10 fathoms, where the bottom is reported to be black mud with good holding.

"Europa Bay"

Chart 3743; entrance: 53°26.75′ N, 128°33.60′ W; position: 53°28.40′ N, 128°41.00′ W (NAD 27)

Alan Reach is entered at its NW end between Walkem Point and Barker Point. Shearwater Point is on the north shore. Active or abandoned logging operations can be found throughout this reach.

Indifferent anchorage can be obtained in 15 to 20 fathoms (27 to 37 m) in the centre of the bight lying NE of Shearwater Point. A logging camp is on the shore of this bight.

A bay 2 miles SE of Shearwater Point has a drying flat and pilings at the head. (p. 113, SD)

Europa Bay is the local name for the bight between Shearwater and Europa points. Anchoring is poor in Europa Bay, due to its uneven rocky bottom, but the bay has the hottest and most artistically-designed hot spring facilities in the area. The structure, built by the Kemano Yacht Club, was buried in a landslide in 1993 but has since been rebuilt. New rock handiwork at the hot springs, and the tasteful structure above it, are located on the west side of the bay about 3 feet above the high-water mark. This is by far the most pleasant hot-spring experience on the North Coast.

Kemano residents have installed two large yellow steel buoys in Europa Bay. You can tie to these buoys or raft with someone who is tied. A camp for workers involved in tree spacing projects is located on the east shore at the ramp and along the east side of the stream. Use or share the yellow buoy or anchor in 6 to 12 fathoms over an irregular rocky bottom with poor holding.

Kiltuish Inlet

Chart 3743; entrance: 53°24.40′ N, 128°31.70′ W; anchor (outside narrows): 53°23.82′ N, 128°30.23′ W (NAD 27)

Kiltuish Inlet, 2 miles SE of Europa Point, has a narrow entrance encumbered with rocks with less than 6 feet (2 m) over them and has drying ledges extending from its shores. Local knowledge is advised to safely navigate this entrance. Kiltuish River enters the head of the inlet over a drying flat. (p. 113, SD)

The Kiltuish Inlet is a narrow, shallow inlet which penetrates 6 miles into the south shore at the east

Kiltuish Inlet, south of Europa Point

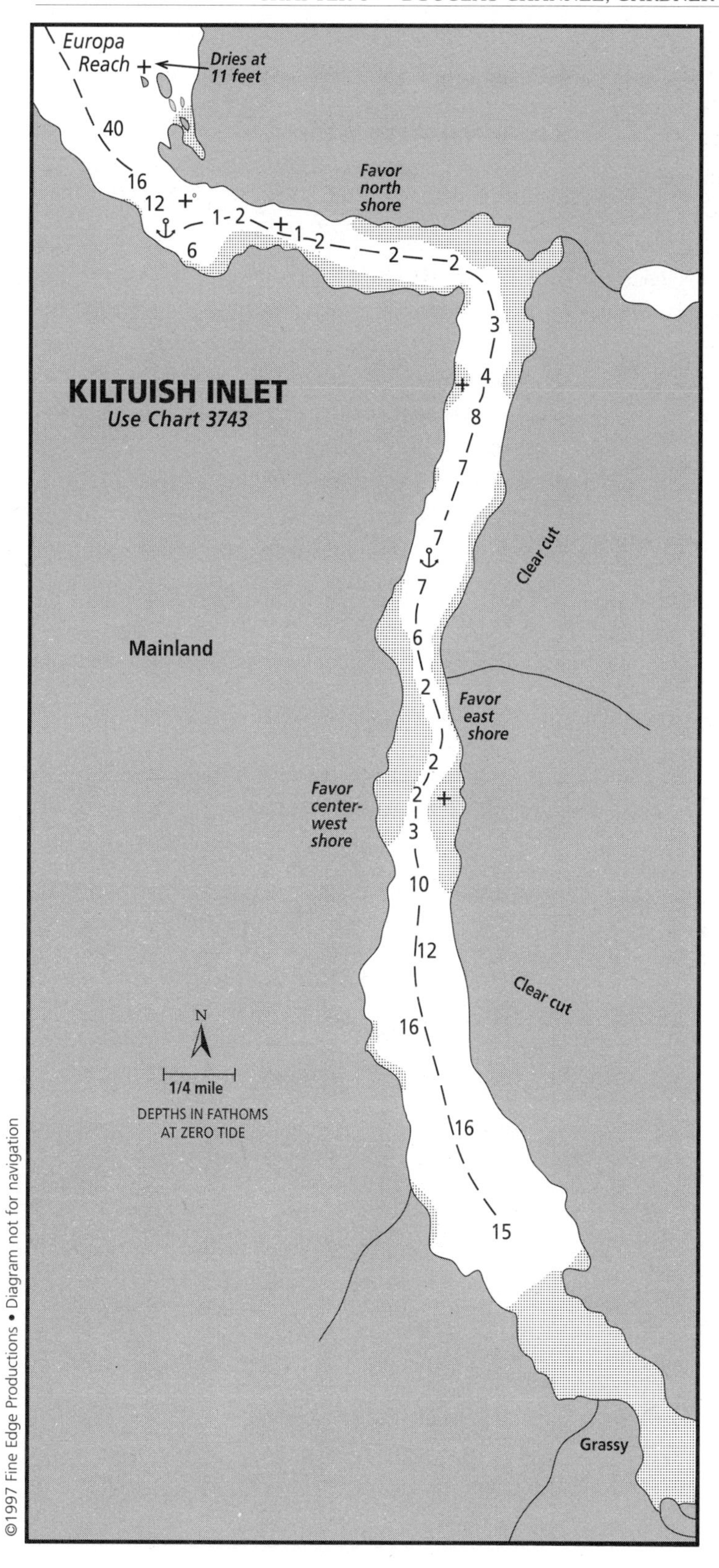

end of Alan Reach. High, snow-covered ridges to the south and east create an attractive setting, combined with a great ice field that runs southeast from the head of the inlet. The south basin in Kiltuish Inlet is surrounded by snow- and icefields on both sides, with a high glacier above Kiltuish River. The current is reported to run at 5 to 6 knots at springs, and the inlet should be entered with care at or near high water, only after proper reconnoitering.

In approaching Kiltuish Inlet, be particularly careful to avoid the rock which reportedly dries at 11 feet about 200 yards northwest of the small islet close north of the north entrance point. You can't see this rock in the glacial water. The submerged rock south of the north entrance point can be detected by the ripple it makes on strong current-flows at lower water.

If you enter the inlet, keep a mid-channel course through the first narrows, favoring the north and east shore slightly. The entrance has an irregular bottom that will give you some anxiety even on high water. We found a minimum depth of about 4 feet at zero tide at the entrance. East of here, the fairway bounces between 2 and 4 fathoms until you reach the deeper sections. The fairway through the second narrows starts from midchannel, then favors the east side near an obvious white rock slab, avoiding the large shoal extending from the west shore. South of the slab, begin to favor the west shore to avoid a shoal and rock along the east shore. The milky-green water has limited underwater visibility.

The recommended anchorage at the entrance is on the south shore just west of the treed point which dries. Anchorage can be found close to shore in a small back eddy in 7 to 9 fathoms with about one knot of counter-current. The bottom is steep but the holding is good. You will swing round and round with the eddy and watch the seals thrashing about feeding on salmon headed upstream.

Kiltuish Inlet has a number of anchorage sites along its 6-mile-length, and there is little chance you will encounter another boat. However, each site should be carefully checked before you anchor in order to properly identify the changing bottom.

A Weather Puzzle

Gardner Canal is a generally-narrow east-west inlet with mountain ranges capped with snow and ice which generate their own microclimate. Normal summer up- and down-slope winds in Douglas Channel tend to peter out before reaching the goosenecks of the canal. Mist and patchy layers of fog with little or no wind are the most prevalent summer condition; bright sunny days are a rare treat.

In general, summer winds are light and variable and only faintly resemble in strength and direction those of the outside. Local boaters tell us that different sections of each arm can have contrary winds, and that winds in Whidbey Reach actually blow from the southeast toward Kemano Bay when, outside, they are blowing from the north. We found that when southeast gales blow in Grenville Channel and Hecate Strait, Gardner Canal experiences little wind. When the low pressure front moved over Kemano Bay during the night, and the barometer rose 6 millibars, a local 20-knot wind blew up Kemano River for about two hours and the yacht club area was lumpy, before returning to its more normal calm condition.

Trees and branches from the wild Kitlope River, frequent mist and fog patches, and opaque glacial water are perhaps the most pressing hazards in the canal. There is no VHF weather reception in the east end of Gardner Canal, and we have been unsuccessful in raising Prince Rupert Coast Guard on either Channel 16 or 22A—or anyone else! There are no nav-aids or signs of civilization as you sail east of Kemano Bay. When you approach the Kitlope, and in Chief Mathews Bay, there are a number of avalanche chutes active into April or May each year, and the amount of snow and ice they deliver into the canal can be as dangerous as icefalls from tidewater glaciers. —DCD

Anchor (outside narrows) in 7 to 9 fathoms over silt, mud and sand with good holding.

Owyacumish Bay

Chart 3745; entrance: 53°29.70′ N, 128°22.00′ W; anchor (waterfall): 53°30.53′ N, 128°22.03′ W (NAD 27)

> *Owyacumish Bay, to the north, is too deep for anchorage.* (p. 113, SD)

Sailing Directions notwithstanding, we feel Owyacumish Bay, known locally as Brim River, is one of the most scenic and enjoyable anchorages imaginable. Located north of Cornwall Point and across from the sharpest of the gooseneck turns, Owyacumish Bay is a delightful place for cruising boats and an excellent haul-out spot for kayakers. It appears to get little direct chop or high winds and should be comfortable in fair weather. The Brim River enters the bay from a low valley on the north. On its northeast side, this valley is backed by an impressive high, sheer granite "half-dome."

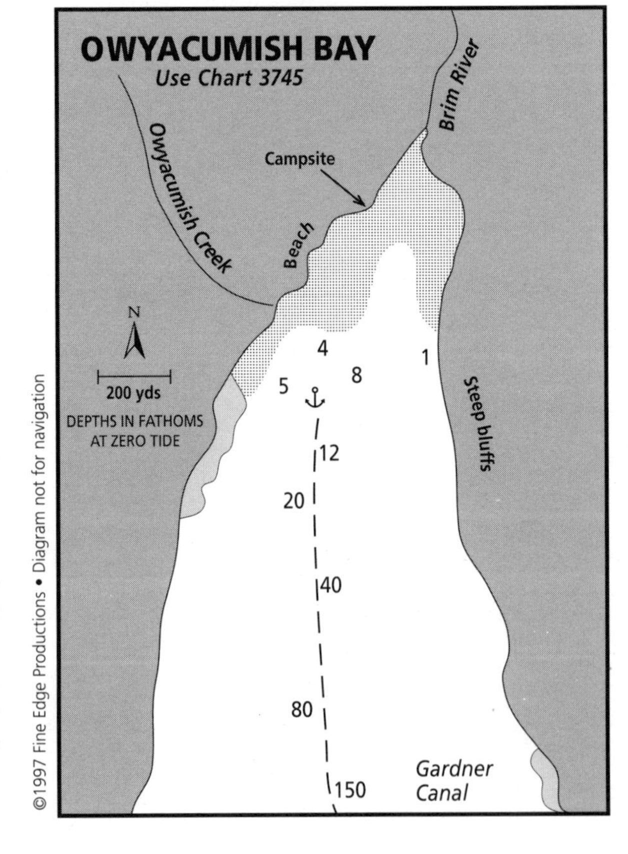

The half-dome is obscured from view in the canal by the abrupt "Wow Ridge" which extends eastward along the banks of the canal. Owyacumish Creek drops into the west side of the bay in a beautiful cascade. In between, there is a grassy shore with little driftwood or storm debris.

In approaching Brim River, avoid the steep-to shoal that extends several hundred yards into the center of the bay and separates the two freshwater courses. Anchorage can be found on the sloping bottom in front of Owyacumish Bay waterfall in about 5 to 7 fathoms or, as locals suggest, against the east wall in appropriate depths. Small boats may be able to take advantage of the 3-foot mud-and-shell shelf on neap tides at the head of the bay on the east side in front of the Brim River.

Anchor (waterfall) in 5 to 7 fathoms over a bottom of silt and soft mud with fair-to-good holding.

Observations from Owyacumish Bay

We were warned that winds in Gardner Canal are brisk, especially in the afternoon, but during our two-week kayak expedition, it was remarkably calm. Tides rose without a ripple, sometimes catching us unaware.

Owyacumish Bay, where we were camped one night, receives so much fresh input from Brim River that we couldn't taste salt at the surface. Much of Gardner Canal is overlaid with an ebbing fresh-water current several feet deep. This has the perverse effect of allowing fresh-water plant life to grow *below* the high-tide line. Judging the high-water mark at a new camp site was a bit dicey. One night my friend Tom looked out from his hammock to find himself swinging over the water.

Overland travel was a big difficulty here. We found it almost impossible to travel up creeks, and life-threatening to try to climb out of the timber to open alpine areas. Our peak-bagging plans, made in the warmth of our livingrooms studying topo maps, became climbs of Himalayan proportions—45-degree slopes, log jams, lethal berry patches that caused our feet to shoot out from under us just as we tried to contour the cliffs. We managed to climb 2,200 feet one day carrying light packs and had just broken out of the timber when we had to bivouac. It rained that night and was socked in by fog the next morning, forcing us to descend with worse footing than before.

—David Scharf, Portland, Oregon

Owyacumish Bay

Kemano Bay

Charts 3736 metric (inset), 3745;
entrance: 53°28.30′ N, 128°08.30′ W;
yacht club entrance:
53°28.79′ N, 128°07.51′ W;
anchor (southeast Entrance Bluff): 53°27.90′ N, 128°07.15′ W (NAD 83)

> *Kemano Bay is the site of port facilities developed by the Aluminum Company of Canada. Entrance Point, on the west side of the bay, is low and ringed by a drying ledge. A spit with depths of less than 6 feet (1.8 m) over it extends 0.2 mile south of Entrance Point and is marked at its south end by port hand buoy "E89". The west and north shores of the bay are fronted by extensive drying flats. Entrance Bluff and most of the east shore of the bay are steep-to.* (p. 113, SD)

Kemano Bay, behind Entrance Point, is somewhat protected from upslope winds in Gardner Canal by the peninsula on the west. The peninsula is an Indian Reserve with a new totem on its far east end and a large log cabin on its south shore.

As you approach from the west, the Alcan dock is hidden by the point. The Alcan complex at the base of Kemano River is private with no public facilities for cruising boats. Fuel and water are available on an emergency basis only.

The Kemano Yacht Club, located in the central part of the complex, has a number of 30-foot slips available for the residents of Kemano. The end-tie on the second finger at the west side is marked "visitors berth," but large pleasure craft of 40 feet or more cannot be easily accommodated. There is a $5.00 per day donation for slip use. Restrooms are located at the head of the gangway, as is an emergency radio that communicates directly with power-station control. No personnel are stationed at the docks. There is no public telephone or any method to obtain weather information. Any assistance you may need is provided by the yacht club volunteers on their own time.

The company town of Kemano is 15 kilometers from the dock, and any visitors to the townsite or the power station must be escorted by employees by prior arrangement. The settlement exists strictly to supply electricity to the Alcan smelter in Kitimat.

Upon approaching Kemano Bay, be careful to keep the green entrance buoy to port. A shoal extends 0.2 mile south of Entrance Point. Temporary anchorage can be taken north of Entrance Point, paying careful attention to water depths and river current.

Anchoring depths are reasonable south of Entrance Point peninsula, with protection from Kemano River current and downslope winds; however, the point is exposed to fickle winds of the main channel. A better temporary anchor site is the shallow bight immediately southeast of Entrance Bluff, east of Kemano Bay which receives less wind and chop than the area around the point.

Anchor (southeast Entrance Bluff) in 10 to 20 fathoms over an unrecorded bottom.

An Engineering Feat: Kemano Power Station

Talk about an engineering feat—the Kemano Power Station built by Alcan takes the prize! The Nechako River, and several major lakes on the east side of the crest which flowed into the Frazer River, were dammed and two 12-mile, horizontal tunnels were driven through the Coast Range to reverse their normal flow. These tunnels provide 2000 feet of head pressure to drive the large pelton wheel generators deep inside the mountain. Built during the height of the cold war, the entire power plant is located 1400 feet inside the solid granite mountain and was built to withstand an atomic attack. Tours of the power plant are not available here at Kemano without prior arrangement. However, once a month during the summer, all-day tours are available through the main offices in Kitimat. You travel by high-speed boat to Kemano, and the tour is well worth taking.

Alcan subsequently spent $250,000,000 dollars to drill two additional tunnels two-thirds of the way through the coast range and install additional high-efficiency generators to double the power output of the plant. In the early 1990s, when word got out about this new project, public opposition began and mounted until the provincial government withheld critical approval; the work was stopped and remains in limbo.

Kemano Bay could be an excellent staging area for visiting and learning about Gardner Canal and the unique Kitlope area, a place of great natural beauty. The Kemano Power Station remains an issue of environmental concern about which you must form your own opinion. (For information contact the Kitimat Visitors Center, tel: 250-632-6294.)

Kemano Yacht Club, private floats for Alcan employees

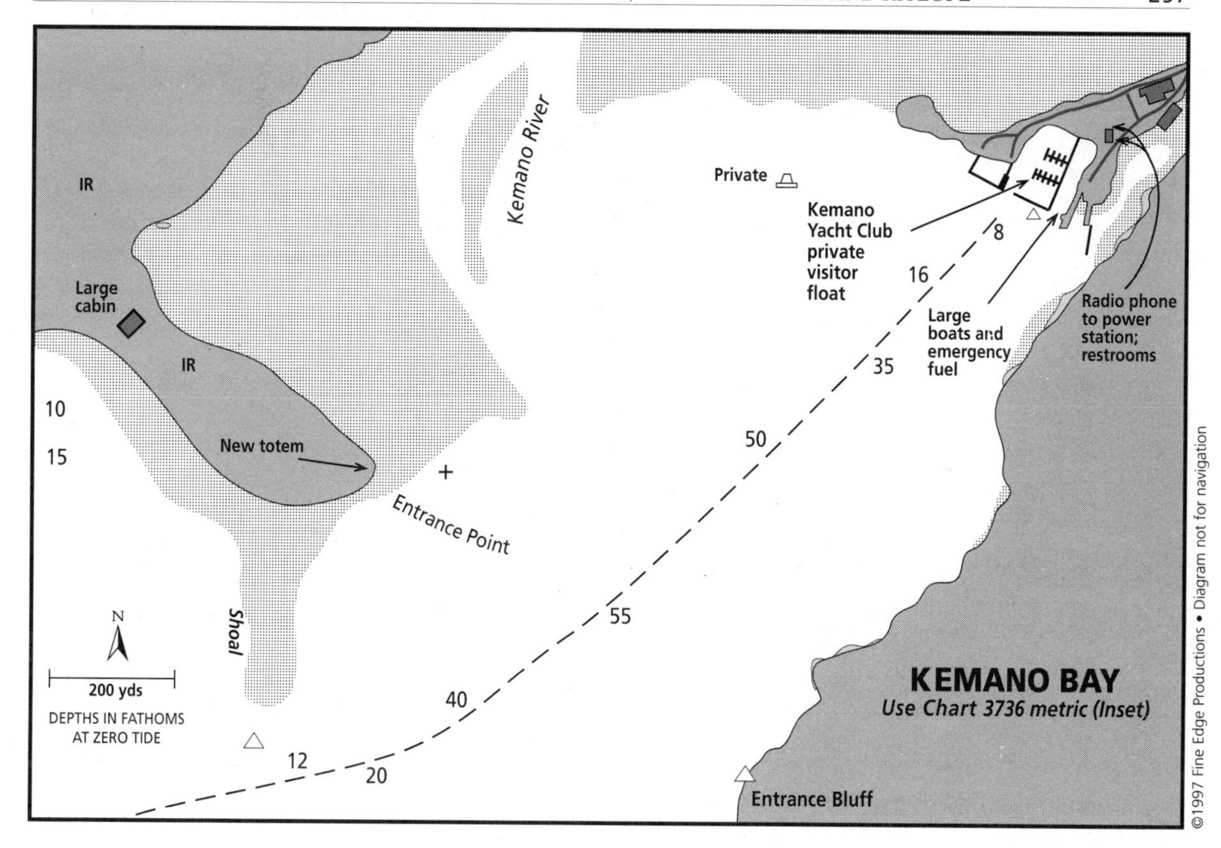

Chief Mathews Bay

Chart 3745; entrance:
53°22.50′ N, 128°03.50′ W (NAD 27)
anchor: 53°20.14′ N, 128°06.00′ W
(NAD 27)

> *Chief Mathews Bay, entered west of Courageux Point, is too deep for anchorage.* (p. 114, SD)

Chief Mathews Bay is in the center of a most beautiful and spectacular part of Gardner Canal. Each spring avalanche chutes clear all vegetation from the high ridges down to saltwater, hanging glaciers tower over the head and sides of the bay, and the sound of waterfalls lulls you to sleep. In 1996, a longhouse was under construction on the southwest corner of the river outlet—the only sign of civilization we encountered east of Europa Hot Springs, except at Kemano Bay. This anchor site or Kemano Bay would be the preferred anchor sites for day trips to the Kitlope area. (Less driftwood, current, exposure to wind and chop than the bitter end of Gardner Canal.)

Chief Mathews Bay is less exposed than Gardner Canal itself; you can find fair shelter on the east shore, south of the rock fall, north of the drying flat at its head. Although locals prefer the 12-fathom area just south of the rockfall (shown as a small blue spot on Chart 3745), we found this place to be steep-to without any flat surface. We prefer a spot about 0.5 miles south where you can anchor in about 10 fathoms, a safer distance from shore if you need to let out some scope.

Anchor in 10 fathoms over a mud bottom with good holding.

Price Cove

Chart 3745; position: 53°16.05′ N, 127°56.80′ W (NAD 27)

> *Price Cove, 3 miles south of Queen Point, on the west side of Egeria Reach, is filled with a drying flat. Small vessels can anchor in 15 to 20 fathoms (27 to 37 m) off the edge of this flat.* (p. 114, SD)

Although Price Cove is steep-to, we were able to

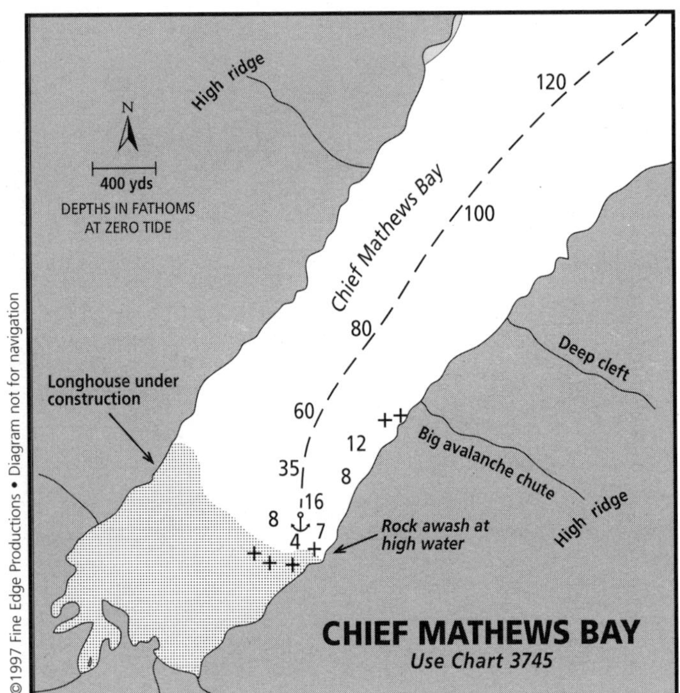

get a good set in about 6 fathoms. With offshore winds, however, holding might be suspect on such a steep shore.

A large glacier west of Price Cove is the source of a number of strikingly beautiful waterfalls that cascade over vertical granite faces, dropping into the saltwater along the west shore of Egeria Reach.

Anchor in 6 to 12 fathoms between the outlet of the creek and the vertical crack on the rock face along shore; the bottom is silt and grey mud with fair-to-good holding.

Chief Mathews Bay enshrouded in fog

Kitlope Bight

Chart 3745; anchor: 53°15.55′ N, 127°54.22′ W (NAD 27)

Kitlope bight, a tiny bight on the east shore, a half-mile from the drying flats of Kitlope River, is reported by locals to be the only reasonable anchorage at the very head of Gardner Canal. This bight is said to receive protection from the river's current and from large trees that frequently wash down the river.

We recorded depths between 10 and 20 fathoms, one to three boat-lengths off the steep rocky cliffs. The opaque glacial water gives only one foot visibility, and we found inconsistencies between the 50KC and 200 KC echo sounders. Some of these readings may be due to the incomplete mixture of fresh and saltwater.

Larger boats that have anchored here reportedly set their anchors in 10 to 30 fathoms using a stern-tie to shore. We found two old cables, indicated on the diagram, which may be useful for stern-ties.

We had trouble getting a good set in the area

Gardner Canal: the Environmentalists' Side

Taking part in the public opposition over the Alcan project was Terry Jack, Vancouver songwriter and owner of *Seasons in the Sun* (both the song and the boat!). Terry, who has spent 18 summers cruising the North Coast, became deeply concerned by what he considered a lack of long-range planning and reckless destruction of habitat in Gardner Canal. He composed a song that became the battle cry of those who opposed the addition to the power plant. His song includes the following refrain:

The Nechako's going down, the future's all been sold
They're draining all the life from her, and greed is in control.
They dammed that mighty river; they brought her to her knees.
They lied to all the people; we've got to set that river free!

—DCD

between the sheer south wall and the creek to the north. The bottom was silt with occasional bumps indicating rocks or stumps, and our anchor brought up a lot of twigs.

Photo by Ron Thiele

The Kitlope River meets Gardner Canal

Kitlope Valley

Chart 3745; drying flat
position: 53°15.00′ N, 128°54.00′ W (NAD 27)

Kitlope Valley, considered the world's largest undisturbed coastal temperate rain forest, lies inland from the mouth of the Kitlope River. In 1994, nearly 700,000 acres (317,000 hectares) were set aside as a reserve to protect this area. The region falls within the Haisla Nation which welcomes visitors and gives guided tours during the summer months. Their name for the valley (Husduwachsdu) means "source of the milky blue waters" and we can attest to that after having seen the outlet of the river.

Visiting the Haisla Peoples

During a recent kayaking trip in Gardner Canal, we had planned to camp at the Haisla ancestral "village" of Kemano on the west peninsula in Kemano Bay. Before beginning our trip we had obtained their permission. However, as we headed down-channel, the day proved to be particularly strenuous and, worn out, we stopped and slept instead on a lovely moss-covered flat short of the ancient village site. The next day we stopped at the "village" to visit Bea and Johnny Wilson. The place we had camped was an ancient burial ground, Johnny told us, and asked how we slept.

I said we slept like babies on the carpet of thick moss.

Johnny said slowly, "They must have accepted you."

We were grateful to have been accepted both by the Ancients and the Wilsons. The place we had camped looked like untouched wilderness, but it was an important place to the Haisla.

—David Scharf, Portland, Oregon

Norm Wagner of Kitimat (see Jesse Falls Sidebar) has this to add: "The battle for this area is far from over. The Nanakila Institute, a Haisla-based organization, also claims Chief Mathews Bay and its river valley as part of the protected area, despite the fact that West-Fraser Forest Company has not given up its harvest right to this valley. Nanakila is in the process of building a modern longhouse on Chief Mathews Bay overlooking the river as an outpost to establish

Saving the Kitlope

The Kitlope area has been found to be *the largest undeveloped coastal temperate watershed in the world.* It was scheduled to be logged, but local community groups and lobbying helped to have 317,000 hectares of land set aside, protected from roads and chainsaws. Work goes on as this is written to extend the protection to the Kowesas and Barrie Creek areas left out in the original set-aside.

During this period the local First Nations opposed the logging of this area, even when offered a share of the profits; they had never recognized the loss of their rights to their ancestral lands. The Haisla were central to the research, planning and lobbying that resulted in saving this priceless treasure, and they are equal partners with the province of British Columbia in its perpetual co-management.

their claim to the area.

Another organization that is based in the Kitlope is the Haisla Rediscovery Society which sets up camp on the beach at Kitlope Lake. The group welcomes youths and adults of all peoples to participate in their rediscovery camp which highlights Haisla culture." (For information, telephone the Haisla Nation Rediscovery Society at 250-632-3308 in Kitimat and see the resources listed in the Appendix.)

Devastation Channel

Chart 3743; south entrance:
53°34.50′ N, 128°48.02′ W; north entrance:
53°46.10′ N, 128°49.50′ W (NAD 27)

> *Devastation Channel has steep-to shores.*
>
> *There is a noticeable difference in current velocities between spring and neap tides in this channel which is not apparent in the adjoining channels, and spring tides increase the rate of both the north-going and south-going streams by as much as 0.5 to 1 kn.* (p. 114, SD)

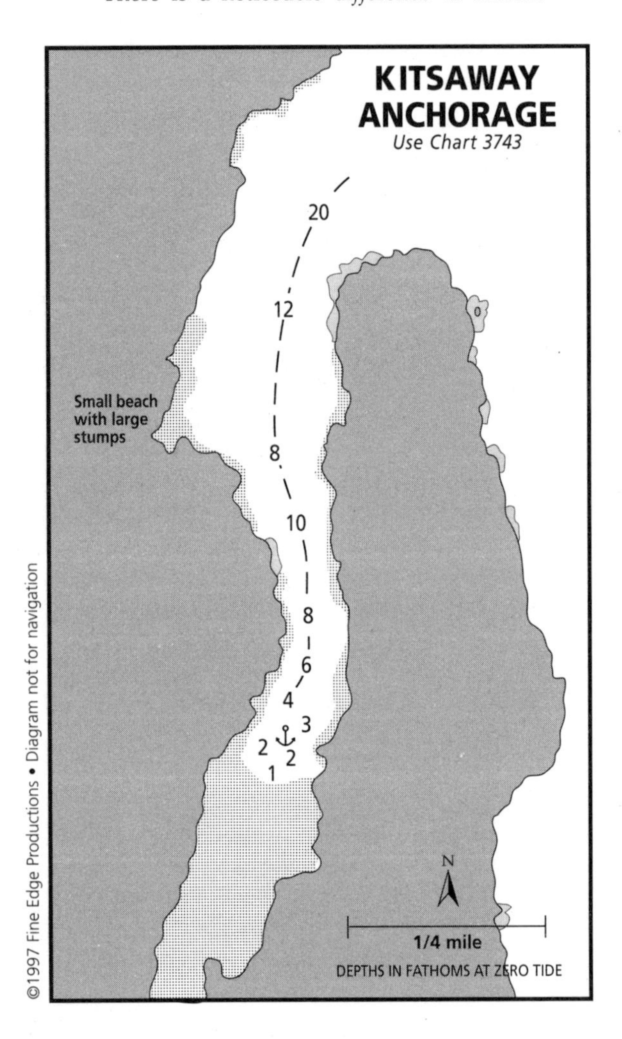

Devastation Channel has very strong tidal flows on spring tides. The large flow of fresh water that comes out of Gardner Canal is, in small part, due to the Kemano power project. The complex hydrology of this region can be studied in the detailed current diagrams shown in *Sailing Directions,* pages 109 to 112.

In Devastation Channel, Kitsaway Anchorage is a good storm port. Excellent sport fishing is reported in the turbulent waters where Ursula Channel and Verney Passage meet.

Kitsaway Anchorage

Chart 3743; entrance: 53°37.80′ N, 128°52.10′ W;
anchor: 53°36.45′ N, 128°52.51′ W (NAD 27)

> *Sheltered anchorage is available in 13 fathoms (24 m) in Kitsaway Anchorage, between the north end of Kitsaway Island and Hawkesbury Island. Small craft can anchor farther south, off the drying bank.* (p. 114, SD)

Kitsaway Anchorage is deep and well sheltered with excellent protection from southerly storms. It appears to be subject to just moderate chop on down-channel williwaws.

We prefer to anchor deep in the bay off the drying grassy flat. The water is opaque, so you need to monitor your echo sounder carefully. Notice the size of some of the old stumps on the small beach halfway down the bay.

Anchor in 2 to 3 fathoms deep in the bay over oozy, soft mud with grass and shells. Use a soft touch when you set your anchor in this soft bottom.

Weewanie Hot Springs

Chart 3743; cove position:
53°41.78′ N, 128°47.30′ W (NAD 27)

> *Weewanie Hot Springs are in a cove about 0.5 mile north of Weewanie Creek; these hot springs have been developed by the Kitimat Yacht Club.*

"I could stay here forever . . ."

> *Two mooring buoys and an old log dump are in the cove.* (p. 114, SD)

For the improvements at Weewanie Hot Springs, we have Kitimat Aquanauts Scuba Club to thank. There is now a Plexiglas window in the hot springs hut that allows you to keep your eye on your boat as you're soaking. There are two tubs side by side, a smaller one for washing yourself, and a larger one for soaking. Protocol calls for opening the valve on the outside of the hut and draining the smaller tub while you're soaking in the larger one. Don't forget to close the valve before you leave so the washing tub fills up again. If you feel the need to take any containers inside, please remember to pack everything out with you, along with any refuse "inadvertently" left by others.

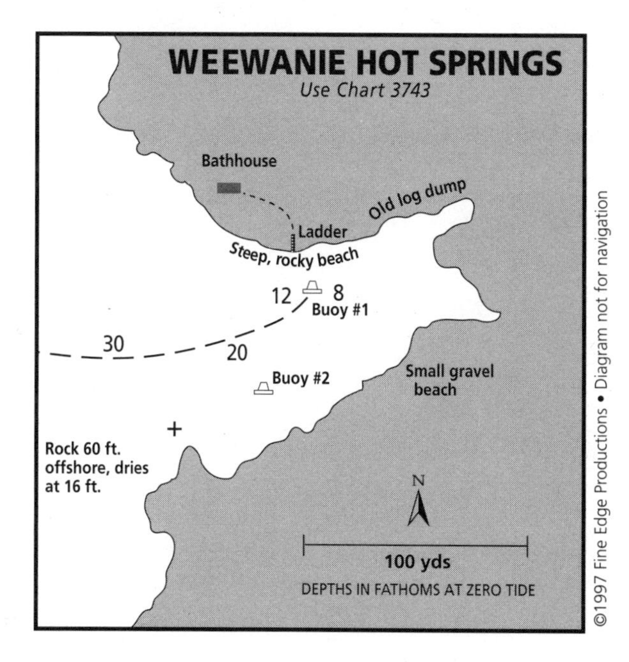

You can land your dinghy on the gravel beach at the head of the cove and take the trail that leads west past a picnic and campsite area to the bathhouse. Or, at high tide, you can take your dinghy to the rocks directly below the bathhouse and tie to a log.

Two small buoys in the cove offer convenient moorage; the one on the south side of the cove gives better protection against southerly chop.

Entering the cove is easy; however, watch for a rock that dries at about 14 feet, 60 feet off the south point.

Anchoring is possible between the buoys and the head of the bay in 6 to 12 fathoms, over a rocky bottom with poor holding.

Sue Channel

Chart 3743; east entrance: 53°43.00′ N, 128°50.00′ W; west entrance: 53°40.80′ N, 128°04.80′ W (NAD 27)

> *Sue Channel has a least depth of 90 feet (27.4 m) through the fairway, encountered about 1 mile within the west entrance. The fairway is narrowed to a width of 0.1 mile, 2 miles within the west entrance, by a gravel bank extending off the mouth of a small stream on the Hawkesbury Island shore. A large conspicuous stump is grounded on the end of this gravel bank. . . .* (p. 116, SD)

Sue Channel, a convenient route for cutting across to Douglas Channel, gives a fast ride down-channel on ebb current, especially with a tailwind. The flip side is that an upslope wind can create a nasty chop.

In case of bad weather, you can find anchoring sites in two places. The first, at the head of the

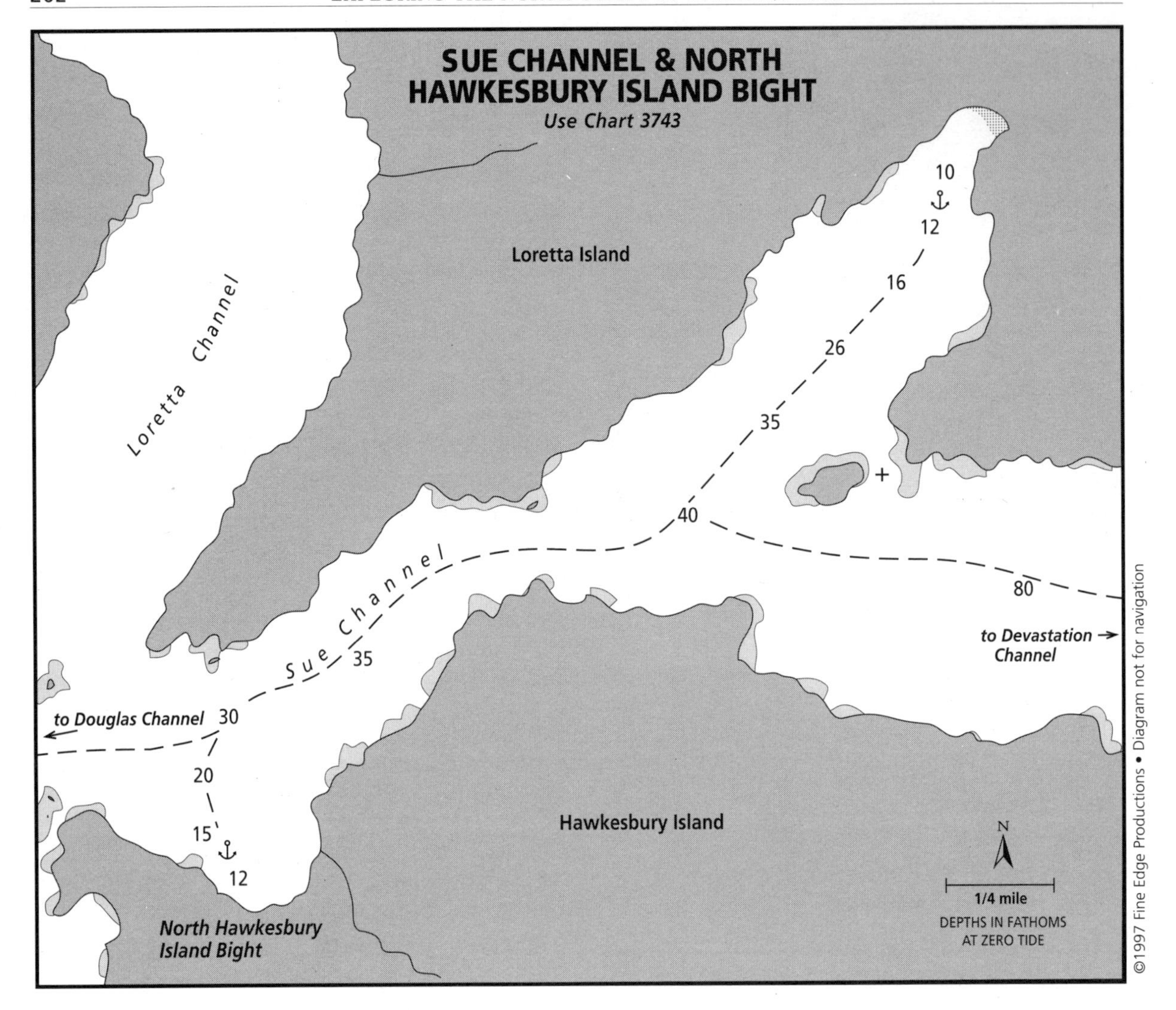

bay on the south side of Loretta Island, is sometimes used for log-boom storage; the second is in Hawkesbury Island North Bight.

"Loretta Island Cove"

Chart 3743; entrance: 53°43.30′ N, 128°51.70′ W; anchor: 53°44.00′ N 128 50.72′ W (NAD 27)

> *Anchorage in 19 fathoms (35 m) can be obtained about 0.5 mile from the head of the bay in Loretta Island. It is well sheltered with good holding ground.* (p. 116, SD)

Very good protection from downslope winds, as well as southeast winds, can be found on the south side of Loretta Island in what we call Loretta Island Cove.

Anchor in 10 to 16 fathoms over an unrecorded bottom.

"Hawkesbury Island North Bight"

Chart 3743; anchor: 53°42.43′ N, 128°53.49′ W (NAD 27)

> *Good anchorage in 19 fathoms (35 m) can also be obtained in the bay on the south shore of Sue Channel, due south of the SW end of Loretta Island.* (p. 116, SD)

Hawkesbury Island North Bight is located directly south of the west tip of Loretta Island. We've tried out this anchorage in a southerly blow and found it almost calm. Although the water is deep, we felt little strain on our anchor.

Anchor in 12 to 15 fathoms over a hard bottom with fair holding

"Stormy Bay"

Chart 3743; entrance: 53°46.50′ N, 128°48.20′ W; anchor: 53°46.39′ N, 128°48.17′ W (NAD 27)

Stormy Bay, the local name for a tiny notch on the north side of Hopkins Point at the entrance to Devastation Channel, offers emergency shelter for small sportfishing boats that need to get out of severe upslope chop or wind. Don Pearson of Moon Bay Marina in Kitimat emphasized the value of both Stormy and Hideaway bays for small boats that get caught out in rough water.

This very shallow notch, which is only about 120-feet wide, has a rock pile at its head, with large drift stumps evidence of strong downslope winds.

We found the bottom to be entirely stony. A couple of sportfishing boats could fit into the middle of the notch over a bottom that nearly dries at zero tide. You may be able to use stern-ties to the small trees on the white rocky shore. A single small cruising boat might find temporary shelter at the entrance in one fathom, but you would need to keep a constant anchor watch and use one or two stern ties to shore.

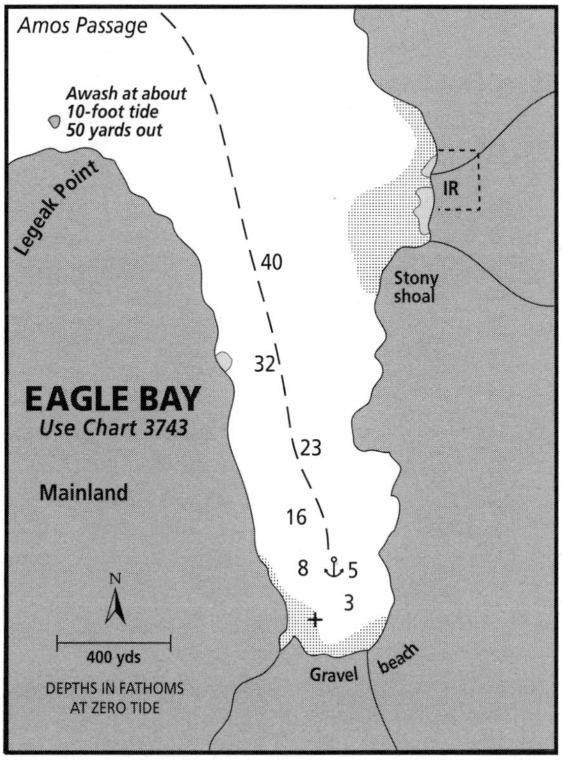

Anchor in 1 fathom over a stony bottom with poor holding.

Eagle Bay

Chart 3743; entrance: 53°49.20′ N, 128°42.80′ W; anchor: 53° 48.11′ N, 128° 42.37′ W (NAD 27)

> *Eagle Bay, on the east side of Amos Passage, is entered between Legeak Point and Steel Point. It offers good anchorage to small craft in 11 fathoms (20 m) about 0.2 mile from its head. A treed islet is close offshore 1.2 miles NNE of Steel Point.* (p. 116, SD)

Eagle Bay is one of our favorite anchorages in Kitimat Arm. The bay gives good shelter and is an attractive anchorage with a view of a high snowy ridge. Small boats can anchor near the head of the bay on a flat 3- to 5-fathom shelf. Larger boats can anchor just outside the shelf with plenty of swinging room. Avoid the rocky bottom on the west shore off the creek outlet.

At the entrance to Eagle Bay, the outflow of a large creek on the east shore creates a shallow flat with stones and mud that makes a good kayak haul-out point. However, give it wide berth if you're going to the head of the bay.

There's a light gravel beach at the head of the bay with a few drift logs where you can land your dinghy. Avoid the rock awash on a 10-foot tide off Legeak Point, approximately 100 feet off the point.

Anchor in about 5 fathoms over dark mud bottom with very good holding.

Kildala Arm

Chart 3743; entrance
53° 51.50′ N, 128° 40.00′ W (NAD 27)

> *Kildala Arm is entered north or south of Coste Island by Amos Passage.*
>
> *Kildala Arm is a log storage area. Dolphins lie along the north and south shores of the arm at various locations.* (p. 116, SD)

Kildala Arm has a striking skyline to the east with several sharp peaks that jut above large permanent snowfields. Closer in, the steep sides are tree-lined to the top. High-tension power-lines for the Alcan smelter in Kitimat cross the head of the arm on their way, and many slopes show the loggers' handiwork. The arm is some-what protected from heavy weather, but the north shore is taken up by log-boom storage.

Gobeil Bay, "Mud Bay"

Chart 3743; entrance: 53°52.00′ N, 128°40.65′ W; anchor: 53°52.63′ N, 128°40.25′ W (NAD 27)

> *Gobeil Bay is on the north side of the entrance to Kildala Arm. Small craft can find indifferent anchorage at the head of the bay. Two shacks are in the next bay east.* (p. 117, SD)

Gobeil Bay, on the north side of Kildala Arm, is known locally as Mud Bay. Although open to the south, it can offer quiet anchorage in fair weath-er in a 6-fathom hole deep in the bay between the west shore and the drying creek delta. Its shores are steep-to and swinging room is limited, so larger boats would need a stern-tie to shore.

The bay is open to wake from passing work boats, but upslope chop is somewhat diminished by the lee formed by Coste Island.

Anchor in 6 fathoms, soft mud bottom with twigs, good holding.

Atkins Bay

Chart 3743; position: 53°50.90′ N, 128°33.60′ W (NAD 27)

> *Atkins Bay, 4.3 miles ESE of Gobeil Bay, affords no anchorage.* (p. 117, SD)

Atkins Bay is steep-to with its beach dropping off at a 45° slope. The only possible anchorage would be with a shore tie along the west shore of the bay. On a clear day, there is a great view to the east of high, snowy peaks. This site offers some shelter from upslope winds behind the peninsu-la. There is a cabin on shore next to the creek..

Kitimat Arm

Chart 3743; entrance: 53°49.00′ N, 128°50.00′ W (NAD 27)

> *Kitimat Arm terminates in low land fronted by an extensive drying flat with the Kitimat port facili-ties on its west side.* (p. 116, SD)

Looking north, Kitimat Arm

Kitimat Arm is the extension of Douglas Channel that extends to Kitimat at the outflow of Kitimat River.

Jesse Falls

Jesse Falls, a prominent landmark for boaters in the Doug-las Channel, is the spectacular end to the world's shortest river. Jesse Lake turns very briefly into a hungry current before roaring 20 to 30 meters down into the ocean.

Recently a young Kitimat teacher underestimated the power of Jesse Falls. Tania Chisholme, outfitted in a wet suit, was enjoying a swim in Jesse Lake near the falls when the current overpowered her and swept her over the main falls. She was spotted just once before she finally came to the surface in the channel off the falls and was rescued. Luckily she lived to tell the tale.

I was in my early teens when I had my first canoeing experience at Jesse Lake. Portaging gear up to the lake across the rock face next to the falls was tough work, but it was well worth it because very few people ever make this trip. My brother and I spent a week exploring the lake and gorging on its trout supply. Most of the lake's shoreline is steep and rocky, yet the trees and brush are quite dense right to the water's edge. A substantial river [Jesse Creek] feeds into the far end of the lake, about 8 kilometers from Douglas Channel. The only feasible campsites with sandy beaches are found at this end. About one kilometer up the river, amongst stands of massive old-growth forest, is Jesse's best kept secret, a most impressive waterfall.

Unfortunately, a logging road will soon lead into this Shangri-la and, although a municipal park has been pro-posed, it's unlikely that the whole lake or river can be saved.

—Norman Wagner, Kitimat Guide

Jesse Falls

Chart 3743; position: 53°50.00′ N, 128°51.50, W (NAD 27)

Jesse Falls, about 1.3 miles north of Hilton Point, are conspicuous. (p. 116, SD)

Jesse Falls is one of the more remarkable waterfalls on the British Columbia coast. The falls are fed from six-mile-long Jesse Lake, held in by a natural rock dike located just above the high-water mark over which massive volumes of water tumble into Douglas Channel. You can carefully land a dinghy and climb up the slippery granite wall on the east side of the smaller of the two waterfalls to watch as it plunges into the Pacific Ocean. *Use extreme caution if you do climb up to the lake; the rocks are slippery!*

Use caution, also, when you motor near the falls; the bottom is uneven and shallow, and the falls cause a strong current and shoal that extends well into Douglas Channel.

Jesse Falls from its lip; Jesse Lake to right, Douglas Channel to left

Emsley Cove ("Old Town" or "Bish Bay")

Chart 3743; position: 53°54.04′ N, 128°46.55′ W (NAD 27)

Emsley Point, on the west side of the arm, forms the east shore of Emsley Cove, which does not afford anchorage and is partially filled with a steep-to stone and gravel drying flat. (p. 117, SD)

Emsley Cove is reported to offer temporary shelter from northerly outflow winds, if you tuck in behind Emsley Point close to the steep-to shore.

The next bay, 1.7 miles north, is reported to provide the same protection as Emsley Cove. Known locally as Old Town or Bish Bay, it has a number of old pilings along shore.

Clio Bay

Chart 3743; entrance: 53°54.75′ N, 128°41.70′ W; anchor: 53°53.74′ N, 128°40.07′ W (NAD 27)

Clio Bay, north of Amos Passage and on the east side of Kitimat Arm, is entered between Clio Point and Raley Point. It is free of dangers and affords anchorage to small craft in depths of 6 to 10 fathoms (11 to 18 m) near the drying bank at its head. Clio Bay is a booming ground. (p. 117, SD)

Well-sheltered Clio Bay is the closest anchorage to Kitimat. Avoid the large steel buoy on the east side of the center of the bay where boomsticks are attached to shore. The head of the bay has a mud flat full of deadheads. Since the area has been used extensively for logging operations, the mud bottom has a lot of slash that could foul your anchor.

Anchor in 5 fathoms over a mud bottom with slash; fair-to-good holding.

Kitamaat Village

Chart 3736 metric (inset); position (floating breakwater): 53°58.06′ N, 128°39.12′ W (NAD 83)

Kitamaat Village, formerly known as Kitimat Mission, is a small community on the east side of Kitimat Arm, close south of Wathl Creek. The post office in this community is known as Haisla. An extensive drying flat, on which there are numer-

Exodus drops off tourists, Jesse Falls

ous large stumps and deadheads, fronts the village and the mouth of Wathl Creek.

Three public floats, 0.7 mile south of the mouth of Wathl Creek, are protected by a floating breakwater. A launching ramp is nearby. (p. 117, SD)

There is a government wharf located in Kitamaat Village, an Indian Reserve, filled mostly with village fishing boats.

Here, the Haisla Canoe Project Society is training a crew to paddle a 40-foot canoe to take part in coastwide festivals; they sometimes take paying guests on their evening practice sessions.

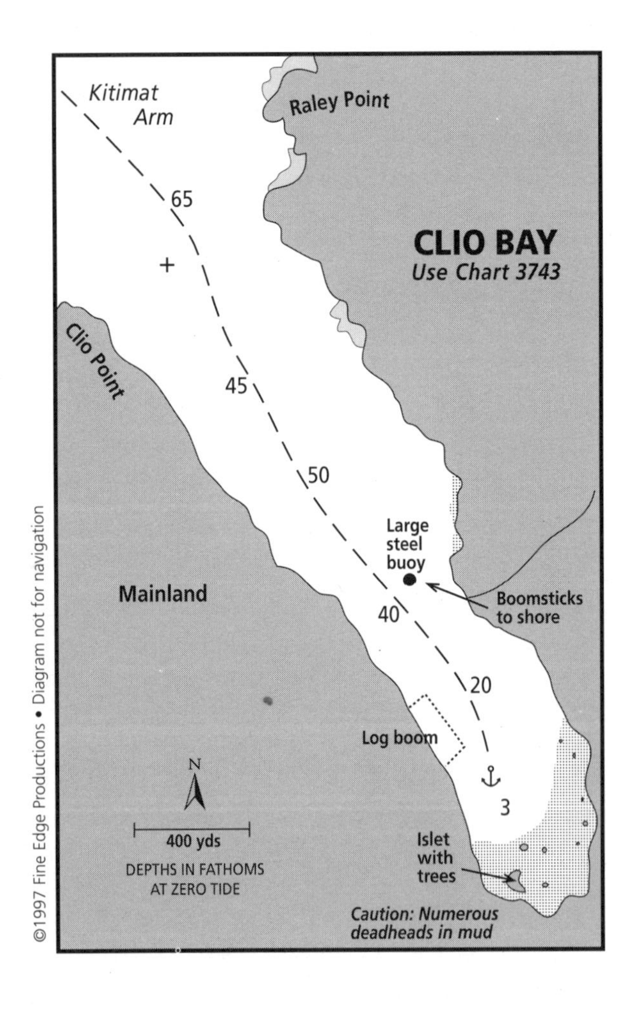

MK Bay Marina

Chart 3736 (inset); entrance:
53°59.04′ N, 128°39.27′ W (NAD 83)

The floats and facilities of MK Bay Marina are on the south shore of a cove about 0.2 mile north of the mouth of Wathl Creek and are protected by a rock breakwater and a short floating log breakwater to the south and by a longer floating log breakwater to the west. The entrance is at the south end of the west breakwater. The marina has charts, gasoline, diesel fuel, water, ice, naphtha, hardware, a tidal grid for vessels to 60 feet (18 m) long, a launching ramp and can do hull and engine repairs. (p. 117, SD)

MK Bay Marina, an upscale marina located on the east side of Kitimat Arm north of Kitamaat Village, can handle pleasure boats of all sizes. Probably the best marina on the North Coast, MK has 125 slips with full amenities that include water and power to the cement floats, laundry and shower facilities, ice, fuel, and a public landline pay telephone. There is waste deposit for boats that pump out their own oil; a boat-launching ramp and large parking lot are available for boaters with trailerable boats.

If you're tired of those high-speed fueling hoses that have no automatic cut-off, you'll be delighted to find that MK's are easy to use; both the slow-delivery gasoline and diesel fuel pumps have valves with automatic cut-off! Wayne Devins and his crew welcome visiting pleasure craft, and do a masterful job of servicing some 200 visiting boats during the summer by "adroit use of hot berthing."

One drawback—the marina is located 11 kilometers from town, a good bicycle ride, but a bit far if you're planning anything other than a marathon walk. Taxi service is available, or you can sometimes hitch a ride with a local. (Telephone: 250-632-6410)

Minette Bay

Chart 3736 metric; entrance:
53°59.40′ N, 128°39.65′ W; position (float):
54°01.60′ N, 128°36.67′ W (NAD 83)

> *Minette Bay, at the head of Kitimat Arm, is obstructed at its entrance by extensive drying flats. The entrance channel, which is accessible only at HW, lies close to the east shore. There are numerous snags and stumps in the area and the channel should be used only with local knowledge. The basin near the head of the bay has depths of 10 to 18 fathoms (18 to 33 m) in it.* (p. 118, SD)

Minette Bay, accessible only at high water, has a private float used as long-term storage for a few commercial and pleasure craft. An active log dump is just south of the float.

Moon Bay Marina

Chart 3736; entrance: 53°59.26′ N, 128°41.77′ W (NAD 83)

Moon Bay Marina, 0.8 mile south of the Eurocan Terminal on the west shore and behind its own causeway, is a working marina that provides shelter for about 60 boats. The operation is a less expensive alternative to the MK Marina across the bay. Limited fuel and water are available. At present, their marina has neither electricity nor a public pay phone, but both are anticipated within the next few years.

Because Moon Bay has a service crane, it's a good place to perform heavy maintenance work

Moon Bay Marina, west side Kitimat Arm

on your boat. The marina is owned and run by Don and Jeanie Pearson (tel: 250-632-4655). Don, who's been around this area for a long time, carries a lot of local knowledge in his head! The marina monitors Channel 16.

Kitimat Harbour

Chart 3736 metric (inset); yacht club entrance:
53°59.96′ N, 128°41.58′ W (NAD 83)

> *Kitimat port facilities, all privately owned, are at the head of Kitimat Arm. Near these facilities, which are on the west shore, is a large aluminum smelting plant operated by the Aluminum Company of Canada and a lumber and pulp mill operated by Eurocan Pulp and Paper Limited. Ocelot Industries Ltd. methanol plant is about 0.5 mile NNE of the Alcan smelter. In 1983 the port handled almost 2,000,000 tonnes of cargo.*
>
> *Kitimat townsite is about 13 km inland from the port facilities, on the NE side of the Kitimat River. It has a population of about 12,000 (1986). The townsite has shopping centres, a liquor store, a post office, a hotel and motels, schools, banks, and a fully equipped hospital. A RCMP detachment is stationed here.* (pp. 116–118, SD)

Kitimat Yacht Club, located just north of the Alcan dock, is a private facility for small sportfishing boats that belong to Alcan employees. There are no personnel stationed at the yacht club, and the float gate is locked.

The community of about 12,000 is quite attuned to outdoor activities, and in the last decade has made a big push to develop tourism

MK Bay Marina, east side Kitimat Arm

for both land- and water-users. Sportfishing is reputed to be some of the best in British Columbia waters (both saltwater and freshwater). Kayaking, whale watching, camping, and hiking are all popular activities in the area, and with the new facilities at MK Marina, visits to the area by pleasure craft are on the increase. For more information about the entire area, contact Kitimat Visitors Centre, tel: 250-632-6294. Their staff is efficient, helpful and friendly! (Please see the Appendix for a more complete listing of sources.)

Douglas Channel

Charts 3743, 3742; north entrance: 53°48.00′ N 128°52.00′ W (NAD 27)

Douglas Channel leads 30 miles north and NE from Wright Sound to the junction of Kitimat Arm and Devastation Channel. Depths in Douglas Channel are great and the shores are steep-to, rising to high mountains a short distance inland. The NW shore is indented by several inlets. Hawkesbury Island separates Douglas Channel from Verney Passage and Devastation Channel.

Tidal streams in Douglas Channel are noteworthy in that the stream is predominantly south-going due to the large runoff of fresh water from the rivers emptying into the channel. (pp. 114–115, SD)

Pacer Chant *hauling bauxite to Alcan smelter, Kitimat*

Douglas Channel deserves serious respect year round. In the summer months, prevailing westerlies funnel up the channel, often reaching gale force and raising seas of 4, 6, or even 8 feet. When inflow conditions are expected (i.e. clear, sunny skies June through September), it is best to transit Douglas Channel before noon. In winter, and sometimes in summer, outflow winds can reach storm force and, with subfreezing temperatures, can cause severe icing on small craft. It's possible for cruising boats to take advantage of a north-setting current of one to 1.5 knots on the west side of Douglas Channel south of Kitkiata Inlet.

Winds in Douglas Channel blow from two directions—in and out. Low pressure over the British Columbia interior plateau, caused by intense summertime heating causes air to rise and winds roar up Douglas Channel. In Squamish or Arctic outflow conditions, the cold interior causes air to flow out of the inlets toward the ocean. Douglas Channel is the termination of a long valley extending northeast from Kitimat to Terrace extending all the way to the interior plateau. Listen for weather conditions at Nanakwa Shoal (one mile east of Jesse Falls). Due to its unique weather patterns, Douglas Channel has its own Marine Weather Forecast Area.

"Hideaway Bay"

Chart 3743; entrance: 53°48.70′ N, 128°53.40′ W; anchor: 53°48.58′ N, 128°53.85′ W (NAD 27)

Hideaway Bay is the local name for the small notch, 0.9 mile southwest of Hilton Point (not to be confused with the larger, deeper cove west of Hilton Point). The roughest water in Douglas Channel can be found at the intersection of Kitimat Arm and Devastation Channel. Hideaway Bay, and Stormy Bay on the east shore, both offer protection from southerly

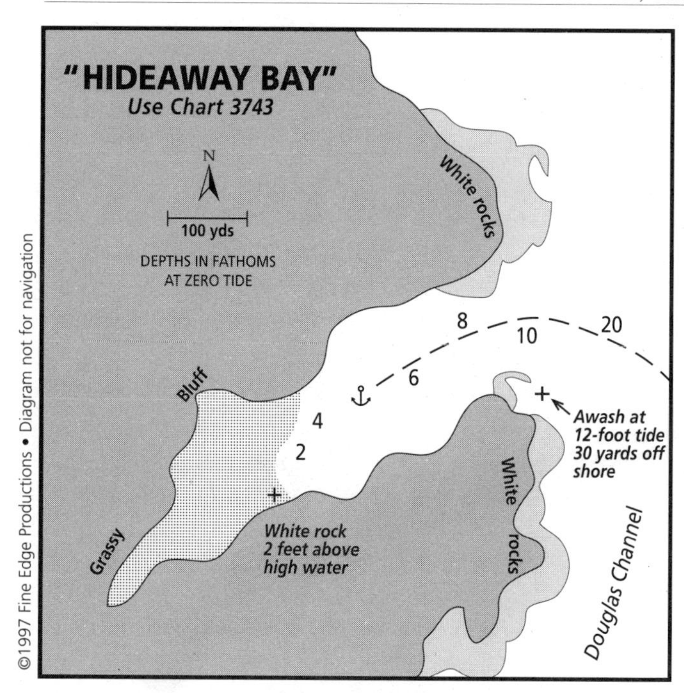

storms or excessive chop in the channel.

White rocks on both sides of the notch mark the entrance point. The head of the notch dries and has a steep-to flat; do not proceed beyond the white-capped rock on the east shore which is 2 feet above high water. The northern half of the bay has a nearly flat 5- to 7-fathom bottom with swinging room for a couple of boats.

Anchor in 6 fathoms over grey mud with shells, good holding.

Miskatla Inlet

Chart 3743; entrance and anchor (fishermen's site): 53°47.85′ N, 128°57.20′ W; anchor (inlet head): 53°51.05′ N, 128°55.10′ W (NAD 27)

Miskatla Inlet has several shoals and drying rocks close to its east shore.

Anchorage can be obtained in mid-channel, about 0.7 mile north of Point Ashton, in 10 to 20 fathoms (18 to 37 m); take care to avoid the shoal water extending from the east shore. The entrance to Miskatla Inlet also affords anchorage in about 15 fathoms (27.4. m). (p. 116, SD)

Miskatla Inlet lies immediately east of Gilttoyees Inlet, and they share a common entrance. The western shore of Miskatla Inlet is high and bold; the eastern shore is lower and flat in places. There may be good anchorage at the head of the inlet in 8 fathoms.

Fishermen report that the charted anchor site at the mouth of Miskatla Inlet provides a pleasant stay during moderate summer weather when there are upslope evening winds.

Anchor (fishermen's site) in 14 fathoms over an unrecorded bottom with good holding.

Gilttoyees Inlet

Chart 3743; entrance: 53°46.20′ N, 128°57.75′ W; anchor (outer anchorage): 53°47.00′ N, 128°57.00′ W (NAD 27)

Gilttoyees Inlet terminates in an extensive drying flat. Gilttoyees Creek flows into the head of the inlet. On the east shore of the inlet, about 0.8 mile north of Point Ashton, shoal water extends 0.2 mile from shore.

Gilttoyees Inlet can be entered on either side of Emilia Island; when using the entrance east of Emilia Island give the 65 foot (20 m) high islet a wide berth to avoid the drying ledge extending SW from it. Small craft can also enter between Point Ashton and the islet. The west shore of Gilttoyees Inlet should be favoured to avoid the shoal water north of Point Ashton. The wooded island, 3 miles north of Point Ashton, should be passed on its west side. (p. 116, SD)

Gilttoyees Inlet is a beautiful inlet with high peaks and steep granite faces above both shores. Snowfields and perpetual icefields hang on the north side of the 4- to 5,000-foot peaks. Alas,

Gilttoyees Inlet

depths in this inlet are too great for convenient anchoring, with little shelter along its sheer walls, although there may be anchorage at the head of the narrow bay halfway up the east shore.

Convenient anchoring can be found in fair weather in the entrance, on a 3-fathom shelf, 0.9 mile north of Point Ashton; protected from downslope winds, this spot is open to the southwest. From here you can conveniently explore Gilttoyees or Miskatla inlets.

Anchor (outer anchorage) in 3 fathoms over a stony bottom with grey silt and broken shells; holding is fair-to-good depending on how well your anchor is set.

Foch Lagoon, Drumlummon Bay

Chart 3743; lagoon entrance:
53°45.85′ N, 129°01.45′ W (NAD 27)

> *Foch Lagoon, at the head of Drumlummon Bay, has a narrow entrance with depths in its fairway of 12 feet (3.7 m). The lagoon can only be entered by small craft at or near slack water; at other times the strength of the tidal streams makes entrance impossible or extremely hazardous. In the entrance to Foch Lagoon HW slack occurs between 30 minutes and 1 hour after HW at Prince Rupert; LW slack can occur as late as 2 hours after LW at Prince Rupert.* (p. 116, SD)

Foch Lagoon, nearly 6 miles long, is one of the largest lagoons on the coast and also one of the best-kept cruising secrets. High granite peaks, with snowfields that melt and cascade into the saltwater, form the backdrop to this lagoon. Islands, islets, cliffs, waterfalls and a major river make Foch Lagoon a destination for cruising boats that want to visit pristine wilderness.

Foch Lagoon, looking out at entrance

The fairway follows a mid-channel course through the narrows, and rocks lie on either side. The very strong currents make control difficult. Arrive early in Drumlummon Bay, anchor, and reconnoiter for slack water for that day's tidal range.

Kitkiata Inlet

Chart 3743; entrance: 53°37.40′ N, 129°14.00′ W (NAD 27)

> *Kitkiata Inlet, 6 miles north of Kiskosh Inlet, is entered between Helen Point and Gertrude Point but most of the inlet is filled with an extensive drying flat. The Quall River flows into the head of the inlet over the drying flat. . . . A waterfall, on the mainland coast about 1.8 miles west of Grant Point, is conspicuous.* (p. 115, SD)

The shore of Kitkiata Inlet is steep-to with little chance for anchoring except off the large drying mud flat. Fishermen report that Kitkiata is an exposed anchorage and not a good choice in doubtful weather. A bridge that crosses the outlet

The Worst Horseflies I've Ever Experienced

I anchored near the mouth of the river in Gilttoyees Inlet in July 1990 and sent a party ashore. While I waited for my crew to return, I used a Dustbuster to vacuum up all the horseflies. By the time Bob and Dan returned, the Dustbuster was full. Even though it was late in the day, I couldn't stand the thought of spending the night there, so we lifted the anchor and moved to the anchorage in the mouth of Miskatla Inlet. As we began to travel, Dan took the Dustbuster to empty it over the side. It was as if he'd opened Pandora's Box. I imagined that I heard the roar of thousands of enraged horseflies as they escaped their prison. What I hadn't imagined was that every one of those horseflies immediately flew back into the wheelhouse and made our lives miserable until they were all in jail again.

But we spent a very pleasant night in Miskatla Anchorage with the summertime breeze blowing up Douglas Channel.

—Captain Kevin Monahan

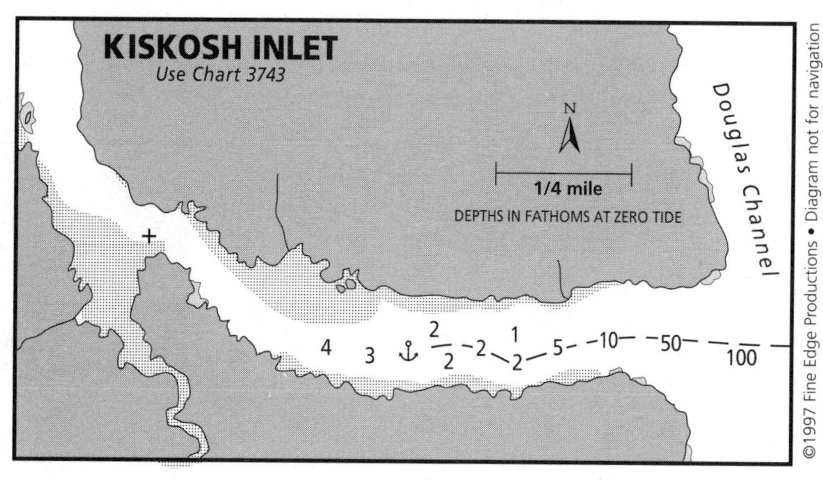

to Kitkiata Creek allows access to the log dump on the north side of the bay.

The waterfall mentioned in *Sailing Directions* is not only conspicuous, it is a majestic sight as it tumbles down, step after step. There is also a perfectly round, U-shaped bowl across the channel from Kihess Creek, and a double waterfall in the next valley north. From Kitkiata Inlet northward, the water in Douglas Channel becomes more opaque from silt and glacier melt.

The Quaal River flows into Kitkiata Inlet's west end. On an 8-foot tide or better, a small outboard-powered boat can travel 8 kilometers upriver; a canoe can travel almost 12; be careful not to get stranded in the river or drying flats on a falling tide. The best time to explore the river is on a rising tide in the morning. And it's worth a visit! It follows a series of oxbows for at least 8 kilometers and its shores are backed by high mountains and bordered by meadows where you might catch sight of a moose.

Kitkiata Inlet is a poor anchorage. At the north side of the inlet, just east of the drying flats, there is an old logging campsite, but it is exposed to up-channel winds.

Kiskosh Inlet

Chart 3743; entrance: 53°30.90′ N, 129°13.90′ W; anchor (on bar): 53°30.86′ N, 129°15.80′ W (NAD 27)

Kiskosh Inlet, with the exception of the first 0.5 mile, is only suitable for small craft. A rock with 6 feet (2 m) over it lies 0.7 mile within the entrance, slightly north of mid-channel. Inside the above-mentioned rock the shores of the inlet are fringed with drying ledges for about 1.5 miles; these drying ledges reduce the channel to less than 0.1 mile wide and the fairway is shallow. A rock with less than 6 feet (2 m) over it lies in mid-channel about 2 miles within the entrance. The inner portion of Kiskosh Inlet widens and depths increase. The entrance to a lagoon at the head of the inlet is choked with drying rocks. (p. 115, SD)

Douglas Channel, as we have said, has only two wind directions—outflow (downchannel) and inflow (upchannel). These winds, along with the strong currents (mostly ebb), can create a sharp, nasty 6-foot chop that makes headway difficult. When this happened to us, we ducked into Kiskosh Inlet and spent a calm afternoon anchored on the inside of the entrance bar.

The inlet is strategically located on the west side of Douglas Channel and provides short-term protection. The entrance bar has a flat 1½- to 2-fathom, sandy bottom. Dropping your lunch hook on the west side of the inlet, just out of the chop, will give you a secure afternoon. When the

Entrance to Kiskosh Lagoon

wind dies or the current lessens, it is easy to move to good shelter in Coghlan Anchorage.

To enter Kiskosh Inlet and cross the 2-mile-long entrance bar, start from a point in the center of the entrance, and head for the far end of the clearcut on the south shore, 1.5 miles. Continue along the treed south shore until you reach the point, avoiding the drying flat that extends halfway from the north shore. (Current here sometimes runs $2^1/_2$ knots or more.) Cross to favor the north shore, heading for a green, brushy patch. Favor the north shore in a northwesterly direction until you reach a clear-cut area and deeper water. This maneuver will avoid the rock and large shoal area on the south shore. Minimum depth in the fairway at the west end of the bay is one fathom at zero tide.

Kiskosh Inlet extends another 4 miles beyond the shallow bar. While the shores have been clearcut near the entrance, there are some outstanding high glacial domes and bowls that make a visit worthwhile.

Anchor (on bar) in about 2 fathoms, sandy bottom with good holding.

"Granite Cove," Kiskosh Inlet

Chart 3743; anchor: 53°33.84′ N, 129°20.76′ W (NAD 27)

The small, remote cove at the foot of a granite bowl southwest of the entrance to the lagoon in Kiskosh Inlet offers shelter from all weather and is a wonderful destination for a wilderness cruising experience. Tucked inside the south point of this cove, you have a magnificent view of the granite mountains towering several thousand feet above. Avoid the uncharted rocks extending about 250 feet from the south point awash on a 9-foot tide.

Kiskosh Lagoon, at the very head of the inlet, becomes a grassy meadow that collects stumps and logs at the foot of another granite bowl. The entrance to the lagoon has a sharp S-shaped turn with rocks that extend to midchannel on both shores. It is a good idea to reconnoiter at low water by inflatable and enter only on slack water when depths are adequate.

Hartley Bay breakwater & public floats

Anchor in Granite Cove in 7 fathoms over a mixed bottom of stones, gravel, and mud, with holding dependent on the set of your anchor.

Hartley Bay

Charts 3711 (inset), 3743; breakwater light: 53°25.44′ N, 129°14.96′ W (NAD 27)

> *Hartley Bay . . . is filled with a drying flat. Hartley Bay Indian settlement has a church and post office. An L-shaped stone breakwater extends over and across the front of the drying flat. A wharf with a small crane and a three fingered float are in a dredged basin behind the breakwater.* (p. 115, SD)

Hartley Bay is a friendly Native settlement with a small but well-protected harbor. Although it is often crowded when the fishing fleet is in, you can raft to other boats. Water is available at the dock; in August 1996, the harbor was beginning a renovation of its facilities, including gasoline and diesel fuel storage tanks and pumps on the dock. The Discovery Coast ferry is scheduled to begin service to Hartley Bay in 1997. There is a fish hatchery at Hartley Bay that you may be able to visit.

Coghlan Anchorage

Charts 3711 (inset), 3742; south entrance: 53°21.90′ N, 129°15.80′ W; north entrance: 53°24.70′ N, 129°14.75′ W; Harbour Rock Light: 53°23.29′ N. 129°16.54′ W; anchor (Otter Shoal): 53°23.82′ N, 129°17.12′ W (NAD 27)

Bella Via *moored in Coghlan Anchorage*

Coghlan Anchorage, on the west side of Promise Island, is entered from Wright Sound between Waterman Point and Thom Point. A drying rock ledge extends about 300 feet (91 m) west from Thom Point.

Anchorage can be obtained near the head of Coghlan Anchorage in 7 to 8 fathoms (13 to 15 m), sand bottom.

Stewart Narrows leads along the north side of Promise Island. Tidal streams in this narrows are strong and the fairway is confined by ledges extending from both shores; it is therefore recommended for small craft only. Public mooring buoys are in the narrows. (p. 112, SD)

Coghlan Anchorage, at the south end of Grenville and Douglas channels, covers a large, loosely defined area that can accommodate a number of anchored craft off the gravel beach on the west side of the channel (Otter Shoal). The bottom is flat at about 5 fathoms with kelp growing along the 2-fathom line. The water is muskeg, and there is little driftwood on shore. Although used principally by fishing boats, we find it convenient on either north- or southbound passages.

If strong southerly winds are expected, you could retreat into Stewart Narrows for more protection against chop. There are currently two public buoys within the narrows that offer good protection from up- or downslope winds; another public buoy is located just north of Brodie Point.

Entry to Coghlan Anchorage can be made from the north via Stewart Narrows or from the south via Wright Sound. South of Brodie Point, avoid Harbour Rock which is passable on either side. Access is easy either day or night, and it's is a good place to wait for correct tide conditions in Grenville Channel.

Anchor (Otter Shoal) in 4 fathoms over sand, gravel, and some kelp with good holding.

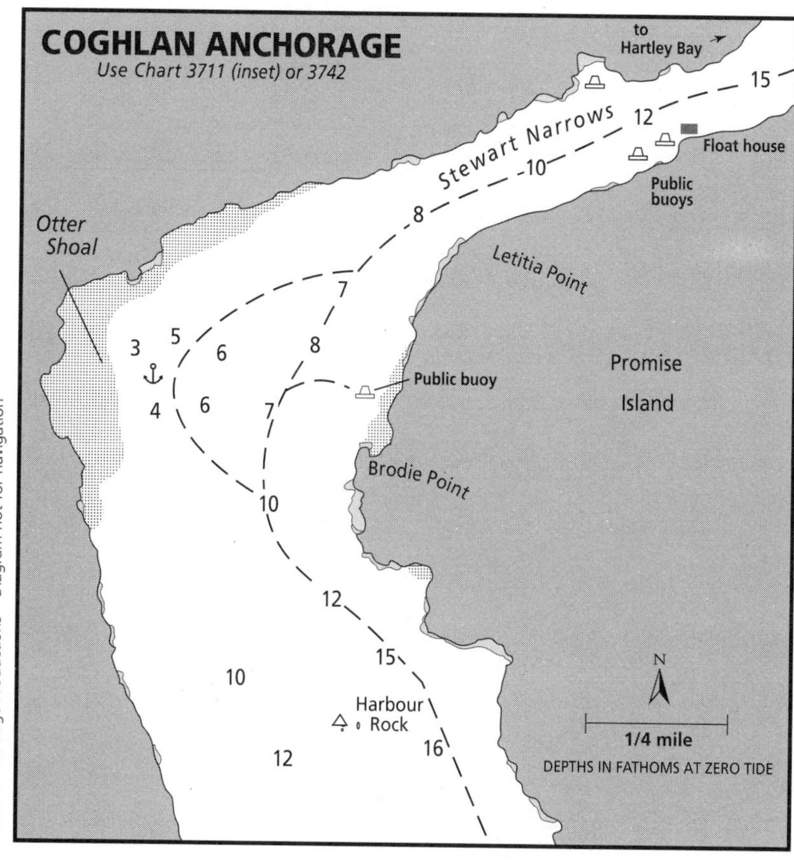

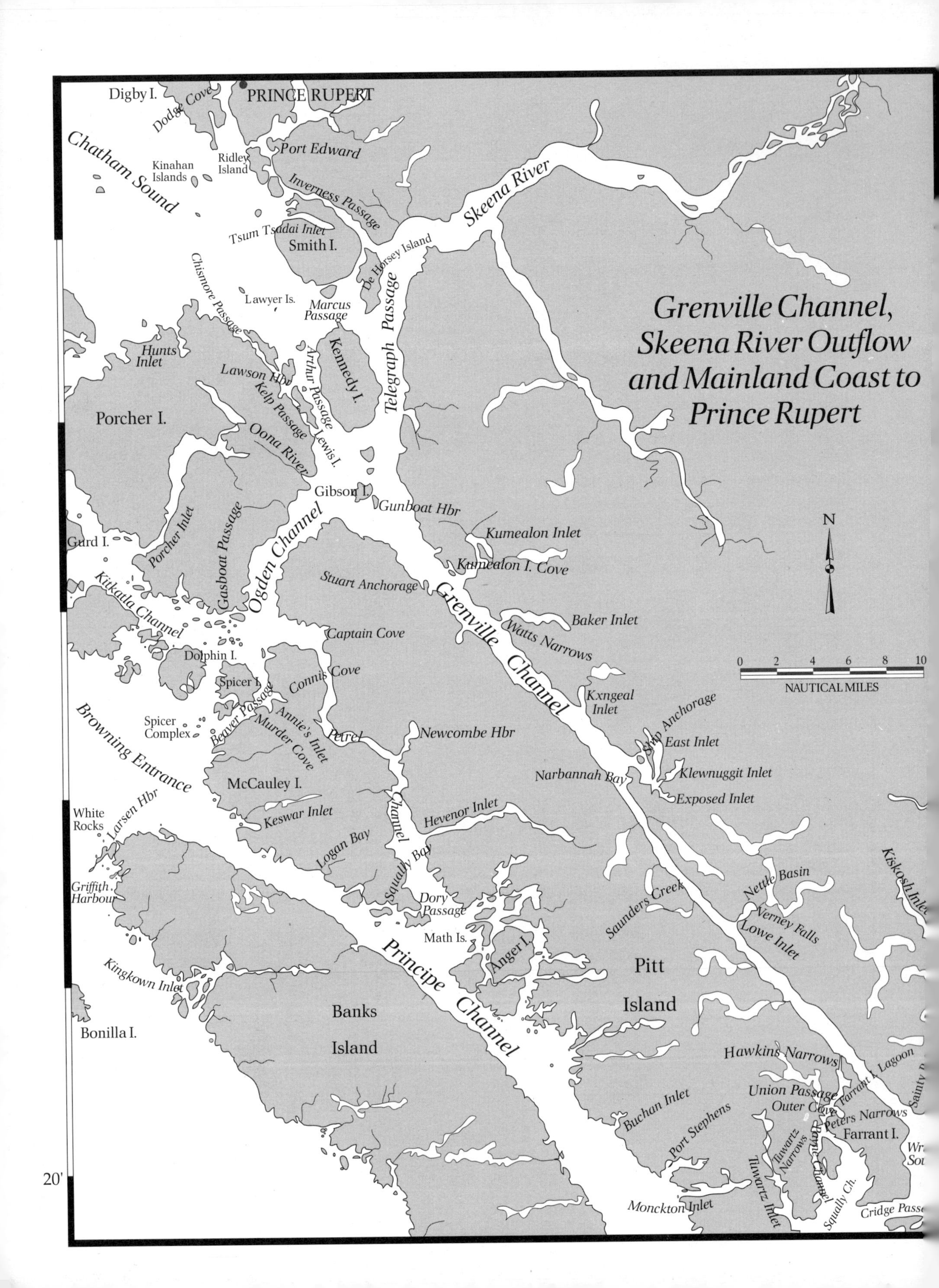

Grenville Channel, Skeena River Outflow and Mainland Coast to Prince Rupert
PRINCE RUPERT
Digby I.
Dodge Cove
Chatham Sound
Kinahan Islands
Ridley Island
Port Edward
Inverness Passage
Skeena River
Tsum Tsadai Inlet
Smith I.
De Horsey Island
Chismore Passage
Lawyer Is.
Marcus Passage
Telegraph Passage
Kennedy I.
Hunts Inlet
Lawson Hbr
Arthur Passage
Kelp Passage
Lewis I.
Porcher I.
Oona River
Gibson I.
Gunboat Hbr
Kumealon Inlet
Kumealon I. Cove
Porcher Inlet
Gasboat Passage
Ogden Channel
Gurd I.
Kitkatla Channel
Stuart Anchorage
Grenville Channel
Baker Inlet
Watts Narrows
Captain Cove
Dolphin I.
Spicer I.
Connis Cove
Kxngeal Inlet
Browning Entrance
Spicer Complex
Beaver Passage
Annie's Inlet
Murder Cove
Petrel
Newcombe Hbr
Ship Anchorage
East Inlet
Klewnuggit Inlet
Narbannah Bay
Exposed Inlet
McCauley I.
White Rocks
Larsen Hbr
Keswar Inlet
Channel
Hevenor Inlet
Logan Bay
Squally Bay
Kiskosh Inlet
Griffith Harbour
Dory Passage
Saunders Creek
Nettle Basin
Verney Falls
Lowe Inlet
Math Is.
Anger I.
Principe Channel
Pitt Island
Kingkown Inlet
Banks Island
Bonilla I.
Hawkins Narrows
Farrant I. Lagoon
Union Passage
Outer Cove
Peters Narrows
Farrant I.
Buchan Inlet
Port Stephens
Tuwartz Narrows
Tuwartz Inlet
Squally Ch.
Moncton Inlet
Cridge Pass
N
0 2 4 6 8 10
NAUTICAL MILES
20'

9

Grenville Channel, Skeena River Outflow and Mainland Coast to Prince Rupert

A crowd-pleaser for passengers of ferryboats and cruise ships, the 45-mile-long Grenville Channel is about as narrow a channel as these large vessels transit on the entire Inside Passage. (The exception is Wrangell Narrows, a man-made, dredged wonder.) Snowmelt from steep, granite peaks feeds waterfalls that tumble a thousand feet, one of the most thrilling sights in upper British Columbia, especially after a heavy rainfall.

Like Johnstone Strait, nearly all traffic travelling this route to and from Alaska must fit into a single channel and, after days of solitude, you may suddenly find yourself in a crowd of vessels. Stay sharp and glance aft frequently to avoid being startled by the sudden blast of a horn! Large commercial and pleasure vessels keep right of center-channel, while low-powered boats normally travel close to the right shore.

As you near Prince Rupert, the waters in Chatham Sound—influenced by the large Skeena River—can be quite choppy. It's a good idea to pre-plot your route across this open stretch in case of decreased visibility.

Wright Sound

Chart 3742; position: 53°20.50′ N, 128°13.00′ W (NAD 27)

> *Wright Sound is the junction of seven channels and forms part of the main Inner Passage leading north toward Alaska. . . . On the north side of Wright Sound, Douglas Channel leads north toward Kitimat and Verney Passage leads NE toward Gardner Canal and Kitimat.* (pp. 108, 112, SD)

Grenville Channel, the "cruise-ship route"

Home Bay

Charts 3740, 3742; anchor:
53°16.29′ N, 129°04.77′ W (NAD 27)

> *Home Bay, in the SE part of Wright Sound, is entered between Swirl Point and Transit Point. A sand flat extends from the head of the bay and a rocky ledge, with above-water heads on it, fringes the south shore.*
>
> *Anchorage for small vessels can be obtained in Home Bay in about 14 fathoms (26 m), sand bottom. . . .* (p. 112, SD)

Home Bay is a large, open bay that offers protection from winds blowing from the south and east quadrants. The bottom is steep-to and the bay is exposed to westerly or northerly winds. It can offer welcome protection in southeast blows.

Anchor in about 10 fathoms over sand and some eel grass with fair-to-good holding.

Fisherman Cove

Chart 3742; position: 53°19.55′ N, 129°16.70′ W (NAD 27)

> *Fisherman Cove, at the north end of Gil Island, lies between Turtle Point and Blackfly Point. Most of the cove dries.*
>
> *Anchorage off the entrance to Fisherman Cove is indifferent and not recommended because of the steep drop-off in depths.* (p. 112, SD)

Fisherman Cove, used by Vancouver over 200 years ago, is open to chop from Wright Sound and offers little protection. It can serve as a lunch stop in fair weather. Large boats can anchor in 15 fathoms off the steep-to beach; small boats can anchor temporarily over the drying mud flat, visible in 12 feet of water. The bottom is composed of small stones, sand, and shells, with some grass; fair holding.

Grenville Channel

Charts 3772, 3773; south entrance: 53°22.00′ N, 129°19.00′ W; north entrance: 53°55.25′ N, 130°11.00′ W (NAD 27)

> *Grenville Channel, which leads 45 miles NW from Wright Sound, is part of the main Inner Passage route leading north toward Alaska.*
>
> *At springs the streams in the narrow portion of Grenville Channel attain 2 kn. The ebb streams continue to run for 1h.30min. after LW by the shore. Strong eddies can be encountered abreast Lowe Inlet with the ebb stream.* (p. 118, SD)

Keep a sharp lookout for logs in Grenville Channel!

Grenville Channel has the appearance of a classic fjord and seldom gets serious seas. However, the ebb currents can be strong. To take advantage of the currents, start your transit on the last of the flood. As you approach Klewnuggit Inlet, pick up the first of the ebb current and let it carry you the rest of the way through Grenville Channel.

Don't let yourself or your crew become overcome by the natural beauty. A large amount of drift logs and debris, as well as shoals near Morning Reef, present lurking hazards.

For sheltered anchorages along the way, Union Passage, Lowe Inlet, East Inlet and Baker Inlet are all popular overnighters. The hike along the trail above Verney Falls in Nettle Basin is worth a stop in itself.

Sainty Point Cove, (known as Camp Point), position: 53°22.43' N, 129°18.30' W, in the southeast entrance of Grenville Channel, has a good kayak haul-out beach on its northwest side and is a good place to wait if current in Grenville Channel is contrary. This is a useful anchorage in northwest winds. The bottom is good.

Mosley Point, 9 miles northwest of Sainty Point, position: 53°28.40' N, 129°29.00' W, offers a very good kayak campsite and haul-out beach.

As Captain Kevin Monahan writes: "Wright Sound, along with Whale and Squally channels, forms an extension of Douglas Channel and its weather systems. Wright Sound can be especially ugly just prior to the approach of a Pacific depression. As pressures fall, offshore outflow conditions are generated in Douglas Channel. As the storm approaches and southeast winds spring up along the outer coast, these southeast winds travel up Whale and Squally channels and meet the continuing outflow winds from Douglas Channel. At these times Wright Sound experiences very confused wind and wave conditions. Strong outgoing tidal currents can add to this and create dangerous seas. The tidal currents are almost always outgoing! Sometime later, as the depression crosses the coast, the winds in Douglas Channel reverse and the conditions in Wright Sound moderate somewhat.

See *Marine Weather Hazards of the B.C. Coast*, published by Environment Canada and available where charts are sold."

Union Passage, Hawkins Narrows

Chart 3722; north entrance:
53°24.74′ N, 129°24.90′ W; anchor:
53°24.90′ N, 129°25.24′ W (NAD 27)

Union Passage, between Farrant and Pitt Islands, leads from the north end of Squally Channel into Grenville Channel.

Hawkins Narrows, at the north end of Union Passage, has a least depth of 7 feet (2.1 m) in the fairway. A shoal rock is in the south entrance of Hawkins Narrows and another is 0.1 mile north. (pp. 187, 188, SD)

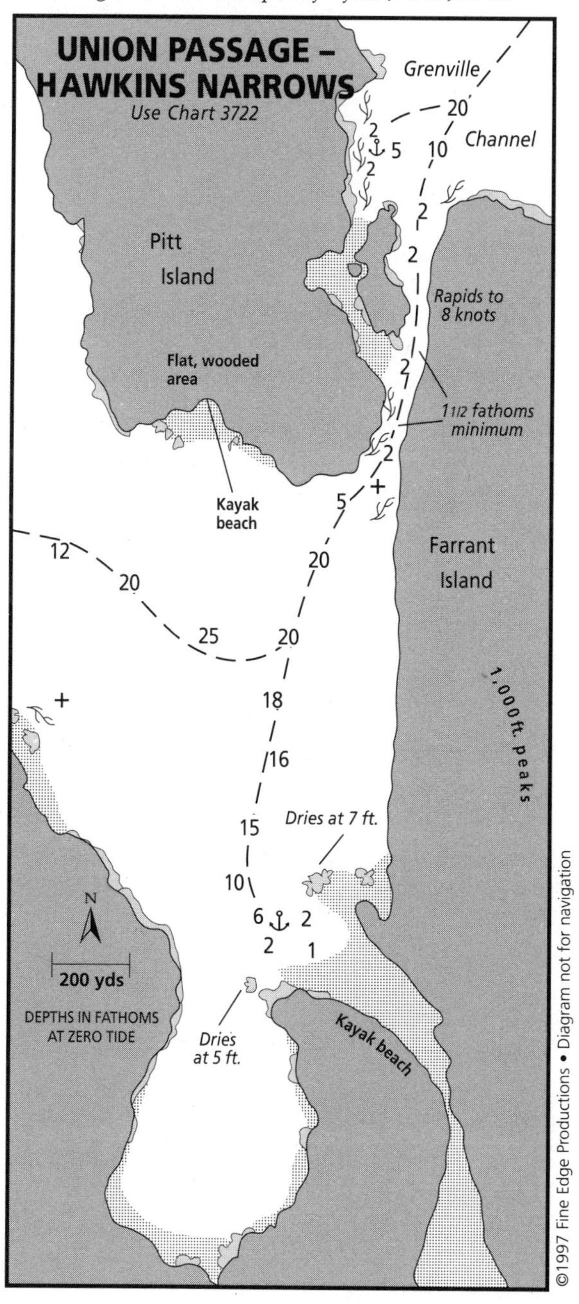

Union Passage is a place few cruising boats visit. Both its northeast and southwest entrances are narrow and shallow, and *Sailing Directions* makes it sound as if you have only five minutes every six hours to enter or exit. While at springs this may be true, we've found that the window of easy access is quite wide most of the month. Since you can see bottom all the way through the narrows itself, it is a good place to head if you're looking for sheltered waters or to do some exploring.

The entry to Hawkins Narrows is difficult to locate because Davenport Point is rather inconspicuous. Farrant Island, on the south shore of the narrows, has a 1,130-foot peak that provides a landmark. Pitt Island, to the north, is a low, flat 200-foot-high peninsula. Hawkins Narrows is the slit that heads back toward the southwest between the two landmarks.

If this is your first visit to the area, you may want to approach Hawkins Narrows on the last of the ebb, which flows north, in order to maintain steerage and be able to back out if you wish. We've found about 1.5 fathoms minimum at zero tide through the fairway.

Favor the east shore in the middle of the narrows, then the west shore as soon as the bay starts to open up. The sides of the narrows are steep-to and the shoal rocks indicated on the chart are not evident.

There is a landing beach with a primitive campsite on the north point where kayakers could pass the night. The shores are covered with old-growth forest and appear to be undisturbed by man. Protection from southerlies can be found against the south shore, as indicated in the diagram.

Anchor in 6 fathoms over a mud bottom with fair holding

Farrant Island Lagoon

Chart 3772; entrance: 53°23.22′ N, 129°26.72′ W;
anchor: 53°22.76′ N, 129°26.03′ W (NAD 27)

The south end of Union Passage, constricted due

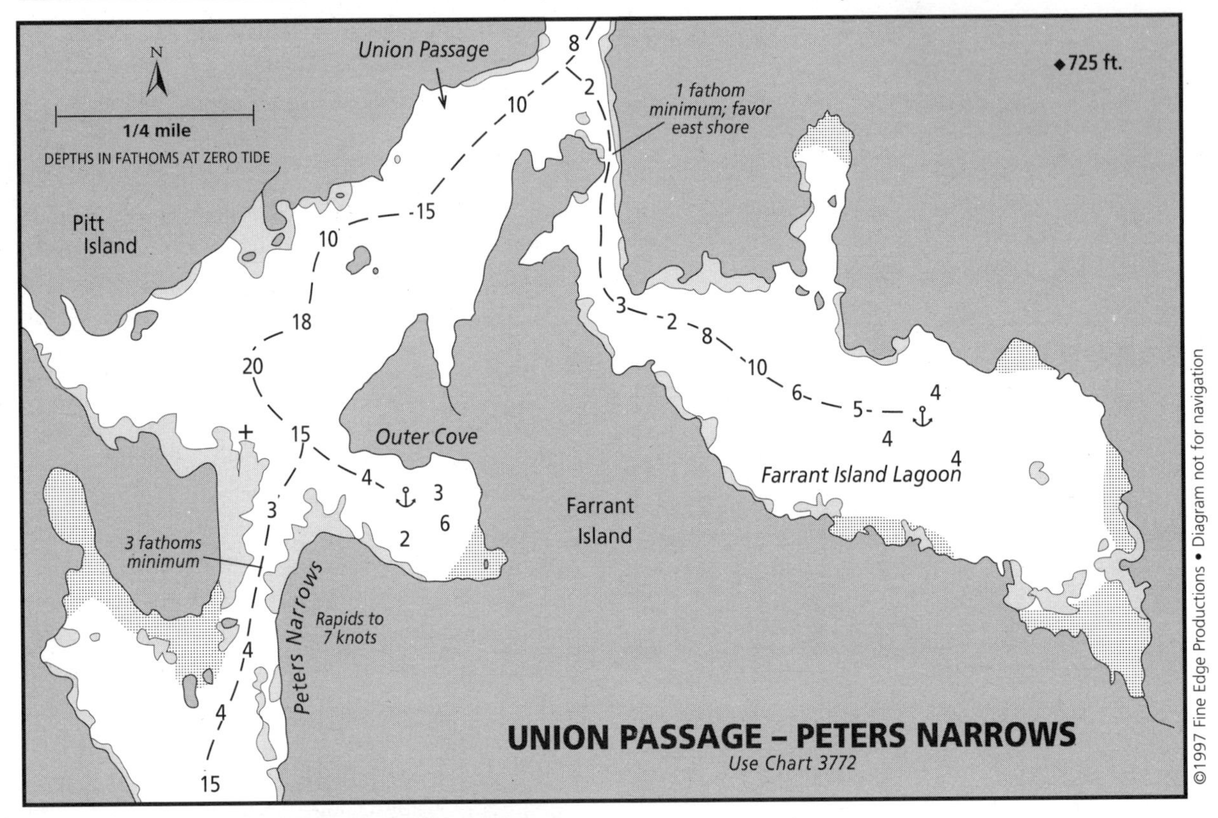

Verney Falls, Lowe Inlet

west of hill 725, has a depth of 6 to 8 fathoms. Just below this constriction, there is a small channel leading due south to Farrant Island lagoon. The tidal currents meet just north of the lagoon.

When entering the lagoon, favor the east shore which is steep-to. Minimum depth in the fairway is about one fathom at zero tide. The channel opens to the east in what must be one of the most remote and sheltered anchorages along the shores of the Inside Passage.

With the exception of a small 10-fathom hole, the entire lagoon has a flat 5-fathom bottom. There is plenty of swinging room, and the level tree branches along the high-tide line indicate that this cove sees hardly a ripple.

Anchor in 5 fathoms over a mud bottom with good holding.

"Outer Cove"

Chart 3772; south entrance:
53°22.39′ N, 129°27.42′ W; anchor (outer cove):
53°22.65′ N, 129° 27.05′ W (NAD 27)

The next cove south, which we call Outer Cove, is easy to enter and offers splendid shelter as well. Avoid the grassy islet in the center of Outer Cove as you enter. The chart indicates that the islet dries at 19 feet, but our observations indicate 15 feet. Logging floats formerly located in the cove were absent in summer of 1996.

The outlet of 2-mile long Tsimtack Lake lies on the west shore, just north of Peters Narrows.

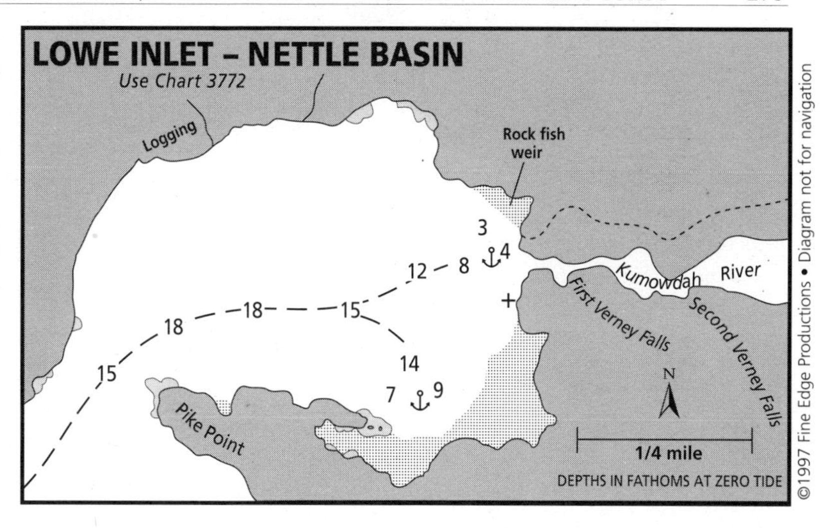

Anchor in 6 fathoms in the center of the cove over sand, mud, and logger's trash (an old pair of Levis!) bottom with good holding.

Peters Narrows

Chart 3772; position: 53°22.62′ N, 129°27.38′ W (NAD 27)

> *Tidal streams in Peters Narrows attain a maximum of about 7 kn and in Hawkins Narrows about 8 kn. Slack water in Hawkins Narrows occurs 15 minutes before HW and LW at Prince Rupert; duration of slack is about 5 minutes. The ebb flows north in Hawkins Narrows and south in Peters Narrows.* (p. 188, SD)

Peters Narrows is very much like Hawkins Narrows, but the flow rate is less.

Nettle Basin, Lowe Inlet (Verney Falls)

Chart 3772; entrance: 53°32.50′ N, 129°35.85′ W; anchor (Verney Falls): 53°33.60′ N, 129°33.93′ W; anchor (Nettle Basin): 53°33.43′ N, 129°34.06′ W (NAD 27)

> *Lowe Inlet is entered between Hepburn Point and James Point. . . .*
>
> *Kumowdah River flows into the east end of Nettle Basin over Verney Falls and drains Lowe Lake.*
>
> *Anchorage can be obtained in Lowe Inlet about 0.2 mile SW of Pike Point in 17 fathoms (31 m). Small craft can anchor close inshore south of Don Point or in Nettle Basin, close to the north side of Pike Point.* (pp. 118, 119, SD)

For years, Nettle Basin in Lowe Inlet has been a popular overnight anchorage for cruising boats. When Verney Falls doubles in height at low tide, you have a spectacular photo opportunity. For a nice hike, you can take the rough but passable trail that starts on the north shore and passes the first and second falls on its way to Lowe Lake.

When you land your dinghy on the north shore, check out the gravel beach where there is an ancient rock fish weir. The lake trail starts from the east side of the beach. Since bears like to poke around the drying flats on the south side of Nettle Basin, keep your binoculars handy. (The first time we went ashore here, we missed the trail and ran smack into a bear's den—empty, thank goodness!)

We like to anchor in the fast-moving stream below the falls for the full view, but the bottom is gravel with just fair holding so we need to set our anchor well. There's a quieter anchorage in the less-exposed south end of Nettle Basin; the bottom there has better holding power. You also get a better view of the wildlife that combs the grassy shore.

Anchor (Verney Falls) in 5 fathoms over a gravel bottom with a strong westerly current and poor-to-fair holding power.

Anchor (Nettle Basin) in 10 to 12 fathoms over a mud bottom with good holding.

Nabannah Bay

Chart 3772; entrance (north):
53°40.75′ N, 129°46.00′ W; anchor (southeast corner): 53°40.30′ N, 129°45.34′ W (NAD 27)

> *Nabannah Bay, 4.5 miles NW of Saunders Creek light, between Evening Point and Morning Point, is fronted by Barrier Rock which has drying reefs extending NW and SE.*
>
> *Morning Reef extends 0.3 mile NW of Morning Point and consists of several drying rocks and some rocks with less than 6 feet (2 m) over them.* (p. 119, SD)

Nabannah Bay, between Morning Point and Evening Point, is largely protected from the chop of Grenville Channel by Morning Reef and Barrier Rock. It makes a convenient lunch stop or a place to wait until the current in Grenville Channel starts to ebb. (The tides meet in this vicinity.)

The safest way to enter Nabannah Bay is from the north, passing just east of the Morning Reef light. The fairway has a minimum of 5 fathoms; however, you need a sharp lookout to avoid the various kelp patches that mark the reef.

You can land a dinghy on the small gravel beach on the east side of the bay, but you need to avoid the uncharted rock about 100 feet from the shore, awash on an 8-foot tide.

A narrow dinghy pass, choked with kelp, about one-fathom deep at zero tide, exists between Evening Point and the southernmost tip of Barrier Rock. This pass can be used by small vessels near high water. Visibility in the water is about 6 feet.

Large boats can find anchorage in the southeast corner of the bay over a flat 10-fathom bottom, while small boats may want to use the nook on the north side between two kelp patches over a 4- to 6-fathom bottom.

Anchor (southeast corner) in 10 fathoms over a mixed bottom of sand, stones, and kelp, poor-to-fair holding.

Anchor (north nook) in 6 fathoms off kayak haul-out and campsite

Saunders Creek, position: 53°36.15′ N, 129°42.39′ W, 4 miles south of Nabannah Bay on the west shore below a high waterfall, has a good haul-out beach and campsite. There are also two campsites on the opposite shore, between one and two miles to the south.

Klewnuggit Inlet

Chart 3772; entrance: 53°41.40′ N, 129°45.20′ W (NAD 27)

> *Klewnuggit Inlet is entered between Rogers Point and Silas Point.* (p. 119, SD)

Where the tidal currents of Grenville Channel meet just outside the entrance to Klewnuggit Inlet, a line of flotsam frequently marks the division point. Morning Reef is a foul area and should be given wide berth.

Ship Anchorage

Chart 3772; entrance: 53°41.20′ N, 129°43.90′ W (NAD 27)

> *Ship Anchorage lies to the east and north of*

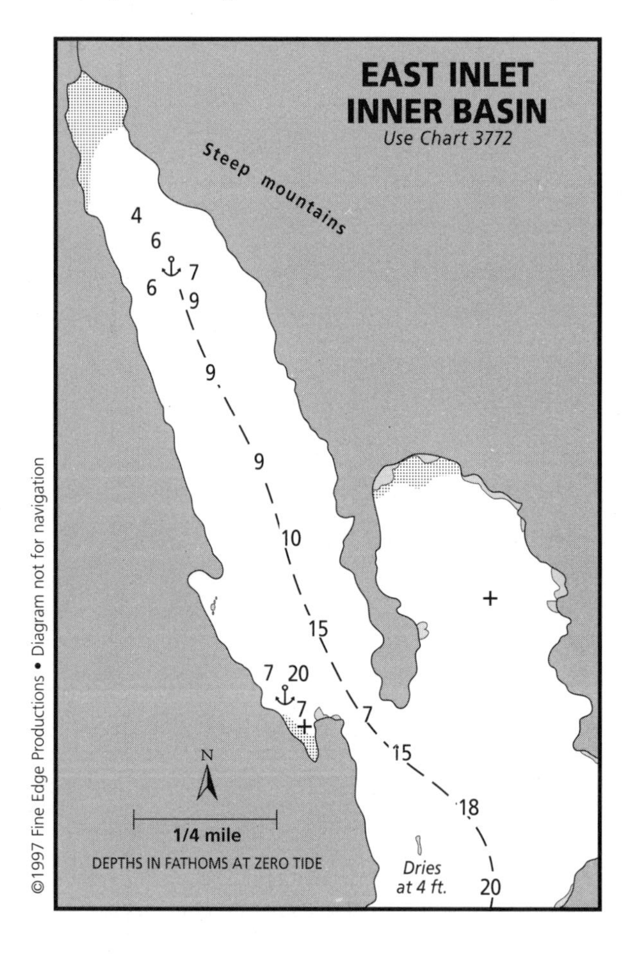

Harriot Island. . . . Small vessels can obtain anchorage in Ship Anchorage off the NE side of Harriot Island in 21 fathoms (38 m), mud bottom. (p. 119, SD)

Since we haven't met a cruising vessel yet that would choose to anchor in over 140 feet of water at high tide, we recommend that you bypass Ship Anchorage and head southeast, then up to the top of East Inlet.

Exposed Inlet

Chart 3772; entrance: 53°40.00′ N, 129°42.90′ W; position: 53°39.80′ N, 129°42.50′ W (NAD 27)

Exposed Inlet, at the south end of Klewnuggit Inlet, terminates in a swamp fronted by drying sand flats. (p. 119, SD)

Exposed Inlet is exposed to prevailing northwest winds but is acceptable in fair weather or southerlies. Take a look at the unusual outlet of Freda and Brodie Lake on the east shore of Exposed Inlet.

East Inlet, Inner Basin

Chart 3772; entrance: 53°40.33′ N, 129°42.96′ W; anchor (inner basin): 53°42.87′ N, 129°43.51′ W (NAD 27)

East Inlet has drying reefs and shoal rocks near the head. When entering, note the shoal water extending from the west entrance point. The basin at the NW end of East Inlet west of a relatively low peninsula; its entrance is about 300 feet (91m) wide with a depth of 46 feet (14m) through it.

Anchorage can be obtained at the south end of East Inlet in 15 fathoms (27.4m). Small craft can obtain well sheltered anchorage in the basin at the head of East Inlet in 9 fathoms (16.5m). (p.119, SD)

The inner basin of East Inlet, protected from channel winds in calm waters, is a natural shelter for cruising boats, and there's enough swinging room for a whole yacht club. The view of the high peaks to the north and the east are splendid but at times williwaws may roar down these mountains, so be prepared to let out plenty of anchor rode if you hear their scream. To obtain shelter from southerly chop, tuck in behind the west point of the narrows.

Entry into the inner basin is easy, and the five miles to the anchor site at the head is a lovely trip. Avoid the rock which dries a quarter-mile southeast of Inner Basin narrows.

Anchor (inner basin) in 7 fathoms over a mud bottom with good holding.

Kxngeal Inlet

Chart 3772; entrance: 53°44.05′ N, 129°49.45′ W; anchor (beach): 53°45.22′ N, 129°49.35′ W (NAD 27)

Ormand Point has a drying reef lying 0.2 mile SE. . . . Kxngeal Inlet is entered east of the above-mentioned reef. . . . Anchorage for small vessels can be obtained in 17 fathoms (31 m) near the head of Kxngeal Inlet. (p. 119, SD)

Kxngeal Inlet is easily accessible from Grenville Channel and offers shelter from north-and south-blowing winds and chop found in the channel. Avoid the dangerous reef mentioned above in *Sailing Directions.* Poorly marked by kelp, it is awash on a 16-foot tide. The fairway north of the rock has a minimum of 11 fathoms.

The inlet can be a welcome relief from the chop of Grenville Channel. Although its shores have been largely clear-cut to the high-tide line in the past several decades, second growth has begun to take hold. On a sunny day, with the high peaks visible above to the east, it can be quite pleasant.

The head of the inlet shows few signs that serious chop enters. Small boats can anchor over the drying flat with appropriate tide level, or on the sloping bottom just off the flat in about 6 fathoms. Larger boats can anchor anywhere in the center of the bay.

Anchor (beach) in 6 fathoms off the steep-to beach in sand, mud, and shells with fair-to-good holding.

Watts Narrows

Chart 3772 (inset); west entrance: 53°48.65′ N, 129°57.23′ W; east entrance: 53°49.00′ N, 129°56.85′ W (NAD 27)

Watts Narrows is about 200 feet (61 m) wide and screened by overhanging trees; the least depth in the fairway is 10 fathoms (18.3 m).

Entrance to Watts Narrows

> *Tidal streams in Watts Narrows attain a considerable rate. HW and LW slack occur about the times of HW and LW at Prince Rupert; the duration of slack water is about 5 minutes.*
> (p. 119, SD)

Watts Narrows, the entrance to Baker Inlet, is a special place to seek beauty and solitude. We seldom pass it without a quick run inside to see our "old friend."

Watts Narrows

Old-growth trees line the shore and create a rich canopy overhead. The winding channel with its turbulent but deep waters flooding in or out is magical. The sides of the channel are fairly steep-to but the rocky shore causes the water to "boil" a bit.

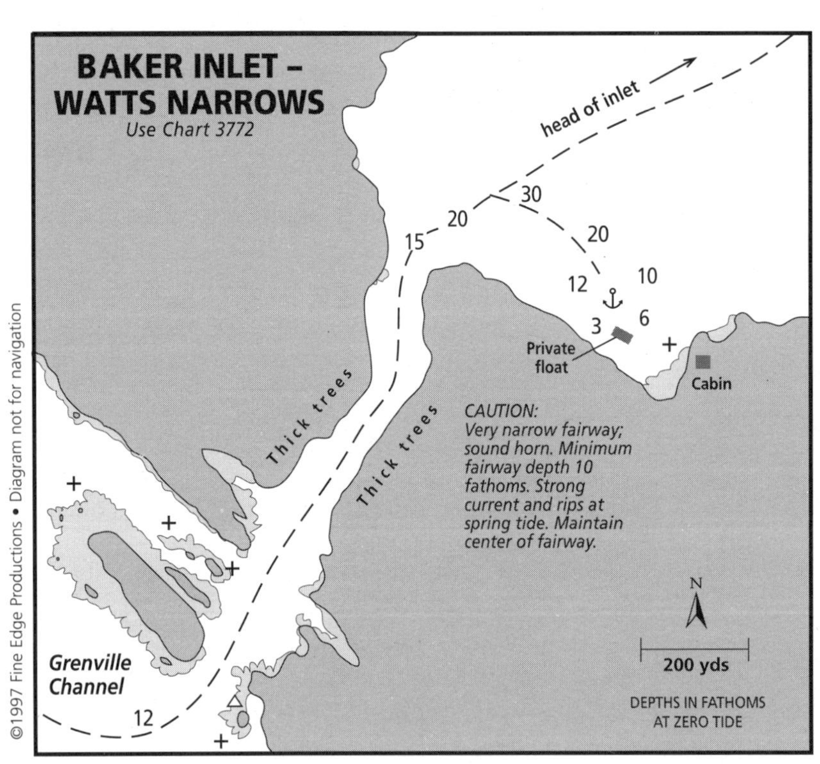

Caution: Watts Narrows has limited visibility and sharply-restricted maneuvering room in the fairway. We always sound our horn upon entering and again halfway through. We also post alert lookouts on the bow and keep a finger on the button of our horn in case we see or hear an opposing boat. While the helmsman must respond quickly to stay in midchannel, no special techniques are required. The minimum depth in the fairway is 10 fathoms and, if the turbulence disturbs the readings of your echo sounder, don't be alarmed; you'll be fine as long as you maintain a near-midchannel route. If you feel anxiety during your approach to the entrance, wait until slack water when you feel more comfortable. Watts Narrows is a memorable experience, but it needn't give you white knuckles!

Baker Inlet

Charts 3772 (inset), 3773; anchor (south bight): 53°48.98′ N, 129°56.65′ W; anchor (inlet head): 53°48.52′ N, 129 51.08′ W (NAD 27)

Baker Inlet is entered close north of Griffon Point by way of Watts Narrows. Anchorage for small craft can be found at the head of the inlet in 11 fathoms (20 m).
(p. 119, SD)

Baker Inlet is one of the most well-protected anchorages in Grenville Channel. You can find shelter from all weather inside this scenic basin. Except for an unattractive clearcut on the south shore near the middle of the inlet, well-developed second-growth trees line the entire inlet. Perpetual snowfields tower high above Alvin Lake to 3,600 feet. At sea level, tree limbs extend over the water in a perfectly horizontal line, giving testimony to the calmness of the basin. At the head of the inlet, behind a treed island, there is a lovely, serene basin where you can look up to glacier-scarred alpine slopes. The head of Baker Inlet is a special place. Wolves howl at night and bears roam the grassy margins of the drying mud flat. A pair of resident loons patrol the shore. The large creek dropping from Alvin Lake lulls you to sleep. To ensure silence, broken only by the rushing creek water, there is no radio reception at the head of the inlet.

While depths in the inlet range from 30 to 50 fathoms, small boats can find many spots to anchor near shore along shoaling banks. This is a perfect place to linger before entering the busy major ports ahead. Avoid the numerous small crab-pot floats.

If you want to be close to Grenville Channel, you can anchor in the small bight to the south just past the narrows, off an old float. Otherwise you can continue to the head of the inlet, behind the treed islet, and anchor off the drying flat. Kayakers will find a good anchor spot across the channel at the outlet of Pa-aat River.

Head of Baker Inlet

Caution: We once snagged our anchor on a nylon line in the south bight.

Anchor (south bight) over a 7-fathom mud bottom with fair holding.

Anchor (head of the inlet) over a 9-fathom mud bottom with good holding.

Kumealon Inlet

Chart 3773; entrance: 53°51.00′ N, 130°01.00′ W; anchor (east shore): 53°51.96′ N, 129°58.27′ W (NAD 27)

When entering Kumealon Inlet from south take care to avoid drying reefs and foul ground extending 0.2 mile offshore south of McMurray Point. An islet, a group of drying reefs, and rocks with less than 6 feet (2 m) over them lie about 1 mile within the entrance.

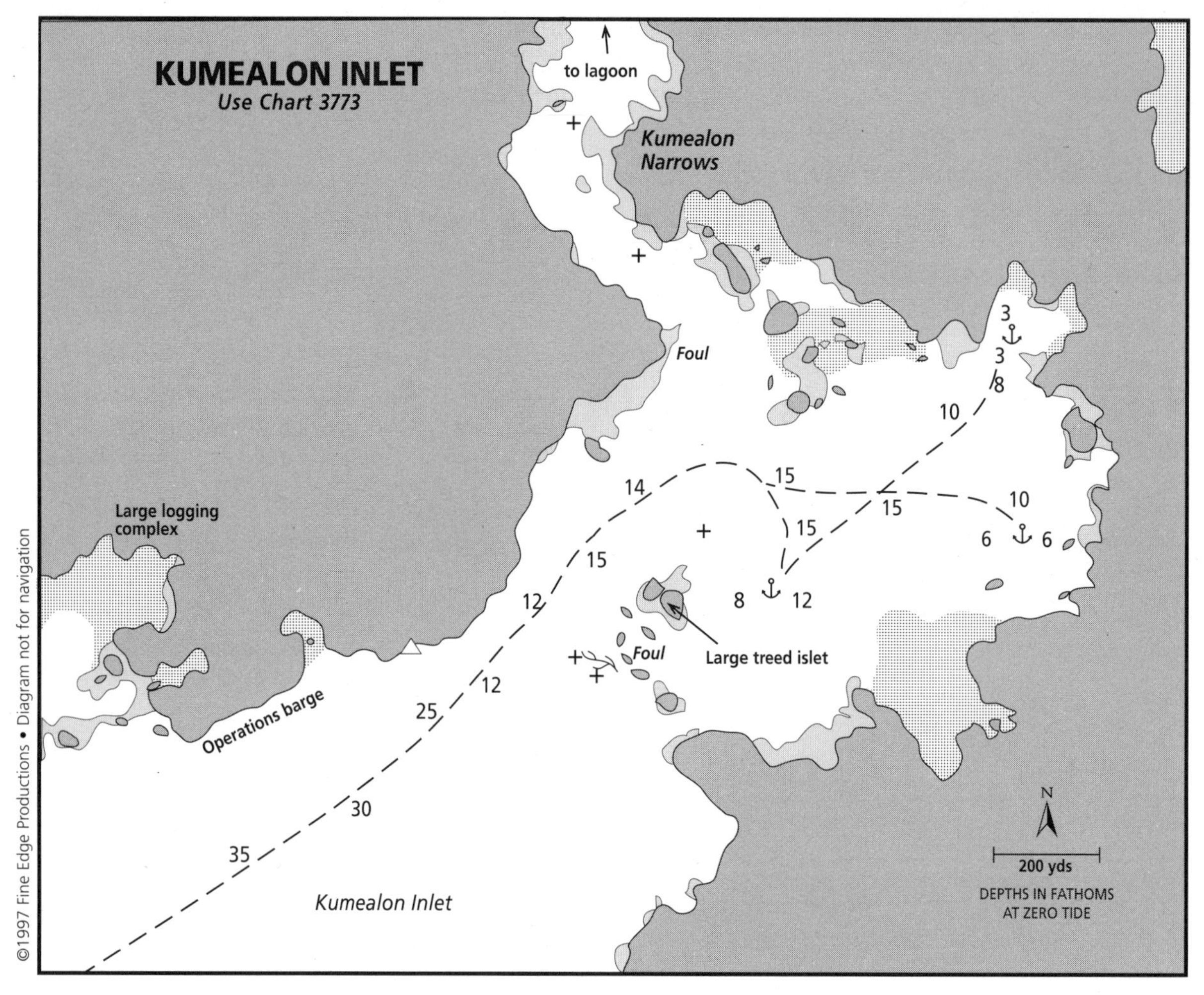

Anchorage can be obtained about 0.8 mile within the entrance of Kumealon Inlet in 30 fathoms (55 m). Small craft can with the aid of local knowledge, proceed past the rocks in mid-channel and anchor near the east end of the inlet.

Kumealon Narrows leads north from the head of Kumealon Inlet into Kumealon Lagoon. The narrows is a shallow and winding channel, encumbered with rocks, with tidal falls at its north end. (pp. 119, 120, SD)

Kumealon Inlet inner basin

Kumealon Inlet, on the northeast corner of Grenville Channel, is a scenic inlet dotted with small tree-covered islands and islets, with an intricate channel into Kumealon Lagoon at its head. The eastern shore of the inner basin provides good protection in most weather. Upon entering the basin at the head of the inlet, favor the north shore until you have passed the treed islet in the center; avoid the group of rocks from the center to the south shore.

Although you could be put off from entering the inlet by the large logging operation that fills the northern cove just inside the entrance, deeper

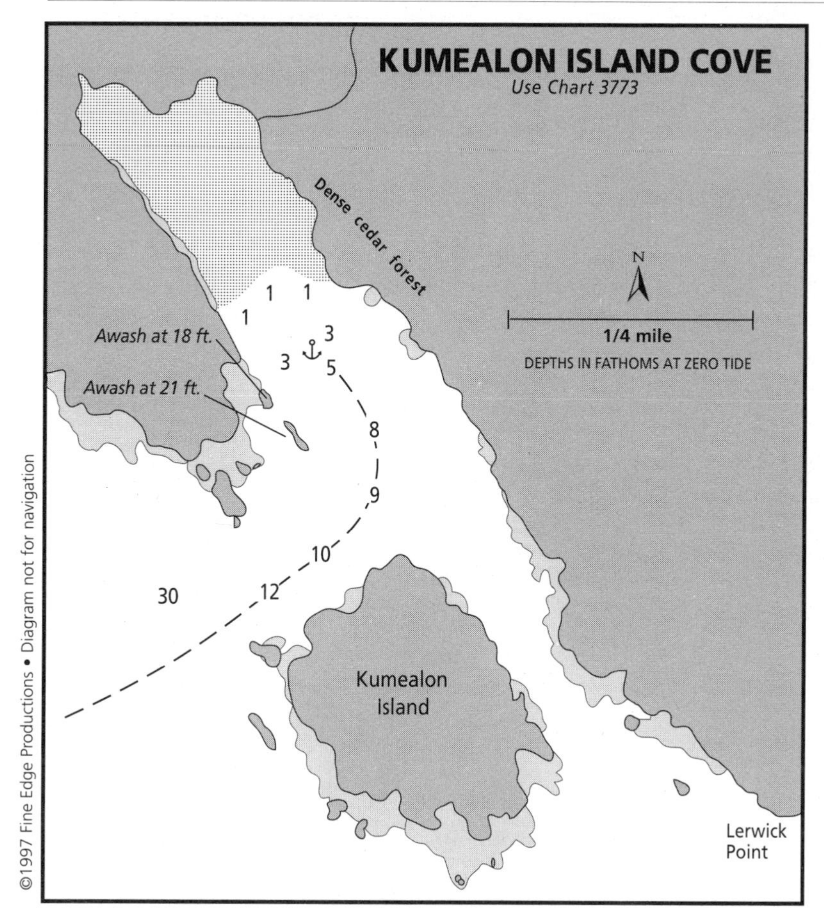

There is a small 5- to 6-fathom shelf on the eastern shore of the basin where one or two boats can find good shelter. Larger vessels can anchor in the center of the basin in 12 to 15 fathoms.

Anchor (east shore) in 5 to 6 fathoms over a grey mud bottom with very good holding.

in the inlet you can quickly find a snug anchorage. Seals swimming in the basin seem unperturbed by the logging camp. The shores of the lagoon have been extensively logged; however, the shores of the inlet remain attractive.

Kumealon Island Cove

Chart 3773; entrance:
53°51.52′ N, 130°01.73′ W;
anchor: 53°51.74′ N, 130°01.53′ W
(NAD 27)

Kumealon Island, 0.3 mile west of Lerwick Point, shelters a small cove to the north which is suitable anchorage for small craft.
(p. 120, SD)

The cove north of Kumealon Island provides excellent shelter from northerly winds and chop and gives good, quiet protection from southerly winds and chop. (One sleepless night, anchored in Kelp Passage Cove, we experienced 50-knot southeast gusts and were hanging on maximum scope. Twenty miles to the southeast, friends anchored in Kumealon Island Cove reported 10- to 20-knot winds and no discomfort.) Kumealon Island Inlet has a large, ongoing logging operation.

Since the head of the cove dries rapidly, allow for a variation of more than 3 fathoms in tide level when you set your anchor.

Anchor in 6 fathoms over a sand and mud bottom with good holding.

Laredo *at anchor, Kumealon Inlet*

Stuart Anchorage

Chart 3773; entrance:
53°51.56′ N, 130°04.27′ W;
anchor (westernmost cove):
53°51.10′ N, 130°04.46′ W (NAD 27)

Stuart Anchorage is 1 mile NW of Bonwick Point and 0.4 mile NW of

Stuart Anchorage

> *Stag Rock. A ridge of foul ground extends 0.3 mile NW of Stag Rock and a drying rock lies 0.1 mile south of it . . .* (p. 120, SD)

Stuart Anchorage provides shelter for large vessels west of Stag Rock next to Pitt Island.

The first cove immediately west of Bonwick Point is fouled by a large center rock and patches of kelp. It can be used only by small boats under 30 feet, and they must use a stern tie to shore on the south side of the center group of rocks.

We prefer the second small cove, west of Bonwick Point against Pitt Island, which offers good shelter from southeast winds or chop that blow up Grenville Channel. There are several isolated rocks in the anchorage that must be avoided; most are well marked by kelp in the summer. Stag Rock, which dries on an 18-foot tide, makes a good leading mark to identify the anchorage as you approach from the north.

This westernmost cove can be used for secure anchorage for two or three small craft. The bottom remains flat at 6 to 8 fathoms for about 400 yards. The head of the cove is grassy, with easy dinghy access and primitive campsites for kayakers.

Anchor (westernmost cove) in 6 to 8 fathoms over a grey mud bottom with very good holding.

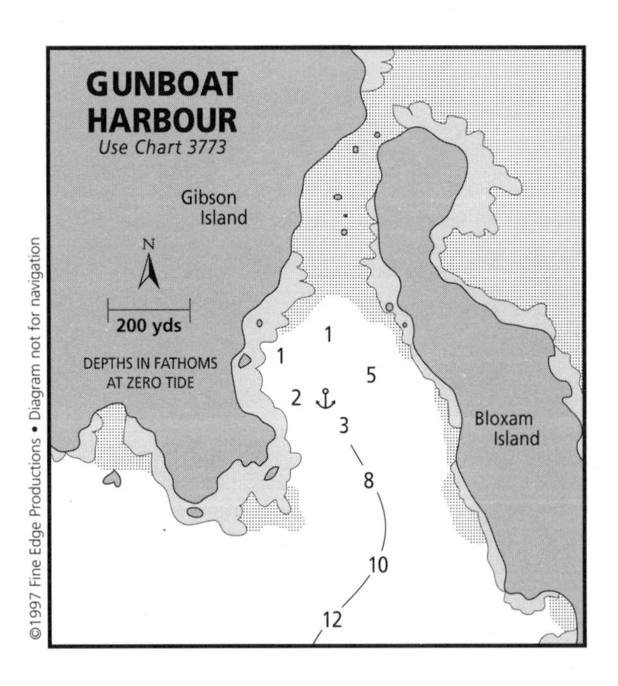

Gunboat Harbour

Chart 3773; entrance: 53°55.18′ N, 130°08.51′ W; anchor: 53°55.38′ N, 130°08.56′ W (NAD 27)

> *Gunboat Harbour lies between the SE side of Gibson Island and Bloxam Island. It affords temporary anchorage to small vessels in about 3 fathoms (5.5m) off the drying flat near its head.* (p. 120, SD)

Gunboat Harbour is a good, short rest stop where you can wait out the chop that occurs 2 miles to the north or find protection from prevailing northwesterlies or northeast outflow winds. Since it's completely open to the south, it would not provide shelter in a southerly storm.

Due to the outflow of the Skeena River from the east, the color of the water in the vicinity of Gibson Island changes to opaque beige. South of Kennedy Island, a moderate southwest wind against the strong, 3-knot ebb current from the Skeena River can cause nasty chop on your beam.

Anchor in 3 fathoms over a sand and gravel bottom with fair holding.

Oona River

Chart 3773; entrance: 53°56.44′ N, 130°14.13′ W (NAD 27)

> *Oona River flows from the interior of Porcher Island. . . . The mouth of the river is filled with a broad drying flat.*
>
> *A large rock breakwater extends from the south shore of the entrance to Oona River. This breakwater shelters a basin that has been dredged to a*

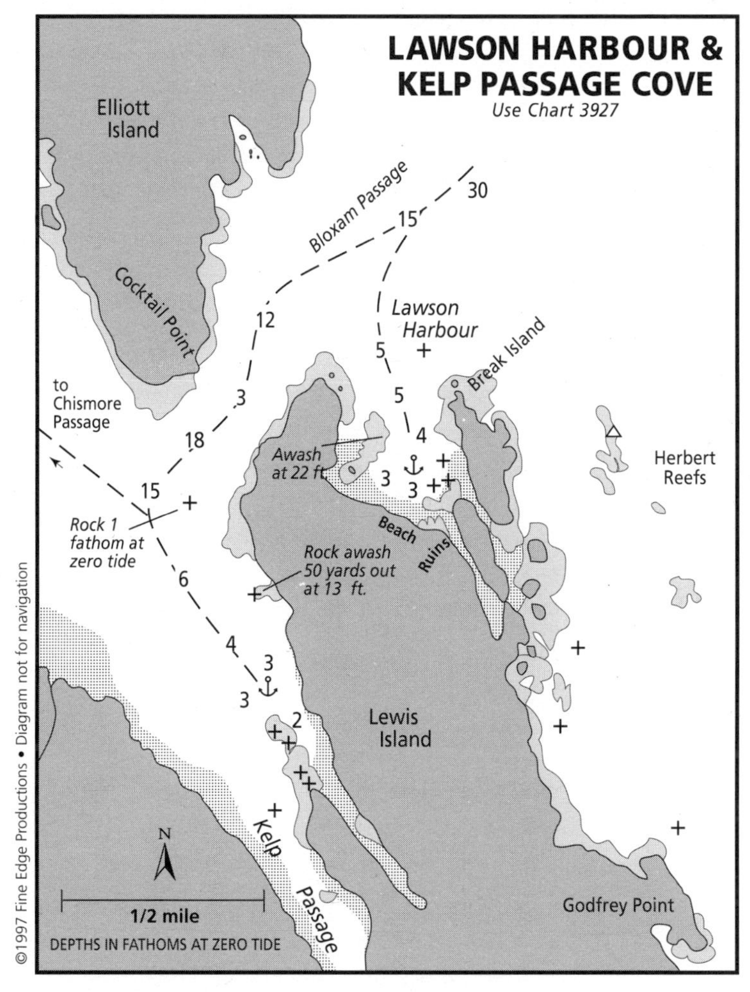

depth of 11 feet (3.4 m) and contains some floats.

Oona River should be entered only at HW and local knowledge is advised to make a safe entrance. If not in possession of local knowledge, moor at one of the mooring buoys and examine the entrance at LW before proceeding into the river entrance on the following HW. (p. 120, SD)

Arthur Passage

Chart 3773; south entrance: 53°57.80′ N, 130°11.90′ W; north entrance: 54°04.50′ N, 130°16.80′ W; Herbert Reefs: 54°01.40′ N, 130°14.23′ W (NAD 27)

Arthur Passage . . . a continuation of the main Inner Passage, connects Grenville Channel, at its SE end, to Malacca Passage, at its NW end. It lies between Kennedy Island, on the east side, and Lewis Island, Elliott Island and McMicking Island on the west side...About 0.5 mile south of Hanmer Island the flood stream attains 2.5 kn. (p. 120, SD)

Arthur Passage, the main route north, avoids the Skeena River flood plain east of Kennedy Island which is shallow and laden with silt. Lawson Harbour, just north of Herbert Reefs, provides good anchorage, and you can pass Herbert Reefs carefully on either side en route.

Lawson Harbour

Chart 3927; entrance: 54°01.83′ N, 130°15.13′ W; anchor: 54°01.40′ N, 130°15.00′ W (NAD 27)

Lawson Harbour is between the north end of Lewis Island and Break Island, close east. Local knowledge is advised for entering this harbour. Anchorage for small vessels can be obtained 0.1 mile within the entrance. The remains of a settlement are on the south shore of the harbour. (p. 121, SD)

Lawson Harbour gives excellent protection from southeast winds and chop from Arthur Passage. However, it is somewhat open to the north and the wake of passing ships.

Entry is easy, as long as you avoid both the underwater rock on the east side of the route, off the northwest corner of Break Island, and the charted reef in the western center of the harbor. Once you pass the Break Island rock, head straight for the narrow slit formed by a small peninsula of Lewis Island. Drop your hook just after you pass the charted mid-center reef, as indicated in the diagram.

Here it's easy to tell you're approaching Prince Rupert, for you can finally pick up an FM broadcast station (CJWF 101.9 FM) and, at night, you can see the glow of Prince Rupert to the northwest.

Anchor in 4 fathoms over a mud bottom with good holding.

Bloxam Passage

Chart 3927; east entrance:
54°01.83′ N, 130°15.13′ W; west entrance:
54°01.33′ N, 130°16.12′ W (NAD 27)

Bloxam Passage separates Lewis Island from Elliott Island and is about 0.2 mile wide.

Anchorage can be obtained about 0.3 mile SW of Cocktail Point in 5 to 10 fathoms (9.1 to 18.3 m). Anchorage can also be obtained in mid-channel about 0.5 mile WNW of Cocktail Point, in 7 to 9 fathoms (12.8 to 16.5 m), NW of the 20 foot (6.1 m) shoal. The holding ground and shelter in these two anchorages are excellent. (p. 121, SD)

Kelp Passage Cove

Chart 3927; anchor: 54°00.88′ N, 130°15.69′ W (NAD 27)

Kelp Passage is a narrow passage, encumbered with reefs, only suitable for small craft. Local knowledge is recommended. (p. 121, SD)

Kelp Passage is a high-water route choked with kelp and reefs and is not recommended except by dinghy. You can take anchorage tucked between the shallow reef and Lewis Island in the northwest corner of Kelp Passage as indicated on the diagram.

Anchor in 3 fathoms over mud bottom with very good holding.

Chalmers Anchorage

Chart 3927; position: 54°02.75′ N, 130°16.35′ W (NAD 27)

Chalmers Anchorage, west of Francis Point, affords anchorage in 24 m (79 ft). Drying reefs lie on the SW side of this anchorage, between Elliott and McMicking Islands. (p. 121, SD)

Chalmers Anchorage provides good holding in southeast winds; however, it is exposed to the northwest. Lawson Harbour, just south, is a better anchorage for cruising boats.

Chismore Passage

Charts 3956 metric, 3717 metric (partial), 3927; north entrance: 54°04.40′ N, 130°20.62′ W (NAD 83)

Chismore Passage separates McMicking and Elliott Islands from Porcher Island and is contracted to about 0.1 mile wide at its north end by drying ledges on both sides. A drying reef, known locally as Elizabeth Rock, lies close off the McMicking Island shore about 1 mile SE of Lamb Point, the north extremity of McMicking Island. Another drying reef lies on the south side of the channel, 0.4 mile south of Lamb Point. (p. 121, SD)

Chismore Passage, a smooth-water route, is well sheltered and provides good anchorage almost anywhere in the south end.

Lawyer Islands

Charts 3956 metric, 3717 metric, 3927; fairway 0.35 mile west of Genn Island light: 54°05.90′ N, 130°18.22′ W (NAD 83)

Lawyer Islands consist of several islands, islets and drying reefs. (p. 121, SD)

Beware: The Lawyers have comfortable red roofs on the island, The Clients grovel in the scruffy reefs to the east, and Bribery Islets to the south catch the unwary.

Chatham Sound

Chart 3957 metric; position:
54°08.00′ N, 130°19.00′ W (NAD 27)

Chatham Sound is the large body of water north of Porcher Island and Lawyer Islands. In our experience, it is either flat calm and featureless in haze or active and lively, with winds on the nose and "square-wave" choppiness unfriendly to boats under 30 feet. More than once, at either end of the sound, we have had to reduce speed because of head seas. The currents are strong in the sound and, with any breeze, it doesn't take long for a nasty chop to pick up.

Entering Chatham Sound, you can head for Prince Rupert by passing to either side of the Lawyer Islands, staying east of Holland Island light, and favoring Kaien Island shore.

We suggest you watch conditions just south of Holland Island light (shoal water and heavy Skeena River outflow), particularly in northwest or southeast winds. If you're unsure about proceeding, call the helpful Prince Rupert Coast Guard by radio to ask if conditions are local or whether there's a general deterioration of the weather. You can always turn back or find temporary shelter. Pay careful attention to all entrance buoys and lights since there are dangerous foul patches off the southeast corner of Digby Island.

Telegraph Passage

Charts 3773, 3927, 3717 metric; south entrance: 53°55.30′ N, 130°05.60′ W (NAD 27)

> *Telegraph Passage can be entered from south between the Gibson Group and the mainland shore, or by way of the channel between Marrack and Kennedy Islands; the latter channel is preferable.*
>
> *The north-going flood stream attains 3 kn and the south-going ebb 4 kn. Abreast the east entrance of Marcus Passage the streams turn 1 hour after HW. In spring, the south-going ebb stream is greatly accelerated at times by freshets.*
>
> *Sand waves with amplitudes up to 1.6 m (5 ft) occur near the junction of Telegraph and Marcus Passages, south and east of Parry Point.*
>
> *The drying and shoal banks in Telegraph Passage are subject to periodical changes. A sharp lookout should be kept for deadheads and other debris, particularly during periods of spring tides and freshets.* (p. 122, SD)

Telegraph Passage is actually the Skeena River east of Kennedy Island. The drying banks in the approaches to the Skeena River are shifting and skippers are cautioned to be vigilant when navigating these waters. When southbound, leaving Eleanor Passage, head across the Skeena River toward Hegan Point. The ebb will carry you downstream, requiring you to crab to port to gain the east shore and carrying you past Robertson Banks with a 3-knot current. Hegan Point is marked with a white lattice marker, and depths in Telegraph Passage appear to be close to charted values in 1996.

Moore Cove

Chart 3927; position: 54°00.15′ N, 130°05.70′ W (NAD 27)

> *Moore Cove, on the east side of Telegraph Passage 1 mile north of Chell Point, is choked by drying flats.* (p. 122, SD)

Moore Cove is a small indentation on the mainland 1.2 miles north of Chell Point. The cove is poorly charted but appears to have an intricate high-water passage which first follows the south shore, then snakes around a small shore and avoids a rocky reef which extends from the north shore and nearly closes the small creek. The inner basin is largely a drying, grassy mud flat; however, old pilings indicate some prior usage.

In our log we noted this as an interesting-looking place. It is a marginal anchorage site, steep-to and subject to heavy ebb currents. Moore Cove is only useful as a temporary lunch stop in fair weather. Anchor inside the current line off the small sandy beach on the north shore. The bottom has one fathom and is composed of rock and gravel with poor holding.

Marcus Passage

Chart 3717 metric; north entrance (0.45 mile NW Hazel Point.): 54°07.20′ N, 130°15.40′ W (NAD 27)

> *Marcus Passage, known locally as Kennedy Gap, connects Chatham Sound to Telegraph Passage. Two bars obstruct Marcus Passage; one extends north from Base Sand and the second extends SW from Parry Point. Marcus Passage enters Telegraph Passage between the north end of Kennedy Island and De Horsey Island; this junction is known locally as Standard Gap.*
>
> *The east-going flood stream attains 3.5 kn and the west-going ebb stream 5 kn. In Telegraph Passage, abreast the east entrance of Marcus Passage, the streams turn 1 hour after HW. In spring, the west-going ebb stream is greatly accelerated at times by freshets.*
>
> *Sand waves with amplitudes up to 1.6 m (5 ft) occur near the junction of Marcus and Telegraph Passages, south and east of Parry Point.*
>
> *The drying and shoal banks in Marcus Passage are subject to periodical changes. A sharp lookout should be kept for deadheads and other debris, particularly during spring tides and freshets.* (pp. 122, 123, SD)

Those proceeding northbound can avoid the strong ebb currents on the Skeena River by taking Marcus Passage west to Chatham Sound.

Inverness Passage, North Pacific Cannery Museum

Inverness Passage

Chart 3717 metric; west entrance
(0.95 mile SE buoy "D18"): 54°09.40′ N,
130°17.65′ W; (course 356° M 2.4 miles to
Mathews Rock Buoy) (NAD 27)

> *Inverness Passage leads from Chatham Sound to the entrance of the Skeena River around the NW, north and NE sides of Smith Island.*
>
> *Tidal streams attain 3 kn off Hicks Point. In spring, the west-going ebb stream is greatly accelerated at times by freshets.*
>
> *The drying and shoal banks in Inverness Passage are subject to periodical changes. A sharp lookout should be kept for deadheads and other debris, particularly during spring tides and freshets.*
>
> *Because of strong tidal streams and floating debris, caution should be exercised when mooring at the floats in Inverness Passage.* (p. 123, SD)

Inverness Passage, which flows between the north shore of Smith Island and the Tsimpsean Peninsula, is part of a smooth-water route that uses the Skeena River to avoid the south end of Chatham Sound. The grassy shore along the passage, once lined with canneries, holds the remains of two canneries: the North Pacific, now a museum, and the Caspaco.

The Smith Island shore is littered with giant stumps which obviously washed down the Skeena River during freshets. De Horsey Passage (known locally as Osland Passage), between Smith and De Horsey islands, leads to the ruined Danish village of Osland. The passage dries 7 feet or more and is subject to very strong ebb currents. It is not recommended that you enter this passage without first reconnoitering a route. The color of the water in Inverness Passage is an opaque pea green with little visibility due to outwash from the Skeena River.

As you pass Osborn Point and De Horsey Passage, you enter Eleanor Passage which connects with the Skeena River 1.25 miles southeast. Avoid Clara Shoal at the east end of Eleanor Passage by favoring the DeHorsey Island shore.

In 1996 we found minimum depths in Inverness Passage of 3 fathoms; in Eleanor Passage, they were approximately 2 fathoms. However, just east of Clara Point, we found a narrow bar with just over one fathom of water at zero tide.

North Pacific Cannery Museum

Chart 3717 metric; position:
54°11.65′ N, 130°13.40′ W (NAD 27)

> *North Pacific, opposite Tatenham Point, is the site of a former cannery. Until 1980 it was used by Canada Packers Limited as a fishing base and for net storage. It is now the North Pacific Cannery Museum, open to the public; marine facilities are planned. It is connected by road to Prince Rupert.* (p. 123, SD)

The North Pacific Cannery, the oldest standing cannery on the west coast and the last in operation, closed its doors in 1981. It has been preserved as a museum where the public can visit the manager's house and the workers' living quarters and mess house. Imagine what life was like when boatloads of salmon were brought in to be packed for shipment around the world! During the summer the museum has demonstrations and tours.

Unfortunately in 1996, the cannery float was under water and there were no accommodations for visiting pleasure craft. The museum can be reached by highway from Prince Rupert.

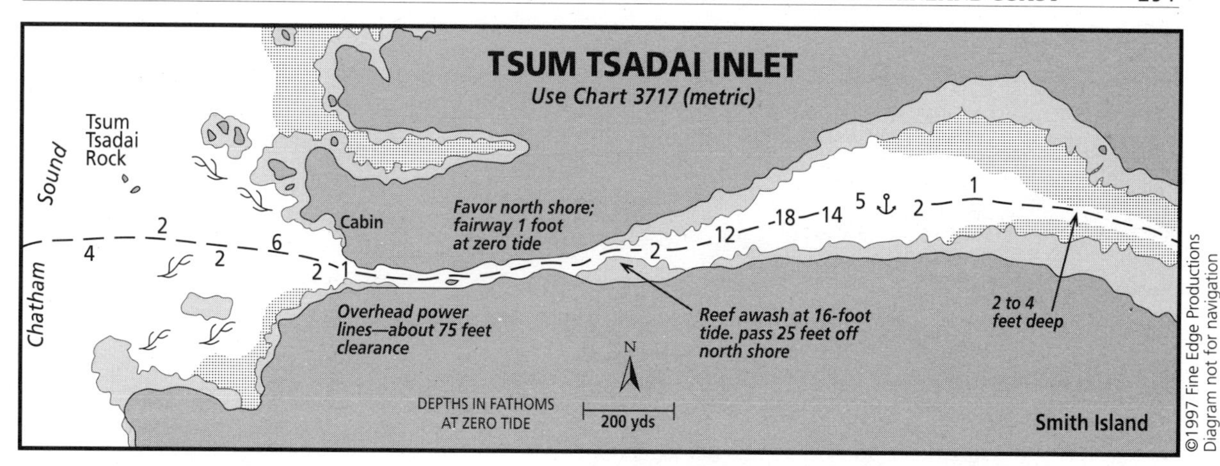

Tsum Tsadai Inlet

Chart 3717 metric; entrance: 54°10.45′ N, 130°16.43′ W; anchor: 54°10.52′ N, 130°14.73′ W (NAD 27)

Tsum Tsadai Inlet has a very narrow and shallow entrance. Tidal streams attain upwards of 5 kn through this entrance channel. The inlet is suitable only for small craft. Local knowledge and entering at or near slack water is recommended. The inlet provides a good, well sheltered anchorage.

Tsum Tsadai Rock, 1.1 miles east of Kitson Island, lies on the east side of the fairway of Inverness Passage. It is the westernmost rock of a group of drying reefs extending from the north entrance point of Tsum Tsadai Inlet. Drying reefs also extend north from the south entrance point of this inlet. (p. 123, SD)

Tsum Tsadai Inlet, on the northwest shore of Smith Island, offers very good protection from all weather and is worth braving the somewhat difficult entrance. The key to entering this inlet is to avoid the charted rocks shown on Chart 3717, and to time your entrance to the narrow channel at or near high-water slack. The minimum depth in the fairway is about one foot at zero tide. This shallow spot lies slightly east of the 18-foot islet with a tall tree. Pass the islet on your starboard.

At the east end of the narrows, about 200 yards from the islet, is a dangerous shoal, awash at 16 feet, which extends past midchannel from the south shore. You can avoid this shoal by favoring the north shore and remaining about 25 feet from shore. Anchor in 2 to 5 fathoms over brown sticky mud with very good holding.

Porpoise Channel

Charts 3955 metric, 3958 metric; entrance range (0.14 mile NW Buoy): 54°11.53′ N, 130°20.50′ W; (course 048° M); middle range (0.09 mile south of buoy "D35"): 54°11.88′ N, 130°30.57′ W (course 015° M); (NAD 27)

Porpoise Channel separates Lelu Island from Ridley Island; the fairway is about 0.1 mile wide.

Tidal streams in the entrance to Porpoise Channel attain 2 kn. At the NE end of Porpoise Channel a very strong set north, during the falling tide, comes from the channel separating Lelu Island from Tsimpsean Peninsula. Great vigilance is necessary while passing through Porpoise Channel. (p. 134, SD)

Porpoise Harbour

Charts 3955 metric, 3958 metric; outer entrance (073°): 54°11.53′ N, 130°20.50′ W; inner entrance (039.5°): 54°11.88′ N, 130°18.58′ W; anchor (north end): 54°14.64′ N, 130°18.67′ W (NAD 27)

Entry to Porpoise Harbour is generally restricted to HW slack during daylight hours, however on some occasions vessels may be piloted in at LW slack.

Anchorage is obtainable at the head of Porpoise Harbour, clear of the submarine pipelines, in 13 to 16 m (43 to 52 ft); the bottom is uneven and caution is necessary. Tidal streams from Zanardi Rapids can also be troublesome.
(pp. 134, 136, SD)

We would consider Porpoise Harbour as an

Prince Rupert Harbour

anchorage in emergencies only, due to industrial noise and pollution 24 hours a day.

Anchor (north end) in 4 fathoms west of Zanardi Rapids.

Prince Rupert Harbour

Chart 3958 metric; south entrance (midchannel between Barret Rock and Buoy "D47"): 54°14.74′ N, 130°20.86′ W (NAD 27)

The main entrance is from south, but it can also be entered from NW through Venn Passage.

Prince Rupert. . . along the SE side of Prince Rupert Harbour, has a population of about 16,000 (1986). It is the terminus of the Canadian National Railway transcontinental system and the centre for extensive mining, lumbering and fishing industries. A modern hospital, with a Poison Control Centre, doctors, dentists, clinics and pharmacies are available. The city of Prince Rupert is equipped with all modern municipal facilities. (pp. 136, 139, SD)

Prince Rupert, located on Kaien Island, is a culturally-diverse city of 18,000 that boasts the third deepest natural harbor in the world. Coal, grain, lumber, minerals, pulp, and fish are exported all over the globe from here. Decidedly attuned to marine life, the city is served by air, highway system, and rail, and full services are available for pleasure craft and commercial vessels.

For vessels heading south from Alaska, this is the first port of entry, and the Canadian Customs office here is open around the clock. Upon your arrival, phone 250-627-3003 to arrange for clearance, then wait aboard until a Customs Officer clears you.

Small craft can find moorage at either of two facilities: The Prince Rupert Rowing and Yacht Club (PRRYC) in Cow Bay, or the public floats at Rushbrooke, one mile north of the yacht club.

The yacht club, a five-minute walk from town, has a pay telephone, water, showers, ice, and garbage disposal. Electricity (15 amp or 30 amp) is available for an added fee. The dock managers of the club are friendly and helpful, and will gladly answer questions if you're unfamiliar with Prince Rupert. Call them on VHF Channel 72 to arrange for a slip as you arrive. Land telephone: 250-624-4317.

Rushbrooke Public Floats, a 20-minute walk from town, has space for up to 400 boats. However, from June through August when the trawlers and gill netters are active, pleasure craft are limited to the three floats at the north end of the marina. Water and power (20 amp/125 volt twist lock) are available; there is a porta-potty at the head of the dock, as well as a pay telephone and garbage drop, but there are no showers. The marina has a free launching ramp. Rushbrooke monitors Channel 10 VHF. Land telephone: 250-624-9400. You can obtain fuel at nearby Whamplers Esso, open seven days a week, where there is a laundromat and showers.

At the south end of Prince Rupert, you can buy fuel at Fairview Petro-Canada (the first fuel dock as you enter the south end of the harbor, open Monday-Friday); in Cow Bay at Petro-Canada and Chevron. Both are immediately east of the yacht club, open Monday-Friday (hours are extended during fishing season).

While we enjoy the convenience of the yacht

club and its proximity to town, many pleasure vessels prefer Rushbrooke because it is quiet and there is less wake from passing vessels.

Safeway, three blocks from the yacht club, has everything a skipper or first mate could possibly want. If you buy more than you can carry, taxi service is convenient and reasonable. For marine supplies, charts and nautical books head to SeaSport Marine at 295–1st Avenue East (tel: 250-624-5337). (PRRYC provides a list of addresses and telephone numbers of businesses that cater to boats, including repairs and parts.)

Other services: In Cow Bay, propane tanks can be filled at Valley Oxygen & Metals one block from the yacht club, and in Rushbrooke at I.C.G., across from B.C. Packers. King Koin Laundromat at 735 W. 2nd offers both self-service and wash-and-fold. Maytag, at 226–7th Street, is self-service. Sassy's Family Hair Styling Centre takes walk-ins at 230–3rd Avenue West (tel: 250-624-9116).

To learn about the cultural history of the area, we recommend a visit to the Museum of Northern British Columbia (tel. 250-624-3207). Of interest to boaters is Mariners Memorial Park, across from the museum, where you can read the names of regional mariners who have been lost at sea—a sadly impressive number! Also on display is the *Kaza Maru,* a small, open Japanese wooden fishing boat that floated across the Pacific and washed ashore on the British Columbia coast; its owner was lost at sea off Japan.

Free brochures and a city map are available at the Tourist Centre. If you're tired of galley cooking, the city map contains a list of the numerous restaurants in town. Smile's Seafood cafe, a "landmark" famous for its fish and chips, and the Breakers Pub are in Cow Bay. For home-made dishes and desserts, try Cow Bay Cafe near the yacht club. If you feel like celebrating in fine style, the dining room of the Crest Motor Hotel (222-1st Avenue West) has consistently good quality food and excellent service. We like to buy freshly-prepared sushi trays from Sea Food Trader, 7 Cow Bay Road. (California roll only, no raw fish, for those who worry.)

There are hotels and motels around town where accommodations can usually be found on short notice.

There is daily air transportation to and from Rupert. Via Rail (1-800-561-8630) provides service two days a week (the western terminus of the trans-Canada railway line). Both the Alaska Ferry (800-642-0066 U.S.; 250-627-1744 local) and B.C. Ferries (1-888-223-3779 B.C. only; 250-624-9627 local) call at Prince Rupert.

Canadian Coast Guard recommends that a sail plan be filed before boats head out to Queen Charlotte Islands. Phone 250-627-3082 with the names of persons aboard, date and point of departure and return, route information, emergency equipment carried, description of your vessel, its make and license or documentation. (Be sure to cancel your float plan on the scheduled date—Canadian Coast Guard takes its responsibilities seriously!)

Casey Cove

Chart 3958 metric; position:
54°16.84′ N, 130°22.58′ W (NAD 27)

> *Casey Cove is entered between Charles Point and Parizeau Point. The ruins of a wharf, some old buildings and wrecks are on the south side of the cove.*
>
> *A submarine cable crosses Casey Cove.*
>
> (p. 137, SD)

Temporary anchorage can be found in Casey Cove out of the tidal stream and chop.

Anchor in 5 fathoms over an unrecorded bottom.

Dodge Cove public float

Dodge Cove

Chart 3958 metric; entrance (to range course 228° M): 54°17.56′ N, 130°22.00′ W (NAD 27)

Dodge Cove is entered between Elizabeth Point and Dodge Island through a narrow channel with drying flats on each side and a least depth of 0.6 m (2 ft).

Digby Island settlement is on the west shore of Dodge Cove. The public wharf consists of five floats, secured end to end, each 24 m (79 ft) long. . . . The depth alongside these floats is 3.7 m (12 ft). . . . The float on the east side of Dodge Cove is used for access to the radio towers. (p. 137, SD)

Good shelter can be found in Dodge Cove. The public floats are generally crowded but rafting is encouraged. The cove is shallow, 1 to 2 feet at zero tide, but there is swinging room for several boats.

Russell Arm

Chart 3958 metric; entrance: 54°19.27′ N, 130°21.54′ W; anchor: 54°19.59′ N, 130°21.62′ W (NAD 27)

Russell Arm is entered between de Stein Point and Russell Point. . . . There are drying flats at the head of the arm. . . . (p. 137, SD)

In Russell Arm the public float and adjacent park are no longer there. Shelter from all but strong southerlies can be found 0.2 mile north of Burrowes Island.

Anchor in 3 fathoms over a mud bottom.

Cow Bay (PRRYC)

Chart 3958 metric; breakwater position: 54°19.73′ N, 130°19.12′ W

The public wharf in Cow Bay is protected by a floating breakwater and has 170 m (558 ft) of berthing space for small craft. The floats of Prince Rupert Rowing and Yacht Club, protected by a floating breakwater, are on the east side of Cow Bay. (p. 139, SD)

The public floats are stuffed *full* during fishing season. See Prince Rupert listing above for marina information.

Rushbrooke Floats

Chart 3958 metric; north end breakwater: 54°19.59′ N, 130°18.27′ W (NAD 27)

Rushbrooke Floats, which are public, are close NE of the B.C. Packers floats and protected by two floating breakwaters. The area between the floats and the breakwaters has been dredged to 2.1 m (7 ft). The north and main entrance to the floats is marked by two daybeacons. . . . These floats provide 1,320 m (4,331 ft) of berthing space for small craft. There is a derrick, fresh water, lights, and a boat launching ramp. The floats manager can be reached on 156.8 and 156.45 MHz, Channels 16 and 9. . . . (pp. 139, 141, SD)

See Prince Rupert listing above for marina information. An old railway line, converted to a walking and cycling trail, connects Rushbrooke floats with Seal Cove, providing a beautiful evening walk along the waterfront.

Seal Cove

Chart 3958 metric; entrance: 54°19.96′ N, 130° 16.70′ W (NAD 27)

Seal Cove is 0.2 mile SE of Ritchie Point. The Coast Guard depot and wharf are on its south side. A seaplane base and the offices of several airlines are at the head of the cove. A series of floats for seaplanes are in the cove. A drying rock is close north of the seaplane floats. (p. 145, SD)

Photo courtesy CHS, Pacific Region

Cow Bay from the air

Photo courtesy CHS, Pacific Region

Rushbrooke floats, aerial view

Fern Passage

Chart 3958 metric; entrance:
54°20.15′ N, 130°16.70′ W (NAD 27)

Fern Passage, entered between Ritchie Point . . . and Pethick Point, leads south through Butze Rapids into Morse Basin. It is part of the Harbour of Prince Rupert. The navigable channel is less than 90 m (295 ft) wide in places and at Butze Rapids it is less than 30 m (98 ft) wide and should only be used by small craft. (p. 145, SD)

Butze Rapids

Chart 3958 metric (inset); position:
54°18.26′ N, 130°14.80′ W (NAD 27)

Butze Rapids, 2.3 miles SE of Ritchie Point, is formed by a number of islets, drying reefs and rocks. The rapids is dangerous and, at times, spectacular; it is only suitable for small craft and should be navigated only at HW slack. Local knowledge is recommended.

Tidal streams flow in and out of Morse Basin through Butze Rapids and the flow is violent during larger tides. HW slack occurs 30 to 45 minutes after HW, and LW slack occurs 1 to 2 hours after LW at Prince Rupert. LW slack is most delayed during very low tides. (p. 145, SD)

Morse Basin

Chart 3958 metric; position:
54°16.00′ N, 130°15.00′ W

Morse Basin can only be entered by small craft, either through Butze Rapids or from Porpoise Harbour by way of Zanardi Rapids, Wainwright Basin and Galloway Rapids. Marine Farms are in Morse Basin. (p. 145, SD)

Butze Rapids is the only entrance to Morse Basin

Photo courtesy CHS, Pacific Region

Butze Rapids from Fern Passage

19-month old Kent Repass waits out a gale in Prince Rupert

suitable for cruising boats and only at slack water. Many small sportfishing boats and some local cruising boats use Morse Basin as a protected and quiet retreat. Some of the more popular attractions are:

Denise Inlet entrance: 54°15.87' N, 130°12.08' W; anchor: 54°16.63' N, 130°09.40' W
Kloiya Bay position: 54°15.06' N, 130°11.78' W
Miller Bay entrance: 54°16.03' N, 130°15.56' W

Tuck Inlet

Chart 3964 metric; south entrance (Tuck Narrows): 54°23.92′ N, 130°15.35′ W (NAD 27)

Tuck Narrows, east of Tuck Point, is about 300 feet (91 m) wide. A drying rock ledge extends about 300 feet (91 m) north from the north side and a wreck lies 0.2 mile SW of Tuck Point.

Tidal streams in Tuck Narrows attain 4 to 6 kn. The times of slack water are the same as those for HW and LW at Prince Rupert; the stream runs out of Tuck Inlet shortly after HW and into it shortly after LW, with very little slack water.

Tuck Inlet has high mountains on either side and a thickly wooded valley at the NW end through which a small stream flows. (p. 146, SD)

Tuck Inlet is located at the northeast end of Prince Rupert Harbour. Landlocked by Tuck Narrows, the inlet is relatively sheltered but seldom visited.

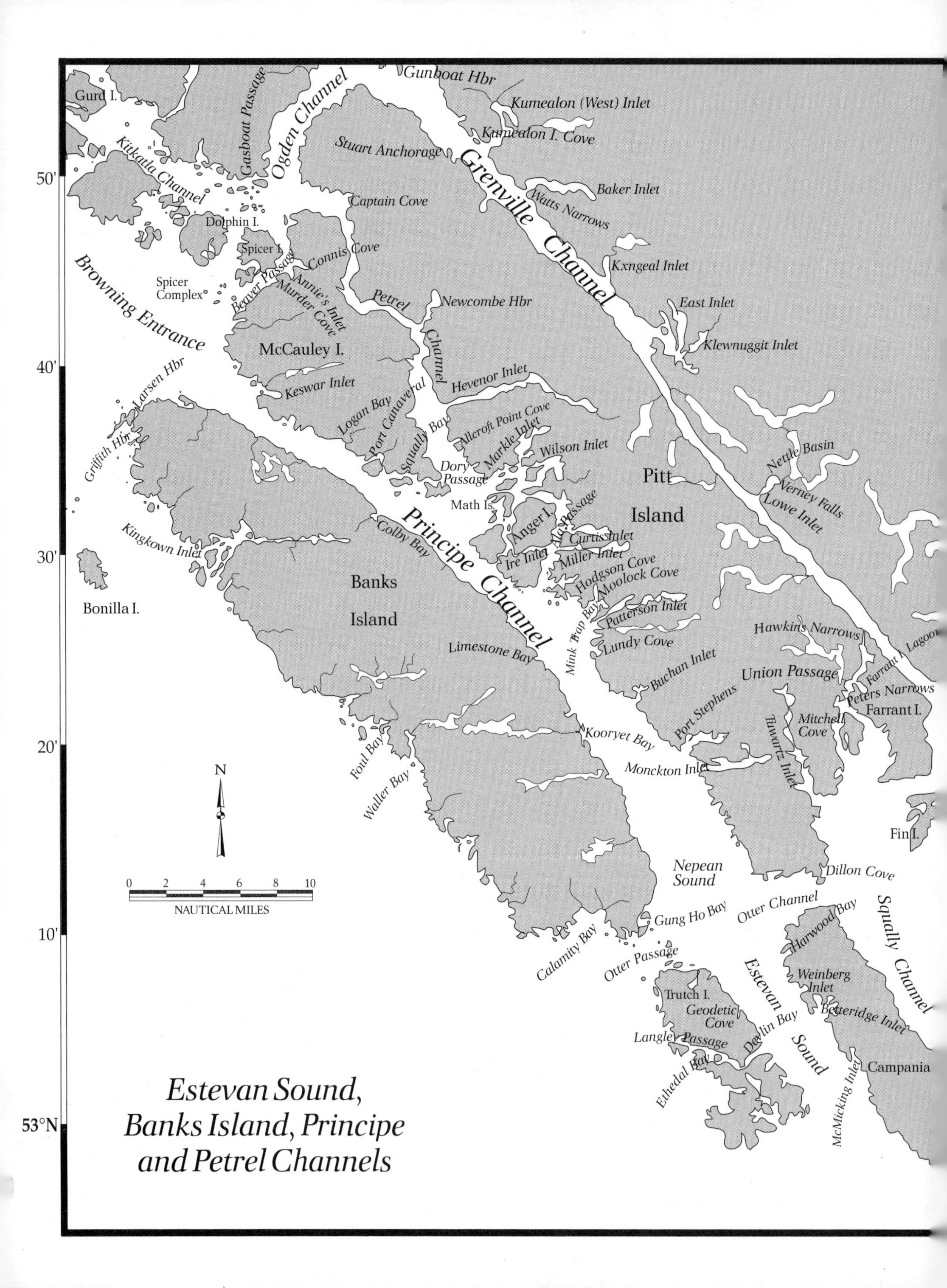
Gunboat Hbr
Kumealon (West) Inlet
Kumealon I. Cove
Gurd I.
Gasboat Passage
Ogden Channel
Stuart Anchorage
Grenville Channel
Kitkatla Channel
Baker Inlet
Watts Narrows
Captain Cove
Dolphin I.
Spicer I.
Connis Cove
Kxngeal Inlet
Browning Entrance
Spicer Complex
Beaver Passage
Annie's Inlet
Murder Cove
Petrel
Newcombe Hbr
East Inlet
Klewnuggit Inlet
McCauley I.
Channel
Larsen Hbr
Keswar Inlet
Hevenor Inlet
Logan Bay
Port Canaveral
Squally Bay
Allcroft Point Cove
Markle Inlet
Wilson Inlet
Nettle Basin
Griffith Hbr
Dory Passage
Pitt Island
Verney Falls
Lowe Inlet
Math Is.
Anger I.
Principe Channel
Colby Bay
Kingkown Inlet
Curtis Inlet
Ire Inlet
Miller Inlet
Hodgson Cove
Moolock Cove
Banks Island
Bonilla I.
Patterson Inlet
Mink Trap Bay
Hawkins Narrows
Lundy Cove
Limestone Bay
Buchan Inlet
Union Passage
Farrant I. Lagoon
Peters Narrows
Farrant I.
Port Stephens
Mitchell Cove
Kooryet Bay
Foul Bay
Monckton Inlet
Waller Bay
N
Fin I.
Nepean Sound
Dillon Cove
0 2 4 6 8 10
NAUTICAL MILES
Otter Channel
Gung Ho Bay
Squally Channel
Harwood Bay
Calamity Bay
Otter Passage
Estevan Sound
Trutch I.
Weinberg Inlet
Geodetic Cove
Devlin Bay
Betteridge Inlet
Langley Passage
Ethedal Bay
McMicking Inlet
Campania
50'
40'
30'
20'
10'
53°N
Estevan Sound, Banks Island, Principe and Petrel Channels

10

Estevan Sound, Banks Island, Principe and Petrel Channels

If you want to experience the "wild" Outer Passage, the area stretching from Estevan Sound north to Petrel Channel is the place to go. Infrequently visited and still natural, the area offers unlimited opportunities for summer cruising and is a viable alternative to the "beaten track" of Grenville Channel. The major bird flyway lies along this route and fishing is excellent; so good that you may be surprised from time to time to encounter a hardy local who's come all the way from Kitimat in a small boat to catch his seasonal quota.

Ranking among the more interesting choices for cruising are the Estevan Group, the west shore of Pitt Island, and Banks Island which has perhaps the most rugged west coast of all the islands. Both Pitt and Banks islands have innumerable lakes, ponds, and muskeg bogs, and the Math Islands and Ala Passage are about as remote and intimate as any area you can find on the British Columbia coast.

The inlets and islands along Principe Channel are largely protected from gales; however, channel waters do kick up when winds oppose the ebbing tide. To avoid these conditions, it's usually best to get an early morning start.

This is wilderness cruising at its best. But along with the thrill of exploration comes marginal radio reception, a lack of navigation aids, and the possibility of strong winds or currents. When you venture along this Outer Passage have fun, but be prepared and vigilant!

Estevan Sound

Charts 3724, 3742; south entrance: 52°57.00′ N, 129°23.00′ W; north entrance: 53°09.50′ N, 129°37.50′ W (NAD 27)

Estevan Sound separates the Estevan Group from Campania Island, and connects Caamaño Sound to Nepean Sound. Tidal streams at the south end of Estevan Sound, between Dupont Island and Estevan Group, set NE on the flood and SW on the ebb. A maximum of 1.7 kn has been observed on the flood; the ebb is generally stronger. (p. 188, SD)

We have found 3 to 3.5 knots on spring ebbs between Hickey Islands, Dupont Island and west to Borwick Rock. Under these conditions, the sound is very lumpy with southwest swells and breaking whitecaps.

Pemberton Bay

Chart 3723 (inset); entrance: 52°56.20′ N, 129°35.40′ W (NAD 27)

Pemberton Bay is entered between Jacinto Islands and Porter Island, 1.7 miles ENE. Pemberton Bay and Gillen Harbour are sparsely sounded, have not been surveyed since 1922 and should be navigated with caution. North of Robertson Rock the east side of the narrow channel leading to Gillen Harbour is fringed with islets and rocks. Do not attempt to enter Gillen Harbour in a gale from SE, except in case of necessity. (pp. 166, 167, SD)

Pemberton Bay, on the southwest side of the Estevan Group, can provide cruising boats with good protection tucked into the far corner of

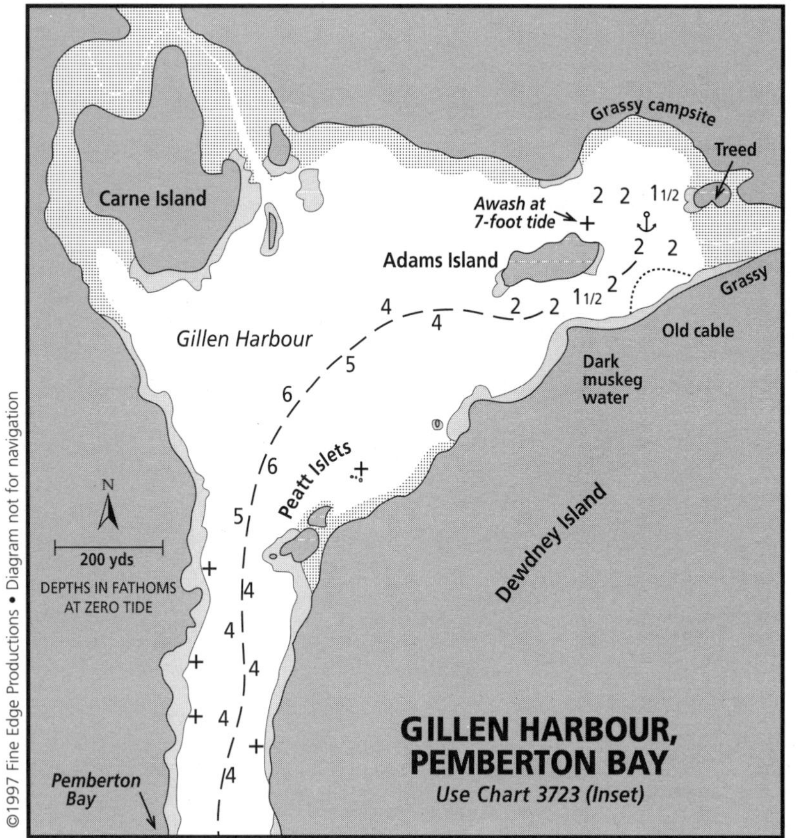

Gillen Harbour

Gillen Harbour. It should be avoided in southerly weather or when a strong ebb is running with wind or southwest swell.

Pemberton Bay (and its sheltered Gillen Harbour) can be a good alternative when crossing from Moresby Island in Queen Charlotte Islands and quick shelter is needed from northwest winds and chop. Jacinto Island on the southwest end of Pemberton Bay has a navigation light that makes a good leading mark when approaching the coast. Note that the exposed south side of Jacinto Island is void of vegetation for 60 to 70 feet above the water due to the pounding it receives during severe storms.

Gillen Harbour

Chart 3723 (inset); entrance (south channel): 52°57.60′ N, 129°35.67′ W; anchor: 52°58.99′ N, 129°35.48′ W (NAD 27)

Gillen Harbour offers sheltered anchorage for vessels of moderate draught. In the channel leading to the harbour there is a least depth of 22 feet (6.7 m). (p. 166, SD)

Gillen Harbour has acquired a major driftwood collection over the decades; however, the far east end is out of the line of fire and offers a calm setting regardless of outside conditions. The flat 2-fathom bottom between Adams Island and the islet to the east is as bombproof as it gets on the west coast. An old cable on the east end of Adams Island can be used for a stern tie for more security. Avoid the small rock pile which dries at 7 feet on the northeast side of Adams Island about 100 feet out. The water is dark brown with poor visibility.

Anchor in 2 fathoms east of Adams Island over a sticky mud bottom with very good holding.

Oswald Bay

Chart 3724; entrance: 53°01.03′ N, 129°41.00′ W (NAD 27)

Oswald Bay is approached between Bland Rocks and Le Jeune Point, 1 mile ESE. Le Jeune Point is steep-to. (p. 167, SD)

Oswald Bay is 3 miles south of the west entrance to Langley Passage. Murray Anchorage is reported to offer good shelter in southeast weather.

Ethelda Bay, Trutch Island

Murray Anchorage

Chart 3724; position: 53°00.78′ N, 129°39.40′ W (NAD 27)

> *Murray Anchorage, on the south side of Oswald Bay, affords good shelter to small craft. Drying reefs extend 0.4 mile west from the east entrance point of the anchorage.* (p. 167, SD)

Murray Anchorage makes a good emergency shelter from southeast winds if you are returning from Queen Charlotte Islands; it can also be used when southeast winds make Gillen Harbour unsafe.

Anchor in 10 fathoms over an unrecorded bottom.

Devlin Bay

Charts 3795, 3724 and 3742; entrance: 53°04.05′ N, 129°35.25′ W; anchor: 53° 03.65′ N, 129° 36.50′ W (NAD 27)

> *Devlin Bay . . . on the north side of Prior Island. Devlin Bay is the entrance to Gillespie Channel, which leads into Langley Passage. An islet in the entrance to Devlin Bay, 0.3 mile off the south shore, has an elevation of about 50 feet (15 m). Foul ground lies between the islet and the south shore. A drying rock is close north, and another is 0.25 mile ESE of the islet. Anchorage for small vessels can be obtained in 8 fathoms (14.6 m) north of the north extremity of Sekani Island.* (p. 189, SD)

Devlin Bay, located on the west side of Estevan Sound on the south side of Trutch Island, offers fair-to-good protection in most weather. Enter north of the wooded islet and avoid the reefs and fast current in the vicinity. A small boat passage

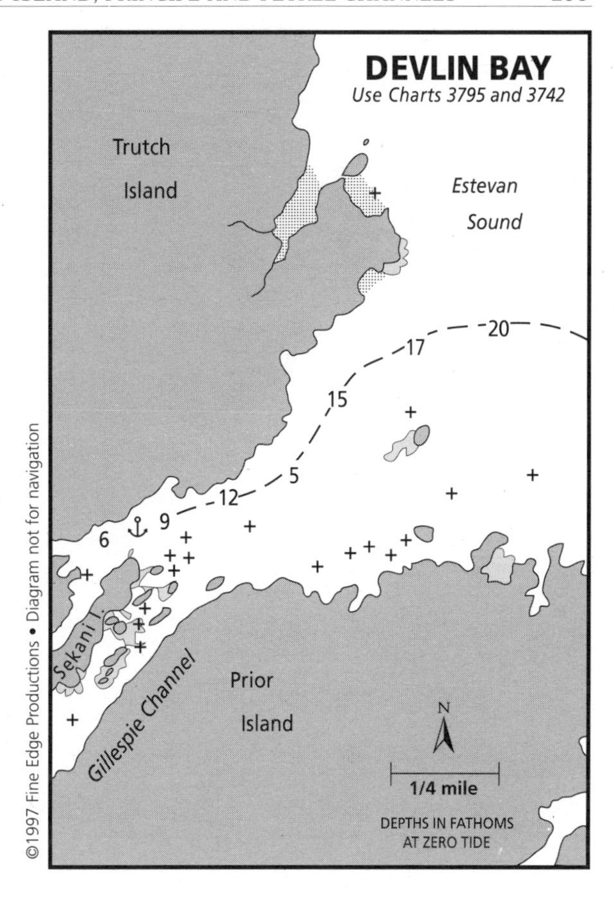

leads west to the outside via Langley Passage.

Anchor in 6 to 8 fathoms, mixed bottom with rocks, fair-to-good holding.

Gillespie Channel

Chart 3795; east entrance 53°03.60′ N, 129°36.22′ W (NAD 27)

> *Gillespie Channel, between Sekani and Prior Islands, is entered SE of Sekani Reef; it should only be attempted at slack water . . . . The narrow fairway through Gillespie Channel lies between the drying reef and islets off the SE shore of Sekani Island and the drying reef and wooded islet close off Prior Island; it has a least depth of 21 feet (6.4 m)*
>
> *Tidal streams in the narrowest part of Gillespie Channel attain at least 7 kn at springs. HW slack occurs 1h.25min. after the time of HW at Prince Rupert. LW slack occurs 30 minutes after the time of LW at Prince Rupert.* (p. 189, SD)

Gillespie Channel has difficult topography and

Visiting the Pollocks, Ethelda Bay

the chart doesn't make it easier. It is not as bad as it sounds if you "read the river" and stay in the fast-moving main channel, avoiding the kelp, breaking water, and turbulence on either side. *Caution:* Buoy "ET2" may have moved west of its charted position.

"Langley Passage Anchorages"

Chart 3795; anchor (0.3 mile southwest of "ET4"): 53°02.82′ N, 129°37.71′ W; anchor Ethelda Bay: 53°03.33′ N, 129°40.50′ W (NAD 27)

> *The west entrance to Langley Passage, on the north side of Nichol Island, is encumbered with drying rocks between which is a narrow shallow passage. . . . It is recommended that any vessel wishing to enter Langley Passage should do so through Devlin Bay in Estevan Sound.* (p. 167, SD)
> *The west entrance to Langley Passage, between the SW end of Trutch Island and the NW end of Nichol Island, is encumbered with drying rocks through which there is a shallow, narrow channel; even in moderate weather the sea breaks across this entrance. This approach to Langley Passage is not recommended. Ethelda Bay affords good anchorage near its head in 14 fathoms (25.6 m), mud bottom.* (p. 190, SD)

Langley Passage is a lovely, intricate passage connecting Estevan Sound with Hecate Strait. Only the east entrance should be used by cruising boats. Its west end, according to Chart 3795, is "not examined," and seas are reported to break across its narrow entrance in moderate weather. Langley Passage is a quiet place with a charm of its own. Wolves and deer roam the islands, and shrimp and crab abound in the passage.

The large antenna structure on the mountain top, on the south side of Trutch Island, can be seen from Estevan Sound. It played an important role in the Cold War as part of the intercontinental ballistic early warning system to protect North America from incoming Russian missiles. The maintenance crew was stationed in Ethelda Bay and the houses, dock, generator station, and helicopter pad remain. Dan and Danielle Pollock purchased the former government property in 1996 to develop an abalone hatchery; they welcome visitors.

There are several good anchoring opportunities in Langley Passage, and we have listed two of the better ones which give protection from both strong northwest and southeast winds.

Anchor (0.3 mile southwest of buoy "ET4") in 10 fathoms, soft bottom; fair-to-good holding.

Anchor in Ethelda Bay in 12 to 14 fathoms over a mud bottom with good holding.

McMicking Narrows

McMicking Inlet

McMicking Inlet

Charts 3719 (inset), 3724, 3742; inner entrance: 53°02.59′ N, 129°26.98′ W; anchor (east cove): 53°04.87′ N, 129°27.89′ W (NAD 27)

> *McMicking Inlet is entered south and east of a chain of islets and drying reefs extending 0.3 mile south from the south end of Jewsbury Peninsula. Several drying reefs and rocks with less than 6 feet (2 m) over them lie in the approach to, and in the entrance of McMicking Inlet. Local knowledge is advised.* (p. 190, SD)

McMicking Inlet is a special place for those up to a navigational challenge. It provides good landlocked protection north of the second narrows. The islands, islets, reefs and rocks which fill its southern entrance effectively kill off any hint of swell.

The water in McMicking Inlet is a dark muskeg color with poor underwater visibility; entering requires careful, good piloting. The inner entrance point we use is located 0.7 miles due east of Logan Rock. Northbound boats can reach the inner entrance point from a southern outer entrance point 0.5 southeast of Cartright Rocks (53°01.10' N, 129°26.50' W). Southbound boats can reach the inner entrance point from an outer entrance point located 0.3 mile northwest of Logan Rock at (53° 02.80' N, 129°28.50' W). A circuitous route using a sharp lookout and responsive helmsmanship is required when entering the inlet. Avoid all breaking water and attached kelp. At the first narrows, favor the west shore (within about 75 feet) since there is dangerous rock awash at 3 or 4 feet on the end of the drying spit, on your starboard hand.

The Canadian Hydrographic Survey has done an unusually detailed job on the mid-section of Campania Island and Chart 3719. Done during World War II, it is a major accomplishment and, as far as we can tell, accurate.

McMicking Inlet, as well as the two inlets immediately north, provide a wonderful natural environment which almost defies imagination. There is a maze of islands and islets where you can easily get confused and turned around. It is a wonderful bird habitat. We watched two rare Sandhill cranes one morning as they fed on the low water mud flat, ruffling their feathers and making their unusual calls. Loons like this place, too, as do many species of gulls. Bright white sand fills the entrance beaches. A quarter-mile hike up the stream bed to the east takes you to a tableland with a peak bog "post-forest" environment, including bonsai-like trees, created after the original forest has died off. An interesting, if speculative, theory postulates that because the lighter-colored mosses reflect sunlight, rather than absorbing it as trees do, the atmosphere will grow colder, contributing to a possible ice age.

There are a number of anchor sites, especially using a stern tie. We prefer the protected anchor site in the small cove, east side of the main basin, west of an island which dries on all sides except the west. The water in the cove is reported to remain smooth even in 60-knot southeast storms. In a southeast storm, since McMicking Inlet faces south, the rocks would be a dangerous lee shore. Weinberg Inlet via Dunn Passage or Anderson Passage would be a safer entrance under such conditions.

Anchor (east cove) in 4 fathoms over a sand and mud bottom with very good holding.

Betteridge Inlet

Charts 3719 (inset), 3742; entrance(Hale Rock): 53°04.93′ N, 129°29.92′ W; anchor: 53°06.18′ N, 129°30.12′ W (NAD 27)

> *Betteridge Inlet, between Jewsbury Peninsula and Finlayson Peninsula, has many islets and drying and below-water rocks encumbering its entrance. The best passage leading into Betteridge Inlet is between Hale Islet and a rock awash 450 feet*

Campania Island beach, south of McMicking Inlet

(137 m) west. Hale Islet is steep-to on its west side and the rock awash is sometimes marked by kelp. (p. 190, SD)

Betteridge Inlet can be a calm-water playground for dinghies or kayaks and a provider of secure anchorages. Between Jewsbury and Finlayson peninsulas, there are dozens of unnamed islands and islets. It can also be confusing, even a nightmare. *Do not attempt to enter Betteridge Inlet without Chart 3719 (inset).* Favor Hale Islet, a major islet with trees; the rock awash mentioned above appears much less than 450 feet away. The entrance is narrow and you should not attempt to enter during strong southerlies or in limited visibility. An alert bow watch is recommended to help avoid the many charted rocks, reefs, and patches of kelp.

There are thousands of silver drift logs along the rocky shores and islets with southern exposure. The northwest shore, in particular, is littered with all sizes of drift logs. The northwest basin can provide shelter or solitude from prevailing northwesterlies during fair weather.

For the adventurous, there is a high-water route which circles east, then south to within 200 yards of the upper end of McMicking Inlet. This basin must be more protected from swells and chop than most of the anchorages on the west coast.

The anchor site listed above is a temporary one for reconnoitering the island maze to the east and south. The depth at this site is 9 fathoms over a soft bottom with poor to fair holding

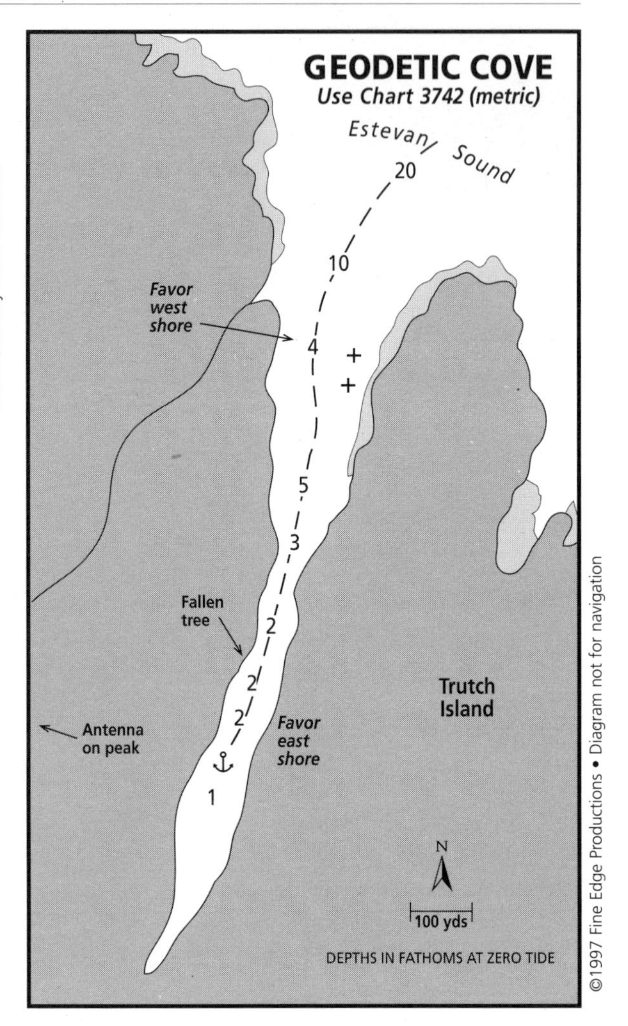

depending on how well you set anchor. Watch spring currents and maintain an anchor watch.

Geodetic Cove

Chart 3742; entrance: 53°06.10′ N, 129°37.35′ W; anchor: 53°05.52′ N, 129°37.68′ W (NAD 27)

Geodetic Cove is 2.3 miles NNW of Devlin Bay. (p. 189, SD)

Geodetic Cove is seldom visited because it is narrow and appears uninviting. On closer inspection, Geodetic Cove offers very good protection for small cruising boats, especially in southeast storms, deep near the head of the cove. Upon entering Geodetic Cove, favor the west shore to avoid a rocky shoal that extends about 50 yards from the east shore, and a fallen tree extending

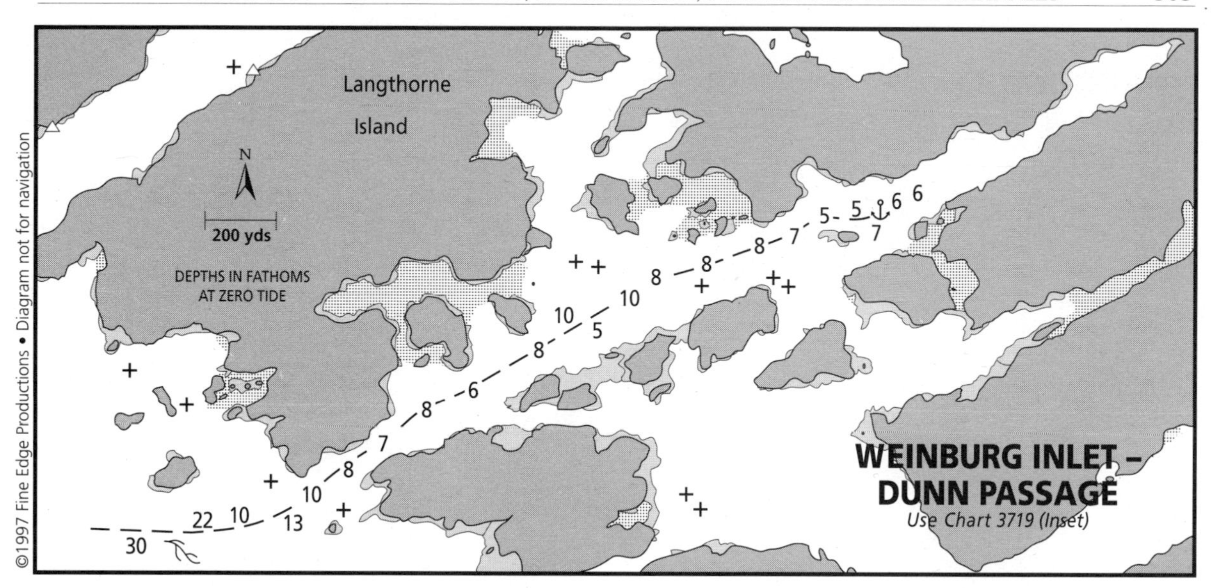

about 60 feet from the west shore. Larger boats may find this cove useful if they use a stern tie to restrict their swinging room. Old growth overhangs the shore on either side of the 200-foot-wide cove. There are no drift logs, the bottom of the cove is flat with no sign of boulders. Several boats in a line can anchor on the slowly sloping bottom.

Anchor in about 2 fathoms over soft brown mud and shells with some kelp. Holding is fair to good.

Weinburg Inlet, Dunn Passage

Chart 3719 (inset); entrance:
53°06.87′ N, 129°32.62′ W; anchor (Weinburg Inlet): 53° 07.52′ W, 129°30.86′ W (NAD 27)

> *Weinburg Inlet can be entered either south or north of Langthorne Island, through Dunn Passage or Anderson Passage.* (p. 190, SD)

Dunn Passage leads into a maze of islets and lagoons that Walt Disney himself would have had a tough time designing. Weinburg and Betteridge inlets to the south—with miniature archipelagos of over a hundred islets—are fun to explore by dinghy or kayak. The islets are all covered with stubby old-growth cedar. You get the feeling you're on a small pond in the midst of the Black Forest. (But be careful, you might get lost!)

The head of Dunn Passage (see diagram) is a bombproof anchorage for small boats. No driftwood or chop enters here. The water is clear and schools of fish passing underneath your keel may make your echo sounder dance. Dunn and Anderson passages can be entered with relative ease in southerly weather.

Dessert time—Geza's preparing Hungarian pancakes!

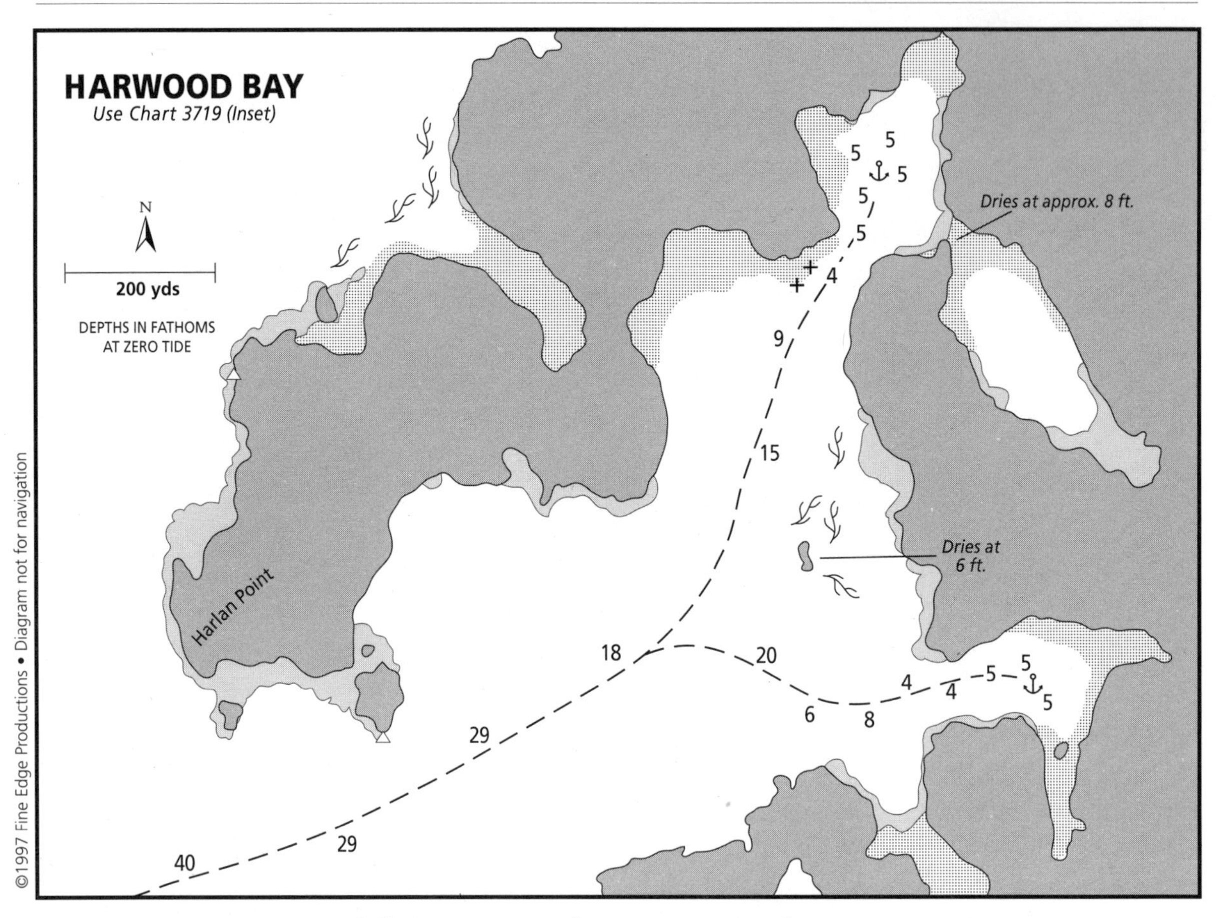

Enter Dunn Passage, carefully staying in mid-channel. The bottom is relatively flat throughout.

Anchor in 6 fathoms over a sand and gravel bottom with good holding.

Anderson Passage

Chart 3719 (inset); entrance:
53°07.53′ N, 129°33.26′ W; anchor (southeast nook): 53°07.94′ N, 129°31.81′ W (NAD 27)

Anderson Passage leads to a large basin, a good anchorage with swinging room for several boats. This is the easiest way to enter Weinberg Inlet in limited visibility and especially for larger boats. Large boats can anchor in the center of the basin north of Langthorne Island in about 13 fathoms. Small boats can anchor in the more scenic and intimate southeast nook.

Anchor (southeast nook) in 5 fathoms over a soft mud bottom with fair-to-good holding.

Harwood Bay

Charts 3719 (inset), 3742; entrance:
53°08.67′ N, 129°33.96′ W; anchor (north basin): 53° 09.14′ N, 129° 33.27′ W; anchor (east basin): 53° 08.82′ N, 129° 33.11′ W (NAD 27)

> *Harwood Bay, 1.2 miles north of Anderson Passage, is open to the SW and too exposed for anchorage.* (p. 190, SD)

Contrary to *Sailing Directions,* we have found that Harwood Bay offers very good shelter for small boats in prevailing northwest summer winds. There is little driftwood in its north basin and none in its eastern basin. We would use it in all conditions except during a strong southwesterly, or a major storm front. If a major storm front is expected, use Dunn Passage.

Harwood Bay is one of the easiest anchorages to enter in Estevan Sound, and the only one to use under a radar approach. We tuck up in either the small far northern or eastern basin as indicat-

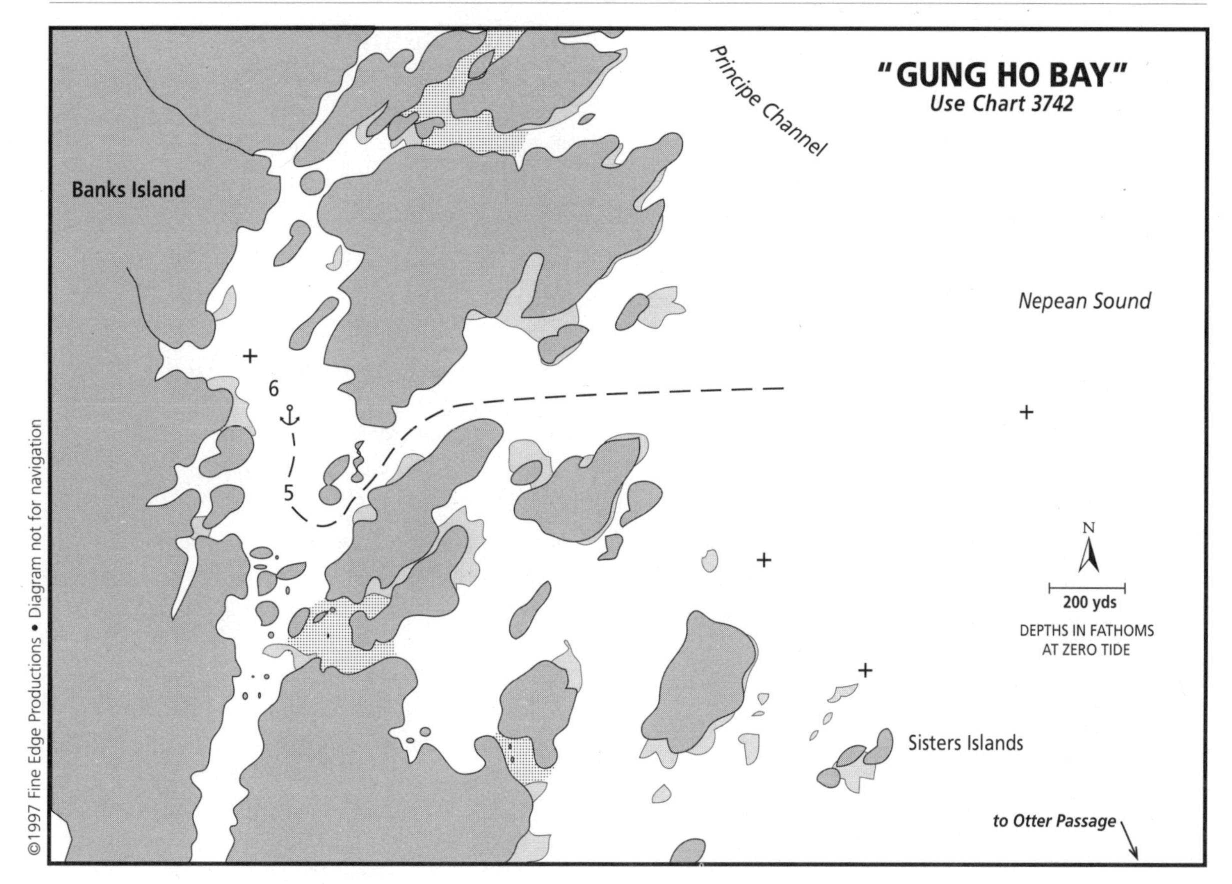

ed in the diagram. The basin is surrounded by old-growth forest, and the water is clear with visibility better than 12 feet.

Anchor (north basin) in 5 fathoms, over a brown sand and mud bottom with good holding.

Anchor (east basin) in 5 fathoms, over a sand and mud bottom with good holding.

Otter Channel

Chart 3742; west entrance:
53°11.50′ N, 129°35.00′ W; east entrance:
53°12.00′ N, 129°29.50′ W (NAD 3742)

Otter Channel leads between Campania and Pitt Islands and joins Nepean Sound to Squally Channel. Tidal streams in Otter Channel attain 1.5 kn on large tides. (p. 190, SD)

Otter Passage

Chart 3742; west entrance:
53°06.85′ N, 129°46.60′ W; entrance:
53°09.40′ N, 129°42.80′ W (NAD 27)

Otter Passage leads from Hecate Strait into Nepean Sound. The fairway is deep and about 0.3 mile wide but because of strong tidal streams and the large number of islands in the passage, local knowledge is recommended.

Tidal streams are strongest in the east part of Otter Passage where the maximum on both the flood and ebb is 6 kn. The flood sets NE and the ebb SW and the duration of slack water is about 11 minutes. Most of the ebb stream from Nepean Sound runs out through this passage and, meeting the ocean swell at the west entrance, produces a turbulent breaking sea.
(pp. 167, 168, SD)

"Gung Ho Bay," Banks Island

Chart 3742; entrance: 53°10.79′ N, 129°45.49′ W;
anchor: 53°10.67′ N, 129°46.55′ W (NAD 27)

Gung Ho Bay is frequently used as an anchorage by sea urchin divers. Gung Ho Bay is the local name for a well-sheltered anchorage deep inside a labyrinth of rocks and islets northwest of Sisters Islands on the southwest tip of Banks Island. A sharp lookout and vigilant navigation are required to safely enter the bay. There is a high-water dinghy route south of the bay directly into Otter Passage. As many as four or five seiners use this bay during fishing openings.

Anchor in 6 fathoms, with fair-to-good holding reported.

Nepean Sound

Chart 3742

> *Nepean Sound is the junction of Estevan Sound, Otter Passage, Principe Channel and Otter Channel.* (p. 190, SD)

Nepean Sound, at the southern end of Banks Island, has little swell action due to the myriad of islets and rocks that protect its western opening. During ebb tides and southeast gales, Nepean Sound can be very ugly due to strong tidal currents.

At this point, you can easily regain Grenville or Princess Royal channels for a smooth-water route north or south. Turn east at Nepean Sound, transiting Otter Channel and Lewis Passage to Wright Sound. Peters Narrows at the south end of Union Passage is a well-protected anchorage.

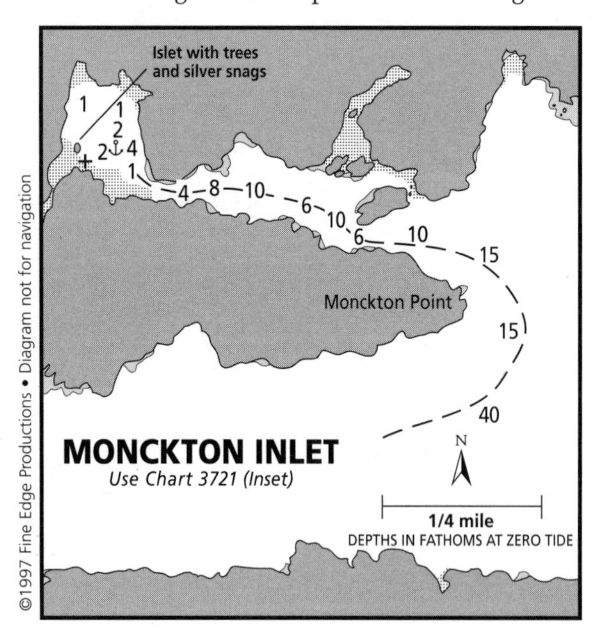

Principe Channel

Chart 3742; south entrance:
53°15.00′ N, 129°42.00′ W (NAD 27)

> *Principe Channel leads along the east side of Banks Island from Nepean Sound to Browning Entrance. Petrel Channel . . . leads NW to Ogden Channel and the Inner Passage.* (p. 190, SD)

Monckton Inlet

Charts 3721 (inset), 3742;
entrance: 53°18.60′ N, 129°41.45′ W;
anchor (lagoon): 53°18.98′ N, 129°39.76′ W;
anchor (0.7 mile north of Roy Island):
53°19.76′ N, 129°36.83′ W; anchor (head of inlet): 53°19.08′ N, 129°34.53′ W (NAD 27)

> *Monckton Inlet is entered north of Cranston Island. A sill across the inlet about 0.8 mile east of Monckton Point has a depth of 11 fathoms (20.1 m).*
>
> *The bay to the east of Monckton Point has a drying reef about 0.1 mile off its east side, and a shoal in the middle of its entrance.*
>
> *Anchorage can be obtained about 0.2 mile SE of Roy Island in 13 to 20 fathoms (24 to 37 m), mud bottom. Anchorage can also be obtained near the head of Monckton Inlet in 11 to 14 fathoms.* (p. 191, SD)

Monckton Inlet, near the southern tip of Pitt Island, carves deep into the island. The trees are laden with moss, and the area looks undisturbed. Within the inlet there are three good anchorages. The first is at the far east end of the inlet; another is in the bay north of Roy Island; the third is in the small lagoon northwest of Monckton Point.

Just a mile inside the entrance to Monckton Inlet, on its north side, a small cove that doubles back to the west around Monckton Point offers excellent protection from all weather. Although the first part of the this cove is roomy enough for two or three boats, we found the bottom to be somewhat irregular and rocky and the holding is poor at best. The lagoon west of this cove, however, can hold one or two small boats and is perfectly bombproof. Enter the lagoon through a narrows that carries a minimum of one fathom at zero tide. Inside the narrows a small 2- to 4-fathom hole provides complete protection from all weather. The steep, rocky shores of the lagoon are covered with lovely old-growth cedar. Anchor just east of the islet with several trees and silver snags, favoring the east shore.

Anchor (lagoon) in 3 fathoms over soft mud bottom with good holding.

Anchor (north of Roy Island) in 4 to 6 fathoms over mud bottom with good holding.

Anchor (head of inlet) in 8 to 10 fathoms over mud bottom with good holding.

Port Stephens

Chart 3742; entrance: 53°19.30′ N, 129°42.50′ W (NAD 27)

> *Port Stephens is entered between Centre and Littlejohn Points. A shoal lies on the east side of the fairway, about 0.4 mile ENE of Littlejohn Point. A prominent bare white patch on a cliff face is on the south side of Port Stephens about 1 mile NE of Centre Point.*
>
> *Anchorage can be obtained in Port Stephens, west of the entrance to Stephens Narrows, in about 20 fathoms (37 m), sand and rock.* (pp. 191, 192, SD)

Port Stephens, located 1 mile north of Monckton Inlet, has a large amount of sheltered water; however, the water is deep and the inner basin and lagoon have restricted passages. We have no local knowledge of Port Stephens; however, the small cove 0.35 mile northeast of Centre Point may offer cruising boats temporary anchorage while exploring Port Stephens.

Stephens Narrows, Leavitt Lagoon

Chart 3721; entrance: 53°20.10′ N, 129°40.82′ W (NAD 27)

> *Stephen Narrows, 2 miles inside the entrance of Port Stephens, has an island at its east end. The narrow boat passages north and south of this island should only be navigated at or near HW slack. At other stages of tide the rapids frequently form a waterfall creating considerable foam in the anchorage.*

Rusty beachcombing on the west coast

> *East of Stephens Narrows there is a basin with a narrow channel at its NE end that is encumbered with below-water rocks; this narrow channel leads into Leavitt Lagoon.* (pp. 191, 192, SD)

Kooryet Bay

Chart 3741; entrance: 53°20.35′ N, 129°51.35′ W; anchor: 53°20.13′ N, 129°51.82′ W (NAD 27)

> *Kooryet Bay is 2.3 miles NNW of Keecha Point. Confined shelter for small craft can be found in its south end, clear of the shoal rocks. Local knowledge is advised. Kooryet Island is off the north entrance to the bay and several islets and drying reefs, south of Kooryet Island, are off the west side of the bay.* (p. 191, SD)

Moderate protection from channel winds and chop can be found in the south end of Kooryet Bay.

Anchor in about 10 fathoms over an unrecorded bottom.

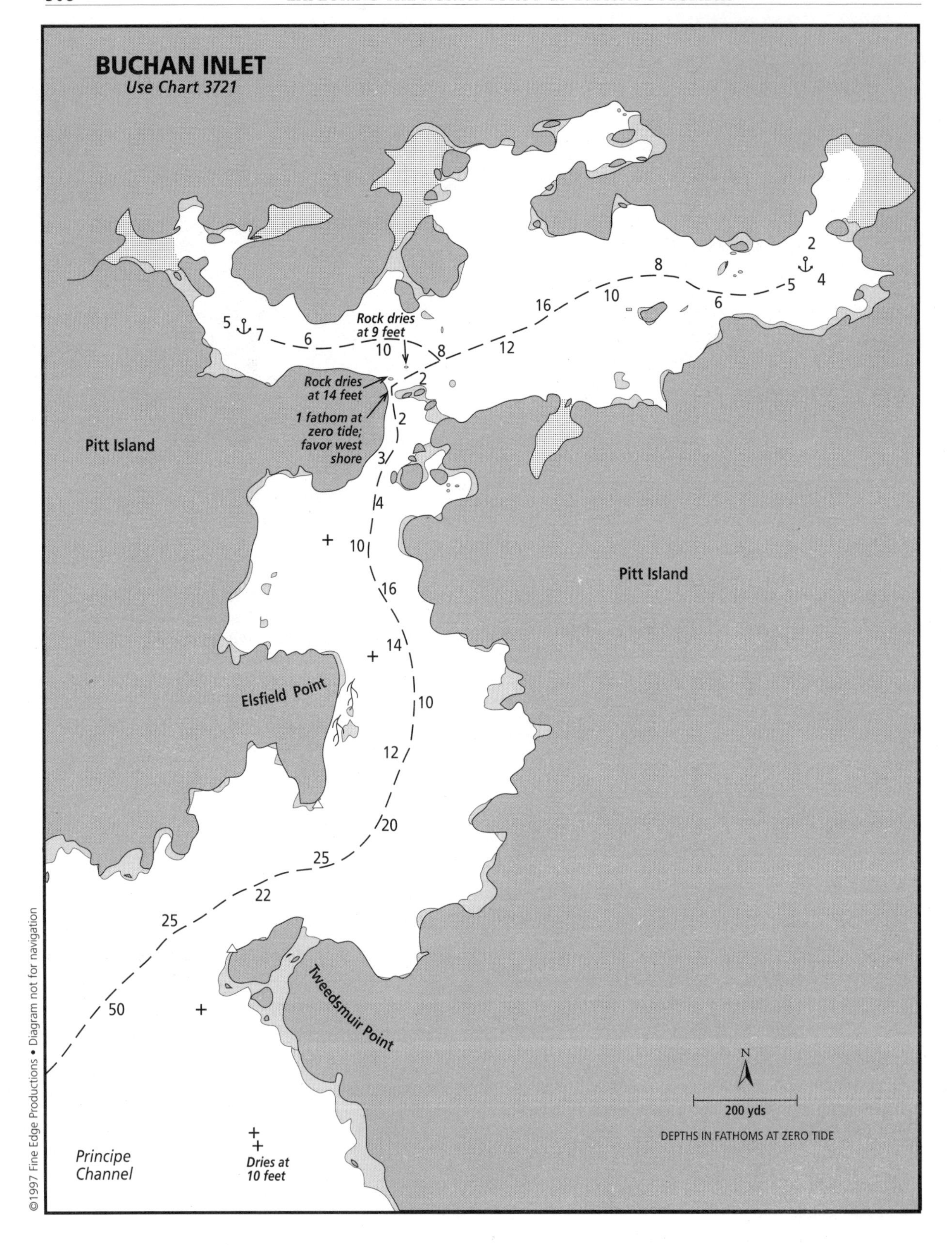
BUCHAN INLET
Use Chart 3721
Rock dries at 9 feet
Rock dries at 14 feet
1 fathom at zero tide; favor west shore
Pitt Island
Pitt Island
Elsfield Point
Tweedsmuir Point
Principe Channel
Dries at 10 feet
N
200 yds
DEPTHS IN FATHOMS AT ZERO TIDE
©1997 Fine Edge Productions • Diagram not for navigation

"Unnamed Inlet," Banks Island

A small inlet, 0.8 mile NNW of Kooryet Island, offers shelter for small craft. An islet lies in the entrance to this inlet; the passage NW of the islet dries but the entrance south of the islet is clear. (p. 191, SD)

This unnamed inlet is similar to Geodetic Cove on the east side of Trutch Island.

Anchor in 7 fathoms with limited swinging room, unrecorded bottom.

Buchan Inlet

Chart 3721; entrance: 53°22.06′ N, 129°47.00′ W (NAD 27)

Buchan Inlet is entered north of an island close off Tweedsmuir Point. . . . This inlet is only suitable for small craft. (p. 192)

Buchan Inlet, cutting deep into Pitt Island, is another intimate and intricate boating paradise, offering good shelter and an environment worth exploring.

Our reported information, received second hand, is shown on the diagram. Caution is advised as the bottom appears to be irregular and may contain uncharted hazards. We welcome your reports and look forward to providing a more complete description in the next edition of this book.

Lundy Cove

Chart 3721 (inset);
entrance: 53°24.95′ N, 129°50.90′ W;
anchor (outer bay):
53° 24.73′ N, 129° 50.24′ W;
anchor (east nook):
53°24.55′ N, 129°49.74′ W (NAD 27)

Drying ledges, on which there are a number of islets, extend across Lundy Cove about 0.5 mile within the entrance. A very narrow boat passage, near the NE end of these drying ledges, leads into the basin at the head of Lundy Cove. Tidal rapids run through this passage and local knowledge is advised to navigate it. (p. 192, SD)

The outer bay of Lundy Cove, adjacent to the pilings, offers quick access to shelter from southerly weather. Additional protection can be found inside the cove south of the tidal rapids.

Inner Lundy Cove offers very good shelter either in the east nook behind the islet on the east shore or at the south end of the cove. The tidal rapids into the inner cove should be transited near slack water. The east nook can be entered from the north by favoring the islet side of the passage.

Anchor (outer bay) in 2 to 6 fathoms over a sand and mud bottom with fair holding.

Anchor (east nook) in 1.5 fathoms over soft mud, broken shells and kelp bottom with poor-to-good holding depending on how well set.

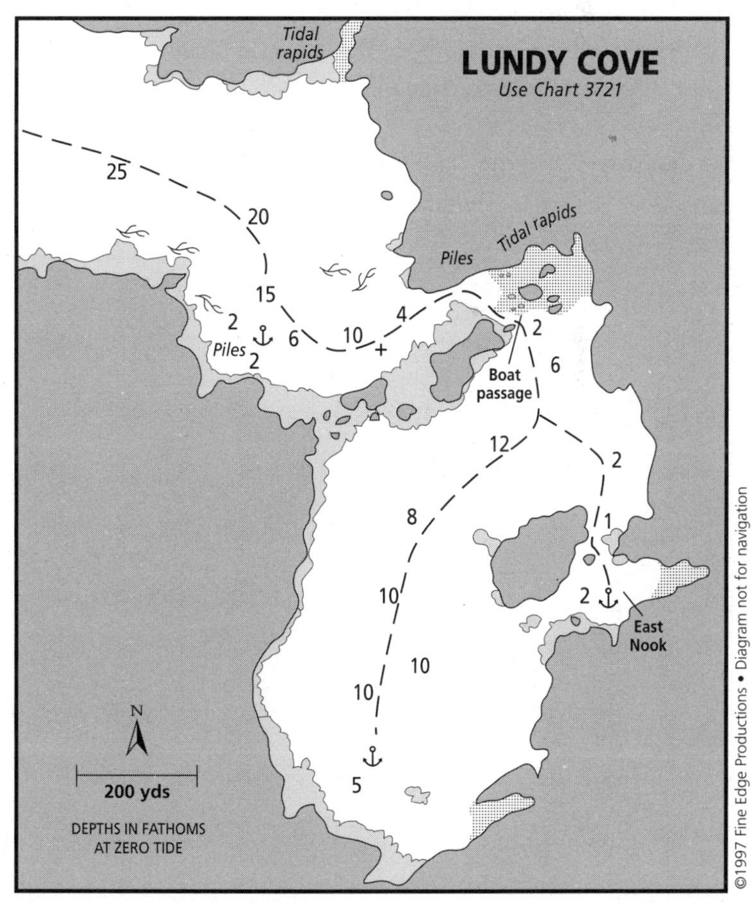

Patterson Inlet

Chart 3721 (inset); entrance:
53°26.00′ N, 129°50.87′ W;
anchor (north basin):
53° 27.42′ N, 129°47.08′ W
(NAD 27)

Patterson Inlet, entered between Annie Point and Rungé Island, is 300 feet (91 m) wide at its narrowest part. The fairway up Patterson Inlet is clear and small craft can find anchorage, mud bottom, near the heads of both arms at its head. (p. 192, SD)

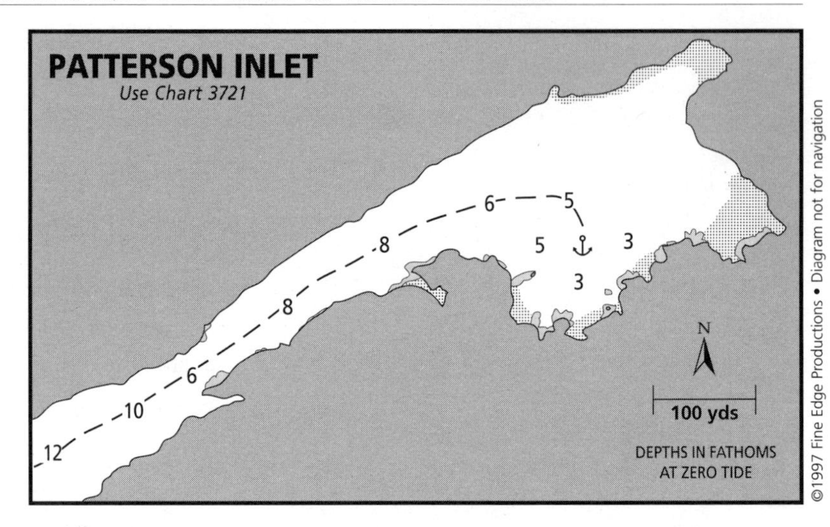

Patterson Inlet has perhaps the most straightforward entry of any anchorage in this area and may be the best choice in foul weather or at night under radar. However, the anchorages are 3 miles from Principe Channel.

Both inlet arms are essentially landlocked and provide very good shelter. The north arm, inner basin, has a large area of shallow water with a mud bottom and room enough for several boats to swing.

Anchor (north basin) in 5 fathoms over a mud bottom with very good holding.

Mink Trap Bay, Burns Bay

Chart 3721; entrance:
53°26.50′ N, 129°51.60′ W
((NAD 27)

Mink Trap Bay, entered north of Rungé Island, has Burns Bay at its head. (p. 192, SD)

Burns Bay is too deep for convenient anchoring unless you use a stern tie. The bay is exposed to the south.

Moolock Cove

Chart 3721 (inset); entrance:
53°27.20′ N, 129°50.25′ W;
anchor (bight):
53°27.12′ N, 129°49.16′ W
(NAD 27)

Moolock Cove is entered through a narrow channel at the NE end of Mink Trap Bay. Drying and below-water rocks encumber the south end of this cove.

Anchorage can be obtained . . . 0.2 mile east of the entrance channel, in 25 fathoms (46 m); the holding ground is indifferent. Small craft can anchor closer to shore. During SE gales furious gusts blow over the narrow neck of land that separates Moolock Cove from Patterson Inlet. (p. 192, SD)

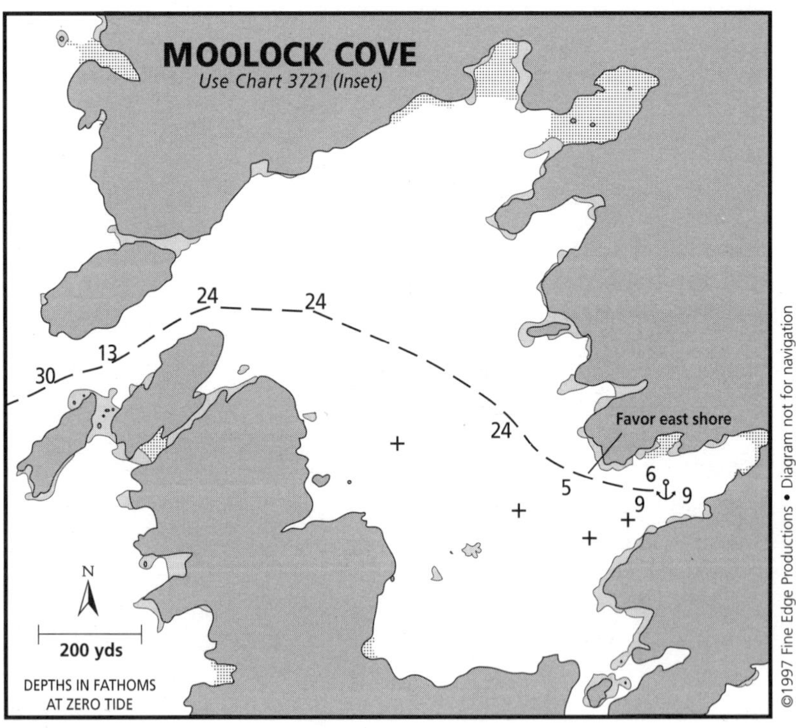

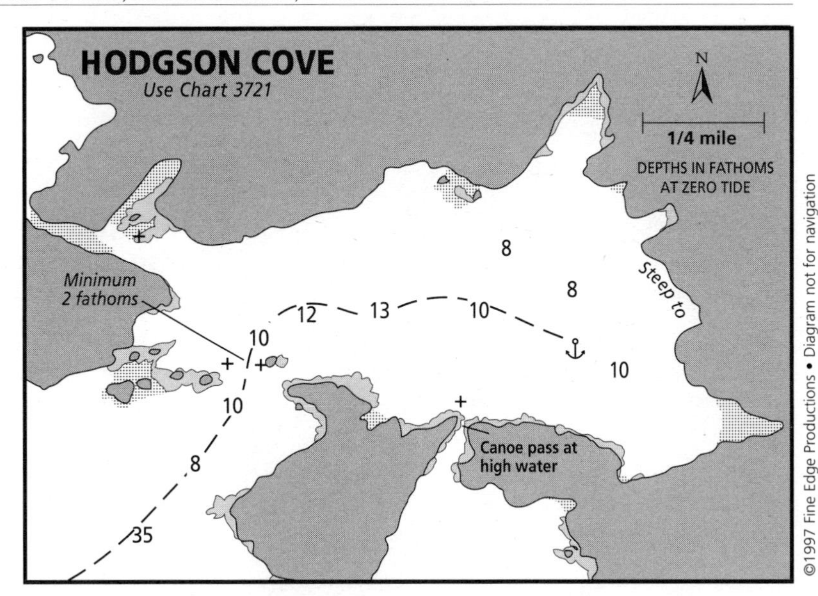

Although Moolock Cove, at the eastern side of Mink Trap Bay, provides good shelter, the water tends to be too deep for convenient anchorage unless you tuck far into its southeast corner. As you enter Moolock, a mountain with an exposed white spot on its south flank makes a prominent landmark. Favor the east shore when you cross the bar at the east end of the cove.

Small craft can anchor in the bight at the southeast corner of the cove, facing the landmark mountain. This bight, northeast of the neck that separates Moolock from Patterson Inlet, is somewhat out of the path of southeast winds. It appears to offer good shelter in all weather. Summer water temperatures in this cove hover in the mid-sixties, providing fertile grounds for hundreds of sea nettles.

Anchor (bight) in 9 fathoms in soft bottom. Holding is good if you set your anchor well.

Hodgson Cove

Chart 3721; entrance (outer): 53°27.00′ N, 129°52.85′ W; entrance (inner): 53°27.40′ N, 129°52.52′ W; anchor: 53°27.48′ N, 129°51.94′ W (NAD 27)

> *Hodgson Cove, 1.5 miles NW of Rungé Island, provides shelter for small craft and is fronted by several large islands. A drying reef with several islets on it extends 0.1 mile east from its west entrance point and a drying reef is about 200 feet (61 m) NW from its east entrance point.*
> (p. 192, SD)

Hodgson Cove has rocky, tree-lined steep-to shores. Its entrance is narrow and shallow, so stay carefully in midchannel between two underwater rocks extending from rocky spits on either shore. Do not enter in poor visibility.

Although the cove is entirely landlocked, giving excellent protection from all weather, on three separate attempts, we were unable to set our Danforth test-anchor satisfactorily in depths of 8 to 9 fathoms. The pattern on our echo sounder indicated soft matter along the fairly flat bottom, over a very hard rock base. Vessels with a different type of anchor and more chain may not experience the same problem. We have talked to others who don't recall having a problem here.

If heavy weather is expected, Patterson Inlet or Monckton Inlet may be better alternatives.

Anchor in 9 fathoms over a very soft bottom; holding may be poor; it depends on your type of anchor and amount of chain.

Ala Passage South

Charts 3721, 3741, 3746; fairway position (west of Peck Shoal): 53°27.86′ N, 129°55.87′ W; (NAD 27)

> *Ala Passage separates Anger Island from Pitt Island. Because of the intricacy of the channels through Ala Narrows and between Ala Narrows and Anger Point the passage is only suitable for small craft. Local knowledge is advised.*
> (p. 192, SD)

Chart 3721 (inset) shows the south entrance to Ala Passage. The somewhat dangerous Peck Shoal is easily avoided by favoring Anger Island until you are directly north of Trade Islets. This passage leads to some great remote waters for

Walking the logs, west coast

intrepid explorers only. *Caution*: Avoid the dangerous midchannel rock 0.3 mile south of the entrance to Ire Inlet. It is awash at mid-tide.

Miller Inlet

Chart 3721 (inset); entrance:
53°28.18′ N, 129°54.63′ W; anchor (inner basin south): 53° 28.43′ N, 129°52.22′ W (NAD 27)

> *Miller Inlet has several coves which could provide shelter for small craft. The narrows, about 0.5 mile within the entrance, has a drying rock near its middle. Several shoal and drying rocks are nearly in the centre of the fairway of Miller Inlet; extra caution is advised. Anchorage for small craft can be found in the basin at the head of the inlet in 8 fathoms (15 m), sand and mud bottom.* (p. 192, SD)

Miller Inlet is off the main Principe Channel, but the inner basin is reported to be bombproof. There is an anchorage at the head of the inlet, but the inner basin on the south shore is more convenient for smaller boats. The entrance is narrow and shallow with several charted rocks.

Anchor (inner basin south) in 4 to 5 fathoms over an unrecorded bottom.

Ire Inlet

Chart 3746; entrance: 53°30.10′ N, 129°54.45′ W; anchor: 53°29.99′ N, 129°56.32′ W (NAD 27)

> *A drying rock, 1 mile north of Lock Island, lies in the middle of the fairway through Ala Passage.*
>
> *Ire Inlet . . . entered NNW of the last-mentioned rock, has a very narrow entrance.* (p. 192, SD) *(NAD 27)*

Ire Inlet is an example of a nearly-perfect anchorage. Although its entrance is narrow, it's landlocked and secure from any weather. The entrance may look daunting, but the fairway is quite deep with a flat bottom. Except for kelp and the 2-fathom bar at the west of the narrows, the entrance is clear. We anchored behind the islet at its west end and felt we were in one of the most remote places in the world.

Anchor in 4 fathoms over a mud bottom with good holding.

Curtis Inlet

Chart 3746 (inset); entrance:
53°30.09′ N, 129°53.66′ W (NAD 27)

> *Curtis Inlet, east of Ire Inlet, has depths in the fairway of 6 feet (1.8 m).*
>
> *Ire Inlet . . . has a very narrow entrance.* (p. 192, SD)

Curtis Inlet has an 8-fathom hole inside its first narrows which appears to offer very good shelter. However, as we approached this hole near low water, our bow lookout observed an uncharted rock in the center of the passage, and we were forced to back out. The inlet is fed by a series of large lakes and looks like a good place to explore. Ire Inlet has equally good shelter and is easier to enter.

Wright Inlet

Chart 3746 (inset); position (Wright Narrows):
53°31.04′ N, 129°52.02′ W (NAD 27)

Wright Inlet, east of Ala Narrows, has a very narrow entrance. Wright Narrows, 0.7 mile within the entrance, is obstructed by a ridge of boulders which dries 10 feet (3 m). Tidal falls occur in Wright Narrows. (p. 192, SD)

Wright Inlet lies behind a fortress of islets and reefs and could be called a lagoon. The entrance to this "end-of-the-world place" defies description. When you study the small-scale chart, you see that it is choked with rocks and reefs. It should be reconnoitered by inflatable before entering. The two small coves and lagoon in the east end of Wright Inlet appear interesting. The narrows has a tidal falls with 7 feet at low water. We have not entered Wright Inlet, but it is the kind of challenge we like. Let us know *your* experience if you enter it.

Authors kayaking during a rain storm on the west coast

Ala Narrows

Chart 3746 (inset); position:
53°31.35′ N, 129°53.51′ W (NAD 27)

Ala Narrows, 1.2 miles north of Curtis Inlet, is about 300 feet (91 m) wide. Numerous drying rocks, rocks awash and rocks with less than 6 feet (2 m) over them are in the south and north approaches to Ala Narrows.

Between Ala Narrows and Anger Point, 1.2 miles north, the fairway through Ala Passage is obstructed by numerous islets, drying and below-water rocks. (p. 192)

Ala Narrows is best transited near slack water when you can make a slow approach with an alert bow lookout. Most of the rocks and reefs are marked by kelp. Study the inset on Chart 3746 and avoid the rock that dries at 7 feet near Anger Island, as well as the kelp and turbulent water. The fairway has a minimum depth of about 3 fathoms.

North of Ala Narrows, the bottom is irregular and you must navigate carefully to avoid the many hazards.

Ala Passage North

Chart 3746; north entrance:
53°32.96′ N, 129°56.78′ W (NAD 27)

Between Anger Point and Logarithm Point, 2 miles west, the fairway through Ala Passage is deep and clear of dangers. (p. 192, SD)

Once you are abeam of Anger Point, the route is clear of dangers. The small cove east of Anger Point has a U-shaped valley, a good leading point when you are southbound through Ala Passage from Logarithm Point.

"Math Islands"

Chart 3746; position: 53°33.50′ N, 129°57.00′ W (NAD 27)

We call this interesting area the "Math Islands" in honor of Sine, Cosine and Tangent islands. In 1949, the first surveyors to chart this maze of islands north of Anger Island faced the challenge of keeping track of their baseline. Visual distances are short and the channels and islands confusing. The survey must have required a lot of triangulation involving trigonometric functions, hence the island names. We are glad to have GPS to help us identify our turning points. In the spring, the area is an important spawning area for herring.

From Principe Channel, the Math Island complex can be entered via Evinrude or Markle passages. While exploring the Math Islands, Wilson and Markle inlets, and Ala Passage, you can find good anchorage on the east side of Clear Passage.

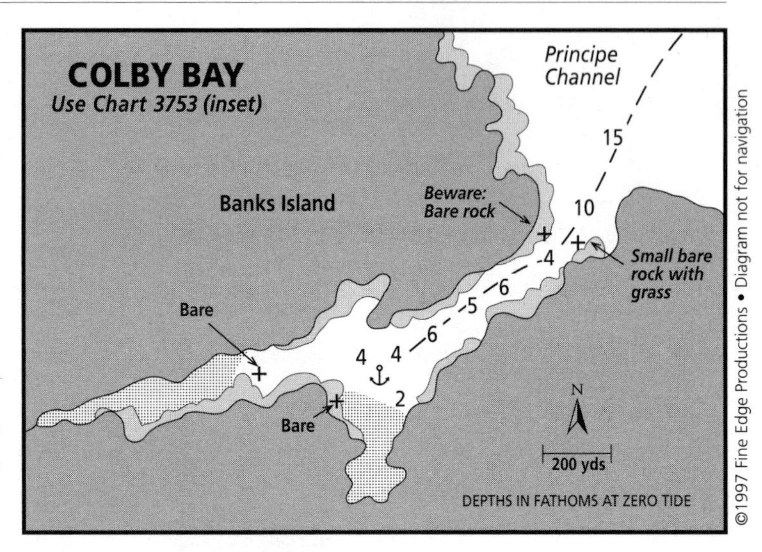

Clear Passage

Chart 3746; anchor (east entrance): 53°33.20′ N, 129° 58.35′ W (NAD 27)

Clear Passage, between Cosine and Sine Islands, is less than 300 feet (91 m) wide and has a least depth of 3 feet (0.9 m). (p. 193, SD)

Very good anchorage is reported just east of the shoal in Clear Passage; this site makes a good base camp from which you can explore by dinghy or inflatable.

Anchor (east entrance) with limited swinging room in about 10 fathoms with good holding reported.

Evinrude Passage

Chart 3746; west entrance: 53°32.23′ N, 129°59.03′ W; east entrance: 53°32.90′ N, 129°57.10′ W (NAD 27)

Evinrude Passage, east of Anger Anchorage, is entered between Azimuth Island and a rock islet 0.2 mile NE. Several drying reefs and shoals are in the south portion of Evinrude Passage, around the south end of Cosine Island. (p. 193, SD)

Anger Inlet

Chart 3746; entrance: 53°31.35′ N, 129°58.40′ W (NAD 27)

Anger Inlet, south of Cosine Island, is encumbered with islands and numerous rocks. (p. 193, SD)

Anger Inlet is intricate, highly convoluted, shallow, and menacingly narrow. Its southern end is less that 100 yards from the head of Ire Inlet. On its southwest corner, it is only 100 yards from Principe Channel backwater. The area is an explorer's dream and a navigator's nightmare.

Wilson Inlet

Chart 3746; entrance: 53°33.45′ N, 129°56.80′ W (NAD 27)

Wilson Inlet, east of Sine Island, has Tangent Island in its entrance. A narrow boat passage along the north side of Tangent Island has a least depth of 11 feet (3.4 m) through it. The main entrance to Wilson Inlet is south of Tangent Point. East of Tangent Island there are a number of islands and rocks. (p. 193, SD)

Wilson Inlet, most easily entered south of Tangent Island, offers very good shelter at its head in 12 to 15 fathoms. Be careful to avoid the rocks shown on the chart.

Markle Passage

Chart 3746; west entrance: 53°33.65′ N, 129°59.75′ W; anchor (island (325) bight): 53°34.38′ N, 129°57.82′ W (NAD 27)

Markle Passage, on the north and east sides of Sine Island, has dangerous detached rocks in mid-channel.

Approaching Ala Passage by way of Markle Passage, round Sine Point at a distance of not more than 0.1 mile to avoid two shoals lying in mid-channel. (p. 193, SD)

Markle Passage connects Petrel Channel to Ala Passage. Good anchorage sheltered from southeast gales can be found in the bight on the west side of island (325), 0.75 mile northeast of Markle Island.

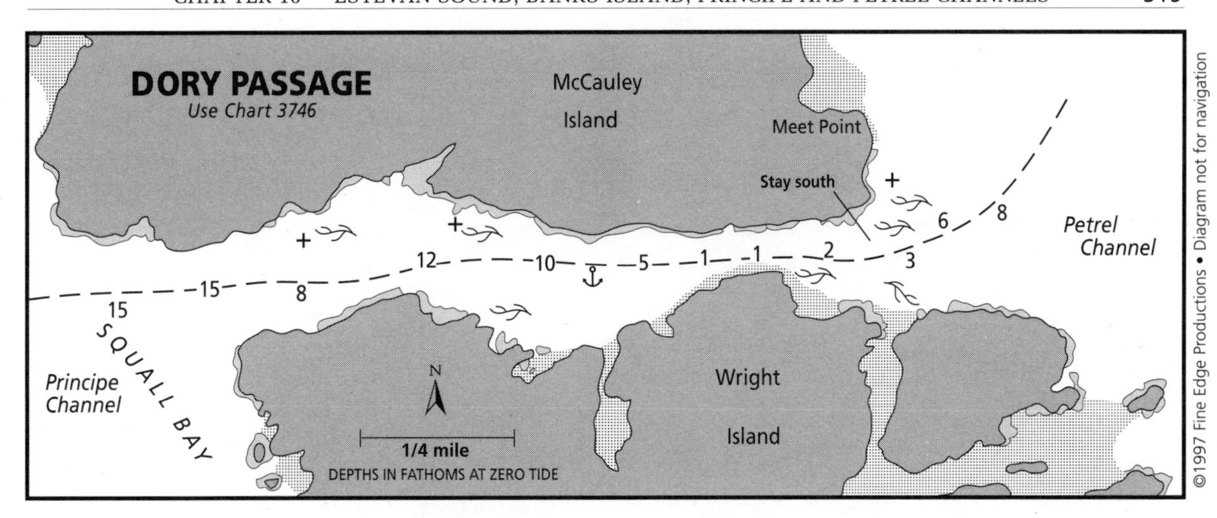

Anchor (island (325) bight) in 14 fathoms with moderate holding.

Markle Inlet

Chart 3746; entrance: 53°34.25′ N, 129°57.12′ W (NAD 27)

> *Markle Inlet has its entrance encumbered with islets, drying reefs and below-water rocks.* (p. 193, SD)

There are several possible anchor sites here for boats able to enter Markle Inlet safely. The eastern cove just inside the entrance looks like a bombproof lagoon. It is best to reconnoiter the inlet before you enter.

Colby Bay

Chart 3753 (inset); entrance: 53°32.15′ N, 130°10.00′ W; anchor: 53°31.82′ N, 130°10.52′ W (NAD 27)

> *Anchorage for small craft can be obtained in 5 fathoms (9.1 m), mud bottom, in Colby Bay, about 300 feet (91 m) south of a prominent point on the north shore and 0.3 mile inside the north entrance point.* (p. 193, SD)

Colby Bay, 2 miles south of Dixon Island, on the east side of Banks Island provides very good protection. The entrance lies between a bare rock extending about 100 feet from the north shore and a small bare rock with some grass on the south shore; minimum depth in the fairway is about 4 fathoms. The shores are edged with old-growth cedar. The bay has swinging room for several boats. Pilings shown on Chart 3753 (inset) are no longer evident.

Anchor in 4 fathoms over a mud bottom with good holding.

Dory Passage

Chart 3746; east entrance: 53°33.82′ N, 130°04.10′ W; west entrance: 53°33.65′ N, 130°06.17′ W (NAD 27)

> *Dory Passage separates Wright Island from McCauley Island; it has a least depth of 6 feet (1.8 m) in the fairway.* (p. 192, SD)

Dory Passage connects Petrel Channel to Squall Bay, located at the southern tip of McCauley Island. Approaching from the north, Dory Passage is not visible. To find the east entrance, head for the grassy flat south of Meet Point until the passage opens up. Kelp marks both the north and south sides of the entrance. Least depth through the narrows is one fathom, with sandy patches, grassy spots, and occasional bull kelp attached to the flat bottom. Locals sometimes use the area just west of Dory Passage shoal for anchorage in 6 to 8 fathoms; this site offers moderate protection from southerlies.

Squall Bay

Charts 3753 (inset), 3746; south entrance: 53°32.95′ N, 130°06.20′ W; anchor (north): 53°34.02′ N, 130°07.26′ W (NAD 27)

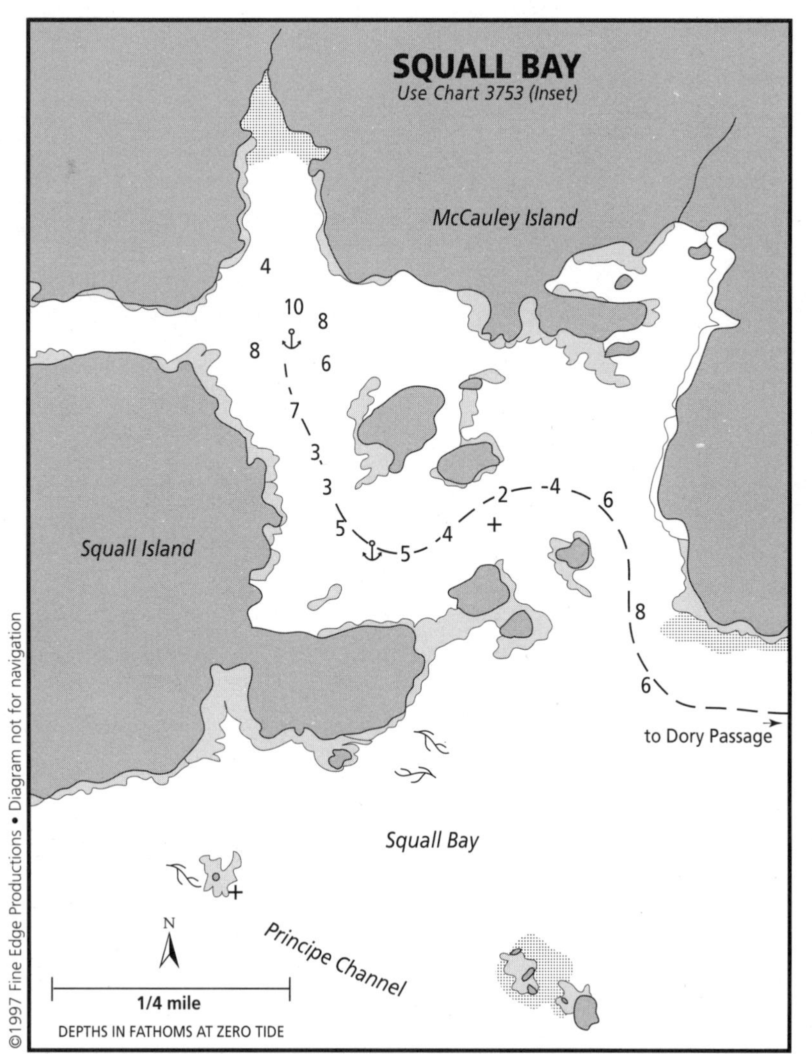

Squall Bay is entered between Wright Island and Cliff Islands, or by way of Dory Passage. Depths throughout the bay are irregular and no good anchorage is afforded. (p. 193, SD)

Squall Bay, east of Squall Island, holds a picturesque group of islets and rocks. It offers temporary anchorage for small boats although its bottom is irregular, hard and rocky, and swinging room is limited. Use the inset on Chart 3753 to enter and post a bow lookout to avoid rocks and kelp patches. The south part of the cove is perfectly calm during a westerly. The 10-fathom hole in the north cove has more swinging room and offers greater protection from southerlies. The intricate pattern of islets and rocks makes this area difficult to enter, and it would be a marginal retreat in a major storm. Colby Bay across Principe Channel provides better shelter and more swinging room than Squall Bay and is the recommended anchorage in foul weather.

Anchor (north) in the 10-fathom hole over a hard rocky bottom; fair holding with a well-set anchor.

Port Canaveral, Canaveral Passage

Charts 3753 (inset), 3746; anchor (nook west end of Canaveral Passage): 53°34.17′ N, 130°08.55′ W; anchor (Dixon Island nook): 53°35.08′ N, 130°10.16′ W (NAD 27)

Port Canaveral, between the NW side of Squall Island and the south side of McCauley Island, is suitable for small vessels but local knowledge is advised.

Anchorage for small vessels can be obtained in Port Canaveral about 0.15 mile SE of Red Point in 14 to 15 fathoms (26 to 27 m), mud bottom. The holding ground is good and the anchorage secure but is uncomfortable in winds from the NW quadrant. Small craft can find anchorage east of Round Islet, near the entrance of Canaveral Passage, and in the basin NE of Dixon Island. (p. 193, SD)

Anchor (nook west end of Canaveral Passage) in about 6 fathoms east of Round Island in 2 to 6 fathoms, unrecorded bottom.

Anchor (Dixon Island nook) in about 6 fathoms, unrecorded bottom.

Logan Bay

Chart 3746; entrance: 53°35.82′ N, 130°14.03′ W (NAD 27)

Logan Bay, 2 miles north of Dixon Island on the

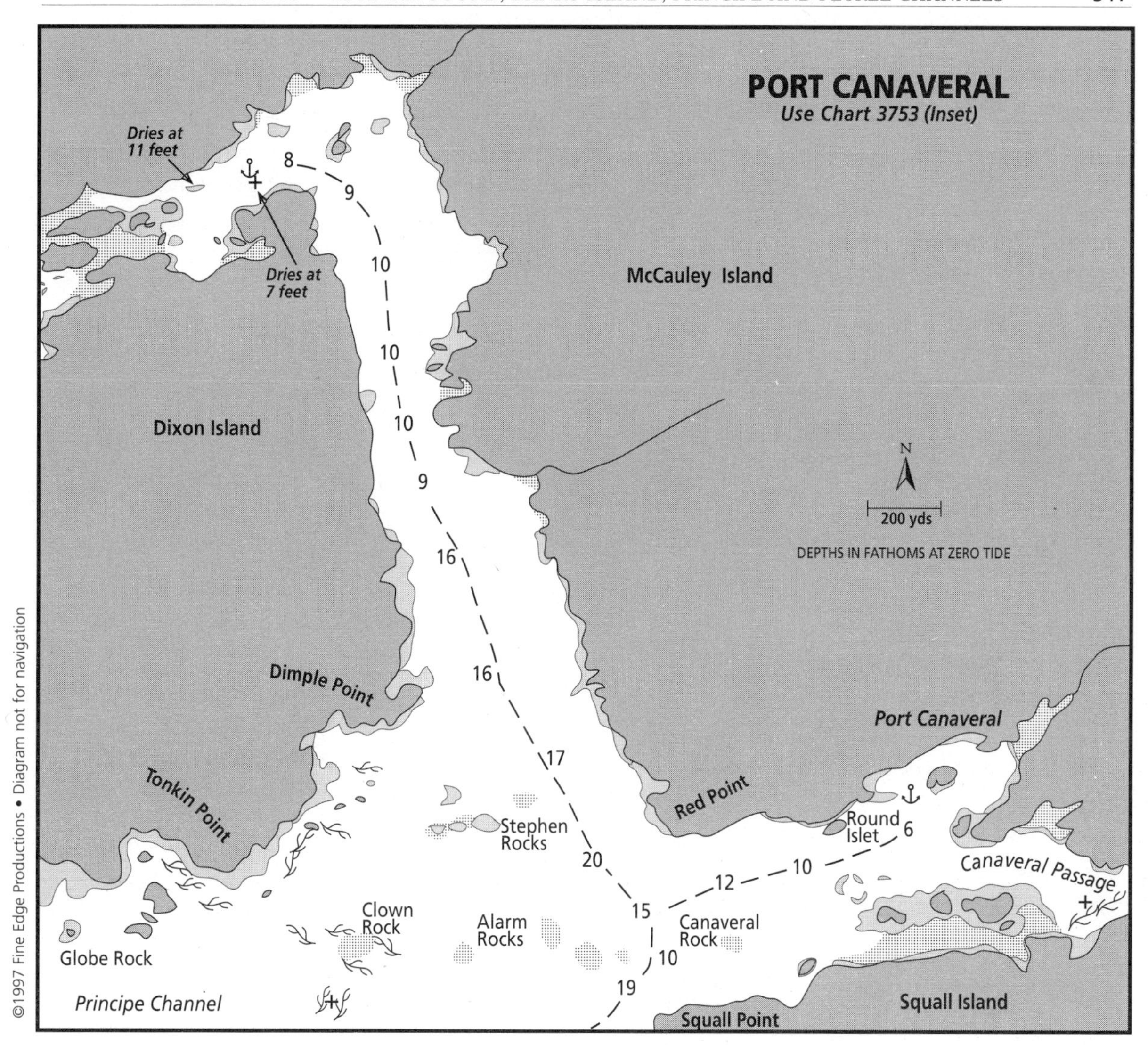

southwest shore of McCauley Island, appears to offer moderate shelter. It is fringed by numerous rocks.

Keyarka Cove

Chart 3747; entrance: 53°36.25′ N, 130°21.40′ W (NAD 27)

> *Keyarka Cove is 1.8 miles south of Keswar Point. End Hill rises 1.6 miles WNW of Keyarka Cove.* (p. 193, SD)

Keyarka Cove, a shallow bight in Banks Island, filled largely with drying flats, is useful only as a fair-weather lunch stop or kayak haulout.

Keswar Inlet

Chart 3747; entrance;
53°38.43′ N, 130°21.76′ W; anchor (inner basin): 53°38.43′ N, 130°20.48′ W (NAD 27)

> *Keswar Inlet, NE of Keswar Point, has several drying reefs in the entrance and within it.* (p. 193, SD)

Keswar Inlet, on the McCauley Island shore at the north entrance to Principe Channel, provides very good shelter in its inner basin in all weather except northwesterly storms. The inner basin which resembles a lagoon, has a nearly flat bottom between 2 and 4 fathoms; there are no driftlogs, and tree limbs create a horizontal line, indicating little chop.

The entrance to Keswar Inlet has an irregular bottom; be careful to avoid rocks by favoring the north shore of island (240). Within the narrows, you can avoid dangerous Pin Rock by hugging island (240) within 75 feet; the rock, which lies midchannel, is marked by kelp and is awash at mid-tide. Moderate current runs through the narrows. The muskeg water limits visibility to about 2 feet.

Anchor (inner basin) in 2 to 3 fathoms over a mud and grass bottom with good holding.

Principe Channel, North Entrance

Chart 3747; Principe Channel (north entrance): 53°39.50′ N, 130° 26.00′ W (NAD 27)
(See Chapter 11 for Browning Entrance and Larsen Harbour.)

Petrel Channel South

Chart 3746; south entrance:
53°33.60′ N, 130°02.00′ W (NAD 27)

Petrel Channel separates McCauley Island from Pitt Island and leads from Principe Channel to Ogden Channel. The fairway through Petrel Channel has a least width of 0.3 mile and is deep . . . (pp. 193, 194, SD)

Just north of Elbow Point, the slopes of Noble Mountain rise 2,885 feet, covered with tundra and glistening slabs of granite. A microwave tower stands on the summit.

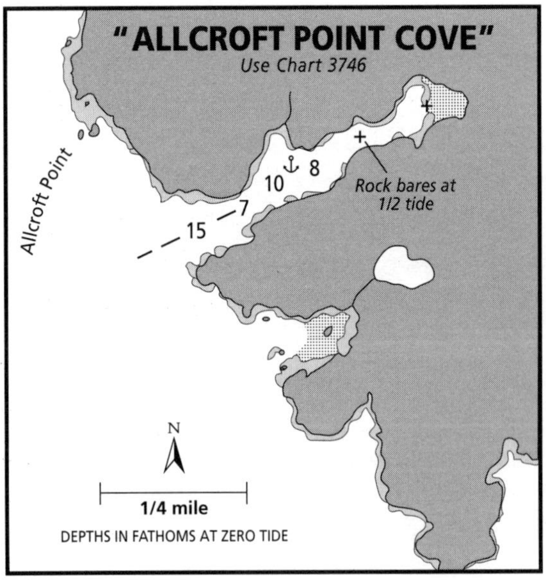

"Allcroft Point Cove"

Chart 3746; entrance: 53°35.65′ N, 130°03.40′ W; anchor: 53°35.76′ N, 130°02.98′ W (NAD 27)

Allcroft Point, 2.8 miles NW of Petrel Point, is prominent. (p. 194, SD)

Allcroft Point Cove, 0.3 mile southeast of Allcroft Point, offers fair-to-good protection in southeasterlies and northerlies, or makes a temporary lunch stop.

Anchor in the middle of the cove in 10 fathoms, with mixed bottom, unrecorded holding.

Hevenor Inlet

Charts 3753 (inset), 3746; entrance (outer): 53°37.60′ N, 130°04.00′ W; entrance (lagoon): 53°38.96′ N, 129°55.33′ W; anchor: 53°39.00′ N, 129°55.50′ W (NAD 27)

Hevenor Inlet is entered between Stark Point and Hevenor Point. Hevenor Islet, 1.4 miles east of Hevenor Point . . . Clark Islet, at the head of the inlet, has a drying rock close south, and shoal rocks 0.2 and 0.3 mile SSE . . . Small vessels can obtain sheltered anchorage at the head of the inlet, east of the last-mentioned rocks . . . Hevenor Lagoon, at the head of Hevenor Inlet, dries 0.4 mile within its very narrow entrance. The lagoon extends 4 miles SE from its entrance. (p. 194, SD)

The high mountains to the east make this an attractive inlet, but clearcutting detracts from its beauty. Fishing boats report there is good sheltered anchorage in an extended 10- to 12-fathom bottom west of the entrance to Hevenor Lagoon.

Anchor in 10 fathoms over an unrecorded bottom.

Newcombe Harbour

Chart 3753 (inset); entrance:
53°41.82′ N, 130°06.11′ W; anchor (east nook): 53°42.27′ N, 130°05.52′ W, anchor (north): 53°42.86′ N, 130°05.08′ W (NAD 27)

Newcombe Harbour is entered east of McCutcheon Point. The entrance is only 300 feet (91 m) wide and a shoal spit extends about 300 feet (91 m) south from McCutcheon Point.

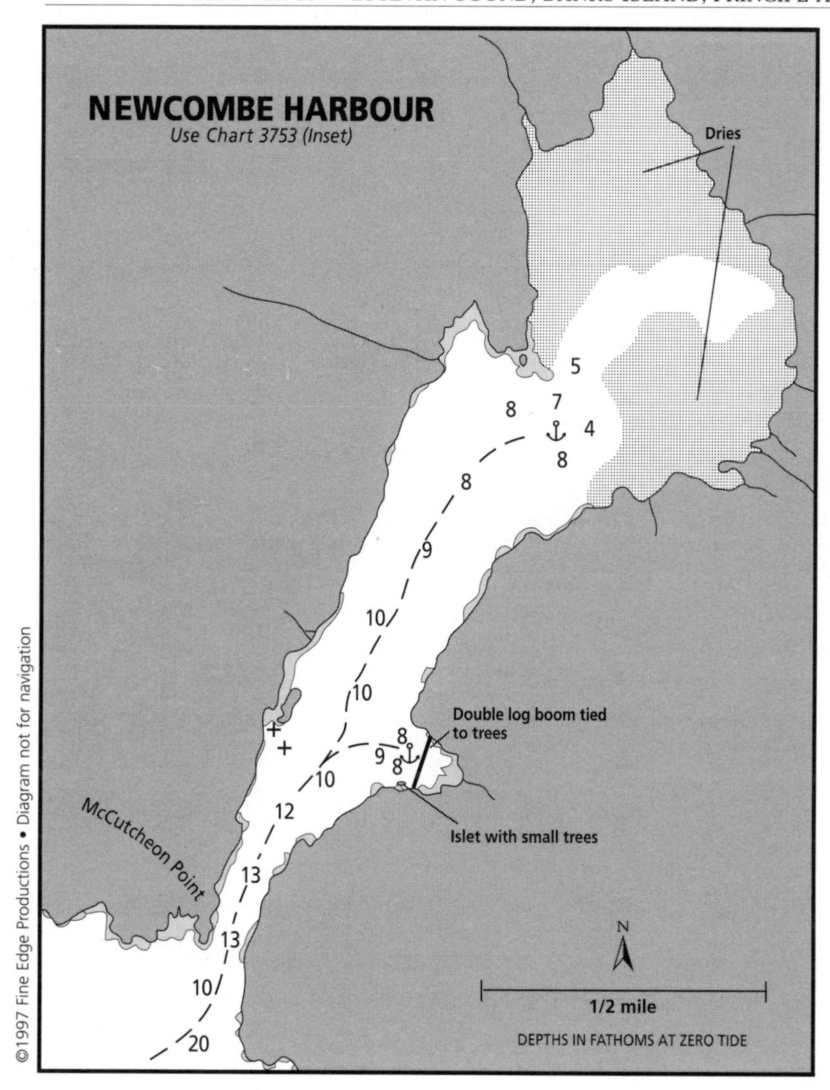

Anchorage for small vessels can be obtained in Newcombe Harbour, 1 mile within the entrance and about 0.2 mile SW of the prominent point, in 8 fathoms (15 m), mud bottom. (p. 194, SD)

Newcombe Harbour offers excellent protection from all weather for small craft transiting Petrel Channel. Enter Newcombe Harbour south of McCutcheon Point, avoiding a shoal on the north side. The shores of the harbor are steep-to and forested, and the absence of driftwood indicates good protection. Several creeks enter the head of the harbor at the north end, creating a large mud flat.

The nook on the east side provides good anchorage for one boat. Small boats can find anchorage in the basin, center of mud flat, north end; larger boats can anchor off the flats in the center of the harbor.

Anchor (east nook) in 9 fathoms over soft grey mud with excellent holding.

Anchor (north) in 7 fathoms over a mud bottom.

Petrel Channel Narrows

Chart 3746; position: 53°42.60′ N, 130°09.00′ W (NAD 27)

Around Elbow Point, the channel turns east-southeast. Due west of Noble Mountain, on the east side of Petrel Channel, several unmarked shoals extend about 100 yards into the channel.

The ebb flows south through here, and the flood flows north. Near Elbow Point, the current may run up to 3 knots. Because of its proximity to the ocean, summer water temperatures tend to be in the low fifties. There is moderate turbulence in the narrows and drift logs sometimes congregate near the Elbow.

Captain Cove

Charts 3753 (inset); entrance: 53°48.73′ N, 130°13.05′ W; anchor: 53°48.65′ N, 130°11.80′ W (NAD 27)

Captain Cove, entered north of Captain Point, is a good harbour, well sheltered from all winds. A drying rock is close west and several islets are 0.5 mile east of Captain Point. All have shoal water in their vicinity.

Anchorage can be obtained in 12 to 13 fathoms (22 to 24 m), mud, at the head of the cove. (p. 195, SD)

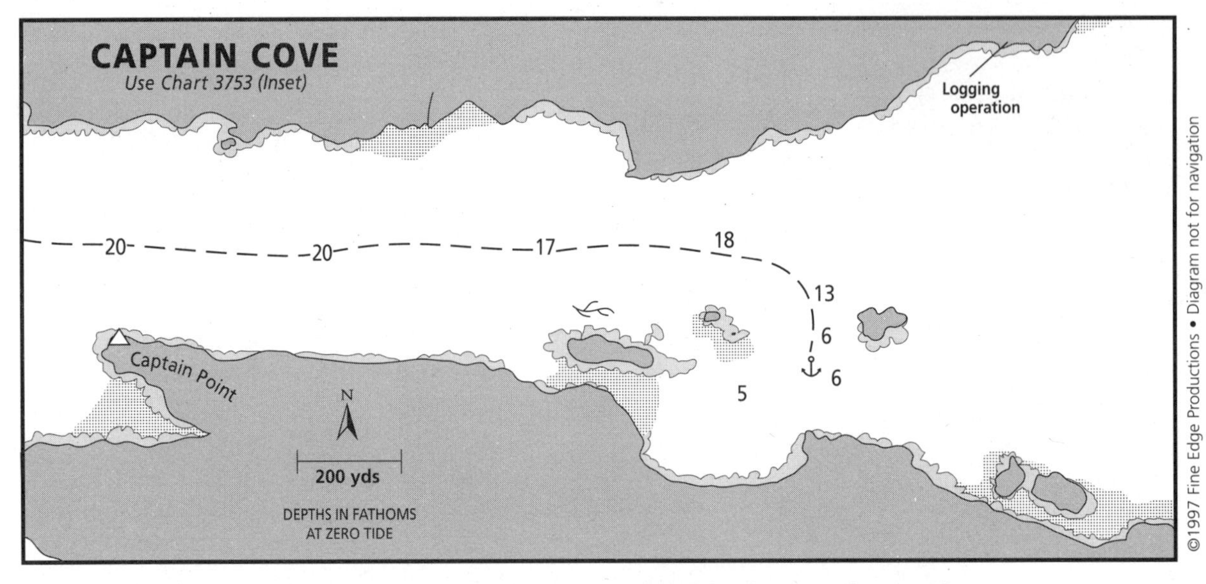

About 2.5 miles deep, Captain Cove offers very good protection. Although pretty, it was home to a noisy 24-hour logging operation.

Small boats can anchor southwest of the last midchannel islet. If a westerly chop picks up, you can tuck up against the western islets in 2 fathoms.

Anchor in 6 fathoms, mud bottom, with good holding.

Petrel Channel North

Chart 3747; north entrance:
53°49.00′ N, 130°18.00′ W (NAD 27)

The west side of Petrel Channel has low, rocky, wooded shores. The east side is mountainous and forested. At the north end of Petrel Channel, you can follow Ogden Channel north to Prince Rupert, west into Kitkatla Inlet, or south into Beaver Passage as described in Chapter 11.

Photographing the Bald Eagle
by Robin Hill-Ward

Bald eagles are abundant in British Columbia, making them easy to photograph. My husband Steve and I are cruising the North Coast waters this summer aboard *Charisma*, our 26-foot Nordic tug. Looking around, you can see the white head and neck feathers of a bald eagle high in the trees. The eagle, known for its keenness of vision, is able to see a mile away. Steve fishes for salmon and halibut, saving a few small fish he would normally use as bait to feed the eagles. Making a small cut at the top of the fish, Steve is careful not to collapse the air bladder causing the fish to sink. Standing on the bow, I grab my camera and pre-focus on the water a few feet from where Steve is in the skiff. He attracts the eagle's attention by waving the fish above his head, then tosses it into the air. In seconds, the eagle swoops down and, with great strength and power, grabs the fish in his talons. I click off several shots as water pours from his feathered legs. Capturing the beauty and grace of such a wonderful bird of prey makes a rare "Kodak moment."

I recommend using 200- to 400-speed film which stops the action and helps on overcast days. Good luck with the perfect shoot!

The eagle goes straight for the fish!

Coastal Bird Occurrences
by Bob Waldon

Photo by Ron Thiele

The magnificent bald eagle surveys the water

Coastal cruising affords marvelous opportunities to expand one's appreciation of birds. You encounter species that land-bound birders never see, and often in numbers that are mind-boggling. An added advantage is that many inshore species are desensitized by the routine presence of boats. They thus allow you to approach quite close before taking evasive action.

As with terrestrial species, the most exciting times of the year for oceanic and inshore species are during spring and fall migrations. Thus, May will give you a chance to see Arctic-bound shorebirds and waterfowl, all decked out in their breeding colors to make identification easier. In August and September you can catch them returning, but many are in their drab fall colors and look frustratingly alike.

In autumn you also have a chance to see pelagic (oceanic) species like shearwaters and storm-petrels that come to inshore waters to feed before heading back out into the open Pacific.

Winter can be more interesting than high summer in coastal waters because species that nest far northward or inland come here to spend their winters. Four species of loons, many species of ducks (including the colorful Harlequin), and the alcids (murres, puffins, guillemots, murrelets and auklets) are winter familiars. Most of the alcids are also year-round residents. Bald eagles, Peregrine falcons and other raptors are also present year-round.

Birds go where their food is most abundant. Tidal flats and river estuaries are rich in shore birds, waterfowl of all kinds, gulls, and the birds like falcons and jaegers (in migration) that prey on them. Locations of heavy tidal upwellings, and the places where migrant feed species like herring and salmon are funneled into restricted passages, are where you'll find the fish-eaters. The excitement of getting close to a "herring ball" and a feeding frenzy of gulls, murres and shearwaters may be accentuated by the presence of a pod of dolphins that add their slapping and thrashing to the din of the excited birds.

A boat is an unsteady platform, but the recent development of binoculars with built-in stabilizers has helped correct this fault. With the push of a button they maintain a steady image. Not only has this helped smooth out wobbles from shaky hands and rocking decks, it has enabled the manufacturers to go well beyond the former 10-power upper limit of hand-held glasses. Some stabilizer binoculars now offer power that matches the lower magnifications of spotting scopes.

All in all, the north coast of British Columbia is a spectacular birding area of unending pleasure.

Bob Waldon, newspaper columnist and author of *Feeding Winter Birds in the Pacific Northwest,* lives in Alert Bay.

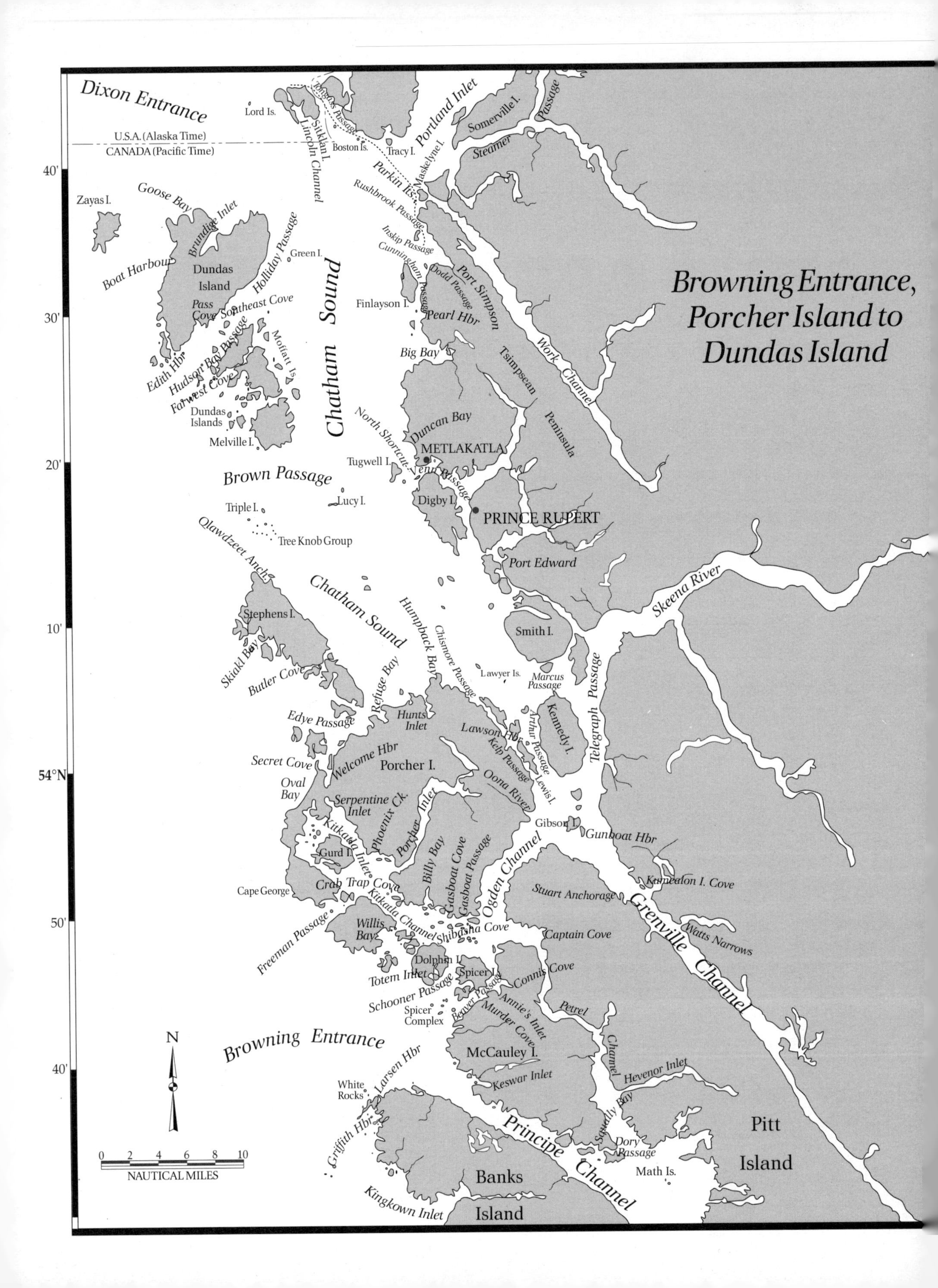

Browning Entrance, Porcher Island to Dundas Island
Dixon Entrance
U.S.A. (Alaska Time)
CANADA (Pacific Time)
Lord Is.
Portland Inlet
Somerville I.
Passage
Steamer
Boston Is.
Tracy I.
Sitklan I.
Lincoln Channel
Parkin Is.
Maskelyne I.
Rushbrook Passage
Inskip Passage
Cunningham Passage
Dodd Passage
Port Simpson
Zayas I.
Goose Bay
Brundige Inlet
Holliday Passage
Green I.
Boat Harbour
Dundas Island
Pass Cove
Southeast Cove
Chatham Sound
Finlayson I.
Pearl Hbr
Big Bay
Work Channel
Tsimpsean
Peninsula
Edith Hbr
Hudson Bay Passage
Moffatt Is.
Farwest Cove
Dundas Islands
Melville I.
North Shortcut
Duncan Bay
METLAKATLA
Tugwell I.
Venn Passage
Brown Passage
Digby I.
PRINCE RUPERT
Triple I.
Lucy I.
Tree Knob Group
Qlawdzeet Anch.
Port Edward
Skeena River
Chatham Sound
Humpback Bay
Chismore Passage
Stephens I.
Smith I.
Skiakl Bay
Butler Cove
Refuge Bay
Lawyer Is.
Marcus Passage
Telegraph Passage
Edye Passage
Hunts Inlet
Lawson Hbr
Arthur Passage
Kennedy I.
Kelp Passage
Secret Cove
Welcome Hbr
Porcher I.
Oona River
Lewis I.
Oval Bay
Serpentine Inlet
Phoenix Ck.
Porcher Inlet
Gibson I.
Gunboat Hbr
Kitkatla Inlet
Gurd I.
Billy Bay
Gasboat Cove
Gasboat Passage
Ogden Channel
Cape George
Crab Trap Cove
Kumealon I. Cove
Stuart Anchorage
Grenville Channel
Kitkatla Channel
Willis Bay
Freeman Passage
Shibasha Cove
Captain Cove
Watts Narrows
Dolphin I.
Totem Inlet
Spicer I.
Connis Cove
Schooner Passage
Beaver Passage
Annie's Inlet
Murder Cove
Spicer Complex
Petrel
Channel
N
Browning Entrance
McCauley I.
Keswar Inlet
Hevenor Inlet
White Rocks
Larsen Hbr
Squally Bay
Pitt Island
Griffith Hbr
Principe Channel
Dory Passage
0 2 4 6 8 10
NAUTICAL MILES
Banks Island
Math Is.
Kingkown Inlet
40'
30'
20'
10'
54°N
50'
40'

11

Browning Entrance, Porcher Island to Dundas Island

The complex of islands from Porcher to Dundas, along Chatham Sound's west side, offers some fine remote cruising grounds seldom visited by cruising boats. There are wonderful opportunities in this area for fishing and exploration. The islands in this chapter provide the first shelter for boats heading south from Ketchikan, Prince of Wales Island, or those crossing Hecate Strait to or from the Queen Charlotte Islands.

Browning Entrance

Chart 3747; west entrance(1.0 mile north of White Rock light): 53°39.10′ N, 130°34.00′ W (NAD 27)

> *Browning Entrance provides a convenient route from Hecate Strait to the Inner Passages. . . . Principe Channel heads southward from Browning Entrance; Beaver and Schooner Passages lead northward. Beaver Passage is marked by lights and is the better of the two channels. . . . Tide-rips are sometimes encountered off Baird Point. . . . Anchorages, with public mooring buoys, are in Larsen Harbour. . . .* (p.170, SD)

Larsen Harbour buoys

Browning Entrance is the jumping-off point for boats headed for the Queen Charlotte Islands.

Larsen Harbour

Charts 3747, 3927; entrance (0.85 mile due west of White Rocks Light): 53°38.10′ N, 130°32.37′ W; inner entrance (100 yards west of QR light): 53°37.76′ N, 130°32.43′ W; anchor (mud flat): 53°37.38′ N, 130°33.00′ W (NAD 27)

> *Larsen Harbour is between the north side of Larsen Island and the islands and drying reefs to the NW. It is only suitable for small craft and local knowledge is advised. The approach is between Larsen Harbour light and the drying reefs 0.1 mile west. Heavy kelp grows on the 4 fathom (7.3 m) bank in the approach to the harbour. . . . Anchorage in Larsen Harbour is rather confined in depths of 12 to 18 feet (3.7 to 5.5 m). . . . Six public mooring buoys with rubber fenders are in Larsen Harbour.* (p. 170, SD)

Larsen Harbour, strategically located on the northwest corner of Banks Island, is a gathering spot for cruising boats waiting to cross Hecate Strait to Queen Charlotte Islands. The six public mooring buoys provide secure mooring and an easy exit in the early morning. Large swells from the northwest can roll into the entrance of Larsen Harbour making it intimidating. Large kelp beds along both sides of the entrance cut the swell and chop substantially as soon as you enter the harbor. The fairway

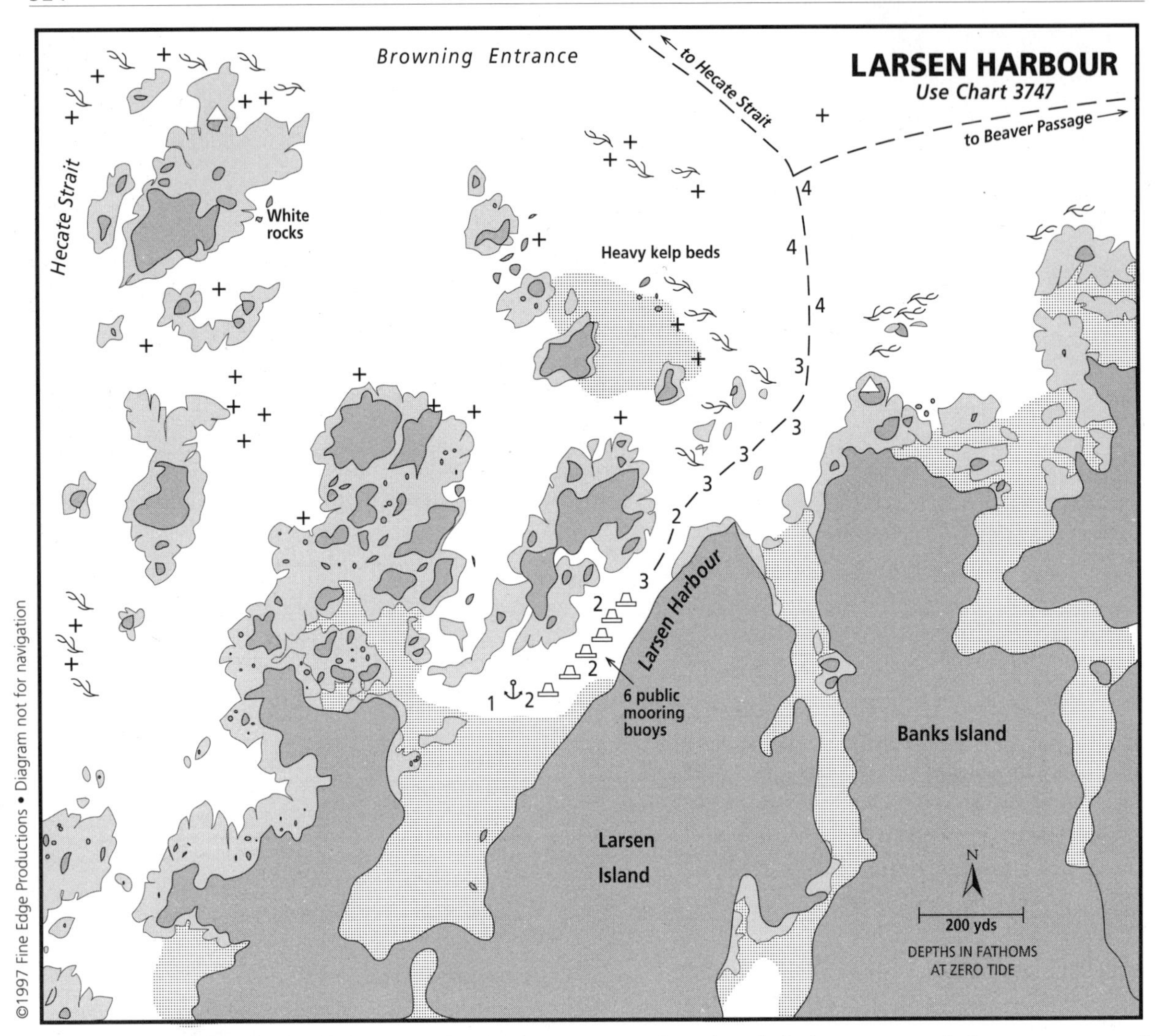

is somewhat difficult to discern and GPS can be useful in determining the point where you turn south toward the Larsen Harbour light. Several boats have bumped a rock or two upon entering Larsen Harbour, and these skippers consider Spicer Anchorage a much better place to hide from the weather before crossing Queen Charlotte Sound.

Larsen Harbour has a wild aspect; the loons moan and the bald eagles scream, and the trees look more like intertwined bushes.

While the trees are stunted and windswept, no swell or chop enters the harbor. Anchorage can be found at the head of the chain of buoys off the drying mud flat with limited swinging room. The public mooring buoys are preferable if available.

Anchor (mud flat) in 1 to 2 fathoms over sand and mud with good holding.

Bonilla Island

Chart 3747; position (Bonilla Island light): 53°29.55′ N, 130°38.10′ W (NAD 27)

Bonilla Island is strategically located close off the northwest corner of Banks Island. The lightstation gives critical reports for weather and sea conditions in Hecate Strait, and the lightkeepers collect and provide weather information for the MAREP program. The passageway between Bonilla and Banks Islands is notorious for nasty chop and swells whenever the currents and wind oppose each other. The west coast of Banks Island is not considered friendly cruising ground because of almost continual rough seas and dangerous unmarked hazards to navigation.

Griffith Harbour

Chart 3723 (inset); anchor (Ford Rock): 53°35.98′ N, 130°32.63′ W (NAD 27)

> *Griffith Harbour is entered between Anderson Rock and Kettle Rock, 0.2 mile east. The fairway, leading NE, is about 300 feet (91 m) wide at its narrowest part and has a least depth of 19 feet (5.8 m) west of Jewsbury Islets. . . . Small vessels can anchor in 9 fathoms (16 m), mud, about 0.15 mile NE of Appleby Island. Small craft can anchor in 5 fathoms (9 m) about 0.1 mile WSW of Ford Rock. The anchorages are sheltered from all winds. Local knowledge is advised for entering Griffith Harbour. Draught permitting, the best time to enter is at or near LW on a rising tide, when most dangers are visible.* (p. 170, SD)

Safely moored in Larsen Harbour before crossing Hecate Strait

Griffith Harbour and Kingkown Inlet, 7 miles to the south, are major spawning grounds for aquatic life, but this is not a human-friendly environment and is seldom visited by cruising boats. The entrance to Griffith Harbour is exposed to the south and has numerous rocks and reefs, making the approach dangerous in anything but calm conditions. The vegetation is highly stressed by the southeast winds that blow through the passage.

Anchor in 6 fathoms over a mud bottom.

Kingkown Inlet

Chart 3753 (inset); entrance (Reverie Passage): 53°28.00′ N, 130°26.00′ W; position (Byers Bay): 53°31.20′ N, 130°22.50′ W (NAD 27)

> *Kingkown Inlet can be entered by Reverie Passage or Allerton Passage but, because of numerous dangers in both passages, local knowledge is advised. Byers Bay, NE of Shadforth Islands, has several islets, drying rocks, and below-water rocks in it. A passage in the SE part of the bay leads to a very narrow arm which is obstructed by drying boulder banks.* (p. 169, SD)

The entrance bar across Kingkown Inlet is, as Captain Monahan says, the world's largest gravel pit, deposited by a glacier terminal moraine. This is not a friendly place and should only be considered by intrepid explorers adequately equipped.

Byers Bay is located in the northeast corner of Kingkown Inlet. Its anchoring potential is said to be marginal.

Beaver Passage

Charts 3747, 3927; west entrance (0.25 mile northwest of Hankin Rock): 53°42.60′ N, 130°25.00′ W; mid-passage turn (0.22 mile east of Connis light): 53°45.48′ N, 130°18.60′ W; north entrance (mid-channel Bully Island and Kitkatla Island): 53°47.85′ N, 130°20.00′ W (NAD 27)

Kingkown Inlet

Kingkown Inlet offers few secure anchorages and the area is filled with drying banks of boulders. When entering Allerton Passage from the north, it is best to wait for lower tides when most (not all) of the dangers are exposed. Reverie Passage, on the east side of Antle Islands, is a less-intimidating entrance; however, it is very narrow and exposed to the south. Be sure to hug the west side of the passage as indicated on Chart 3753 (inset). The area between Bonilla Island and Kingkown Inlet is almost always rough and in even moderate conditions vicious tide rips make this a dangerous area for small vessels. Kingkown Inlet looks like a giant's gravel pit. It is desolate. In fact, the west coast of Banks Island is no place for the timid.

—Captain Kevin Monahan

Beaver Passage is entered from the south between Hankin Rock and Ralph Islands. . . . Tidal streams flood north and ebb south. . . . The rate is 2 to 3 kn in the south approach and north entrance and 4 kn within the passage. (p. 171, SD)

Beaver Passage is the shortest route for those crossing Hecate Strait to the protected waters of the Inside Passage. The ferryboat route from the town of Queen Charlotte, however, uses Edye Passage on the north side of Porcher Island.

"Spicer Island Complex" ("Spicer Anchorage")

Charts 3747, 3927; entrance (southwest): 53°44.7′ N, 130°21.71′ W; anchor (unnamed island nook): 53°44.88′ N, 130°21.57′ W (NAD 27)

Spicer Island and South Spicer Island separate Beaver Passage from Schooner Passage. The passage separating Spicer and South Spicer Islands is narrow and intricate but suitable for small craft. (p. 171, SD)

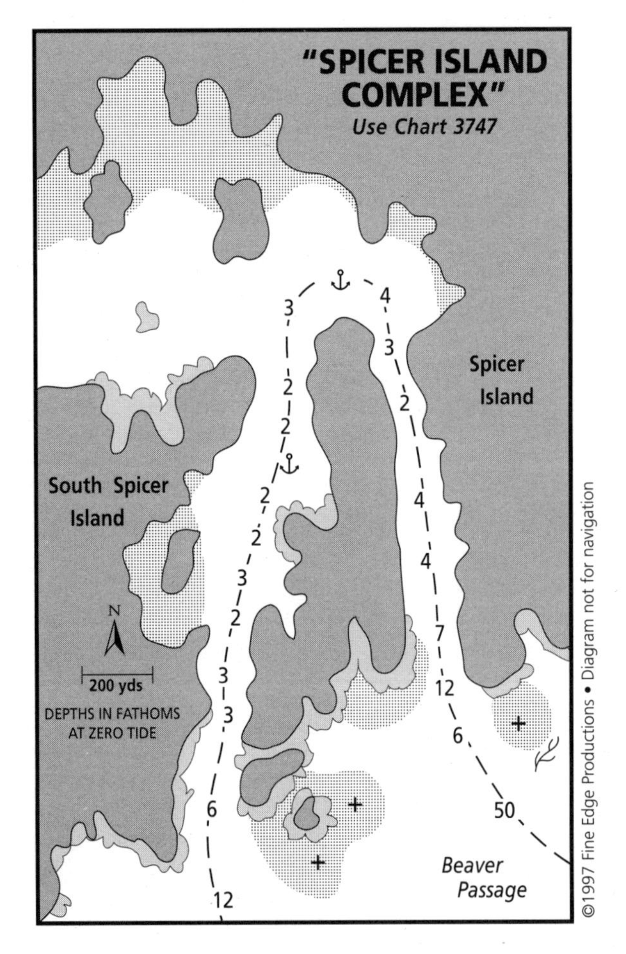

The wonderful landlocked passage between Spicer Island and South Spicer Island is well sheltered and offers cruising boats very good anchorage out of all swells and chop. There are no drift logs and grass grows along the rocky shore. Mergansers, bald eagles and other waterfowl frequent this Spicer Island Complex. The anchorage at the elbow of the passage is called "Spicer Anchorage" by fishermen who frequent it.

Anchor (unnamed island nook) in 1 to 2 fathoms over a soft grey mud bottom with shells and kelp. Holding is very good if you set your anchor well.

Murder Cove

Charts 3747, 3927; anchor: 53°44.26′ N, 130°19.44′ W (NAD 27)

Murder Cove is 1.2 miles SW of Connis Islet on the SE side of Beaver Passage. A waterfall flows into its south side. (p. 171, SD)

Murder Cove is a small indentation on the south shore of Beaver Passage. It can be used as a convenient lunch stop; however, it has limited swinging room for anything but one or two small vessels. The cove is full of floating rockweed and there are no logs on shore, indicating good protection from southerly weather. Favor the north shore on entering to avoid a shoal area.

Anchor off the small waterfall in 2 to 3 fathoms over a sand gravel bottom with fair holding.

Annie's Inlet

Charts 3747, 3927; entrance: 53°44.80′ N, 130°18.30′ W; anchor: 53°44.51′ N, 130°18.23′ W (NAD 27)

We call this small, unnamed inlet Annie's Inlet where *Baidarka*'s First Mate can find relief from the last of the swells in Hecate Strait and Browning Entrance. This is a well-protected anchor site for a small boat. You are surrounded by old-growth cedar and silver snags; nothing manmade is in sight. You will enjoy watching the huge green sun stars in the clear water. There are no logs on the beach, no surf, and cedar branches kiss the saltwater at high water. Dall porpoises swim just outside the inlet and harbor seals play inside. This is an intimate and scenic place.

Favor the west side upon entering; there are uncharted rocks on the east side that dry at 8 and 10 feet.

Anchor in 3 fathoms over a mud, grass and shell bottom with very good holding.

Calm anchorage, Porcher Island

Connis Cove

Charts 3747, 3927; entrance:
53°45.40′ N, 130°18.00′ W; anchor:
53°45.20′ N, 130°17.77′ W (NAD 27)

> *Connis Cove, east of Connis Islet, is almost filled with drying flats. . . . Anchorage for small craft can be obtained in Connis Cove, about 0.1 mile NE of a small wooded islet off the south entrance point of the cove. However, the depth in this anchorage is 16 fathoms (29 m).* (p. 171, SD)

Connis Cove is exposed to the north, but fair protection can be found from most weather if you tuck in behind the wooded islets on the south shore. River otters are busy on these islets and the large drying flat off the creek is a favorite resting place for Canada geese.

Anchor in 5 fathoms over mud and sand with some kelp; fair holding.

Ogden Channel

Charts 3773, 3927; south entrance:
53°49.60′ N, 130°18.70′ W; north entrance:
53°55.40′ N, 130°14.50′ W (NAD 27)

> *Ogden Channel separates Pitt Island from Porcher Island and leads north from Beaver Passage and Petrel Channel to Grenville Channel and Arthur Passage. It is deep and free of dangers in the fairway.* (p. 195, SD)

Skene Cove

Charts 3773, 3927; entrance:
53°50.90′ N, 130°20.25′ W (NAD 27)

> *Skene Cove is 1 mile north of Sparrowhawk Point and Peter Point is 2 miles farther NNE. Bareside Point, 1.7 miles NE of Peter Point, rises steeply to the summit of Bareside Mountain.* (p. 195, SD)

The tiny nook in the south shore may be useful to small boats as a lunch stop or emergency shelter.

Alpha Bay

Charts 3773, 3927; position:
53°51.95′ N, 130°17.10′ W (NAD 27)

> *Alpha Bay, 2.3 miles north of Comrie Head, is between Fish Point and Alpha Point; it is filled with drying flats which front the mouth of Alpha Creek.* (p. 195, SD)

Alpha Bay is a very deep open bight and is steep-to. Fishing boats sometimes anchor off the drying shoal.

Schooner Passage

Charts 3747, 3927; south entrance:
53°44.50′ N, 130°25.30′ W; north entrance:
53°47.20′ N, 130°23.20′ W (NAD 27)

> *Schooner Passage, between Spicer and Dolphin Islands, is entered from the south between Christie Islands and Boys Point. . . . Tidal streams in Schooner Passage attain 1 to 2 kn in the south entrance and from 3 to 4 kn in the north entrance, where it is much narrower. The flood sets north and the ebb south.* (p. 172, SD)

Schooner Passage is used as a shortcut from Browning entrance to Kitkatla Inlet.

Porcher Island, crabs on the way to market

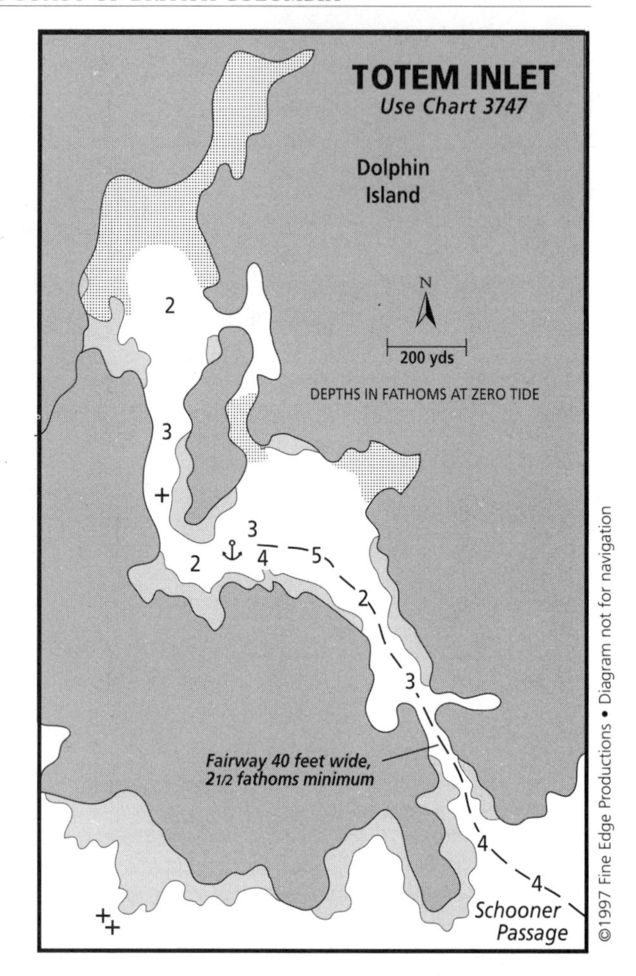

Shaman Cove

Charts 3747, 3927; entrance:
53°45.15′ N, 130°25.65′ W; anchor:
53°45.54′ N, 130°36.03′ W (NAD 27)

> *Shaman Cove, close NE of Boys Point, is encumbered with rocks; it offers shelter to small craft but local knowledge is advised.* (p. 172, SD)

Anchorage can be found at the head of Shaman Cove; however, it is exposed to the southeast. Totem Inlet, immediately to the north, provides superior shelter for cruising boats.

Anchor in 2 fathoms over an unrecorded bottom.

Totem Inlet

Charts 3747, 3927; entrance:
53°45.38′ N, 130°24.89′ W; anchor:
53°45.75′ N, 130°25.48′ W (NAD 27)

> *Totem Inlet, 0.3 mile NW of Letts Islets, is entered through a narrow passage with a least depth of 27 feet (8.2 m) in the fairway. It offers shelter to small craft but local knowledge is advised.* (p. 172, SD)

Totem Inlet, on the southeast corner of Dolphin Island, is a scenic, landlocked inlet providing good shelter for cruising boats. There is adequate room for several boats to anchor here. The entrance is about 40 feet wide with about 2 1/2 fathoms minimum in the fairway. The first basin is perfectly calm with grassy margins along the shore and rockweed floating in still waters. The inner lagoon can best be explored by dinghy.

It could be difficult to enter Totem Inlet during times of heavy southwest swells. Under such conditions it would be easier to head 1.5 miles north to Shibasha Cove.

Anchor in 3 fathoms over soft mud bottom with good holding.

"Shibasha Cove"

Charts 3747, 3927; entrance:
53°46.80′ N, 130°28.83′ W; anchor:
53°46.98′ N, 130°24.43′ W (NAD 27)

Shibasha Island is connected to the NE end of Dolphin Island by a drying bank. A drying ledge extends 0.1 mile south from the south end of the island. . . . Anchorage for small craft can be found in the sheltered cove SW of Shibasha Island. It is entered through a narrow passage with a least depth of 15 feet (4.6 m) which leads south of the above-mentioned drying ledge. (p. 172, SD)

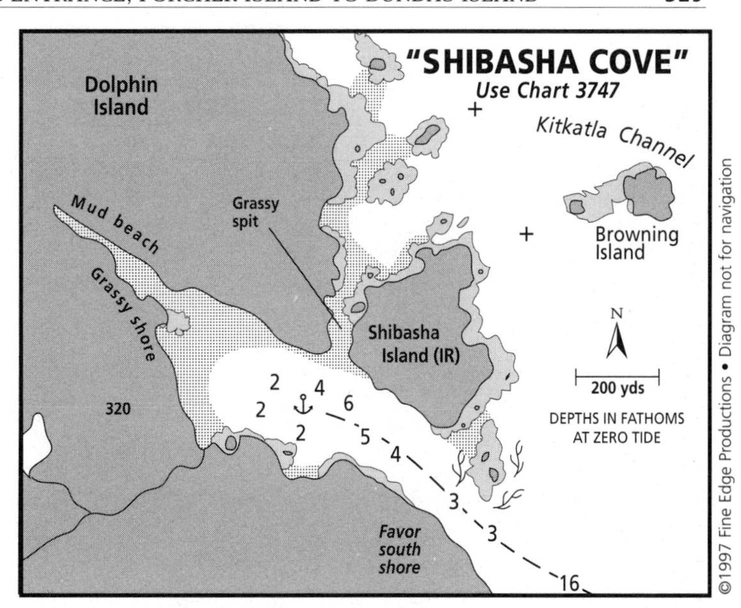

Shibasha Island, on the northeast corner of Dolphin Island, provides good protection in all weather. A large, dangerous reef in the middle of the entrance is awash on an 18-foot tide. You can easily avoid this reef by favoring the south shore with 2 fathoms in the fairway. The reef is well-marked with a large patch of kelp. There is swinging room for up to six boats. Anchorage can be taken anywhere in the cove off the drying flat.

Anchor in about 3 fathoms over soft grey mud with kelp and wood debris; good holding.

Willis Bay

Charts 3761, 3747, 3927; entrance:
53°47.00′ N, 130°32.20′ W; mooring buoys:
53°48.31′ N, 130°32.27′ W (NAD 27)

Willis Bay, on the east side of Goschen Island, and 1 mile north of Moore Island, affords shelter during west winds. . . . Two public mooring buoys are in Willis Bay . . . Shakes Islands, east of Willis Bay, are separated by narrow and intricate channels obstructed by numerous drying reefs and foul ground. No attempt should be made, even by small craft, to pass from Browning Entrance into Kitkatla Channel through any of these channels. . . . The narrow and intricate channel between Prager Islands and Shakes Islands is only suitable for small craft and local knowledge is advised. The SW coast of Dolphin Island, east of Prager Islands, is fronted by numerous islets, drying rocks and below-water rocks. (p. 172, SD)

Kitkatla Pass is used by locals to connect Willis Bay to Kitkatla Channel. The north end is very tricky and must be done with a good bow lookout. Sheltered anchorage is reported on the south side of Shakes Islands, in a small basin next to Porcher Island, in about 13 fathoms.

Dolphin Lagoon

Charts 3747, 3927; entrance:
53°46.68′ N, 130°28.23′ W (NAD 27)

Dolphin Lagoon penetrates the west side of Dolphin Island; its entrance dries. (p. 172, SD)

Dolphin Lagoon is filled with a sizable island and several islets. Its cruising potential is unknown.

Freeman Passage

Charts 3761, 3927; west entrance:
53°49.40′ N, 130°39.75′ W; east entrance:
53°51.10′ N, 130°34.20′ W (NAD 27)

Freeman Passage, between the NW side of Goschen Island and the SE side of Porcher Peninsula, is narrow and intricate. The fairway is about 300 feet (91 m) wide between the dangers on each side. It is only suitable for small vessels and local knowledge is advised. . . . The flood sets NE and the ebb SW through the fairway and the maximum rate is 4 kn. (p. 173, SD)

Freeman Passage is the western entrance to Kitkatla Inlet. Public mooring buoys can be found in a small cove on the northwest shore.

Another lagoon to explore!

Freeman Passage Mooring Buoys

Charts 3761, 3927; position:
53°50.49′ N, 130°38.59′ W (NAD 27)

> *Four public mooring buoys with rubber fenders are in a narrow bay on the north side of the west end of Freeman Passage. A rock, with less than 6 feet (2 m) over it, lies 0.3 mile SE of the entrance to the narrow bay.* (p. 173, SD)

On the northwest shore of Freeman Passage is a small cove with four public mooring buoys. The cove is well sheltered from all weather.

"Absalom Cove'

Charts 3761, 3927; entrance:
53°50.42′ N, 130°36.54′ W; position:
53°51.18′ N, 130°37.25′ W (NAD 27)

> *Absalom Island, with a group of islets close SW of its south point, and Coquitlam Island, are on the NW side of the east end of the fairway through Freeman Passage. A shoal rock is close south of, and drying and below-water rocks fringe, the east side of Coquitlam Island; between this foul ground and that which fringes Goschen Island the fairway is at its minimum width.* (p. 173, SD)

Absalom Cove is useful as an anchor site when the mooring buoys in Freeman Passage are crowded, or as a base camp for exploring the surrounding islets and reefs.

Kitkatla Channel

Charts 3747, 3761, 3927; south entrance:
53°47.10′ N, 130°20.80′ W; north entrance:
53°51.50′ N, 130°32.75′ W (NAD 27)

Kitkatla Channel connects Kitkatla and Porcher inlets to Beaver Passage. The village of Kitkatla is located on the south shore.

Kitkatla

Charts 3761, 3747, 3921; public floats:
53°47.74′ N, 130°26.18′ W (NAD 27)

> *Kitkatla is an Indian settlement on a point of land on the north side of Dolphin Island. It has a post office (V0V 1C0), a mission and a large church with a spire. Fresh water and provisions are usually available. . . . The public wharf and floats at Kitkatla . . . are protected by an islet and breakwater and have 643 feet (196 m) of berthing space. A least depth of 8 feet (2.4 m) lies along the outside of the main float. . . . Anchorage for vessels of moderate size can be obtained about 0.3 mile NW of Kitkatla in depths of 10 to 18 fathoms (18 to 33 m). The anchorage is indifferent with a mud bottom and strong tidal streams.* (p. 173, SD)

Kitkatla is a thriving village with its mission church spire clearly visible.

Gasboat Passage

Charts 3761, 3927; east entrance:
53°49.60′ N, 130°20.30′ W; west entrance:
53°49.60′ N, 130°25.00′ W (NAD 27)

> *Gasboat Passage separates Pelham Islands from Porcher Island. The fairway has a least depth of 42 feet (12.8 m) but drying rocks north of Pelham Islands restrict the channel to less than 0.1 mile wide and make it suitable only for small craft.* (p. 173, SD)

Cruising boats should experience no problem using Gasboat Passage; however, there are a number of submerged rocks on the south side of the passage at its west entrance.

"Gasboat Cove"

Charts 3761, 3927; entrance:
53°49.86′ N, 130°25.26′ W; anchor:
53°50.22′ N, 130°24.84′ W (NAD 27)

Gasboat Cove is what we call the small L-shaped cove on the northwest end of Gasboat Passage. It offers very good protection deep in the eastern part of the cove over a shallow, flat bottom. You are surrounded by scenic old growth here. On

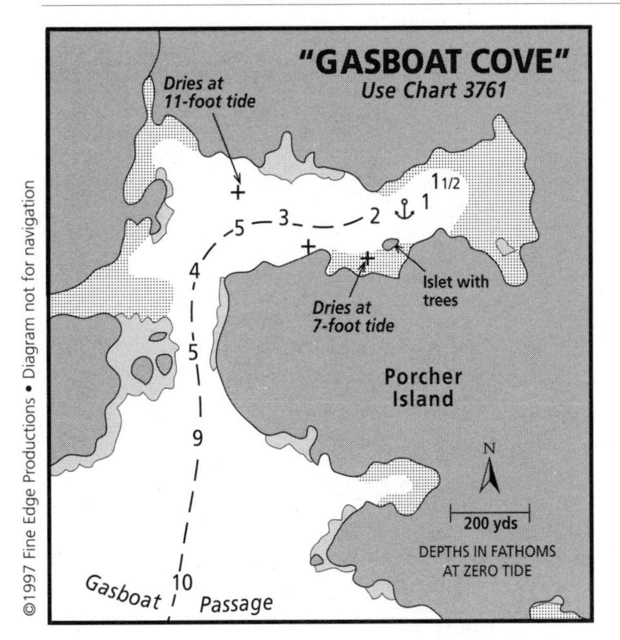

entering Gasboat Cove, avoid the rocks on the west shore and the rock at the elbow which extends 150 feet from the north shore, awash at 11 feet. Also avoid the two rocks awash on 7 feet off the south shore of the inner cove. Anchor north of the uncharted wooded islet.

Anchor in 1 to 2 fathoms over soft grey mud bottom with fair-to-good holding.

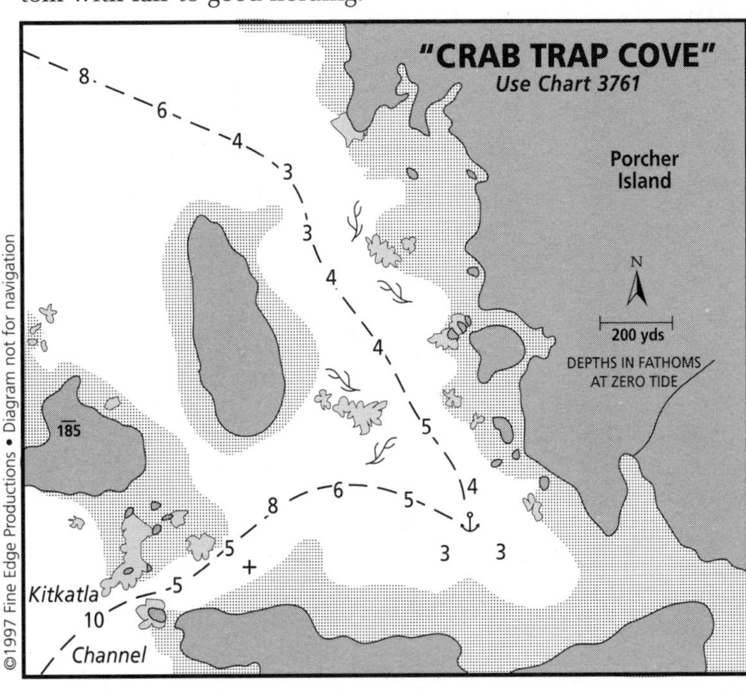

Billy Bay

Charts 3761, 3927; entrance: 53°49.83′ N, 130°25.80′ W; anchor: 53°50.43′ N, 130°25.97′ W (NAD 27)

> *Billy Bay is encumbered with drying rocks and only suitable for small craft.* (p. 173, SD)

Billy Bay offers good shelter in the eastern section of the cove. Avoid the rock awash at 3 feet near the elbow at midchannel. We prefer Gasboat Cove, a half-mile to the east, because it is more intimate.

Anchor in 4 fathoms over an unrecorded bottom.

"Crab Trap Cove"

Charts 3761, 3927; south entrance: 53°50.97′ N, 130°30.91′ W; north entrance: 53°51.80′ N, 130°31.40′ W; anchor: 53°51.07′ N, 130°30.00′ W (NAD 27)

> *Small vessels can obtain well sheltered anchorage, in about 7 fathoms (12.8 m), about 0.3 mile ENE of the 110 foot (34 m) high islet at the NW end of Cessford Islands.* (p. 173, SD)

The Cessford Islands, at the north end of Kitkatla Channel, provide a well-sheltered basin to the east which we call Crab Trap Cove. The flat mud and grassy bottom of Crab Trap Cove is a favorite crabbing location of fishermen. The northern entrance to the cove is more accessible; however, sand spits extend from both shores and must be avoided. The south entrance is usable, but very narrow with several reefs, some marked by kelp. In both cases a very slow entrance speed is prudent. There is a large, flat area with plenty of swinging room in the middle of the cove to accommodate several boats.

The westernmost Cessford Island has a bright, white sandy beach which makes an excellent kayak haul-out and campsite.

Anchor in 3 to 4 fathoms over soft mud with grass bottom with very good holding.

Porcher Inlet

Charts 3761, 3927; entrance:
53°52.70′ N, 130°30.70′ W (NAD 27)

Porcher Inlet has generally steep-to shores and depths too great for anchorage, except near its head. It is only suitable for small craft because of the numerous reefs in its narrow entrance; entry should be attempted only at or near HW slack. (p. 174, SD)

Porcher Inlet nearly cuts Porcher Island in two. Its entrance is encumbered with a shallow bar with many isolated rocks. Porcher Narrows, 2 miles northeast of the entrance, has tidal streams which reach 7 knots on spring flood and ebb. The entrance to Salt Lagoon at the head of the inlet has a convoluted channel that dries. The narrows has an irregular bottom with several drying rocks on both sides.

Kitkatla Inlet

Charts 3761, 3927; entrance:
53°51.50′ N, 130°32.75′ W (NAD 27)

Anchorage can be obtained almost anywhere in Kitkatla Inlet. Depths in the inlet are generally less than 25 fathoms (46 m) with a mud bottom. (p. 174, SD)

Kitkatla Inlet is a horseshoe-shaped basin on the west side of Porcher Island with Gurd Island in the center. Gurd Inlet is on the south side of Gurd Island; Serpentine Inlet is in the northwest corner of the basin and Dries Inlet is in the north corner of the basin. Kitkatla Inlet is exposed to southeast winds and chop.

Captain Kevin Monahan adds: "There is only one place in Kitkatla Inlet to even consider during a southeast blow. That is along the northwest side of Gurd Island. Anchor near 53°54.70' N, 130°39.10' W over a mud bottom with moderate holding close under the lee of Gurd Island, the closer to the island the better. I have anchored here in a 60-knot southeast wind and it is tolerable, but a close anchor watch must be maintained. Better get anchor and stern tie to the beach. In a normal southeast gale, this anchorage is fine; but remember that when it is blowing southeast 60 knots in Hecate Strait, it is also blowing southeast 60 knots in Kitkatla Inlet. In three years of working on the *Bahine Post*, this was the only time I ever dragged anchor. Anywhere else

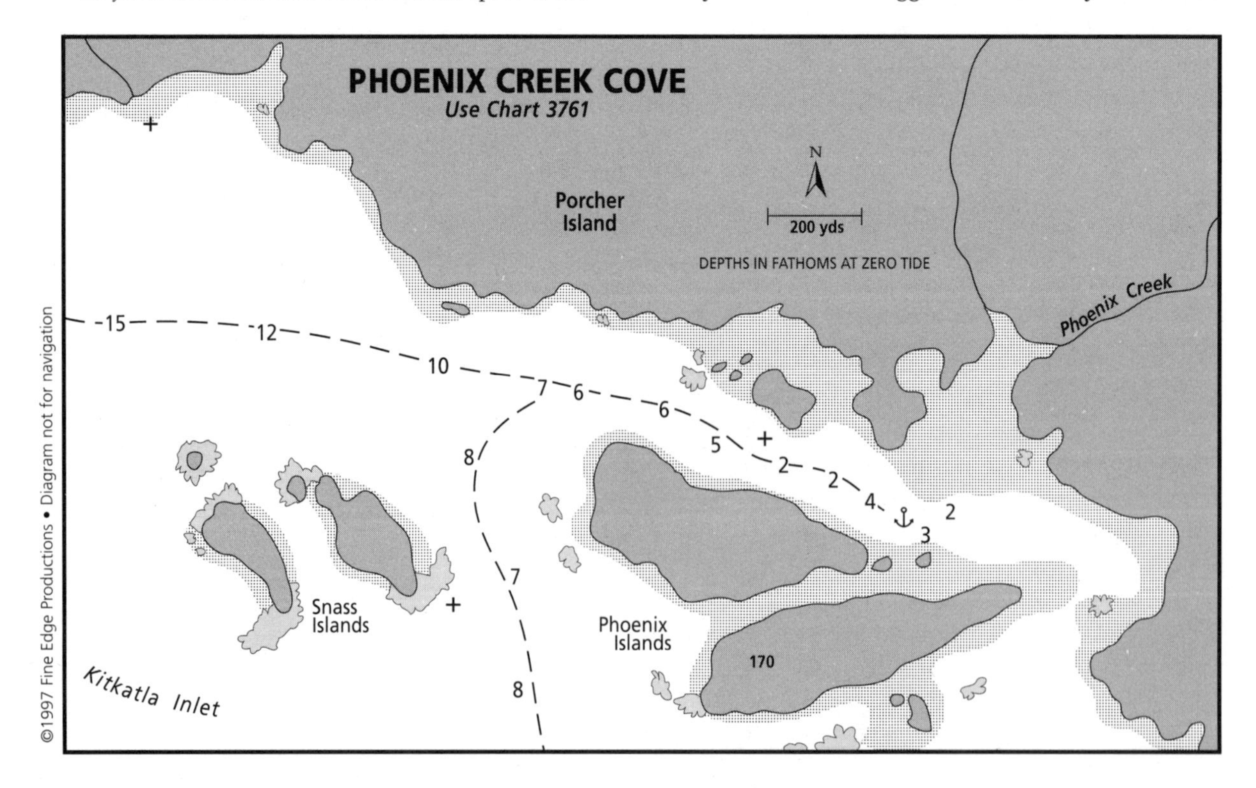

in Kitkatla Inlet proper is totally untenable in southeast gales."

Photo courtesy Kevin Monahan

Seiner at work in the fog

"Phoenix Creek Cove

Charts 3761, 3927; west entrance: 53°53.65′ N, 130°31.40′ W; anchor 53°53.53′ N, 130°30.77′ W (NAD 27)

We call the narrow passageway between Phoenix Islands and the outlet of Phoenix Creek Phoenix Cove. This scenic, well-protected spot is a favorite of loons and eagles. It has grassy campsites on shore and is a generally quiet retreat. Anchorage can be found in the passage off the drying flat of Phoenix Creek.

Anchor in 2 to 3 fathoms over sand and mud bottom with good holding.

Gurd Inlet

Charts 3761, 3927; entrance: 53°53.28′ N, 130°39.16′ W; anchor: 53°53.18′ N, 130°37.55′ W (NAD 27)

Gurd Inlet is entered 0.5 mile SE of Robert Island. Its narrow entrance dries at LW; at other stages of the tide there are rapids through it. The inlet is accessible only to small craft at HW slack.
(p. 174, SD)

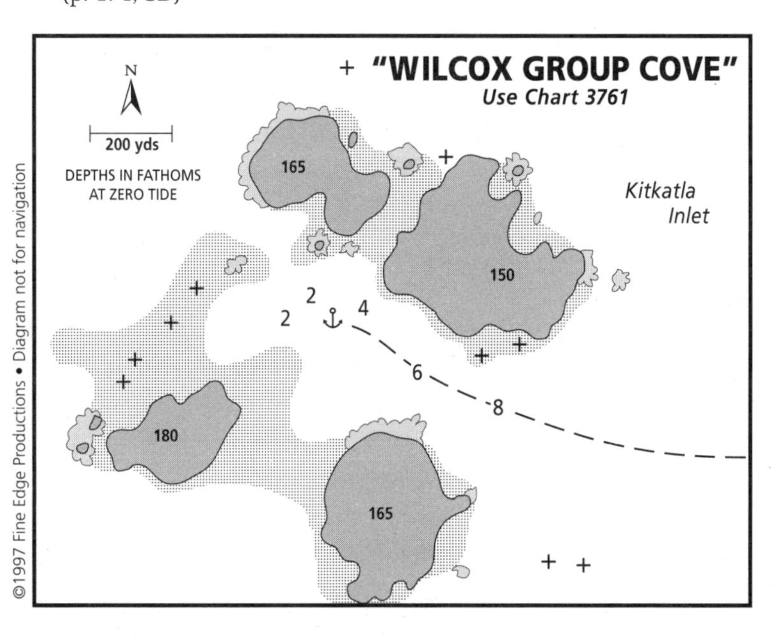

Gurd Inlet is well sheltered and is reported to have 5 to 7 fathoms at the east end of the inlet. The entrance to Gurd Inlet is encumbered with a number of rocks and reefs and should be entered near high-water slack with alert bow lookouts.

"Wilcox Group Cove"

Charts 3761, 3927; anchor: 53°55.17′ N, 130°39.88′ W (NAD 27)

The Wilcox Group, with Clamshell Island and other islets, drying reefs and below-water rocks, extend 2 miles south from the entrance of Serpentine Inlet.
(p. 174, SD)

The Wilcox Group consists of several islands on the northwest side of Gurd Island. Approaching from the east, you can anchor in the center of the Wilcox Group. At high water, there is some chop in this cove; however, the reefs at low water form a natural breakwater. This cove is useful in stable weather only.

Anchor in 3 fathoms over soft mud with shells and weed bottom with fair-to-good holding.

Serpentine Inlet

Charts 3761, 3927; entrance:
53°56.02′ N, 130°40.24′ W; anchor:
53°56.65′ N, 130° 40.80′ W (NAD 27)

> *Serpentine Inlet, 2 miles west of Dries Inlet, is very shallow and almost filled with drying flats.* (p. 174, SD)

Serpentine Inlet is badly exposed to southeast winds and should be used as a fair weather anchorage only. The entrance is narrow with drying flats on either side; caution and close coordination with the tide tables is advised. Temporary anchorage can be found at the head of the inlet off a small grey-pebble beach. There are several abandoned cabins at the north end of the inlet. The sandy beach at Oval Bay is less than a half-mile away. We understand there may be a trail across to the beach but we have not been able to find it.

Anchor in 1 to 2 fathoms over a soft bottom with fair-to-good holding.

Dries Inlet

Charts 3761, 3927; entrance:
53°56.25′ N, 130°37.00′ W (NAD 27)

> *Dries Inlet, at the head of Kitkatla Inlet, has extensive drying sand and gravel flats fronting its shores. Camp Creek flows into the inlet at the SE entrance.* (p. 174, SD)

Dries Inlet is a large, shallow area exposed to winds, especially from the south. Temporary anchorage can be taken anywhere short of the drying flats in 2 to 3 fathoms over a soft bottom.

Chatham Sound, Western Side

Charts 3956, 3957, 3959, and 3960

The western side of Chatham Sound, extending from the north end of Porcher Island to Dundas Island, offers remote cruising with scenic and isolated anchorages. The three main passages between Chatham Sound and Hecate Strait and Dixon Entrance to the west are Edye Passage, north of Porcher Island, Brown Passage in the center, and Hudson Bay Passage on the south side of Dundas Island. Currents can be strong in all of these passages. Nasty chop can be found in Chatham Sound as well as in the passages when wind opposes the current.

Humpback Bay, Porcher Island

Chart 3956; entrance: 54°05.50′ N, 130°23.20′ W;
anchor: 54°05.26′ N, 130°23.99′ W (NAD 83)

> *The remains of a jetty extend ENE from the settlement across the north end of the mud flats in Humpback Bay.* (p. 121, SD)

Humpback Bay, on the northeast corner of Porcher Island, once held an active fishing cannery known as "Porcher Island." Only the pilings, old cannery buildings, and the ruins of houses remain. The large flat south of the cannery dries at low water. The shore along the bay is lined with cabins and derelict fishing boats.

Humpback Bay provides good shelter from most weather, especially southeasterlies, in the narrow channel between the old pilings and the two islands on the north side.

Anchor in 4 fathoms, over mud and gravel bottom with fair holding.

Hunt Inlet

Charts 3909 metric (inset), 3956 metric;
entrance: 54°05.16′ N, 130°27.25′ W; public
float: 54°04.12′ N, 130°26.68′ W; anchor:
54°02.78′ N, 130°26.32′ W (NAD 83)

> *Hunt Inlet has drying ledges on both sides which should be given a good berth. Drying reefs lie off the east side of the inlet, about 0.5 mile north of the public wharf. The settlement Hunts Inlet, about 0.7 mile from the entrance, is used as a base during the fishing season. Houses lie along the shore south of the public wharf. . . . The public wharf, consisting of a pier and floats, offers 64 m (210 ft) of berthing space. There is a depth of 3 m (10 ft) at the outer end of the floats.* (p. 131, SD)

Hunt Inlet, two miles long, indents the north end of Porcher Island. It lies between the Creek Islands on the west and a large group of unnamed islands, rocks and islets off the north end of Porcher Island. Use the inset on Chart 3909 to identify the hazards.

Hunt Inlet offers welcome protection from the vagaries of Chatham Sound. Well-sheltered anchorage can be found in the middle of the inlet. You can, however, experience a nasty chop near the entrance when a strong northwest blows against an ebb tide. There's a small public dock, largely filled with locals, with traditional red railings, and a number of nice-looking homes with large wood sheds. The remote, quiet atmosphere of Hunt Inlet exudes a sleepy vitality.

The inner basin has a very narrow channel with a least depth of one fathom, nearly chock full of kelp east of treed islet (18). At the bitter end, there is a private float. The inner basin is landlocked and offers total shelter over a large area.

Anchor in the inner basin in 2 fathoms, mud bottom with good holding.

Refuge Bay

Charts 3909 metric (inset), 3956 metric; anchor: 54°03.24′ N, 130°32.44′ W (NAD 83)

> *Refuge Bay, entered between Pearce Point and Table Point, has a sand flat extending 0.5 mile from its head. Both entrance points, and both sides of the bay, are fringed with drying ledges and foul ground. . . . Anchorage for vessels of moderate size can be obtained in the middle of Refuge Bay in 14 to 16 fathoms (26 to 29 m), sand bottom. During SE gales strong squalls are experienced in this anchorage and with north winds a heavy swell sets in.* (p. 131, SD)

Refuge Bay is easy to enter and offers quick relief in nasty southeast chop. It is rather open for small boats. During fishing season a fish-buyer barge is located here for commercial boats. Useless Bay (the next bay west) is well-named because it completely dries on low tides. South of Useless Point is a long, sandy beach which can be used by kayakers.

Edye Passage

Chart 3956 metric; west entrance: 54°03.30′ N, 130°39.75′ W; east entrance: 54°04.20′ N, 130°33.20′ W (NAD 83)

> *Edye Passage is deep in the fairway, with reefs on both sides, and easily navigated at all stages of the tide. This passage affords a convenient route for entering the south portion of Chatham Sound from the north end of Hecate Strait. . . . Tidal streams flood east and ebb west through Edye Passage at 2 kn. The streams are probably stronger in the narrow part, abreast Pearce Point. There are heavy tide-rips at times over the bank extending south from the east end of Arthur Island.* (p. 131, SD)

Crab for dinner anyone?

Approaching Edye Passage from the east, it looks like a landlocked dead-end until you are well south of Arthur Island. The Queen of Prince Rupert ferry uses Edye Passage on its crossing to Queen Charlotte Islands.

Welcome Harbour

Chart 3909 metric (inset); north entrance: 54°02.00′ N, 130°37.45′ W; anchor: 54°00.14′ N, 130°39.67′ W (NAD 83)

> *Welcome Harbour is entered from Edye Passage between the east side of Henry Island and Edwin Point. This harbour does not offer a welcome to the stranger, being obstructed by numerous drying reefs and below-water rocks. Small craft can also enter Welcome Harbour from Oval Bay, by way of Secret Cove, previously described; this route is very shallow and intricate.* (p. 131, SD)

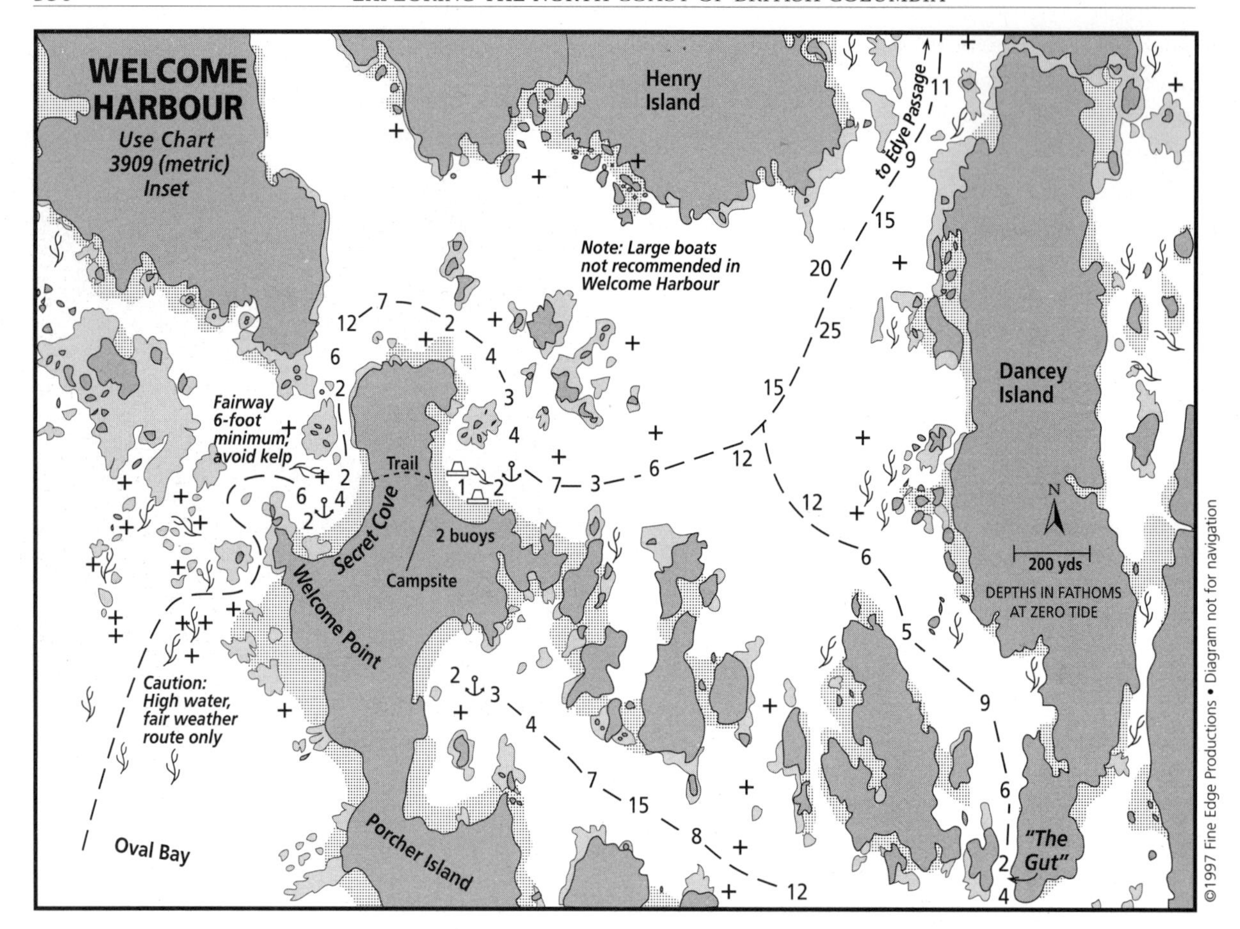

Welcome Harbour, in the northwest corner of Porcher Island, is well named. It is composed of a labyrinth of islands, islets, and reefs with no navigational aids or identifying features. There must be at least 100 islets and reefs in an area less than five miles square. Entering can be a nightmare to the newcomer on a first visit, or in poor visibility. The bottom is irregular and echo sounders record a ragged pattern. Consider entering on a low tide rising when rocks and kelp are more easily seen. Plotting your course on the inset of Chart 3909 is necessary. Careful dead reckoning or judicious use of GPS to help identify turning points is vital; we recommend both.

Because of its intricate layout, Pacific swell does not enter Welcome Harbour; chop is present only in the strong tidal current off the northwest corner of Dancey Island or when very strong winds are blowing. There is an almost unlimited number of crooks and crannies where anchorage may be taken, especially using a stern-tie. The area 0.8 mile west of the center of Dancey Island has been designated by the B. C. Forest Service as Welcome Harbour. The placement of two orange public mooring buoys and development of the campsite on the peninsula were carried out by the Forest Service with help from the Prince Rupert Boy Scouts and the North Coast Cruising Association. A primitive trail starts behind the campsite and leads about 150 yards to the stone beach in Secret Cove. During the day you can hear crows, ravens, and bald eagles, and at night you may hear wolves howl.

Welcome Harbour has been almost entirely the playground of Prince Rupert residents. When cruising boats learn about its fascinating geography, solitude, pristine hemlock and cedar forest, and nearby sandy beaches, Welcome Harbour will become a major boating destination. The bay south of Welcome Harbour is known locally as Campbells Place and is entered by way of "the gut" along the southwest corner of Dancey Island. The very narrow channel is chock full of bull kelp and has rocks and reefs at both ends. Secret Cove, the small outer bight with an extraordinary view of the exposed outer coast, is entered as noted below.

Anchor east of the mooring buoys in 6 fathoms over a sand, stone and seaweed bottom. Holding can be poor to good depending on how well your anchor is set.

Secret Cove

Chart 3909 metric (inset); west entrance (Henry Island): 54°00.64′ N, 130°41.37′ W (NAD 27); anchor: 54°.00.10′ N, 130° 40.10′ W (NAD 83)

> *Secret Cove, close NE of Welcome Point, can be entered by small craft through a narrow passage, encumbered with rocks, between the above-mentioned chain of islands and Henry Island; it can also be entered through a narrow, winding channel close west of Welcome Point. Local knowledge is advised to safely navigate both channels. A shallow, narrow channel leads from the north end of Secret Cove into Welcome Harbour....* (p. 130, SD)

Secret Cove lies on the exposed west side of Porcher Island, but is surprisingly well sheltered by a complex of reefs and rocks which act as a breakwater at low tides, making the cove essentially landlocked. Large stumps and old drift logs line the gravel beach. The shore bank has been eroded by storms, and the beach is steep-to. A trail that crosses from Welcome Harbour requires a descent by rope tied to a log on the north shore of the cove.

Although this can be an interesting anchorage, or a good lunch stop, at low spring tides the rocks and reefs off Welcome Point (the "breakwater") largely disappear underwater, and the anchorage becomes quite rolly.

When entering Secret Cove from Welcome Harbour, avoid the rocks off the north end of the peninsula by favoring the Henry Island shore. Proceeding south, favor the east shore close to Porcher Island while passing east of the off-lying reefs. The narrow 40-foot-wide, or less, fairway has a minimum depth of about 1.5 fathoms. Kelp and rocks are on either side. Avoid patches of attached bull kelp since they indicate shoals or uncharted rocks. Moderately strong currents run in the fairway and flood tends to cross the reef, setting you on the island.

Photo by Robin Hill-Ward

A mink combs the shore looking for dinner

During a moderate southerly gale, breakers smash on the rocks and reefs to the west, but only occasional strong puffs enter the almost-calm cove. We would not recommend that you enter or anchor in Secret Cove except during fair weather; enter on a low tide rising so rocks and reefs can be more easily identified. Entering from Hecate Strait along the Henry Island shore or from Oval Bay to the south is not advised unless you reconnoiter first, and only under ideal conditions. We have seen one 40-foot fishing boat use the Oval Bay route at mid-tide. Approaching this coast from seaward would be hazardous under most conditions.

Oval Bay, one mile south of Secret Cove, has a beautiful long sandy beach which is best visited by hiking across from the protected anchorage on the east side of the peninsula, or taking a fast inflatable from Welcome Harbour.

Butler Cove, Stephens Island

Chart 3956 metric; entrance: 54°06.30′ N, 130°41.30′ W; mooring buoys: 54°06.73′ N, 130°39.87′ W (NAD 83)

> *Butler Cove, between the south side of Stephens Island and Joyce Island, is sheltered except from south or SW winds when a heavy swell sets into the cove. . . . Anchorage for small craft can be obtained in the NE end of Butler Cove in 22 m (72 ft), mud bottom. When entering Butler Cove give the drying rocks at the SW end of Joyce Island a good berth, then favour the Joyce Island shore to avoid the rock 0.3 m (1 ft) high near the middle of the cove. Four public mooring buoys are in Butler Cove.* (p. 130, SD)

Stephens Passage

Chart 3956 metric; position (drying passage): 54°07.10′ N, 130°08.80′ W (NAD 83)

> *Stephens Passage, separating Stephens Island from Prescott Island, dries 1.2 m (4 ft) in the narrowest part of the fairway. Local knowledge is advised for navigating this passage.*
>
> *Tidal streams in Stephens Passage attain 4 kn.* (p. 130, SD)

We understand Stephens Passage is only used by skiffs near high water. We would strongly recommend reconnoitering before use by cruising boats since, from the chart, it looks very challenging.

Skiakl Bay

Chart 3956 metric; entrance: 54°07.30′ N, 130°46.90′ W; position (northeast basin): 54°08.80′ N, 130°46.50′ W (NAD 83)

> *Skiakl Bay, entered west of Skiakl Island, has drying ledges and rocks on all sides. The NW arm of the bay, and the arm entered west of Ludlam Point, are only suitable for small craft.* (p. 130, SD)

The entrance to Skiakl Bay is exposed to the south. It is reported to offer shelter in the basin north of Ludlam Point.

Qlawdzeet ("Squatterie")

Chart 3909 metric (inset); entrance: 54°13.00′ N, 130°46.50′ W; anchor: 54°12.47′ N, 130°45.87′ W (NAD 83)

> *Qlawdzeet Anchorage is a useful anchorage when seeking shelter from strong SE winds, prevalent in this area. It is open to NW winds, but these are usually light.*
>
> *Anchorage for vessels of moderate size can be obtained in about 22 m (72 ft), mud and sand. . .* (p. 129, SD)

Qlawdzeet Anchorage, a fisherman's favorite, is located on the extreme northeast end of Stephens Island. Called locally "Squatterie" (emphasis on the last two letters), it is reported to offer very good protection for small boats deep in the inner basin south of Dunn Island, tied to one or more of the old pilings or dolphins. Larger boats anchor southwest of Dunn Island in about 8 to 10 fathoms.

Tree Nob Group

Chart 3957 metric; position: 54°15.19′ N, 130° 48.53′ W (NAD 83)

> *Tree Nob Group separates Brown Passage from Bell Passage to the south and consists of numerous islands, islets, drying reefs and rocks. Do not attempt to pass between the islands of this group without the aid of local knowledge; the whole area is foul and tidal streams are strong.* (p. 127, SD)

Temporary anchorage can be found in the Tree Nob Group on the east side of Rushton Island, 3 miles northwest of Squatterie. A large, flat area southwest of bell buoy "D72" can be used as an anchorage in fair weather. This is a useful anchorage as a lunch stop or for exploring the interesting rocks and islets of the Tree Nob Group, but it provides inadequate shelter from weather.

Anchor in 5 to 7 fathoms over an unrecorded bottom.

Brown Passage

Chart 3957 metric; west entrance: 54° 15.19′ N, 130°55.40′ W (NAD 83)

> *Brown Passage is the main approach channel to Chatham Sound for large vessels coming from*

Dixon Entrance or Hecate Strait. . . . In the vicinity of Triple Islands the tidal streams are strong and irregular . . . [and] are greatly affected by prevailing winds. (pp. 126–127, SD)

Triple Island is a key lightstation on the south side of Brown Passage, 3 miles northwest of Rushton Island. The weather reports from Triple Island are an important indicator of conditions in Dixon Entrance.

Dundas Islands

Chart 3959 metric; west entrance (Hudson Bay Passage): 54°25.50′ N, 130°58.50′ W; east entrance: 54°33.00′ N, 130°45.00′ W (NAD 83)

Three channels north of Brown Passage pass through Dundas Islands. The passage between Melville and Dunira Islands is narrow, shallow, and filled with reefs; it is not recommended. The narrow channel between Dunira Island and Baron Island is usable by small vessels but local knowledge is advised. Hudson Bay Passage, between Baron Island and Dundas Island, is suitable for small vessels. (p. 126, SD)

Dundas Islands consists of hundreds of small islands in an intriguing pattern. Relief can be found from northeast chop in Chatham Sound during outflow gales in Portland Inlet. It is a great place to explore.

"Farwest Cove"

Chart 3959 metric; position (Farwest Point): 54°25.50′ N, 130°50.00′ W; entrance (cove): 54°25.94′ N, 130°48.70′ W (NAD 83)

Farwest Cove is what we call the basin 1.5 miles northeast of Farwest Point, on the west side of Dunira Island. This cove is located on the west side of Coast Mound, a 700-foot cone-shaped peak; it appears to be well-sheltered in most weather. The entrance is encumbered by a number of reefs and rocks.

Clam Inlet

Chart 3959 metric; entrance: 54°29.95′ N, 130°47.30′ W; anchor: 54°29.48′ N, 130°47.19′ W (NAD 83)

Clam Inlet is on the NE side of Baron Island. (p. 147, SD)

Photo by Robin Hill-Ward

See what the west coast offers?

In the August 1994 issue of *Pacific Yachting,* Anne Vipond described a picturesque anchorage in Clam Inlet on the north side of Baron Island. Sheltered by Randall Island, it is a favorite anchorage in settled summer weather. Many anchorages in the Dundas and Moffatt islands remain to be explored.

Anchor in 2 to 4 fathoms at the head of the inlet.

"Hudson Bay Passage Cove"

Chart 3959 metric; entrance: 54°30.96′ N, 130°50.48′ W; anchor: 54°30.90′ N, 130°50.94′ W (NAD 83)

Hudson Bay Passage, along the SE side of Dundas Island, is encumbered with numerous islands, reefs and shoals. The fairway narrows to 0.2 mile between Dundas Island and Nares Islets and is suitable for small vessels. (p. 147, SD)

Hudson Bay Passage Cove is what we call the nice nook on the south side of Dundas Island opposite the Nares Islets. When current and northeast wind

Ready for fishing?

and chop combine to make life miserable in Chatham Sound, we head for Hudson Bay Passage Cove and wait for morning and a smooth passage into Alaskan waters. This small cove has room for two or three boats out of the nasty chop and winds blowing outside.

Anchor in 6 to 8 fathoms over mud bottom with good holding.

Edith Harbour

Chart 3959 metric; entrance:
54°27.60′ N, 130°56.75′ W; mooring buoys:
54°28.03′ N, 130°56.98′ W (NAD 83)

> *Edith Harbour, entered 1.8 miles NE of Chearnley Islet, offers good shelter. The upper part of the harbour is best accessed close off the west side of the 14 m (46 ft) islet. . . . Anchorage for small vessels can be obtained in Edith Harbour.*
> (p. 147, SD)

Edith Harbour is a narrow, landlocked passage on the extreme southeast corner of Dundas Island, well protected from the "slop" in Dixon Entrance. The two public mooring buoys are frequently used by commercial fishermen.

Brundige Inlet

Chart 3909 metric (inset); entrance:
54°36.86′ N, 130°50.73′ W; anchor (bitter end):
54°35.30′ N, 130°53.50′ W (NAD 83)

> *Brundige Inlet is entered east of Prospector Point. Fitch Island, 1 mile SW of Prospector Point, has a drying rock 0.1 mile west of it. A rock shoal, 0.6 mile SW of Fitch Island, lies in the middle of the fairway leading to the head of the inlet. . . . Anchorage can be obtained in midchannel NW of Fitch Island in 27 m (89 ft). Anchorage for small craft can be obtained at the head of Brundige Inlet in 16 m (52 ft).*
> (p. 200, SD)

Brundige Inlet, a narrow, 3-mile-long channel on the north side of Dundas Island, affords excellent shelter from all outside swells and chop. When you're anchored deep in the inlet, everything is still, and it's difficult to tell whether a tempest is blowing outside or not. Brundige Inlet has long been a favorite refuge for both north- and southbound cruising boats.

The only negative we've heard is the presence of pesky black flies when winds are slight or nonexistent. However, we've been so thankful for this shelter after a rough crossing of Dixon Entrance that we didn't notice the flies or they weren't there. There are no deer on Dundas Island because it is said the black flies drain them of all their blood.

Although entering is not difficult, if you're coming from the north it's easy to overshoot the entrance. It helps to take a fix on Prospector Point. Stay midchannel for the entire 3 miles but then favor the west shore at the beginning of the last narrows; there is a rock midchannel with about 6 feet over it at zero tide. The entrance is quite narrow and Chart 3909 is helpful for entering.

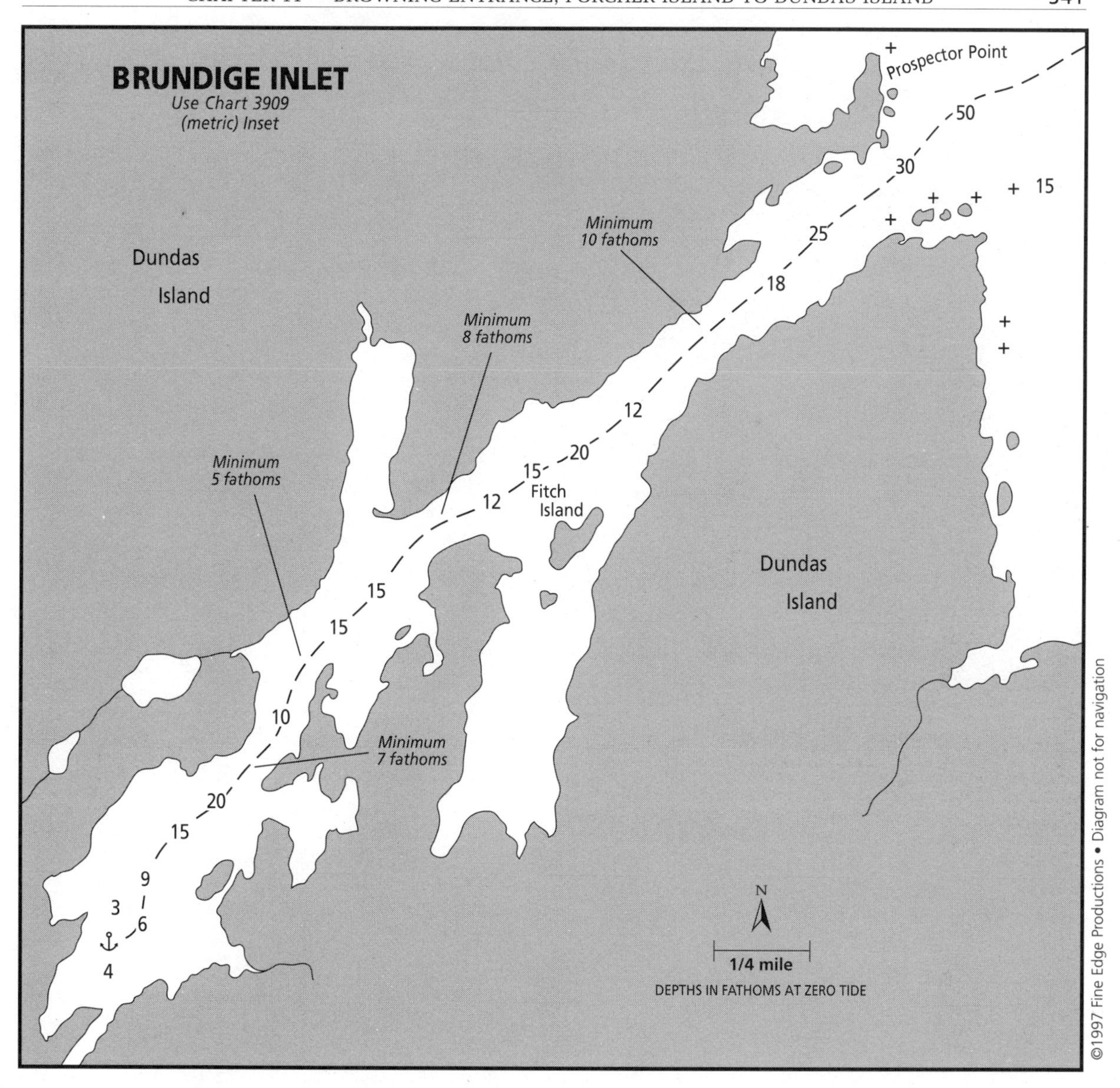

We have stayed at the bitter end of the inlet and been perfectly comfortable during a major blow. There is shallower water and more swinging room on the south side of the lagoon south of Fitch Island.

Anchor (bitter end) in 4 to 6 fathoms over a mud bottom with very good holding.

Green Island

Chart 3959 metric; position (light): 54°34.10′ N, 130°42.40′ W (NAD 83)

Green Island, 3.6 miles NNE of Whitesand Island, is a grassy island 11 m (36 ft) high with two hummocks connected by a low shingle beach. Foul ground extends 0.3 mile north from the island. An overhead cable extends from Green Island to the islet close NW. . . . The fog signal consists of one blast on a horn every 30 seconds. (p. 148, SD)

Green Island is an important weather observation station for boats crossing Dixon Entrance. Most small boats pass west of Green Island in Holliday Passage, using the lee of Dundas Island to avoid the westerly swells found in Dixon Entrance.

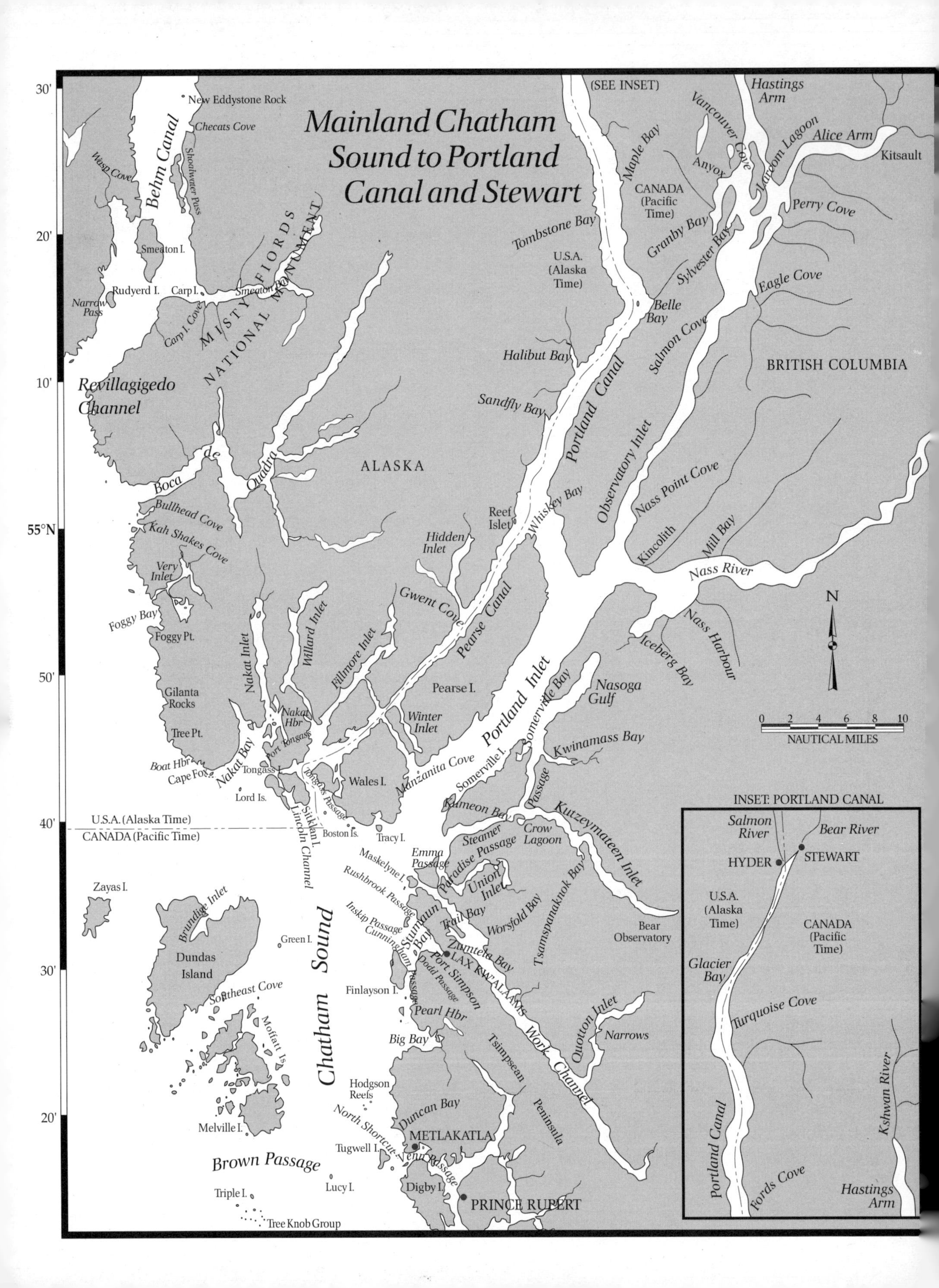

Mainland Chatham Sound to Portland Canal and Stewart
(SEE INSET)
Hastings Arm
New Eddystone Rock
Checats Cove
Behm Canal
Shoalwater Pass
Wasp Cove
Vancouver Cove
Maple Bay
Anyox
Lagoon Lagoon
Alice Arm
Kitsault
CANADA (Pacific Time)
Perry Cove
Granby Bay
Sylvester Bay
Tombstone Bay
U.S.A. (Alaska Time)
MISTY FIORDS NATIONAL MONUMENT
Smeaton I.
Smeaton
Rudyerd I.
Carp I.
Carp I. Cove
Narrow Pass
Eagle Cove
Belle Bay
Salmon Cove
Halibut Bay
BRITISH COLUMBIA
Revillagigedo Channel
Sandfly Bay
Portland Canal
Observatory Inlet
Boca de Quadra
ALASKA
Nass Point Cove
Bullhead Cove
Whiskey Bay
Reef Islet
55°N
Kah Shakes Cove
Hidden Inlet
Kincolith
Mill Bay
Very Inlet
Nass River
Gwent Cove
Foggy Bay
Foggy Pt.
Willard Inlet
Nakat Inlet
Fillmore Inlet
Pearse Canal
Nass Harbour
Iceberg Bay
N
Pearse I.
Portland Inlet
Somerville Bay
Nasoga Gulf
Gilanta Rocks
Nakat Hbr
Winter Inlet
Tree Pt.
Port Tongass
Kwinamass Bay
0 2 4 6 8 10
NAUTICAL MILES
Boat Hbr
Cape Fox
Nakat Bay
Tongass I.
Tongass Passage
Wales I.
Manzanita Cove
Somerville I.
Passage
Lord Is.
Sitklan I.
Khutzeymateen Inlet
Kumeon Bay
Crow Lagoon
INSET: PORTLAND CANAL
U.S.A. (Alaska Time)
CANADA (Pacific Time)
Lincoln Channel
Boston Is.
Tracy I.
Steamer Passage
Paradise Passage
Emma Passage
Maskelyne I.
Salmon River
Bear River
HYDER
STEWART
Rushbrook Passage
Union Inlet
Zayas I.
Brundige Inlet
Inskip Passage
Cunningham Passage
Stumaun Bay
Trail Bay
Worsfold Bay
Tsamspanaknok Bay
Bear Observatory
Green I.
Zumtela Bay
Dundas Island
Chatham Sound
LAX KW'ALAAMS
Port Simpson
Dodd Passage
Glacier Bay
Southeast Cove
Finlayson I.
Pearl Hbr
Quottoon Inlet
Turquoise Cove
Moffatt Is.
Narrows
Big Bay
Work Channel
Tsimpsean
Hodgson Reefs
Kshwan River
Duncan Bay
Peninsula
North Shortcut
Melville I.
METLAKATLA
Tugwell I.
Venn Passage
Brown Passage
Lucy I.
Digby I.
Triple I.
PRINCE RUPERT
Tree Knob Group
Fords Cove
Hastings Arm
30'
20'
10'
50'
40'
30'
20'

12

Mainland Chatham Sound to Portland Canal and Stewart

Portland Canal, a long and narrow inlet, is perhaps the longest fjord on the entire North American continent. Measured from Dixon Entrance to Stewart, it is more than 100 miles long. The canal was named by Vancouver after William Bentinck, duke of Portland. The international boundary between Canada and Alaska runs mid-channel through Pearse and Portland Canals, north to Stewart. Largely pristine, and seldom visited, the shorelines of Portland Canal have stunning scenery. Floating trees or flotsam, common north of Fords Cove, call for caution. North of Hattie Island, the water becomes progressively more opaque, with very limited underwater visibility. Between Blue Point and Glacier Bay, the water in Portland Canal is an unusual and outstandingly bright turquoise blue. The upper end of the canal has high snowcapped peaks and several hanging glaciers. Fog patches form in thin streaks where cold streams reach the warmer saltwater and when atmospheric conditions are favorable.

The passage, narrower and more intimate than Alaskan fjords, generally requires less challenging navigation, although anchorages are somewhat marginal and far apart. Portland Canal is remote and has little if any radio reception. At its entrance and central section, you can receive weather broadcasts but only on 21B (on some receivers Weather Channel #8); north of "Glacier Bay" there is no reception. (See Stewart Marine Rescue under Stewart.) Locals report that upslope winds predominate in the summer, and downslope winds in the winter. The winds tend to die off as you near Stewart; this phenomenon becomes apparent near Hattie Island or a little farther north. Most summer nights are quiet and calm. Other than a few Stewart sportfishing boats and the twice-a-month Alaska ferry, which calls on Stewart in summer only, you are unlikely to see any other boats.

Venn Passage and Metlakatla Bay

Charts 3955 metric, 3958 metric; east entrance: 54°18.68′ N, 130°22.88′ W (NAD 27); south entrance (Metlakatla Bay): 54°18.40′ N, 130°30.40′ W (NAD 83)

> *Venn Passage, known locally as Metlakatla Passage, connects Metlakatla Bay to Prince Rupert Harbour. The passage should be used only by small vessels. Local knowledge is recommended. . . . Tidal streams in Venn Passage, between Dundas Point and Verney Island, attain 3 kn on the flood and ebb; the stream turns about 1 hour before HW.* (pp. 143–144, SD)

Venn Passage is a good small-boat route from Prince Rupert to Chatham Sound. It is marked by a couple of ranges and several buoys. Note that buoys in Venn Passage are often dragged out of position after being hit by tows. Make sure of your route before attempting the passage. Use Chart 3955 to identify turning points and line up with the range marks. There is shoal water on both sides of the fairway. Slow down to no-wake

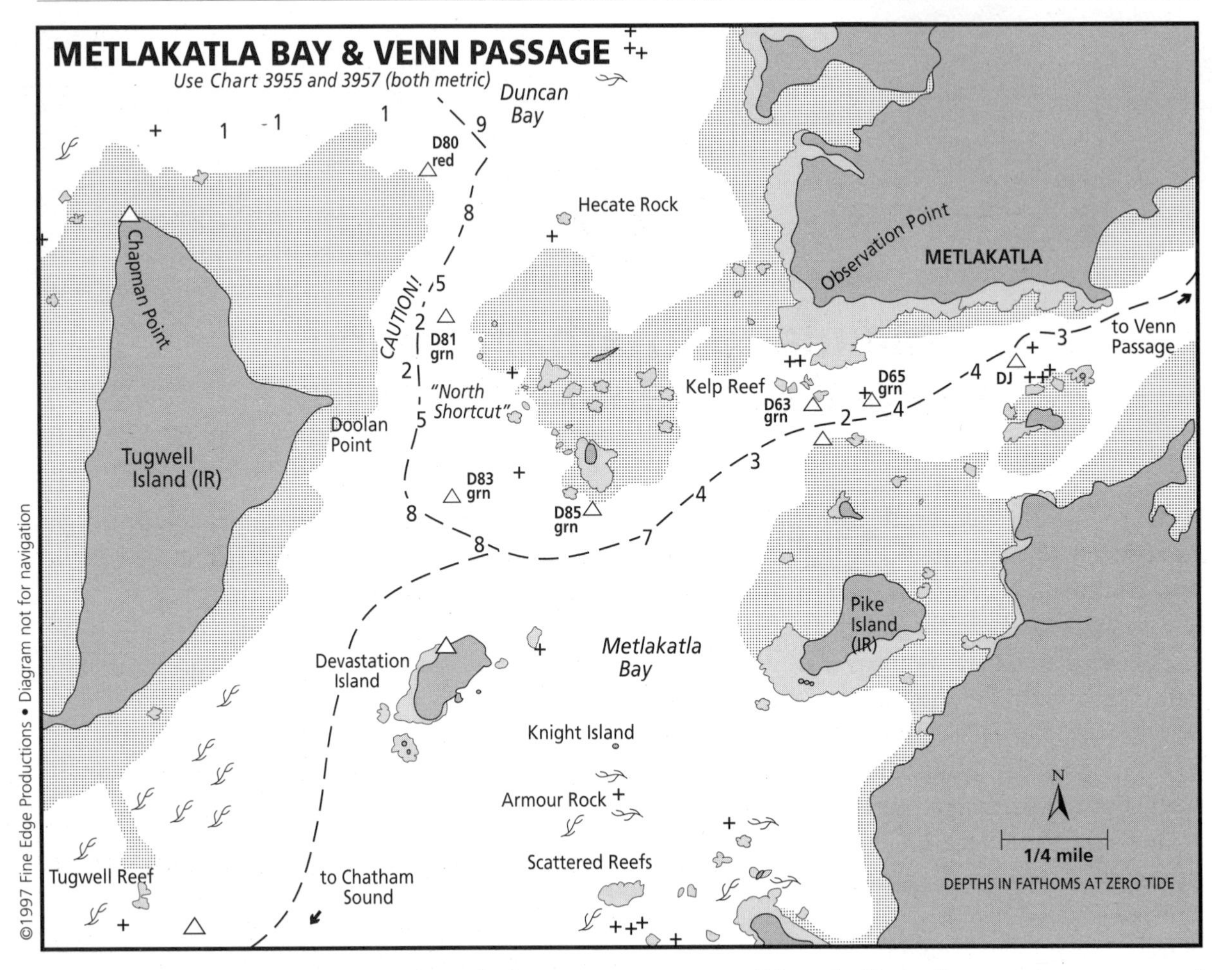

speed when you pass the airport ferry dock at Du Vernay Point, and again off the Metlakatla float.

In summer, after a favorable weather forecast, there is frequently an early morning exodus (0400 to 0500) of boats heading north from Prince Rupert. Although Venn Passage is narrow and intricate with strong currents, it greatly shortens the route to Chatham Sound for northbound boats.

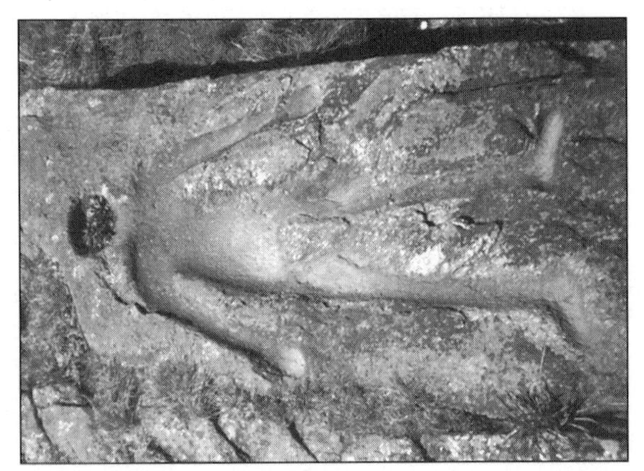

Fallen Human, Venn Passage

If you leave Prince Rupert near or ahead of high water, you will have favorable current all the way to Green Island. The north shortcut (explained below) saves another half-hour or so.

"Fallen Human Bay"

Chart 3955 metric; entrance:
54°19.00′ N, 130°22.70′ W; anchor:
54°19.53′ N, 130°23.88′ W (NAD 27)

> *A bay lying east and north of this drying flat has Pillsbury Cove, which dries on the north side.*
> (p. 145, SD)

Fallen Human Bay is our name for the bay north of Anion Island. A petroglyph of "The Man Who Fell From Heaven" is located near Robertson Point. The museum in Prince Rupert has an attractive replica of this petroglyph and the story associated with it.

Anchor in 5 fathoms over a mud bottom with good holding.

"Carolina Island Anchorage"

Chart 3955 metric; entrance: 54°20.24′ N, 130°25.52′ W; anchor: 54°20.47′ N, 130°25.72′ W (NAD 27)

Anchorage for small craft can be obtained in the bay NE of Carolina Islands; this bay has extensive drying ledges on all shorelines. Scott Inlet and Bencke Lagoon, on the east side of this bay, dry. (p. 144, SD)

This anchorage is well sheltered and out of the current and busy traffic of Venn Passage.

Anchor in 4 fathoms over mud bottom with good holding.

"Gribbell Islet Anchorage"

Chart 3955 metric; entrance: 54°20.00′ N, 130°26.35′ W; anchor: 54°19.92′ N, 130°26.42′ W (NAD 27)

Gribbell Islet, 0.5 mile east of Shrub Island light, together with Isabel Islet, 0.1 mile NE of it, lie on a detached drying sand bank on the south side of the fairway. Drying rocks are close off the north edge of this sand bank and a rock awash is in the middle of the fairway 0.1 mile NW of Isabel Islet. Port bifurcation buoy "DJ" is close west of the rock awash. . . . Four mooring buoys are on the south side of the fairway between Isabel Islet and Auriol Point. (p. 144, SD)

Gribbell Islet Anchorage, across the channel from Metlakatla village, is a good base camp to use for exploring by dinghy the petroglyphs on or near Pike Island, one mile to the southwest. Avoid the telephone cable near the mooring buoys. Anchorage can be found just west of the drying flat of Gribbell Islet.

Anchor in 1.5 fathoms over a sandy bottom with fair holding.

"North Shortcut"

Charts 3957 metric, 3955 metric; south entrance: 54°19.63′ N, 130°29.38′ W; north entrance: 54°20.57′ N, 130°29.15′ W (NAD 83)

You can gain a half-hour when northbound by leaving the west end of Venn Passage and entering Duncan Bay, using a shortcut across the sand bar. We call this route "North Shortcut." Larger yachts may find this route too shallow and/or narrow for use; however, smaller yachts can safely cross the bar during the upper half of most tides, staying close to the buoys and monitoring the echo sounder carefully.

To enter the North Shortcut, turn north at buoy "D83" on the east side of Tugwell Island, due north of Devastation Island, and pass close on the west side of buoy "D81" which marks the shallow spot. Continue north and pass just east of buoy "D80" as you enter Duncan Bay. Minimum depth on the bar is about $1^1/_2$ fathoms at zero tide. However, the channel is narrow and subject to shoaling or shifting. When northbound, don't cut west until 0.25 mile north of buoy "D80," since the Tugwell Island shoal extends well over a half-mile from shore. If you are southbound, red buoy "D80" is hard to see until you are fairly close. Its position is about 54° 20.46' N, 130° 29.30' W.

On the Duncan Bay side, the shoal extends well out from Tugwell Island, so avoid turning west too soon. Avoid the shoals 1.2 miles off Ryan Point as well as Hodgson Reefs north of Duncan Bay. (If you plan to follow the mainland route north, see the latter part of this chapter.)

Duncan Bay

Charts 3955 metric (inset), 3957 metric, 3959 metric; west entrance: 54°21.20′ N, 130°30.50′ W; anchor (0.12 mile south Hecate Rock): 54°20.33′ N, 130°28.20′ W (NAD 83)

Duncan Bay is entered between Chapman Point and Ryan Point, 1.6 miles NNE. Drying ledges fringe the bay and drying and shoal rocks, including Hecate Rock, lie off the shores and near the middle of the bay. The outer edge of the reef SW of Ryan Point is marked by starboard hand buoy "D82". Starboard hand buoy "D80" marks the edge of the drying bank east of Chapman Point and the entrance to a buoyed channel leading south to Metlakatla Bay. . . . Anchorage can be obtained in 12 to 15 m (39 to 48 ft), mud bottom, in Duncan Bay. (p. 148, SD)

Duncan Bay is a good place to hide from southerly chop in Chatham Sound or wait for adequate tide level in North Shortcut.

Anchor in 7 fathoms over mud and shell bottom.

Hodgson Reefs

Chart 3959 metric; south end of reef: 54°22.35′ N, 130°31.73′ W (NAD 83)

> *Hodgson Reefs, 1 mile west of Swamp Island, consist of several drying reefs and below-water rocks.* (p. 148, SD)

Caution: If you head directly for buoy "D84" from Duncan Bay, you will cross the south part of Hodgson Reefs; pay close attention to pass south of Hodgson Reefs.

Mainland Route across East Dixon Inlet via Portland Inlet

(Recommended during conditions of northeast outflow winds in Portland Inlet.)

When strong winds funnel down Portland Inlet and kick up a nasty chop in Chatham Sound and East Dixon Entrance, consider hugging the mainland coast for a smooth-water route. Although longer than the direct route, this route is more scenic and interesting. If you stay in Port Tongass, divide your trip to Ketchikan into two easy segments. Rough water on this route is reduced to about 3 miles crossing the entrance to Portland Inlet, and convenient layovers can be taken on either side of the inlet to allow for an optimum crossing time.

Leaving Prince Rupert via Duncan Bay, from a point 0.25 miles west of buoy "D82," located 0.7 miles southwest of Ryan Point, head north (about 344° magnetic) for Slippery Rock light via the channel inside Hodgson Reefs. As you approach Slippery Rock, head for buoy "D86" at about 320° magnetic. From "D86," head for buoy "DK" at Sparrowhawk Rock off the south end of Finlayson Island, avoiding Ripple Bank and Escape Reefs in Big Bay. Pass north of buoy "DK" and turn directly for the white triangle on the mainland shore near Redcliff Point. When you have safely passed Pender Rock and Centre Rock, turn north (about 346° magnetic) into Cunningham Passage, passing east of Finlayson Island, bound for buoy "D88" off Hankin Reef and the entrance to Dodd Passage, then to Port Simpson.

From Port Simpson, exit via Inskip Passage or Rushbrook Passage, and pass east of Parkin Islets to the west side of Maskelyne Island. The lee of Maskelyne Island is the last smooth water until you cross Portland Inlet to the lee of Wales

Fouled Prop—A High-Latitude Emergency

It was getting dark, which in Glacier Park, Alaska is almost tomorrow. Crab pots littered the anchorage. The engine gave a strangled cough and died. The pots were catching more than crabs tonight. A morning dive was a chilling prospect.

Making do with what I had, I donned a thin wet suit (1/8 of an inch is not enough), a light jacket, quilted hood, boots, and sailing gloves. My accessories included mask, snorkel and a fanny-pack of zinc weights.

We rigged a guide-line under the boat, rafted the dinghy as a work float, taped a hose to the snorkel, and went in. The water was the temperature of a martini with visibility like milk. Scary stuff. The snorkel kinked. No air. Straighten the snorkel and try again. No air. Shorten the hose. Still can't get air below 2 feet. Bag the snorkel.

The guide-line curves into the darkness. No prop here. We move the line three times before a shadowy prop materializes. Dive, search the murk for the rope end, unwrap a loop. One dive per wrap. After each dive the crew dumps very hot water (feels lukewarm) inside my wetsuit. Finally there is enough line free to bring the end to the surface. Heavy duty, expensive stuff; just like on our boat. Funny they would use it for crabbing. Hello??!! This isn't a crab pot float line. We ran over our own gib sheet. Crab fishermen aren't so bad after all. More hot water. Back down. I fantasize about hot showers. Only icebergs are comfortable here. My average dive lasts 10 seconds. Up on the dinghy, hot water down the wetsuit, drag myself down the guide-line. My lungs tell me to stop. Back to the dinghy for more blessed water. Only six more wraps to go. Last wrap. Warm up the champagne. Let's celebrate!

—Lachlan and Becky McGuigan,
S/V *Xephyr,* Landfall 48

Island. If Portland Inlet looks forbidding, wait and watch from the south side of Maskelyne Island, or return to Port Simpson for shelter.

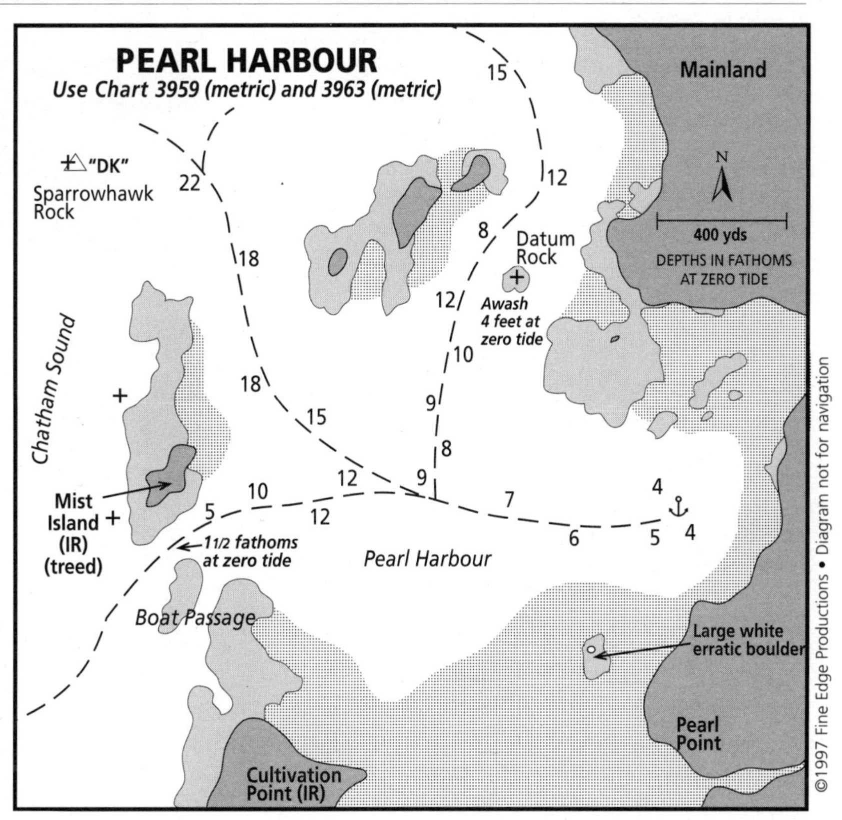

Big Bay

Charts 3959 metric, 3963 metric; entrance (south passage): 54°27.45′ N, 130°30.00′ W; anchor (Salmon Bight): 54°27.50′ N, 130°25.00′ W (NAD 83)

> *Big Bay affords good protection in all winds with little swell. The three recommended anchorages are as follows. Haycock Island . . . Swallow Island . . . south of Swallow Island.* (p. 149, SD)

Enter Salmon Bight at the extreme east end of Big Bay, between Curlew Rock and Swallow Island. Avoid the reef on the north side of Curlew Rock which extends northeast about 350 yards. You can find anchorage anywhere off the drying flat east of Curlew Rock, due south of One Foot Rock. One Foot Rock is a good guide when entering near high water.

Anchor (Salmon Bight) in 5 fathoms over sand and mud bottom.

Pearl Harbour

Charts 3959 metric, 3963 metric; entrance (Boat Passage): 54°30.16′ N, 130°28.30′ W; anchor: 54°30.29′ N, 130°26.83′ W (NAD 83)

> *Good anchorage can be obtained near the middle of Pearl Harbour in 20 m (66 ft), mud. . . . Anchorage can also be obtained at Otter Anchorage, about 0.2 mile north of the NE end of Flat Top Islands, in 31 m (102 ft), mud.* (p. 149, SD)

Very good protection from northeast winds can be obtained in the east side of Pearl Harbour. After clearing Sparrowhawk Rock, enter Pearl Harbour via the deep-water route on the west side of Flat Top Island. Small boats can use narrow Boat Passage, but the reef south of Mist Island must be identified and avoided. If passing north of Mist Island, be careful to avoid the drying spit to the north. Many boats have gone aground there, expecting the reef to terminate farther south. Stay close to Buoy "DK."

Anchor in the far east side of Pearl Harbour, due north of Pearl Point. The "pearl" in Pearl Point is a large glacial boulder 200 yards northwest of the point.

Anchor in 4 fathoms, sand and mud bottom, fair-to-good holding.

Cunningham Passage

Charts 3959 metric, 3963 metric; south entrance (0.10 mile north of buoy "DK"): 54°30.90′ N, 130°28.40′ W; north entrance: 54°34.40′ N, 130°28.40′ W (NAD 83)

> *Cunningham Passage is unsuitable for large vessels because of Pender and Centre Rocks. . . . Tidal streams in Cunningham Passage attain*

about 1 kn but are probably somewhat accelerated in the narrow parts; the flood sets south and the ebb north. . . . Caution. Shoals in the entrance to and within Cunningham Passage are steep-to and kelp may not always be visible on them; soundings will give little warning. (p. 149, SD)

Cunningham Passage is the easy, smooth-water passage for cruising boats on the east side of Finlayson Island. The white triangle near Redcliff Point provides the leading point for the fairway between Pender and Centre rocks, both underwater. Avoid the reefs at the north end of Cunningham Passage.

Dodd Passage

Charts 3959 metric, 3963 metric; west entrance: 54°33.72′ N, 130°27.25′ W (NAD 83)

Dodd Passage lies north of Hankin Reefs and One Tree Islet and separates them from Harbour Reefs. This passage is only suitable for small vessels and local knowledge is advised. . . . The fairway through Dodd Passage is marked by starboard hand buoy "D88" and port hand buoy "D89." (p. 150, SD)

Dodd Passage is the shallow and narrow smooth-water route into Port Simpson. Pass north of buoy "D88" and south of buoy "D89" on a generally northeast heading. When you are north of One Tree Islet, round slowly for the Port Simpson breakwater. *Note*: We once found that buoy "D88" had drifted 200 or 300 yards southeast of its charted position!

Port Simpson (Lax Kw' Alaams)

Charts 3963 metric (inset), 3959 metric; breakwater light: 54°33.71′ N, 130°25.71′ W (NAD 83)

Port Simpson harbour, at the north end of Cunningham Passage, is fronted by Harbour Reefs and Birnie Island; it is one of the most spacious harbours on the north part of the British Columbia coast. The harbour is well sheltered from all but west winds and is easy of access, having no strong tidal streams. (p. 150, SD)

There are three finger-floats for small boats on the south side of the Port Simpson breakwater, but they are frequently crowded with sportfishing and commercial boats. Avoid the shallow water east and south of the floats (see inset in Chart 3963). Fuel and propane are available on a part-time basis, good water can be obtained from a hose at the foot of the gangway; electricity is available for a reasonable fee. The village has a grocery store. New fuel docks are under construction.

Public floats, Port Simpson (Lax Kw'Alaams)

Stumaun Bay

Chart 3963 metric; position: 54°33.70′ N, 130°23.44′ W (NAD 83)

Stumaun Bay, at the head of the harbour, has an extensive drying flat at its head. The south shore is an active logging area (1988) with log dumps, a large booming ground and mooring buoys. (p. 150, SD)

Good protection from southeast blows can be found off the drying flat east of the log booms in 12 fathoms.

Rushbrook Passage

Chart 3963 metric; entrance (south): 54°36.08′ N, 130°26.62′ W; entrance (north): 54°36.30′ N, 130°26.95′ W (NAD 83)

Rushbrook Passage . . . is encumbered by drying reefs and below-water rocks. It is only suitable for small vessels and local knowledge is advised. (p. 150, SD)

The narrow fairway through Rushbrook Passage is midway between two sets of reefs northeast of Birnie Island. This route helps you avoid chop in Chatham Sound.

Dudevoir Passage

Chart 3963 metric; west entrance:
54°37.86′ N, 130°26.71′ W ; east entrance:
54°38.29′ N, 130°26.93′ W (NAD 83)

> *Dudevoir Passage has a least depth of 0.9 m (3 ft). The passage is very narrow and only suitable for small craft. A drying spit, about midway through the passage, projects north from the south shore; it is reported to be subject to change.* (p. 151, SD)

Dudevoir Passage is useful to cruising boats for avoiding the turbulent waters off the entrance to Work Channel. However, the passage has considerably less water than indicated on the chart, perhaps as much as 6 feet less. It is only useful near high water. The bar is stony and you can see the bottom readily. There are two old cabins at the north entrance on the Work Channel side. Temporary anchorage can be found just inside either entrance from which to reconnoiter the shoal area. The bottom is flat with isolated patches of bull kelp, indicating a stone-and-gravel bottom.

Work Channel

Chart 3963 metric; entrance:
54°39.00′ N, 130°26.70′ W (NAD 83)

> *Work Channel extends 28 miles SE along the NE side of the Tsimpsean Peninsula. The shores of Work Channel are generally steep-to and rise to mountains with elevations in excess of 914 m (3,000 ft). . . . Tidal streams in Work Channel attain 3 to 4 kn. Considerable tide-rips, dangerous to small craft, are encountered in the vicinity of Sager Rock, and in the entrance of Work Channel.* (p. 207, SD)

Heading for Alaska, Chatham Sound

We have seen breaking waves extending a half-mile from the entrance during spring ebb tides, when there were strong outflow winds blowing down Portland Inlet. Trail Bay and Zumtela Bay, 7 miles inside Work Channel, provide good summer anchorages.

Whales Watching Us!

Exploring the north coast of British Columbia is richly rewarding. Since 1980, we've seen wonderful whales who've watched us just as much as we've watched them.

Our first adrenaline rush is recorded in the 1982 ship's log of our 22-foot Bayliner, *Sundancer*. While we were sightseeing one afternoon in golden sun, a huge humpback whale surfaced along our port beam, eyeball to eyeball; we're still not sure who was the most startled. What a great surprise! On a steady course, our friendly whale kept an eye on us by resurfacing three times before continuing to other waters. We became hooked on all forms of British Columbia sea life, especially friendly whales. We've never been disappointed.

In 1985, aboard our 35′ Uniflite, *Sea Señor II*, a once-in-a-lifetime show erupted from the depths. Traveling at cruising speed, ahead off the bow, we saw what appeared to be dynamite charges exploding repeatedly. Slowing, we discovered what we'd seen only in movies. Two huge, frolicking whales were leaping remarkably high, again and again. We watched, completely in awe, never-tiring. Finally, in order to anchor for the night, we were forced to part company. If we never saw another whale in our lives, we'd be happy.

However, as whales "watching us" goes, we never have long to wait. Another day, while trolling slowly, a spectacular orca suddenly surfaced across the course of our bow. We were on a collision course. We stopped. The bobbing eyes of this mammoth creature registered as much surprise as we felt. Needless to say, our friendly orca took a dive. Whales can literally take your breath away!

Recently, friends chatting with us aboard our 45′ *Sanctuary,* told us of their expedition in a much larger Hatteras. While trolling, their whale show turned into a giant whale lifting! The damaged stern told the tale.

Cameras in hand, we wait and we ask ourselves: when will the next whales watch us?

by Linda and Jack Schreiber,
Sanctuary, Greeley, Colorado

Paradise Passage, looking toward Work Channel

Paradise Passage

Chart 3963 metric; south entrance: 54°37.85′ N, 130°23.60′ W; north entrance: 54°38.90′ N, 130°23.38′ W (NAD 83)

> *Paradise Passage separates the SE side of Hogan Island from the mainland and connects Emma Passage to Work Channel. It is very narrow and only suitable for small craft; local knowledge is advised. The fairway leads on the east side of the drying rock 0.4 mile south of Emma Point. . . . Tidal streams in Paradise Passage attain up to 3 kn.* (p. 208, SD)

Paradise Passage, connecting Work Channel to Emma and Steamer passages, continues the smooth-water route north. Emma Passage can be transited during most phases of the tide; avoid kelp patches, however, in the vicinity of the islet. There is about one fathom in the fairway of the narrows east of the islet. Favor the east shore, avoiding the kelp. The islet, covered with rockweed, dries on about a 17-foot tide and is about 45 feet across. The ebb flows northward in Paradise Passage.

Trail Bay

Chart 3963 metric; entrance: 54°34.28′ N, 130°20.22′ W; anchor: 54°35.31′ N, 130°22.25′ W (NAD 83)

> *Trail Bay, 6 miles SE of Maskelyne Point, is entered between Grace Point and Trounce Point. . . . Anchorage can be obtained in Trail Bay, 1 mile NW of Grace Point, in 40 m (131 ft), sand and gravel bottom.* (p. 208, SD)

Trail Bay, surrounded by old-growth cedar and silver snags, offers very good protection from prevailing west and northwest winds. It is out of the brunt of southerly winds, unless they are storm-force. Large boats can find good anchorage over a wide, flat area of 7 to 9 fathoms, south of a predominant point on the north shore. Small craft wanting more "intimate" shelter can tuck in behind the north point in 4 fathoms with a stern-tie.

Anchor in 8 fathoms over a mixed bottom of sand, gravel, and soft grey mud patches with fair holding.

Zumtela Bay

Chart 3963 metric; entrance: 54°34.85′ N, 130°21.75′ W; anchor: 54°34.95′ N, 130°22.37′ W (NAD 83)

> *Zumtela Bay is a small cove on the west side of Trail Bay. . . . Small craft can obtain well sheltered anchorage in Zumtela Bay in 12 m (39 ft), sand bottom, about 0.1 mile from shore.* (p. 208, SD)

Zumtela Bay offers slightly more protection than Trail Bay with a wide, flat bottom of 7 to 9 fathoms. Anchor off the small gravel beach at the head of the bay.

Anchor in 8 fathoms over a sand and gravel bottom with fair holding.

Worsfold Bay

Chart 3963 metric; position: 54°34.10′ N, 130°17.85′ W (NAD 83)

> *Worsfold Bay, on the east side of Work Channel and 1.5 miles east of Grace Point, is deep and not suitable for anchorage.* (p. 208, SD)

Worsfold Bay holds a large float camp with a two-story building. You may be able to obtain some protection from southeast winds here, but it is exposed to prevailing northwest winds.

"Quottoon Narrows Cove"

Chart 3963 metric; entrance (Quottoon Inlet): 54°24.75′ N, 130°06.45′ W; anchor: 54°28.20′ N, 130°04.18′ W (NAD 83)

> *Quottoon Inlet, 5 miles SE of Sarah Creek, is entered between Reservation Point and Quottoon Point. The shores of the inlet are bold and steep-to*

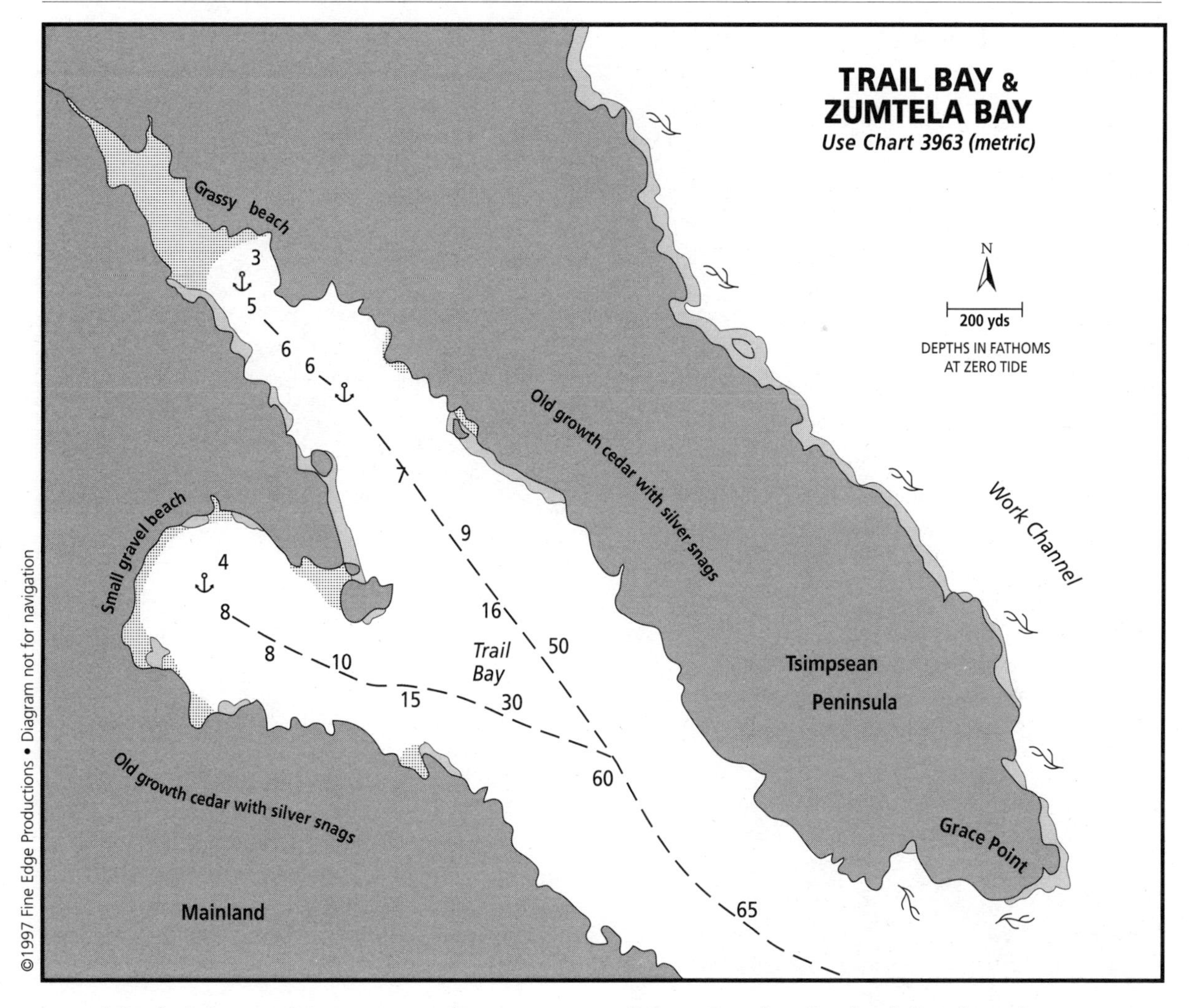

and backed by precipitous mountains. . . . Anchorage is reported to be available in the cove close NE of Quottoon Narrows. (p. 208, SD)

The Quottoon Narrows Cove appears to be the only anchor site in the general area.

Anchor in about 10 to 15 fathoms over an unrecorded bottom.

Portland Inlet

Chart 3994; entrance: 54°41.00′ N, 130°27.50′ W (NAD 27)

Portland Inlet leads about 22 miles NE from Dixon Entrance to its junction with Observatory Inlet and Portland Canal. (p. 209, SD)

If Portland Inlet is choppy, cruising boats can follow a smooth-water route from Wales Passage to Pearse Canal to Portland Canal; or, for more protection, use Steamer Passage as far north as Trefusis Point. Somerville Bay and Winter Inlet are two of the more protected anchor sites in the center of Portland Inlet.

Wales Passage

Chart 3994 ; south entrance: 54°45.60′ N, 130°25.80′ W; north entrance: 54°50.50′ N, 130°27.60′ W (NAD 27)

Wales Passage, which is free of dangers, leads NW from Portland Inlet to Pearse Canal. (p. 209, SD)

When there's a blow in Portland Inlet or Pearse Canal, the water is generally smooth in Wales Passage. This passage frequently contains a number of crab pots marked by small floats.

Manzanita Cove

Chart 3994; entrance:
54°45.65′ N, 130°26.10′ W; anchor:
54°45.44′ N, 130°26.18′ W (NAD 27)

> *Manzanita Cove, on the west side of the south entrance of Wales Passage, is entered north of Swaine Point; it affords anchorage for small vessels.* (p. 209, SD)

Manzanita Cove, South Cove, Wales Island

Manzanita Cove has a steep-to bottom with depths inconvenient for anchoring and no flat areas. The little nook on the south side, immediately west of Swaine Point, is protected in most weather and is useful for one or two small craft, using a stern-tie to shore.

At the head of the nook, you can see one of the four original stone masonry cabins built for the initial surveys of the Alaska border in 1896, under the direction of Captain Gaillard, U.S. Army Corps of Engineers. A stone plaque on the north corner of the ruined building says " . . . property, Do not Injure." The U.S.-Canada border was established north of Wales and Pearse islands by a later tribunal and, since then, someone chiseled out the "US" in the stone marker. In contrast with the fairly well-maintained building that marks the Hyder-Stewart border, the roof, floor, and door at this site are missing, and brush and moss have taken over inside its walls.

Exploring the former U.S. Customs House, now on Canadian soil (Manzanita Cove)

Anchor in 6 fathoms, rocky bottom, poor holding, with a stern-tie to shore recommended.

"Wales Cove"

Chart 3994; entrance: 54°46.75′ N, 130°25.70′ W;
anchor: 54°47.00′ N, 130°25.60′ W (NAD 27)

Wales Cove is what we call the small bay in Wales Passage, on the south side of Pearse Island.

Sign on Customs House, U.S. has been obliterated

Temporary shelter may be found here when downslope winds are blowing in Portland Inlet. Depths in the cove are irregular, indicating a rocky bottom. Winter Inlet, just north, provides superior all-weather protection.

Anchor in about 6 fathoms over a largely rocky bottom with poor-to-fair holding.

Steamer Passage

Chart 3994 south entrance:
54°41.30′ N, 130°22.35′ W; north entrance:
54°47.50′ N, 130°11.30′ W (NAD 27)

> *Steamer Passage separates Somerville Island from the mainland SE.* (p. 209, SD)

Steamer Passage is a smooth-water route from Chatham Sound to Portland Canal. Its steep shores are lined with white and grey granite cliffs, mostly forested. There are several striking examples of climax avalanches along both the south and north shores. The upper reaches of Steamer Passage, previously clearcut, are just beginning to show re-growth of small alders and bushes.

Kumeon Bay

Chart 3994; anchor: 54°42.56′ N, 130°14.57′ W (NAD 27)

> *Kumeon Bay, on the south side of Steamer Passage, has a gravel drying bank on its west side extending 0.1 mile north into Steamer Passage. . . . Anchorage for small vessels, with fair holding ground of sand and mud, can be obtained in Kumeon Bay in about 12 fathoms (22 m); take care to avoid the gravel drying bank described above.* (p. 209, SD)

An attractive creek flows out of a lake just west of Kumeon Bay; the shoal lies directly off that creek. On the west side of the creek is a log dump, and a road that extends into the interior of the mainland. Two hundred yards into the bay, a large log acts as a breakwater of sorts. There are no drift logs on shore in Kumeon Bay, indicating good protection in most weather.

The west side of Kumeon Bay has a steep-to mud flat that rises rapidly to just 100 feet offshore. Rusting cables secured to a tree along the south shore indicate earlier use of the bay.

The best anchorage appears to be just west of the avalanche bluff. You can easily land your dinghy on the gravel beach and explore the pile of red fire-bricks at the south end of the bay. Possibly the bricks fell off a barge that was carrying them to Anyox for construction.

Anchor in the center of the bay in 5 fathoms, sand and gravel bottom with good holding.

Somerville Bay

Chart 3994; entrance: 54°47.75′ N, 130°12.40′ W; anchor: 54°46.50′ N, 130°13.48′ W (NAD 27)

> *Somerville Bay, entered between Start Point and Yakaskalui Point, 0.5 mile SE, is sometimes used as a base for fishing operations during the salmon fishery. . . . Anchorage for small vessels can be obtained near the head of Somerville Bay in 12 fathoms (22 m), sand.* (p. 209, SD)

Excellent protection can be found at the far head of the bay on the west side, tucked in behind the point. A stern tie would make this anchorage bombproof. Long used by fishermen, the central part of the bay is reported to have old rope and nets along the bottom which could foul an anchor.

Anchor in 2 to 3 fathoms over a mud bottom with grass and kelp; fair-to-good holding. Check your anchor to make sure it is not fouled.

Khutzeymateen Inlet

Chart 3994; entrance: 54°43.20′ N, 130°13.30′ W (NAD 27)

> *Khutzeymateen Inlet, on the SE side of Steamer Passage, has mainly steep-to shores rising to high wooded mountains.* (p. 209, SD)

Poplar III *anchored in Somerville Bay*

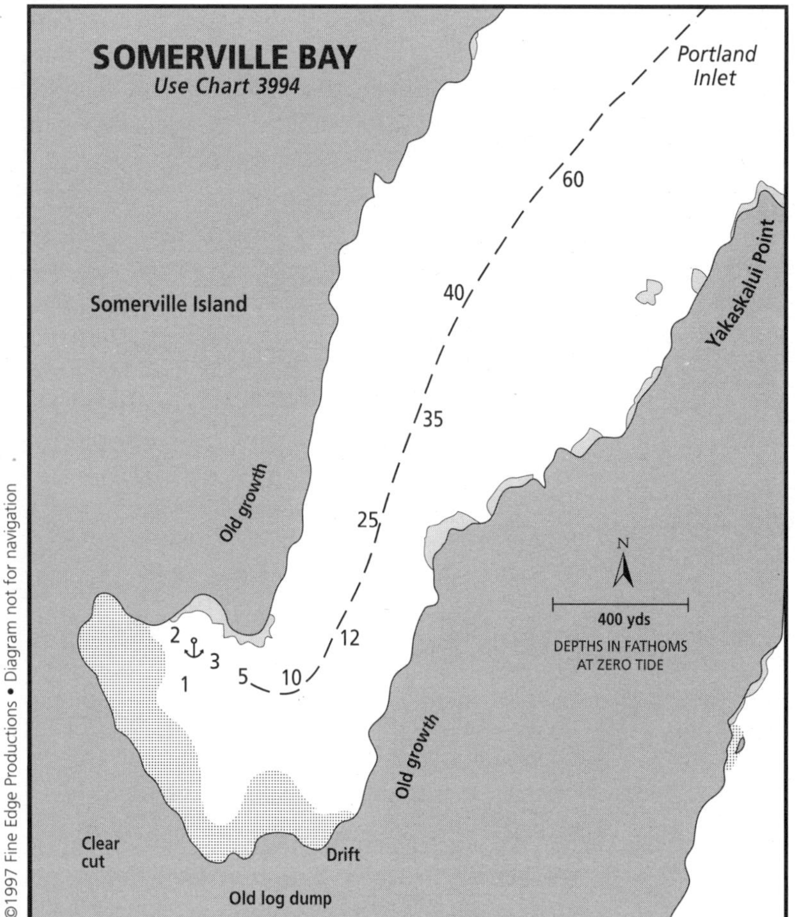

Khutzeymateen Inlet is scenic, with deep water and few options for anchoring. The inlet area, which holds the largest concentration of grizzlies along the British Columbia coast, is a designated sanctuary and an area of extreme sensitivity. Boaters wishing to view the bears are asked to sign up with one of the two authorized guide services. (Please see Appendix for sources.)

Crow Lagoon

Chart 3994; outer entrance: 54°42.90′ N, 130°12.80′ W (NAD 27)

Crow Lagoon, 0.5 mile SSE of Keemein Point, has a drying flat extending across its entrance on which there is a drying rock and another drying rock lies in the centre of its narrow entrance. (p. 209, SD)

Crow Lagoon is an amazing geological feature. It can only be entered on high-water rising due to the shallow mud flat. The steep, rocky cliffs surrounding the steep-sided volcanic crater produce good echoes. We can only guess what the reverberations are like inside the lagoon when outside channel winds blow by its tiny entrance and set the lagoon howling.

The lagoon is entirely landlocked but, unfortunately, too deep for convenient anchoring. No weather of any kind reaches Crow Lagoon except a few circular gusts. You can tie temporarily to the boomsticks or to the old float in the southeast corner of the lagoon. We have passed the center rock in the narrows on its north side; however, you should reconnoiter the channel before entering since it may be subject to change.

Tsamspanaknok Bay

Chart 3994; entrance: 54°40.75′ N, 130°06.40′ W; anchor: 54°40.00′ N, 130°05.87′ W (NAD 27)

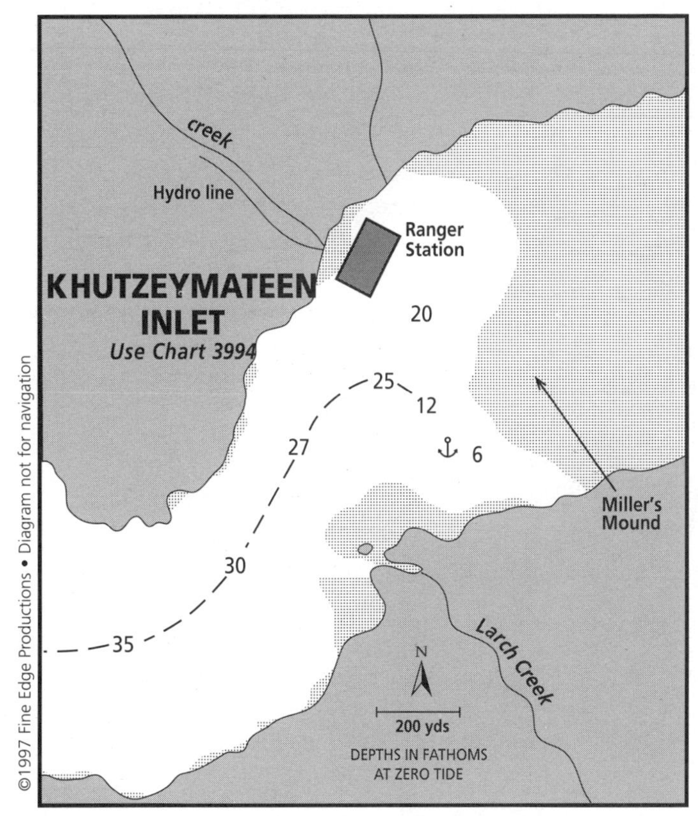

Tsamspanaknok Bay, 5 miles within and on the south side of Khutzeymateen Inlet, provides anchorage for small craft about 0.1 mile off the edge of the drying flat at the head of the bay. Shoal water projects from both sides of the bay, 0.4 mile from the head. (p. 209, SD)

Anchorage can be found off the drying flat; however, the beach is steep-to. The shore, which has been logged on the east side, shows no driftwood or stress from chop. Weather reception on VHF is poor.

Anchor in 11 fathoms over sand, stone and grassy bottom with fair holding.

Khutzeymateen Inlet Head

Chart 3994; anchor: 54°36.30′ N, 129°55.90′ W (NAD 27)

Khutzeymateen River, 8 miles SE of McGregor Point, and Larch Creek flow into the head of Khutzeymateen Inlet over an extensive drying flat. (p. 209, SD)

The seasonal ranger station in Khutzeymateen Inlet is moored off the north shore at the head of the inlet. Visiting boats are asked to register at the ranger station where information is available on the Khutzeymateen Grizzly Reserve.

The Khutzeymateen River has a large drying flat which has changed shape over the years. Anchorage must be confined to a narrow sector south of the ranger station, along the south shore, between the drying flats from Larch Creek and the Khutzeymateen River. Avoid the sand bar to the east which is called Miller's Mound in honor of Skipper Warren Miller who, if the tale be told, kissed the mound with *Sacalaurie*.

Anchor in about 10 to 15 fathoms over a sand, mud, and shell bottom with fair holding.

Kwinamass Bay

Chart 3994; position: 54°47.05′ N, 130°10.04′ W (NAD 27)

Kwinamass Bay is at the north end and on the east side of Steamer Passage. Gadu Point is the south entrance point to the bay and drying flats,

Three-year-old grizzly in Khutzeymateen Inlet

Photo by Ron Thiele

formed by the Kwinamass River, fill the major portion of the bay. (p. 209, SD)

The south shore of Kwinamass Bay behind Gadu Point is steep-to; the bottom shoals rapidly on the north shore as well. The head of the bay at the outlet of Kwinamass River is filled with deadheads. The inlet does not appear as charted, and should be entered only after reconnoitering with a dinghy. The water is opaque, with visibility limited to a foot or two. There are about a half-dozen cables along the north shore formerly used for shore ties. On the north shore of Kwinamass Bay, next to the fishing triangles, you can see where a climax avalanche started from the top of the ridge, scoured everything to bare rock, and dumped rocks and trees at the bottom along shore.

Temporary shelter can be obtained off the north shore along the steep granite cliffs, northwest of the old log dump, in 2 to 3 fathoms; sand bottom with poor holding.

Nasoga Gulf

Chart 3933; entrance: 54°49.70′ N, 130°10.00′ W; anchor: 54°53.70′ N, 130°04.00′ W (NAD 27)

Anchorage can be obtained near the head of Nasoga Gulf, about 0.2 mile from the north shore, in 10 to 18 fathoms (18 to 33 m), gravel bottom. (p. 209, SD)

Nasoga Gulf, a five-mile-long inlet on the east shore of Portland Inlet, offers good protection from downslope winds. The head of the gulf is a deep U-shaped valley. Chambers Creek, which drains the land basin, flows northeast into Iceberg Bay on the Nass River. As you enter the gulf, you can see high snowy peaks on the north side of Nass River. A two-story float house was at the head of the bay in 1996.

If you're headed up Portland Inlet, be aware that depths are about 7 fathoms in the fairway between the tip of Mylor Peninsula and the drying rock north of Ranger Islet. Stay about 50 yards off Trefusis Point on the tip of the peninsula.

Anchor in 10 fathoms over a gravel bottom with fair holding.

Nass River

Chart 3920 metric; entrance: 54°59.30′ N, 130°00.50′ W (NAD 83)

Nass River flows into the NE part of Nass Bay; its mouth is encumbered by numerous drying sand flats. The channels in Nass River are subject to annual changes caused by freshets; local knowledge is advised. (p. 211, SD)

Nass River is entered between Low Point on the south and Nass Point on the north. Vigilant navigation is required. A number of old pilings lie off Low Point, with stumps and logs along the shore.

Head up the river on a rising tide since the water, already opaque and light green, becomes increasingly more milky and pale. If you're attempting to head up Nass River from Double Islet Point, the 2-knot current on springs could set you onto Ripple Tongue, which dries at a minimum of 6 feet on zero tide, and is marked by overfalls. Take the depths listed on Chart 3920 with skepticism. We found many discrepancies in the area between Governors Bar and Ripple Tongue. A high-speed inflatable with echo sounder is the best way to explore the river.

The name Nass comes from a Tlingit word meaning "stomach," since the river was the source of their food. Although Vancouver was the first to document the name, his men did not explore more than four miles beyond the entrance, but you can explore what they considered to be an "insignificant river." Landslip Mountain, south of Stevens Point, is an impressive half-dome of grey granite. Its west-leading face appears to have been shaped by a huge cleaver.

Kincolith

Chart 3920 metric; boat harbour entrance: 54°59.83′ N, 129°58.66′ W NAD 83

Kincolith, 1.2 miles ESE of Bay Point at the mouth of Kincolith River, is a settlement with an area population of 354 (1986), a post office (V0V 1B0), two stores and a medical station with resident nurses . . . The public float at Kincolith is usable only at certain stages of the tide; caution should be exercised in approaching it over Governors Bar due to the presence of snags. (pp. 210–211, SD)

Kincolith's small-boat harbor is crammed with local fishing boats and is not large enough for anchoring.

Mill Bay

Chart 3920 metric; anchor (Mill Bay):
54°59.60′ N, 129°53.63′ W (NAD 83)

Mill Bay, 1 mile ENE of Fort Point, is the site of an abandoned cannery. . . . Mill Bay light (755.6), on the north shore 1.1 miles NE of Fort Point, is shown from a tower with orange vertical stripes. (p. 211, SD)

Mill Bay is a shallow bay, out of the river's current on a drying flat. As you approach this area, the water becomes almost pure grey. In 1996, a logging camp with trailers, trucks, and other equipment was located on the east side of the bay. A sign just west of Mill Bay light warns that this is a blasting area. Old pilings below Fort Point light are the remains of a cannery.

Windswept trees on shore indicate that strong downslope winds occur here in winter. Large logs and stumps that move with the river's current can create a hazard.

Temporary anchorage can be taken in Mill Bay, out of the river current in a backeddy. It is also possible to anchor temporarily a few hundred yards east of Fort Point in a 6-fathom hole, but do some reconnoitering first.

Marine life

Anchor (Mill Bay) in 2 fathoms over soft, grey mud bottom with good holding.

Iceberg Bay

Chart 3920 metric; entrance:
54°57.50′ N, 129°56.50′ W (NAD 83)

Iceberg Bay is entered between Double Islets and Jaques Point, 1.3 miles south. (p. 211, SD)

If you wish to go into Iceberg Bay, you should remain on the south side of the Nass River entrance, along Mylor Peninsula.

Nass Harbour

Chart 3920 metric; position:
54°56.30′ N, 129°56.10′ W (NAD 83)

Nass Harbour, on the east side of Jaques Point, has an extensive drying sand flat at its head. (p. 211, SD)

A classic U-shaped valley, with snow-covered peaks to the south, makes a lovely background to Nass Harbour. Wilp Syoon, an attractive new fishing lodge that opened in August 1996, is located on the east shore of Nass Harbour. The lodge is accessible only by boat or float plane from Prince Rupert.

The inner bay dries at the narrowest part and currents are strong within the bay. The lodge has its own log breakwater to provide protection for its boats.

Anchorage can be taken inside the harbor between the lodge and the drying flat in 2 fathoms, sticky grey mud with very good holding. Larger boats are asked to anchor between Jaques Point and the lodge.

Echo Cove

Chart 3920 metric; anchor:
54°55.67′ N, 129°57.00′ W (NAD 83)

Echo Cove, on the east side of Iceberg Bay, and the drying flat east of Nass Harbour are booming grounds. (p. 211, SD)

Lovely Echo Cove is the site of an abandoned cannery; you can see the remains of the wharf dolphins at the head of the cove. When strong

Salmon Cove, Observatory Inlet

upslope winds blow in Portland Inlet, winds from Nasoga Gulf whip across Chambers Creek. However, when there is a large logboom on the south side of the cove against the steep cliff, little chop enters the cove. The cove has grassy margins with granite cliffs on either side of its head and a low pass that leads to Nass Harbour.

Anchor in 4 to 5 fathoms, between the island and the south shore, in sticky grey mud with very good holding.

Observatory Inlet

Chart 3933; entrance; 55°00.70′ N, 130°01.60′ W (NAD 27)

> *Tidal streams in Observatory Inlet seldom exceed 2 kn with the greatest rates occurring during early summer when land drainage runoff is at its maximum.* (p. 211, SD)

Observatory Inlet was named by Vancouver because he made his astronomical observations in Salmon Cove, about six miles to the north.

"Nass Point Cove"

Chart 3933; anchor:
55°03.10′ N, 129°59.00′ W (NAD 27)

> *A small bay on the east side of Observatory Inlet, about 2.5 miles north of Nass Point, has depths of 30 fathoms (55 m), sand bottom, about 0.3 mile off the head of the bay. The north entrance point to the bay has a shoal spit extending 0.3 mile SSW from it. Local knowledge is advised before anchoring in the bay.* (p. 211, SD)

What we call Nass Point Cove, 2.5 miles north of Nass Point, provides welcome relief from strong downslope winds. However, it is exposed to upslope winds, as evidenced by the many large stumps and old logs at the upper edge of the beach. An attractive, sizable creek enters the cove from a U-shaped valley fed by a small lake on the north side of Mt. Tomlinson. *Caution:* Avoid what we call Two-Foot Rock at the end of the western spit; it has about 2 feet of water at zero tide. Also avoid the fast-shoaling flat off the creek. Good protection from downslope winds can be found near the west end of the beach. We have stayed here overnight in fair weather, hanging on our lunch hook with little concern.

Anchor in 2 to 3 fathoms over sand with fair-to-good holding.

Salmon Cove

Chart 3933; anchor (north side):
55°16.23′ N, 129°50.75′ W (NAD 27)

> *Salmon Cove, 6.5 miles NNE of Observatory Inlet light, has a sand flat extending 0.2 mile from its south shore. . . . Anchorage can be obtained in the entrance of Salmon Cove in depths of 31 to 35 fathoms (57 to 64 m), mud and stones.* (p. 211, SD)

Tidal ponds, Salmon Cove

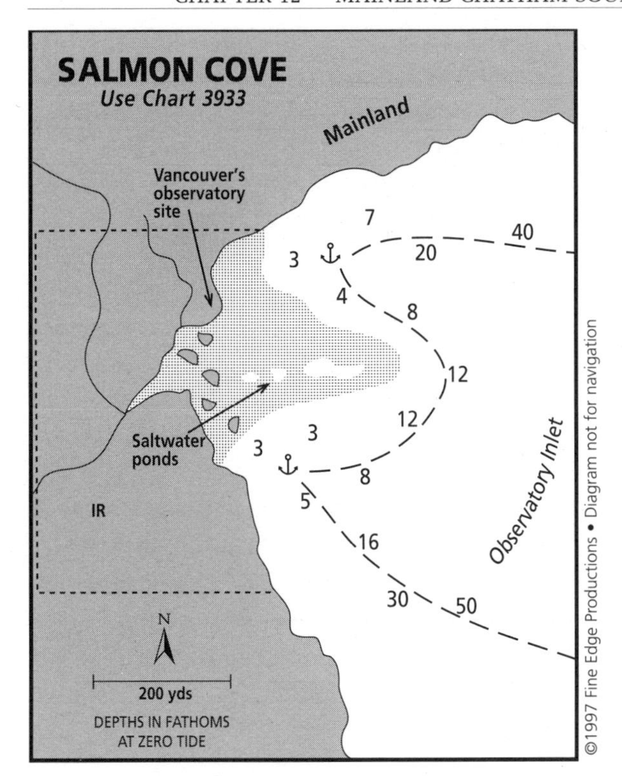

Salmon Cove, named by George Vancouver, is the site where *Discovery* anchored while his men were exploring Observatory Inlet, Hastings Inlet, and Alice Arm. He established a base camp on the beach behind the drying flat where he made astronomical observations in order to check the latest Kendall chronometer.

The shoreline reveals a great variety of marine creatures: colonies of leather stars, barnacles, mussels, and small clams. On the west side, landward of the shore, are two small ponds lined with rocks at their lower edges, which appear to be old fish weirs.

The cove provides some protection from downslope winds on its north side, and upslope winds on its south side. As you proceed north of Salmon Cove, low islands at the head of the inlet come into view, along with high, snowy peaks rising on either side of Hastings Arm.

Large vessels can anchor off the mouth of the creek in 20 fathoms, much like Vancouver did; small craft can anchor on a shallow spot next to the rock walls on either extreme of the extensive drying flats. A major creek divides the drying flat. The north side of the cove is rocky and steep-to, but you can conveniently use a shore tie to hold your boat in position.

Anchor (north side) in 3 fathoms over a mixed bottom of stones, sand, gravel and mud; good holding if you set your anchor well.

"Eagle Cove," Stagoo Creek

Chart 3933; anchor:
55°17.65′ N, 129°45.02′ W (NAD 27)

The cove off Stagoo Creek, 2.5 miles northeast of Dawkins Point, is a haven for eagles and seals. The raptors perch on the many snags and stumps on shore, while a dozen or more seals make their home in the harbor. This cove, which we call Eagle Cove provides good protection from upslope winds. This substantial creek drains a wide area which you can explore on foot.

Large boats can anchor in 16 fathoms; small craft can anchor, using a stern-tie, along the rocky shore at the southwest side of the cove.

Anchor in 4 to 16 fathoms over a mud and shell bottom with good holding.

Juggins Bay

Chart 3920 metric; position:
55°21.92′ N, 129°47.17′ W (NAD 83)

> *Juggins Bay, on the west side of Observatory Inlet opposite Brooke Island, has three drying reefs in its centre. The bay affords shelter for small craft but local knowledge is advised.* (pp. 211–212, SD)

Juggins Bay can offer temporary protection from downslope winds; however, its shore is lined with large drift logs, indicating its exposure to southerlies. The bay is shallow, and anchorage can be taken north of the rocks in the middle of the bay.

Anchorage is reported in 3 fathoms over an unrecorded bottom

Alice Arm

Chart 3920 metric; entrance Liddle Channel:
55°23.60′ N, 129°41.50′ W (NAD 83)

> *Alice Arm, at the north end of Observatory Inlet, has the settlements of Alice Arm and Kitsault at*

Moving a pick-up truck from Kitsault to Alice Arm

> *its head. . . . There are no recommended anchorages in the vicinity of Alice Arm or Kitsault. Small vessels can find temporary anchorage in about 27 m (15 fms) 0.3 mile NNE of Pearson Point, or about 0.15 mile ENE of the same point in 18 m (10 fms); neither anchorage is recommended and the holding ground is poor.* (p. 212, SD)

Alice Arm is a steep-sided fjord that trends 10.5 miles northeast to its head. Along the north shore of Alice Arm, the 5,000-foot peaks of Chaloner Ridge are just a mile and a half above saltwater. Alice Peak, with its permanent ice field, is the source of a number of impressive waterfalls that tumble over forested granite slabs to the inlet below.

The head of the arm, a large U-shaped valley, is fed by four major streams: Kitsault River, Wilwauks Creek, Illiance River and Lime Creek. A gravel logging road from Kitsault, now a ghost town, leads 130 kilometers to Terrace. With prior arrangement, the locked gate 6 miles up-canyon can be opened for vehicles wishing to reach Alice Arm.

Alice Arm Settlement is located on the west shore at the outlet of Kitsault River. A substantial public dock and float at the head of the bay are a mile away from the village via a good gravel road. The public float is used for local skiffs and workboats, and rafting is the norm.

The Dolly Varden silver mine, whose ore was reported to be 85% pure, opened in the early years of the 20th Century. Located 18 miles up the Kitsault River, it was served by a narrow-gauge railroad that ran from Alice Arm Settlement to the mine. You can hike a short portion of this old road to Falls Creek (known locally as Bug Creek), where you can see salmon spawning in late summer and spot black bear in search of easy prey. A primitive trail paralleling its west side leads to beautiful falls

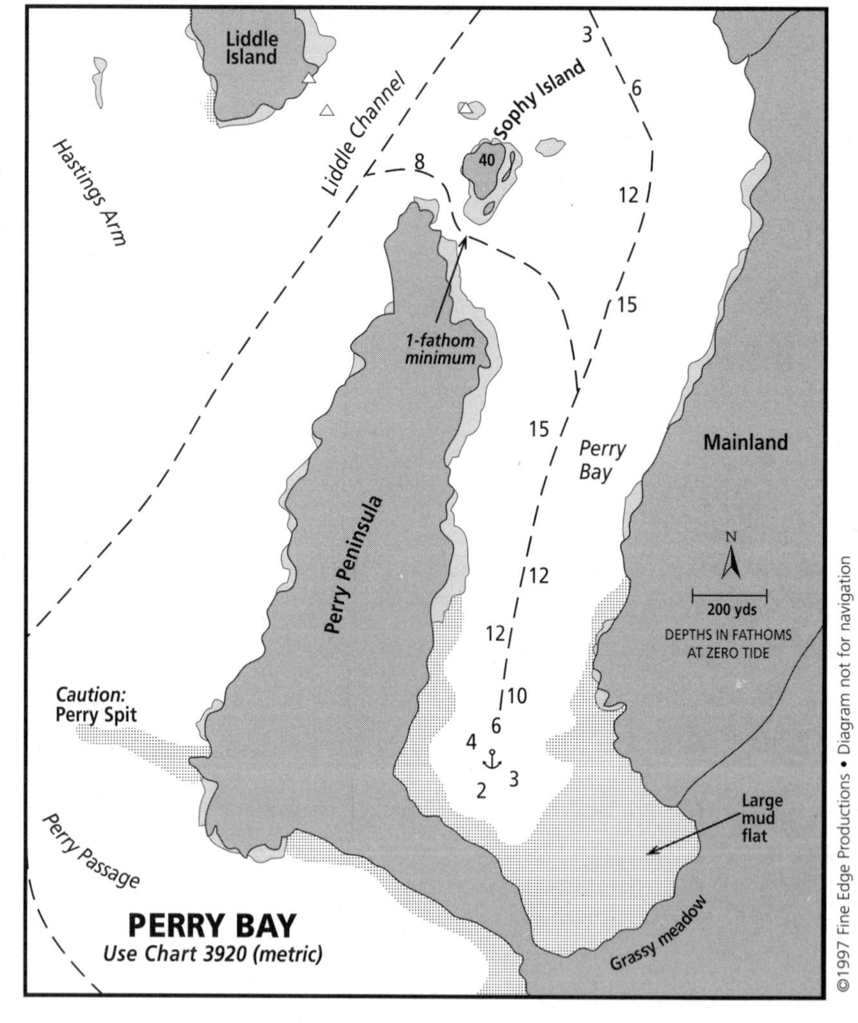

whose source is the ice fields of Alice Peak; the creek is full of glacial "flour."

Anchorage is reported along the west shore between the public dock and a white house located on the bluff above the road to the village; locals says that this part of the bay gets less wind and chop than any other. Pay attention to depths and tide levels, and anchor in about 40 feet. The area south of the Alice Arm public dock is used as a log boom storage area; you can tie temporarily to the boomsticks.

Perry Bay

Chart 3920 metric; entrance (north): 55°23.90′ N, 129°40.90′ W; anchor (shelf): 55°22.77′ N, 129°40.90′ W (NAD 83)

> *Perry Bay, on the east side of Perry Peninsula, is obstructed in its entrance by a shoal spit extending about 0.3 mile WSW from its east entrance point and by the drying reef close east of Sophy Island; its navigable entrance, between these two shoal areas, is very narrow with a least depth of 5.5 m (18 ft) in the fairway. . . . Anchorage can be obtained in Perry Bay, about 0.2 mile SE of Sophy Island, in 24 m (13 fms), mud bottom.* (p. 212, SD)

Perry Bay, one of the best anchorages at the head of Observatory Inlet, offers good protection from southeast storm winds or upslope winds. The head of the bay has a large, drying grassy flat. With no drift logs, the bay appears to offer calm shelter in most weather.

In addition to the entrance noted above in *Sailing Directions*, you can enter between Perry Peninsula and Sophy Island, carefully staying midchannel between the two bodies of land. Depth in the fairway is a minimum of one fathom.

Large boats can anchor anywhere in Perry Bay in 16 fathoms; small boats can anchor over a 3- to 4-fathom shelf at the south end of the bay just north of a large tree stump on shore. Good landing beaches and campsites can be found at the southeast corner of the bay.

Anchor (shelf) in 4 fathoms over a mixed bottom of sand, mud, gravel and stones, with poor-to-fair holding; good if your anchor is well set.

Kitsault

Chart 3920 metric; position: 55°27.57′ N, 129°28.88′ W (NAD 83)

> *Kitsault, on the east side of Alice Arm about 0.7 mile ENE of Pearson Point, is a mining settlement operated by Amax of Canada Ltd. . . . A siren is on the gate at the float to alert the security staff to visitors.* (p. 212, SD)

The former mining town of Kitsault, on the north shore of Lime Creek, is entirely private property and closed to the public. Mining operations at Kitsault ceased in the early 1980s when the price of molybdenum made further operation unprofitable. Only a small crew remains, off-loading mining equipment from the mine 6 miles up Lime Creek, and maintaining the modern apartments and outbuildings. No one lives in Kitsault, and visitors are not welcome. Visiting boats are not allowed to tie up to the small floating dock on the east end of the waterfront; the dock is closed to all but Amax personnel. Amax is reportedly seeking a purchaser to take over the town which "has everything for 2,500 people."

Access to Alice Arm is either by private boat or vehicle via a gravel road from Terrace. There is a locked gate 6 miles from Kitsault; campers or trailer-boaters may make prior arrangements with Amax mine personnel to be admitted.

Alice Arm Settlement

Chart 3920 metric; wharf position: 55°28.28′ N, 129°29.72′ W (NAD 83)

> *The public wharf, 1 mile NNE of Pearson Point and on the west side of Alice Arm, has a wharfhead, 30 m (100 ft) long, with a depth of 7.3 m (24 ft) alongside. . . . Floats are attached to the south side of the wharf, part of one float is reserved for aircraft.* (p. 212, SD)

Alice Arm is a part-time settlement that consists of a few small homes, log cabins, and dilapidated buildings with just one or two families remaining year-round. In its heyday, the village was a thriving community with a school, medical facility, and fire station whose residents worked in mining, fishing and logging activities.

Hastings Arm: cabin, north end

Today, its summer residents enjoy the fine growing-climate, quiet fishing and hunting. During salmon runs the river outlet is known for its large concentration of grizzlies.

A section of Alice Arm's old public float is used these days to ferry vehicles across the arm; several outboard skiffs push the float like little tugs guiding a large ship into port.

To visit the shore, raft to local boats that are tied to the public float.

Hastings Arm

Chart 3920 metric; entrance (west fairway at Vadso Rocks): 55°22.87′ N, 129°45.90′ W; entrance (east fairway at Brooke Shoal): 55°23.00′ N, 129°43.50′ W (NAD 83)

> *Hastings Arm is entered between Bocking Peninsula and Davies Point. Larcom Island divides the entrance.* (p. 212, SD)

As you proceed northward into Hastings Arm, the water turns to the milky green of glacial runoff, and water runs down every crevice and canyon of the western side. The weather becomes increasingly misty and rainy, and fog wafts up and down the mountainsides. This inlet is a spectacular treat!

There are a number of good anchor sites at the south end of Hastings Arm. At the north end of Hastings Arm, there are two old cabins on the east shore. Be careful as you approach the outlet of Kshwan River; the bottom shoals rapidly, and visibility is limited to about 3 inches in the glacial-melt water!

Strombeck Bay

Chart 3920 metric; entrance: 55°22.90′ N, 129°46.90′ W; anchor: 55°22.42′ N, 129°47.00′ W (NAD 83)

> *Strombeck Bay, between the north side of Aiskew Island and Fortier Point, is encumbered with drying and below-water rocks. . . . Anchorage can be obtained off the entrance of Strombeck Bay, about 0.2 mile west of Aiskew Point, in 37 m (20 fms).* (p. 213, SD)

Strombeck Bay, although open to the north, can provide good protection from southerlies if you anchor deep in the bay. You can easily land a dinghy on its gravel beaches and comb the grassy shores, but be careful to watch for bear. South of the cluster of mid-bay rocks, there is a flat bottom of 6 fathoms with swinging room for several boats. Avoid these rocks by staying within 200 feet of the west shore. There is an uncharted rock 100 feet off the southwest beach that dries only at low water.

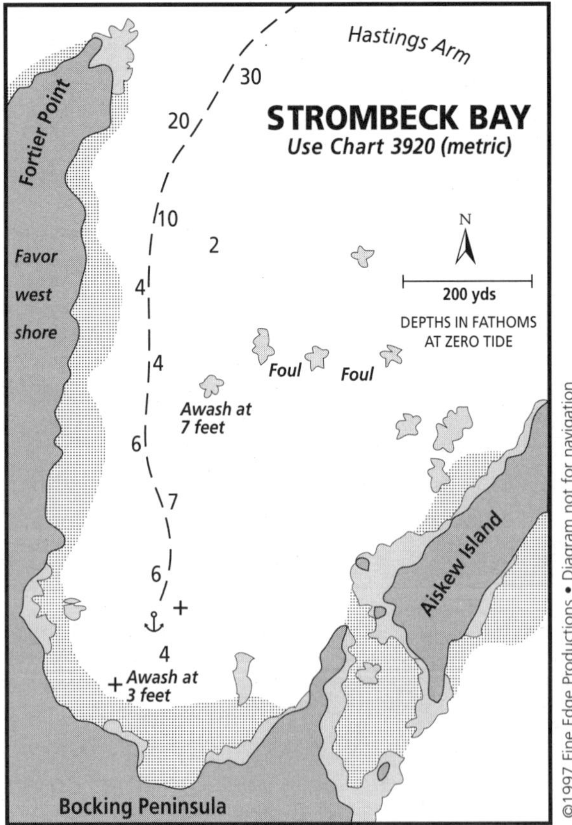

Anchor on a line between the 2.7-meter rock on the west shore and the 3.7-meter rock on the east shore.

Anchor in 5 fathoms, sand bottom with good holding.

Sylvester Bay

Chart 3920 metric; entrance:
55°23.20′ N, 129°47.20′ W; anchor:
55°21.74′ N, 129°48.42′ W (NAD 83)

> *Sylvester Bay lies between Bocking Peninsula and Granby Peninsula and is entered between Fortier Point and Cane Rock, which is surrounded by several shoals. Drying rocks and shoals encumber the SE part of Sylvester Bay. A small cabin is on the NE shore close south of Fortier Point.* (p. 213, SD)

Sylvester Bay, with its grass- and tree-covered shores, is well protected from southeasterlies and up-channel winds, and makes a wonderful anchorage for pleasure craft. There are no drift logs along shore. You can often spot bears combing the shores, and get a rare glimpse of a marten or two. To the west, you have a magnificent view of a hanging glacier whose valley is drained by Cascade Creek.

After you pass south of Cane Rock and Fortier Point, favor the west shore to avoid the rocks shown on the chart two-thirds of the way down the bay. There is plenty of swinging room for a number of boats near the head of the bay. The bottom is flat over an extensive area.

Anchor in 4 fathoms, sand, mud, and shell bottom with good-to-very-good-holding.

Larcom Lagoon

Chart 3920 metric; entrance:
55°23.26′ N, 129°45.14′ W; anchor:
55°23.87′ N, 129°44.42′ W (NAD 83)

> *Larcom Lagoon, in the SW part of Larcom Island, is entered 0.5 mile NE of Vadso Island through a narrow channel that almost dries. Several drying rocks lie within the lagoon and local knowledge is advised to enter.* (p. 213, SD)

Larcom Lagoon gives the best all-weather protection in upper Observatory Inlet. When a blustery southerly is blowing outside, no chop penetrates the lagoon. Because the fetch is minimal, southerly winds and gusts raise little threat. The lagoon can be entered only at adequate tide levels and by careful piloting, using the detail on Chart 3920.

Larcom Lagoon has a very narrow entrance channel and the current runs at considerable strength. On a blustery south wind and ebb current, there are small standing waves just outside the entrance. West of the entrance, there are two isolated rocks awash at about 2 feet. Stay close to the south shore to avoid these rocks.

Favor the south shore of the entrance narrows; the fairway is fairly steep-to and composed of gravel and stone. On a 3.5-foot tide, there are no

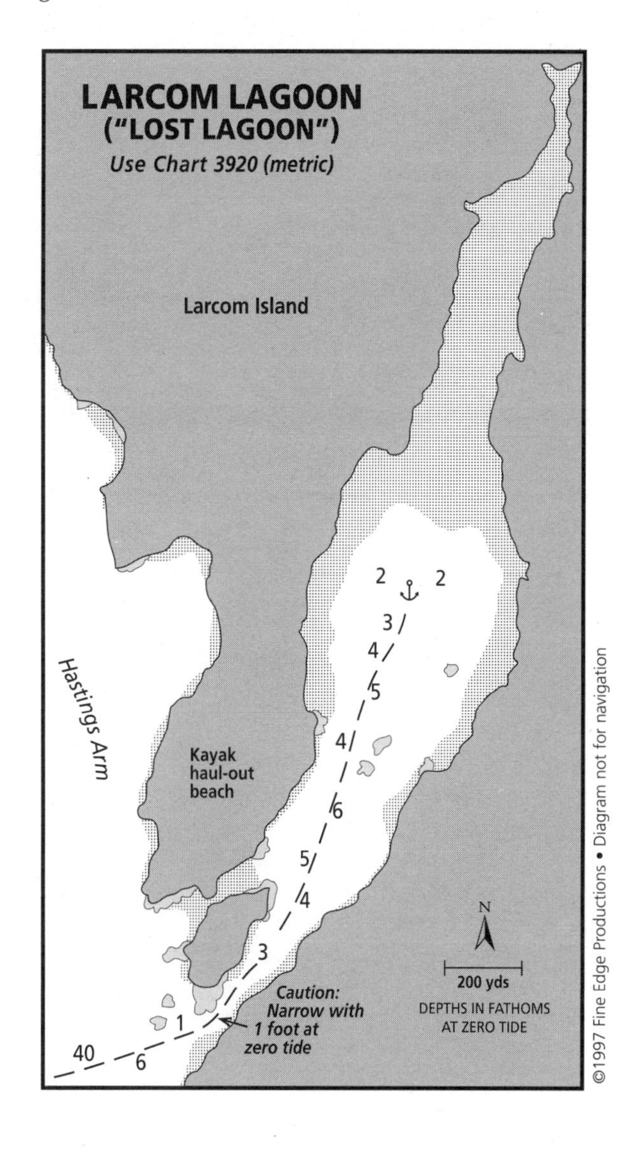

visible isolated rocks. There is about a foot of water in the center of the fairway in the narrows at zero tide, so you should enter only at mid-tide or better. Slack water is within a few minutes of Prince Rupert. Avoid the rock connected to the entrance island which extends to midchannel at high water. At low water the fairway passes about 20 to 30 feet east of this rock.

Inside the lagoon, there is ample swinging room for a number of boats. Avoid the charted rocks in mid-lagoon by favoring the west shore. Larger boats and those wanting plenty of swinging room will find convenient anchorage over a very large flat area of 3 to 4 fathoms in the center of the bay. Small boats can find good shelter in the small nook between the north end of the entrance island and Larcom Island, protected by a wide grassy spit.

Anchor in 3 to 4 fathoms in the west center of the bay; mud bottom with very good holding.

Anyox: remains of old smelter

Anyox (pronounced annie-ox)

Anyox, whose short history follows the pattern of so many other mining communities in British Columbia, was a thriving town of 1500 in the early part of the 20th Century. In 1913, the town boasted a hospital, electricity, a telegraph station and complete telephone system, as well as docks that could accommodate three or four freighters—remarkable facilities when you consider how remote the town was. Destroyed by fire in 1923, the town was completely rebuilt and, within a few years, was producing 35 million pounds of copper annually, in addition to gold and silver. During the Depression copper prices declined, and operations became unprofitable. The mine and the town were closed for good in 1934. When you study the destruction of vegetation along the western shores of Granby Bay, you can't help but wonder what effect years of breathing noxious smelter gas had on the lungs of the residents.

Anyox

Chart 3920 metric; position:
55°25.10′ N, 129°48.73′ W (NAD 83)

> *Anyox, west of Graves Point, is the site of a copper smelter and mine that were abandoned in the late 1930s. . . . The slag dump charted south of Smith Bluff has been partially removed (1988) exposing a conspicuous black face with a single pile in front.* (p. 213, SD)

Two lovely old brick chimneys on Graves Point mark the site of a former copper smelter. Unfortunately, the chimneys are the only attractive part of the once-vast operation. The old buildings between Graves Point and the slag pile resemble a bombed-out village. Two additional stacks and ruined buildings lie along Anyox Creek. In August 1996, the barge conveyor,

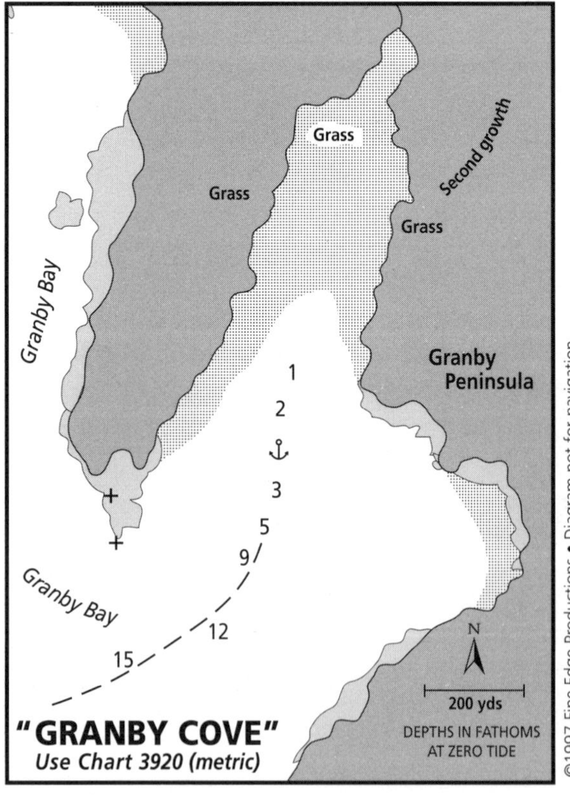

Adams, was moored off the slag pile, loading barges for hauling away the slag to be used in manufacturing cement aggregate.

Keep a sharp lookout as you pass Anyox. The drying flat off large Anyox Creek extends into the bay, and you could easily be distracted while studying the ruins.

"Granby Cove"

Chart 3920 metric; entrance:
55°22.85′ N, 129°49.05′ W; anchor:
55°22.98′ N, 129°48.81′ W (NAD 83)

> *Granby Bay is entered between Granby Point and Johnson Point, 0.6 mile NNE. Anyox Rock, 0.4 mile SE of Granby Point, has drying reefs close north and south of it. . . . Drying flats extend from the west shore of Granby Bay at Hidden Creek, Anyox Creek, Bonanza Point, Tauw Creek and Cascade Creek. . . . Depths within Granby Bay are too great for satisfactory anchorage. Vessels up to 76 m (250 ft) long have obtained temporary anchorage 0.15 mile SW of Graves Point in about 66 m (36 fms). Good anchorage for small vessels is reported to be close off the slag dump in about 20 m (66 ft).* (p. 213, SD)

Granby Cove (from Granby Consolidated Mining Company) is situated halfway down Granby Peninsula at its narrowest point. The only convenient anchorage for small craft in Granby Bay, this cove is calm in all weather, as shown by the grassy shores without drift logs. Snowy peaks to the north and west provide a beautiful backdrop for your anchorage.

Anchor in 5 fathoms, mud bottom with good holding.

"Vancouver Cove," Doben Island Passage

Charts 3920 metric; anchor (north side of the two islets): 55°26.93′ N, 129°46.37′ W (NAD 83)

> *Carlson Islets and Doben Island are west of the north end of Larcom Island. The passages on both sides of Doben Island are scattered with shoal and drying rocks, making them navigable only with local knowledge and by small craft.* (p. 213, SD)

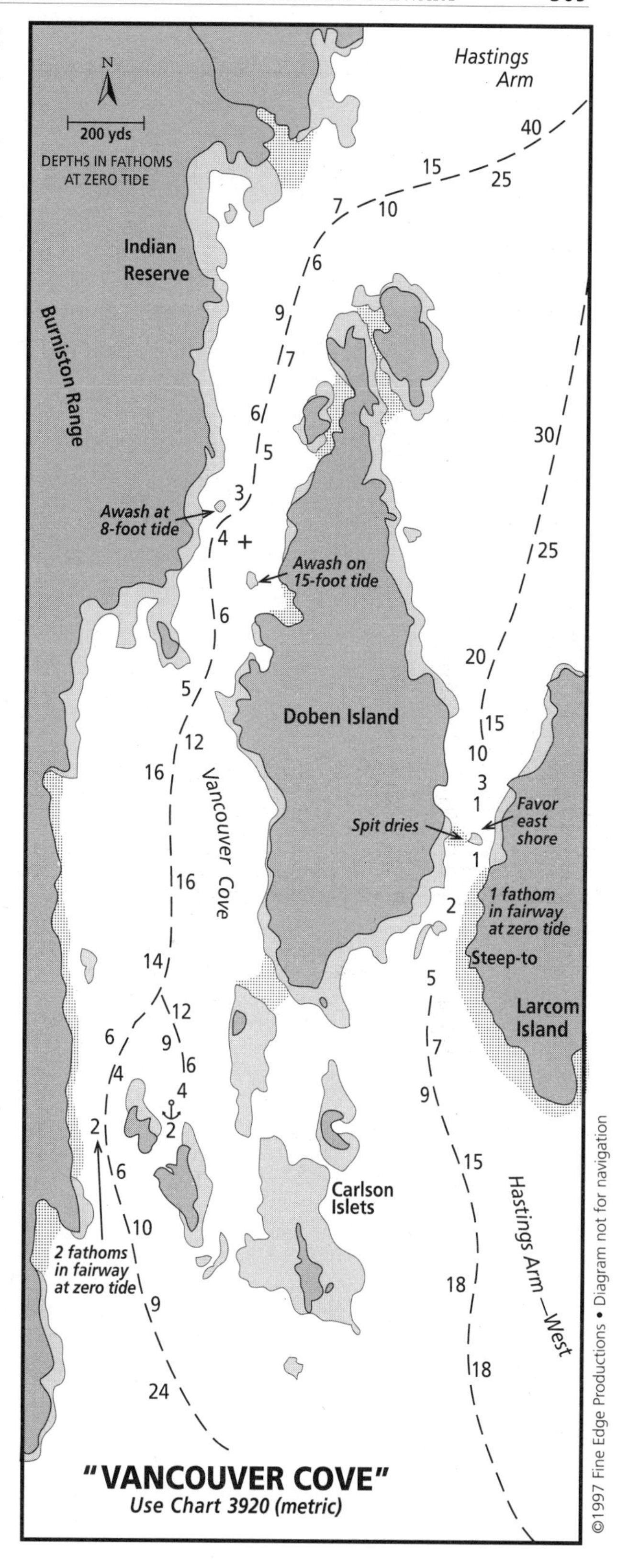

There is no cove named after George Vancouver, as far as we know, but we understand that he and his men liked the area between Salmon Cove and these islands. Hence, we call this calm, quiet place, west of Doben Island and Carlson Islets, Vancouver Cove. This quiet cove is the calmest anchorage we've found in Observatory Inlet, and its grassy shores attest to the fact that very little wake or chop enters these waters. This is bird heaven; we sighted dozens of tufted puffins, old-squaw, loons, and small gulls. We also saw a large wolf combing the beach on Larcom Island.

To enter Vancouver Cove from the north, find the narrow fairway west of Doben Island, about 50 feet to the west of the rock that dries at 5.5 meters. The south entrance to Vancouver Cove, east of Carlson Islets, has a minimum of 2 fathoms in the fairway.

The passage on the east side of Doben Island, known as "The Narrows," has a fairway of about one fathom east of the drying rock. Favor the steep-to east shore to pass through the narrows. In Vancouver Cove, large craft can anchor in several places, including the center, in 12 to 15 fathoms over a gravel bottom. We prefer to anchor on the north side of the two southwesterly Carlson Islets that are connected by a spit.

Anchor (north side of the two islets) in about 2 fathoms over a mud and stone bottom with fair-to-good holding.

Kshwan River

Chart 3933; position: 55°37.40′ N, 129°48.48′ W (NAD 27)

> *Kshwan River, 4.5 miles north of Olh Creek, flows into the head of Hastings Arm across an extensive drying flat.* (p. 213, SD)

Kshwan River enters at the head of Hastings Arm. This area can be a very misty and mystical place. If you're lucky enough to arrive when the sky clears, you will get a view of a snow-covered peak, dramatic in its sharpness, that lies directly north of the river delta. The peaks here rise to 4,000 to 6,000 feet. We have heard reports of petroglyphs near the river's outlet but have not been able to locate them.

There is a large steep-to mud flat, the extent of which is difficult to gauge because of the opaque water. Use caution when proceeding beyond the two cabins located on the east shore. There is no convenient anchorage.

Portland Canal

Chart 3933; entrance: 54°58.80′ N, 130°07.80′ W (NAD 27)

> *Portland Canal is a deep, narrow inlet extending 60 miles north from its junction with Portland Inlet and Pearse Canal. The towns of Stewart, B.C. and Hyder, Alaska, are at the head of the inlet. . . . Tidal streams in Portland Canal have an estimated maximum of 2 kn on the flood and 3 kn on the ebb, diminishing toward the head of the inlet. The streams by the shore turn shortly after HW and LW.* (pp. 214–215, SD)

Portland Canal is a long, narrow inlet, perhaps the longest on the entire North American continent. When measured from Dixon Entrance to Stewart, it is more than 100 miles long. Portland Canal is deep with sheer sides and a rugged wilderness appearance.

Anchorage is marginal at best and depends entirely on the weather. VHF weather reports are

Photo courtesy CHS, Pacific Region

Portland Canal, looking north at head

Portland Canal: heading south from "Glacier Bay"

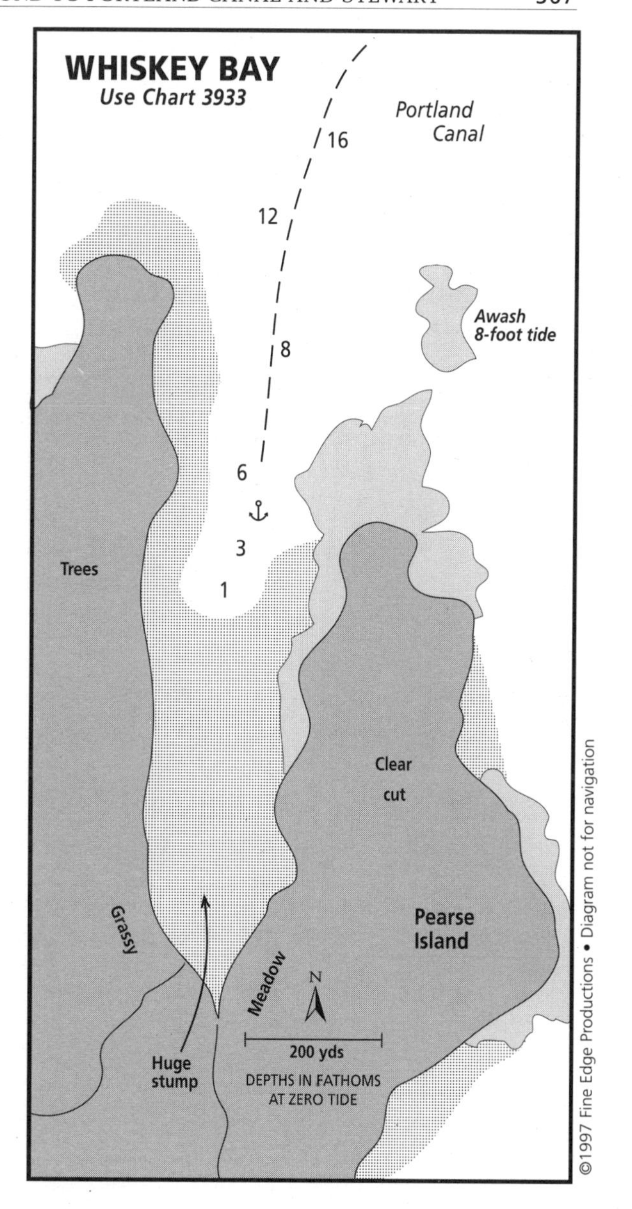

difficult to receive; VHF Channel 21B is useful in the central part of Portland Canal.

Whiskey Bay

Chart 3933; anchor: 55°01.98′ N, 130°10.09′ W (NAD 27)

> *Whiskey Bay is 3.5 miles NNW of Stick Point and near the north extremity of Pearse Island.*
> (p. 215, SD)

Whiskey Bay is a good lunch stop, or an overnighter, if no downslope winds are expected. At the head of the bay is a grassy meadow with a huge stump; the shoreline has a constant slope which can be used as a kayak haul-out. Upon entering, avoid the rocks awash on the east side of the bay and anchor in convenient depths.

Anchor in 4 to 6 fathoms over sand and mud with good holding.

Reef Island

Chart 3933; anchor (south cove): 55°04.76′ N, 130°12.53′ W; anchor (west Reef Island): 55°04.93′ N, 130°12.32′ W (NAD 27)

> *Two coves, west of Reef Island, have sandy beaches and small craft can find shelter in them.*
> (p. 215, SD)

Reef Island, on the west side of Portland Canal, has two coves that provide some relief from downslope winds, but both are exposed to the south.

The south cove is steep-to and temporary anchorage can be taken in 6 to 8 fathoms off the drying beach near a drift tree with limbs still attached.

Small craft can also find some protection directly west of Reef Island, off the stony beach, where there is a 100-foot-long tree lying onshore. The fairway on the west side of Reef Island has a minimum depth of about one fathom. There is a 1- to 2-fathom area in the passage between Reef Island and the shore. The level of the tree limbs indicates that the area is mostly free of chop. If you anchor in this passageway, a stern-tie to shore may be effective.

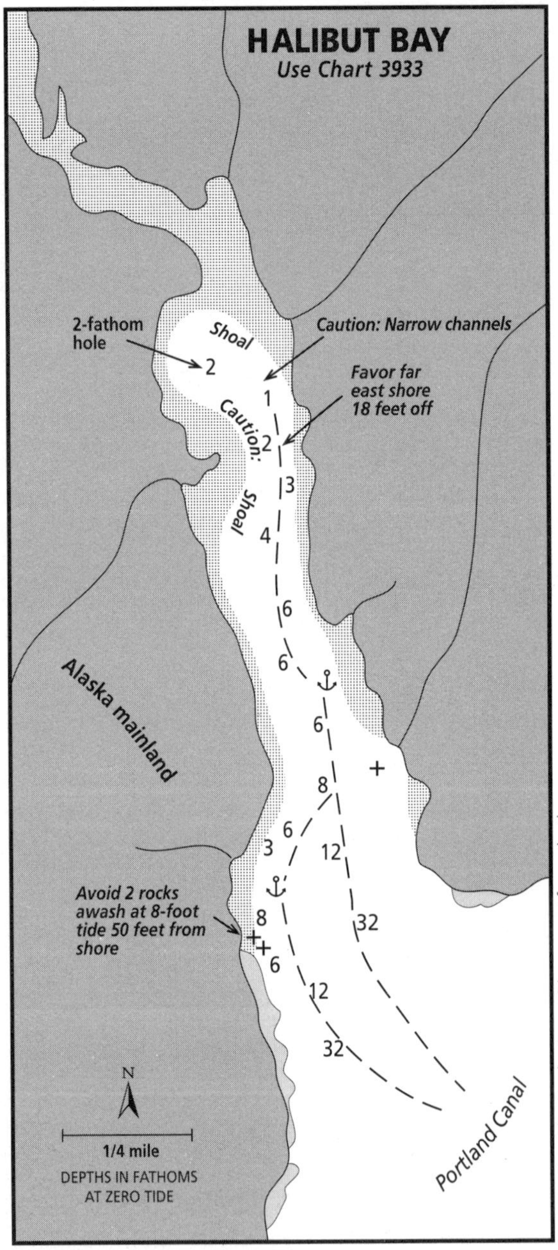

Anchor (south cove) in 6 to 8 fathoms. The bottom is sand, stones and iridescent seaweed; fair holding.

Anchor (west Reef Island) in about 3 fathoms, mixed bottom, predominantly sand; fair-to-good holding.

Sandfly Bay

Chart 3933; anchor: 55°09.80′ N, 130°09.08′ W (NAD 27)

> *Sandfly Bay, 1 mile WNW of Dickens Point, is useless as an anchorage.* (p. 215, SD)

Some temporary protection from downslope winds can be found in scenic Sandfly Bay. It is a good place for small craft to anchor only in fair weather. Sandfly Bay is steep-to off the creek outlet; the foreshore slope is less steep on the west side of the bay. Its grassy margins have little driftwood to indicate severe weather or chop. Avoid the charted rocks near the east shore.

Anchorage can be found about 100 yards from the white granite rocks on the west shore, 50 yards south of the drying gravel flat. This spot can provide reasonable anchoring for one or two boats in fair weather. There is easy landing access.

Anchor in 3 to 5 fathoms; sandy bottom with fair-to-good holding.

Halibut Bay

Chart 3933; entrance (east cove): 55°13.75′ N, 130°05.65′ W; anchor (west shore): 55°13.20′ N, 130°05.85′ W (NAD 27)

> *Halibut Bay, on the west side of Portland Canal, is entered between Halibut Point and Astronomical Point. Its shores are generally bold, but on each side near the entrance are sandy beaches with shoal water extending 240 feet (73 m) offshore, and low, grassy land, extending back for 300 feet (91 m). Near the head of the bay drying flats

extend from the west shore nearly all the way across, leaving a narrow channel close to the east side, through which a depth of 5 feet (1.5 m) can be carried. The narrow basin north of this passage is only suitable for small craft and has a depth of 24 feet (7.3 m). . . . Anchor in mid-channel about 0.3 mile within the entrance in 6 to 10 fathoms (11 to 18 m), mud bottom. (p. 215, SD)

Halibut Bay affords the best protection between Whiskey Bay and Maple Bay or Fords Cove. Convenient anchorage can be found in the entrance on the east shore, just off a tiny creek and stony beach, or on the west shore between a small creek and the rocky point. While the bay is open to the southeast, most of the summer up- and downslope winds blow by the entrance.

In the inner bay, there is a 3-fathom hole north of the large creek. The passage to this hole is very shallow. We found as little as 2 feet in the fairway at zero tide, with rapidly-shoaling flats on either side. There was a small float house moored to the west of this hole. In 1996, we found it necessary to travel within a few yards of the east wall until we were abeam the low point north of the west creek. We would not recommend inner Halibut Bay until it is more fully charted. Chart 3933 is not a reliable guide to the shoals.

Anchor (east shore) in 8 fathoms; sand, gravel and stone bottom with good holding.

Anchor (west shore) in 6 fathoms off a tiny creek; sand, gravel and stone bottom with good holding.

Belle Bay

Chart 3933; position: 55°17.45′ N, 129°56.70′ W (NAD 27)

Belle Bay, east of Hattie Island, does not afford anchorage. (p. 215, SD)

Belle Bay lies at the foot of a U-shaped valley. It is steep-to, with depths dropping 45 degrees to 30 fathoms. Temporary protection from southerlies might be obtained at the south end of the beach with a stern-tie to the trees, or from northerlies at the far north end of the beach, with a stern-tie to the drift logs on shore. However, upwind chop blows into both sites, making them quite rolly. Belle Bay Creek flows from high lakes which lie just 1.5 mile from the lower end of Granby Bay in Observatory Inlet.

Temporary protection in southerlies may be possible off the northeast corner of Hattie Island, avoiding the charted rock.

Car Point Notch

Chart 3933; position: 55°20.30′ N, 130°00.00′ W (NAD 27)

The head of the notch at Car Point holds a wonderful surprise—a stunning waterfall that tumbles vertically over somber, angular, grey and rust granite. Although we encountered many lovely cascades along the eastern shore of Portland Inlet, this one got raves from all the crew. As we approached the notch, the water grew calm and we were able to come within 10 feet of the waterfall. Ferns and delicate white flowers grow out of every small crevice, while hemlock and spruce sprout from unlikely vertical faces.

At the south end of Portland Canal, the water is tea-colored but becomes progressively greener as you proceed northward.

Tombstone Bay

Chart 3393; float position:
55°24.38′ N, 130°33.13′ W (NAD 27)

Tombstone Bay, 3 miles north of Breezy Point, has rocks in the entrance of its south bight. A wooded valley extends SW from the head of the south bight. . . . Temporary anchorage can be obtained by small craft near the head of the north bight of Tombstone Bay in 8 fathoms (15 m). (p. 215, SD)

On the north side of Tombstone Bay are overhanging cliffs from which hemlock and cedar grow. The bottom is steep-to with a rocky beach. This bight could offer shelter from north winds with an anchor placed close to the drying flat at its head.

The south end of Tombstone Bay is the watershed for an unnamed creek flowing from a perfect, U-shaped valley. On the north side of the south bight is a large steel ball with a 30-foot float attached. There is a house with its own dock and

Sea Chief *in Tombstone Bay*

In 1996 there were three mobile homes on logs floats moored in the bay. An old cabin and pilings from a former pier are located at the north end of the bay. Several streams and waterfalls drop from snow on Mt. Tourney.

Anchor in 3 fathoms off the edge of the drying bank; stone and gravel bottom with poor holding. Be sure to check the set of your anchor.

some small outbuildings located along the shore of the creek and the float is probably private. Protection from southerly weather can be obtained; however, avoid the charted rocks and the drying flat off the creek.

Anchor off the drying flat, in the vicinity of the float, in about 10 fathoms over an unrecorded bottom.

Maple Bay

Chart 3393; entrance: 55°25.40′ N, 130°00.90′ W; position: 55°25.20′ N, 130°00.55′ W (NAD 27)

> *Maple Bay, NE of Tombstone Bay, and entered between Columbia Point and Maple Point, has two drying rocks in it. The bay has a moderately shelving foreshore of stones and gravel and is the site of a former mining camp; ruins of a jetty and the remains of a few houses are all that is left of the camp. . . . Anchorage for small craft can be obtained about 0.15 mile from the south shore of Maple Bay in 9 fathoms (16 m).* (p. 215, SD)

Maple Bay lies 1.5 miles north of Tombstone Bay at the foot of Mt. Tourney. The bay offers good protection from southerlies if you tuck just inside Columbia Point on the south end, and moderate protection from northerlies behind Maple Point on the north end.

Hideaway Lodge

Chart 3933; dock position: 55°36.14′ N, 130°06.38′ W (NAD 27)

The Hideaway Lodge, located 0.2 mile south of Bay Islet on the east shore, is 1.5 miles south of Fords Cove. The lodge is highly recommended by townspeople in Stewart. Owned by Richard and Bebe Lemieux, the lodge caters to people who are seeking good sportfishing or a pristine wilderness experience. Both can be obtained here, along with good food and other amenities, including a hot tub. The lodge has a float at the end of a substantial dock and a log breakwater which reduces wind chop.

As you leave the bay and resume your northward travel, you can see a beautiful hanging glacier in the Halleck Range, 2 miles from the saltwater, several thousand feet above the canal.

Fords Cove float & Green Islets

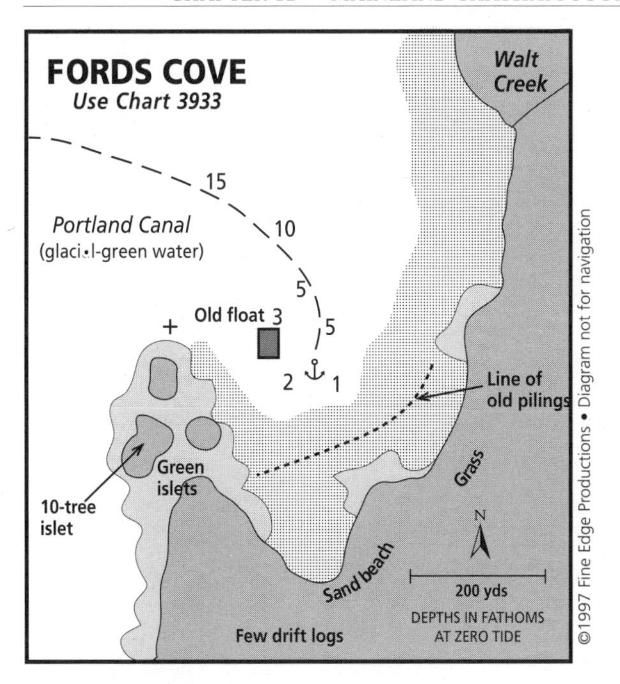

Fords Cove

Chart 3933; entrance: 55°37.78′ N, 130°05.80′ W; anchor (small boats): 55°37.67′ N, 130°05.65′ W (NAD 27)

> *Fords Cove, east of Green Islets, affords fair shelter from south winds but none from north winds. The south part of the cove is shoal for about 450 feet (137 m) offshore. Only old piles and a float in ruins remain of a former logging camp in Fords Cove (1988). . . . A fair anchorage can be found in Fords Cove, about 0.2 mile from Green Islets and the same distance from the east shore, in 16 fathoms (29 m).* (p. 215, SD)

Fords Cove, directly west of the hanging glacier described above, affords good protection in southerly weather. An old wooden float lies several hundred yards east of Green Islets; small boats may be able to tie to this float.

Small boats can also anchor between the float and the sandy beach in 3 fathoms; larger boats can anchor just outside the float in 5 to 7 fathoms.

Anchor (small boats) in 3 fathoms, sand bottom, very good holding.

"Turquoise Cove"

Chart 3933; entrance: 55°45.35′ N, 130°08.05′ W (NAD 27)

The cove on the east side of Portland Canal, 0.5 mile south of Round Point, can provide anchorage for one small boat only. You will be out of the southerly chop, and have good protection from most summer weather. The V-shaped cove is deep with constant shoaling to the small beach at its head. A stern tie to shore is recommended.

The color of the water is an exquisite light turquoise, hence we call it Turquoise Cove. Water visibility is about a foot. You have a first-class view of high snowfields on the mountains to the west.

Anchor in the head of the cove in about 5 fathoms, soft silt bottom, with fair holding.

"Glacier Bay and Cove"

Chart 3933; entrance: 55°48.95′ N, 130°07.60′ W; anchor (east cove): 55°49.38′ N, 130°06.93′ W; anchor (west bay): 55°49.45′ N, 130°07.56′ W (NAD 27)

The large bay south of Glacier Point, known locally as Glacier Bay, has two possibilities for anchorage in stable weather or in downslope winds. The

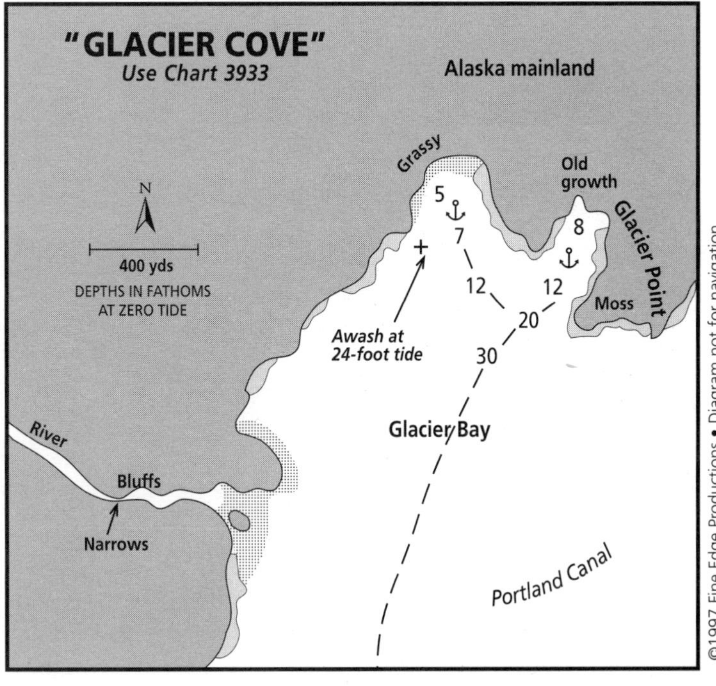

The signs say it all for the Baidarka *crew*

easterly cove, just behind Glacier Point, is steep-to close to a rocky shore with room for one or two boats in about 7 fathoms. Here a stern-tie to shore can be used effectively.

The western part of the bay is steep-to and more open, with swinging room for a number of boats. Water visibility is limited to about a foot. Both anchor sites are completely open to the south.

An unnamed river enters the south end of Glacier Bay through a 40-foot cleft in a 100-foot-high cliff. It's an impressive sight to view from a dinghy. *Caution:* shoal water exists a quarter-mile off the shore of the river, contrary to what is indicated on Chart 3933.

The waters of Glacier Bay take a close second in beauty to the turquoise of "Turquoise Cove."

Anchor (west bay) in 7 fathoms over sand or glacial silt, with fair holding.

Anchor (east cove) in 9 fathoms over sand or glacial silt, with fair holding.

Marmot Bay

**Charts 3794, 3933; position:
55°53.08′ N, 130°00.33′ W (NAD 27)**

> *Marmot Bay, on the north side of Lion Point, has the ruins of a pier in its NE part. Mooring dolphins and booming grounds are south of the ruins.* (p. 216, SD)

Marmot Bay, on the British Columbia side of Portland Canal, is 2 miles south of Stewart. It offers some protection from downslope winds; however, the bay is largely filled with a number of log booms, float houses, and steel dols. Consider temporary moorage tied to the boomsticks. This is a place to stay only if fog develops and you have no radar, or if you don't want to approach Hyder or Stewart in poor visibility.

Hyder float dock

Hyder, Alaska

Chart 3794; float position:
55°54.24' N, 130°00.56' W (NAD 27)

> *Hyder is a community on the United States side of the boundary. It is connected by road to Stewart. . . . A causeway extends 2,100 feet (640 m) SE from the community of Hyder across the mud flats; a trestle extends a further 1,250 feet (381 m) from its outer end to the extreme edge of the mud flats. A small craft float, 150 feet (46 m) long, is at the outer end of the trestle.* (p. 217, SD)

Hyder advertises itself as the friendliest ghost town in Alaska. The orthodox church with its golden ornaments is the only attractive building in town. There are a couple of sourdough saloons. The town, with its pot-holed road, largely exists as a duty-free zone for Stewart residents, and a waypoint for Salmon Glacier, some 30 miles up the Salmon River. Ketchikan, Alaska has the nearest Customs and Immigration facilities. There are none in Hyder.

Hyder has two floats. One is a small float on the south side of the bitter end of the causeway. The outside of the float is frequently vacant; however, in 1996, there was a float house at the outside of the float on the south end which protruded about 12 feet. This main float does not appear to offer good protection when chop is running in the channel. It should be considered a fair-weather moorage only.

The small-craft float is located north of a ramp on the north side of the causeway. There is a floating walkway which extends out about 100 yards to the float, largely filled with small local sportfishing boats. This walkway and the area immediately offshore dries at low water, at which time the marina can be entered only at the north end of the floats. A log breakwater on the north side serves as a barrier to chop.

Stewart

Chart 3794; Stewart Yacht Club public float:
55°55.03' N, 130°00.52' W (NAD 27)

> *Stewart, at the head of Portland Canal, is a settlement with a population of 858 (1986). . . . The principal industries are mining, logging and tourism. It has a small hospital with resident doctor, a visiting dentist, a RCMP detachment, several stores and hotels, a pharmacy, a liquor store, a post office and an airfield. . . . Ice forms at the head of Portland Canal, in the vicinity of Stewart, from November to February; it is never heavy enough to stop shipping but can be troublesome to*

Stewart signpost

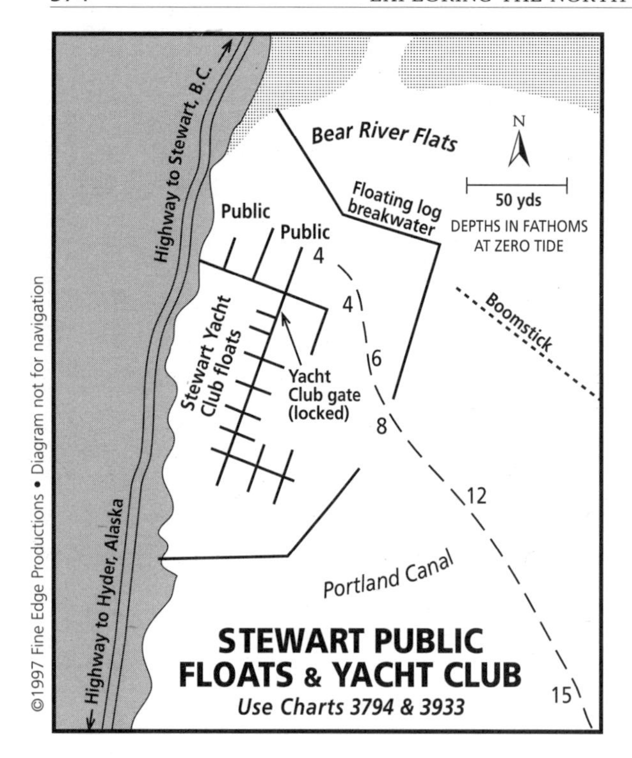

small craft. . . . A public float north of the public wharf has 150 feet (46 m) of berthing space with a depth of 16 feet (4.9 m). The east end of the float is reserved for aircraft. The Stewart Yacht Club has two floats attached to the south side of the public float. Power is laid on the floats and they are protected by floating log breakwaters. . . . The town of Stewart is connected by paved road to the main highway that connects Prince Rupert to Prince George. (p. 217, SD)

The beautiful settings of Stewart and the upper canal make the lengthy cruise up Portland Canal worthwhile. The mountains are more precipitous, more glaciers are visible, and waterfalls increase. As you approach the head of the canal and pass Marmot Bay, Bear Glacier comes into view, looming high over the town and harbor.

The Stewart Yacht Club and public wharf lie just off the delta of Bear River. The Yacht Club has a locked gate with barbed wire fence; if you wish to stay there, make prior arrangements. Electricity is available, but no water. Large vessels sometimes tie up at the north end of the public wharf to avoid interfering with the Alaska ferry which calls twice a month. There are no amenities at the wharf. However, it's a short walk to town where a large variety of goods and services are available. Stewart Marine Rescue, which handles land and marine communications 24-hours a day, and monitors Channel 16, can arrange for transportation to town for pleasure-craft crews. There is no VHF weather reception at the north end of Portland Canal, but Mike and Wendy Clark of Stewart Marine Rescue can provide weather forecasts.

Pearse Canal

Chart 3994; north entrance:
55°02.20′ N, 130°12.60′ W (NAD 27)

Pearse Canal leads about 23 miles along the NW sides of Wales and Pearse Islands and connects Tongass Passage to Portland Canal. Fillmore Island and the mainland of Alaska form its NW side. . . . The SW end of the fairway through Pearse Canal, between Wales and Fillmore

Stewart: private floats south of public float

Stewart: public dock & yacht club floats

Islands, is encumbered with rocks and shoals; great care is required when navigating this portion of the fairway. The NE end of Pearse Canal between Pearse Island and the mainland of Alaska is deep in the fairway. (p. 214, SD)

Pearse Canal is narrower and more sheltered than Portland Inlet. It offers interesting places to explore at its southern entrance.

Hidden Inlet

Chart 3994; entrance:
54°56.80′ N, 130°19.75′ W; anchor:
54°57.14′ N, 130°20.22′ W (NAD 27)

Hidden Inlet, entered between Gwent Cove and Hidden Point, is of no value as an anchorage and can only be entered at slack water. The main body of the inlet is about 4 miles long; depths vary from 30 to 73 fathoms (55 to 134 m). The entrance is less than 450 feet (137 m) wide and has a depth of 15 feet (4.6 m). . . . Tidal streams set through the entrance of Hidden Inlet at 8 to 10 kn, forming swirls that extend well into Pearse Canal. (p. 214, SD)

Hidden Inlet is located on the west side of Pearse Canal, 8 miles north of Winter Inlet. The entrance is narrow, set back from the canal, and is easy to miss. The tree-covered Yelnu Islets, 300 yards off the west shore, are a leading mark.

Enter the inlet on or near slack, staying mid-channel. The fairway is quite wide, but favor slightly west of center at the south entrance, and east of center in the narrows. The fairway has a fairly even bottom, bouncing between 3 and 5 fathoms. One hour after a low water of 6 feet, the flood current was 2 knots. Thirty minutes later, it had increased to 3 plus knots, with moderate turbulence forming.

Just beyond the narrows, on the west side of the inlet, is a grassy shore, off which lies a 2- to 3-fathom shoal where temporary anchorage can be found. The bottom is rocky and there are kelp patches on either side of the beach area. The shores are steep, with rocky slabs, and high peaks can be seen nearby.

Anchor in 3 fathoms over a rocky bottom with kelp; poor holding

Hidden Inlet entrance

Gwent Cove, old cannery

Gwent Cove

Chart 3994; entrance: 54°56.55′ N, 130°19.70′ W; anchor: 54°56.57′ N, 130°20.00′ W (NAD 27)

Gwent Cove, 0.6 mile north of Yelnu Islets, is the site of an abandoned cannery and ruined wharf. (p. 214, SD)

Gwent Cove, off the south entrance to Hidden Inlet, provides fair-weather anchorage directly in front of the old white cannery building with two smoke stacks. There is a 5-fathom flat area off the old wharf and small private float. The float is sometimes used as a sportfishing outstation.

The head of the cove shoals rapidly west of the wharf and, as the water is dark brown muskeg, you can't see more than a foot or two.

Anchor in 5 fathoms over sand and mud with shells; good holding.

Winter Inlet

Chart 3994; entrance: 54°50.50′ N, 130°27.60′ W; anchor: 54°48.30′ N, 130°25.83′ W (NAD 27)

Winter Inlet affords secure anchorage for small craft; the holding ground is good and there is ample swinging room in the widest part of the inlet. . . . A wooded islet fronted by a drying reef lies on the west side of Winter Inlet, about 1.3 miles inside the entrance. (p. 214, SD)

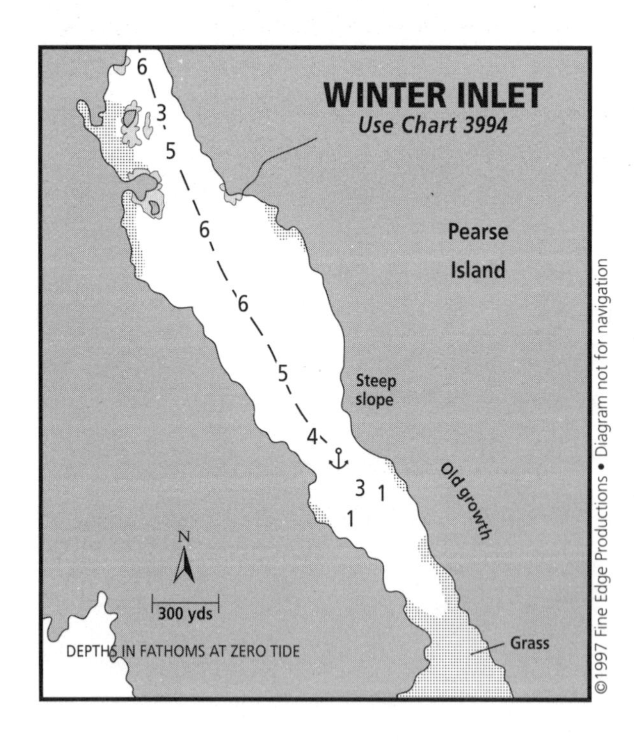

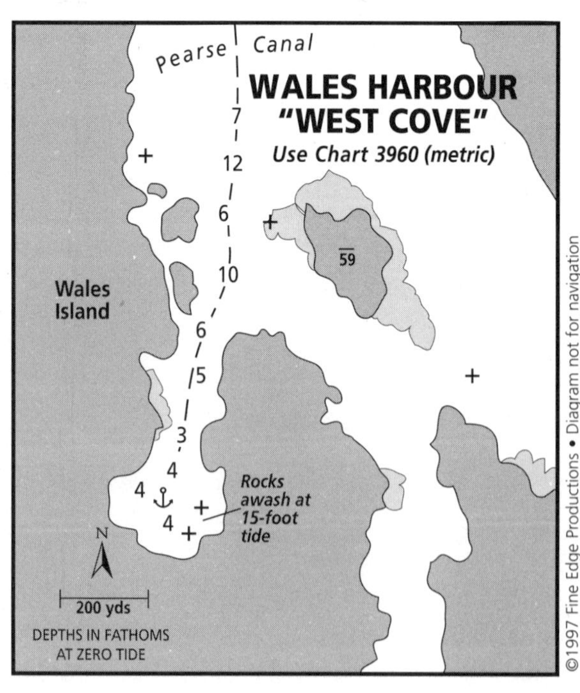

Winter Inlet is one of the most well-sheltered anchorages east of Dixon Entrance. It is a long, scenic inlet and total protection can be found anywhere in reasonable depths past the small west shore islets with trees. Porpoises and seals like to play in the strong currents off the entrance. The creek outlet on the east shore has grassy margins, and the head of the inlet is a large grassy meadow.

Anchor in 3 to 5 fathoms over black sticky mud, small broken shells and wood debris; very good holding.

Bryce Gillard hooks his own birthday present

Wales Harbour, "West Cove"

Chart 3960 metric; entrance: 54°46.60′ N, 130°36.80′ W; anchor: 54°45.28′ N, 130°35.78′ W (NAD 83)

> *At the head of the harbour are three arms; the middle and longest one is unsurveyed and the west arm is shallow. . . . Wales Harbour affords good anchorage in 89 to 108 feet (27 to 33 m), soft bottom and is reported to have good anchorage for small craft in the eastern arm.* (p. 214, SD)

The West Cove of Wales Harbour is shaped like a keyhole and offers very good protection from southerly weather. Intimate West Cove has room for one or two boats over a flat bottom with steep, rocky shores.

Anchor in 4 fathoms, soft bottom, with good holding.

Tongass Passage

Chart 3960 metric; south entrance: 54°43.50′ N, 130°37.70′ W (NAD 83)

> *Tongass Passage separates Sitklan Island from Wales Island and connects Dixon Entrance to the west end of Pearse Canal. It is entered between Island Point, the SE extremity of Sitklan Island, and Haystack Island. Rocks awash are reported to lie 0.1 mile west of Haystack Island. . . . The International Boundary Line runs down the centre of Tongass Passage.* (p. 213, SD)

The channel between Protector and Boston islands is clear and well protected. Both sets of islands have beautiful sandy beaches for excellent kayak haul-outs and campsites. The head of the bay, on the south end of Wales Island, offers protection from downslope winds from Portland Inlet.

BEARS AND BOATS

by Roderick Frazier Nash and Honeydew Murray-Nash

Viewing bears is one of the highlights of a visit to northern British Columbia, and a cruising boat offers the best opportunity for an encounter with minimal stress to either party. Indeed, your chances of seeing a bear other than from a boat are close to zero. Just as is the case with rhinos and big cats in Africa, bears fear humans on foot. Remember these guys are wild, not the campground Yogi-bears adept at raiding ice chests next to your tent. So your boat is your Land Rover safari vehicle. Bears don't associate it with danger nor do they think of the sea as the direction from which a threat might come.

Watching a grizzly find his dinner, Khutzeymateen Inlet Photo by Ron Thiele

Here are some tips that have helped us and *Forevergreen*'s crew see an abundance of bears in the areas covered in this cruising guide.

1. *Maintain a constant shoreline watch.* Every time you round a point make it a habit to scan the shore carefully with binoculars. You'll see a hundred stumps and rocks that you will *swear* are bears. But suddenly one of those dark lumps will move and you are watching a bear.

Although they can come in a wide range of colors, including pure white, most British Columbia bears are startlingly blue-black. They have a distinctive long-legged profile that becomes easy to recognize. But movement is your litmus test, and bears on shore patrol are always on the move. With the binoculars you will know in a few seconds if you have the real thing.

2. *Let them come to you.* Since bears move most of the time, your chances of a sighting are good if *you* stay in one place; that is, at anchor. Keep looking around a full 360 degrees, and take advantage of the fact that north of Cape Caution in the summer, there is twilight most of the night. This means that you could sight a bear around the clock. When we wake up to use the head or check the anchor, we routinely take a look around. Tell your crew to do the same. On one occasion a friend woke us at 5 a.m. to see a female black bear and her two cubs

working the shoreline rocks for crabs. They were only 50 feet away and totally oblivious to our presence. With amazing dexterity, the mother flipped rocks over and lapped up the goodies. Eventually they worked down the beach and into the timber. It was a peaceful moment in sharp contrast to the usual panicky human-bear encounters. We felt privileged to have witnessed this normal activity.

If bears are a priority, select an anchorage at the head of an inlet (they love the grassy flats) or off the mouth of a river or stream.

3. *Approach quietly and stealthily.* If you spot a bear while underway, slow your engine and ease in toward shore. Bears are not threatened from the sea, and chances are good that he will not even look up until you are less than a hundred yards away. He may stare at you a moment and go right back to the food patrol. One trick we have used with great success is to position the boat in the direction the bear is moving, kill the engine and drift in to close range.

Once, with the engine killed, we watched in awe as a big male grizzly walked directly past our position no more than 50 yards away. We were so close we could hear his 3-inch claws tap-tapping on the stones. The beach ended in a steep cliff and there was a sharp 30-foot cutbank right before it. We wondered if the big guy would wade around and turn back the way he had come. Instead, he scrambled right up the bank in a shower of dirt and gravel. The sight of his big haunch muscles bunching as he powered uphill is one we will always remember. It was especially nice to know that he was not fleeing from us but just doing his thing. It hardly needs saying that such undetected, close-up sightings of grizzly are rare. Once again—the magic of a cruising boat!

4. *Shore encounters.* Your boat is your castle, but on land it is a whole new ball game. Now you *are* perceived as a threat—or as food! The basic axiom in dealing with bears on land is *no surprises.* Let large animals know you are coming and give them a chance to express their natural fear of you and flee. We normally carry an air horn—found in many pilothouses for marine signaling—and make several blasts before walking into the forest. A whistle or a can with some pebbles or merely talking and singing loudly will also do the trick.

If a confrontation should occur, remember that when a bear rears on its hind legs, it is simply trying to gain a better vantage point to figure out what you are. Let him know. Stand still, speak in a normal voice, do not look directly at him. If there are several people in your group, stand together to increase your apparent size and hold packs or raingear over your heads. If the bear does not run off (which he almost always will) back away slowly. Never run.

Pepper spray specially designed for bears would be a last-ditch deterrent in the event of a charge. You can wear a can in a holster on your belt. The problem is that carrying pepper spray into Canada is a violation of customs regulations. Use your own judgment as to whether the bear or the customs agent is the greater threat!

Finally, if you are near the mainland between Kynoch and Khutze inlets, think twice about landing. The bears in this region are so-called "problem" animals that have been trapped and relocated from the communities of Terrace and Kitimat. They are not afraid of people and have a taste for garbage. Since they are decidedly smarter than the average bear, give them a wide berth!

Close encounters of the bear kind are a special treat in northern British Columbia. Good luck!

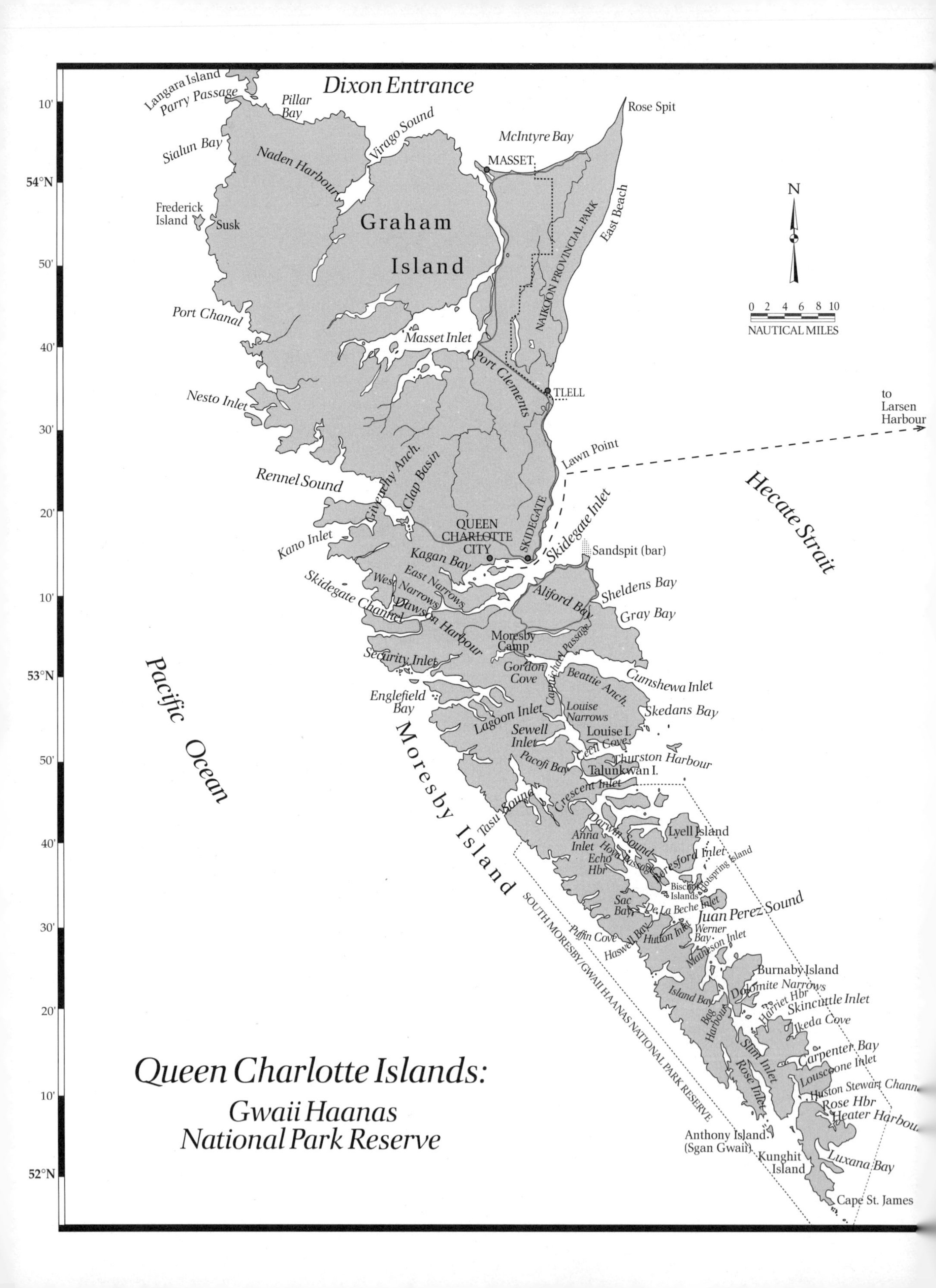

Dixon Entrance
Langara Island
Parry Passage
Pillar Bay
Rose Spit
Virago Sound
Sialun Bay
McIntyre Bay
Naden Harbour
MASSET
Frederick Island
Susk
Graham Island
NAIKOON PROVINCIAL PARK
East Beach
N
0 2 4 6 8 10
NAUTICAL MILES
Port Chanal
Masset Inlet
Port Clements
TLELL
Nesto Inlet
to Larsen Harbour
Lawn Point
Givenchy Anch.
Clap Basin
Rennel Sound
Hecate Strait
SKIDEGATE
QUEEN CHARLOTTE CITY
Skidegate Inlet
Kano Inlet
Sandspit (bar)
Kagan Bay
East Narrows
West Narrows
Skidegate Channel
Aliford Bay
Sheldens Bay
Dawson Harbour
Gray Bay
Moresby Camp
Carmichael Passage
Security Inlet
Gordon Cove
Beattie Anch.
Cumshewa Inlet
Pacific Ocean
Englefield Bay
Louise Narrows
Skedans Bay
Lagoon Inlet
Sewell Inlet
Louise I.
Cecil Cove
Moresby Island
Thurston Harbour
Pacofi Bay
Talunkwan I.
Crescent Inlet
Tasu Sound
Darwin Sound
Lyell Island
Anna Inlet
Echo Hbr
Hoya Passage
Beresford Inlet
Hotspring Island
Bischof Islands
Sac Bay
De La Beche Inlet
Juan Perez Sound
SOUTH MORESBY/GWAII HAANAS NATIONAL PARK RESERVE
Puffin Cove
Haswell Bay
Hutton Inlet
Werner Bay
Matheson Inlet
Burnaby Island
Dolomite Narrows
Island Bay
Harriet Hbr
Skincuttle Inlet
Bag Harbour
Ikeda Cove
Carpenter Bay
Slim Inlet
Louscoone Inlet
Rose Inlet
Huston Stewart Channel
Rose Hbr
Heater Harbour
Anthony Island (Sgan Gwaii)
Kunghit Island
Luxana Bay
Cape St. James
10'
54°N
50'
40'
30'
20'
10'
53°N
50'
40'
30'
20'
10'
52°N
Queen Charlotte Islands:
Gwaii Haanas National Park Reserve

13

Queen Charlotte Islands: Gwaii Haanas / South Moresby National Park Reserve

The historic Queen Charlotte Islands, an archipelago of 150 islands, lie across Hecate Strait, 60 miles from the nearest point of the mainland coast. Often referred to as the "Hawaii of Canada" for its diverse ecosystem, the archipelago has one of the finest remaining old-growth rain forests as well as some of the highest densities of sea birds, eagles and falcons on the Pacific Coast. Scientists believe that portions of the islands escaped glaciation during the last ice age, providing refuge for flora and fauna that might otherwise have been eliminated. Gwaii Haanas, the Haida name for the Queen Charlottes, means beautiful islands, and indeed, as you cruise through the pristine waters of South Moresby Island, you are aware of this unique beauty. Misty inlets, snow-capped mountains, and abandoned Haida village sites offer unforgettable experiences for cruising boats.

The exposed nature of a Hecate Strait crossing, the remoteness of the islands, and the wildness of rugged, seldom-visited shores demand careful planning and vigilant seamanship. If you're accustomed to sailing in protected, well-charted waters, you need to approach the Queen Charlottes with care and preparation; this is an area where weather can change rapidly and charts may not show all the hazards.

Boats wishing to visit Gwaii Haanas/South Moresby National Park Reserve must make advance reservations and complete an orientation course (about an hour long), in Queen Charlotte City. Reservations may be made from the first of March by phoning the Parks Office (250) 559-8818. Park visitation fees may be instituted in 1998, and we expect that waters around South

Advice from a Local Expert

For sailors not fettered by a tight schedule—and adequate time is often synonymous with safety—the west coast of the Queen Charlotte Islands offers solitary magnificence and seafaring challenge. Weather and sea conditions may change abruptly. Shorelines, horizontal and vertical, change with random abandon from beaches of gleaming surf-smoothed sand to bare, blunt wave-scoured rocks, over 100 feet in height, crowned with silvered drift logs cast by deadly breakers. There are days when one can safely enjoy this North Pacific in a small rowboat; on other days, sailors pray for a snug harbor.

Weather forecasting is not a precise science, sources of information are not always available, and occasionally a local gale will develop without warning. Accept all the information available, then use your seaman's judgment. In winter months, west coast waters may be flat for days, due to islands sheltering the sea from the force of cold northeasterly winds. In summer, the coastal waters may be roughened for many successive days—even weeks—by northwesters blowing some 15 knots at night, building to 45 knots or more from mid-morning onward. Any sunny day will see the convection wind raise whitecaps before noon. Exquisite rainbows are a specialty of the Charlottes.

—by Neil Carey, a recognized authority on the islands, and Betty Carey, who has paddled the Queen Charlottes in a dugout canoe

Moresby will become a Marine Park sometime in the future. Cruising season is generally restricted to June, July and August.

Hecate Strait

Charts 3853, 3902, 3802; position (Bonilla Island Light): 53°29.55′ N, 130°38.10′ W; position (White Rocks Light): 53°38.10′ N, 130°38.80′ W (NAD 27)

> *Queen Charlotte Islands, an archipelago of about one hundred and fifty islands and islets, form the south side of Dixon Entrance and are separated from the mainland by Hecate Strait. The two largest islands are Graham Island, in the north, and Moresby Island, in the south. . . . In general, the flood coming in from Dixon Entrance meets the flood coming up Hecate Strait from the south in the vicinity of Porcher Island. In late summer, mid July to mid September, they meet some 25 or 30 miles farther south. . . . At springs, or during bad weather, the tide-rips caused by the meeting of the streams are sometimes so great as to convey an appearance of broken water.* (p. 218, SD)

The shortest and most direct crossing of Hecate Strait, 55 miles, begins at Browning Entrance. Larsen Harbour, on the north end of Banks Island, is a well-protected anchorage used frequently as a convenient jumping-off place. Beaver Passage, east of Banks Island, also has a number of coves where you can wait for favorable weather to make the crossing. With the new CANPASS program, U.S. small craft who pre-qualify may cross directly from southeast Alaska via Dixon Entrance, approximately 110 miles. This route avoids going to Prince Rupert for Customs check-in, and thereby saves you nearly 100 miles.

Some boats prefer to cross Queen Charlotte Sound directly to the south end of Moresby Island—a distance of 110 miles from Cape Scott to Cape Saint James—or cross from Ivory Island to the south end of Moresby—also 110 miles. Since these southern routes are exposed to swell and changing sea conditions, they are more appropriate for offshore sailboats.

If you have a trailerable boat, you can take the ferry from Prince Rupert to Skidegate Landing, then across to Alliford Bay, and then drive on logging roads to the launching ramp at Moresby Camp on Cumshewa Inlet.

Before you cross Hecate Strait, carefully monitor the weather forecasts, wait until the combined swell and sea height is expected to be one meter or less, then leave very early in the morning. That way you can anticipate a much smoother ride. During your crossing, monitor on-going weather reports from the North or South Hecate weather-buoys, Bonilla Island Lighthouse, and Sandspit. If conditions deteriorate, you can turn around before the halfway point. Bonilla Island, a MAREP station, is happy to give you updates when they are monitoring Channel 69.

Before heading out, be sure your vessel is in proper condition and that you are self-sufficient for your stay. Fuel is only available at Skidegate Landing or Massett; shopping is limited to Queen Charlotte City; telephones are few; and water can be easily obtained from only one float, once you enter the Gwaii Haanas National Park. In August 1996, a new Coast Guard repeater station became operational on South Moresby Island, and we found that in crossing from Larsen Harbour, and later from Cape Saint James to Ivory Island, we had excellent VHF communication with Prince Rupert Coast Guard on both Channels 16 and 25. We were also happy to discover that, near the halfway point, our hand-held VHF transceiver reached the Coast Guard without difficulty.

Neuron II *approaching Lawn Point*

Prince Rupert Coast Guard (telephone: 250-627-3082) is willing to take a detailed sail plan from you for the duration of your stay in the Charlottes. Be sure to close your sail plan on completion, or notify the Coast Guard of any change in your plans—they take their monitoring duties seriously.

Fuel dock, Skidegate

During the summer, in Prince Rupert or along Moresby Island, it is easy to meet other small craft interested in rendezvousing with you to make the crossing a little safer for both of you. The Dogfish Banks are regularly fished day and night by a sizable commercial fishing fleet and their numerous floats and fishing maneuvers need to be avoided. However, their presence is reassuring when you are out of sight of land. If they all head for shore at the same time, you may want to do the same.

Skidegate Inlet to Lawn and Rose Points

Charts 3902, 3802; position (Lawn Point Buoy "C14"): 53°25.54′ N, 131°53.10′ W (NAD 27)

> *The coast between Lawn Point and Rose Point, the NE extremity of Graham Island, is fronted by the shoal flats of Dogfish Banks and should be approached with caution. There is no harbour or protected cove for small craft.* (p. 243, SD)

Lawn Point is the leading mark when heading for Skidegate Channel and Queen Charlotte City from the north end of Hecate Strait. Close off Lawn Point, marked by a series of buoys, is the entrance channel leading south behind the shallow 10-mile spit which protrudes north from Sandspit. *Caution*: The Prince Rupert Ferry and other high speed traffic going both to and from Queen Charlotte City all converge at Lawn Point.

Ferrying between Alliford Bay and Skidegate

We found the currents in Hecate Strait somewhat confusing as to direction, but not excessively so. During prevailing northwest summer winds, you will find a smooth lee extending for several miles east of Graham Island.

Skidegate Landing

Chart 3890 metric; entrance: 53°14.70′ N, 132°00.50′ W (NAD 27)

> *Skidegate, a small settlement known locally as Skidegate Landing, is at the SE extremity of Graham Island, in a cove between Image Point and Haida Point. . . . A public wharf with a depth of 10.5 m (34 ft) along side has a landing float for small craft on its west side.* (p. 236, SD)

The small public float is close to shore and largely hidden by the ferry dock. *Caution:* The float has shallow water alongside, and prop wash from the Alliford Bay ferry to the east and Prince Rupert ferry to the west can create serious turbulence. The fuel dock is located on the east side of the

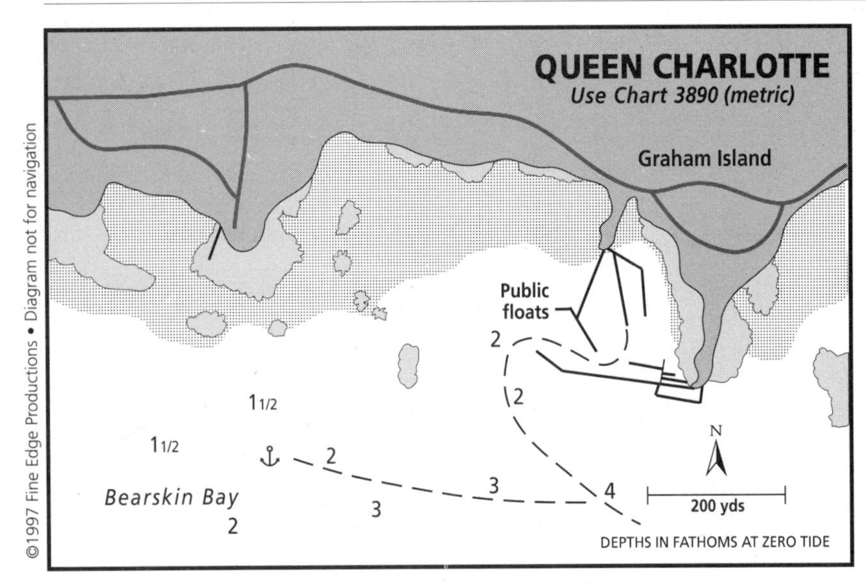

cove, halfway to Image Point. It is a short walk from here to the attractive Haida Museum and Cultural Center less than a kilometer to the east.

Queen Charlotte City, Bearskin Bay

Charts 3890 metric (inset), 3894; entrance: 53°14.60′ N, 132°02.00′ W; Queen Charlotte breakwater: 53°15.16′ N, 132°04.35′ W; anchor: 53°15.10′ N, 132°04.60′ W (NAD 27)

> *Queen Charlotte, known locally as Queen Charlotte City, the principal settlement in Skidegate Inlet, is on the north shore of Bearskin Bay. . . . The breakwater protects a boat harbour to the north with three public floats about 60 m (120 ft) long connected to a pier at the southern end of a causeway.* (p. 238, SD)

Queen Charlotte City is the administrative hub for the Queen Charlottes. The public floats offer a visiting yacht the chance to resupply, visit Park Headquarters, and receive a briefing on visiting the park. The main shopping center and credit union, ATM, post office, RCMP and churches are west of the floats. Public telephones are on the wharf at the head of the floats. Car rentals for visiting Graham Island are available here, and a number of guide services offer tours to out-of-the-way attractions. (Please see Appendix for suggested guide services. Neil Carey's *Guide to the Queen Charlottes,* 11th Edition contains the most comprehensive tourist information.)

Public floats, Queen Charlotte City

If the floats in Queen Charlotte City are full, rafting is encouraged. There is adequate space for anchoring in Bearskin Bay over a wide, flat bot-

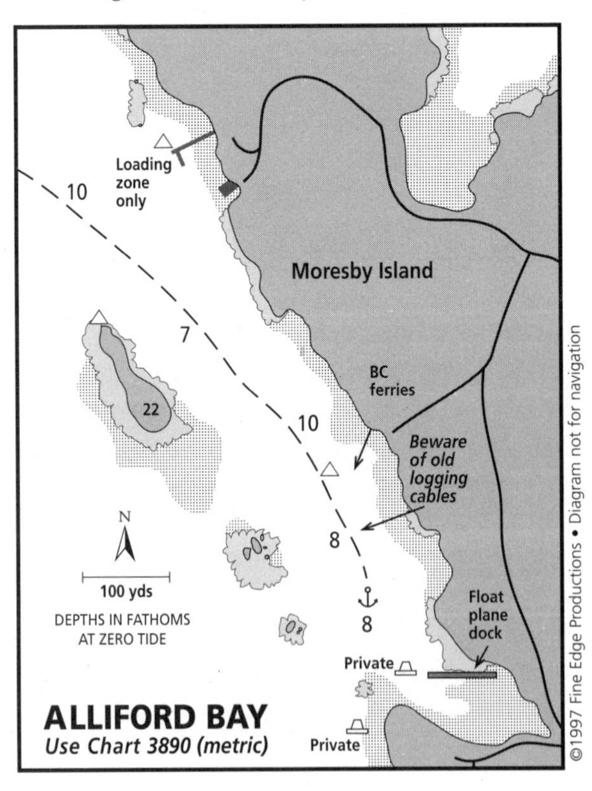

Secord *anchored in Bearskin Bay, Queen Charlotte City*

tom, 0.2 mile southwest of the end of the breakwater, avoiding the shoal west of the breakwater.

Anchor in 2 fathoms, mud and shell bottom with good holding.

Hope is alive in Queen Charlotte City

Alliford Bay

Chart 3890 metric (inset); entrance: 53°12.90′ N, 131°59.60′ W; anchor: 52°12.62′ N, 131°59.21′ W (NAD)

Well sheltered anchorage can be obtained almost anywhere within Alliford Bay; the best position for a large vessel is in the middle of the bay in about 15 m (49 ft), mud. Small vessels can anchor closer inshore. Caution: It is reported that these anchorages are fouled by old logging cables. (p. 238, SD)

The public wharf and float are marked as loading zones only; no moorage is allowed. One quarter of a mile south of the public float is the ferry dock. There are several runs a day to Skidegate. Anchor south of the ferry dock, avoiding the several private mooring buoys and the float plane dock.

Anchor in 6 fathoms, clear of float plane area and mooring buoys, over an unrecorded bottom.

Sandspit

Chart 3890 metric (inset); entrance: 53°14.53′ N, 131°51.72′ W; position (public wharf): 53°15.26′ N, 131°49.30′ W (NAD 27)

Sandspit, on the SE shore of Shingle Bay, has a post office, a hotel with a restaurant, stores, a bank and a liquor store. A public wharf, 49 m (160 ft) long along its head, is about 0.35 mile south of Spit Point. Depths alongside range from 6.4 m (21 ft) at the north end to 5.5 m (18 ft) at the south end. A notice on the wharf states that it is inadvisable to berth overnight. A launching ramp is close north of the wharf. (p. 236, SD)

A new, small-boat harbor, located 1.7 miles south of Spit Point on the east side of Haanas Creek in Shingle Bay, is scheduled to open in 1997. Plans call for 80 berths, 10 of which are for boats up to 70 feet, plus a 100-foot dock, dredged to 3 meters in the harbor and 5 meters at the outer dock. A 5-ton crane is planned at the unloading dock and the berths will have electrical outlets, fresh water and a sewage pump. Boaters will have access by foot or taxi to the Sandspit airport, store and hotel. Fuel may be obtained from a tank truck or in Skidegate Landing.

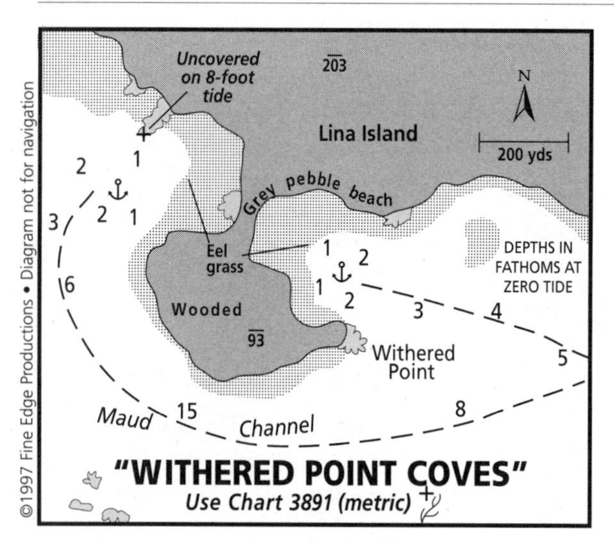

Haida war canoe on display in museum

"Withered Point Coves," Lina Island

Chart 3981 metric; anchor (east of spit): 53°13.22′ N, 132°08.32′ W; anchor (west of spit): 53°13.33′ N, 132°08.88′ W (NAD 83)

Lina Island separates Bearskin Bay from Kanga Bay, both of which have a number of anchor sites. Lina Island is on the southwest side of Bearskin Bay. It has private homes on its east end, one of which is marked by a modern totem on the beach. Kanga Bay, to the west of Lina Island, has a number of anchor sites. Two petroglyphs are on tidal rocks on the west side of Lina Island.

You can find good protection during prevailing northwesterlies in the small, shallow cove just north of Withered Point, on the southwest tip of Lina Island. There's a 200-foot wooded hill on the south side of this cove, connected to Lina Island by a low, narrow spit with a landing beach of grey pebbles, sand and mud. In its shallow portion, east side of the spit, the flat bottom of 1 to 2 fathoms is covered with eel grass. There is nothing manmade in sight. There is room for two to three moderate-sized boats; avoid the shallow drying portions of both coves. If there is southeast chop, anchorage can be found on the opposite (west) side of the spit.

Anchor (east of spit) in 1.5 fathoms, sand bottom with grass, very good holding.

Anchor (west of spit) in 1 to 2 fathoms, mud bottom, very good holding.

Kagan Bay

Chart 3891 metric; entrance: 53°12.85′ N, 132°08.60′ W (NAD 83)

> *Kagan Bay and its entrance . . . are encumbered by islands, rocks and shoals. Access to the bay*

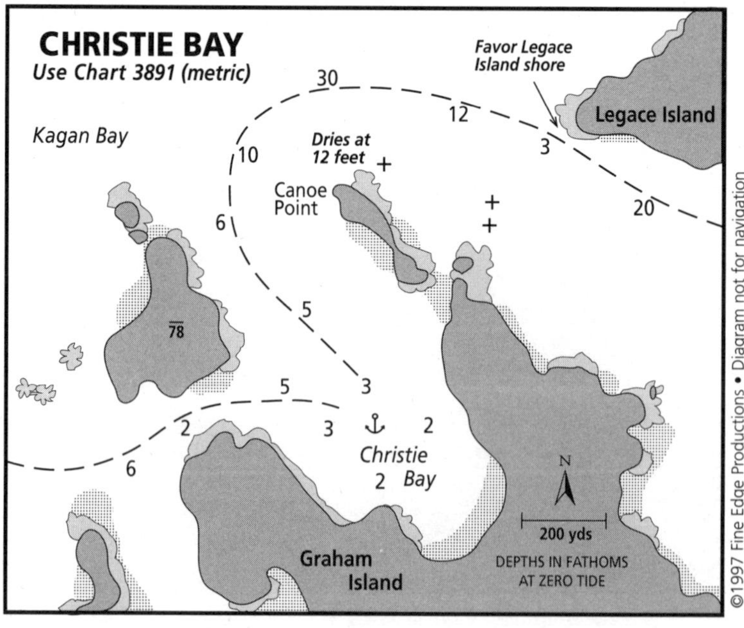

is confined to narrow passages suitable only for small vessels. (p. 238, SD)

Kagan Bay connects Bearskin Bay to the east, and Skidegate Channel to the south, with Long Inlet to the west. This is an area of smooth water, full of intimate anchorages and abundant wildlife. Graham Island to the north is slowly recovering from extensive clearcutting done years ago. The northeast quadrant of the bay is still used as a log booming area. Slatechuck Creek to the west has a quarry where the Native People gather argillite—usually obtained in Slatechuck Mountain—for their carvings.

Christie Bay

Chart 3891 metric; entrance:
53°12.60′ N, 132°13.25′ W; anchor:
53°12.32′ N, 132°12.85′ W (NAD 83)

Christie Bay offers the best protection for small craft in Kagan Bay. It is well protected from all weather, with great views of the high peaks to the northwest. There is swinging room for several boats. The easily-accessible landing beach of sand and cobblestones is backed by second-growth trees. Christie Bay and the mud flats to the south are favorite "hangouts" for ducks and shore birds.

The main entrance to Christie Bay lies south of Canoe Point. The small passage to the west can be used by moderate-sized vessels; minimum depth is approximately 2 fathoms. Entering from the east is a small-boat passage immediately west of Legace Island. Stay within 75 yards of its west end with 3 fathoms minimum.

Anchor in 2 fathoms, black sand and mud bottom, very good holding.

Anchor Cove

Chart 3891 metric; anchor:
53°12.38′ N, 132°14.67′ W (NAD 83)

Anchor Cove, a small bight between Pier Point and Random Point on the far west side of Kagan Bay, provides good protection from strong westerlies. The small landing beach is steep-to.

Anchor in 2 fathoms over a soft grey mud bottom with shells; good holding.

"Hallet Island Cove"

Chart 3891 metric; entrance:
53°12.95′ N, 132°14.30′ W; anchor:
53°13.14′ N, 132°14.35′ W (NAD 83);

We call the shallow, flat-bottomed cove between Hallet Island and the drying flat south of the outlet to Saltchuck Creek, "Hallet Island Cove." Anchor on the west side of the wooded island. This is a good place from which to explore the surrounding islets and flats at the outlet of the creek. The cove is somewhat exposed to south winds.

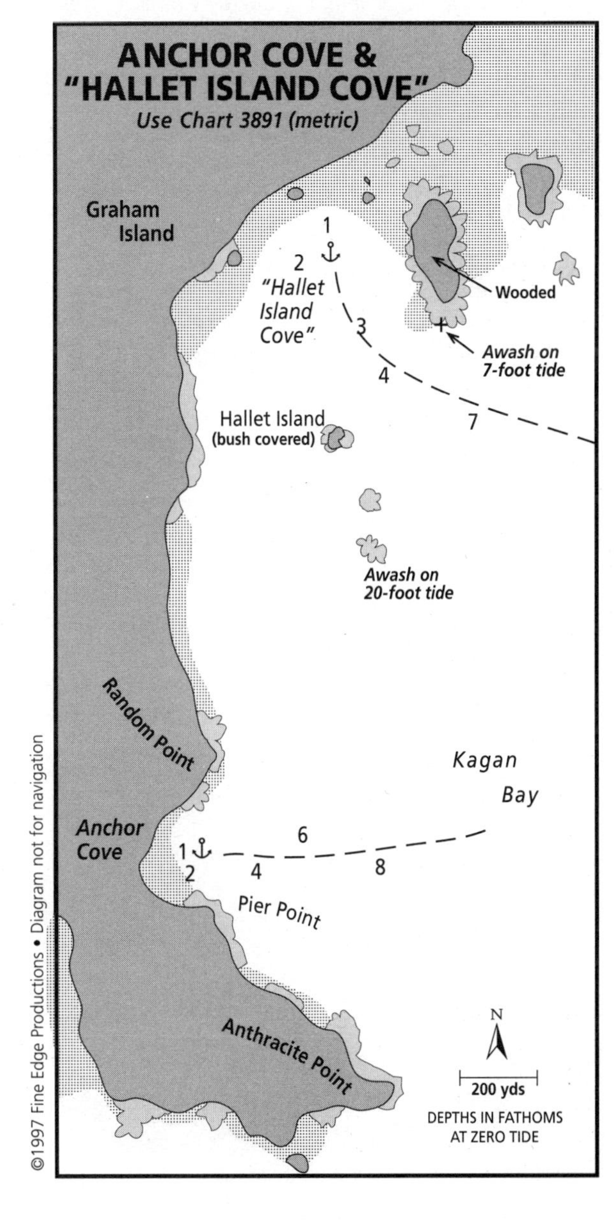

Skidegate Channel, east end of narrows looking west

Anchor in 2 to 3 fathoms over a bottom of mud, shell, and patches of cobble and grass; holding is fair to good.

Long Inlet

Chart 3891 metric; entrance:
53°12.10′ N, 132°14.00′ W (NAD 83)

The head of Long Inlet is deep and steep-to with excellent views of the jagged peaks to the northwest. The entrance to Long Inlet is encumbered with a number of small islands, reefs, and rocks, with drying flats along the shore. It's a good area to explore by kayak or dinghy. Temporary fair-weather anchorage can be found along either side of the entrance.

Saltspring Bay

Chart 3891 metric; anchor:
53°11.88′ N, 132°12.97′ W (NAD 83)

Skidegate Channel, East Narrows

Saltspring Bay offers little in the way of protection; however, in fair weather, you can anchor temporarily just off the drying flats. The flats here and to the north and south are excellent places for viewing the local bear population. At low tide you can often find a mother bear with her cubs, combing the beach and turning rocks over, teaching the cubs to look for "goodies."

Anchor in one fathom or less over a combination of sand, gravel and mud; fair-to-good holding.

Skidegate Channel

Chart 3891 metric; east entrance:
53°09.90′ N, 132°08.60′ W; west entrance:
53°09.80′ N, 132°34.50′ W (NAD 83)

> *East Narrows, the central portion of Skidegate Channel, is narrow and winding with strong tidal streams. . . . it is recommended only for mariners with local knowledge. West Narrows, although shallow, is deeper, less winding and has weaker tidal streams than East Narrows.* (p. 240, SD)

Skidegate Channel can be entered south of Sandilands Island or through the shallow passage west of Maude Island. Using the passage west of Maude Island, stay midchannel and pass close west to red-green-red buoy "CA" in a minimum depth of 4 fathoms.

The channel is used by local sportfishing and commercial fishing boats headed for the rich fishing grounds on the west coast of the Queen Charlottes. Both East and West Narrows have 2 to 3 feet at zero tide with a meandering course difficult to discern, with steep-to mud flats on either side. Many boats have gotten into trouble here because of the strong and unpredictable currents and the poorly-defined channel.

The flood tide coming from Hecate Strait to the east has a tidal range roughly twice as high as that coming from the Pacific to the west. This creates some interesting tidal dynamics, and we recommend taking any predictions of slack water time with a grain of salt. In our limited experience, two transits on two different days, we found the currents flowing in directions and strengths that differed substantially from the chart, *Sailing Directions*, and local advice. Furthermore, since the ranges in East Narrows are designed for use in returning eastbound from the Pacific, on a westbound passage it is easy to overshoot your turning points.

East Narrows, Skidegate Channel

Chart 3891 metric (inset); east entrance: 53°08.72′ N, 132°13.60′ W; west entrance: 53°09.26′ N, 132°18.02′ W (NAD 83)

East Narrows, Skidegate Channel, should not be attempted unless you have Chart 3891 metric (Inset), and have studied the tidal information, top of Chart 3891, as well as pages 240 to 243 of *Sailing Directions* (North Portion), Volume 2. You must feel comfortable in risky situations requiring high performance and be willing to make your own judgments.

If you arrive early at the east end of Skidegate Channel to observe tidal conditions, take advantage of the rusty public mooring buoy 0.6 mile east of East Beacon (53°08.63' N, 132°12.97' W), or anchor temporarily midchannel at the east end of the narrows. For more protection, you can anchor temporarily in what we call "Donkey Cove."

"Donkey Cove"

Chart 3891 metric; entrance: 53°09.10′ N, 132°12.12′ W; anchor: 53°09.24′ N, 132°12.12′ W (NAD 83)

The eastern part of Skidegate Channel is used extensively in logging operations; temporary anchorage can be found, avoiding these operations, west of a chain of islets and reefs on the north shore, east of the narrows.

Moderate-sized vessels can anchor midchannel between the grassy islet to the east and an old float with a rusting steel "donkey" on the west shore.

Temporary anchorage can also be found, if needed, near the center of East Narrows, immediately east and slightly south of the point with the easternmost set of range markers, out of the main current. Eastbound vessels transiting East Narrows can wait for favorable conditions by anchoring 0.4 mile west of West Beacon, along the north shore.

Photo courtesy CHS, Pacific Region

Skidegate Channel, mid-beacon at low water

Anchor (Donkey Cove) in 2 to 3 fathoms over an irregular bottom with poor-to-fair holding.

West Narrows, Skidegate Channel

Chart 3891 metric (inset); east entrance: 53°08.92′ N, 132°20.30′ W; west entrance: 53°08.76′ N, 132°22.10′ W (NAD 83)

The currents in West Narrows are approximately half those found in East Narrows; the challenge here is extensive kelp. Stay midchannel between the 14-meter islet on the north and two small rocks off the northeast corner of Downie Island. From this point, head due west toward a marker on shore, favoring the Graham Island side, and avoiding shoals and a dangerous reef off Downie Island.

While awaiting proper conditions, temporary anchorage can be taken on the east side of West Narrows along the north shore, west of the 28-meter island, or on the southeast side of Downie Island. The latter, however, can be exposed to chop from strong westerly winds.

Photo courtesy CHS, Pacific Region

Skidegate Channel, West Narrows, looking east

A Thirty-year Perspective from Puffin Cove

Kayakers, singly or in groups, men and women, have visited us in Puffin Cove while paddling around Moresby Island. None ever mentioned that their trip was anything less than an extremely satisfying and memorable experience. Betty has rowed much of the Charlotte's coast in her trusty and durable 14-foot dugout. As a family of four, we crossed Hecate Strait and cruised around the Charlottes in a 19-foot codfish dory powered by an outboard. For thirty years Betty and I have cruised the Charlottes during all months, especially the west coast, experiencing the joy of flat seas and the demands of savage storms, always thankful to return to the safety and calm of our cabin in Puffin Cove on Moresby Island's enticing west coast.

There are more than two dozen bays or inlets on the Charlotte's west coast where you can find shelter for mooring or anchoring. These vary greatly in safety, depending upon the wind's direction and velocity, and the size of your craft. We have used all of these and more. Though our converted 26-foot lifeboat would usually stay put with a 35-pound Danforth, 50 feet of 3/8-inch chain and fathoms of line, we sometimes found it necessary to add, on the same cable, a 35-pound CQR anchor. And when we started to drag, I'd slide a 25-pound lead down until it was stopped by the cable/chain shackle. We have endured gales and storms tied bow and stern to trees near an indentation in the rocky shore, our skiff alongside as a fender while the anchor (or anchors) held us off. Most storms pass within a complete tidal cycle. A few last longer. It never ceases to amaze me how fast the sea can change from an angry killer to a pacified friend. *Heavy anchor gear is necessary on the west coast.* You should also have long, strong lines for tying to the shore if all else fails.

Ashore you encounter beaches littered or piled with logs lost from forest harvests; occasionally a redwood from California, a Douglas fir from Vancouver Island, or a Sitka spruce from Alaska. Most logs are local spruce, red cedar, and hemlock. Treasures to pick up are the Japanese glass fishing floats of assorted sizes and shapes, bamboo from the Philippines, some item lost from a shipping container wrenched from the decks of a storm-wrecked vessel, even a message in a bottle cast overboard months or years past.

—Neil and Betty Carey are modern pioneers of the Queen Charlotte Islands. You can read about their adventures on the west coast of Moresby Island in their classic book, Puffin Cove. *(Please see Bibliography.)*

Armentieres Channel

Chart 3891 metric (inset); north entrance: 53°07.70′ N, 132°23.90′ W; anchor (buoy): 53°06.65′ N, 132°23.50′ W (NAD 83)

If you want to fish or explore the west coast of the Queen Charlottes, Armentieres Channel offers the closest and most bombproof anchorage on the west side of Skidegate Channel. Although three public buoys at the south end of the channel are noted on the chart, there was only one buoy in the summer of 1995.

Sportfishing boats headed south along Moresby Island coast use the uncharted Chaatl Narrows and Buck Channel near high water. No vessel should attempt Chaatl Narrows, known locally as Canoe Pass, without local knowledge.

Anchor (buoy) north of the drying flat midchannel in 4 to 6 fathoms, mud and shell bottom, good holding.

Dawson Harbour

Chart 3891 metric (inset); entrance: 53°09.75′ N, 132°29.10′ W; Dawson Harbour mooring buoy: 53°10.27′ N, 132°26.48′ W (NAD 83)

> *Dawson Harbour, which extends east from Dawson Inlet, is too deep for good anchorage. A public mooring buoy is in Yovanovich Bight on the north side at the head of the harbour. A fresh water hose is on a logboom which connects the mooring buoy to shore.* (p. 253, SD)

The first well-protected anchorage on the west coast north of Skidegate Channel is Dawson Harbour on the eastern part of Dawson Inlet. In addition to the mooring buoy mentioned above, anchorage is reported near the islet on the south shore, halfway to the head of the harbor.

The next well-sheltered anchorages along the northwest coast of Graham Island are found in Givenchy Anchorage in Kano Inlet and Clap Basin (53°18.10' N, 132°25.80' W) in Rennell Sound.

The first well-protected anchorage south of Skidegate Channel on the Moresby Island coast is Security Cove (at approximately 53°03.30' N, 132°16.80' W). This is a beautiful spot in the head of Security Inlet. The anchor site is reported to be in the middle of the cove in 6 fathoms. Neil Carey told us he has dragged from west to east here; this was also experienced by the Fisheries Patrol Vessel *Sooke Post*. For this reason, you may want to check the set of your anchor and use more than normal scope.

Skidegate Inlet to Cumshewa Inlet

Charts 3890 metric, 3894

When you leave Skidegate Inlet heading for South Moresby and the National Park Reserve, you must carefully negotiate the classic, shallow bar that extends north from Sandspit all the way to Lawn Point. If you have a large vessel or one with deep draft, you may want to exit Skidegate Inlet by heading north to Lawn Point, then due east with 3 fathoms minimum depth. Others may want to cross farther south with a more comfortable depth.

If you head east from buoy "C19," 5 miles northwest of Spit Point, you will cross the shoal in a little over 2 fathoms at zero tide. We have also crossed from a point 3.5 miles northwest of Spit Point (position: 53°18.50' N, 131°52.20' W) with just over one fathom at zero tide. The bar is steep-to and is essentially flat. There are a few isolated rocks, so check Chart 3890 metric carefully and watch your drift or cross track error. GPS is very useful for identifying your turning points and route, since there is as much as 2 knots running on the shoal and no visual signs to guide you. The route south follows the 6-fathom curve as far as Gray Point, then stays offshore a mile or so, in 8 to 15 fathoms, until reaching Cumshewa Island and turning into Cumshewa Inlet. Avoid the rocks north of Gray Point.

Although Sheldens Bay appears to offer good temporary relief from southerly weather, its entrance is encumbered by two sets of rocks and reefs. For this reason *Sailing Directions* does not recommend it. Gray Bay, 3 miles south, has a nice sandy beach, and appears to offer relief from southerly chop; however, the bay is shallow and chock full of kelp.

Note: The caution on Chart 3894 states: *Mariners are urged to exercise extreme caution when navigating inside the 6 fathoms contour on this chart in the area north of Cumshewa Head, as uncharted shoals may exist.*

Cumshewa Inlet and Approach

Chart 3894; entrance: 53°01.40' N, 131°35.50' W (NAD 27)

Cumshewa Inlet is entered between Cumshewa Island and Cumshewa Rocks to the southeast. Favor the north shore to clear Fairbairn, McLean, and Davies shoals on your port. This is done by passing Red Buoy "C8" close to starboard and heading due west; when off McCoy Cove, follow the range lights, passing the green buoy on McLean Shoal to port. The large kelp beds on Fairbairn Shoals do a good job knocking down southerly chop, and make Cumshewa Inlet a welcome haven in southerly weather.

McCoy Cove

Chart 3894; entrance:
53°02.25' N, 131°39.55' W (NAD 27)

> *McCoy Cove, 1.3 miles NW of Kingui Island, has a drying bank extending 0.2 mile from its head with some rocks 0.2 mile further off. The cove offers temporary anchorage, in fine weather, at its entrance on the edge of the tidal stream.* (p. 234, SD)

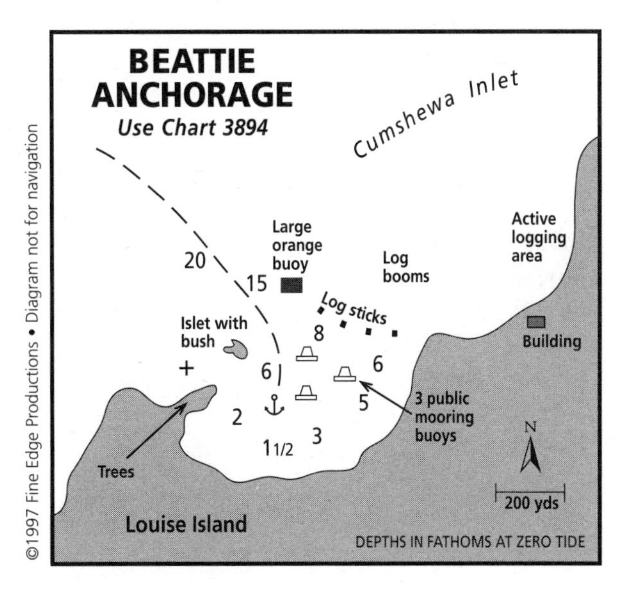

This is a stop for an emergency or in fine weather, but better anchor sites beckon 10 miles to the west. McCoy Cove can be rolly on a change of tide.

Captain Kevin Monahan reports: "Good anchorage and protection from southerly weather can be found 3 miles southwest of McCoy Cove, 1.5 miles east of Mathers Creek. Anchor away from the kelp beds in 14 fathoms; otherwise, you will have difficulty getting the anchor to hold or difficulty breaking loose from the kelp. Once, in a 150-foot yacht, I had to cut at least 2 tons of kelp free from the anchor before we could get it housed."

Beattie Anchorage

Chart 3894; entrance: 53°01.55′ N, 131°54.35′ W; anchor: 53°01.33′ N, 131°54.25′ W (NAD 27)

> *Beattie Anchorage is about 1.3 miles SW of Renner Point. . . . Beattie Anchorage has a logging camp with a log storage area marked by buoys connected by cables to the bottom. Small craft can find good shelter at the head of the anchorage, south of the islets. Two public mooring buoys are in Beattie Anchorage.* (p. 234, SD)

Beattie Anchorage, at the northwest corner of Louise Island, has the first safe anchorage in Cumshewa Inlet in the bight behind the large logging operation. Small craft will find very good protection from southerly weather; moor on a public buoy or anchor nearby in the islets to the west. The logboom helps break northerly chop. The surroundings are clear-cut, with a noisy logging operation on the east side. The landing beach is gravel.

Anchor in 2 fathoms over a mixed bottom of unknown holding.

Moresby Camp Dock, Gordon Cove

Chart 3894; entrance: 53°02.90′ N, 132°00.90′ W; anchor: 53°02.50′ N, 132°01.50′ W (NAD 27)

> *Gillatt Arm affords anchorage in 16 fathoms (29 m), mud, in midchannel about 0.5 mile from the head. . . . Small craft can obtain anchorage with good shelter in the middle of Gordon Cove in 6 fathoms (11 m), mud. A public mooring buoy and a float are in the cove.* (p. 234, SD)

Gordon Cove is a bombproof anchorage; the preferred anchor site is at the head of the cove clear of the buoys. The cove is calm and quiet, with tree limbs extending over the water and no drift logs along the shore. Moresby Camp is out of sight to the northwest. The seven Fisheries buoys offer excellent convenience and security. Gordon Cove has great views in all directions of the tall peaks of Moresby Island. The cove is surrounded by virgin forest with a service road approaching the beach on the southwest corner. It is a good place to stretch your legs. There are also public mooring buoys along the south shore of Gillatt Arm.

Anchor in about 4 fathoms over an unrecorded bottom.

Carmichael Passage

Chart 3894; north entrance: 53°00.85′ N, 131°56.50′ W; south entrance: 53°56.10′ N, 131°54.10′ W (NAD 27)

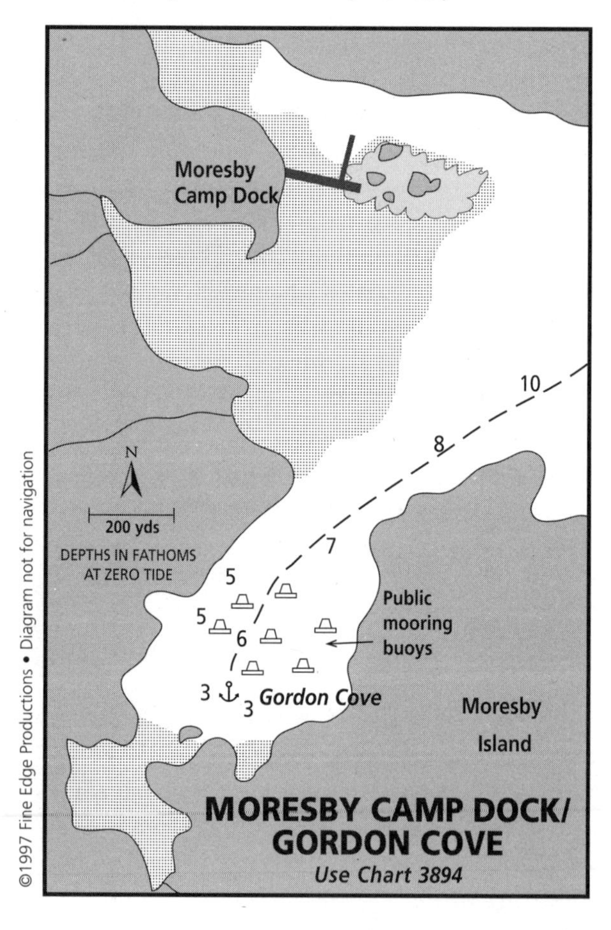

Carmichael Passage leads from the north end of Selwyn Inlet to the west end of Cumshewa Inlet between mountains rising steeply from its shores. (p. 231, SD)

Carmichael Passage is the first of several small-craft passages which provide a smooth-water route along the east side of Moresby Island, leading to the National Park Reserve. We have found Carmichael Passage to be near-calm when southeast winds blow on the outside of Louise Island.

Four public mooring buoys on the east side and three buoys on the west side, about a half mile north of Louise Narrows, provide very good protection in all weather. There is also a small float closer to the narrows, but the water hose was inoperative in 1995. Water can be obtained from a nearby stream. The view from this spot is simply wonderful. There are high peaks in all directions, thickly forested except for their crowns; you can imagine you are cruising on saltwater in a small-scale Yosemite Valley.

Louise Narrows

Chart 3894; north entrance:
52°57.60′ N, 131°54.15′ W; south entrance:
52°56.57′ N, 131°54.04′ W (NAD 27)

Louise Narrows is the narrow drying section of Carmichael Passage about 0.8 mile long. Except for a dredged channel the narrows is filled with shingle and stones which dry as much as 11 feet(3.4 m). This channel passes east of a wooded islet inside the narrows. At HW the west side of this islet could be mistaken as a passage. Bends in the channel obscure vision of approaching traffic. (p. 232, SD)

Photo courtesty CHS, Pacific Region

Louise Narrows, north end looking south

Louise Narrows

Louise Narrows, the small-boat passage between the west side of Louise Island and Moresby Island, is an interesting, narrow traverse in which the bottom can be followed visually all the way. The channel has a least depth of about one foot at zero tide abeam the islet, and is about 30 feet wide throughout. The recommended time for a traverse is on a rising tide, when the top of the banks are still visible; you will have a clearly-defined dredged channel, more like a ditch, that can be easily followed. We have found the last of the flood flowing south at about 3 knots at the north end, slowing to about half that near the islet. There is a painted arrow on the islet to remind you to pass to the east side. A starboard hand daybeacon is at the south entrance and a daybeacon on the islet.

Be sure to make a security call on Channel 16 announcing your transit intentions before entering Louise Narrows, as you cannot turn around and there is insufficient passing room. Your bow watch will see a fine collection of many-colored

Photo courtesty CHS, Pacific Region

Louise Narrows, south entrance

Louise Island, looking southwest

lagoon with an extensive drying flat at its head. Tidal rapids are formed in the narrows and entry to the lagoon should be effected only by small craft at HW slack, which occurs at about the same time as HW at Prince Rupert. A rock 4 ft (1.2m) high, with a rock which dries 7 feet (2.1 m) close WNW, are 0.2 mile ESE of the narrows. . . . Small craft can obtain anchorage within the lagoon in 8 to 10 fathoms (15 to 18 m) but caution should be observed as heavy squalls can be expected from the valley at the head during periods of bad weather.
(p. 231, SD)

starfish on the bottom, and large fish milling around, in a beautiful natural setting.

Lagoon Inlet

Chart 3894; entrance:
53°55.70′ N, 131°54.30′ W; anchor (near pier):
53°55.68′ N, 131°56.70′ W; anchor (lagoon):
52°56.10′ N, 131°57.60′ W (NAD 27)

Lagoon Inlet ...A very narrow obstructed passage about 1.5 miles within the entrance leads to a

S/V Takooli *waits to pass into south entrance, Louise Narrows*

Lagoon Inlet, located immediately south of Louise Narrows, offers a place to wait for proper conditions in the narrows; it offers fairly-good protection along the south shore when southeasterlies are blowing further south in Selwyn Inlet. This is a beautiful natural environment with little sign of man's impact. The cannery is gone except for a few remnants and part of an old pier. There is an abandoned 30-foot wooden boat on the shore near the pier. Temporary anchorage can be found off the flat in front of the pier in about 8 fathoms.

The lagoon, west of the bottleneck and tidal rapids, appears to be almost bombproof; a land-locked anchorage for small boats able to enter safely. It offers sufficient swinging room for several boats, even if the williwaws come hurdling down the surrounding 3- to 4,000-foot peaks. The tidal rapids are shallow, rocky and crammed with bull kelp. Entrance should be attempted at high-water slack only. The bottom in front of the lagoon entrance is irregular and should be sounded by dinghy before entering.

Anchor (near pier) in 7 fathoms over sand, gravel and mud bottom with fair holding.

Anchor (lagoon) in 4 to 7 fathoms near the head of the lagoon, on the south side, over an unrecorded bottom.

Lagoon Inlet, tidal rapids at high water

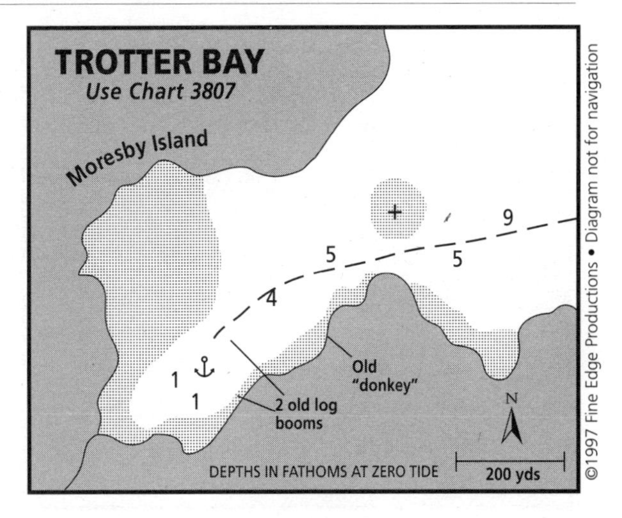

Sewell Inlet

Chart 3894; entrance: 52°54.10′ N, 131°53.90′ W (NAD 27)

Sewell Inlet, like Lagoon Inlet, runs west, deep into Moresby Island's spine. Its head is less than 3.5 airline miles from the saltwater in Newcombe Inlet on the west coast. The large complex of Western Forest Products Ltd. is located on the south shore near the head of the inlet. Some facilities are located here such as telephone and post office; however, supplies are said to be available on an emergency basis only. The head of the inlet is often completely filled with log-booms and offers little interest to cruising boats at this time.

Trotter Bay

Chart 3807; entrance: 52°53.10′ N, 131°52.60′ W; anchor: 52°52.90′ N, 131°53.02′ W (NAD 27)

> *Trotter Bay . . . has a shoal in its south approach, a rock with less than 6 feet (2 m) over it in the middle of its entrance and a drying bank at its head. The bay is suitable only for small craft.*
> (p 231, SD)

Trotter Bay is a small, cozy bay on Moresby Island that is slowly reverting to its natural condition since the log dump was abandoned. There is slash, a couple of logs tied to shore, and some underwater logs or cables left behind. With a southeaster blowing outside, low clouds scud along the north shore heading west, swaying old-growth trees. You will find an old "donkey" near the entrance on the south shore. The small beach area is backed with alder trees.

Small craft can find good protection from westerlies, and some protection from all but strong southeast gales, deep in the cove close along the south shore. You can avoid most chop by anchoring just off the drying flat on the south side of the cove. Avoid the shoal on the west and north sides, and patches of kelp. Watch for possible discarded cables. (We found none.)

Anchor in 1 to 2 fathoms over a mixture of soft mud, grass and small rocks. Holding is good if anchor is well set.

Selwyn Inlet

Chart 3807; entrance: 52°50.70′ N, 131°40.00′ W (NAD 27)

Selwyn Inlet is the east-west route on the south side of Louise Island, connecting Laskeek Bay and Hecate Strait with Carmichael and Dana passages. Cecil Cove and Pacofi Bay, southwest of Point Selwyn, offer anchorage, as do Rockfish Harbour on the north and Thurston Harbour on the south.

Cecil Cove

Chart 3807; entrance: 52°51.30′ N, 131°51.50′ W; anchor: 52°51.64′ N, 131°52.15′ W (NAD 27)

> *Cecil Cove is entered 0.5 mile SW of Selwyn Point. A reef is on the south side of the entrance to the cove. . . . Small craft can obtain anchorage in Cecil*

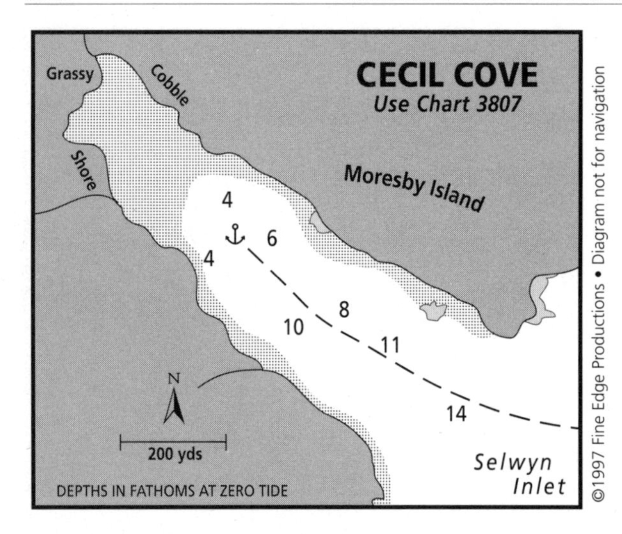

Cove in 4 to 9 fathoms (7 to 17 m) near the drying flat at the head. (p. 231, SD)

Cecil Cove, one-half mile southwest of Selwyn Point, is a convenient anchorage in prevailing westerlies. In strong southerlies, however, 2- to 3-foot chop funnels into the cove along with gusts. In easterly winds, favor the north shore to minimize chop.

You can anchor anywhere in 4 to 6 fathoms off the drying mud flats, or farther out in 8 to 10 fathoms The drying flat has a cobble shore and grassy beach. Watch for occasional deadheads.

Anchor in 4 to 6 fathoms over a mud bottom with good holding.

Pacofi Bay

Chart 3811(inset), 3894; entrance: 52°50.50′ N, 131°51.60′ W; anchor: 52°50.10′ N, 131°52.65′ W (CHS states NAD unknown)

Pacofi Bay has a number of rocks and shoals. Consult the inset on Harbours in Queen Charlotte Islands, Chart 3811, to avoid these hazards. Note that the footnote on Chart 3811 states that the horizontal datum is unknown and a GPS reading may be in error by as much as 0.2 mile.

Pacofi Bay is a large, wide bay open to easterlies. The roomy, attractive two-story South Moresby Lodge is located on the south side of Pacofi Bay. *This is the last possible emergency communication and transportation connection for southbound boats.* We have seen fishing boats take shelter from southeast storms, anchoring at the northwest corner of Dana Passage on the south side of Beatrice Shoal in about 6 fathoms.

Anchor (north of Locke Shoal) in 5 to 10 fathoms over a mud bottom with unrecorded holding.

Rockfish Harbour

Chart 3811 (inset); entrance: 52°52.93′ N, 131°46.50′ W; anchor: 52°52.95′ N, 131°48.98′ W (CHS states NAD unknown)

Small vessels can obtain anchorage in Rockfish Harbour in 9 to 12 fathoms (16 to 22m) about 0.5 mile from the head. It is not recommended except as a fair weather anchorage. (p. 231, SD)

Rockfish Harbour, on the southeast corner of Louise Island, is reported to be a good anchorage with good fishing nearby and in the harbor. We have noticed, however, a propensity for a strong easterly component of southeast gales to blow through the harbor and across the low spit at the head of the bay. If the white caps in upper Selwyn Inlet to the west are any indication, the easterly chop could be substantial in the harbor under these circumstances. Chart 3811 has an unknown horizontal datum and the above anchor position could be in error by as much as 0.2 mile.

Anchor in 6 to 8 fathoms over a mud bottom with good holding.

Thurston Harbour

Charts 3811 (inset), 3894; entrance: 52°50.40′ N, 131°43.00′ W; anchor: 52°50.50′ N, 131°44.88′ W (CHS states NAD unknown)

Good anchorage can be obtained in about 16 fathoms (29 m), mud, about 0.25 mile SE of Thompson Point, or in about 13 fathoms (24 m) 0.2 mile SW of the same point. Small craft can anchor in about 10 fathoms (18.3 m) 0.5 mile west of Thompson Point. Five mooring buoys are at the head of the harbour. (p. 229, SD)

Thurston Harbour, with its excellent public

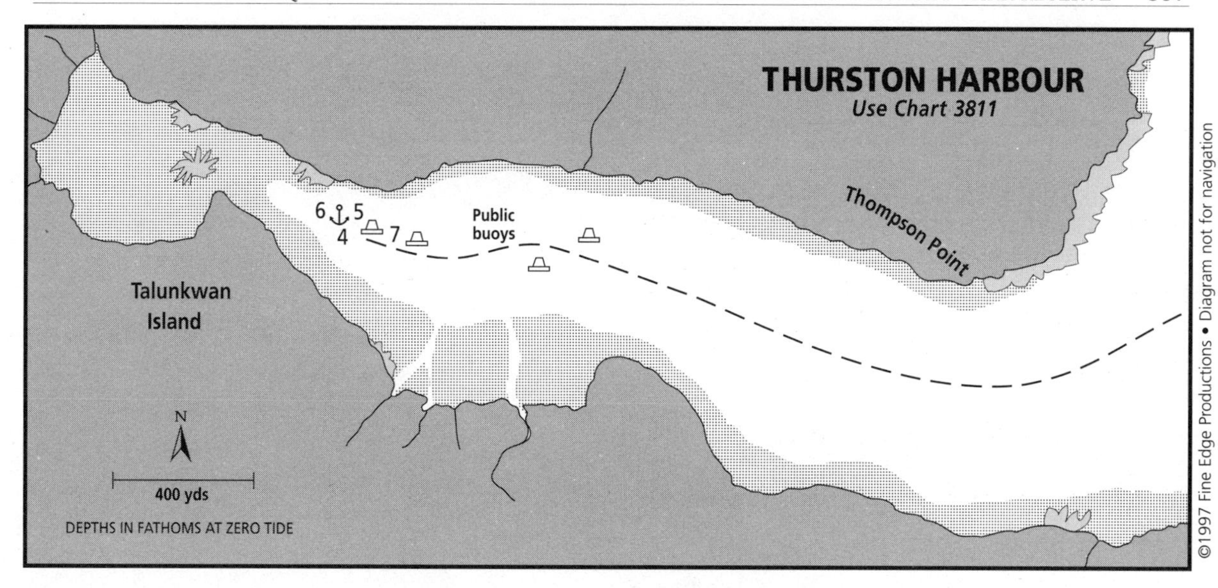

buoys, is one of the safer anchorages for small craft between Gordon Cove on the north and Crescent Cove to the south. Moor to a buoy or anchor just inside the west public buoy. *Caution*: Chart 3811 has an unknown horizontal datum and the above anchor position could be in error by as much as 0.2 mile. From our GPS readings, it appears the datum is close to NAD 27.

On August 18, 1995, we ran into Thurston Harbour at 1300 hours after the barometer fell about 4 millibars in the morning. We sat out what became an unpredicted front crossing with easterly storm force winds of 50-plus knots. The 2- to 3-foot easterly chop and strong wind gusts blew foam that nearly covered the buoys for short periods. This was nothing compared with the 10- to 12-foot chop off Protector Rocks we had encountered on our beat into the harbor. While Thurston Harbour was noisy and bouncy, we didn't feel particularly uncomfortable. The next morning was flat calm! Rapid change in weather can occur during any month.

The mountainsides of Thurston Harbour are recovering from prior logging activities and their overgrown roads can be used to stretch your legs; enjoy the views!

Anchor in 6 fathoms over a sand and mud bottom with good holding.

Skedans Bay

Chart 3894; north entrance:
52°57.50′ N, 131°35.40′ W; position:
53°56.75′ N, 131°37.55′ W (NAD 27)

> *Skedans Bay, SE of Skedans Islands, has an extensive drying ledge with two above-water rocks on it projecting from its north shore. An islet, 233 feet (71 m) high, is on the south side of a sandy beach at the head of the bay. Several drying rocks lie up to 0.4 mile easterly from this islet. Drying and sunken rocks marked by kelp lie in the approaches to Skedans Bay. A large waterfall, visible for some distance, marks the location where Skedans Creek enter the bay.* (p. 232, SD)

Skedans Bay can be used as a temporary anchorage while you visit the Haida Historic Site, located just west of Skedans Point, one mile north of the bay. Listen for the "Drums of Skedans" when northeast seas beat into a sea cave on the east side of Skedans Bay.

Dana Passage

Chart 3807; north entrance:
52°50.25′ N, 131°51.00′ W; south entrance:
52°49.10′ N, 131°49.80′ W; anchor (center of passage): 52°49.80′ N, 131°50.35′ W (NAD 27)

Dana Passage is a narrow, scenic passage between Talunkwan and Moresby islands, easily navigated by small craft at all tide levels. The narrows are about 100 yards wide with a minimum depth of about 5 fathoms.

The passage is seldom penetrated by high winds or chop and has an average depth of around 10 fathoms. Temporary anchorage can be taken along the shore almost anywhere in the passage.

Along the east shore, just north of the point, midway along the narrows, are the remains of a burned barge. It is reported that local fishing boats sometimes find overnight or storm shelter in this shallow bight. A stern tie to shore may be a good idea.

Anchor (center of passage) in 3 to 5 fathoms over an unrecorded bottom.

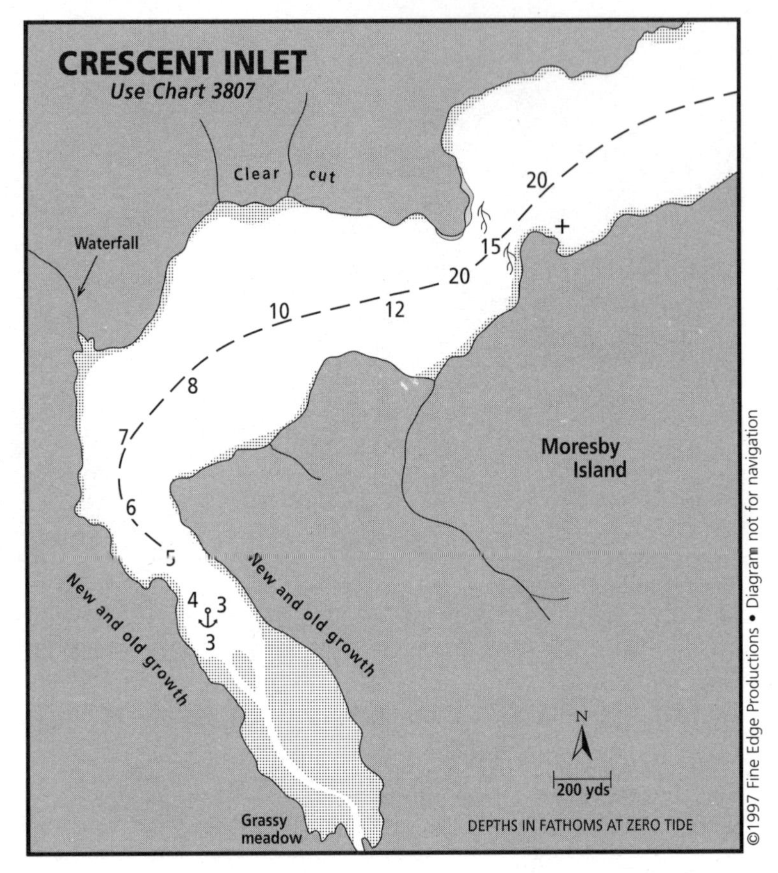

Gwaii Haanas/ South Moresby National Park Reserve

Chart 3807; Dana Inlet entrance: 52°49.20′ N, 131°38.80′ W; Logan Inlet entrance: 52°47.50′ N, 131°38.90′ W (NAD 27)

The northern boundary of Gwaii Haanas/South Moresby National Park Reserve, is passed as you transit the eastern terminus of Tangil Peninsula. As you pass Porter Head, you may feel some swells from Laskeek Bay and Hecate Strait to the east. As soon as you enter Logan Inlet, these swells die off. If approaching from Hecate Strait directly into the park, do not confuse Helmet Island and Dana Inlet for the similar-sized Flower Island in Logan Inlet. You can pass on either side of both islands, avoiding any kelp patches.

In Logan Inlet, the shallow bight on the north side of Tanu Island can be used, tucked up close to shore, for temporary protection from southerlies. During times of prevailing northwest winds, Stalkungi Cove can provide a central anchorage; however, there are a number of well-protected anchorages for the next several miles on Moresby Island proper.

Stalkungi Cove

Chart 3807; entrance: 52°45.70′ N, 131°44.55′ W; anchor: 52°46.00′ N, 131°44.80′ W (NAD 27)

If approaching from the north, avoid the large reef off the point on the west side of the cove. This reef dries on about a 17-foot tide and is a major seal haul-out spot.

The small landing beach is steep-to and a prominent burned-out stump, 9 feet wide, is behind the beach in dense trees. At this anchor site, use a stern tie to a log on shore. These logs are a sign that you don't want to be here in a strong southeast wind.

Anchor in about 5 fathoms over a gravel and sand bottom with fair-to-good holding.

Crescent Inlet

Chart 3807; entrance: 52°45.00′ N, 131°47.90′ W; anchor: 52°44.85′ N, 131°52.83′ W (NAD 27)

Anchorage can be obtained in 8 to 12 fathoms (15

to 22 m), mud bottom, in the basin SW of the narrows. Small craft can obtain anchorage in about 26 feet (8 m) about 0.1 mile NW of the mud flat at the head. (p. 237, SD)

Crescent Inlet is an attractive, winding inlet which offers isolation and a scenic environment deep in Moresby Island. We consider it the best bombproof anchorage south of Gordon Cove.

The far head of the inlet offers solitude, a great view of old growth on all sides, a half-mile drying flat with flowing stream, a grassy meadow, and high peaks in all directions. It should be an excellent place for wildlife viewing. There is some beautiful old growth along the shore, but also indications of clearcutting, and a road to the southwest.

At high water, it's easy to confuse the recommended anchor site. There are two small points which stick out from the west shore. The first, about 0.5 mile south of the prominent waterfall on the west shore before you turn southeast, has two trees growing nearly horizontal to the water. Look for the anchor site south of this point, as the drying flat before the second point is steep-to and dries at low water.

There may be williwaws off the peaks to the south, but chop should be minimal except at high tide when the fetch grows considerably. There is no visible sign of chop damage or driftwood along the shore.

Anchor in 3 fathoms over a flat mud bottom, steep-to, with very good holding.

Anna Inlet

Chart 3807; entrance: 52°42.98′ N, 131°49.60′ W; anchor: 52°42.22′ N, 131°50.43′ W (NAD 27)

Anna Inlet, at the head of Klunkwoi Bay, has an islet connected to the west shore by a drying bank in its entrance. The passage on the east side of this islet is about 200 feet (61 m) wide with a least depth in the fairway of 35 feet (10.7 m)

Sheltered anchorage for small craft is available near the head in about 8 fathoms (15 m), mud bottom. (p. 227, SD)

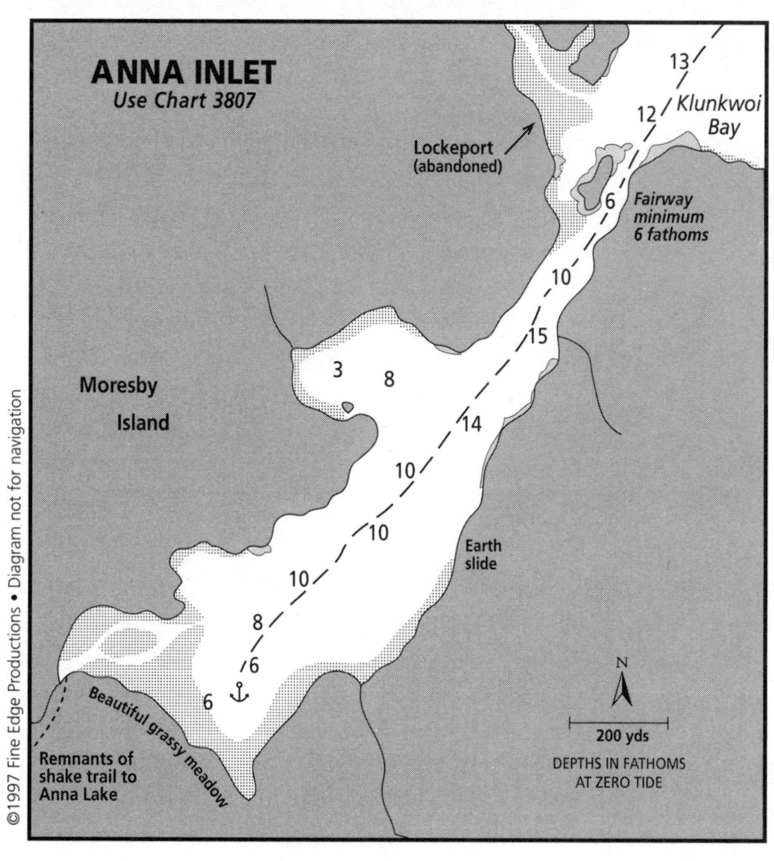

Anna Inlet is a beautiful, small inlet custom-made for cruising boats. There are good views of the high peaks in all directions. Tall alders grow among the old-growth evergreens along the shore, and the drying flat turns into a grassy meadow.

In mid-bay, the Klunkwoi Rocks are marked with a private cement pillar not indicated on the chart. The narrow entrance is navigated without difficulty, and there is swinging room for a large number of boats. The bottom is a little deep, 10 fathoms, until you approach the steep-to shore. Fifty feet from shore you can be in 20 feet of water, so a stern tie can be used. The cove in the west shoreline is well protected, but proved to have a rocky bottom with poor holding.

The old shake trail to Anna Lake

is near the stream on the northwest shore. Just northeast of the entrance to Anna Inlet is a small bay, site of the abandoned settlement of Lockeport.

Anchor in 6 fathoms or so over brown mud bottom with shells; very good holding.

McEchran Cove

Chart 3807; entrance: 52°42.85′ N, 131°48.80′ W (NAD 27)

> *McEchran Cove is not recommended as an anchorage.* (p. 227, SD)

McEchran Cove, immediately east of Anna Inlet, is full of rocks, reefs and kelp. Nevertheless, it is an interesting place to explore by dinghy or kayak.

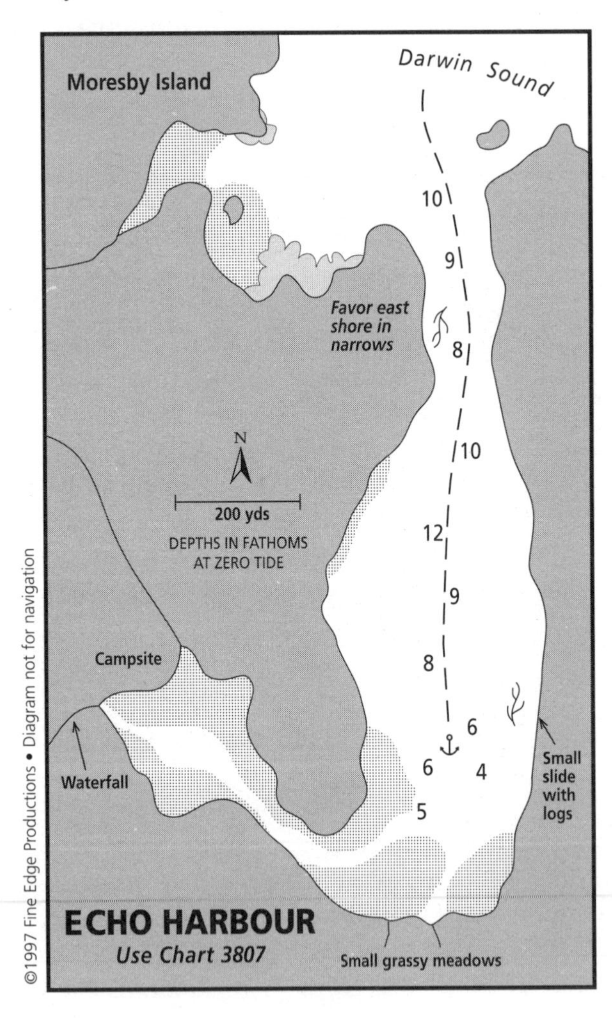

Photographing the waterfall at Echo Harbour

Echo Harbour

Chart 3807; entrance: 52°42.10′ N, 131°45.80′ W; anchor (harbor): 52°41.51′ N, 131°45.72′ W (NAD 27)

> *The harbour affords good anchorage for small vessels in about 8 fathoms (15 m) near the head; the bottom is soft mud and good holding ground.* (p. 227, SD)

Well-protected Echo Harbour makes a very good stop because it is on the smooth-water route south and there is easy access. It is a scenic place to poke around. The high peaks are picturesque and the landlocked inner cove is charming. While some small boats may stay overnight in the inner cove, paying due regard to tide levels, most stay outside and row in for a look.

You can find evidence of an old homestead and several apple trees. The forest behind the apple trees is open and you can enjoy a walk in the rain forest. *Caution*: Bears are very active in the mud flats; evidence of their presence will be found

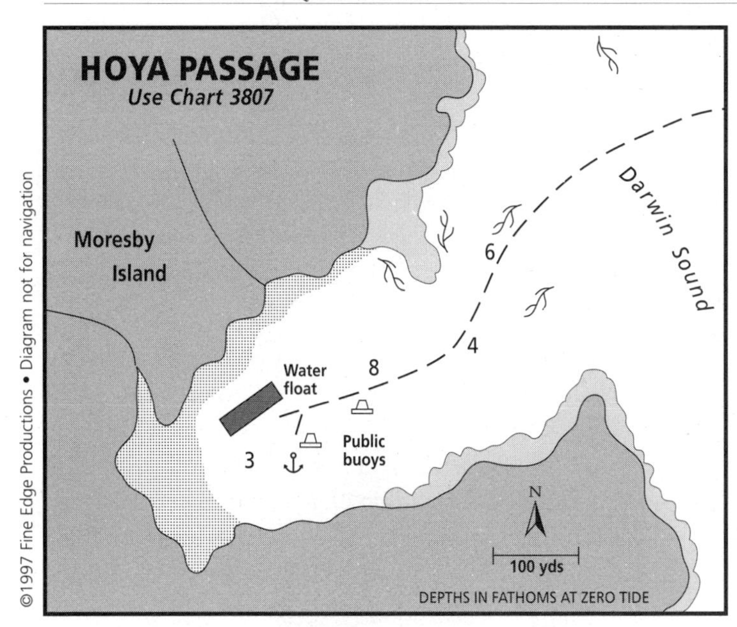

everywhere. They probably fish the small waterfall at the head of the cove when salmon are running.

When entering the harbor, favor the east shore in the narrows as the west shore is shoal. The depth of the east shore is 8 to 10 fathoms. The mud flat at the head of the bay is steep-to with small grassy margins.

Anchor (harbor) in 6 fathoms over a mud bottom with good holding.

"Freshwater Cove," Hoya Passage

Charts 3807, 3808; entrance:
52°40.10′ N, 131°43.30′ W; anchor:
52°39.93′ N, 131°43.60′ W (NAD 27)

Two mooring buoys are in a cove on the west side of Hoya Passage, 0.5 mile within the north entrance. Fresh water is obtainable from a hose at log floats on the north shore of the cove. (p. 227, SD)

We call the Hoya Passage cove, "Freshwater Cove," because of the welcome, tasty water continuously flowing out of two large hoses on the sizable detached cement float on the west side. This is the only convenient place to get water south of Skidegate Inlet. Freshwater Cove is a must stop; it may be the only time you tie to a float in Gwaii Haanas. If staying long or overnight, consider clearing the float and staying at one of the two public buoys, or anchor just inside the southern buoy. Fishing, charter and cruising boats are likely to stop for water at any time.

Anchor in about 6 fathoms over an unrecorded bottom.

Lyell Bay

Chart 3808; entrance:
52°39.45′ N, 131°39.85′ W; anchor
52°38.95′ N, 131°38.70′ W (NAD 27)

The bay affords anchorage for small vessels in about 15 fathoms (27 m) about 0.5 mile from the head. This anchorage is not recommended during SE gales as the wind draws strongly through it from Beresford Inlet. (p. 227, SD)

Lyell Bay is an indentation on Lyell Island on the east side of Shuttle Passage. Anchor near the head of the bay, avoiding the rocks and kelp.

Rain forest interior, Echo Harbour

Anchor in about 8 fathoms over an unrecorded bottom.

Bigsby Inlet, Darwin Sound

Chart 3808; entrance: 52°36.90′ N, 131°41.50′ W (NAD 27)

> *Bigsby Inlet...depths are to great for anchorage.* (p. 226, SD)

Darwin Sound connects Hoya and Lyell passages to Juan Perez Sound and Hecate Strait. Bigsby Inlet, to the west, is steep-sided and deep throughout.

Reportedly, a back-up source of water is the stream which empties into Darwin Sound one mile northwest of Bigsby Point. This stream is said to be approachable at high water, and can be found in the southwest corner of the unnamed cove.

Kostan Inlet

Chart 3808; entrance: 52°35.30′ N, 131°40.50′ W; anchor: 52°34.82′ N, 131°42.25′ W (NAD 27)

> *Kostan Inlet...A shoal rock lies in the middle of the fairway about 0.5 mile within the entrance. The inlet narrows to about 100 feet (31 m) about 0.6 mile within the entrance, where the least depth is 4 feet (1(1.2 m) . Tidal streams in the narrows attain 2 to 4 kn. Passage through the narrows is advised only for small craft at or near HW slack. Sheltered anchorage can be obtained in about 4 fathoms (7.3 m) off the sandy beach at the head of the inlet.* (p. 226, SD)

Kostan Inlet is the first of a number of very beautiful, intimate, and intricate inlets and coves between Darwin Sound and Dolomite Narrows. South of Darwin Point, you begin to feel a residual swell from Juan Perez Sound. With winds from the southeast, this can be uncomfortable until you reach the lee of Burnaby Strait. Kostan Inlet is very well protected and appears to be bombproof, with no sign of chop or serious winds. Gusts may drop from the surrounding high peaks but, in general, you will never know what is happening outside. The outer inlet has an irregular bottom with isolated patches of kelp.

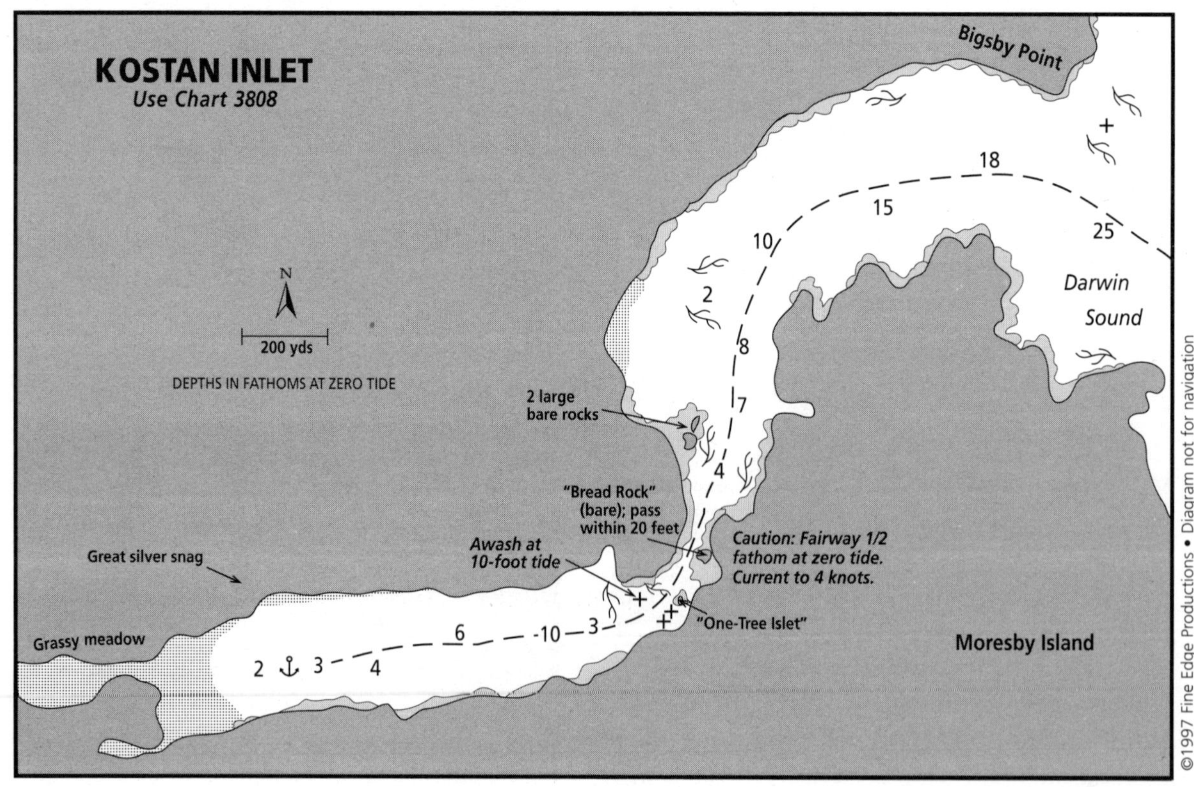

The inner inlet is totally landlocked and feels like an inner sanctum. The narrows is navigable for most cruising boats at upper half of neap tides, and near high-water slack at spring tides. We found a narrows-flooding current of 1.5 knots, 2 hours after a neap tide low water.

Approaching the narrows, stay midchannel, avoiding the kelp off the two large bare rocks on the west shore. Head for what we call "Bread Rock" (it looks like an uncut loaf of bread). Pass within 20 feet of Bread Rock on a heading to pass midchannel between "One Tree Islet" and a rock to starboard, awash on a 10-foot tide. We found a minimum fairway depth of about one-half fathom just north of Bread Rock. There is a gradual deepening to 3 fathoms as the inlet opens up. The depths are reasonable for anchoring anywhere in the inlet, and we prefer to anchor midchannel near the head, abeam a giant silver snag with a split top which is on the north wall.

Inside Kostan Inlet, you will find a dramatic wilderness of striking proportions. Tall peaks with bare, slate-grey slopes and wind-carved bushes testify to strong westerlies on the San Christoval Range and Barry Inlet, less than 3 miles away on the west coast. If it is perfectly calm, the shoreline rocks are mirrored in the water, creating fascinating patterns and designs. In the stillness, you can hear many distant streams hidden in the rain forest, as they tumble down the steep mountainsides. In the evening, you may see Sitka deer grazing on the bank of the grassy meadow.

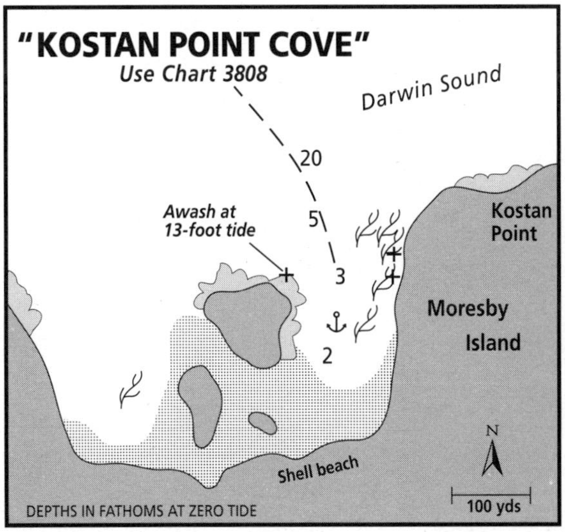

Anchor in 2 to 3 fathoms over brown mud bottom with big clam shells; very good holding.

"Kostan Point Cove"

Chart 3808; entrance: 52°35.00′ N, 131°40.35′ W; anchor: 52°34.94′ N, 131°40.10′ W (NAD 27)

"Kostan Point Cove" is what we call the small cove immediately west of Kostan Point. This cove is open to the north, but somewhat protected by a line of kelp stretching from the island to the east shore. The cove, generally out of the southeast swell of Juan Perez Sound, is useful only as a temporary stop in fair weather. This is a very good place to wait for optimal tide conditions before entering Kostan Inlet.

An alternative, Stevenson Cove, one mile to the southeast, is very deep, steep-to, with no flat bottom or shelf as shown on the chart. Stevenson Cove might be useful in a southeast storm, if you had a strong shore tie to a big tree.

Anchor in a 2-fathom hole just off the drying flat over a bottom of sand, kelp and eel grass with poor-to-fair holding

Juan Perez Sound

Chart 3808; north entrance: 52°34.30′ N, 131°36.30′ W (NAD 27)

For many cruising boats, Juan Perez Sound is the heart of Moresby Island There is plenty of interesting cruising and exploring and a real wilderness feel among the several inlets. The refreshing hot springs of Hotspring Island are on the east side of the sound. Afternoon or gale southeast winds can kick up a chop or southeast swell, but you are never more than a few miles from sheltered waters. The tide tables for Juan Perez Sound are referenced on Bella Bella and the differences are given for Section Cove and Sedgwick Bay in Tide Tables, Volume 6.

"One Foot Rock Cove," Bischof Islands

Chart 3808; entrance (west): 52°34.37′ N, 131°34.04′ W; anchor ("One Foot Rock"): 52°34.48′ N, 131°33.40′ W (NAD 27)

> *Bischof Islands...consisting of one large and several small islands, all wooded, together with numerous above water and drying rocks, lie off Richardson Point, the SW extremity of Lyell Island.* (p. 226, SD)

Bischof Islands are grouped in a small cluster and are fun to explore by dinghy, kayak and/or skin diving. The rocks, reefs and kelp beds are full of marine life. The anchor site is only for fair weather, and can be used to wait for optimal tide conditions before entering Beresford Inlet. Keep a careful lookout; the bottom is irregular and swinging room is limited. Some boats prefer the north nook, entered from the east, as shown in the diagram.

Anchor southeast of "One-Foot Rock" in about 3 fathoms over a rocky kelp-and-sand bottom; poor-to-fair holding.

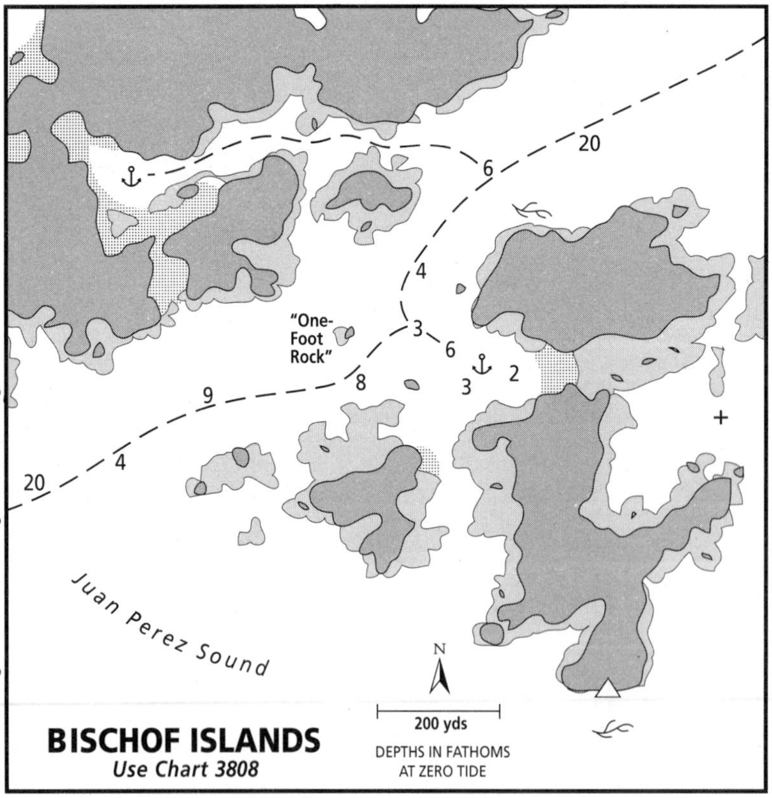

"One-Foot Rock"
Juan Perez Sound
200 yds
DEPTHS IN FATHOMS AT ZERO TIDE

BISCHOF ISLANDS
Use Chart 3808

Beresford Inlet

Chart 3808; entrance: 52°35.35′ N, 131°34.10′ W; anchor: 52°38.03′ N, 131°37.10′ W (NAD 27)

> *Beresford Inlet is about 300 feet (91 m) wide at its narrowest point, which is almost completely blocked by above-water and drying rocks. A shoal rock, marked by kelp , is 0.3 mile SE of the east entrance point of Beresford Inlet. Entry should be attempted with caution, by small craft only at or near HW. Tidal streams attain a 2 to 3 kn in the narrowest part of Beresford Inlet; slack water occurs about the times of HW and LW.* (p. 226, SD)

Beresford Inlet is one of those places that appeals only to intrepid explorers looking for an experience we call "anchor at the ready" or "heads-up bow watch." The transit is not technically difficult, but information is minimal and the surroundings austere and foreboding. It may not be easy to retreat if you change your mind. The Careys, in typical understatement, simply call it "a unique experience." We found no indication of man's having been in Beresford Inlet before, and it is solitude *par excellence*.

The long, narrow inlet has a straight, mile-long drying section which is relatively easy to navigate with sufficient tide. Its flat bottom of mud and large clam shells is clearly visible most of the time. However, remain alert and use caution at the north end of the flat where a wooded islet and a number of rocks choke the fairway. On a 15-foot tide, we found the minimum depth of the fairway to be 11 to 12 feet.

The course we followed was to approach the wooded islet, avoiding the two rocks off the eastern point on the starboard shore, pass about 75 feet east of the wooded islet, then resume a generally northeast course, reaching deeper water about 100 yards north of the islet. The rocks and reefs on the west side of the islet appear intricate and dangerous. We found little or no current in the inlet at high-water slack. The inlet could handle a number of boats with ample swinging room.

Hotspring Island, temporary anchorage, east side

Small cedars interspersed with old silver snags line the shores of Beresford Inlet. The inner basin is pure wilderness with plenty of places to anchor. We anchored on the western side at the head of the inlet across from the two rocks on the east side. There may be a strong draw of southeast winds across the low pass to Lyell Bay to the northwest, but we found little evidence of strong winds or any chop in the inner basin. The winds mentioned in *Sailing Directions*, referring to Lyell Bay, may occur aloft through this section of Beresford Inlet.

Anchor in 4 fathoms over a brown mud bottom with shells and twigs with good holding.

Murchison Island

Chart 3808; entrance: 52°35.90′ N, 131°27.60′ W; buoys: 52°35.63′ N, 131°27.96′ W (NAD 27)

> *Three public mooring buoys are in the cove on the west side of Murchison Island, 0.5 mile west of the 473 foot (144 m) hill.* (p. 226, SD)

Murchison Island, 3 miles east of the Bischof Islands, one mile northwest of Hotspring Island, has a well-protected and scenic cove on its north shore. The cove is surrounded by rocks and reefs and should be carefully entered from the northeast. The public mooring buoys offer secure moorage in foul weather.

Photo courtesy CHS, Pacific Region
Hotspring Island, west beach

Hotspring Island

Chart 3808; position (springs): 52°34.45′ N, 131°26.42′ W; anchor (east side): 52°34.64′ N, 131°25.90′ W (NAD 27)

Hotspring Island has several of the most wonderful hot springs found on the Pacific Coast of North America. Located on the south side of the island, these springs have been developed and maintained by the Haidas of Skidegate. In small groups, they take turns as watchmen camping on the west shore. There are a number of tasteful, natural rock-lined hot pools, some farther up the beach, with unusually fine views and isolated surroundings. Become friendly with one of the Haidas, and he or she may guide you to some of the outlying pools. Your guide may explain how they clean and rebuild the rock-lined pools and dry fish over an open campfire when staying on the island. The watchman will gladly stamp your visitor card.

Visiting boats anchor temporarily off the south shore in an exposed and rocky area. This is the only way to be close-to and keep an eye on your

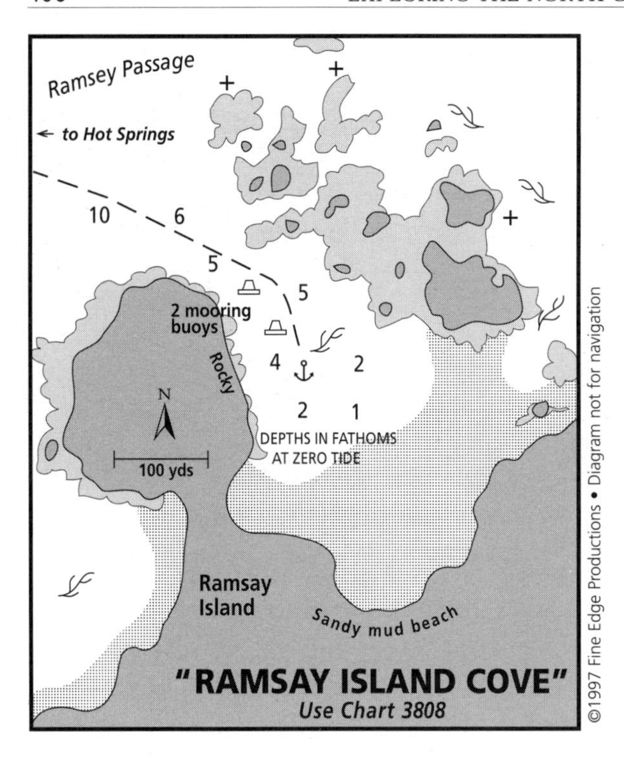

boat; however, water may become rough at change of tide. A more protected spot is located in the shallow area between Hotspring and House islands on the east side of the island. Visiting float planes land in this shallow passage, so watch for planes. Ramsay Passage Cove (see below) is the most protected place to leave your boat, but you have to travel the mile and a quarter to the hot springs by outboard.

An excellent trail through the center of the island leads directly to the springs; the walk itself is worthwhile. The trail starts near the center of the eastern beach, and is marked here and there with white clamshells.

Anchor (east side) in 4 fathoms over a stone and gravel bottom with poor-to-fair holding.

Moresby Explorers' Fishing Lodge, De la Beche Lagoon

"Ramsay Passage Cove"

Chart 3808; entrance: 52°34.52′ N, 131°24.05′ W; anchor: 52°34.35′ N, 131°23.76′ W (NAD 27)

> *Ramsay Passage ...Anchorage in the coves on the SE side of Ramsay Passage is only suitable for small craft. Two public mooring buoys are in the cove on the east side of the promontory 1.3 miles SW of Andrew Point.* (.p. 225, SD)

The reefs, rocks and kelp beds on the north side of Ramsay Passage Cove create good anchoring protection when you want to visit Hotspring Island. There are two public Fisheries mooring buoys off the northeast corner of the peninsula in 5 fathoms of water. Small craft can work their way closer to shore through some kelp patches and find a clear 1.5-fathom hole. The beach is marked by eel grass at the one-fathom contour.

Anchor in 1.5 fathoms over a sand, mud and grass bottom with fair-to-good holding.

De la Beche Inlet

Chart 3808; entrance: 52°32.35′ N, 131°38.70′ W (NAD 27)

> *The approach to De la Beche Inlet has irregular depths and is encumbered by drying and sunken rocks in the passages north and south De la Beche Island. Entry should be attempted with caution and by small vessels only. The inlet is narrowest at its entrance where the fairway is reduced to about 0.1 mile wide by islets and rocks extending from the north side. The head of the inlet is narrow and foul. . . . Sac Bay, on the south side of the inlet, is very narrow and obstructed by sunken and drying rocks at its entrance.* (p. 225, SD)

De la Beche Inlet contains lots of surprises. Skittagetan Lagoon and the head of the inlet are especially interesting to explore by kayak and dinghy. Sac Bay has its own special environment.

Sac Bay

Chart 3808; entrance: 52°32.40′ N, 131°40.10′ W; anchor: 52°31.97′ N, 131°40.38′ W (NAD 27)

> *Sac Bay, on the south side of the inlet, is very narrow and obstructed by sunken and drying rocks at its entrance.* (p. 225, SD)

"After a rain, Sac Bay's dark waters—on the southwest side of rocky and baroque De la Beche Inlet—are brightened by mounds of foam riding seaward like miniature icebergs from two chattering waterfalls. The shore is rimmed with black lichen-covered rocks, decorated with golden rockweed. On windless days the still water mirrors the steep hillside, surrounding your boat with trees that appear to be standing on their delicate tops."—*A Guide to the Queen Charlotte Islands* by Neil G. Carey

Sac Bay, deep in the east side of Moresby Island, has much in common with the rugged Patagonian coast: high, black granite walls with stunted trees that struggle to survive in vertical and horizontal crevices. The trees hang on for dear life up to 1,800 feet, then give way to knobs of somber grey granite. This is a brooding place where the perpetually dark muskeg-colored water is made darker by the long shadows of the San Christoval Range. The mountains form a dinosaur ridge where Moresby Island narrows at its southern tip. Look up and try to imagine hiking conditions and the trail to the southwest, where hikers climb, crossing to Puffin Cove on the west coast!

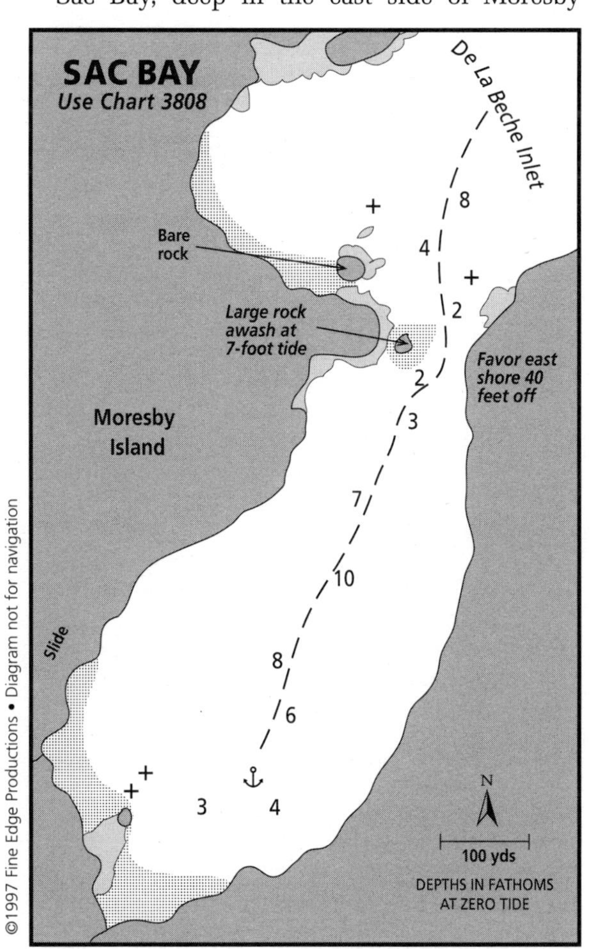

Sac Bay is similar to Kostan Inlet. The narrows is tight and shallow. The western side of the narrows is largely a dangerous reef which dries on about a 7-foot tide. As you approach the narrows, after passing a bare rock midchannel on the west side, move smartly to the east side and stay about three-quarters of the way to the east shore where you will find a narrow channel. This channel, at its narrowest part, is only 40 feet off the east shore, and over 2 fathoms deep at zero tide.

Because the entire Sac Bay is of moderate depth, you can anchor anywhere. We like the small bight just east of a small spit that extends from the head of the bay. (It lies east of the two waterfalls that tumble down the granite slopes at the south end of the bay.) Winds occasionally sweep down from the surrounding high peaks, so don't be lulled into complacency when checking your anchor set.

Anchor in 5 fathoms over a mud bottom with good holding.

"De la Beche Cove"

Chart 3808; east entrance:
52°32.15′ N, 131°37.85′ W; anchor:
52°32.18′ N, 131°38.36′ W (NAD 27)

"De la Beche Cove" is what we call the unnamed cove formed by a bight in the south shore of De la Beche Inlet; it is landlocked by a moderate-sized unnamed island on its north side. The west entrance isn't much more than a kayak passage;

however, the eastern passage appears safe enough with 2 fathoms or more on the south side. The north side of the east passage has a shoal which dries at about 11-foot tide; pass south of the shoal by favoring the south shore (about 15 feet off).

In the summer, this well-protected cove is home to the Moresby Explorers guide outfit which anchors a float bunkhouse on the south shore. The Explorers run clients down and back to Anthony Island in one day, using high-speed inflatables.

Although the bottom of the cove is somewhat irregular, indicating a rocky bottom, we found the northwest corner to be flat at about 4 fathoms with adequate holding.

Anchor in 4 fathoms over a sand and mud bottom with fair-to-good holding.

Haswell Bay

Chart 3808; entrance: 52°31.45′ N, 131°36.15′ W; anchor: 52°30.53′ N, 131°36.93′ W (NAD 27)

> *Haswell Bay affords good anchorage for small craft in 7 fathoms (12.8 m) near the head. . . . Fresh water is obtainable year round from the stream 1 mile SSW of Hoskins Point.* (p. 225, SD)

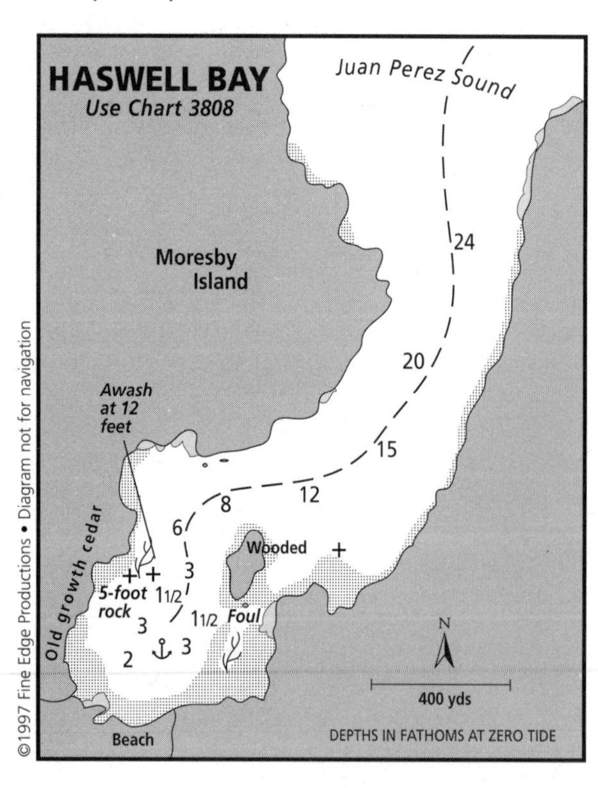

Haswell Bay is easily accessed from Juan Perez Sound and well sheltered from all weather. You can anchor, as *Sailing Directions* recommends, in 7 fathoms or continue deeper into the bay, crossing a bar and its kelp patch into a flat-bottom mud hole. There you will barely move, no matter how badly it's blowing outside.

The bar, depth about 8 to 13 feet at zero tide, extends from the west shore to the unnamed wooded island and the drying flat to its south. The mud hole has 3 fathoms of water with room for a couple of boats to anchor.

Less intimidating than Sac Bay, Haswell Bay has good views of the tall peaks to the south and its shores are surrounded by old-growth cedar in every direction. You can frequently see a mother bear and her cubs browsing along the landing beach.

Anchor in 3 fathoms over a soft, brown mud bottom with clam shells; very good holding.

Hutton Inlet

Chart 3808; entrance: 52°31.50′ N, 131°31.90′ W; anchor: 52°30.00′ N, 131°34.08′ W (NAD 27)

> *Anchorage for small vessels can be obtained in about 7 fathoms (12.8 m), mud, 1 mile from the head of the inlet.* (p. 224, SD)

Hutton Inlet is a long, straight inlet which gradually shallows to a long drying flat. Off the drying flat, you can select your depth with plenty of swinging room.

Anchor in 5 fathoms over a recorded bottom.

"Hutton Island Cove"

Chart 3808; anchor: 52°30.88′ N, 131°31.43′ W (NAD 27)

A small cove, frequently used as a campsite by kayakers, is close to good fishing around Marco Island and the passage along the Moresby Island shore. It is located at the south side of the entrance to Hutton Inlet, 0.3 mile southeast of Hutton Island, and we call it Hutton Island Cove.

The cove is open to the north but provides shelter from all other directions. It has easy access to Juan Perez Sound and is a good base for exploring the surroundings by kayak or dinghy.

Avoid one bare and two wooded islets on the west side of the cove, and anchor off the steeply-sloping landing beach.

Anchor in about 4 fathoms over a sand, shell and kelp bottom with fair-to-good holding

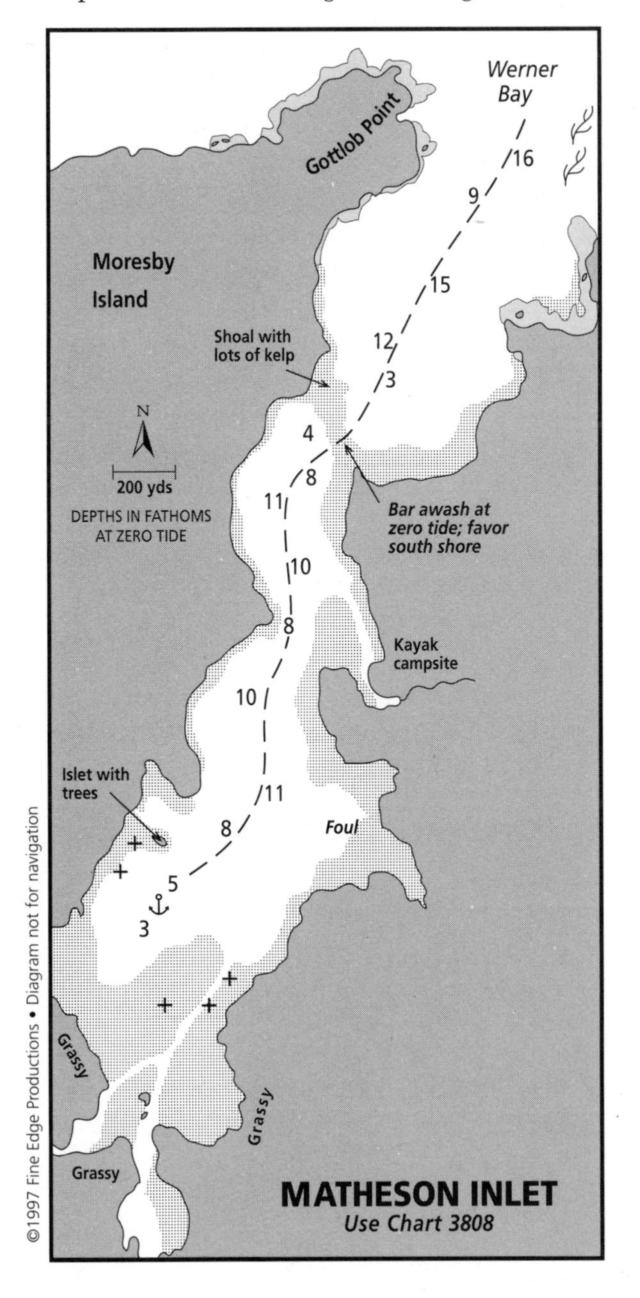

Marshall Inlet

Chart 3808; entrance: 52°28.70′ N, 131°27.90′ W; anchor: 52°28.00′ N, 131°30.36′ W (NAD 27)

> *Marshall Inlet has a drying rock and a shoal, both marked by kelp, in the middle of its entrance.*
> (p. 224, SD)

Marshall Inlet is an east-west channel off Werner Bay, west of the interesting tree-covered "All Alone Stone" in Juan Perez Sound. The inlet appears to offer fair protection in all but easterly winds. At the head of the inlet is a large 5-fathom flat which makes a good anchor site; however, the gravel beach is steep-to with depths going from 5 fathoms to 1 fathom in two boat lengths.

Avoid the shoal midchannel in the entrance by passing on either side. Note that the high rock bluffs at the entrance are washed clean by waves from southeast storms. The swells and chop appear to diminish as you proceed west in the inlet. There is evidence that strong northwest winds funnel through the low valley to the northwest. Note that the south shore has predominately old-growth cedar with silver snags, while the south-facing north shore is a vibrant mix of all kinds of trees and plants.

Anchor in the center of the 5-fathom flat, over a mud and shell bottom with good holding.

Matheson Inlet

Chart 3808; entrance: 52°28.40′ N, 131°27.90′ W; anchor: 52°27.06′ N, 131°28.51′ W (NAD 27)

> *Matheson Inlet...A shoal is on the east side of the entrance and the inlet is obstructed by a bar with 4 feet (1..2 m) over it 0.5 mile within the entrance. About 0.4 mile farther south the fairway is reduced to less than 300 feet (91 m) wide by drying banks on each side....Matheson Inlet provides sheltered anchorage for small craft near its head.*
> (p. 224, SD)

Matheson Inlet, immediately south of Marshall Inlet, offers better shelter, but it is more difficult to enter than its northern cousin. A bar extends from the west shore, marked during the summer by large kelp patches. The fairway across the bar

Canoeists in Burnaby Strait

favors the east side, passing the kelp patches to starboard. Stay in midchannel to avoid the drying banks in the narrows.

Secure anchorage can be found just beyond the small wooded island on the west shore, near the head of the inlet. Avoid the inshore rocks and the large reef across on the east shore. A kayak campsite is on the east shore south of the bar. Wildlife can be found in the grassy margins. This area offers excellent fishing for Coho (silver) and Chinook (king) salmon.

Anchor in 4 fathoms over soft, brown mud with eel grass; fair-to-good holding.

Burnaby Strait

Charts 3808, 3809

> *The strait between its south entrance and Dolomite Narrows is encumbered by drying and sunken rocks, most of them marked by kelp, and is suitable only for small craft, navigated with great caution.* (p. 222, SD)

Burnaby Strait continues the smooth-water route south along the Moresby Island coast, sheltered by Burnaby Island. Because of the drying flats at Dolomite Narrows, which require careful timing, boats heading directly to Anthony Island may find it faster to follow Juan Perez Sound around the north side of Burnaby Island.

Section Cove

Chart 3809; entrance: 52°25.50′ N, 131°21.70′ W; south buoy: 52°25.10′ N, 131°22.70′ W (NAD 27)

> *Section Cove is sheltered to the west by Section Island. . . . Anchorage can be obtained in Section Cove in 17 fathoms (31 m). Three mooring buoys are in the cove.* (p. 223, SD)

Section Cove is a convenient anchorage at the north end of Burnaby Strait. It has three mooring buoys well sheltered from southerly weather.

Skaat Harbour

Chart 3809; north entrance: 52°26.40′ N, 131°24.70′ W; anchor: 52°23.05′ N, 131°26.33′ W (NAD 27)

> *Anchorage can be obtained in about 12 fathoms (22 m), generally mud bottom, west of Wanderer Island (or at 12 fathoms, mud) about 0.6 mile from the head of the harbour. Small vessels can anchor in shallower depths closer to shore. The anchorage at the head of the harbour provides the best shelter from all but northerly winds.* (p. 223, SD)

Skaat Harbour is a good place to wait for tidal conditions in the narrows or use as a base camp for the general area. It has easy access and protection from southerlies is very good. On the west shore, just north of the 110-foot island, is a grassy rock. Next to that is a low bare rock which is a favorite haul-out rock for dozens of harbor seals.

We found harbor depths somewhat different than charted. Most of the southern part of the harbor is 7 to 8 fathoms and is steep-to right up to the shore. We found a 2.5-fathom ledge just south of the wooded islet and the bare rock, north of the drying flat and landing beach, which provided a scenic and convenient anchor site.

Anchor in 2.5 fathoms over a sand and mud bottom with fair-to-good holding.

Photo courtesy CHS, Pacific Region

Dolomite Narrows, looking north

Dolomite Narrows, "Burnaby Narrows"

Chart 3809; north entrance:
52°21.90′ N, 131°21.05′ W; south entrance:
52°21.00′ N, 131°20.80′ W (NAD 27)

> *The navigable channel dries, is about 0.3 mile long and has three sharp bends. Vessels up to 70 feet (20 m) long with a draught of 9 feet (2.7m) regularly use the narrows. Local knowledge is advised. Passage should be made on a rising tide, at half tide or better, when most dangers can be seen. The bottom throughout the narrows is rock. . . . Tidal streams; . . . with in Dolomite Narrows the streams are relatively weak and seldom exceed 1.5 knots.* (p. 223, SD)

Burnaby Narrows, as Dolomite Narrows is called locally, is a challenge and should be carefully studied before attempting passage from either direction. *Note:* There has been no channel cut through this drying flat! *Sailing Directions* mentions four private daybeacon ranges, but the only ones we noticed are noted in the diagram; they were in need of maintenance. *Our diagram is the only one we know of which has been published; it may contain errors or omissions and you should not use it without independent verification of its accuracy.*

The currents in the narrows may be moderate but, if the current is with you, you will find the rocks moving faster than you would like. The trickiest part of the transit is passing the reef with two bare rocks west of the range mark point on the east shore. This is the narrowest part with the most current. If the tide level covers most of the reef, the south-flowing current will tend to set you on the reef. The water is shallow at either end of Burnaby Narrows, and we recommend you get in position early, anchor midchannel, observe the flooding current, and get the lay of the land. During high water, our friends in the dive boat *Clavella* are frequently found diving these rocks, enjoying their beauty and charm. This is an excellent place to observe marine life.

M/V Clavella *dive boat in Dolomite Narrows*

Bag Harbour

Chart 3809; entrance: 52°20.88′ N, 131°20.96′ W;
anchor: 52°20.80′ N, 131°21.80′ W (NAD 27)

> *Bag Harbour affords sheltered anchorage to small craft over mud bottom in a basin near its head. A shoal lies in the approach to the bay about 0.2 mile east of the entrance and a rock with less than 6 feet (2 m) over it lies 0.1 mile from the head* (p. 223, SD)

Bag Harbour is an excellent small-boat harbor and offers good protection and welcome relief for those completing the southbound narrows transit. It is a convenient place to wait for correct conditions on a northbound trip.

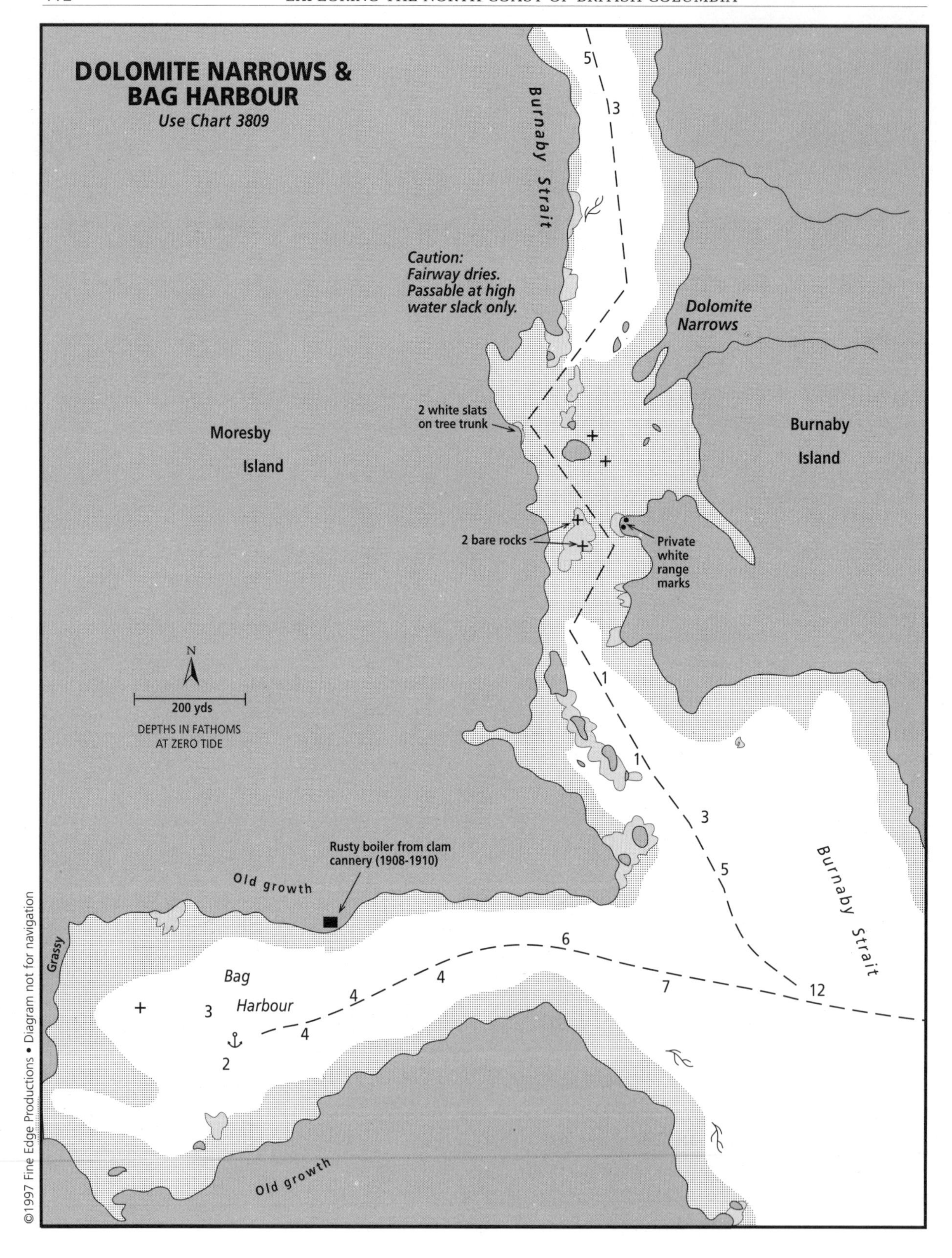

DOLOMITE NARROWS & BAG HARBOUR
Use Chart 3809
Burnaby Strait
Caution: Fairway dries. Passable at high water slack only.
Dolomite Narrows
2 white slats on tree trunk
Moresby Island
Burnaby Island
2 bare rocks
Private white range marks
N
200 yds
DEPTHS IN FATHOMS AT ZERO TIDE
Rusty boiler from clam cannery (1908-1910)
Old growth
Grassy
Bag Harbour
Burnaby Strait
Old growth
5
3
1
1
3
5
6
4
4
4
7
12
3
2

Grassy margins surrounding the harbor indicate that little chop penetrates here. With the flat bottom, it can be used by many boats, anchoring anywhere in the basin. The forest is all old growth with several small creeks entering the west end. Except for a rusty boiler hidden in the brush on the north shore, this is a quiet and peaceful place with nothing manmade in sight.

Anchor in 2 fathoms over a soft mud bottom with good holding.

Slim Inlet

Chart 3809; entrance: 52°17.85′ N, 131°19.35′ W; anchor: 52°17.08′ N. 131°19.23′ W (NAD 27)

> *Slim Inlet...is only 300 feet (91 m) wide between the 3 fathom (5.5 m) lines and has a drying flat at it head. Drying rocks and shoal reef extend up to 0.3 mile off the east and west shores at the entrance . . .* (p. 222, SD)

In our estimation, Slim Inlet is underrated. We found it peaceful, scenic and intimate. Many deer graze on the grassy margins and we liked the feel of the place.

At the entrance, avoid the submerged rocks to the north northwest, as well as all the poorly-defined isolated rocks and shoals en route to and from Dolomite Narrows. The entire shore line of Slim Inlet is composed of grey sand and gravel or cobble beaches. We saw no indication of strong southerly winds here; however, the low pass to the south leads to Louscoone Inlet on the west coast, which means gusts could blow during southerly storms. Since there are only low hills near the inlet, the chance of williwaws is greatly reduced. It is easy to land anywhere along the shoreline.

Anchor in 3 fathoms over a grey mud and shell bottom with very good holding.

Jedway Bay

Chart 3809; entrance: 52°18.10′ N, 131°15.80′ W; anchor: 52°17.25′ N, 131°15.43′ W (NAD 27)

> *Jedway Bay . . . Small craft can obtain anchorage in 5 to 6 fathoms (9 to 11 m) in the indentation on the east side of the bay close south of Kankidas*

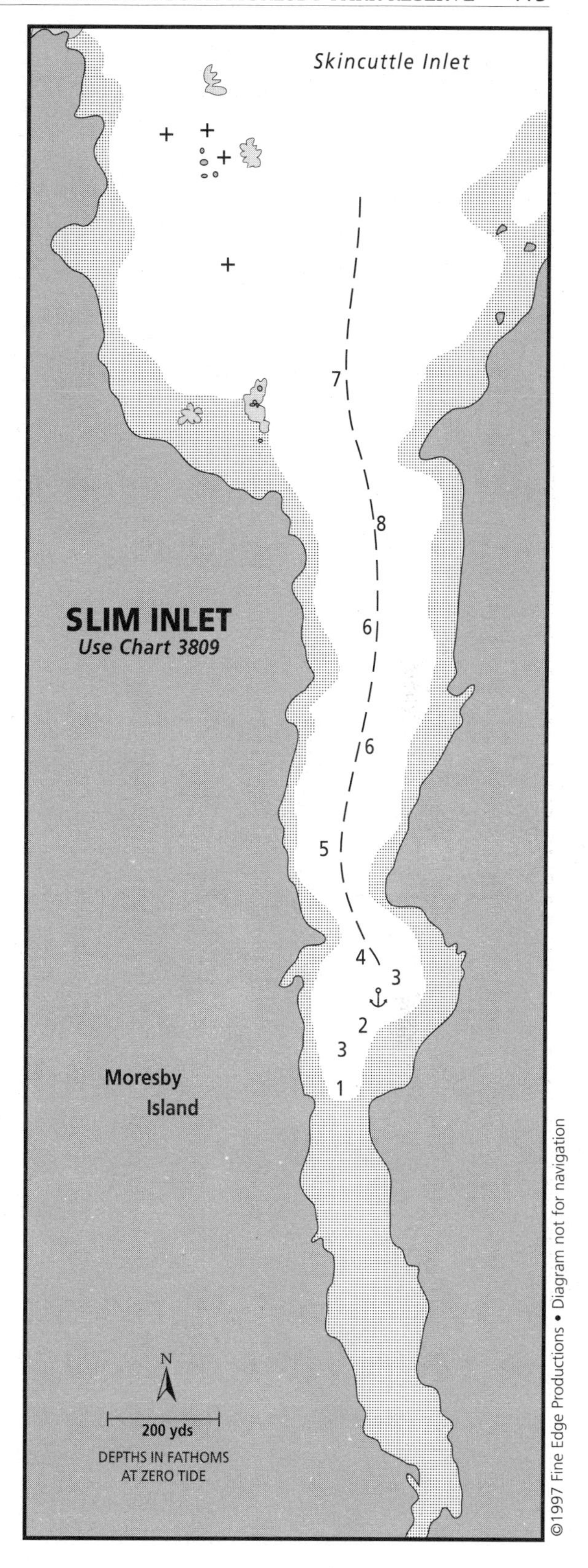

Point, or at the head of the bay, clear of the rock with less than 6 feet (2 m) over it. (p. 222, SD)

We found Huston Inlet much too large and open for our comfort. Jedway Bay or Harriet Harbour are better choices, and we prefer Slim Inlet or Ikeda Inlet. (See the caution about the entrance to Ikeda Inlet below in *Sailing Directions.*)

At the head of Jedway Bay was a source of piped running water; however, in 1995 we found that the pipe, located on the log float, was not functioning. There is a public mooring buoy near the log float.

Anchor in 5 fathoms over a mixed bottom with unrecorded holding.

Harriet Harbour

Chart 3809; entrance: 52°18.40′ N, 131°13.90′ W; anchor: 52°17.85′ N, 131°13.30′ W (NAD 27)

During strong southerly gales Harriet Harbour is subject to heavy squalls from the valley at its head which induce violent yawing. A slight swell enters the harbour with north to NE gales. (p. 222, SD)

Landing beach & temporary anchorage, Anthony Island

Harriet Harbour houses the abandoned Jedway mining ruins on Funter Point. This moderate-sized bay has fair-to-good protection in all but strong northerlies. The roads along the east shore

Cleaning the memorial poles, Ninstints

Sgan Gwaii World Heritage Site, Anthony Island

East beach, Anthony Island

can be used for hiking. Be on the lookout for open or hidden tunnels or pits.

Anchor in 4 fathoms over a sand, mud and gravel bottom with unrecorded holding.

Ikeda Cove

Chart 3809; entrance:
52°18.80′ N, 131°08.00′ W; anchor:
52°17.80′ N, 131°09.30′ W (NAD 27)

> *Anchorage can be obtained in 6 to 7 fathoms (11 to 13 m) near the head of Ikeda Cove. During normal weather this anchorage is satisfactory, but a sharp watch is necessary during strong southerly gales, as the cove is subject to heavy squalls from the valley at its head, which cause considerable down draughts from the surrounding hills. The holding ground is reported to be good. . . . Caution: During SE gales there is considerable turbulence, accompanied by heavy seas dangerous to small vessels, in the entrance to Ikeda Cove.* (p. 221, SD)

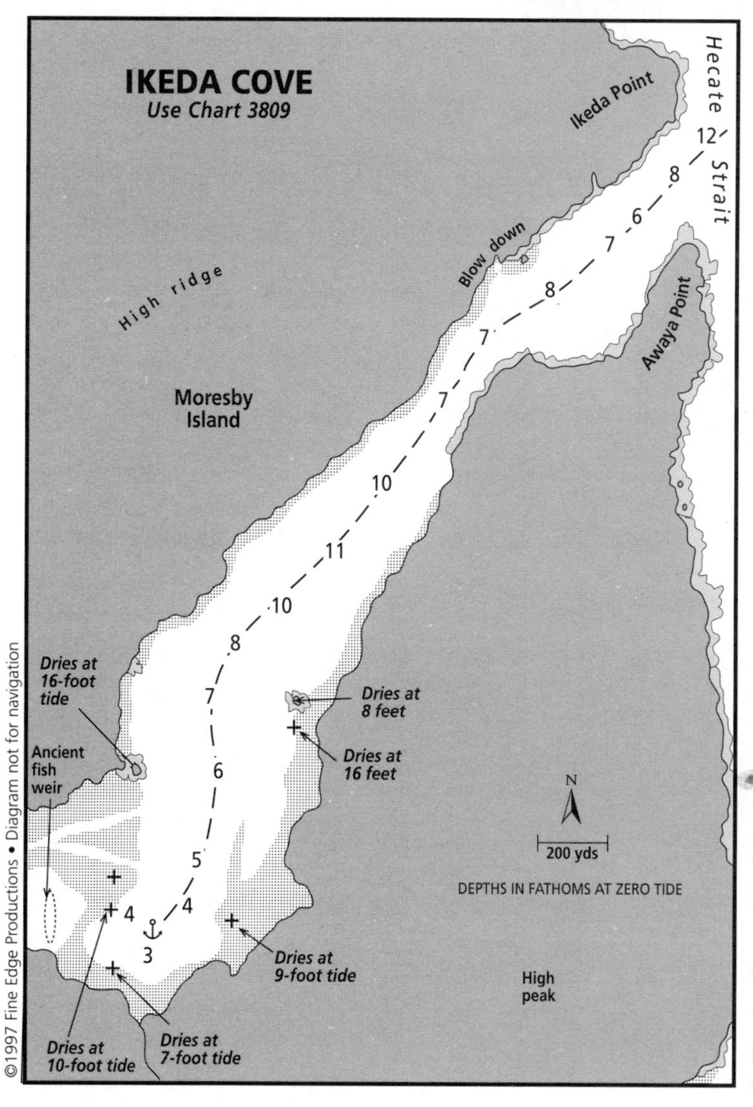

Ikeda Cove is a well-protected anchorage, subject to the above-mentioned limitations. We have found it quite comfortable and secure. Because of the strong currents along this coast, the entrance to Ikeda Cove may be treacherous during times of gales, confirmed by the rock wall on Ikeda Point that is washed bare and the wind-felled trees to the immediate west. The south side of the bitter end of the cove appears to be secure and, except for the williwaws off the high ridges, should get little chop.

The shore is fairly steep-to, but it might be possible to anchor close enough for a shore tie, if southerly gales are expected. We find Ikeda Cove a convenient summer stopping place

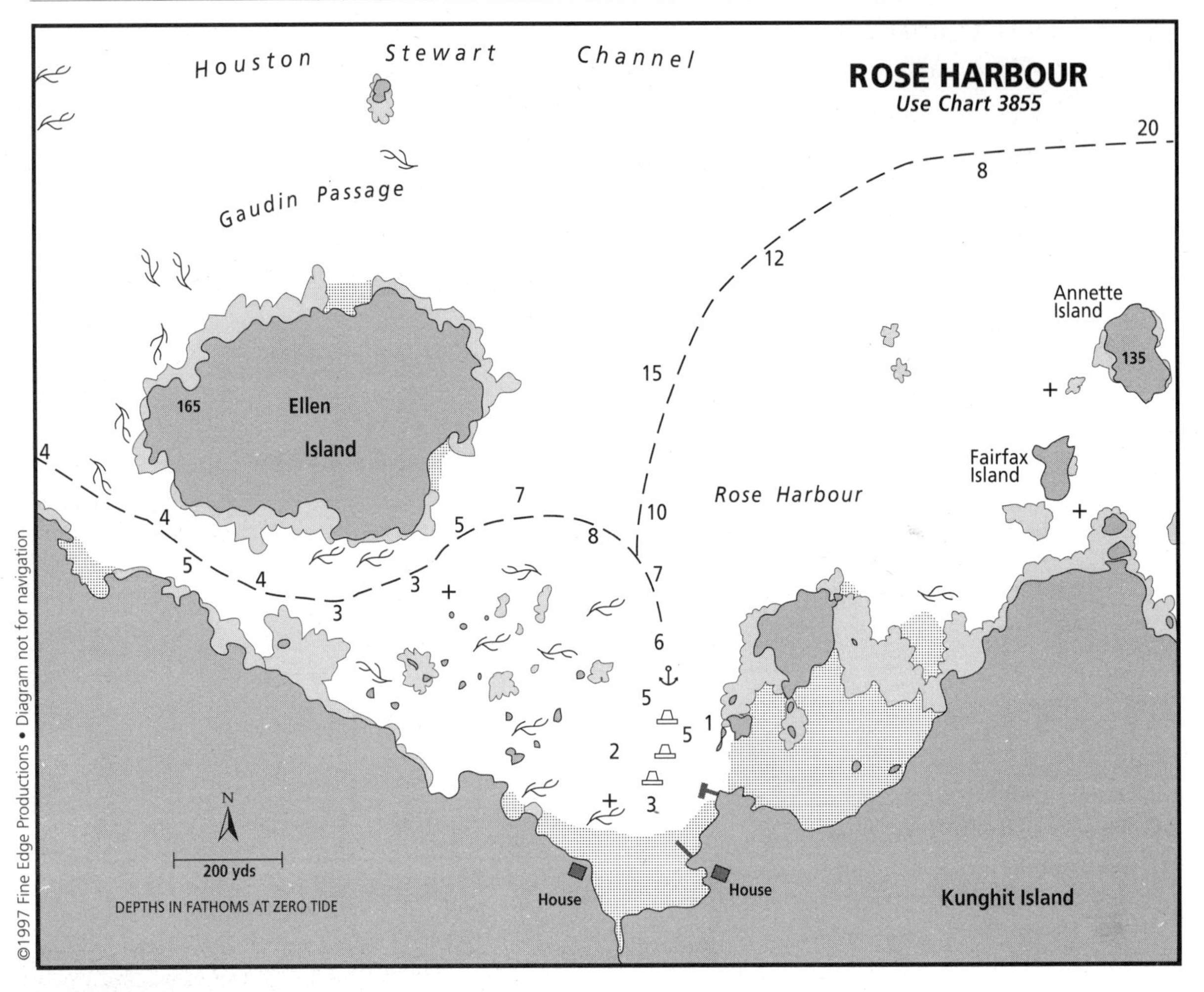

Looking northeast from beach at Ninstints village

on the way to Anthony Island via Houston Stewart Channel.

What appears to be an ancient fishing weir is at the head of the basin. Deer are found grazing on the large grassy meadow in the mornings, and at the creek outlet in the evenings. The tailings on the ridge and service roads are scars left from the mining operation in Jedway many years ago. The water temperature in the summer is a rather balmy low sixties. You may find thousands of moon jellyfish so densely packed they give the appearance of a reef.

Anchor in 4 fathoms over sticky brown mud with large clam shells; good-to-excellent holding.

Houston Stewart Channel

Chart 3855; east entrance:
52°09.55′ N, 131°02.30′ W; west entrance:
52°06.65′ N, 131°09.50′ W (NAD 27)

> *Caution: Because of the strong streams and numerous dangers, Houston Stewart Channel lying east of Hornby Point should be taken only during daylight and at slack water.* (p. 246, SD)

Houston Stewart Channel is the protected route between Moresby and Kunghit islands. It allows entry to the west coast of Moresby Island without going around Cape St. James. Houston Stewart Channel has well-protected Rose Harbour on its south side, a good place for boats to stay when visiting Anthony Island.

Rose Harbour

Charts 3855, 3825; entrance:
52°09.40′ N, 131°05.00′ W;
outside mooring buoy:
52°09.12′ N, 131°05.06′ W (NAD 27)

> *Rose Harbour . . . has numerous above-water and drying rocks in its SW part. A drying bank with an island at its NW extremity fills the SE part . . . A campsite, the ruins of a whaling station and three public mooring buoys with finders are at the head of the harbour. . . . N to NE gales funnel down a valley and into the anchorage.* (p. 246, SD)

Rose Harbour and the area near the three public mooring buoys are out of the strong currents found in Houston Stewart Channel. The cabins on shore are occupied; the mooring buoys are sometimes busy and rafting is encouraged. It may be possible for small boats to anchor in 2 fathoms near the buoys; however, swinging room is severely cramped because of the shoals and kelp nearby. The narrow passage on the south side of Ellen Island can be carefully navigated by small craft and used as an overflow anchor site, out of the main current.

Anthony Island Provincial Park, Sgan Gwaii World Heritage Site

Chart 3825

> *Anthony Island . . . 335 feet (102 m) high with some white cliffs on its west side, is on the west side of the approach to Houston Stewart Channel and Louscoone Inlet. On the east side of the island there are a few totem poles marking the site of a former Indian village...Park-Anthony Island is a provincial park and a caretakers cabin is near the site of the old village. Written permission must be obtained prior to landing. . . .*
> (p. 245, SD)

For most tourists, a visit to abandoned Ninstints village on Anthony Island (Sgan Gwaii) is the highlight of the Queen Charlotte Islands. Original memorial poles still standing in the former village site are kept in a state of arrested decay. Summer caretakers carefully remove moss from the poles in an effort to minimize decay of the wood. As you walk along the path viewing these giants, you can't help being moved by their originality and authenticity. Visitors are asked to remain on existing paths and not to touch or handle any standing or fallen wood.

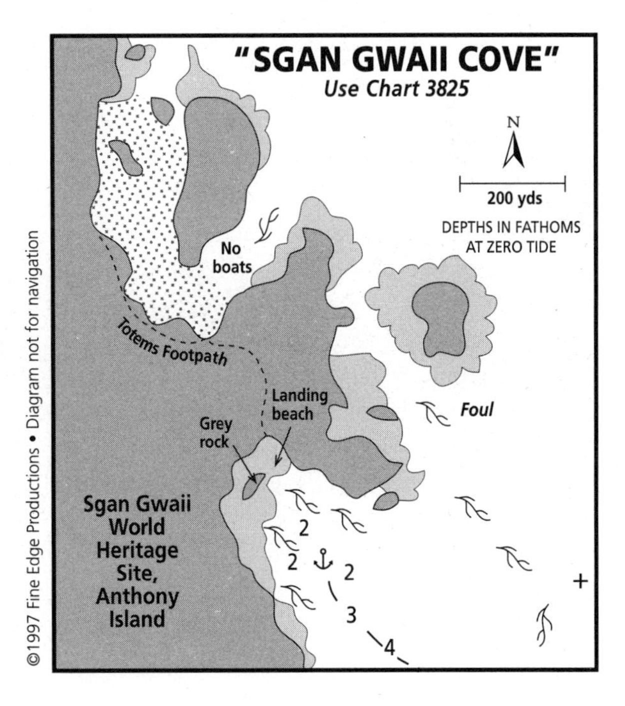

Carefully cleaning the moss from a memorial pole, Ninstints

Anthony Island Cove

Chart 3825; entrance: 52°05.57′ N, 131°12.28′ W; anchor (small east bight): 52°05.77′ N, 131°12.76′ W (NAD 27)

Three or four small craft can anchor in the small bight on the east shoreline just south of Totem Park. This site is a fair-weather anchorage only and is completely open to south winds. Entry into the basin should be made from the south, to avoid the rocks and kelp off the small grey rock point forming the east side of the cove. The west shore is composed of rocky bluffs where oyster catchers wade and otters play in the adjacent waters. A small but effective landing beach is in the northeast corner of the bight; the short trail to the historic site is located there.

In an emergency, the nearest protected anchorage is 4.5 miles north of Anthony Island on the east side of Louscoone Inlet, 0.6 mile north of Etches Point. The shelter lies between two unnamed islands; a public mooring buoy is reportedly located there. It is also reported that the site has a good mud bottom with protection from both north and south winds. Neil Carey tells us that this unnamed cove is pretty and has a small stream nearby. Shelter may also be found 2.75 miles north in Small Cove, east of Crooked Point, but it is reported to be too close to the entrance of Louscoone Inlet for satisfactory anchorage in rough weather.

Nearby Flatrock Island, northeast of Anthony Island, is known for its large concentration and variety of nesting birds. Gordon Island has a nice beach. Temporary anchorage may be taken on the east side of Gordon Island (position: 52°05.92' N, 131°08.52' W).

Anchor (small east bight) in 2 to 4 fathoms over a rocky bottom with some sand and kelp with poor-to-fair holding.

Heater Harbour

Chart 3825; entrance: 52°07.50′ N, 130°59.85′ W; buoy: 52°07.50′ N, 131°02.50′ W (NAD 27)

> *Anchorage can be obtained in 11 to 13 fathoms (20 to 24 m), mud, in the basin forming the inner part of Heater Harbour. Small craft can obtain anchorage near the west end of the harbour. One public mooring buoy is in the north part of the harbour. Anchorage may be preferable to moorage during NE gales as a slight swell enters the harbour and the buoy has no fenders.* (pp. 219–220, SD)

Heater Harbour, located on the east side of Kunghit Island, provides good protection from westerlies and southerlies, and moderate protection from easterlies. This is the site where the lighthouse tender for Cape St. James waits out storms. Small boats will find the buoys in Rose Harbor superior to Heater Harbour.

Appendices and References

APPENDIX A
Distance Tables

Port Hardy to Prince Rupert

Inside Passage via Milbanke Sound via Jackson Pass . . . add 14 miles

#	Location	1	2	3	4	5	6	7	8	9	10	11	12	13	14	15	16	17	18	19	20	21	22	23	24	25	26	27	28	29	30	31
1	**PRINCE RUPERT (Fairview)**																															
2	Genn Island	13																														
3	Watson Rock	25	12																													
4	Kumealon (Entrance)	32	19	7																												
5	Morning Reef	46	33	21	14																											
6	Lowe Inlet	57	44	32	25	11																										
7	Sainty Point	71	58	46	39	25	14																									
8	Point Cumming	78	65	53	46	32	21	7																								
9	Kingcome Point	86	73	61	54	40	29	15	8																							
10	Butedale	97	84	72	65	51	40	26	19	11																						
11	Khutze Inlet	105	92	80	73	59	48	34	27	19	8																					
12	Sarah Head	116	103	91	84	70	59	45	38	30	19	11																				
13	Split Head	129	116	104	97	83	72	58	51	43	32	24	13																			
14	**KLEMTU**	134	121	109	102	88	77	63	56	48	37	29	18	5																		
15	Jorkins Point	144	131	119	112	98	87	73	66	58	47	39	28	15	10																	
16	Ivory Island	155	142	130	123	109	98	84	77	69	58	50	39	26	21	11																
17	Idol Point	161	148	136	129	115	104	90	83	75	64	56	45	32	27	17	6															
18	**BELLA BELLA**	170	157	145	138	124	113	99	92	84	73	65	54	41	36	26	15	9														
19	Pointer Island	181	168	156	149	135	124	110	103	95	84	76	65	52	47	37	26	20	11													
20	**NAMU**	194	181	169	162	148	137	123	116	108	97	89	78	65	60	50	39	33	24	13												
21	Kelpie Point (East Hakai)	203	190	178	171	157	146	132	125	117	106	98	87	74	69	59	48	42	33	22	9											
22	Safety Cove	216	203	191	184	170	159	145	138	130	119	111	100	87	82	72	61	55	46	35	22	13										
23	Dugout Rocks	227	214	202	195	181	170	156	149	141	130	122	111	98	93	83	72	66	57	46	33	24	11									
24	Egg Island	234	221	209	202	188	177	163	156	148	137	129	118	105	100	90	79	73	64	53	40	31	18	7								
25	Cape Caution	239	226	214	207	193	182	168	161	153	142	134	123	110	105	95	84	78	69	58	45	36	23	12	5							
26	Storm Islands	247	234	222	215	201	190	176	169	161	150	142	131	118	113	103	92	86	77	66	53	44	31	20	13	8						
27	Pine Island	251	238	226	219	205	194	180	173	165	154	146	135	122	117	107	96	90	81	70	57	48	35	24	17	12	4					
28	Scarlett Point	260	247	235	228	214	203	189	182	174	163	155	144	131	126	116	105	99	90	79	66	57	44	33	26	21	13	9				
29	Duval Point	268	255	243	236	222	211	197	190	182	171	163	152	139	134	124	113	107	98	87	74	65	52	41	34	29	21	17	8			
30	**PORT HARDY**	271	258	246	239	225	214	200	193	185	174	166	155	142	137	127	116	110	101	90	77	68	55	44	37	32	24	20	11	3		
31	Pulteney Point	283	270	258	251	237	226	212	205	197	186	178	167	154	149	139	128	122	113	102	89	80	67	56	49	44	36	32	23	19	16	
32	Cape Scott	271	258	246	239	225	214	200	193	185	174	166	155	142	137	127	116	110	101	90	77	68	55	44	37	32	29	28	36	40	42	54

APPENDIX A
Distance Tables

Bella Bella to Kitimat

Route including Bella Bella and McInnes Island is via Milbanke Sound

No.	Location	1	2	3	4	5	6	7	8	9	10	11	12	13	14	15	16	17	18	19	20	21	22	23	24	25	26	27	28	29	30	31	32
1	**KITIMAT**																																
2	Nanakwa Shoal	11																															
3	Loretta Anchorage	18	6																														
4	Staniforth Bank	25	14	9																													
5	Europa Bay	38	27	22	13																												
6	**KEMANO**	55	45	40	31	18																											
7	Kitkiata (Old Town)	30	19	16	24	37	55																										
8	**HARTLEY BAY**	43	32	27	24	36	54	13																									
9	Sainty Point	49	38	33	26	39	57	19	6																								
10	Peters Narrows	56	45	40	33	46	64	26	13	8																							
11	Tuwartz Narrows	60	49	46	35	48	66	30	17	13	9																						
12	Man Islet, Otter Passage	71	60	57	50	63	81	41	28	24	22	18																					
13	Gillen Harbour	85	74	69	63	76	94	53	40	36	34	30	16																				
14	Barnard Harbour	66	55	50	45	58	76	36	23	21	28	24	29	23																			
15	Duckers Islands	78	67	62	57	70	88	45	32	28	28	25	27	16	12																		
16	Evinrude Inlet	87	76	71	66	79	97	54	41	37	37	34	38	22	21	9																	
17	Ramsbotham Islands	93	82	77	72	85	103	60	47	43	43	40	40	28	27	15	6																
18	Kettle Inlet	93	82	77	72	85	103	59	46	42	42	39	36	21	27	15	16	21															
19	Weeteeam Bay	117	106	101	96	109	127	84	71	67	67	64	66	41	51	39	30	24	20														
20	Point Cumming	50	39	33	24	37	55	21	8	8	19	17	28	32	15	26	35	40	40	65													
21	Bishop Bay	44	33	27	18	31	49	37	27	28	39	37	48	52	35	46	55	60	60	85	20												
22	Kingcome Point	62	51	45	23	49	67	33	17	16	47	47	36	40	22	34	43	48	48	73	8	12											
23	Butedale	73	62	56	34	60	78	44	28	27	58	58	47	43	32	44	53	59	66	84	19	23	11										
24	Khutze inlet	77	66	60	51	64	82	48	35	35	46	44	55	51	40	52	61	67	72	92	27	31	19	8									
25	Sarah head	89	78	72	63	76	94	60	47	47	58	56	67	71	53	65	74	45	79	52	39	43	31	20	12								
26	Split Head	102	91	85	76	89	107	73	60	60	71	69	80	61	67	48	39	32	56	39	52	56	44	33	25	13							
27	**KLEMTU**	107	96	90	81	94	112	78	66	65	76	74	85	66	72	53	44	38	61	44	57	61	49	37	30	18	5						
28	Wingate Point	104	98	106	97	110	128	74	61	80	55	52	46	40	39	27	18	12	35	18	72	76	64	54	46	34	21	26					
29	Wilby Point	105	99	107	98	111	129	75	62	83	56	53	47	41	40	28	19	13	32	15	75	79	67	57	49	37	24	29	3				
30	Quigley Creek	104	98	106	97	110	128	74	61	83	55	52	46	40	39	27	18	12	33	21	75	79	67	57	49	37	24	29	3	6			
31	Kipp Islet, West Higgins Pass	109	103	111	102	115	133	79	66	86	60	57	51	45	44	32	23	17	30	14	81	85	73	63	55	43	30	35	9	6	12		
32	McInnes Island	136	125	110	110	123	141	90	77	90	73	70	70	61	57	45	36	30	38	20	81	86	74	63	55	43	30	49	22	19	26	14	
33	**BELLA BELLA**	171	131	125	116	129	147	112	101	100	111	109	102	88	84	72	63	57	65	47	92	96	84	73	65	53	40	35	49	46	52	41	27

APPENDIX B
Procedures Used in Documenting Local Knowledge

1. Coves, bays or bights which seemed to offer full or limited protection from different weather situations were identified and visited by our boat.
2. Routes were sketched and photographed.
3. Perusal of a possible anchor site was made with a dual-frequency recording echo sounder to identify major underwater obstacles and to check the depth and flatness of the bottom over the expected swinging area. These depths were recorded on the sketches.
4. Once an anchor site was selected, a sample anchor test was made of the bottom by using a small "lunch hook" attached to light line and six feet of chain for maximum responsiveness and to facilitate a feel of the bottom.
5. The response of the anchor to the bottom was noted (i.e. soft or hard mud, sand, gravel, rocky, etc.; digging power, bounce, foul with kelp, pull out, etc.)
6. Additional line was let out to fully set the anchor.
7. A pull-down with the engine in reverse was made against the anchor to test holding power of the bottom (see definitions below).
8. Upon retrieving the anchor, we inspected the residue on its flukes to verify bottom material, as well as the type of grass, kelp, etc.
9. Discussions were held with local residents and fishermen about anchorages, names, etc., and their comments were noted on the sketches. In some cases rough drafts of the manuscript were sent to experts for review.
10. The information gathered from our procedures, or that submitted by local experts was consolidated and edited and became the local knowledge we have presented in our diagrams and text.

Definitions used for holding power

Excellent—very good holding
Anchor digs in deeper as you pull on it—the preferred bottom in a blow, but a rare find—usually thick sticky mud or clay.

Good holding
Generally sufficient for overnight anchorage—anchor digs in but may drag or pull out on strong pull. Common in mud/sand combinations or hard sand.

Fair holding
Adequate for temporary anchorage, but boat should not be left unattended. Bottom of light sand, gravel with some rocks, grass or kelp. Anchor watch desirable.

Poor holding
Can be used for a temporary stop in fair weather only. Bottom is typically rocky with a lot of grass or kelp, or a very thin layer of mud and sand—insufficient to properly bury anchor. Anchor watch at all times is recommended.

Steep-to
Depth of water may decrease from 10 fathoms to $1/2$ fathom in as little as one boat length! Dead-slow speed approach recommended. use shore tie to minimize swinging and to keep anchor pulling uphill.

APPENDIX C
Sources for Fishing Regulations

British Columbia is home to some of the most productive fishing waters in the world, and opportunities for quality fishing are endless. For current Canadian fishing regulations, request a free copy of *British Columbia Tidal Waters Sport Fishing Guide*, published by the Fisheries and Oceans. Write to: Fisheries, Ministry of the Environment, 780 Blanchard St., Victoria, B.C. V8V 1X5; telephone 250-363-3252, or call the Fisheries and Oceans Field Office: Nanaimo 250-754-0230; Campbell River 250-287-2101.

Toxic paraplegic shellfish warnings, as well as local fishing closures and openings, are given on the continuous weather broadcasts on VHF radio.

APPENDIX D
Canadian Holidays

The following holidays are observed in British Columbia:

New Year's Day
Good Friday
Easter Monday
Queen's Birthday (by proclamation)
Canada Day (July 1)
Civic Holiday (first Monday in August)
Labour Day (first Monday in September)
Thanksgiving Day (by proclamation)
Remembrance Day (November 11)
Christmas Day
Boxing Day (first working day after Christmas)

APPENDIX E
Sources of Charts, Books, & Information

Your ship's chandlery and nautical bookstore can supply you with nautical charts and books listed in the Bibliography. The following sources are those we have used for quick and reliable mail orders:

Armchair Sailor
2110 Westlake Ave North
Seattle, WA 98109
Tel: 800-875-0852, 206-283-0858; fax: 206-285-1935

Carries extensive selection of nautical books, including cruising guidebooks for the world; chart coverage for the Pacific and Caribbean, as well as U.S. charts in black and white.

Ecomarine Ocean Kayak Centre
1668 Duranleau Street
Vancouver, B.C. V6H 3S4
Canada
Tel: 604-689-7575; fax: 604-689-5926;
email: cladner @direct.ca

Collection of nautical charts and publications for the B.C. coast; extensive book selection on marine and natural history.

Kitsilano Marine Supply Ltd.
1530 West 2nd Avenue
Vancouver, B.C. V6J 1H2
Canada
Tel: 604-736-8891; fax: 604-732-8176

Full selection of nautical charts and books.

Nanaimo Maps and Charts
8 Church Street,
Nanaimo, B.C. V9R 5H4
Canada
Tel: 800-665-2513, 250-754-2513;
fax 800-553-2313

Carries one of the largest selections of NOAA and Canadian Charts north to the Arctic.

Shipwrite Productions
P.O. Box 5041 Station "B"
Victoria, B.C. V8R 6N3
Canada
Tel: 250-360-2717

Publisher of Higgins Passage, Kitasu Bay and maps incorporating the best local knowledge available. Kevin's Notes is a book of tables of useful information concerning the north coast.

Tanners Books and Gifts
2436 Beacon Street
Sidney, B.C. V8L 4X3
Canada
Tel: 250-656-2345; fax 250-656-0662

Full selection of nautical charts and books.

TOURIST OFFICES

Kitimat Chamber of Commerce
P.O. Box 214
Kitimat, B.C. V8C 2G7
Tel: 250-632-6294; 800-664-6554;
fax: 250-632-4685

North by Northwest Tourism Association
P.O. Box 1030
Smithers, B.C. V0J 2N0
Tel: 250-847-5227; 800-663-8843;
fax: 250-847-7585

Tourism British Columbia
Parliament Buildings
Victoria, B.C. V8V 1X4
Tel: 800-663-6000

Travel Infocentre
P.O. Box 669 (NW)
Prince Rupert, B.C. V8J 3S1
Tel: 250-624-5637, 800-667-1994;
fax: 250-627-8009

Travel Infocentre
Queen Charlotte City
Tel: 250-559-4742

BRITISH COLUMBIA PROVINCIAL MARINE PARKS

British Columbia has 54 outstanding Provincial Marine Parks, most of which offer recreational sites for cruising boats free of charge, and eight of which have mooring buoys. Most of these parks are located in the South Coast and along Vancouver Island. The Penrose-Walbran Islands complex on the Central Coast is an undeveloped marine park. A map showing the Coastal Marine Parks of British Columbia is available on all B.C. ferries and at Visitors Centers. For further information or to request a map, contact:

Ministry of Environment, Lands & Parks
2nd Floor, 800 Johnson Street
Victoria, B.C. V84 1X4
Tel 250-387-5002; fax 250-387-5757

Hakai Recreation Area; Penrose & Walbran Islands Marine Park
B.C. Parks
Cariboo District
181 First Ave. North
Williams Lake, B.C. V2G 1Y8
250-398-4414

(This is also the address for the Tweedsmuir Park east of Bella Coola.)

Gwaii Haanas / South Moresby National Park Reserve
P.O. Box 37
Queen Charlotte City, B.C. V0T 1S0
Tel: 250-559-8818; fax: 250-559-8366;
e-mail:Gwaiicom@island.net

GUIDE SERVICES

Kitimat, Garnder Canal, Kitlope
Norman Wagner:
Exodus Sailing Adventures
49 Braun Street
Kitimat, B.C. V8C 2J1
Tel: 250-639-9650; fax: 250-632-5619

Kitlope, Queen Charlotte Islands
Duen Sailing Adventures
Michael & Manon Hobbis
c/o 876 Westview Crescent
North Vancouver, B.C. V7N 3Y2
Tel & fax: 604-474-0569

Kutzeymateen Grizzly Bear Reserve
Ecosummer: 800-465-8848
or 250-669-7741
Sunchaser Charters (Dan Wakeman):
250-624-5472

Queen Charlottes
John De Groete, M. V. *Clavella*
Magna Yachting Ltd.
P.O. Box 866
Nanaimo, B.C. V9R 5N2
Tel: 250-753-3751, fax: 250-755-4014

Sail Secord
P.O. Box 181
Bowen Island, B.C. V0N 1G0
Tel: 250-947-2413, fax: 250-947-0633

Moresby Explorers
Tel: 250-637-2215

Queen Charlotte Adventures
Tel: 250-559-8990

APPENDIX E (continued)

Haisla Nation Kitlope Declaration

(used with permission of the Haisla Nation)

We, the Henaaksiala (Haisla People) of Hudusdawachsdu (the Kitlope), have known, loved and guarded the Kitlope Valley for untold, uncounted centuries. Here our people have been born, have lived out their lives, and returned to the Earth, at one with the land.

For we do not own this land so much as the land owns us. The land is part of us, and we are part of the land.

It is given to us only as a trust: to live within its boundaries in beauty and harmony, to nourish our bodies and spirits with its gifts, and to protect it from harm.

We have a solemn, sacred duty to keep faith with those who came before us, who guarded and protected this land for us; we must do no less for ourselves and for those who come after.

Long before, our people set down laws to protect the land, the waters, the animals, the fish and the forests. These laws are embodied in our ancient title to the land, a title which has never been surrendered or extinguished, and which remains in full force for us today.

These laws require that we make it known to all:

To those who would despoil our land; we will oppose any proposals or acts that threaten the lands, waters and living creatures of the Kitlope. You will find us implacable, for we are protecting the very core of our existence as a people.

To those who would approach us in friendship and harmony, who would join us in wonder and respect for this place; our laws require that we make you welcome, and share our most precious gifts with you. You are welcome here; we know that once you have seen and felt this place, you cannot leave here unmoved and unchanged.

—*Chief Council Gerald Amos on behalf of the Haisla Nation*

For more information on the Kitlope phone the Nanakila Institute in Kitimaat Village 250-632-3308 or Ecotrust Canada 604-682-4141.

Sources for Information on the Kermodei (Spirit Bear)

Both Charles Russel's book *Spirit Bear: Encounters with the White Bear of the Western Rain Forest* (1994) and Jeff and Sue Turner's documentary film can be obtained from the Great Bear Foundation, Box 2699, Missoula, Montana, 59806, phone 406-721-3009. Another organization working hard for wilderness in British Columbia is the Valhalla Wilderness Society, Box 224, New Denver, British Columbia VOG ISO, phone 250-358-2333. Both groups have interesting newsletters and are worthy of support. Be aware that if you have cruised in northern British Columbian waters, you have gained first-hand credibility that could be valuable in the campaign to extend environmental protection. Let the politicians know how you feel after seeing the land and sea involved in the Spirit Bear idea.

APPENDIX F
Key VHF Radio Channels

Emergency
16—Calling and distress
22A—Working Channel
06—Ship-to-ship safety
13—Bridge-to-bridge
Search & Rescue Telephone Numbers
B.C: 800-742-1313

Weather Channels
WX-1—Alert Bay, Comox, Klemtu
WX-2—Calvert I., Seattle
WX-3—Victoria, Cumshewa, Kitimat, Vancouver
21 B—Vancouver, Victoria, Alert Bay, Mt. Hays

Canadian Marinas & Yacht Clubs
68—South of Campbell River
73—North of Campbell River

Marine Telephone Operators
02—Cape Caution
03—Rivers Inlet
23—Courtenay, Vancouver, Calvert I.
24—Port Hardy, East Thurlow Island, Douglas/Grenville Ch., Prince Rupert
25—Vancouver, Port Angeles, Bella Bella
27—Campbell River, Victoria, Ganges, Prince Rupert
64—Ganges, Campbell River
85—West Vancouver, Sechelt, Alert Bay, Dundas I., Smith Sound
86—Sechelt, Alert Bay
87—Nanaimo, Swindle I., Bellingham, Whidbey I.
88—Vancouver

Ship-to-Ship
68, 69, 72, 78

Vessel Traffic Services
11—Vancouver, Sector 1 (southern Strait of Georgia)
11—Prince Rupert, Cape Caution to north end of Grenville Channel
12—Vancouver, Sector 3 (Vancouver Hbr)
14—Seattle
71—Vancouver, Sector 4 (north of Strait of Georgia)
71—Prince Rupert, north of Grenville Channel
74—Vancouver, Sector 2 (Fraser River)
74—Tofino (west coast of Vancouver Island)

APPENDIX G
Summer Wind Reports

The following wind reports show percentages of wind speeds for May through September for typical Inside Passage areas:

Herbert Island *(North of Goletas Channel near Pine Island where Queen Charlotte Strait meets Queen Charlotte Sound)*

May, winds less than 20 knots 88%; 20 to 33 knots 8%; winds greater than 34 knots 3%
June, winds less than 20 knots 94%; 20 to 33 knots 6%
July, winds less than 20 knots 97%; 20 to 33 knots 3%
August, winds less than 20 knots 97%; 20 to 33 knots 3%
September, winds less than 20 knots 94%; 20 to 33 knots 5%; winds greater than 34 knots 1%

Egg Island *(Queen Charlotte Sound, east)*

May, winds less than 20 knots 92%; 20 to 30 knots 8%; winds greater than 34 knots 1%
June, winds less than 20 knots 94%; 20 to 30 knots 5%; winds greater than 34 knots 1%
July, winds less than 20 knots 96%; 20 to 30 knots 3%; winds greater than 34 knots nil
August ,winds less than 20 knots 95%; 20 to 30 knots 4%; winds greater than 34 knots nil
September, winds less than 20 knots 92%; 20 to 30 knots 7%; winds greater than 34 knots 1%

Bonilla Island *(B.C. coast, central, west of Banks Island)*

May, winds less than 20 knots 75%; 20 to 30 knots 23%; winds greater than 34 knots 2%
June, winds less than 20 knots 82%; 20 to 30 knots 17%; winds greater than 34 knots 1%
July, winds less than 20 knots 88%; 20 to 30 knots 11%; winds greater than 34 knots nil
August, winds less than 20 knots 86%; 20 to 30 knots 13%; winds greater than 34 knots 1%
September, winds less than 20 knots 77%; 20 to 30 knots 22%; winds greater than 34 knots 1%

Triple Island *(Dixon Entrance, east of Dundas Island)*

May, winds less than 20 knots 84%; 20 to 30 knots 15%; winds greater than 34 knots 1%
June, winds less than 20 knots 87%; 20 to 30 knots 13%; winds greater than 34 knots nil
July, winds less than 20 knots 92%; 20 to 30 knots 8%; winds greater than 34 knots nil
August, winds less than 20 knots 91%; 20 to 30% 9%; winds greater than 34 knots nil
September, winds less than 20 knots 85%; 20 to 30 knots 14%; winds greater than 34 knots 1%

Cape St. James *(off South Moresby Island)*

May, winds less than 20 knots 71%; 20 to 33 knots 26%; winds greater than 36 knots 3%
June, winds less than 20 knots 74%; 20 to 33 knots 24%; winds greater than 36 knots 2%
July, winds less than 20 knots 75%; 20 to 33 knots 24%; winds greater than 36 knots 1%
August, winds less than 20 knots 79%; l 20 to 33 knots 20%; winds greater than 36 knots 1%
September, winds less than 20 knots 74%; 20 to 33 knots 23%; winds greater than 36 knots 3%

Bibliography & References

Anderson, Hugo. *North to Alaska.* Anacortes: Anderson Publishing Company, 1993.

________ *Secrets of Cruising The New Frontier, British Columbia Coast and Undiscovered Inlets.* Anacortes: Anderson Publishing Company, 1995.

Brower, Kenneth. *The Starship and the Canoe.* New York: Harper & Row, 1978.

The Call of the Coast. Edited by Charles Lillard. Victoria: Horsdal & Schubart, 1992.

Canadian Tide and Current Tables, Pacific Coast, Vols. 5 and 6 [issued annually]. Ottawa: Department of Fisheries and Oceans, 1993.

Capt'n Jack's Current Atlas, Pacific Northwest: Queen Charlotte Strait south to Puget Sound. Port Ludlow, Washington: Marine Trade Publications, Inc., published annually.

Carey, Neil G. *A Guide to the Queen Charlotte Islands.* Vancouver: Raincoast Books, 1995.

Carey, Neil G. *Puffin Cove, Escape to the Wilderness of the Queen Charlotte Islands.* Surrey, British Columbia: Hancock House Publishers Ltd., 1989.

Chappell, John. *Cruising beyond Desolation Sound.* Surrey, B.C.: Naikoon Marine, 1979, revised edition 1987.

To the Charlottes. George Dawson's 1878 Survey of the Queen Charlotte Islands. Edited by Douglas Cole and Bradley Lockner. Vancouver, UBC Press, 1993.

Chittenden, Newton H. *Exploration of the Queen Charlotte Islands.* Burnaby, British Columbia: Fireweed Enterprises Inc., 1984, first published in Victoria, British Columbia,1884.

Conner, Daniel, and Miller, Lorraine. *Master Mariner.* Vancouver: Douglas & McIntyre, 1978.

Dalzell, Kathleen E. *The Queen Charlotte Islands 1774–1966 (Volume 1).* Queen Charlotte City, British Columbia: Bill Ellis, Publisher, 1988.

Dalzell, Kathleen E. *The Queen Charlotte Islands, Places and Names (Volume 2).* Madeira Park, British Columbia: Harbour Publishing, 1993.

Dawson, Will. *Coastal Cruising.* Vancouver: Mitchell Press, 1959.

Douglass, Don. *Exploring Vancouver Island's West Coast, A Cruising Guide.* Bishop, California: Fine Edge Productions, 1994.

Douglass, Don, and Hemingway-Douglass, Réanne. *Exploring the Inside Passage to Alaska—a Cruising Guide.* Bishop, California: Fine Edge Productions, 1995.

_________. *Exploring the South Coast of British Columbia, Gulf Islands and Desolation Sound to Port Hardy & Blunden Harbour.* Bishop, California: Fine Edge Productions, 1996.

Fox, William T. *At the Sea's Edge.* New York: Prentice Hall Press, 1983.

Graham, Donald. *Lights of the Inside Passage.* Madeira Park, British Columbia: Harbour Publishing Co. Ltd., 1986.

Harbo, Rick M. *Guide to the Western Seashore.* Surrey, British Columbia: Hancock House Publishers Ltd., 1988.

Hill, Beth and Ray. *Indian Petroglyphs of the Pacific Northwest.* Saanichton, British Columbia: Hancock House Publishers Ltd., 1974.

Horn, Elizabeth L. *Coastal Wildflowers of the Pacific Northwest.* Missoula: Mountain Press Publishing Company, 1994.

The Journals and Letters of Sir Alexander Mackenzie. Edited by W. Kaye Lamb. Cambridge: The Hakluyt Society, 1970.

Kozloff, Eugene N. *Plants and Animals of the Pacific Northwest.* Seattle: University of Washington Press, 1976.

Large, R. Geddes. *The Skeena, River of Destiny.* Surrey, British Columbia: Heritage House Publishing Company Ltd., 1996.

Lawrence, Iain. *Far-Away Places, 50 Anchorages on the Northwest Coast.* Victoria: Orca Book Publishers, 1995.

Lillard, Charles. *Just East of Sundown, the Queen Charlotte Islands.* Victoria: Horsdal & Schubart, 1995.

Loudon, Pete. *Anyox, The Town That Got Lost.* Sidney, British Columbia: Gray's Publishing Ltd., 1973.

MacDonald, George F. *Ninstints: Haida World Heritage Site.* Vancouver: University of British Columbia Press, 1983.

Marine Weather Hazards Manual, a guide to local forecasts and conditions, 2nd Edition. Vancouver: Environment Canada, 1990.

Nehls, Harry B. *Familiar Birds of the Northwest.* Portland: Portland Audubon Society, 1981.

Northwest Boat Travel. Anacortes: Anderson Publishing Company, published annually.

Pacific Coast, List of Lights, Buoys and Fog Signals. Canadian Coast Guard, Marine Navigation Services, 1992.

Paterson, T.W. *British Columbia Shipwrecks.* Langley, British Columbia: Mr. Paperback, 1983.

Renner, Jeff. *Northwest Marine Weather, from the Columbia River to Cape Scott.* Seattle: The Mountaineers, 1993.

Rogers, Fred. *Shipwrecks of British Columbia.* West Vancouver: J.J. Douglas Ltd., 1973.

Sailing Directions—British Columbia Coast (North Portion). Ottawa: Department of Fisheries and Oceans, Vol. 2, Twelfth Edition, 1991.

Sailing Directions —British Columbia Coast (South Portion), Ottawa: Department of Fisheries and Oceans, Vol. 1, Fifteenth Edition, 1990.

Small Fishing Vessel Safety Manual. Ottawa: Minister of Supply and Services, 1993.

Snively, Gloria. *Exploring the Seashore.* West Vancouver: Gordon Soules Book Publishers Ltd., 1978, sixth printing, 1985.

Thomson, Richard E. *Oceanography of the British Columbia Coast.* Ottawa: Department of Fisheries and Oceans, Fisheries and Aquatic Sciences 56, 1981.

Upton, Joe. *Journeys through the Inside Passage.* Bothell, Washington: Alaska Northwest Books, 1992.

________. *The Coastal Companion, A Guide for the Alaska-Bound Traveler.* Bainbridge Island, Washington: Coastal Publishing, 1995.

The Voyage of George Vancouver 1791–1795. Volumes I–IV. Edited by W. Kaye Lamb. London: The Hakluyt Society, 1984.

Walbran, Captain John T. *British Columbia Coast Names.* Vancouver: Douglas & McIntyre, 1971.

Waldon, Bob. *Feeding Winter Birds in the Pacific Northwest.* Seattle: The Mountaineers, 1994.

Wise, Ken C. *Cruise of the 'Blue Flujin'.* Fowlerville, Michigan: Wilderness Adventure Books, 1987.

Index

Please Note: Names in italics refer to sidebars

Aaltanhash Inlet, 204
About the Authors, 431
Absalom Cove, 330
Ada Cove, 97
Adams Harbour, 110
Addenbroke Light Station, 79
Addenbroke Point Cove, 77
Admiral Group, 127
Advice from Local Expert , 381
Ahclakerho Channel, 56
Ala Narrows, 313
Ala Passage North, 313
Ala Passage South, 311
Alarm Cove, 99
Alexander Inlet, 201
Alexander Mackenzie Rock Provincial Park, 150
Alexandra Passage, 48
Alice Arm, 359
Alice Arm Settlement, 361
Alison Sound, 39
Allard Bay, 71
Allcroft Point Cove, 318
Alliford Bay, 385
Allison Harbour, 22
Alpha Bay, 327
Alston Cove, 221
Anchor Bight, 53
Anchor Cove, 387
Anchor Cove, Quascilla Bay, 57
Anchor Islands Cove, 42
Anderson Passage, 304
Anger Inlet, 314
Angler Cove, 248
Anna Inlet, 399
Annie's Inlet, 326
Anthony Island Cove, 418
Anthony Island Provincial Park, 417
Anvil Cove
Anyox, 364
Argyh Cove, 232
Aristazabal Island, West Coast, 227
Armentieres Channel, 390
Around the Next Point, 238
Arthur Island, Cove Northwest of, 189
Arthur Passage, 287
Atkins Bay, 264
Bachelor Bay, 143
Back Door Anchorage, 120
Bag Harbour, 411
Bainbridge Cove, 157
Baker Inlet, 283
Baker Point, 227
Bamford Lagoon, 355
Banks Island, Gung Ho Bay, 305
Banks Island, Unnamed Inlet, 309
Barnard Harbour, 238
Bay of Plenty, 222
Bears and Boats, 378
Bearskin Bay, Queen Charlotte City, 384
Beattie Anchorage, 392
Beaumont Island, 157
Beaver Passage, 325
Belize Inlet, 36
Bella Bella, 99
Bella Coola, 144
Belle Bay, 369
Bent Harbour
Bentinck, North Arm, 143
Bentinck, South Arm, 145
Beresford Inlet, 404
Berry Inlet, 104
Betteridge Inlet, 301
Bibliography & References, 425
Big Bay, 347
Big Bay, Desbrisay Bay, 193
Big Frypan Bay, 65
Bigsby Inlet, Darwin Sound, 402
Billy Bay, 331
Bischof Islands, One Foot Rock Cove, 404
Bish Bay, Emsley Cove, 265
Bishop Bay Hot Springs, 248
Bitter End Cove, 87
Bitter End, Roscoe Inlet, 161
Blair Inlet, 210
Bloxam Passage, 288
Blunden Bay, 47
Blunden Harbour, 20
Boat Inlet, 187
Bob Bay, 126
Boddy Narrows, 130
Bolin Bay, 198
Bombproof Anchorage, 120
Bone Anchorage, 234
Bonilla Island, 324
Borrowman Bay, Turtish Harbour, 230
Boswell Cove, 59
Boswell Inlet, 58
Bottleneck Inlet, 195
Boukind Bay, 160
Brant Bay, 243
Bremner Bay, 114
Briggs First Narrows, 167
Briggs First Narrows Cove, 165
Briggs Inlet, 165
Briggs Lagoon, 169
Briggs Lagoon, Southeast Cove, 169
Briggs Second Narrows, 168
Broad Bay, 55
Brown Cove, 201
Brown Passage, 338
Browning Entrance, 323
Brundige Inlet, 340
Brydon Anchorage, 116
Brydon Channel, 116
Bryneldson Bay, 147
Buchan Inlet, 309
Buie Creek, 222
Bull Cove, 54
Bulley Bay, 190
Bullock Channel, 170
Bullock Channel North Cove, 171
Bullock Channel, Island (35) Cove, 171
Bullock Channel, Island (45) Cove, 171
Bullock Channel, Mouth of Bay, 171
Bullock Spit Cove, 170
Burke Channel, 137
Burke Channel, Upper (above Cathedral Point), 142
Burnaby Narrows, Dolomite Narrows, 411
Burnaby Strait, 410
Burnett Bay, 44
Burns Bay, Mink Trap Bay, 310
Butedale, 205
Butedale Restoration Project, 205
Butler Cove, Stephens Island, 338
Butze Rapids, 295
Calvert Island, 110
Cameron Cove, 239
Campania Sound, 236
Campbell Island Inlet, 123
Canadian Holidays, 422
Canal Bight, 99
Canaveral Passage, Port Canaveral, 316
Canoe Cove, 76
Cape Calvert, 76
Cape Caution, 45
Captain Cove, 319
Car Point Notch, 369
Carlson Inlet, 154
Carmichael Passage, 392
Carolina Island Anchorage, 345
Carter Bay, 197
Cascade Inlet, 151
Casey Cove, 293
Catala Passage, 211
Cathedral Point Cove, 141
Cavin Cove, 100
Cecil Cove, 395
Chalmers Anchorage, 288
Chappell Cove, 25
Chapple Inlet Lagoon, 235
Chapple Inlet, Doig Anchorage, 234
Chapple Inlet, Kiln Bay, 235
Charlotte Bay, 29
Chatham Sound, 288
Chatham Sound, Western Side, 334
Cheenis Lake, Cove East of Chettleburgh Point Cove, 234
Chief Mathews Bay, 257
Chief Nollis Bay, 40
Chismore Passage, 288
Choked Passage, 110
Christie Bay, 387
Clam Inlet, 339
Clarke Cove, 236
Clatse Bay, 159
Clear Passage, 314
Clement Rapids, 239
Clifford Bay, 229
Clio Bay, 265
Clothes Bay, Klemtu Anchorage, 194
Coastal Bird Occurrences, 321
Cockle Bay, 188
Codville Lagoon, 95
Coghlan Anchorage, 272
Colby Bay, 315
Collins Bay, 251
Commando Inlet, 226
Connis Cove, 327
Convoy, Patrol, Fairmile, Souvenir and Sweeper Island Passages, 79
Cooper Inlet, 98
Corney Cove, 216
Cornwall Inlet and Drake Inlet, 239
Cougar Bay, 201
Cougar Inlet, 25
Cousins Inlet, 148
Cove East of Cheenis Lake, 182
Cove East of Westcott Point, 21
Cove Northwest of Arthur Island, 189
Cove Southeast of Latta Island , 122
Cow Bay (PRRYC), 294
Cowards Cove , 217
Crab Cove, 92
Crab Trap Cove, Porcher Island, 331
Crack, The, Upper Burke Channel, 142
Crane Bay, 242
Crescent Inlet, 398
Crow Lagoon, 354
Croyden Bay, 142
Culpepper Lagoon, 193
Cultus Bay, 122
Cultus Sound, 120
Cumshewa Inlet and Approach, 391
Cunningham Passage, 347
Curlew Bay, 242
Curtis Inlet, 312
Dana Passage, 397
Darby Channel, 69
Darwin Soound, Bigsby Inlet, 402
David Bay, 199
Dawson Harbour, 390
Dawsons Landing, 70
De Cosmos Lagoon, 94
De Freitas Islets, 189
De la Beche Cove, 407
De la Beche Inlet, 406
Dean Channel, 147
Dearth Island Cove, 163
Deep Anchorage, 120
Denise Inlet, 295
Desbrisay Bay, Big Bay, 193
Devastation Channel, 260
Devlin Bay, 299
Dillon Bay, 242
Discovery Coast, 137
Discovery Cove, 165
Distance Tables, 420
Dixon Inlet, East, 351
Doben Island Passage, Vancouver Cove, 365
Dodd Passage, 348
Dodge Cove, 294
Dodwell North Cove, 123
Dodwell South Cove, 123
Doig Anchorage, Chapple Inlet, 234
Dolomite Narrows, Burnaby Narrows, 411
Dolphin Lagoon, 329
Domestic Tranquility Cove, 114
Don Peninsula Inlet, 173
Donkey Cove, 389
Dory Passage, 315
Double Eagle Cove, 29
Douglas Channel, 268
Drake Inlet and Cornwall Inlet, 239
Draney Inlet, 71
Draney Narrows, 71
Dries Inlet, 334
Drumlummon Bay, Foch Lagoon, 270
Dsulish Bay, 51
Dsulish Bay, East Cove, 52
Dudevoir Passage, 349
Duncan Bay, 345
Duncanby Cove, 61
Duncanby Landing, 62
Dundas Island, Brundige Inlet, 340
Dundas Islands, 339
Dundivan Inlet, 104
Dunn Bay, 156
Dunn Passage, Weinburg Inlet, 303
Dyer Cove, 209

Eagle Bay, 263
Eagle Cove, Stagoo Creek, 359
East Anchorage, Ellerslie Bay, 178
East Cove, Dsulish Bay, 52
East Inlet, Inner Basin, 281
East Narrows, Skidegate Channel, 389
Echo Cove, 357
Echo Harbour, 400
Eclipse Narrows, 32
Edith Harbour, 340
Edward Channel, 112
Edye Passage, 335
Egg Island, 48
Elcho Harbour, 150
Eliza Bay, 60
Elizabeth Lagoon, 83
Ellerslie Bay, 178
Ellerslie Bay, East Anchorage, 178
Ellerslie Falls, 179
Ellerslie Lagoon Entrance, 180
Ellerslie Lagoon, First Narrows, 179
Ellerslie Lake,
Ellis Bay, 30
Emily Bay, 167
Emily Carr Cove,
Emily Carr Inlet, 235
Emsley Cove, "Old Town" or "Bish Bay", 265
End of the World Inlet, 128
Engineering Feat: Kemano Power Station, 256
Estevan Sound, 297
Ethelda Bay, 300
Ethel Cove, 56
Eucott Bay, 151
Europa Bay, 252
Europa Hot Springs, 252
Evans Inlet, 96
Every Nook and Cranny, Gildersleeve Bay, 80
Evinrude Inlet, 226
Evinrude Inlet Bight, 226
Evinrude Passage, 314
Exploring the West Coast, 227
Exposed Anchorage, 65
Exposed Inlet, 281
Fairmile Passage, 79
Fallen Human Bay, 344
Fancy Cove, 97
Fannie Cove, 98
Farrant Island Lagoon, 277
Farwest Cove, 339
Fern Passage, 295
Fifer Bay, 78
Fifer Cove, Laredo Inlet, 221
Finis Nook, 59
Finlayson Channel, 194
Finn Bay, 70
First Narrows Cove, Briggs Inlet, 165
First Narrows, Ellerslie Lagoon, 179
Fish Egg Inlet, 79
Fish Trap Bay, 87
Fish Weir Cove, Spiller Channel, 177
Fisher Channel, 95
Fisher Point, The Watchmen, 105
Fisherman Cove, 276
Fishhook Bay, 71
Fishing Regulations, Sources, 422
Fishtrap Bay, Verney Passage, 250
Fitz Hugh Sound, 75
Five Meter Hole, 174
Five Window Cove, 67
Fjordland, 185, 201
Float Camp Cove, 70
Flotsam & Jetsam Cove, 231
Fly Basin, 54
Foch Lagoon, Drumlummon Bay, 270
Fords Cove, 371
Forit Bay, 156
Fougner Bay, 139
Fouled Prop—A High Latitude Emergency, 346
Fox Islands, 42
Frederick Bay, 31
Frederick Sound, 32
Freeman Passage, 329
Freeman Passage Mooring Buoys, 330
Freshwater Cove, Hoya Passage, 401
Frigate Bay, Safe Entrance, 65
Frypan Bay, 65
Fury Bay, Aristazabal Island
Fury Cove, Schooner Retreat, 63
Gale Passage, 105
Gale Passage Landlocked South Cove, 135
Gardner Canal, 250
Gardner Canal: The Environmentalists' Side, 258
Gasboat Cove, 330
Gasboat Passage, 330
Gee Whiz Nook, 85
Geodetic Cove, 302
Gildersleeve Bay, Every Nook & Cranny Lagoon, 80
Gill Net Cove, 55
Gillatt Arm, Gordon Cove, 392
Gillen Harbour, 298
Gillespie Channel, 299
Gilttoyees Inlet, 269
Glacier Bay and Cove, 371
Goat Cove, 196
Goat Harbour, 248
Gobeil Bay, Mud Bay, 264
Goldstream Harbour, 89
Good Hope, 72
Goodlad Bay, 115
Goose Bay, Rivers Inlet, 62
Goose Group, 119
Goose Island Anchorage, 119
Goose Point Cove, 25
Goosenecks of the Roscoe, 161
Gordon Cove / Moresby Camp Dock, 392
Gosse Bay, 156
Graham Island, 383
Granby Cove, 365
Granite Cove, Kiskosh Inlet, 272
Grant Anchorage, 215
Great Salt Lake Anchorage, 120
Green Bay, 143
Green Inlet, 203
Green Island, 341
Green Island Anchorage, 87
Grenville Channel, 276
Gribbell Islet Anchorage, 345
Grief Bay, 76
Griffin Passage, North Entrance, 197
Griffin Passage, South Entrance, 191
Griffith Harbour, 325
Gullchuck, Kakusdish Harbour, 101
Gunboat Harbour, 286
Gunboat Lagoon Cove, 156
Gunboat Passage, 155
Gung Ho Bay, Banks Island, 305
Gurd Inlet, 333
Gwaii Haanas / South Moresby National Park Reserve, 398
Gwent Cove, 376
Haaksvold Point, 139
Hague Point Lagoon, 219
Hakai Passage, 109
Hakai Recreation Area, 107
Half-Dome Waterfall, 39
Halibut Bay, 368
Hallet Island Cove, 387
Hampden Bay, 156
Hardy Inlet, 73
Harlequin Basin, 93
Harriet Harbour, 414
Hartley Bay, 272
Harvell Islet Cove, 29
Harwood Bay, 304
Hastings Arm, 362
Haswell Bay, 408
Hawk Bay, 243
Hawkbury Island North Bight, 262
Hawkins Narrows, Union Passage, 277
Heater Harbour, 418
Heathorn Bay, 193
Hecate Strait, 382
Helicopter Logging, 154
Helmcken Inlet, 225
Hemasila Inlet, 69
Henderson Bay, 80
Hevenor Inlet, 318
Hewitt Island, 202
Hickey Cove, 58
Hidden Inlet, 375
Hideaway Bay, 268
Hideaway Lodge, 370
Hiekish Narrows, 201
Higgins Lagoon, 214
Higgins Passage, 212
High Waves on Ivory Island, 211
Hochstader Basin, 128
Hochstader Cove, 128
Hodgson Cove, 311
Hodgson Reefs, 346
Holmes Point Cove, 33
Home Bay, Rivers Inlet, 61
Home Bay, Wright Sound, 240, 275
Hoop Bay, 48
Horsefly Cove, 203
Hotspring Island, 405
Hot Springs, Eucott Bay, 152
Houston Stewart Channel, 417
Hoya Passage, Freshwater Cove, 401
Hudson Bay Passage Cove, 339
Humpback Bay, Porcher Island, 334
Hunt Inlet, 334
Hunter Channel, 122
Hunter Channel Complex, 125
Hurricane Anchorage, 117
Huston Inlet, 414
Hutton Inlet, 408
Hutton Island Cove, 408
Hyder, Alaska, 373
Iceberg Bay, 357
Ikeda Cove, 415
Illahie Inlet, 87
Indian Island, 53
Ingram Bay, 183
Inner Basin, East Inlet, 281
Inner Warrior Cove, 92
Intersection Anchorage, 120
Inverness Passage, 290
Ire Inlet, 312
Ironbound Islet, 155
Iroquois Cove, 132
Island (35) Cove, Bullock Channel, 171
Island (45) Cove, Bullock Channel, 171
Ivory Island, 210
Jackson Narrows, 191
Jackson Passage to Klemtu, 191
Jacobsen Bay, 143
James Bay, 192
Jane Cove, 98
Jeannette Islands, 20
Jedway Bay, 413
Jenny Inlet, 150
Jesse Falls, 265
Jesse Falls, 264
Jesus Pocket, 31
Joassa Channel, 130
Joe's Bay, 83
Johnson Channel, 157
Johnston Bay, 71
Jones Cove, 50
Jorgensen Harbour, 215
Juan Perez Sound, 403
Juggins Bay, 359
Kagan Bay, 386
Kakushdish Harbour, Gullchuck, 101
Kayak Cove, 120
Keith Anchorage, 108
Kelp Passage Cove, 288
Kemano Bay, 255
Kemano Power Station, An Engineering Feat, 256
Kent Inlet, 224
Keswar Inlet, 317
Kettle Inlet, 229
Key VHF Radio Channels, 424
Keyarka Cove, 317
Khutze Inlet, 203
Khutzeymateen Inlet, 353
Khutzeymateen Inlet Head, 355
Kid Bay, 197
Kilbella Bay, 72
Kildala Arm, 263
Kildidt Inlet and Lagoon, 115
Kildidt Narrows, 115
Kildidt Sound, 113
Kiln Bay, Chapple Inlet, 235
Kiltik Cove, 94
Kiltuish Inlet, 252
Kimsquit Bay, 155
Kincolith, 356
King Bay, 28
Kingkown Inlet, 325
Kingkown Inlet, 325
Kingsley Point Coves, 129
Kinsman Inlet, 122
Kisameet Bay, 95
Kiskosh Inlet, 271
Kiskosh Inlet, Granite Cove, 272
Kitamaat Village, 265
Kitasu Bay, 217
Kitimat Arm, 264
Kitimat Harbour, 267
Kitkatla, 330
Kitkatla Channel, 330
Kitkatla Inlet, 332
Kitkiata Inlet, 270
Kitlope Bight, 258
Kitlope Valley, 259
Kitlope, Saving the Kitsault, 259
Kitsaway Anchorage, 260

Kittyhawk Cove, 116
Kiwash Cove, 92
Klaquaek Channel, The Lake, 65
Klekane Inlet, 205
Klemtu Anchorage, Clothes Bay, 194
Klemtu Passage, 194
Klewnuggit Inlet, 280
Kliktsoatli Harbour, 100
Kloiya Bay, 295
Koeye River, 90
Kooryet Bay, 307
Kostan Inlet, 402
Kostan Point Cove, 403
Kshwan River, 366
Kumealon Inlet, 283
Kumealon Island Cove, 285
Kumeon Bay, 353
Kwakshua Channel, 107
Kwakume Inlet, 89
Kwakume Point, 89
Kwatna Bay, 140
Kwatna Inlet, 140
Kwinamass Bay, 355
Kxngeal Inlet, 281
Kynoch Inlet, 193
Kynumpt Harbour (Strom Bay and Cove), 103
Labouchere Channel, 146
Lady Trutch Passage, 188
Lagoon Inlet, 394
Lama Passage, 97
Langford Cove, 212
Langley Passage Anchorages, 300
Lapwing Island, 92
Larcom Lagoon, 363
Laredo Channel, 222
Laredo Inlet, 219
Laredo Sound, 217
Larkin Point Basin, 217
Larsen Harbour, 323
Larso Bay, 146
Lassiter Bay, 28
Lawn Point, 383
Lawson Harbour, 287
Lawyer Islands, 288
Lax Kw'Aalams, Port Simpson, 348
Leavitt Lagoon, Stephens Narrows, 307
Leckie Bay Cove, 113
Leroy Bay, 52
Lewall Inlet, 112
Lime Point Cove, 197
Lina Island, 386
Little People, The, 122
Little Thompson Bay and Cove, 134
Lizzie Cove, 99
Local Knowledge, Procedures Used in Documenting, 422
Lockhart Bay, 104
Lockhart Bay, Rait Narrows, 132
Logan Bay, 316
Long Inlet, 388
Long Point Cove, 95
Loretta Island Cove, 262
Louisa Cove, 209
Louise Channel South, 134
Louise Narrows, 393
Lowe Inlet, Nettle Basin (Verney Falls), 279
Lucy Bay, 60
Lundy Cove, 309
Lyell Bay, 401
MacDonald Bay, 240
Mackenzie Rock Provincial Park, Sir Alexander, 150
Magee Channel, 68
Mainland Route across East Dixon Inlet via Portland Inlet, 346
Mantrap Inlet, 80
Manzanita Cove, 352
Maple Bay, 370
Marcus Passage, 289
Margaret Bay, 56
Markle Inlet, 315
Markle Passage, 314
Marmot Bay, 372
Marmot Cove, 205
Marsh Bay, 20
Marshall Inlet, 409
Martins Cove, 100
Mary Cove, 195
Math Islands, 313
Matheson Inlet, 409
Mathieson Channel, 187
Mathieson Narrows, 194
Maunsell Bay, 32
MAYDAY—Griffin Passage, 191
Maze Cove, 123
McBride Bay, 55
McClusky Bay, 82
McCoy Cove, 391
McEchran Cove, 400
McInnes Island Light Station, 211
McKay Bay, 151
McKay Reach, 247
McKinnon Lagoon, 35
McLoughlin Bay, 99
McMicking Inlet, 301
McNaughton Group Anchorages, 120
McRae Cove, 215
Mellis Inlet, 222
Mereworth Sound, 37
Metlakatla Bay and Venn Passage, 343
Meyers Narrows, 215
Meyers Narrows Cove, 216
Meyers Passage, 215
Middle Cove, Fish Egg Inlet, 83
Milbanke Sound, 208
Miles Inlet, 44
Mill Bay, 357
Millbrook Cove, 51
Miller Bay, 295
Miller Inlet, 312
Minette Bay, 267
Mink Trap Bay, Burns Bay, 310
Minnis Bay, 245
Miskatla Inlet, 269
Mitchell Cove, Payne Channel, 245
MK Bay Marina, 266
Monckton Inlet, 306
Monk Bay, 218
Moolock Cove, 310
Moon Bay Marina, 267
Moore Cove, Telegraph Passage, 289
Mooring Buoys, Freeman Passage, 330
Morehouse Bay, 162
Morehouse Passage and Lapwing Island, 92
Moresby Camp Dock, 392
Morgan Bay, 70
Morris Bay, 188
Morse Basin, 295
Moses Inlet, 73
Mosquito Bay, 176
Moss Passage, Sloop Narrows, 188
Mouat Cove, 104
Mouth of Bay, Bullock Channel, 171
Mud Bay, Gobeil Bay, 264
Muir Cove, 212
Murchison Island, 405
Murder Cove, 326
Murray Anchorage, 299
Murray Labyrinth, 23
Mussel Bay, 200
Mussel Inlet, 198
Mustang Bay, 113
Nabannah Bay, 280
Nakwakto Rapids, 26
Nalau Inlet, 111
Nalau Passage, 112
Namu Harbour, 93
Narrows Cove, 85
Nascall Bay, 153
Nascall Island and Rocks, 154
Nash Narrows Cove, Spiller Channel, 178
Nash Passage, 177
Nasoga Gulf, 356
Nass Harbour, 357
Nass Point Cove, 358
Nass River, 356
Nautical Titles from Fine Edge, 431
Naysash Bay, 58
Naysash Inlet, 57
Neekas Cove, 176
Neekas Inlet, 176
Nenahlmai Lagoon, 35
Nepean Sound, 306
Nettle Basin, Lowe Inlet (Verney Falls), 279
Newcombe Harbour, 318
NFG Cove, 114
Ninstints, 417
No Name Bay, 40
Noble Lagoon, 228
Nook, The, Little Thompson Bay, 134
Norman Morrison Bay, 130
North Bentinck Arm, 143
North Pacific Cannery Museum, 290
North Shortcut, 345
Northwest Hecate Island Cove, 111
Nowish Cove, 194
Nugent Sound, 33
Nugent Sound Cove, 34
Oatswish Bay, 199
Observations from Owyacumish Bay, 255
Observatory Inlet, 358
Obstruction Islet, 39
Ocean Falls, 149
Ochwe Bay, 251
Odin Cove, 103
Ogden Channel, 327
Old Town, Emsley Cove, 265
Oliver Cove, 186
One Foot Rock Cove, Bischof Islands, 404
One of the Worst Nights in My Life, 233
Oona River, 286
Open Bight, 60
Ormidale Harbour, 102
Oscar Passage to Klemtu, 190
Osment Inlet, 218
Oswald Bay, 298
Otter Channel, 305
Otter Passage, 305
Outer Cove, Union Passage, 278
Outer Narrows, Slingsby Channel, 42
Owyacumish Bay, 254
Oyster Bay, 87
Pacofi Bay, 396
Palmer Anchorage, 219
Paradise Passage, 350
Parsons Anchorage, 218
Passage Cove, 186
Passages from Smith Sound to Rivers Inlet, 59
Patrol Passage, 79
Patterson Inlet, 310
Pearl Harbour, 347
Pearse Canal, 374
Peck Shoal, 311
Peet Bay, 41
Pemberton Bay, 297
Penn Harbour, 232
Penrose Island, 63
Perceval Narrows, 187
Perry Bay, 361
Peter Bay, 128
Peters Narrows, Union Passage, 279
Petrel Channel Narrows, 319
Petrel Channel North, 320
Petrel Channel South, 318
Philip Inlet, 77
Philip Narrows, 224
Phoenix Creek Cove, 333
Photographing the Bald Eagle, 320
Pictograph Passage, 127
Pictographs, 40
Piddington Island, 127
Pierce Bay, East Cove, West Cove, 69
Poison Cove, 200
Porcher Inlet, 332
Porcher Island,
Porcher Island, Humpback Bay, 334
Porpoise Channel, 291
Porpoise Harbour, 291
Port Blackney, 185
Port Canaveral, Canaveral Passage, 316
Port John, 97
Port Simpson (Lax Kw'Aalams), 348
Port Stephens, 307
Portland Canal, 366
Portland Inlet, 351
Potts Island Hideaway, 130
Power Wash Waterfall, 39
Price Cove, 257
Price Inlet, 214
Primordial Wolf Calls, 240
Prince Rupert, Prince Rupert Harbour, 292
Princess Royal Channel, 202
Princess Royal Island, 185, 207
Principe Channel, 306
Principe Channel, North Entrance, 318
Protection Cove, 48
PRRYC, 294
Pruth Bay, 108
Puffin Cove, 390
Purcell Rock and Ironbound Islet, 155
Qlawdzeet, Squatterie, 338
Quartcha Bay, 161
Quascilla Bay, 57
Queen Charlotte City, Bearskin Bay, 384
Queen Charlotte Islands, 381
Queen Charlotte Sound, 19
Queens Sound, 118
Quigley Creek Cove, 220

Quottoon Narrows Cove, 350
Racey Inlet, 233
Rait Narrows, 132
Rait Narrows, South Cove, 131
Ramsay Passage Cove, 406
Ramsbotham Islands, 224
Rattenbury Point, 148
Raven Cove, 162
Raymond Passage, 129
Raymond Passage Cove, 129
Reba Point Cove, 130
Reef Island, 367
Refuge Bay, 335
Reid Passage, 185
Remotesville Cove, Waterfall Inlet, 85
Rescue Bay, 190
Restoration Bay, 140
Return Channel, 162
Ripley Bay, 159
Rivers Inlet, 60
Rivers Inlet, South Shore, West Home Bay, 72
Rock Inlet, 93
Rockfish Harbour, 396
Rocky Bay, 65
Roderick Cove, 195
Roscoe Creek, 161
Roscoe Inlet, 158
Roscoe Inlet, Bitter End of, 161
Roscoe Narrows, 160
Rose Harbour, 417
Rose Point, 383
Rowley Bay, 28
Rudolf Bay, 217
Rupert Island Passage, 113
Rushbrook Passage, 348
Rushbrooke Floats, 294
Russell Arm, 294
Sac Bay, 407
Safe Cove, 31
Safe Entrance, Frigate Bay, 65
Safety Cove, 76
Sagar Lake Trail, 96
Salmon Arm, 33
Salmon Bay, 190
Salmon Cove, 358
Saltspring Bay, 388
Sanctuary, The, 142
Sandell Bay, 72
Sandfly Bay, 368
Sandspit, 385
Sans Peur Passage, 122
Saving the Kitlope, 259
Schooner Channel, 24
Schooner Passage, 327
Schooner Retreat, 65
Schooner Retreat, Fury Cove, 63
Schwartzenberg Lagoon, 34
Scow Bay, 205
Sea Otter Inlet, 91
Sea Otter South Arm, 91
Seaforth Channel, 102
Seal Cove, 294
Secret Cove, 337
Section Cove, 410
Secure Anchorage, 65
Security Bay, 59
Selwyn Inlet, 395
Separation Point, Split Head, 200
Serpentine Inlet, 334
Sewell Inlet, 395
Seymour Inlet, 27
Seymour River, 33
Sgan Gwaii Cove, 417
Sgan Gwaii World Heritage Site, Anthony Island, 417
Shack Bay, 159
Shaman Cove, 328
Shearwater, 101
Sheep Passage, 197
Shelter Bay North, 21
Shibasha Cove, 328
Ship Anchorage, 280
Shotbolt Bay, 72
Silvester Bay, 45
Skaat Harbour, 410
Skedans Bay, 397
Skeena River Outflow, 275
Skene Cove, 327
Skiakl Bay, 338
Skidegate Channel, 388
Skidegate Channel, East Narrows, 389
Skidegate Channel, West Narrows, 389
Skidegate Inlet to Cumshewa Inlet, 391
Skidegate Inlet to Lawn and Rose Points, 383
Skidegate Landing, 383
Skowquiltz Bay, 188
Skull Cove, 23
Sleepy Bay, 70
Slim Inlet, 413
Slingsby Channel, 41
Slingsby Channel, Outer Narrows, 42
Sloop Narrows, Moss Passage, 188
Smith Inlet, 56
Smith Sound, 59
Smithers Island Cove, 225
Somerville Bay, 353
Sources of Charts, Books & Information, 423
South Bentinck Arm, 145
South Moresby, Gwaii Haanas National Park Reserve, 398
Southeast Lagoon Cove, Briggs Lagoon, 169
Southgate Island, 22
Souvenir Passage, 79
Spicer Island Complex, Spicer Anchorage, 326
Spider Anchorage, 116
Spiller Channel, 172
Spiller Channel, Fish Weir Cove, 177
Spiller Channel, Nash Narrows Cove, 178
Spiller Inlet, 182
Spiller Inlet, Weeping Woman, 182
Spitfire Channel, 117
Spitfire East Cove, 117
Spitfire Lagoon, 118
Spitfire West Cove, 118
Split Head, Separation Point, 200
Squall Bay, 315
Squally Channel, 240
Squatterie, Qlawdzeet, 338
St. John Harbour, 209
St. John Lagoon, 209
Stagoo Creek, Eagle Cove, 359
Stalkungi Cove, 398
Steamer Passage, 353
Steamer Passage, Somerville Island, 353
Stephens Island, Butler Cove, 338
Stephens Narrows, Leavitt Lagoon, 307
Stephens Passage,
Stewart, 373
Stewart Inlet, 115
Storm in Bishop Bay, 250
Stormy Bay, 263
Strachan Bay, 38
Strom Bay, 103
Strom Cove, 103
Strombeck Bay, 362
Stryker Island Nook, 133
Stuart Anchorage, 285
Stumaun Bay, 348
Sue Channel, 261
Sulphur Arm, 84
Summer Wind Reports, 425
Summers Bay, 41
Sunshine Bay, 66
Superstition Point, 118
Superstition Point Cove, 118
Surf Inlet, 232
Surf Inlet Head, 233
Swanson Bay, 203
Sweeper Island Passage, 79
Swordfish Bay, 118
Sylvester Bay, 363
Takush Harbour, 53
Tallheo Hot Springs, 146
Tankeeah River, 172
Target Bay, 113
Tate Cove, 231
Taylor Bay, 68
Telegraph Passage, 289
Thirty-Year Perspective, Puffin Cove, 390
Thistle Passage, 219
Thompson Bay, 132
Thompson Bay, Little, 134
Thompson Cove, Little, 134
Thurston Harbour, 396
Tolmie Channel, 200
Tom Bay, 189
Tom's Cove, 55
Tombstone Bay, 369
Tongass Passage, 377
Totem Inlet, 328
Towry Point East Cove, 32
Towry Point West Cove, 32
Trahey Inlet, 220
Trail Bay, 350
Treadwell Bay, 41
Tree Knob Group, 338
Tribal Group, 132
Triumph Bay, 251
Trotter Bay, 395
Troup Narrows (Deer Passage), 164
Troup Narrows Cove, 164
Trout Bay, 194
Tsamspanaknok Bay, 354
Tsum Tsadai Inlet, 291
Tuck Inlet, 295
Turnbull Inlet, 111
Turquoise Cove, 371
Turtish Harbour, Borrowman Bay, 230
Tuwartz Inlet, 243
Tuwartz Lagoon Cove, 244
Tuwartz Narrows, 243
Underhill Island Coves, 112
Union Passage, Hawkins Narrows, 277
Union Passage, Peters Narrows, 279
Unnamed Cove, Keith Anchorage, 107
Unnamed Cove, Laredo Inlet, 220
Unnamed Inlet, 34
Unnamed Inlet, Banks Island, 309
Upper Burke Channel (above Cathedral Point), 142
Ursula Channel, 247
Vancouver Cove, Doben Island Passage, 365
Venn Passage and Metlakatla Bay, 343
Verney Falls, 279
Verney Passage, 249
Verney Passage, Fishtrap Bay, 250
Vigilance Cove, 43
Village Cove, 38
Visiting the Haisla Peoples, 259
Walbran Island, 63
Wales Cove, 352
Wales Harbour, West Cove, 377
Wales Passage, 351
Wallace Bay, 149
Wallace Bight, 196
Wallace Islands, 21
Walsh Rock, 223
Ward Channel, 111
Warner Bay, 31
Watchmen, The, 105
Waterfall Inlet, Remotesville Cove, 85
Watson Bay, 195
Watt Bay, 114
Watts Narrows, 281
Waump Creek, 41
Wawatle Bay, 30
Weather Puzzle, 254
Weeping Woman, Spiller Inlet, 182
Weeteeam Bay, 227
WeewanieHot Springs, 260
Weinburg Inlet, Dunn Passage, 303
Welcome Harbour, 335
Weld Cove, 221
West Home Bay, Rivers Inlet, South Shore, 61
West Narrows, Skidegate Channel, 389
Westcott Point, Cove East of, 21
Westerman Bay, 37
Whale Channel, 238
Whales Watching Us! 349
Whelakis Lagoon, 36
Whirlwind Bay, 93
Whiskey Bay, 144
Whiskey Bay, Pearse Island, 367
Whisky Cove, 100
Wide Awake Cove, 127
Wigham Cove, 163
Wilcox Group Cove, Kitkatla Inlet, 333
Wilkie Point Cove, 44
Willis Bay, 329
Wilson Bay, 68
Wilson Inlet, 314
Windsor Cove, 139
Windy Bay, Fjordland, 143
Windy Bay, Sheep Passage, 198
Winter Inlet, 376
Withered Point Coves, Lina Island, 386
Woods Lagoon, 35
Work Bay, 196
Work Channel, 349
World War II Names, 116
Worsfold Bay, 350
Worst Horseflies I've Ever Experienced, 270
Wright Inlet, 312
Wright Sound, 275
Wyclees Lagoon, 58
Yeo Cove, 173
Zumtela Bay, 350

About the Authors

Over the past twenty-five years Don Douglass and Réanne Hemingway-Douglass have sailed from 60° N to 56° S latitude—from Alaska to Cape Horn—logging 150,000 miles of offshore cruising. They consider the cruising grounds of British Columbia some of the finest in the world and an unending source of excitement and pleasure. They now spend summers on their diesel trawler, *Baidarka,* cruising in British Columbia and Alaska.

Don Douglass began exploring Northwest waters in 1949 when he circumnavigated Guemes Island in a skiff. He has sailed the Inside Passage on everything from a 26-foot pleasure craft and a commercial fishing boat to a Coast Guard icebreaker. Don holds a BSEE degree from California State University, Pomona, and a Masters in Business Economics from Claremont Graduate School. He is the author of *Exploring Vancouver Island's West Coast* and, co-authored with Réanne the acclaimed *Exploring the Inside Passage to Alaska* and *Exploring the South Coast of British Columbia.* Their articles have appeared in *Pacific Yachting* and other outdoor magazines. In Valparaiso, Chile, Don was given an honorary membership in the International Association of Cape Horners. He has written several skiing and mountain biking guidebooks and, as a father of the sport, was elected to the Mountain Biking Hall of Fame in Crested Butte, Colorado.

Réanne Hemingway-Douglass holds a degree in French from Pomona College. She attended the University of Grenoble, France, and Claremont Graduate School. A former French instructor, Réanne is now an editor and writer. Her book, *Cape Horn: One Man's Dream, One Woman's Nightmare,* which describes their pitchpoling 800 miles northwest of Cape Horn, and their self-rescue in the seas and channels of Patagonia, has been well received nationally and in South America and is currently being translated into French. Réanne led the first women's team to bicycle across Tierra del Fuego.

Authors at Ellerslie Falls

In addition to their sailing experience, the Douglasses have kayaked extensively in the Northwest, and together they founded International Mountain Bicycling Association (IMBA), a non-profit foundation. Their company, Fine Edge Productions, publishes outdoor guidebooks and detailed topographical maps.

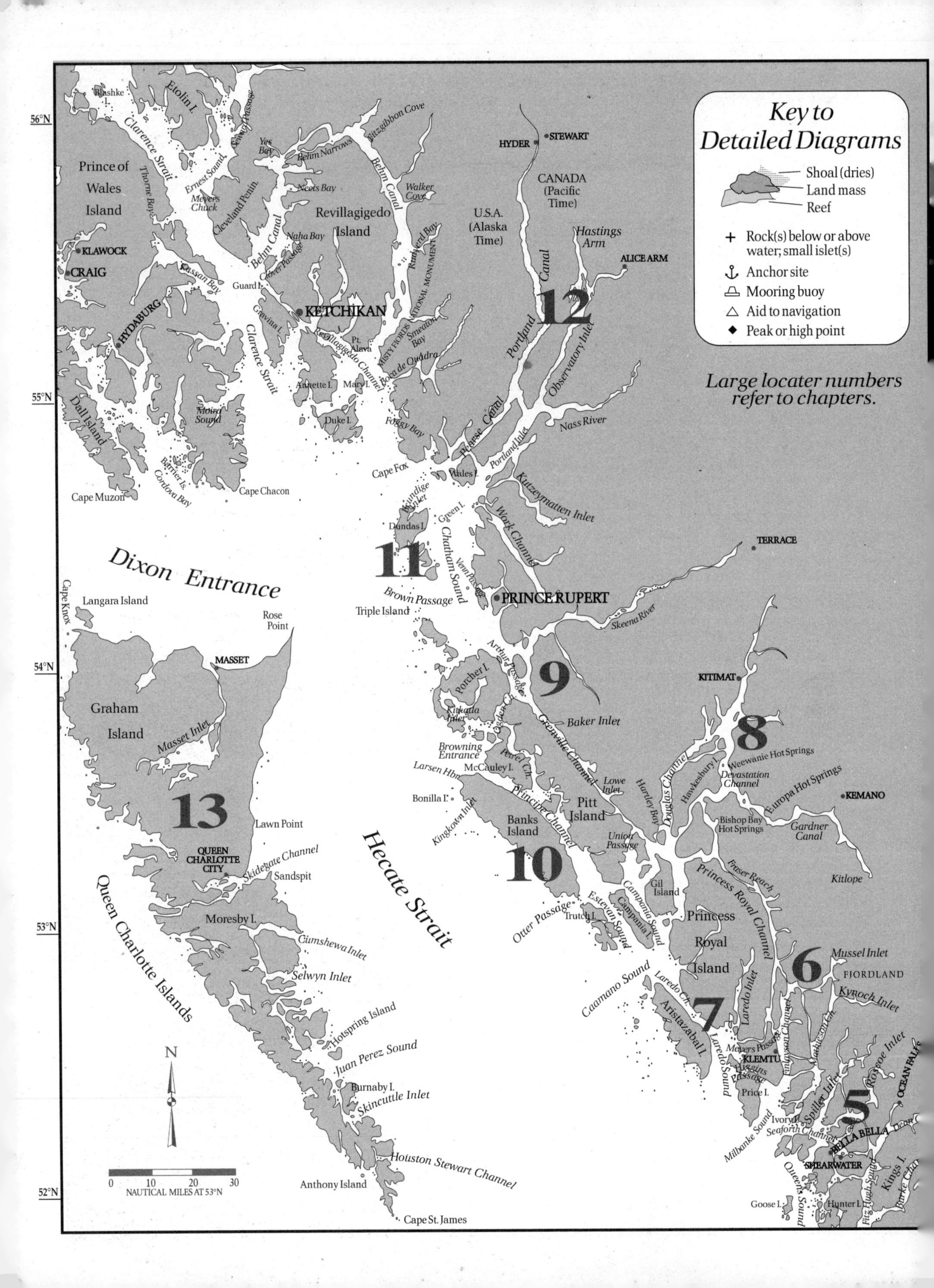

Key to Detailed Diagrams
Shoal (dries)
Land mass
Reef
Rock(s) below or above water; small islet(s)
Anchor site
Mooring buoy
Aid to navigation
Peak or high point
Large locater numbers refer to chapters.
56°N
55°N
54°N
53°N
52°N
Etolin I.
Clarence Strait
Prince of Wales Island
Thorne Bay
Ernest Sound
Meyers Chuck
Cleveland Penin.
Yes Bay
Behm Narrows
Fitzgibbon Cove
Neets Bay
Behm Canal
Walker Cove
Revillagigedo Island
Naha Bay
Clover Passage
Rudyerd Bay
MISTY FIORDS NATIONAL MONUMENT
KLAWOCK
CRAIG
Kasaan Bay
Guard I.
KETCHIKAN
HYDABURG
Gravina I.
Revillagigedo Channel
Pt. Alava
Smeaton Bay
Boca de Quadra
Annette I.
Mary I.
Dall Island
Moira Sound
Duke I.
Foggy Bay
Barrier Is.
Cordova Bay
Cape Muzon
Cape Chacon
Cape Fox
Wales I.
HYDER
STEWART
CANADA (Pacific Time)
U.S.A. (Alaska Time)
Hastings Arm
ALICE ARM
Portland Canal
12
Observatory Inlet
Pearse Canal
Portland Inlet
Nass River
Kutzeymatten Inlet
Dundas I.
Green I.
Chatham Sound
Work Channel
11
Venn Passage
Dixon Entrance
Cape Knox
Langara Island
Rose Point
Brown Passage
Triple Island
PRINCE RUPERT
TERRACE
Skeena River
MASSET
Arthur Passage
Porcher I.
9
Graham Island
Masset Inlet
Kitkatla Inlet
Ogden Ch.
Baker Inlet
Grenville Channel
KITIMAT
8
Browning Entrance
Petrel Ch.
Larsen Hbr.
McCauley I.
Lowe Inlet
Hartley Bay
Douglas Channel
Hawkesbury I.
Weewanie Hot Springs
Devastation Channel
Europa Hot Springs
KEMANO
Bonilla I.
Principe Channel
Pitt Island
Banks Island
Kingkown Inlet
13
Lawn Point
Hecate Strait
Bishop Bay Hot Springs
Gardner Canal
Union Passage
QUEEN CHARLOTTE CITY
Skidegate Channel
Sandspit
10
Fraser Reach
Kitlope
Gil Island
Campania Sound
Campania I.
Estevan Sound
Princess Royal Channel
Otter Passage
Truth I.
Princess Royal Island
Queen Charlotte Islands
Moresby I.
Cumshewa Inlet
Mussel Inlet
6
FIORDLAND
Caamano Sound
Laredo Ch.
Selwyn Inlet
Laredo Inlet
Kynoch Inlet
Aristazabal I.
7
Hotspring Island
Meyers Passage
KLEMTU
Mathieson Ch.
Roscoe Inlet
Laredo Sound
Higgins Passage
Juan Perez Sound
OCEAN FALLS
Price I.
Burnaby I.
Skincuttle Inlet
5
Spiller Inlet
Milbanke Sound
Ivory I.
Seaforth Channel
BELLA BELLA
SHEARWATER
Houston Stewart Channel
Queens Sound
Fitz Hugh Sound
Kings I.
Anthony Island
Goose I.
Hunter I.
Cape St. James
N
0 10 20 30
NAUTICAL MILES AT 53°N